THE TIMES HISTORY OF OUR TIMES

EDITOR MARCUS CUNLIFFE

WEIDENFELD AND NICOLSON
5 WINSLEY STREET LONDON W1

ISBN 0 297 00492 1

Designed by Trevor Vincent

Printed in England by Jarrold and Sons Ltd, Norwich

JACKET ILLUSTRATIONS

Front: view of earth from *Apollo 11* (UPI); poster of
Mao Tse-tung (William Sewell); explosion of 'A' bomb
(Black Star); President Kennedy (Camera Press);
John Lennon (Camera Press)
Back: Nigerian scene (Keystone Press); Berlin Wall
(Suddeutscher Verlag); used cars (Camera Press); May Day
parade in Moscow (Keystone Press)

Contents

Part Two
Nations and Frontiers

Foreword

The conception of this book was a joint one between *The Times* and the publishers, Weidenfeld and Nicolson. In the editorial planning, however, *The Times* has had no part. The responsibility for this has been entirely that of Professor Cunliffe, who was appointed editor by the publishers and *The Times*, since it was felt by both parties that an outsider would make the most suitable editor. He has been free to invite contributors of his choosing with or without any connection with *The Times* or any other newspaper. It follows that *The Times* does not necessarily agree with all the views expressed in this book. An attempt to impose a collective viewpoint by *The Times* would not have served the project as originally planned.

Marcus Cunliffe

The Scope of Our Times

This is a volume of world history, at least in so far as such a thing is possible. How much, from 1945 to 1970, could we be said imaginatively to inhabit one world? And – a related question – who are 'we'? What are *our* times? *One World* was the title of a book published in 1943 by the American politician Wendell Willkie, who had challenged Franklin D. Roosevelt in the presidential campaign of 1940. He sought to present a view of the contemporary and future scene as broad and sanguine as that of President Roosevelt. The notion of one world was characteristic of the last phase of the war, when the Western powers and Russia could feel confident that at last victory was in sight. Soon there would be an end to the years of killing and destruction. There was a yearning for peace and a readiness, indeed a psychological necessity, to believe that the postwar world would be a better world. The creation of the United Nations Organization in 1945 was a symptom of the same mood. Oneness, unity were in the air. The immensity of the war had itself stimulated such largeness of conception. Some historians argue that it ought not to be called the Second World War, since the 1914-18 War was less far-reaching and so (according to this opinion) not properly designated as the First World War. Whether or not the 1939-45 conflict was the first real world war in history, there was no dispute that it was in every way a giant affair. Few nations were able to remain neutral. Scores of millions of men and women were put into uniform or involved in quasi-military work. Hundreds of millions, in Asia, Africa and Europe, witnessed the struggle at first hand. Theirs was the freemasonry of the ration-card and the air-raid siren, the bomb, the shell and the bullet. The commanders on both sides had to plan strategy and mobilize resources on a global level; on both sides the manifold problems of coalition warfare had to be faced – even if they were not always overcome.

In important respects the postwar world did seem to become increasingly aware of itself as *one* world. The UN served as a kind of world parliament, and it absorbed or founded a cluster of specialized agencies whose names sufficiently indicate their global range: the Universal Postal Union (UPU), the World Meteorological Association (WMO), the Food and Agriculture Organization (FAO), the International Refugee Organization (IRO), the World Health Organization (WHO), the International Bank for Reconstruction and Development (IBRD; also known as the World Bank), the International Monetary Fund (IMF), the United Nations Educational, Scientific and Cultural Organization (UNESCO), and so on. UNESCO, for example, undertook an ambitious world cultural history of mankind, with an international team of editors and contributors, and launched an associated *Journal of World History* – these coordinated by a Swiss scholar, Guy Métraux, who had grown up in the Argentine and obtained a Ph.D. in the United States.

The UN also by force of circumstance on several occasions furnished a sort of world police. The first of these, in Korea from 1950 to 1953, was also the most equivocal, since the enterprise was initiated and dominated by the United States, which provided nearly ninety per cent of the non-Korean troops under the aegis of the UN. Nevertheless, fifteen other nations did offer to send forces, and thirty-seven others volunteered various supplies and services. The next occasion, in 1956, was a more genuine instance of an international peace-keeping move conceived within the UN. In the midst of the Suez crisis Lester B. Pearson of Canada introduced an emergency resolution, unanimously approved by the General Assembly, for the dispatch of a United Nations Emergency Force (UNEF) to the Middle East. Working with great speed, Pearson and the UN secretary-general, Dag Hammarskjöld, improvised a miniature army of 6,000 men and, with the consent of Colonel Nasser, interposed it as a buffer between Egypt and Israel. In diversity of origins the UNEF far surpassed the coalition armies of 1939-45. No less than ten nations – Brazil, Canada, Colombia, Denmark, Finland, India, Indonesia, Norway, Sweden and Yugoslavia – were represented, and fourteen others had offered contingents.

The third emergency arose in 1960-1, when Belgium suddenly conceded independence to its Congo colony and pulled out its own armed forces. It was obviously necessary to help the new Congo republic to maintain order, and a UN Congo Force (ONUC) was quickly assembled and eventually grew to a body of 20,000 men drawn from nearly thirty nations, a majority of them African. ONUC operated under extremely difficult conditions. A Katanga secession movement developed, and the UN became caught up in the intricate national, tribal and personal rivalries exemplified by the Congolese president, Joseph Kasavubu, the prime minister, Patrice Lumumba, and the Katanga leader, Moïse Tshombe. UN troops found themselves mixed up in some bitter skirmishes; and Hammarskjöld himself was killed in a plane crash in September 1961, *en route* to a meeting with Tshombe. However, these experiences did not deter the UN from a further peace-keeping endeavour in 1964. The independence of Cyprus in 1960 had not cured latent communal tension, and fighting between Greeks and Turks flared up; once more a UN emergency force was gathered. The existing British garrison of 3,000 men passed under the UN flag (a useful way of making them more universally acceptable), and was joined by 4,000 other troops from Canada, Sweden, Ireland and Finland; a Finnish diplomat was appointed by the UN to act as mediator between the Greeks and the Turks.

In the quite different realm of sport a similar gathering of nations was apparent. The quadrennial Olympic Games brought together athletes from almost every country in the world. Football (soccer) likewise grew prodigiously in popularity – the United States, Canada and Japan were soon the only major nations not caught in the game's contagion – and by the 1960s its fever had acquired a regular cyclical peak in the shape of the World Cup contest: a prize gained by England in 1966 and by Brazil in 1970. As with the Olympics, the World Cup fixtures were relayed live to a prodigious world audience. The game of tennis generated a lesser yet far from negligible international excitement. In such athletic milieux, players and trainers moved round the globe with dazing rapidity; star performers seemed willing to transfer their domicile from one country to another. In a more limited sphere, car rallies seemed to make light of national boundaries. In the most famous of all, the Monte Carlo Rally, it was not unusual for the driver of a car to be of a different nationality from his navigator, and for their vehicle to be from a third country. The unity of mankind seemed to be symbolized when the first two men to stand on the summit of Mount Everest happened to be a Sherpa (Tensing) and a New Zealander (Edmund Hillary); a subsequent successful ascent of this highest mountain in the world was made by a Japanese climbing party. Sometimes the symbolism was more deliberate, as with the amazingly polyglot crew that Thor Heyerdahl selected for his 1970 voyage across the Atlantic on a craft made of reeds to prove that the Egyptians might have discovered the New World.

Styles in the arts also often seemed to transcend the familiar frontiers of nation and language. Knowledge of the world's art heritage had become widespread and omnivorous. Thanks to photographic reproduction there was now, in the phrase of André Malraux, an 'imaginary museum' available to everyone with access to even a modest library, indeed even a rack of postcards in an art-shop. Modern styles appeared to grow more and more 'international': this became a designation of style itself, at any rate in architecture, where the same materials and idioms were employed all over the world with only minor (and sometimes tourist-orientated) concessions to local tradition or – as Le Corbusier complained of the naked tower-block of the UN headquarters in New York – to climate. Wherever painting, sculpture and music were allowed to develop without state direction, they responded to world trends. Thus, Abstract Expressionism or Action painting, the main concern of the fifties, yielded to Pop Art, this to Op Art, this to Minimal Art, and so on. The pace was set by a few leaders, who might happen to be congregated in a particular metropolis (after the war New York for a while replaced Paris as the main innovative centre). The work of each renowned artist – that for instance of a Jackson Pollock, a Willem de Kooning or a Claes Oldenburg – was instantly recognizable for its special 'signature'. But the signature, the personal solution to the somewhat hermetic art problems of the moment, had little to do with the artist's nationality. An unsophisticated visitor to international exhibitions such as the Venice Biennale would have had the greatest difficulty in guessing the national provenance of the works on display. For more knowing spectators, so swift was the pace of innovation in the visual arts, the country (or capital) of origin might well be classified according to criteria of relative modishness: Paris, say, might be deemed a year behind New York and six months behind London, and Brussels a year behind Paris. In literature, language and ideological barriers made more of a difference. But there too translation moved swiftly, and while certain authors like certain wines did not 'travel' well, others – Beckett, Borges, Brecht, Camus, Grass, Mailer – easily surmounted linguistic obstacles. Another new international prize, the Prix Formentor, was established to supplement the pioneering enterprise of the Nobel awards. Even poetry, the least translatable of the literary genres, spoke across frontiers, especially when the poets themselves read their lines in public. World poetry festivals in London, for instance, attracted large ecstatic gatherings, and the audience seemed to divine the sense of what was being said as readily as if they were listening to the abstractly international language of the music of Cage or Stockhausen.

This eagerness to meet the performer half-way, this intuitive comprehension (as if within the words and sounds was secreted some universal language, a Morse code of sensibility) was still more evident in the youth-dominated realm of pop music and balladry. Again, a few nations provided the lead, and others banned or frowned upon the manifestations of youth culture. But the movement was both unconsciously and consciously international – or perhaps non-national is the more accurate designation. The Beatles and the Rolling Stones were British groups, yet their singing accents were midatlantic and their techniques frankly and cheerfully eclectic (the Beatles began their career with a German engagement, in Hamburg). The 'Woodstock Nation' – the vast assembly of the young held in rural New York – represented not a nation state at all in the usual sense but a global tribe, prelapsarian and universalist in spirit. The chief newspaper of this tribe bore a significant name: IT, standing for 'International Times'. One of the wittiest and most inventive of associated tribes, the Provos of Amsterdam, devised a brilliant frontier-ignoring symbol: a painted white line, endless, curly and wayward, writhing along pavements, up and over buildings, to disappear from Holland down a street-drain – and to reappear and continue its mysterious life via a manhole in England (and maybe other countries).

Styles of affront and of revolt – no doubt imitatively, through the medium of mass communications – also became extraordinarily identical. Marches, sit-ins, teach-ins, confrontations, hardly varied in vocabulary or tactics round the universities of the world. The first aircraft hijacking (who now recalls where and when the practice started?) was almost overnight re-enacted on a score of international routes. Ransom kidnappings, usually of foreign diplomats in order to secure the release of political prisoners, were pioneered in Latin America; and though in 1970 the *tupamaros* of Uruguay remained masters of this method, it had spread several thousand miles north, into Canada. Protest-suicide by setting fire to one's petrol-soaked clothing, a gesture introduced by Buddhists in South Vietnam, was soon adopted by young men in half a dozen countries: for despair too was a universal emotion, and petrol was a universal fluid.

Simultaneity of transmission through newsprint, radio and television (rendered easier and more spectacular by the introduction of communication satellites) created an illusion of a world audience. Whatever the hour of day or night, untold millions listened to and watched the enactment of a presidential assassination in Texas, a football match in London or Rio de Janeiro, an earthquake catastrophe in Peru or Yugoslavia, a moon landing. A traveller in the privileged enclaves of airport lounges and 'international' hotels could be forgiven for becoming confused as to which country he was in. Whether produced in the United States or Russia, Britain or France, the jet aircraft visible beyond the airport windows obeyed a common functional necessity; and the downtown view of steel-glass skyscrapers, from his hotel room, revealed the same conventions of ubiquitous modernity. Maps of air-routes reduced the earth's dimensions to a mere diagram, densely criss-crossed with lines of routinized motion. In the muted, matter-of-fact atmosphere of such enclaves, the drama inherent in travel yielded to fatigue and boredom. Space exploration served to rekindle excitement, and to supply more staggering reminders that the airport travellers were inhabitants of one world. Seen from a moon-rocket, the earth was a little, mottled, grey-white marble. At its best, the rise of science-fiction extended man's imaginative range, and carried the humane message that we were all passengers on what Buckminster Fuller called 'Space-Ship Earth'. Human squabbles dwindled to insignificance, for example, in the novels of the American Kurt Vonnegut (*Cat's Cradle, The Sirens of Titan*). In 1945, as a prisoner of war in Dresden, Vonnegut had survived the terrible fire-storm of an Allied air-raid that caused as many deaths as at Hiroshima and Nagasaki. A quarter of a century later, in *Slaughter-House Five*, he still could not quite render the experience directly; but he achieved a healing detachment by linking his central character with another civilization from outer space.

Global prophets such as Fuller, Marshall McLuhan and Lewis Mumford sought to perceive our planet as an entity. Historians like the Englishman Geoffrey Barraclough, who argued that we now inhabited a 'post-modern' world, insisted that it was no longer adequate to confine the record to the affairs of Europe, still less those of single nations; they attempted to restore the balance, retrospectively, by delving into the past of China, India, Africa, and endeavouring to orchestrate the whole. There was a fresh emphasis on the idea of comparative history – impressively demonstrated in David B. Davis's analysis of slavery as a world institution, or in Barrington Moore's *Social Origins of Dictatorship and Democracy* (1966). Scholars in other disciplines responded to the same impulse. In *Five Families* (1959) and *The Children of Sánchez* (1961), for example, the American anthropologist Oscar Lewis investigated the lives of the poor, the lumpenproletariat, in non-primitive societies. He suggested that 'the culture of poverty has some universal characteristics which transcend regional, rural-urban, and even national differences'; there were 'remarkable similarities', he felt from his work, 'in family structure, interpersonal relations, time orientations, value systems, spending patterns, and the sense of community in lower-class settlements in London, Glasgow, Paris, Harlem, and Mexico City'.

Divisions – Old and New

At various levels, then, the years from 1945 to 1970 might be taken to reveal a deep and a growing awareness of the essential unity of mankind. But no one who lived through the era and retraced its crises would be likely to accept so simple a portrait. One might of course ask whether the phenomena described were in fact so new, at least within Christendom. Latin had once provided a universal language for the educated. Later, for *salon* and for diplomatic discourse, French had almost fulfilled the same function. Where was the equivalent in our supposedly international times? Esperanto was a brave but nearly abandoned monument to an earlier hope. English was perhaps dominant in the Western world. But the claims of French, German and Spanish could hardly be ignored, nor those of Russian,

Chinese and Japanese. To the extent that there were cultural unities, these had arguably long existed – again within the Western world. Architecture, painting and sculpture, costume, the opera, ballet: such features appeared much the same from country to country a hundred or two hundred years ago, allowing for regional variations.

But leaving aside this point, more important reservations remain. *Was* there one world in this quarter of a century? The UN may have been fashioned in a mood of fairly robust optimism. Its history, however, seemed to many observers to be of growing frustration and futility. Most contemporaries would probably not regard the Korean venture as an authentic display of UN authority, but rather as an indication that the UN was an instrument of United States policy. The Middle East force of 1956 was ignominiously withdrawn at Colonel Nasser's insistence, and so unable to prevent a further outbreak of fighting between Israel and the Arab states. Several influential commentators, including the Irish diplomat Conor Cruise O'Brien, regard the intervention in the Congo as a disastrous error, pro-Belgian in implication and leading to the alienation of several African states (which withdrew their contingents in protest). In 1970 – when mainland China was still excluded from membership – the meeting of the General Assembly coincided with the twenty-fifth anniversary of the UN. But, in contrast to the electric atmosphere of the 1960 meeting (attended among others by Nikita Khrushchev and Fidel Castro), the 1970 Assembly was distinctly a second-rank affair. Some journalists and delegates might feel that the secretary-general, U Thant of Burma, lacked the stature necessary to uphold the institution. But the decline of the UN from major polemics to minor squabbles could not fairly be blamed upon one man. There was a widespread and depressing suspicion that the UN might die of inanition – and lack of funds. It seemed to some of its weary denizens to have become a talking-shop, the length of whose speeches was in inverse proportion to their substance – a permanent exhibit of the inveterate jealousies and hostilities of a fragmented world. Even the less controversial activities of UNESCO suffered from the divisiveness and parochialism of member states; the completion of the world-history project no doubt entailed prodigies of revision and placatory compromise in order to avoid offence to national susceptibilities.

If the UN and its agencies, seen in this light, seemed to act as a forum for chauvinism and big-power manœuvres, this was no less conspicuous an aspect of international sporting competitions. Despite the ceremonies of fraternity and the fluttering of flags, it could be felt that the element of nationalist fervour was predominant. Nation vied with nation; the emphasis tended to be more upon the competition than upon the sport. With the World Cup, whole countries plunged into mourning and recrimination at the defeat of their teams, or exploded with pride at the news of a victory.

As for the unity of styles in art and design, and technology, this could be interpreted as often merely imposed by one of the top-dog nations, especially the United States. True, this was not an unprecedented situation. In the eighteenth century France had spread its styles through the world, as Britain was to do in the nineteenth century. But *le défi Américain* seemed more alarming in scale; the giant American corporations, operating all over the world, had assets and incomes exceeding those of most *nations*. The appearance of universality might thus really connote the virtual monopoly of certain products, or the obligation of rival producers in other countries to compete by imitation.

Certainly the world after 1945 began to coalesce into multi-national groupings, which could be viewed as a step towards the achievement of the wartime dream of one world at harmony with itself. Western Europe came together in the EEC, Egypt and Syria came together in the UAR (United Arab Republic), the newly independent African nations in the OAU (Organization of African Unity). Yet their significance was equivocal. Their purpose was frequently military-strategic (NATO, SEATO, CENTO, the Warsaw Pact): they were expressions, that is, of solidarity for combative reasons. They were not primarily *for* fraternity, but *against* potential enemies. Often, a cynic might feel, they were also exercises in self-deception. During the war, it was remarked that the vocabulary of idealism underwent a progressive deflation. There was for example much talk in Britain and the United States of the 'liberation' of the occupied countries. These countries were undoubtedly pleased to be liberated, and the cost in Allied lives was sometimes heavy. But in the process, thanks in large part to the British-American strategy of bombardment from the air, the price of freedom was wholesale destruction. In the soldiers' slang of 1944-5, to say that a town such as Caen or Le Havre had been 'liberated' came to mean that much of it had been laid flat. By the same token, in the postwar world a sceptical observer might learn to attribute an ironical reversal of meaning to certain key terms. Organizations professing 'unity' might in fact be confessing an acute lack of this estimable element. 'Brotherhood' could be read (cf. 'Muslim Brotherhood') as a euphemism for a tendency to fratricide. During the 1960s the word 'community' possibly acquired something of this ambiguity, at least in certain contexts. At best, our cynic could maintain, it was a quality to be aspired to, though not yet attained: at worst, an admission that there never would be a community in any genuine sense.

It is not necessary to be a cynic to point out that in some extremely important respects the one world envisaged during the war was becoming two inimical worlds even before the war ceased. Two years after the collapse of Germany and Japan, the cold war between the superpowers, the USSR and the USA and their associated nations, was taking shape. For the next fifteen years or so this division into two blocs shaped the thought and the energies of much of the globe. In the textbook parlance of that time, there was the 'free world' and there was the 'communist world'. Within a few more years, India and several other nations who were reluctant to fall into either camp were organizing as 'non-aligned' powers. Soon these were referred to collectively as the 'Third World'. And during the 1960s there were widening rifts inside the so-called free world and in the communist one. Logically, of course, this nomenclature is absurd. It is tautological to speak of 'one world' – how could there be more than one? – and even more meaningless to speak of several worlds. Still, it is too late in the day to raise such quibbles. The fundamental factor, for our purposes, is that for every instance of an underlying identity of outlook in the postwar world there is a contrary instance of dissonance and division. Indeed, even discounting the major ideological cleavages, one may doubt whether the mass of mankind developed more than a hazy and intermittent appreciation of the globalism expounded by McLuhan. Most people, even in the more prosperous nations, moved about the world rather less than they might have done in wartime service. Most people spoke only one language. Their everyday 'world' was not the world, but their home, their family, their place of employment, their village or suburb or city. As immemorially in human history, their allegiances diminished upward in intensity. Except for special moments of emotional transfiguration, they cared more for their children than for their neighbours, more for their locality than for their nation. Their collective consciousness, in some ways powerful, was in other ways fitful and ephemeral. The co-ordinates of time and space tended to cancel one another out. Those born around or after 1945 might have a more open appreciation than their elders of the world context; yet the young might have very little comprehension of the movement of history during their early lifetimes.

In theory, the intelligent citizen seeking to make sense of the era could not fail to acquire an understanding of the emergence of what might be termed a world consciousness. But such understanding was blocked and countered by various considerations. Ideologies barred the free movement of tastes, opinions, sensibilities. There was actual censorship in many corners of the world, and a greater or lesser degree of conformist pressure in most places. Those living in so-called 'capitalist' societies could find out something about existence in the communist areas of the world. They might even be surprised and impressed, for instance, by the seriously humane poetry written under the aegis of social realism by some of the younger Russians, or by a Herbert in Poland, a Holub in Czechoslovakia, a Popa in Yugoslavia. But they could not find out much, with – we might say – the best will in the world. Albania was more mysteriously sealed-off, more conjectural than the coast of Bohemia had been to William Shakespeare. China was about as impenetrable to Westerners as it had been in the eighteenth century. Russia, relatively, was an open book; and every non-Russian concerned with literature was full of admiration for the talent revealed by a Boris Pasternak or an Alexander Solzhenitsyn – both awarded Nobel prizes. But for Russians these books were closed; and so were many others, and many manifestations of Western life, through official edict. While such hindrances persisted it was idle to expect that the sophisticated portion of mankind in all countries would arrive at a unified world-view; for a world knowledge must come first. In the era of 1945-70 it seemed that among the fields of human inquiry only science and technology had an entry visa valid for all countries.

The barriers set up by the communist areas were not the only ones. These others were more defensible, and in a way more complex. Despite the challenge of communist ideology, the Western capitalist nations still remained culturally more dynamic. They might be unsure of their own cultural heritage, and eager to absorb cultural insights from the rest of the world. But this eclecticism, this willingness to synthesize, coupled with their considerable economic prosperity, reinforced rather than weakened sundry aspects of the Western dominance which had been so marked a feature of the world in the nineteenth century. In everything from dress to nuclear physics – pop music, cinema, theatre, literature, automation, medicine, business administration – with Japan in a collateral relationship, the West was far more of an exporter than an importer. The aggregate of Western styles and techniques offered something like a universal, a one-world set of a contemporary *summa* or encyclopædia. They were not the only innovators, but they were the most inquisitive, the most open, the most vigorous. The undoubted talents of Russia were in comparison occluded.

Yet this continued, dynamic dominance on the part of the white West was as dangerous as it was unattractive to the new nations of Africa and Asia. To some extent their distaste was traditional: Western ways were alien. To some extent they disapproved of what they took to be unwholesome tendencies in Western society: miniskirts and bearded wandering students aroused intense antagonism in some non-Western countries. In any case, their need was to define their own identity, in necessarily non-Western terms. This led to paradoxes and problems that might seem comical if they were not so serious to the nations concerned. None could afford to reject all Western influence, or for that matter could possibly determine where 'Westernness' ended and – for example, in technology – 'world' culture began. Professor Ali Mazrui of Uganda in a recent article furnished a vivid illustration of the dilemma, as it affected Kenya. Kenya as a sensitive new nation wished to promote the wearing of native as distinct from Western costume. But in local instances this might mean nudity – itself of course a form of costume – and nudity was unacceptable according to the generalized *mores* of independent Kenya.

The determination of the new, ex-colonial nations to avoid 'neo-colonialism' was heightened by a new militant anger – typified in books like *The Wretched of the Earth* by the Martinican Frantz Fanon – against the white sector of the world. The celebration of blackness, which some would call a form of reverse racialism, meant that its arguments tended to run counter, not only to orthodox (and hateful) white prejudice, but also to much more well-intentioned attempts to define universal values and problems. Oscar Lewis, who died in 1970, was an exceptionally sensitive scholar; his work and his life merged into one, and he developed an intimate comradeship with his families of the poor in Mexico. But his suggestion that there was a universality of culture derived from deprivation, linking Harlem with other districts of city-poor round the world, would almost certainly now be rejected by black spokesmen in the United States – much as they rejected the view that the sufferings of the Jews in world history might be equivalent to their own. Here, in short, was another alignment of the world into segments – this one based on colour, and capable of generating passion of ideological intensity.

The attempt of a hypothetical earthman, possessed of intelligence and goodwill, to envisage one harmonious world was still further confused by a trend that became marked during the 1960s. We have seen that there was an undoubted tendency towards larger agglomerations in the quarter of a century; the move towards European unity was perhaps the most remarkable of all these. But the process of decolonization or self-determination (as in the case of the Austro-Hungarian Empire, at the end of the First World War) sometimes entailed the fragmentation of larger previous units. In the nineteenth century new nations such as Germany and Italy, as the word 'unification' implies, might grow by agglomeration. After 1945, many of the new nations appeared by fission rather than fusion – some of them tiny in area, population and resources, though they sought internal cohesion. In this era there were thus simultaneous impulses towards both fusion and fission. Nor was the latter tendency confined to the activity of nation-building. Among the older nations, strategic and economic motives induced them to merge centripetally into bigger groupings such as the Common Market. Yet they also experienced quite unexpected centrifugal tendencies, in the shape of a revived localism or regionalism, or – more controversially – of buried and presumably extinct nationalisms. In Britain, Scottish and Welsh nationalism took on militant new life. There was bitter disagreement between the Flemish and the Walloon areas of Belgium. In the United States there were demands for the separate nationhood of Afro-Americans and ('Red power') of the American Indians. In Canada, French-Canadian nationalism became vehement. In Yugoslavia, though the federal structure allowed plenty of autonomy, the old separatisms of Slovene, Serb, Croat and so on proved far from dead.

In the new nations, sometimes burdened with artificial boundaries bequeathed from old imperial demarcations, tribal rivalries might be fanned into secessionist drives. Such was the case with Katanga in 1960-1, though this particular movement was soon abandoned; with feuding between Arab and African in Zanzibar, which led in January 1964 to the merging of Zanzibar and Tanganyika in the new state of Tanzania; with Nigeria, where the secession of Biafra brought about a protracted civil war; and with a succession of other internal hostilities in such countries as Ethiopia, Kenya and Uganda. Perhaps, in the quasi-global atmosphere of 1945-70, at least through the news media, the new nations imbibed something of the internal divisiveness of their former imperial managers. Perhaps, the other way round, Welsh or Flemish or French-Canadian nationalists were stirred by the news from Biafra – if so, the eventual defeat of Biafra might have disheartened them.

The Great Divide

So much for the world seen spatially. In some respects it could be thought to present a unity: to have universal aspects, perceived as such by many if not all men. In other respects it could be seen as set into large, mutually hostile blocs according to ideology, race and degree of affluence. In yet other respects it presented neither a unity nor a massing of blocs, but an almost infinite number of local areas with local preoccupations. Each of these was a part of the truth; collectively they perhaps brought us close to a grasp of the psychological components of 'our' world.

A further aspect, the time-dimension, has so far only been touched upon. How sensible is it to seek to view the world framed within this particular segment of time? Does the segment appear to possess a beginning and an end, or manageable subdivisions? The answer must appear both obvious and oracular. All portions of chronology are arbitrary, sliced from the continuum like a saw-cut log from a tree-trunk: the rings and the grain run before and after. However, some portions are more well defined than others. For a beginning date 1945 is unusually definite – we might say, more like a main branch or joint of a tree. The terminal date of 1970 is of course simply neat and convenient, a *terminus ad quem* sealing off the duration of our fragment and a quarter of a century. Yet within this span comes a half-way point, or great divide, which does help a good deal to make sense of the era. Naturally it too is something of a mental construct, and it cannot be assigned any precise date. Yet it may have as much reality as 1945 or 1970, and its significance becomes more clear with each year that passes. Somewhere around the late 1950s the postwar era came to an end, and another began whose lineaments could by 1970 be provisionally sketched even if their outcome was naturally still conjectural. The middle-aged and elderly in 1970 tended to have their imaginative horizons bounded by the limits of the earlier period. Conversely, the young often showed an inability to move backwards in time beyond their latter-day fragment of time – mentally to re-enter the earlier world of Churchill and Stalin, Roosevelt and Truman, Chiang Kai-shek and Mahatma Gandhi, King Farouk and Juan Perón, Anthony Eden and John Foster Dulles. They refused to see a connection between their universe and that prior one; and in a way they were correct to insist that the two periods had quite different sets of assumptions.

The key events of the first period were largely bound up with postwar reconstruction and with the tensions of the cold war. The Yalta and Potsdam Conferences of 1945, the Truman Doctrine and the Marshall Plan (1947), the formation of NATO, the creation of the Chinese People's Republic and the establishment of two Germanies (1949), the Japanese peace treaty (1951) and the creation of the European Defence Community (1952), the retirement of the UN secretary-general, Trygve Lie (1952) and the death of Stalin (1953), the fall of Dien Bien Phu and of Senator Joseph McCarthy (1954), the resignation of the British prime minister Winston Churchill (1955): these entrances and exits punctuated the ten to fifteen years following the end of the Second World War. A few tough old survivors from the epoch carried on into the second phase of our times, and even made their mark upon them: Konrad Adenauer remained chancellor of West Germany until 1963, Jawaharlal Nehru prime minister of India until his death in 1964; and Charles de Gaulle dominated French life until near the close of the 1960s. But they were exceptional.

With the late 1950s there were signs of another order of world history. Some of these, such as the 1956 riots in Poland and the rising in Hungary, or the Anglo-French-Israeli assault upon Egypt, proved to be abortive – mere portents of future crises. But one spectacular new departure was the launching by the Soviet Union of *Sputnik 1* in October 1957. A second Russian satellite, this time carrying a dog, was put into orbit a month later. The shock to American pride was enormous, though the United States managed to fire two satellites into orbit within the next few months. Ostensibly these operations fitted into a world programme for the International Geophysical Year. But the competition between the superpowers was the prime issue in most people's minds, including those of the American and Russian leaders. From a preoccupation with the Bomb, with something of the effect of a *détente* they turned to a preoccupation with rocketry and outer space – though there were reminders of the awesome fertility of superpower rivalry, such as the first submarine crossing of the North Pole, under the icecap, by the US nuclear submarine *Nautilus* in August 1958. But the rhythms of space rivalry seized the headlines. In 1959 the Russians sent *Lunik 1* out on a 90-million-mile journey to orbit the sun. In April 1961 they scored another astounding success by launching and safely retrieving a spacecraft manned by the cosmonaut (a new word in the world vocabulary) Yuri Gagarin. Three weeks later the United States countered, a good deal less dramatically, by firing *their* astronaut Alan B. Shepard into a 115-mile trajectory. Later in the year, however, the Russians proclaimed their lead by sending a man round the earth on no less than seventeen orbits. Not until February 1962 did the United States succeed in putting one of their own astronauts into orbit. They repeated the feat in May of the same year, but were once more outshone when in August two manned Soviet satellites operating in tandem achieved sixty-four and forty-eight orbits. Further developments continued rapidly; in 1965, for example, an American spacecraft transmitted photographs of Mars. But the main American endeavour, announced by John F. Kennedy near the start of his presidency, was to land a man upon the moon by 1970; and this sensational feat – perhaps less soundly conceived than the Russian concentration upon unmanned devices – was duly achieved. In the meantime, though without resounding effects, the two nations unobtrusively signified their joint anxiety to avoid the risk of a nuclear war. One symbol was the establishment in June 1963 of a direct 'hot line' teleprinter link between the White House and the Kremlin; appropriately the instrument at the Washington end was coloured red. They made gestures towards nuclear disarmament, and – more significantly – were at pains to evade head-on disagreements over such issues as the suppression of the Dubček regime in Czechoslovakia. One reason of course was the new position of Maoist China as the declared leader of genuine world communism. In December 1962 Khrushchev publicly criticized Chinese incursions across the Himalayan frontier with India as threats to world peace; and the Chinese retaliated with the to-them dreadful accusation that Soviet Russia was attempting 'peaceful coexistence' with the West.

Another large shift in the world emphasis came with the new wave of decolonization. There had been a previous Asian phase, when in 1947-9 India, Pakistan and Indonesia achieved independence. The next wave began in 1956, as Morocco and Tunisia emerged as new nations. Ghana followed in 1957; several more French colonies chose independence or autonomy through the referendum of 1958; de Gaulle proposed a similar referendum for Algeria in 1959; and in 1960 Nigeria and the Congo joined the throng. An ideologically related event, at the beginning of 1959, was the overthrow of President Batista in Cuba by Fidel Castro and his followers. Castro became prime minister, though so conventional a title failed to convey the scope and *brio* of his activity. Despite initial cordiality from the Americans, he and they were soon angrily at variance with one another. And within the United States, young negroes in 1960 staged the first 'sit-in' at a North Carolina lunch-counter. In England the Campaign for Nuclear Disarmament (CND) was by now attracting as many as 50,000 sympathizers for its annual Easter convergence upon Trafalgar Square. A radical minority wished to do more than march. In the words of the London *Economist*: 'For the first time since the days of the militant suffragettes a group of people are actively seeking to be sent to prison as a means of political protest.' In 1961 the new satirical magazine *Private Eye* delighted the irreverent with its deliberate outrageous mockery of what was soon to be known as the 'Establishment'. In the following year a wider public was amazed, and occasionally scandalized, by the BBC's weekly 'send-up' programme, *That Was The Week That Was*.

All over the world the moral and intellectual climate was changing. In its own eyes, at any rate in the Western world, the 1950s were post-ideological. The atmosphere of the decade was brilliantly conveyed in *The End of Ideology* (1960), a book of essays by the American sociologist Daniel Bell. The passions and aspirations of the previous era had been betrayed by evils such as Stalinism, and confounded by benevolent modifications to capitalism such as the Welfare State. For the radical intelligentsia, said Bell, 'the old ideologies have lost their "truth" and their power to persuade'. In Western scholarship and political life the notion of 'consensus' was dominant. It was assumed that all dramatic expedients had been tried and found wanting. Extremism simply did not work, and almost never had worked in world history. Certainly it was not the recipe for steady progress and prosperity.

But around the end of the decade the fatigued anxieties and the cautious optimism of the postwar phase began to modulate into a new radicalism. In retrospect it appeared that the 1950s were also, or perhaps more truly, pre-ideological. Bell had indeed noted some elements in this apparent reversal. While Western ideology was exhausted, 'the rising states of Asia and Africa are fashioning new ideologies with a different appeal for their own people'; and in the West, 'the young intellectual is unhappy because the "middle way" is for the middle-aged, not for him; it is without passion and is deadening.' The new radicalism spread rapidly, much influenced by its interpretation of events in the non-Western world. It acquired new heroes, sometimes young as in the case of Castro and Che Guevara, sometimes venerable warriors as with Ho Chi Minh and Mao Tse-tung. It acquired a miscellaneous new heraldry: the CND symbol, red and black anarchist flags, lapel badges ('Make Love, Not War'; 'I Am A Human Being: Do Not Fold, Spindle, or Mutilate' – this a reference to the instructions to students whose registration was being carried out with the aid of IBM cards).

The shift, the passage over the great divide, was reflected in a wholesale alteration of vocabulary. The word 'liberation', formerly tarnished, was refurbished ('National Liberation Front'). 'Confrontation', which hitherto had usually meant a disagreement between the superpowers, now came to mean a clash between dissidents and authority. Instead of 'reconstruction', the talk was of 'revolution'. Talk of 'productivity' and of the gross national product now began to seem 'gross' in the unfavourable sense of the word; the emphasis changed to talk of 'environment', 'ecology', 'pollution'. 'Negro' metamorphosed into 'Black', 'civil rights' into 'Black power'; Martin Luther King seemed to the militants an outmoded figure in comparison with Malcolm X or Eldridge Cleaver. Instead of 'representative' democracy, the cry was for 'participatory' democracy; instead of 'neighbour-hoods', 'communes'. Pornography, previously peddled and deplored, was now flaunted and recommended. In the United States, according to the critic-novelist Leslie Fiedler, there was a profound shift under way from the 'whisky' culture to the 'marijuana' culture, from the old Protestant ethic to the new hedonism. There was much indignation on the part of the old, some of it pompous, and much rhetoric on the part of the young, some of it shrill. It was really too simple to speak of two sides, aligned merely by age-group. Many of the middle-aged and elderly, who had not felt enthusiastic about the postwar years, were sympathetic; many of the young remained circumspect, or probably had no more than a superficial attachment to the causes they proclaimed. Nevertheless, there was a general conviction that the times had changed, with a vengeance.

Part One

One World

STOP NUCLEAR SUICIDE CAMPAIGN FOR NUCLEAR DISARMAMENT 2 CARTHUSIAN ST LONDON EC1

François Duchêne

War and Peace
in a Nuclear Age

It is impossible to write of war and peace between 1945 and 1970 without the mind being conditioned by the image of cold war. In some ways this is misleading, because it reduces the very varied developments of a generation to the single theme of the confrontation between two superpowers and their respective alliance systems. Yet in other ways 'cold war' is a brilliant phrase, which captures the tense quality of a period of neither peace nor war, or more precisely of a period that knew both a high degree of peace and a high degree of war. All the sound and fury of the Korean War, of the two major crises around Berlin and of the nuclear crisis in Cuba cannot obscure the fact that the industrial countries of the northern hemisphere, from Tokyo via New York and Berlin to Vladivostock have experienced a generation of unprecedented growth, prosperity and, despite everything, peace. For nearly a quarter of a century forty per cent of the land surface of the earth and one-third of humanity lived free of war and the imminent threat of war. On the other hand, some researchers maintain that elsewhere there were more bloody conflicts during that twenty-five years than at any other time during this turbulent century. In a famous speech to the American Society of Newspaper Editors in Montreal in May 1966, the then American defense secretary, Mr Robert McNamara, said 'in the last eight years alone there have been no less than 164 internationally significant outbreaks of violence. . . . The planet is becoming a more dangerous place to live on – not merely because of a potential nuclear holocaust, but also because of the large number of *de facto* conflicts and because of the trend of such conflicts growing rather than diminishing.' In a paper using a narrower definition of conflict, Mr David Wood, for the ISS (Institute for Strategic Studies), found that there had been 128 conflict situations in the seventy years between 1898 and 1968 of which no less than 84, or two-thirds, came after 1939. Moreover, some of the violence unleashed in minor wars equalled or surpassed standards recently applicable to major ones. The Americans dropped a bomb tonnage on Vietnam between 1965 and 1969 that was more than twice as great as that dropped by them during the whole of the Second World War, an awesome comparison when one recalls the destruction wreaked on Germany and Japan. Even in the Six-Day War of 1967 more tanks were committed to the Sinai battle between tiny Israel and poverty-stricken Egypt than by the Axis Powers and Allies together at the key battle of El Alamein in 1942. It is, then, equally possible to claim that 1945-70 was a period of greater peace and of greater violence than ever before: it depends where one looks.

The key to the paradox is the highly varied effects of the staggering material and technological growth of civilization during this century. It has often been pointed out that since the eighteenth century, major wars have become rarer but progressively more destructive. Major wars are, almost by definition, fought between the most powerful nations or on their periphery. Logically enough, the industrial nations of Eurasia, along with China as Japan's victim, bore the brunt of the 50-60 million deaths caused by the Second World War. War weariness undoubtedly played a vital role during the postwar years in maintaining peace in the industrial world despite the tensions which might have torn it apart. Moreover, the industrial nations, having the strongest reasons to dread war, also had the strongest ones to enjoy peace. The technological advances, not least in methods of government, of the twentieth century have made possible, or at least far easier, the rapid material development of vast states like the USSR and the USA

The shadow of the bomb: the CND movement in the early sixties grew out of a background of cold war, wholesale atmospheric nuclear tests and inadequate safeguards against holocaust by accident

Hiroshima, the beginning of the Nuclear Age;
paradoxically the prospect of massive mutual destruction
between the US and the USSR was to enforce peace and
the cold war's indirect, localized conflicts

The postwar attempt at a world society grew from 51
founder-members in 1946 to 135 in 1970. For a short
time – until the early sixties – it looked as if the UN
might prove an effective peacekeeping force in
the Third World

UNITED
NATIONS
DAY
October 24

whose resources of men and materials were only beginning to be mobilized in nineteenth-century conditions. They have also led to the increasingly efficient administration of the international economy, which was a major weakness of capitalism between the wars. The West's postwar conversion to the precepts of Lord Keynes and the planned ambitions of the socialist powers of the Soviet bloc have together more than doubled the historic rate of economic growth of societies since the Industrial Revolution. The energies of the peoples of the temperate zones have been concentrated on the reality, or hope, of mass liberation from ancestral poverty and the creation in the luckier ones of the mass consumer society. The millennial emotions which at other times went into conflict have been for almost a generation devoted to the unprecedentedly successful and widespread pursuit of Guizot's maxim: 'enrichissez-vous'. It is no exaggeration to say that in the process a large part of the world has passed from one stage of civilization into another. This has not been an option open to the much poorer, pre-industrial countries of the sub-tropical and tropical zones which have had to struggle, despite rapid rates of growth, with appallingly high birthrates eating up wealth almost at the rate it is produced.

Such factors have had a far greater influence on the postwar dispensation than it has been fashionable to recognize. At any rate the contrast between social quiescence in the rich countries and turbulence in the poorer ones, so important to the distribution of peace and war since 1945, cannot be explained purely in terms of the structure of international power. However, this structure has also played a manifest role; and it too is based on economic and technological progress. The relative decline of Europe has not been due to a failure of vitality, likely as this seemed after the war when only Marshall Aid funds from the United States apparently protected the West European birthplace of modern civilization from political and material collapse. The economic ebullience of the region in the face of lost empire has abundantly proved this. The major reason has been that modern conditions made possible the emergence of powers, of whom the USA and the USSR are no doubt only the first, built on a scale out of all proportion to the norms of the past. The US and the USSR have maintained a direct control over Western and Eastern Europe and Japan, which seemed to them vital to the balance of power, present and future. Their involvement in the more 'remote' and peripheral areas elsewhere has been more sporadic and on the whole less intense, but for that very reason more apparent and feverish.

What postwar system these factors alone would have produced is impossible to tell, because stability has been sealed by the most spectacular technological innovation of all – the advent of nuclear weapons. The atomic

A Soviet picture of British and Russian soldiers meeting in 1945 – suspicion soon ended an alliance of convenience
Below British and American aid in the Greek civil war resulted in communist defeat in 1949; over 45,000 lives were lost

The Berlin airlift in 1948, when tons of supplies were dropped every day in response to the Russian stranglehold on the city; Berlin became the initial focus for cold war tensions

explosion, 'brighter than a thousand suns,' has, along with the idea of cold war itself, dominated the contemporary imagination. Although the fire-storms over Dresden and Tokyo in 1945 killed far more people by 'conventional' means than the two nuclear explosions over Hiroshima and Nagasaki, fission and above all fusion (hydrogen) weapons have changed all the traditional calculations of force. The maximum radius of destruction of a 'blockbuster' bomb in the Second World War was one-tenth of a mile. The radius of intensive destruction of a one-megaton nuclear warhead current on US Minuteman and Polaris missiles at the end of 1970 was 4·32 miles. Destruction on such a scale has virtually destroyed the idea of 'victory' in war. This was being eroded by the horrors of the industrialization of war well before nuclear weapons appeared on the scene. It was not mere euphemism which changed the 'ministries of war' of pre-1914 days into the 'ministries of defence' of post-1945 days; or that in the 1950s changed the notion of defence itself into one of 'deterrence' or prevention. These semantics are directly correlated with the growing consciousness of the cost of war by whole societies, rulers and ruled alike. By making this cost astronomical and nightmarish, nuclear weapons have had the curious result of inhibiting the use of force by major powers against others of their kind. Immediately after the war, the American monopoly of nuclear bombs neutralized the natural military advantages enjoyed by the USSR as the dominant land-power in Eurasia. Later on, with the arrival in the late 1950s of intercontinental missiles which introduced the science-fiction age of push-button warfare, the mutual nuclear terrors of the USA and the USSR led to the 'balance of prudence' which consisted in their damping down confrontations which might entail even the risk, as in Cuba in 1962, of nuclear tests of will between them. A nuclear, and more generally military, stalemate between the two superpowers has developed. This has turned force from its traditional role as the last appeal from international political competition into an ambiguous factor within that competition itself. In the core areas of the balance of power, such as Europe, the inhibitions on the use of force have become so much the accepted context that a slow but real shift from military to political relations seems to be under way. In less central and more volatile regions, the superpowers often become sucked into local quarrels which they both stoke up and damp down, caught as they are between their own rivalries and the passions of their clients, and their fear of nuclear confrontation. Here, as in the Middle East, they tend to figure as international political faction leaders in quarrels that are potentially dangerous for world peace but which the common interest of the superpowers tends to circumscribe within their local bounds. As a result there seems to have been a definite shift since the war along the spectrum of conflict from the higher to the less intense bands on the scale.

Violence: the imposition of will

Violence can be seen as a complete range passing from major, now nuclear, war through local inter-state wars to civil wars to the ballot-box of the Eatanswill variety in *Pickwick Papers* to the polite but not invariably accepted codes of majority rule in a parliamentary system: they are all forms of imposition of will in a process of decision-making. Seen in this light, the nuclear era seems to have concentrated conflict in the middle and lower ends of the register, in half-fulfilled regional conflicts and civil wars of various degrees of intensity, depending on their particular context. This does not necessarily exclude future major wars. The nineteenth-century European system knew two longish periods of relative calm, between 1815 and 1854 and between 1871 and 1912, both of which led to intensely warlike phases. There is some similarity between these phases and the post-1945 one in that great-power stability combined with overseas competition and 'Balkan' conflicts has been a common feature. But the nuclear and perhaps other inhibitions on the resumption of war seem far greater now than then. It is, therefore, no longer fanciful to imagine that the world may, reluctant and unbelieving as it is, be entering into a state of uncertain and riotous *confederalism*. Confederalism is neither a state of international still less of

The strategic balance in the 1960s

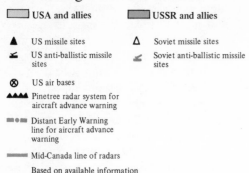

▭ USA and allies	▭ USSR and allies
▲ US missile sites	△ Soviet missile sites
US anti-ballistic missile sites	Soviet anti-ballistic missile sites
⊗ US air bases	
▲▲▲▲ Pinetree radar system for aircraft advance warning	
▬▬▬ Distant Early Warning line for aircraft advance warning	
▬▬ Mid-Canada line of radars	
Based on available information	

Strategic nuclear delivery systems 1969

Intercontinental ballistic missiles	Intermediate and medium-range ballistic missiles
submarines	strategic bombers

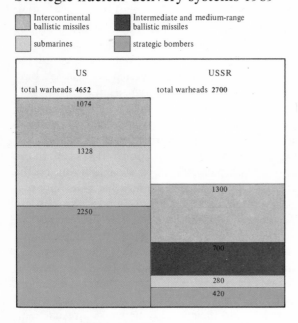

US	USSR
total warheads 4652	total warheads 2700
1074	
1328	1300
2250	700
	280
	420

Military balance 1950-68

▭ 1950   ▭ 1968

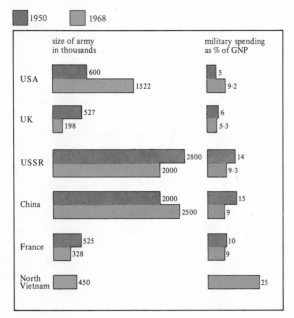

	size of army in thousands	military spending as % of GNP
USA	600 / 1522	5 / 9·2
UK	527 / 198	6 / 5·3
USSR	2800 / 2000	14 / 9·3
China	2000 / 2500	15 / 9
France	525 / 328	10 / 9
North Vietnam	450	25

supranational government, nor of peace; during the six centuries of its existence, confederal Switzerland suffered five wars between its member states, and these ended only with the coming of federation. What confederation implies, though, is a system in which there is a limit to violence. In such a system, the political process tends slowly, with ups and downs, to become more important and the logic of military power to become less so, as it is circumscribed by other factors, social, economic and generally civilian. Since the war, the day-to-day international politics of the world have turned into something which is not much further from traditional ideas of turbulent and even violent politics within a state than it is from traditional ideas of what constitute inter-state wars.

The extraordinary growth of man's power to control nature has shaped not only the structure of the world system since 1945, but the power relations between peoples. Here the time-scale for understanding has to be stretched much beyond 1945; it covers in fact the whole era of the Industrial Revolution. The received image of international relations is still permeated by nineteenth-century experiences. It is customary to think of 'great powers', 'balances', 'concerts' and 'imperialisms'. These ideas may still apply to some extent, but they have been profoundly affected by socio-cultural changes vital to the nature of peace, conflict and war.

The European great powers of the nineteenth century can be regarded as early *populist* states. They were only beginning to transform the peasantry of the pre-industrial civilization, scratching the soil near the subsistence level (there were sixteen *general* famines in a country as rich as France as late as the eighteenth century) into urbanized proletarians and *petit-bourgeois*. Such a society naturally inherited attitudes from its previous existence. At the top were to be found oligarchic, landowning and often military and bureaucratic traditions, a notion of the state as master and *owner* of lands and people. At the bottom, the first stage of what Jung has called from another point of view 'individuation', among men and women used to think of themselves as subjects on week-days and souls only on Sundays, with the most narrow local and humble horizons, was to look to the nation as the heir to the king as potential source of justice and focus for loyalty. It was this hope which made nationalism a radical force in early nineteenth-century Europe. This combination of traditional paternalism tinged with militarism at the top, and of nationalism as a primitive form of democratic and egalitarian feeling at the bottom, goes far to explain the mobilized aggression of the late nineteenth-century European states, once Germany began to threaten the mid-Victorian balance. In Europe, this aggression was inhibited, and for a long time delayed, by nationalism itself: it was a risky enterprise to violate the sense of nationality of a whole people. The contrast with the eighteenth century can be seen in the fate of Lorraine. In 1740 the French crown inherited Lorraine (a partly German-speaking province)

The US aircraft carrier *Saratoga* refuelling at speed
in the Mediterranean; (*below*) *Krokodil* cartoon, 1960, of
the US leading its unwilling allies to the brink

Moscow 1965: the USSR parades its nuclear strength

without fuss. In 1870 the annexation of Alsace-Lorraine by the German
Reich created endless trouble (even though the parts of Alsace-Lorraine
absorbed into Germany were German-speaking). Nineteenth-century
Europe was rich in successful people's wars, from the Spanish resistance to
Napoleon to the Irish resistance to Britain.

Outside Europe, however, the early populist, psychologically mobilized,
state found totally different conditions. The areas the Europeans reduced to
colonial or semi-colonial status were, in European terms, notoriously 'under-
administered', ranging from huge empires like the Chinese down to tribal
constellations in Africa. It was not just Europe's superior weapons and
techniques which loaded the dice against these societies. So did their own
habit of regarding any but local authorities as a kind of distant fate, like the
weather which looms so large in the peasant consciousness. The imbalance
between the newly mobilized European-style nation and the varieties of
old-style societies in which most of the people hardly participated, between
early industrialism and a range from Stone Age pastoralism to the higher
agrarianism, was so great that European empires were almost a form of
nature's abhorrence of a vacuum. In the later nineteenth century Britain
held India with an army of 65,000 Europeans and 75,000 Indian sepoys.

The situation has now changed at both ends of the power scale. The mass
consumer societies of today have reached a point where they present symptoms, though in ways a Marxist would hardly recognize, of a gradual
withering of the state. It is, of course, more all-embracing than ever before,
but in stretching out to cover the whole of society, it is becoming more and
more a transparency of that society. As such the state reflects both the growing multiplicity of organized group interests, and the varied individual
perceptions of interest, within it. General de Gaulle, though he seemed to
foreigners to possess an almost magic charisma, proved utterly helpless in
the face of social pressures in his own country. This was just as true at the
height of his career, with the miners' strike of 1963, as it was with the shop-
keepers' agitation on the eve of his second self-exile from power in April
1969. Much the same happened to the supposedly totalitarian regimes of
Hungary and Czechoslovakia as they collapsed from within during 1956
and 1968. One does not have to cite extreme examples such as these to see
how primitive national loyalties are giving way to more critical and varie-
gated public attitudes, attitudes which in some sense collectivize individual
rather than hierarchical conceptions of human relations. One can hardly
doubt, for instance, that between 1914 and 1970, amilitarism made enormous strides throughout the highly industrialized world. So did the belief
that all peoples have a right to self-determination. Such feelings played an
immense part both in Britain and in France in the process of decolonization
as indeed in the process which led up to colonial revolt: for the man over
whom one wished to continue to rule also had, on democratic principles,

War in Korea: (*top*) June 1950; the communist-backed North begins its push towards Pusan
Above American marines during the landings at Inchon in September 1950

Below The conference table at Panmunjom: an uneasy truce followed the armistice of 26 June 1953

to be given the kind of education which would lead him to rebellion. The sub-national community problems in Quebec, Ulster, Flanders and elsewhere are also related to stages of emancipation of under-privileged groups. The picture is further complicated by the growth of currents of transnational migration and consciousness in the industrial world especially between, say, businessmen, scientists, engineers, students, pilots, radicals and others. In short, in advanced industrial societies, the process of 'individuation' has reached a point where it makes harder once again for the state to mobilize its citizens, not because of their isolation, but because of the standards of individual self-interest they have learned in the suburbs.

At the same time, many of the once-colonized peoples have been moving out of the various forms of pre-industrial parochialism into the stage which many of the European states knew in the nineteenth century. It is difficult not to see in the revolutions of many of the developing countries, from Yugoslavia and China to Algeria, Vietnam and Biafra since the war, examples of that proto-populism, often highly authoritarian, which sometimes goes under the name of 'nation-building'. The poorer nations are beginning to develop a will to collective self-determination at a time when the richer ones are tending to move beyond that stage to one of more individual self-determination.

The changing face of empire

It follows that while the rich powers continue to be in the temperate zones and the poor in the tropical ones, so that there is a geographical continuity to the interplay of power, the nature of these relations has profoundly altered. The visible sign is the decline of the administrative landowning empires of the Europeans, confined by 1970 to their Portuguese, Spanish and settler relics, and the quite new kind of dominance exercised by the Americans in particular. This is a dominance much more of economic dynamism, cultural influence and strategic shaping of the milieu than of direct interference in the internal lives of nations and peoples. This is often called 'imperialism' and certainly carries connotations of domination and subordination. But the inadequacy of the traditional mental associations of the term are shown up by numerous paradoxes. Thus the countries that are most closely shaped by the economic dynamism, cultural influence and military framework of the United States – those of Western Europe – tend to have the least sense of being oppressed by them. This is because the internal adaptation of these nations to the American-dominated system and the partial but real exercise of joint responsibilities in international organizations common to them and the United States, are both highly developed: the Europeans are more aware than poorer countries of the United States as a diverse society, resembling their own, and less as an alien culture, backed by a state, which forces or inhibits their own development. Accordingly, it is customary to speak less of empire (though some, like President de Gaulle, have done so) than of rapidly growing and trans-national relations between industrialized societies.

There are other paradoxes. Russia, despite or because of its revolution, seems a prime example of a country where the state, heavily influenced by Tsarist tradition, is still typical of early populism and almost uniquely powerful in relation to a society with a relatively weak sense of self-determination. It may well be because Russia is, for practical international purposes, a state rather than a society, while Czechoslovakia is a society rather than a state, that the invasion of 1968 succeeded, at least in the short run, so completely. Conversely, it may be because the United States is, for international purposes, very much a society as well as a state, while Vietnam is discovering itself as a nation, that the Americans have had difficulties, to the point of virtual failure, in keeping up the war in Vietnam.

As with violence, the different societies in the world must be viewed as spreading along a spectrum of collective and individual self-determination, and not as simply of different kinds. There are, therefore, no neat patterns in their relationships. Nevertheless, whatever the wealth of variations, a world ranging from pre-industrial and early populist nation states to mass consumer societies is bound to have constellations of power utterly different from the nineteenth-century system of tribes to early populist states which still tends to govern the imagination. This socio-cultural substratum has been as important as the structure of power, with its nuclear pinnacle, in determining the nature of peace and war since 1945.

Effects of the Second World War on the world power structure

War may not solve problems, but it is certainly apt to change them. The Second World War is a particularly telling case in point. It produced at least four major changes in the system of power.

The first was that the 'defeated powers', Germany, Italy and Japan, constituted the radical right of the prewar international system. The elimination of their fascist regimes in effect left the postwar ideological stage to the reformist and revolutionary wings of the prewar system, represented by the Anglo-Americans on one side and the USSR on the other. These promptly fell out and became, in a purely political sense, the 'conservatives' and 'radicals' of the new order. The fact remained that the more neurotic prewar regimes were excised by the war and that in both West and East reform was a marked feature of the postwar generation.

The second major change was that the 'old' nations of the ruined European system, Britain and France, were in fact almost as much defeated as the official losers of the war. The effect of this was to end the European domination of world politics and create a vacuum. The expulsion of the Japanese from South-east Asia modulated almost without a break into wars of independence in Indo-China and Indonesia against France and the Netherlands; and in 1947 the British Labour government gave up the jewel in the crown of empire by according independence to India. The European retreat continued rapidly until by 1962 the grant of independence by France to Algeria at the end of six years of war wound up all the main colonial administrations of Britain, France, Belgium and Holland. The transformation was all the greater because the Europeans were not directly replaced; the end of their empires meant the end of the nineteenth-century system of colonial administration in the traditional property-owning sense. In 1914 there were only seven independent nations outside the European system. By 1970 the United Nations, which had 51 founder-nations in 1946, had swollen to 135 states. The end of the European empires was a major step towards the creation of a genuine world society.

The third change wrought by the Second World War was to leave the United States and the Soviet Union as the only two real victor nations. They emerged as world powers on a scale which dwarfed any of their predecessors. The Russian 'hordes' were matched by the new nuclear power of the United States. By 1949 the Russians too possessed nuclear weapons; and by 1953 both 'superpowers' had exploded hydrogen devices. The disparity between the resources of these two powers, in military and in the case of the United States also economic, terms and all other powers, gave the postwar system for a time a bipolar character. The East-West conflict was in part a reflection of the 'dual hegemony' of the United States and the Soviet Union as a result of the defeat of the Western European powers and Japan.

The fourth change produced by the Second World War showed, almost from the beginning, that the days of this structure of world power might be numbered. China during the war, much like Russia during the First World War, was a pre-industrial state caught in the toils of a gigantic conflict between industrial states. Like Russia in the First World War, the Chinese regime that entered the Second World War collapsed under the strain. In 1949 the communists under Mao Tse-tung finally defeated the Kuomintang government of Chiang Kai-shek, which took refuge on Taiwan, and introduced a revolutionary regime with ambitions to wipe out China's nineteenth-century humiliations at European hands and join the ranks of the superpowers. In 1970, twenty-one years after its revolution, China was far from having the international power the Soviet Union had acquired by 1938 after a similar span of time from Lenin's seizure of power. Nevertheless, the Chinese revolution, in reaction against the West, along with the spectacular

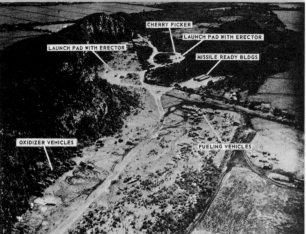

MEDIUM RANGE BALLISTIC MISSILE BASE IN CUBA

SAGUA LA GRANDE

CHERRY PICKER

LAUNCH PAD WITH ERECTOR

LAUNCH PAD WITH ERECTOR

MISSILE READY BLDGS

OXIDIZER VEHICLES

FUELING VEHICLES

The Cuban crisis, 1962: (*top*) one of the US air pictures that led to Kennedy's demand for the withdrawal of Soviet missiles in October; (*above*) the Soviet ship *Kasimov* under way to Cuba – fuselage crates were opened for US air inspection

NATO and the Warsaw Pact

☐ NATO members   ■ Warsaw pact countries

1	Belgium	9	Luxembourg
2	Canada	10	Netherlands
3	Denmark	11	Norway
4	France	12	Portugal
5	West Germany	13	Turkey
6	Greece	14	UK
7	Iceland	15	USA
8	Italy		

16	Bulgaria
17	Czechoslovakia
18	East Germany
19	Hungary
20	Poland
21	Roumania
22	USSR

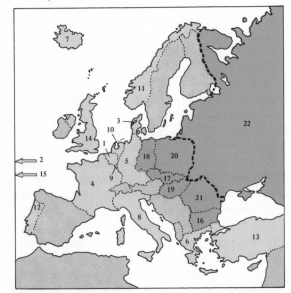

West German army parade at the Nurburgring in 1969 for the twentieth anniversary of NATO
Below A rare four exposure picture of a Russian nuclear missile being elevated to firing position

growth of Japan during the 1950s and 1960s in adaptation to it, held out the prospect of a partial and eventual shift of the world balance of power back to Asia after four centuries of European dominance.

The postwar generation, however, belonged largely to America and Russia. Similar in their huge size and victory over Germany, in all else they were a study in contrasts. The USA which shook off isolationism at the end of the war as it had not in 1919, entered the world scene from a background of 150 years of isolation and security behind the shields of the Atlantic and the British navy. The United States was immune to bombing or invasion in the war: Russia lost 20 million people in four years of terrible destruction. The United States was an island power, ruling the seas and the air: its bases were soon to ring the Eurasian land mass. The Soviet Union was land-locked in its north Eurasian heartland and, for all its power and ideological appeal, strangely isolated in its 'socialist sixth of the earth'. The United States was a society before being a state; Russia had one of the most solidly entrenched traditions of arbitrary power in the world, worthily represented by Stalin. The United States was the richest nation on earth, accounting by itself for nearly half the world's industrial output in 1948. The Soviet Union was still a backward giant struggling to catch up on a diet of Five-Year Plans. It was not altogether surprising that the one took the head of the 'satisfied' powers of the old system, now reduced to its core as the 'West', and that the other became the champion of radicals the world over in the political struggle against 'monopoly capitalist imperialism'.

Both had a postwar programme of dramatic change. That of the United States was liberal in the Anglo-American tradition, evolutionary in method and reformist-conservative in temper. The specific weaknesses of the prewar system were to be remedied to make 'the world safe for democracy'. Collective security, backed (as it had not been between the wars) by the US itself was to inhibit the vices of inter-state anarchy which had produced two wars: the United Nations set up by the San Francisco Charter in 1946, was to maintain peace through a concert of five great powers (America, Russia, Britain, France and China) in the Security Council. A new slump was to be prevented by the repair of the world's faulty international economic mechanisms: international institutions to promote free trade (the General Agreement on Tariffs and Trade, or GATT) and a world central banking system (the International Monetary Fund, or IMF) were established. The aftermath of colonialism, poverty, was also to be tackled internationally, and a series of United Nations special agencies were set up for food, health, aid and so on. All this flurry of institution-making was to have a profound and on the whole beneficial effect on the postwar system, constituting the most ambitious effort at international organization yet attempted. On the other hand, its accompanying ideology of 'one world' was soon to seem ironic in the face of what actually followed.

From the Russian point of view, a great deal of this was window-dressing in the interests of the dominant capitalist and imperialist power which was bound sooner or later to clash with the proletarian revolution, led by the Soviet Union. It is hard in the West to gauge the driving motives in Moscow at the time. In retrospect the problem seems to have been to secure the triumphant but shaken base of the world revolution and, wherever it was safe, to help ripen the conditions for the overthrow of capitalist regimes. These two aims were far from identical and in practice Stalin again and again chose to seize local power advantages rather than pursue universal aims in the Trotskyist manner. The Soviet Union recognized the Kuomintang regime in China and did nothing to help the communists come to power in 1949. The postwar takeover of Eastern Europe was carried out with ruthless single-mindedness, but the Russians did little to challenge the American sphere of influence in Western Europe although the war and its aftermath for the first time gave communist parties a mass constituency – between twenty-five per cent and thirty per cent of the electorate – in France and Italy respectively. Nevertheless much of Western Europe was in a semi-revolutionary state politically and in a parlous one materially and the sheer ideological force of communism thrust the United States, for all its material superiority, very much on the political defensive. In addition, while the Western Allies rapidly disarmed after the war, the Soviet Union maintained its forces under arms. The result was extreme tension in Europe, the only continent where the superpowers physically met and the one which both regarded as the only reservoir of industrial power which could potentially challenge their own. This was particularly the case with Germany, which was still seen as an obvious challenger for future world power. The cold war which soon followed was essentially a struggle over Germany seen as the key to Europe and Europe as the key to the balance of power.

Stalin, Roosevelt and Churchill had agreed at the Yalta Conference of February 1945 that after the defeat of Nazi Germany the area east of the Elbe would be a Russian sphere of influence and the area to the west an Anglo-American one. But the traditional Anglo-American notion of a sphere of influence did not include the tight control the Soviet Union established over Eastern Europe from March 1945 onwards. The civil war in Greece which began in 1946, the insurrectionary strikes organized in France and Italy in 1947 by the communists and above all the communist *coup d'état* in Czechoslovakia, the one Eastern European state regarded as desirably democratic in the West, all contributed to a panic fear of Stalin's ambitions in Europe. The Prague coup of February 1948 led to the signing of the Atlantic Alliance, which gave a formal American guarantee of protection to Western Europe: its aim was to complete in the security field the bolstering up of the West European regimes begun in the economic field by Marshall Aid the previous year. However, the clash which precipitated the cold war came over Germany. Originally all the wartime allies had agreed Germany should be kept as a postwar power vacuum. But economic reality and gathering storms in Europe soon impelled the Americans to begin building up the economy of the Western-occupied two-thirds of Germany, including the industrial heartland of the Reich's old war-machine, the all too symbolic Ruhr. In June 1948 the Anglo-Americans carried out the currency reform designed to get the West German economy moving again on capitalist lines and by the same token integrated it definitively in the Western system. This was the breaking-point with Russia and the Russian blockade of the Western enclave in Berlin immediately followed.

The cold war

The cold war flared up at once to incendiary heights of political violence

The divided city: (*above*) an East German poster in 1958 to celebrate the tenth anniversary of East Berlin

Below Checkpoint Charlie: the Wall stopped the flow of refugees to the West in August 1961

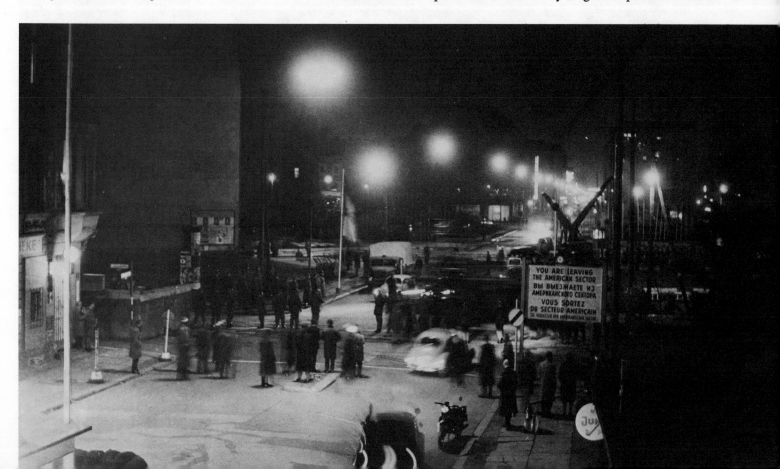

Twilight of Empires

A persistent source of unrest in the postwar
world was the break up of the great European-
ruled empires. In particular, Britain and
France showed that they no longer had the
strength or the will to preserve their empires
in the face of general hostility. Yet both
allowed themselves repeatedly to be forced into
confrontations such as Indo-China, Algeria,
Cyprus or Aden which could only end in
withdrawal. Probably the most significant
event in the post-imperial history of both
countries was the attempted occupation of the
Suez Canal zone which finally emphasized
that world opinion had turned decisively
against the methods and ideas which had
built the great empires.

Right A British soldier
searches a Jewish terrorist
suspect in the closing
months of the Palestine
Mandate, 1947

Below The British under
fire during the 1956 Suez
invasion, conducted with
all the ethics of gunboat
diplomacy but none of
its conviction

French troops towards the
end of the Indo-Chinese
War in 1954: part of
the pattern of European
losses against determined
guerrilla resistance in
South-east Asia

Left Determined British soldiers haul in a stone-throwing schoolboy during 1955 demonstrations in Cyprus

Far left Kenyan police search for Mau Mau terrorists

Left Victims of the Algerian War, brought to an end by de Gaulle in March 1962

Above Aden, 1967: Arab terrorism accompanied British reluctance to give up the military base
Left Wounded in Dien Bien Phu, 1954; the French were totally outmanœuvred by Ho Chi Minh in the only pitched battle of the war

US forces in Vietnam

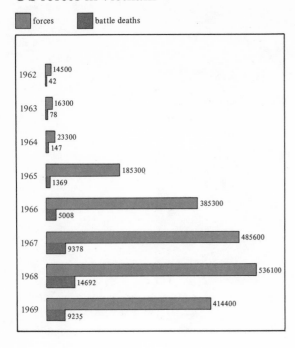

	forces	battle deaths

1962 — 14500 / 42
1963 — 16300 / 78
1964 — 23300 / 147
1965 — 185300 / 1369
1966 — 385300 / 5008
1967 — 485600 / 9378
1968 — 536100 / 14692
1969 — 414400 / 9235

The undeclared war in Vietnam became the longest sustained military engagement in US history. From the late fifties it was a story of growing involvement; hundreds of 'advisers' became thousands, then, officially, troops; defence of the democratic South gave way to direct bombing raids on the North; (*below*) bitter fighting around Hué, February 1968

which belied its adjective. Exploiting capitalism's image with much of the left as the ultimate cause of war, the Russians branded the Americans as 'warmongers'. Many believed them: fears of an American 'preventive war' were widespread even in a West Europe weary of war and power politics, especially as waged by others. Significantly, the famous dove on communist banners all over the world symbolizing the 'peace-loving' forces was designed by the most famous of all Western painters, Picasso. America's Rooseveltian New Deal image was further smirched by the domestic anti-communist witch-hunts whipped up by Senator Joseph McCarthy on the New World's first shock at being exposed to the insecurities of world power. Yet the tyranny of Stalin, successfully defied by the radical but independent-minded communists of Yugoslavia in 1948, discredited the political primitivism of the Soviet Union with all but a dwindling band of 'fellow travellers'. In this intense ideological warfare, artists and scientists often made the headlines as spies, renegades and refugees.

Yet political violence was a substitute in many ways for military risks that were not taken. There was room for doubt about this when Soviet-backed North Korea invaded American-backed South Korea in June 1950 and brought the cold war to its climax. Yet in retrospect the outstanding feature of cold war trials of strength, even during this nerve-racking phase, was the moderation of the superpowers. Both in Berlin and Korea the United States aimed merely at the 'containment' of Soviet expansion, recommended in an influential article by George Kennan published in *Foreign Affairs* in October 1947. Similarly, the Russians never pressed their advantage in the blockade of West Berlin to the point of interfering with the massive and vulnerable Allied airlift which broke the siege after a year. The Soviet Union, assumed to be the ultimate instigator of the Korean War, never actually entered the fray. Moreover, the war took place precisely because Asia was regarded as peripheral to the central issue in Europe and the US secretary of state, Mr Dean Acheson, in a speech in January 1950, had inadvertently left the impression Korea might be peripheral even to 'containment' in Asia. The central rule of the nuclear era, that armed force should be used only indirectly in the pursuit of political advantage, was paramount from the outset.

On the whole, American 'containment' succeeded both in Europe and in Korea. More accurately perhaps, Stalin's strategy failed. In retrospect it seems to have been too threatening for its caution and too cautious for its threats. The dictator's ruthlessness in Eastern Europe, his menacing postures in Central Europe, and his encouragement to aggression in Korea, united the potential opposition to his policies without overawing it. West European majority opinion swung behind Atlantic-orientated governments and the Americans returned in force to Europe: by 1959 there were over 3 million armed men in Europe (excluding Russia), a statistic which alarmed those who assumed armaments solicit war, but which in the event stabilized the continent. In Korea the US had no difficulty in gathering small contingents from many allies round its skirts in the name of the UN and collective security. By 1953, on the eve of the Korean armistice, the impetus of Stalin's policy was spent, the time was ripe for a change and, symbolically, at this juncture, the dictator died. His successors, particularly his ultimate residuary legatee in power, Nikita Khrushchev, promptly inaugurated a policy of 'peaceful coexistence', later explained to signify all-out political and economic competition short of war. This meant, on the one hand, declared nuclear prudence and an acceptance of *faits accomplis* in stabilized areas like Europe; and, on the other, the exploitation, far more subtle than Stalin's, of positions of political instability. Taking a new tack, in 1955, the Soviet Union sold a vast arsenal of arms at concession rates to Egypt, humiliated by Israel in the first Jewish-Arab War of 1948. By this one stroke it became the champion of the Arabs against Israel, broke the West's monopoly of power in the Middle East and initiated a new strategy of influence in areas beyond those contiguous with its own frontiers.

The new strategy implied that the colonial world, as it freed itself from its European masters, would become the Achilles' heel of the West, without

Top A dead North Vietnamese regular. Despite their tenacity and determination the North Vietnamese have suffered savage losses
Above A child in an individual bomb shelter in Hanoi. The US has dropped more than twice the bomb tonnage on Vietnam that it dropped during the Second World War
Below US marines in a training course; involvement in Vietnam has demoralized all sections of American society and created a massive financial burden

the superpowers having to confront one another directly. The European retreat from empire raised all kinds of uncertainties about upheavals and reversals of alignment in the ex-colonial world. This seemed highly plausible as the Dutch in Indonesia (1946-9) and the French, first in Indo-China (1947-54) and then Algeria (1954-62), failed to hold imperial bastions in long wars against indigenous guerrilla armies. Resulting expectations of crisis duly made parts of the Third World indirect battlegrounds between the superpowers themselves.

Battlegrounds for the superpowers

One such area was the Middle East, because of the virulence of the regional civil war between the Jewish settler state of Israel, victorious in three lightning campaigns of 1948, 1956 and 1967, and its defeated and humiliated but far more numerous Arab besiegers. This made it easy for the Soviet Union to gain influence as the champion of Arab irredentism and radicalism against Western 'neo-colonialism'. By 1970, with some 20,000 soldiers in the key country, Egypt, it had attained a position there almost comparable with that of the old British 'protecting' power.

The other area enmeshed constantly in cold war was Vietnam, for twenty years involved in first a war of national independence against the French from 1947 to 1954 and then a civil war between the nationalists who partitioned the country into a Northern, communist half and a Southern, anti-communist one. From the beginning, in 1954, the Americans became the patrons of the anti-communist South and by 1965 the civil war there was going so badly for the regime that they entered the fray themselves. By 1968, 500,000 American troops were involved. Like the French, they found regular armies a poor instrument for guerrilla war, so that Vietnam had an immense influence in the growth of the guerrilla mystique in the later 1960s. Yet Vietnam was in some ways an anachronism: it is doubtful that an America not committed to Vietnam at the height of the cold war in 1954 would have committed itself there ten years later.

Despite the special nature of these major cases of cold war infection, they were far from isolated. In the 1950s the communist Tudeh Party was one of the main backers of the anti-Western Iranian nationalist, Dr Mossadeq, in his abortive attempt to nationalize British oil assets in his country; and the Soviet Union gave its usual visiting card – large consignments of arms – to President Soekarno's Indonesia and to Syria and Iraq when their regimes moved to the left. The United States riposted by backing anti-communist coups which reinstated the Shah of Iran in 1955 and anti-communists in Guatemala in 1954. In the 1960s the Soviet Union tried, and failed, to gain a footing in the Congo, sold arms to the federal government in the Nigerian civil war and, throughout the decade, protected the revolutionary Cuban regime of President Fidel Castro on America's doorstep. The US helped to organize counter-insurgency campaigns to suppress communist guerrillas in Venezuela and Bolivia and in 1965 occupied the Dominican Republic to prevent an imaginary communist coup. It also backed the Indonesian generals who, in 1965, overthrew Soekarno and massacred the powerful communist party (by then China-orientated).

All this gives the impression of a non-industrial world dominated by cold war rivalries between the superpowers and indeed of a cold war dominated by their struggles in the Third World. While this competition always lay in the background, the reality was far more complex. For one thing West Europe, far from being undermined by the loss of empire, went from economic strength to strength while the process was under way. One of the revelations of the period was how little the industrial world depended, except for oil, on the non-industrial areas. Far from the loss of empire threatening peace through the ruin of Europe, it gradually looked more likely to do so through the indifference of the rich to the poor.

Moreover, in the non-industrial world itself, much of the emancipation from European rule has been carried out peacefully, particularly in British possessions and in black Africa, and without immediate cold war complications. France, for instance, failed to persuade its NATO allies of the cold

Top A new standard of guerrilla fighting brought the Cuban revolution to power in January 1959
Above Castro's chief lieutenant, Ernesto 'Che' Guevara, the Argentinian Marxist who later preferred to spread the revolution in Latin America rather than consolidate it in Cuba

Below Cuban-style freedom fighters in Rhodesia

war relevance of the struggle for Algerian independence (1954-62). Indeed, the third grand design of the postwar period was largely an attempt by the newly independent Afro-Asian powers to remove their problems from the cold war arena.

This first surfaced at the Bandung Conference of 1955, where the twenty-nine participants proclaimed the 'non-alignment' most prominently preached by India's first prime minister, Pandit Jawaharlal Nehru. The Afro-Asians and their Western sympathizers pinned many of their hopes on a new form of crisis management: peace-keeping by the UN. This reached a climax when Belgium suddenly vacated the Congo in 1960 without preparing the colony for independence so that it promptly collapsed into a chaos of competing ethnic regions. The majority in the UN pressed for UN intervention and for four years, to begin with under its energetic Swedish secretary-general, Mr Dag Hammarskjöld, the UN held the ring – and even entered it – during the transition to a more stable regime.

This vision was already becoming moribund when Mr Hammarskjöld died in an air crash in September 1961, although peace-keeping forces were still to prove useful in less controversial crises (e.g. Irian 1962, Cyprus 1964). The central obstacle has been that in crisis situations peace itself is not neutral; and neutrals who tend to support 'peace-keeping' are keen also not to take sides. This became evident when on the eve of the third Arab-Israeli War of 1967 President Nasser demanded that UNEF be withdrawn from Sinai and the UN hastily complied. Moreover, as the newly independent nations multiplied and generated their own quarrels they grew less keen for external supervision: the UN's good offices were not requested in the Nigerian civil war of 1968-70, nor indeed in the Algero-Moroccan, Indonesian-Malaysian or Sino-Indian wars of the early 1960s, all of which were short-lived but together destroyed the vision of a Third World consensus.

The Third World vision was not the only one to be in a parlous state by the early 1960s. So were the postwar grand designs of both East and West. This first became evident with the East, both economically and politically. In 1945 many, even in the West, were inclined to agree that communist-type planning might be the wave of the economic future. But by the 1960s socialist states began to find that their very progress was producing complex industrial societies increasingly ill at ease with rigid centralized planning and politics *à la russe*. Thus, while after the war politics were influenced by expectations of a renewed capitalist slump or the loss of empires and as late as 1960 Mr Khrushchev was still promising to 'overtake' the USA, by 1970 the Soviet Union itself was admitting to a technology gap with the West.

The political reversal of prestige was equally serious. The turning-point came in 1956 when Mr Khrushchev in a secret session of the Twentieth Congress of the Communist Party of the Soviet Union, denounced Stalin's 'crimes' and 'cult of personality'; then the overthrow of Stalinist regimes in Poland and Hungary exploded, in Hungary, in a revolution suppressed, after much hesitation, by Soviet tanks. The revelation of these two skeletons in Moscow's cupboard undermined its previously almost religious authority over world communism. China in particular began to challenge Moscow's ideological leadership, and Albania in Europe followed its lead. By the mid-1960s, an internally Stalinist country and member of the Warsaw Pact like Roumania could afford to flaunt its neutrality between China and Russia in ideological terms and its semi-autonomy between East and West in diplomatic ones. This poetic licence was not allowed to strategically and politically more crucial countries, as Czechoslovakia found to its cost when its experiment in liberal socialism 'with a human face' was crushed in 1968, once more, after some hesitation, by Soviet tanks. Henceforth, the Soviet Union's power in Eastern Europe was openly military, for lack of the economic and cultural magnetism the United States had exerted so naturally since the war. Radicals the world over turned finally to other gods: Maoism, Castro, the *guerrilleros*.

In the late 1950s it seemed that Western evolutionary reformism might be more successful than revolutionary Soviet rigidity: European integration,

Atlantic 'partnership' and international cooperation for the capitalist world economy seemed to go harmoniously hand in hand. This dream too did not last. Most West European powers, wanting American protection against the Soviet Union, did not follow President de Gaulle in his anti-American diplomacy of 1963-8, apparently designed to revive a continental European concert of powers under Franco-Russian patronage. But in 1969 West Germany, under a new and predominantly Social Democrat government led by Chancellor Willy Brandt, recognized the futility of hoping for reunification with East Germany on its own terms and began to 'normalize' relations with the socialist states. Though operating from under the American nuclear umbrella, this new *Ostpolitik* hinted at an increasingly individual 'European' diplomatic style. So did the efforts of West European countries to cooperate in building up their defence industries (especially aerospace) and reduce their dependence on American supplies. By 1970 there were ominous signs of a revival of protectionism between the increasingly competing economies of North America, Western Europe and Japan, after a generation of internationalism and freeing of trade.

The grand climacteric of all these cumulative changes can be isolated as 1962-3. That one year destroyed all the visions and shibboleths of cold war. The border war between China and India destroyed the notion of a coherent Third World. The veto by President de Gaulle of France on British entry into the European Common Market, expressly addressed against all forms of Western 'supranationalism' under the 'American protectorate', destroyed the hope of Western integration. Mr Khrushchev's public attack on communist China for 'warmongering' broke the idea of communist unity as the base for world revolution. In a few months all the grand designs of the immediate postwar period had been laid in ruins: history has rarely been so neat.

What has taken their place was certainly much less tidy. It is sometimes said that nationalism emerged from the maelstrom as the major force. But even this is far too simple, since many developments, such as the autonomist movements in various countries, were sub-national; while others, such as the consciousness of youth, seemed increasingly trans-national. What does seem true is that the new period was marked by attempts to adapt to changing trends rather than to construct vast blueprints, and by the emergence of

Palestinian guerrillas; in September 1970 they hi-jacked and exploded three civil aircraft and held the passengers hostage, utilizing the media in a new way to draw attention to their cause

Burning aircraft at Beirut Airport after an Israeli reprisal raid

In Portuguese Angola terrorists kill Africans who remain loyal to their white employers

Below Whites were caught up in the butchery of inter-province war in the Congo which followed independence in 1960 and the over-hasty Belgian withdrawal
Bottom Biafrans recruit for their own war of independence from Nigeria in 1968 which had its roots in pre-colonial tribal enmities

new social processes and values rather than of clear-cut policies. The post-war rites of spring seem to have come to an end in the 1960s: a new normalcy, ambiguous and evolving, took their place.

The changing face of the cold war

One of its features was the hope of gradually outgrowing the cold war between East and West. It was striking that instead of renewing the cold war, the invasion of Czechoslovakia by the Russians in 1968 was followed only a year later by Soviet negotiations with the US on Strategic Arms Limitations (SALT) and the Middle East, and with West Germany on the complex of issues dividing Europe. A major factor in this change was the growing awareness by both superpowers of the constraints placed upon them by their own nuclear weapons. 'Peaceful coexistence' *à la* Khrushchev was from the first largely motivated by the realization, once both powers had fusion weapons about 1953, that they must reach an understanding, if only of prudence. This led to the fashion for summit meetings between the leaders of the superpowers: Mr Khrushchev met President Eisenhower twice and President Kennedy once before 1961. These meetings generated clouds of cordiality soon dispersed by whiffs of verbal grape-shot, yet laid the ground for more substantial discussion after the Cuban missile crisis of October 1962. In that year the Soviet Union placed nuclear missiles in Cuba, ruled by the revolutionary regime of Fidel Castro and, in a breathless week, was forced to withdraw them under American pressure. This greatest of post-1950 crises so alarmed the contestants that it led them, by reaction, to symbolize their desire for peace by sponsoring the Treaty for the Ban of Nuclear Tests in the Atmosphere signed by 110 states by November 1963. This, and the Nuclear Non-Proliferation Treaty (NPT) which followed later cost the superpowers little, since they placed restrictions on countries reaching the nuclear threshold rather than on those, including the minor nuclear powers, Britain, France and China, which had already crossed it. The SALT talks which opened in 1969, were more significant, because if successful they would imply self-denial by the superpowers themselves and, even if unsuccessful, would be the first purely bilateral negotiations between them on matters of world-wide interest.

The superpower dialogue, slow to develop and punctuated by crises, nevertheless had great cumulative impact. First, the decision of the USSR to place nuclear caution before revolutionary zeal seems more than anything else to have focused the Sino-Soviet quarrel. By 1969 there were serious and highly publicized border incidents between the two communist giants and the Russians even hinted at nuclear strikes directed at China's nuclear potential. Second, the anxiety of the superpowers to freeze the nuclear *status quo* by the NPT was not only denounced by China and France but also created potential rifts with powers, like India and Japan, which might aspire to acquire their own nuclear deterrents. Third, the super-powers' fears of nuclear confrontation also led them to inhibit the military effects of political quarrels, as in the Middle East, which they themselves espoused. As a result, both in Europe where the political situation was relatively stabilized, and in the Middle East where it was not, the United States and Soviet Union seemed to have established ultimate, though limited, control of the context. Little by little they had elaborated a code of rules for political competition in the nuclear age which tended to create a framework for the world system and to change the political climate within it. This was particularly noticeable in Europe where the stable balance of the 1960s generated a growing desire to break down cold war barriers and restore more cordial relations.

Yet this was a far cry from the 'dual hegemony' of the superpowers which some claimed to see developing. One of the many reasons why a dual hegemony was unlikely, was the competition which remained at the heart of their 'limited adversary relationship', and that can clearly be seen in the strategic arms race of two decades. For ten years after the war America's nuclear primacy was barely challenged by the Soviet Union's limited bomber force. The spectacular success of *Sputnik I* in 1957 changed everything. It

Indo-Pakistani War in 1965: an attempt to settle once and for all the problem of Kashmir, the state that couldn't make up its mind whether to join India or Pakistan after partition in 1947

The 1967 Arab-Israeli War; perhaps the most important single symbolic gain for the Israelis was the old Jordanian sector of the holy city, Jerusalem

inaugurated the era of the intercontinental missile and of 'push-button' warfare in which distance becomes irrelevant, and showed that the Soviet Union had, or soon would have, the ability to hit American cities. This posed two problems for the USA. One was the profound shock of a successful foreign challenge to America's technological primacy and the unprecedented vulnerability of America itself. The other was the doubt that a vulnerable America would dare use nuclear weapons to defend Western Europe against a Soviet land attack. The instinctive solution to both problems was to build up an enormous lead in nuclear missiles. Duly achieved from 1962 to 1965, this was to restore the image of American 'superiority', threaten Soviet nuclear forces with near-total destruction and so deter the Soviet Union from taking any political chances. Yet the lead thus regained became eroded after 1965 precisely because the Americans began to judge 'superiority' to be an illusion. For in operational terms, a balance had been reached in which neither side could prevent the other from inflicting the apocalypse on its cities, even if it landed a surprise blow first. Theoretically, and at great cost, technical advances in missiles in the 1970s might give an absolute advantage to the surprise attacker. But such highly uncertain innovations were open to both superpowers, so that rather than conferring supremacy on either they simply made both more vulnerable. In the circumstances it was safer to maintain the balance of mutual vulnerability which already inhibited both sides from military adventure and even seemed sufficient to protect Western Europe so long as sizeable ground forces, American and European, were stationed there to deter an easy Soviet land attack. The United States had virtually resigned itself to conceding 'parity' to the USSR if that would produce agreement in the SALT talks. 'Parity' also loomed – more remotely – at sea, where the Soviet Union had been building up its once outclassed navy. Despite lack of air cover, this gave it a potentially global presence it lacked at the height of cold war. In short, the Soviet Union had eroded American nuclear and naval supremacy without losing its own superiority on land. It was not plain what effect this would have on world politics. Would the Soviet Union be able to use armed power for political purposes in areas contiguous to its own frontiers more effectively than the US, disenchanted with the role of world policeman, across the seas?

The diffusion of power

Another reason for scepticism about a dual hegemony was the rapid diffusion and diversification of power during two decades of unprecedented growth throughout the world. No state would be able to challenge the nuclear supremacy of the superpowers in the next decade. But China could have a modest force of intercontinental missiles by the mid-1970s and Japan a sizeable force within ten years of deciding to deploy one. It was plain the superpowers would not control Asia as they did Europe or even the Middle East. Moreover, the nuclear stalemate between the superpowers itself tended to give more importance to other, more civilian or political, forms of power where the relative hierarchy might be quite different from the military one. Economic centres like West Europe and Japan, for instance, were exerting an increasing pull, the one on the Mediterranean and Africa, the other on South-east Asia. There were also minor but fiercely independent centres, such as Yugoslavia, Algeria and Vietnam, that were not easily susceptible to great-power pressures. Other states had an ideological magnetism, so that not only China but small countries like Cuba or Peru could for a while exert a strong pull. This in turn was an expression of the social forces, sub-national and trans-national as well as national, which might gradually transform the system from within. They burst on the world as a new force in the mini-revolutions which swept the university campuses of many countries in 1968.

All such 'crises de civilisation' as André Malraux called this, are in some sense mysterious. But part of the story is probably that a generation which, in the industrial world, had dreamed of socialism and, in the colonized areas, of the sunlit era after liberation, was rapidly disillusioned by the

Russian cartoonists in the early sixties made full use of anti-nuclear demonstrations in the West

realities of Stalinism and independence. Radicals the world over had been deprived of their expected consummations. Significantly, it was in Latin America, with its exquisite frustration of feeling colonial without being actually colonized, that the tide began to turn with the advent of Castro, the romantic radical guerrilla, seizing power in Cuba in 1959 and thereafter singeing the beard of Uncle Sam. Guerrilla prestige was further swelled after 1965 by the success of the Vietnamese in bogging down the United States in a war which destroyed the American sense of omnipotence which followed on victory over Russia in the Cuban missile crisis. The success of the radical and youthful opposition in America to the Vietnam War in effectively forcing President Johnson to abdicate added a new technique to the guerrilla appeal. The next step was radicalism for the TV flash, and the fashion for hijackings and kidnappings of diplomats, both techniques devised in Latin America. A new style of international radical politics was borne on the invisible waves of modern communications: Vietnam has been dubbed the 'first television war'.

Although by 1970 the style and consciousness of the New Left seemed universal, the 'low-level violence' associated with it can hardly be viewed as a coherent phenomenon. The many successful military coups in Africa were the sign of the lack of any other structure of relatively equitable administration: they were part of nation-building. The numerous wars between hill tribes and central governments, particularly in South-east Asia, seemed a form of resistance precisely to 'nation-building'. Violence in some parts of Latin America, on the other hand, was beginning to seem socially purposive in nations which had already plunged relatively strong roots: about the same time had elapsed since Bolívar as between the effective unification of Britain and France under absolute monarchy and their great revolutions. The regional civil wars of the Middle East and Southern Africa were something else again: the mutual rejection symptoms of local civilizations and the alien settler communities left behind by the ebb of European empire. None of these really seemed to resemble the conditions behind urban and student violence in industrial countries. All these distinctions between different forms of violence might be academic for world security if their effects were tending to converge, and it was sometimes assumed they were. But this might not be so. Much of the evidence suggested they might actually be diverging.

British CND marchers to Aldermaston: under a peace umbrella the movement became a focus for a wide variety of social protest

UN forces temporarily stabilized the situation in Cyprus in 1964, when violent rioting between the Greek and Turkish communities brought Greece and Turkey to the verge of war

Kennedy signing disarmament legislation: the US and USSR agreed in July 1963 to ban all but underground nuclear tests. By 1970 it seemed clear that an effective means of banning nuclear proliferation had yet to be found

Regional civil wars, revolving round exotic settler states, could be major threats to world security. This is probably not the case with hill-tribe wars and perhaps not even with Latin American violence. Paradoxically, Latin American nationalism seems so well rooted that it is harder for the United States to impose its own will and also less necessary for it to fear the Soviet Union might do so. In fact, despite the guerrilla mystique, the trend in many non-industrial countries seems to be towards a preoccupation with efficiency or to a radical nationalism by-passing the guerrillas. Che Guevara, the archetype of the anarchist guerrilla terrorizing reaction at home and a great power abroad, or Mao Tse-tung leading the young into the second, 'cultural', revolution in China against his own bureaucrats, may be folk-heroes for the New Left throughout the world. But Guevara died in the Bolivian jungle in 1967 because he could not rouse the peasants, and even radicals have interpreted the move to urban terrorism in Latin America as a retreat. Recent change has come either from the top, with the new military regime in Peru since 1968, or through the ballot-box as in Chile in 1970. The fact that at the end of 1970 General Franco in Spain and the courts in Russia reprieved in the one case Basque autonomists and in the other Jewish hijackers who would probably have been executed not so long since may be a sign that the national and world-wide restraints on state power are beginning to erode even the most authoritarian regimes. But this may mean the very contrary of revolution: it may mean evolution.

Cold war pointers to the future

The very presentation of the rich confusions of the 1960s depends on one's interpretation of the postwar period. It is common ground that the world is becoming increasingly interdependent and shaped by technologies which respect no frontiers, cultural or material. But from there on, many views are possible. One is that the caution instilled by nuclear weapons, the increasingly widespread rejection of war in industrial societies and the limitation of conflict within certain bounds, mean that while turmoil will continue, it will resemble conflict as known in the past within nations rather than 'war' between states as accepted since the days of Louis XIV. The struggle for justice and greater equality, even as 'low-level violence', will not spell the breakdown of the international system so much as introduce a new and more political phase: historically, social violence has been associated at least as much with change inside states as with war across frontiers. For all the turmoil that remains, this represents progress of a kind.

Another view, however, might be that depression, Nazism and world wars were symptoms of the failure to elaborate effective international institutions for what was already a highly interdependent world. The early postwar period, reacting to this, produced the greatest step forward to such institutions the world has yet known. This was partly rooted in a revulsion from the aberrations of the prewar period, and so was closely related to the lack of violence within industrial societies. Now time has passed, and the very progress of the world has produced new forces to strain the system to the utmost. Violence at the level of political habit could combine with the latent anarchy of a renewed great-power concert to produce nationalism, imperialism, breakdowns and even major war. Were it not for the inhibitions of nuclear weapons, the present trend could seem to resemble the process which led the Victorian era, so full of hope, blindly towards 1914. Can nuclear weapons alone cancel imbalances inherent in such a system?

The experience of the postwar period cannot answer the question. What it does suggest, however, is that interlocking hierarchies of international arrangements, each appropriate in aims, means and membership to the particular task in hand, and all forming a kind of architecture, however baroque, of rules and institutions, will be needed to turn the technological peace of nuclear terror into a political peace of accepted political process. The issue is not to end conflict, which is inherent in life itself, but to civilize the frame within which it is pursued. From this point of view, and despite all the caution events have taught us, the quarter of a century after the terrible failure represented by two world wars does give grounds for hope.

Peter Worsley

Problems of the 'Have-not' World

The divisions of a unified world

The 'haves' and the 'have-nots': what simpler and more realistic model of the world could there be? Yet the model is problematic, for it is a dichotomous view of the world, which, for all its usefulness, is only one of a number of ways of cutting up the same reality. To say this is not to spin academic conceptual webs for their own sake, for nothing is more real, nothing more of an institutionalized fact, shaping the lives of all of us, than the other major dichotomy that we experience and use as a way of dividing up the world: the distinction between the capitalist and communist countries – the 'First' and 'Second' Worlds.

Here, then, are two different dichotomies: rich and poor, capitalist and communist. Each is clearly useful, and in the past they have coincided. Before the 1950s, communist countries were poor countries (though few poor countries were communist); rich countries, capitalist countries. This is no longer so: there is now an advanced communism and the communism of the 'world's countryside', as Lin Piao called it – the communism of the USSR and Eastern Europe on the one hand, and that of China on the other. Lodged uneasily between these two giant variants is a further set of state communisms in poor countries: those of North Korea, North Vietnam and Cuba (which significantly do not closely identify themselves with small communist powers, such as Czechoslovakia, when these latter are both industrialized and European – as, notoriously, when Cuba supported the USSR over the latter's invasion of Czechoslovakia).

Most poor countries are not communist; many are strongly anti-communist. Despite this division, both sets of countries continue to share common interests that derive from a colonial past that only ended in the 1960s for many of them, and from a continuing present condition of underdevelopment. 'Ex-colonialism' still provides a common identity for countries which are now constitutionally independent, but which – as the term 'neo-colonialism' implies – have not yet seriously acquired the same degree of control over their economic situation that they have over their internal political institutions. Economic and political ties still connect them not only to the former metropolitan imperialist countries, but also to the other new states that were formerly subject to the same imperial power. There are still French troops in independent Chad, British administrators in independent Kenya, Belgian businessmen in the independent Congo republic, as well as Congolese students at Louvain, Ivoriens at the Sorbonne, and Sudanese at Manchester.

In discussing world society, we normally consider only international relations, assuming the crucial unit always to be the society or country. More accurately, we should speak of 'inter-societal' or 'inter-state' relations, for nationality, or ethnic identity, by no means necessarily coincides with the state. There are nationalities, and so-called 'tribes', within state boundaries – usually discounted and sometimes suppressed. And there are other relationships that transcend the nation-state, notably ties of religion (particularly Buddhism, Christianity and Islam) and those of 'continental' identity, since whole continents have shared closely in the parallel experience of conquest, colonization, and the achievement of independence, and remain linked together by common economic and political life-situations. Thus Latin American governments associate, partly due to their common roots in Spanish and Portuguese conquest and their common liberation in the early nineteenth century, but much more because their contemporary

Famine in the Dahomey: the sixties saw an ever widening gap between the 'haves' and 'have-nots'. The major powers spent twenty-five times as much on arms as on official aid

43

Development line 1970

■ mechanized rich ■ rural poor

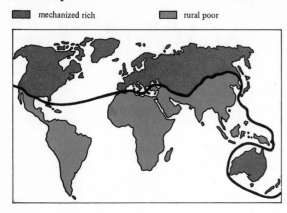

identity is shaped *vis-à-vis* the United States, to which governments look for support against a rising revolutionary tide, and against which revolutionaries contend, seeing the USA as the common enemy of all, and dreaming of the liberation of the whole continent: a second stage of the liberation achieved under Bolívar. An African continent is emerging from a past of slavery and colonization with a new self-consciousness of African identity that extends to the descendants of Africans now living in Harlem or Trinidad. Such identities are by no means merely nostalgic or abstract sentiments: they are real enough to support an Organization of African Unity, and to drive a middle-class Argentinian doctor, Che Guevara, to immerse himself in the revolutionary struggles of Guatemala, Cuba and Bolivia.

Many of these memberships overlap. Most African countries are both 'poor' and 'non-communist'; most rich countries 'capitalist' and 'Christian'. In the high colonial era, if you were high on the totem-pole on one criterion, you tended to be high on all others – and vice versa. Life was simplified, and its dimensions congruent with one another. The whole system was standardized on the basis of the 'uniform of colour' stamped on the body. The diversity of past cultures: of historic empires, feudal regimes, Asiatic despotisms, tribes, crusading world-religions and local cults, all became reduced to this simple, de-historicized common denominator. As Jean-Paul Sartre put it: 'Not very long ago, the earth numbered two thousand million inhabitants: five hundred million men, and one thousand five hundred million natives.'

The brief era of Euro-American imperial domination of the world was thus a very simple order: a world in which the 'Lords of Human Kind', as V.G.Kiernan has called the white colonizers, conquered the world and reduced the conquered to a common dehumanized denominator, no longer Mahrattas, Trobrianders, Sioux or Vietnamese, but an homogenized product: the Native. A 'product', because as one of them, Frantz Fanon, has said so ragingly: 'The settler and the native are old acquaintances. In fact the settler is right when he speaks of knowing "them" well. For it is the settler who has brought the native into existence and who perpetuates his existence.'

Since the Second World War, however, older cultural identities have been revived and invested with new significance: religious ones (such as Islam), ethnic ones (*négritude*), historic-cultural (the rebirth of Ghana, Mali or Zimbabwe, or the identification of young intellectual urban guerrillas in Uruguay with Tupac Amaru, the leader of an Indian revolt against the Spaniards in far-off Peru in the distant eighteenth century). In place of the monolithic orthodoxy imposed on Eastern Europe, Roumania, Poland, Czechoslovakia, and even nationalities within the USSR once more flex their limbs.

Today nation and state usually coincide, but nationalism often precedes statehood, and 'submerged nationalities' continue to struggle for self-determination within states whose authority they reject. The 'established' nationalism – the nation-state – has become the dominant unit of action in the modern world. Many new states are equally new nations.

But if the nation-state is the chief structural unit of analysis and action, the stage on which the action takes place is by no means set by the frontiers of states, for both the newly independent and the long-established find themselves part of world-wide political and economic structures. Cultures, as well as organized structures, also easily leap across national boundaries: the appeals of communism, for instance, transcend the more parochial appeals of mere nationalism, powerful as the latter are. When yoked together, the ensuing mixture has proved especially powerful. Communism, however, exists in institutionalized, as against purely ideological, forms: as a set of states as well as a set of movements or parties within non-communist polities. The major communist powers have claimed an authority that also overrides purely national limits, as the Czechs and the Hungarians have come to know only too well, for countries on the marches of the USSR constitute a communist Russian sphere of influence, recognized by NATO,

Frantz Fanon (1925-61): author of *The Wretched of the Earth* and advocate of Third World freedom from the West; 'for it is the settler who has brought the native into existence and who perpetuates his existence'

The Third World rejects the others
Above Biafrans protest at both British and Russian involvement in the war with Nigeria
Left In practice Afro-Asian solidarity often means anti-Americanism (Malagache cartoon)

Below In Dar-es-Salaam a pro-Tanzania demonstration against Britain and the US; but in the first five years of independence Tanzania accepted economic aid from all quarters

a kind of *de facto* semi-'empire', different in kind from the imperialism described by Lenin or Hobson in that its *raison d'être* is the maintenance of a set of defensive outworks which are a striking reverse-image of the *cordon sanitaire* created by the imperialist powers after 1917. Equally, American imperialism has come to exhibit increasing impatience with the niceties of national rights or international law within its spheres of influence, whether the country concerned be the Dominican Republic, Cambodia or Laos.

Indeed, nothing could be further from the plans of these giant powers, for all their colossal resources of materials, population and internal market, than archaic notions about 'autarky' or 'isolationism'. Economically, they know that they need the outside world. Since 1945, they have both been engaged in a struggle for world hegemony. But one new factor has emerged: neither wants a world war in which both would be destroyed.

Though the nation-state may be the typical actor, the action of the play is going on in Djakarta, Algiers, Washington, Moscow and Lima simultaneously. The world has become what it never was before the nineteenth century – a single social system. The process of unification began with the 'booty capitalism', to use Max Weber's term, of the mercantilist age: the international brigandage, 'primitive accumulation', loot and piracy on a magnificent scale, of a Cortés or a Pizarro; but it reached its climax with modern imperialism, when societies based on machinofacture, as Marx called it, turned outwards in the search for markets, cheap labour and materials, and, later, as loci for investment and profitable returns on capital.

In our day, the whole process of world unification has been further speeded up by virtue of changes other than the specifically political and economic, important, indeed central as these latter remain. The arrival of vastly more efficient and speedy means of communication has turned the whole world into what Marshall McLuhan has graphically called a 'global village'. This very night, hundreds of thousands of villagers in the most remote corners of Tanzania will be listening to music, comedy, and to world news, just as tens of millions of Europeans and North Americans watched the Battle of Hué from the comfort of their living-rooms, directly, as it was being fought. Television and radio are not just furniture of the house, but furniture of the mind. They make men part of a new social world. Few today could refer to Cuba or Vietnam in the way that Mr Chamberlain, prime minister of Britain in 1938, referred to the conflict between Czechoslovakia and Nazi Germany as 'a quarrel in a faraway country between people of whom we know nothing'.

The Third World

If, since 1945, technology has unified the world, politics, economic interests, history and culture still divide it. Communism and capitalism – the First and Second Worlds – were familiar enough before 1939.

In the immediate postwar years, five major events took place, four of them in Asia, which foreshadowed the pattern of subsequent decades: India, Burma and Ceylon became peacefully independent; Indonesia fought a successful revolution of independence against the Dutch; Indo-China's revolution began and remained uncompleted; and communism came to power in China, the largest country on earth. Finally, in 1952, Nasser deposed King Farouk and forced Britain finally to abandon its political grip on Egypt, joining other independent states like Saudi Arabia, and newer ones like Syria and the Lebanon, in outright hostility to an Israeli state founded in 1948.

The emergence of newly independent ex-colonial states and of world-wide nationalist and revolutionary independence movements shifted the whole focus of world events out of Euro-America, made Korea, Vietnam and Cuba the flashpoints, and brought into being a novel entity, the 'Third World'. Where, then, did the 'have-nots' of the Third World locate themselves, and where have we put them? Significantly, French usage differs from the English: in francophone countries, the *Tiers Monde* embraces all underdeveloped countries *including* communist states; in Anglo-American usage, it has usually referred to the 'non-aligned' countries, i.e. those which

have recently won independence, for the most part, but which are not communist. The concept of the Third World has always continued this ambiguity: at the Bandung Conference of 1955 China was most prominent, other members were anti-communist, and a third set 'neutralist'.

And there have been sub-groupings of non-aligned powers: the unlikely association of a Muslim Middle Eastern country, the United Arab Republic – a defector from the imperialist bloc – with Yugoslavia, not a recently ex-colonial power, but a European country defecting from Russian communism. India was the third member of this grouping, which thus cut across continents, ethnic divisions, political ideologies and social systems.

No single timeless model of the Third World, will do, then; neither will any absolute model of world society, whether it be a dichotomous one of 'rich' versus 'poor', 'capitalist' versus 'communist', or a trichotomous one of three 'worlds' – capitalist, communist and Third World.

The communist world has become split between the two major varieties of communism, advanced-industrial (Russian) and agrarian-revolutionary (Chinese) – the communism of the rich and the communism of the poor. Nor have we been able by any means to ignore the smaller communisms, in a world where Cuba has inspired a whole generation of Guevarist-Castroites across the world, and established a lighthouse of revolution off the coast of Latin America, and where North Vietnam and the NLF, in a country of some 37 million peasants, has fought the greatest power in the history of the world to a standstill.

Any viable model of the changing system has to include all these inter-secting memberships and take account of the fact that different member-ships become relevant in different situations. Thus Arab identity (more widely, Muslim identity) has been regularly activated *vis-à-vis* Israel. But where communism has been the issue, those who are friends over Israel have parted company: King Hussein retaining his Western links, the UAR its association with Russia, and the Palestinian guerrillas taking support from China.

Those hostile to the concept and practice of 'non-alignment' have had an easy time demonstrating that this group of powers has been internally divided by all kinds of rivalries, general and specific. Of course any group of powers, such as NATO or the Warsaw Pact, exhibits internal divisions; on a higher level of abstraction, all social systems are inherently differentiated, and there is no neat 'fit' between the component parts in every situation. Nevertheless some societies are more consistent than others: to be black in South Africa also means to be poor, to be excluded from trade unions, churches and political parties, to have little if any formal education, etc.; to be white is to be comfortably off, well educated, to have the vote, and so forth. In inter-societal terms, despite internal divisions, NATO and the Warsaw Pact act effectively in concert, whereas the Afro-Asian powers do not: the First and Second Worlds have been blocs, politically, economic-ally and militarily coordinated. The Third World has not so much been a bloc as a 'grouping'.

It has not, for example, been able to create customs unions, common markets or standing armies. Its political activities have been its most visible aspect, but conferences of the non-aligned have been few and far between, and there has been no effective continuing infrastructure of a secretariat (though sets of Third World countries have established such machinery for coordinating policy, e.g. the Organization of African Unity). Finally, attendance even at the periodic conferences of the non-aligned has become increasingly unimpressive, and there has been a tendency for the serious disputes either to result in splits or non-recognition of one or the other party, withdrawal or avoidance. In the extreme, internal tensions became so great that the conference planned for Algiers in 1965 was abandoned.

There has been an underlying pattern, however, to these successive splits over particular issues, for they have all tended to fall along the same line of cleavage: that between the 'militants' and the rest. The militants have tended to look for aid, material and spiritual, to the communist countries.

Top 'Peoples of the world unite' (Chinese poster)
Above Nehru, the key figure in early Afro-Asian movements, speaks at an Asian conference in Delhi (1949) to discuss Dutch 'police actions' in Indonesia
Below A Dutch cartoon shows a wolfish Chou En-lai listening to Soekarno at Bandung in 1955

Top In Belgrade, 1961, Nehru, Nasser and Tito; Nehru attempted to extend the group of non-aligned countries into Europe and to make peace rather than colonialism the conference issue

Above A Ghana stamp issued to mark an Organization for African Unity meeting in 1965, two years after its foundation

A Cuban poster for Third World unity

They have not necessarily been familiar with dialectical materialism, nor necessarily highly enamoured of the idea of eliminating private ownership. Their main current problems are not the shortcomings of remote communist countries, but their own pressing internal problems of economic development, as primary producers largely trading within the capitalist world. In such a situation, a friend who responds to need is a friend indeed.

The non-militants, conversely, have stayed close to their former masters. The most powerful links holding them together are no longer the apparatus of direct political control, i.e. colonial institutions, but the invisible bonds (and chains) of the market. For raw materials-producing colonies which have become politically independent have not been similarly able, overnight, to modernize agriculture, develop industry or alter the world price for cocoa. However much internal political power has become concentrated in the hands of the new élites, even in single-party or military regimes, most of the decisions which vitally affect the fortunes of the country are not taken by them, but by men in Washington, London, Paris, Brussels and Amsterdam. They are part of a world-market system in which they are very small fry indeed.

The world system which has emerged since 1945, then, has been very much a *political* economy, dominated by the struggle between two major blocs, each, in turn, dominated by a single superpower, with China coming up on the rails as an independent force of immense potential.

The Gallic use of the term 'Third World' to include all the poor countries, communist and otherwise, is a usage which captures a very important part of the relationship between the rich and the poor, i.e. that this is a major geological fault, at times far more important than differences of ideology, social and political system.

When China speaks of the 'world's countryside', it is precisely this concept she is expressing: that of an identity shared by all the 'wretched of the earth', not merely by communist revolutionaries. It is an identity which explains the strange phenomenon of military élites flirting with China, or quite conservative political leaders in the Third World using the rhetoric of Marxism. More than this, this common identity has revealed itself in practical situations where the common interests of the underdeveloped countries stand opposed to those of the wealthy powers. The most crucial arena where this has occurred has been at the sessions of the United Nations Conference on Trade and Development, where the '75' (later '77') poor countries have repeatedly voted together against the USA and the UK.

This economic pressure has been the major indication of the collective presence of the Third World on the international stage in recent years. In the 1950s and early 1960s their common interests were political rather than economic: the struggle for colonial independence was the prime preoccupation of the Third World states, governments-in-exile and pressure groups which gathered at the United Nations. Political pressure is still being exerted concerning the remaining colonial territories, though more particularly those independent states like South Africa and Rhodesia where white minority rule displays the basic social and political features of the classic colony. But despite all this, coordinated political action by Third World countries has not been notable, and the divisions within the Third World have perhaps been more evident. For ex-colonial countries which have themselves achieved their political independence are now primarily concerned with their problems of economic development. UNO itself is no longer the vital forum for international relations that it was in the early 1960s. The last major General Assembly session was that of 1960 at which Khrushchev slammed his shoe on the desk and Fidel Castro's retinue made themselves at home in Harlem.

Meetings of the non-aligned themselves now take place virtually unnoticed, a decline as real as it has been secular since the highpoint of Bandung in 1955, when it seemed to some that a new balancing force between the superpowers might be coming into existence.

Finally, to cap this story of decline and fall, the sixties were the decade of the most significant failure in terms of collective efforts on an international

Above CARE a voluntary US relief organization launched in the early 1950s sent food and gifts overseas from Americans on a personal basis
Below Uncle Sam the hypocrite: a Pakistani caricature of American aid

Below A Colombo Plan conference session in Singapore; during the fifties the Plan provided for economic aid to Asian states from the US, Japan, Britain and Commonwealth countries

scale to abolish world poverty without fundamental transformation of established political and social structures, for this was the 'development decade' that never took place. Nor is there any good reason to assume that the second 'development decade' will be any more effective.

Aid and development

In so far as this failure has been a failure of aid policy, some examination of the philosophy and practice of aid is called for. It is no vulgar cynicism to observe that aid is not philanthropy. It is a form of social exchange, to understand which the economists' way of working out the costs and benefits is quite inadequate. What is exchanged certainly includes capital, material goods and services; what is much more crucial is the maintenance or creation of an interdependence, both economic and political, that has consequences for the future. In the extreme, grants may be given to poor countries, free of interest, with no conditions imposed that they be spent in purchasing goods of the donor country; here, the crucial exchange may be a flow of material aid in one direction, and a flow of quite immaterial political support, a sense of obligation, even gratitude, in the other direction, all of which constitute powerful political gains for the donor country.

Aid generates economic as well as political dependence. More aid is now taking the form of grants, not loans (at the end of 1970 grants made up about sixty per cent of official aid; loans forty per cent). Those loans which are given at rates of interest below normal commercial rates of course contain a 'grant' element to that extent. But most do not. Loans have to be repaid; they are no more charity than is money-lending. And they have to be repaid with interest. The result is that interest charges on past loans have accumulated over time to the extent that underdeveloped countries are now spending the equivalent of ten per cent of their export earnings in servicing loan-debts.

The 'donor' country further exercises politico-economic influence over the recipient in so far as some or all of the credits have to be expended in the donor country, thus providing a powerful stimulus to the export trade of that country. Some sixty per cent of official aid is 'tied' aid of this kind. About half of the aid in official statistics, too, is made up of private investment. A good deal of direct or indirect influence is also exercised in the very process of implementing the loan. The donor country does not simply hand over a cheque: it insists on feasibility studies to see if the monies that it is being asked to provide will be put to good use: pre-investment surveys are usually carried out to examine the economic and social viability of a set of specified projects, rather than a merely general indication that the loan will be expended on 'agricultural development'. Such surveys are particularly meticulous where the operation proposed is a large-scale one, such as the building of a hydro-electric dam, the setting up of a medical school or a family-limitation campaign. The negotiation of a general loan between an underdeveloped country and a rich one may involve an 'opening of the books' of the poor country to an extent which seems degrading to countries super-sensitive about their newly found independence, but which now find themselves visited by experts from the very powers, often, whose direct rule they have escaped from. In mounting pre-investment surveys (usually with some – often quite token – representation of experts from the country whose projects are being studied), and because they are in a position to approve or disapprove of the proposed investment in the end, the donor power obviously exercises considerable influence over crucial economic decisions, whatever the constitutional or *de facto* internal political strength of the government seeking the aid.

It is common for loans to cover a long list of named projects. It is equally common to label such a list of projects a 'Plan'. A 'Plan', however, may be anything from a mere putting together on paper of dozens of separate projects, to an interrelated set of projects, deliberately designed to be launched together so as to take the economy and society in a specified direction. Again, 'Plans' vary according to the degree to which they are, at one pole, merely 'indicative' – either indicating the areas in which the

Krokodil gives the Russian view of emerging Africa (1960)

In Ghana under the Nkrumah regime (1957–66) Chinese instructors trained potential revolutionaries for other Asian and African nations

government would *like* to see investment or in which concessions (e.g. in the form of tax concessions) or inducements are used to encourage the desired kind of investment – or, at the other, highly centralized, rigidly planned specifications of production-targets for every branch of industry and each unit of production. The latter type of planning, of course, was characteristic of the Stalin era in the Soviet Union. It has not been imitated in the new communist countries outside Europe, since these turned to communism largely after the Stalin era and were well aware of the short-comings of this over-bureaucratized mode of economic organization, as well as the unacceptable social, political and human consequences entailed. Thus Cuba found Czech methods of running a planned economy to be disastrous and rapidly terminated the experiment.

But non-communist underdeveloped countries have still been faced with the same need to modernize quickly; this spells state planning, for they are attracted by the 'demonstration effect' of the USSR and of China as agrarian countries which have lifted themselves up by their own bootstraps. However much many of the new regimes have feared, even abhorred, communist society, they could not fail to be impressed by the emergence of the Soviet Union as the second greatest power in the world in just over thirty years, and the even more relevant emergence of agrarian China as a major power in only twenty years.

In the immediate post-independence period, a set of short-term crises occurs. A major one arises because there are usually too few nationals capable of filling gaps left by expatriate administrators.

To people in the developed countries, the presence of British nationals working in the inner sanctums of Nigerian or Malawian ministries is taken to be quite unremarkable: it is merely a continuation of a tradition that goes back into the history of the colonial era. But it is precisely this connection that rankles. The British would be unlikely to accept, without twinges of suspicion or wounded pride, Greeks or Turks, let alone Malawians or Nigerians, working on contract in their sacred ministries in Whitehall. And where an 'unacceptable' country provides the Third World with precisely similar services – as with the Chinese on the Tanzania-Zambia Railway – indignant allegations of political influence and photographs of those foreign nationals at work in Africa are to be found in all the newspapers. To the nationals of the states in question, of course, Chinese are not more or less 'foreign' than are Canadians or Israelis. The training of hundreds of indigenous future higher civil servants thus becomes an early priority. But short-term answers have been found to these short-term problems: the shortfall has usually been met by swallowing national pride and hiring expatriates on contract or by recruiting them from countries other than that of the former colonial power.

Once trained, such administrators have usually been engaged in laying the foundations, on paper at least, for planned development, and specialized planning machinery is set up. Where costly capital-intensive projects are called into being, as with the Volta River Dam Project in Ghana, many different branches of government, and the lives of large numbers of people, are affected in many different ways. Thus dam-construction – a large enough operation in itself – further involves electricity generating and the rational economic use of such energy (whether industrial or domestic); the use of water to irrigate unused arid lands; the relocation of population from the flooded areas and the moving of other populations to newly usable land; the building of access and feeder roads, and a thousand and one other major and minor operations.

Whether the project be large-scale or small-scale, however, the donor country remains a significant force even when the investment has actually taken place, for the equipment will normally come from the donor country and will continue to be serviced from there. It makes sense in terms of economies of scale and cutting overhead costs to buy more of the same, if the equipment is technically satisfactory. Military equipment is the most obvious case, where weapons are not standardized internationally, and Russian tanks will not take American shells. Personnel are further required

49

The Brazilian FURNAS hydro-electric project, one of the largest in Latin America during the sixties, was financed with the help of World Bank loans

Below In northern Thailand Japanese experts in lacquer manufacture have brought ILO technical assistance
Bottom A British VSO volunteer helps Indians drill wells

to do servicing or maintenance on the spot. Those countries whose supply of modern machinery spares and replacements gets cut off – notably the case of Cuba, a country formerly heavily dependent on American suppliers – experience acute problems of substitution.

The reference to military supplies should remind us that the greater part of aid has not contributed seriously to maximizing either production or consumption directly. World aid figures usually exclude or conceal the flow of purely military aid. But a whole vocabulary of motives needs to be spelt out before we accept the assumptions lying behind the very distinction between 'military' and 'non-military' or 'political' aid and 'aid without strings', for quite humane programmes to improve the health or the food-consumption of the civilian population may, at one level, be part of a general strategy of winning over such a country as an ally, or, by enabling it to put its house in order internally, to make it a more effective political or military ally. Finally, there is usually a direct connection between the provision of aid and the geopolitical strategic interests of the disbursing countries. Conversely, there is no coherent relationship between the pattern of aid-flow and the extent to which the internal political and social systems of the recipient countries coincide with that of the donor. In the game of international patronage, hard cash is exchanged for political support, and ideals are treated as subsidiary variables, something with which political romantics can afford to delude themselves, but not politicians. Western aid has by no means gone to the more democratic states in the Third World: it has flowed strongly towards such authoritarian regimes as South Korea, Thailand, and South Vietnam in Asia; in Latin America, to Brazil and Argentina, where military regimes have displaced parliamentary-democratic ones; and even in Europe, to Greece and Spain. Equally cynically the Chinese People's Republic has supported 'feudal' or military regimes in Burundi and Pakistan, and the USSR has poured money and armaments into the UAR, where indigenous communists languish in gaol.

Revolution

Aid programmes of this kind are unlikely to diminish the social inequalities that give rise to political protest. For the poor countries, faced with an ever-widening gap between themselves and the rich countries, the prospects for revolution might appear to be as right as Chou En-lai declared them to be for Africa in 1964. Subsequent events have not borne out his predictions. In most of black Africa, military regimes have displaced single-party states. If the political swing has been unmistakably to the right, the difference on the ground has not been remarkably great. Despite the weakening of non-alignment and of the UN, despite the failure of the 'development decade' and the arrival of the military, no corresponding sharpening of revolutionary resistance can be chalked up on the other side of the account. There has been one very good reason for this, well expressed by one in a strategic position to reflect on revolutionary mistakes, for it was Régis Debray himself who declared that 'Cuba has raised the material and ideological level of imperialist reaction in less time than that of the revolutionary vanguard.'

Outside Africa, military regimes have been much more overtly counter-revolutionary, particularly in Indonesia, where the largest communist movement in the non-communist world was cut to ribbons in the slaughter of several hundred thousand communists after the *coup d'état* in 1965.

Since the Second World War though, 'revolution' has been a much more inclusive term than the term 'communist'. Not a single one of the armed revolutionary movements in Africa in the past two decades – with the exception perhaps of that in Portuguese Guinea – has been either socialist or communist either in ideology or leadership. Algeria, Mau Mau, the guerrilla movements in Angola and Mozambique, and lesser movements operating against South Africa, have predominantly been nationalist movements. Like non-revolutionary independence movements, they have often used left-wing rhetoric and vocabulary, but when they have arrived in power, have created precious little socialism or communism in practice. 'Nationalization', for instance, has generally meant the replacement of expatriate

Left The symbol of the Food and Agriculture Organization of the UN, which provides personnel and information for developing countries. In Kenya (*right*) the UK section has been responsible for initiating a rice crop on the slopes of Mount Kenya, irrigated by local rivers. Average income of Africans farming the area rose from about £10 to £142 a year

In Libya FAO experts advise on tractor maintenance at the Garabulli Farm Training Centre

local executives of state enterprises, new and old, by indigenous nationals: the presence of representatives of the state on the boards of 'mixed', public/private, national/foreign enterprises, or a 'token' indigenous director or two on the boards of international companies, means little in terms of hard power, however striking the symbolism.

The language of revolution in our time is Marxism, as it was once the language of the Bible. Nearly all radical movements, therefore, even those simply seeking political power without any accompanying social transformation, have used this language (and hence provided their enemies with a stick with which to beat them). It is hard to recall now that Nkrumah and Kenyatta were once seriously labelled 'communist'. There have been socially conservative and anti-communist nationalists, too, like the early Chiang Kai-shek or Algeria's Boumédienne, as well as anti-communist *radical* nationalists, like Gamal Abdul Nasser, who did not simply secure the final exodus of the British, but who also carried through a land-reform programme, nationalized a great deal of industrial and commercial enterprise and associated his country with the USSR. It is too early to judge whether the new Peruvian left-wing military regime, or the advent of a democratically elected (Russian-type) Marxist as president of Chile, are the first examples of novel forms of revolutionary innovation. Nor can the potential demonstration effect of Tanzanian socialism be evaluated at this stage.

There is one exception to the record of revolutionary setback, however, that outweighs all these failures. For the tiny agrarian society of revolutionary Vietnam has provided an extraordinary example to the rest of the world's revolutionaries and potential revolutionaries that, given the will and some external help, it can be done.

The effects of revolution are not just demonstrations of how to seize power. Once the revolutionary state is established it becomes a model of development also. Inimitable as the history of Russia or China may be for the population of small-scale peasant societies, they constitute 'utopias', to use Mannheim's term, which are not only powerful sources of inspiration, but also are sources of material assistance as well.

Revolutionary models of development are particularly powerful because they are composed of several overlapping elements, each one of which would be powerful enough if it occurred separately. Taken together, they seem to provide decisive answers to a set of related problems. In the first place,

Comparison of company sales and national revenues 1969

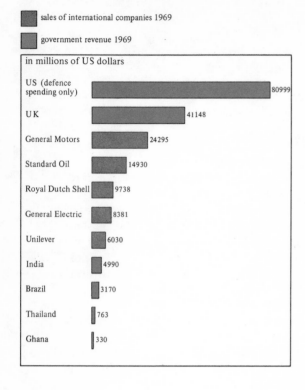

■ sales of international companies 1969

▨ government revenue 1969

in millions of US dollars

US (defence spending only)	80999
UK	41148
General Motors	24295
Standard Oil	14930
Royal Dutch Shell	9738
General Electric	8381
Unilever	6030
India	4990
Brazil	3170
Thailand	763
Ghana	330

In Tanzania, President Julius Nyerere's Arusha declaration of self-reliance in 1967 pointed the way to economic development through hard work by the Tanzanians themselves rather than dependence on foreign capital

the revolutionary doctrine provides an intellectual map of the world, an explanation of how it works, and a specification of its main components: it tells men they are victims of 'imperialism'. Secondly, the revolutionary ideology locates the actor or potential actor within this world: it provides him with an identity which he shares with others like him: he belongs to a 'class'. Further, it tells him who he is, not simply in structural terms, but also in ethical terms: he is a 'downtrodden worker' or an 'exploited peasant'. The identity he is thus provided with is new and disturbing, even exciting: he is no longer simply a 'Thai', a member of the x clan, a 'Buddhist' or a 'villager'. Next, the identity of his friends and enemies is pointed out to him (the 'middle peasantry' and the 'Soviet people', or the 'rich peasants' and the 'American imperialists', respectively). The revolutionary ideology also provides a set of goals: the alternative society towards which one should aim, and a programme to be followed in order to reach these goals. Finally, above all, ideology and programme do not simply float around in some disembodied form. They are communicated, and the agency that does the communicating is the party itself. But the party has not been merely an agency of communication; it has also been the organization which translates that ideology into action, by mobilizing people.

China

The postwar era has seen at least one major revolution of world-historic significance: the coming to power of the Communist Party in China in 1949. The dynamic of this revolution, both internally and externally, is not so much exhausted as scarcely begun, and it requires no particularly fertile imagination to foresee that the emergence of China as the greatest power in the world is a matter for the not very remote future, in a world that is likely to see the emergence of countries such as Brazil and Australia as major powers also. Nor, ultimately, can the conversion of India's and Indonesia's natural and human resources into even greater political power be long delayed.

However, at present China remains a singularly poor country; North Vietnam, racked by war, is even poorer. Gabriel Chaliand has described how every household keeps a record of its purchases from the state, checked by government officials, in which the purchase of a needle, a box of matches or a cake of soap, is recorded.

But war itself affects the pattern of development. It is likely that the rapid growth of North Korea would be emulated in a postwar North Vietnam also, since in both countries revolution and war have produced high levels of efficiency and morale in the population. At present, even in China, allocations to defence – especially nuclear weapons – have been heavy enough to hold back both economic development and initiatives outside her borders. The blockade, military, political and economic, has produced a counter-intransigence, suspicion and isolation. Never in history has so major a power been so effectively sealed off from the outside world.

On two occasions in the postwar period China struck out: in each case on her borders, in each case defensively. The first was in 1950 when General MacArthur's Korean strategy brought him to the very border of China, on the Yalu, and when the prospect of the nuclear bombing of Manchuria seemed a distinct possibility.

Tibet we must by-pass, for – however much the claim is disputed – the Chinese view of Tibet is simply that this was the reassertion of both title and effective authority over a territory long part of China, but where effective control, because of national decay and imperialist intervention, had weakened that authority.

There remains the other major Chinese border affair: the India-China border war of 1962. Virtually without exception, the Western Press interpreted this as unprovoked aggression. Yet the first serious study of that war to be published in the West, in 1970, entirely rejects this interpretation, places the blame for vainglorious aggressiveness on an inept Indian government and Indian High Command, and depicts China as the party which actively sought a positive and peaceful solution and only resorted to arms under the severest provocation.

Chinese attempts at setting up small 'backyard' industries in the 1958 'Great Leap Forward' proved economically disastrous

Below On independence Algerians faced the severe problems of modernizing traditional agricultural methods
Bottom Cuban May Day; the Russians bailed out the Cuban economy after the 1962 failure of hasty industrialization policies

To discuss China's presence in the world outside her borders in simply military terms would be to omit the crucial impact China has made in her bid for leadership of the world's revolutionary forces. Her success has not been very marked. Not a single foreign communist party of any size has abandoned the Soviet camp: the typical unit identifying with China is a *groupuscule* of intellectuals, or a micro-breakaway from orthodox Soviet-type communist parties. In terms of influence on foreign states, only two or three countries in the whole of Africa have exhibited any interest in positive ties with China, none in Latin America apart from Cuba, whose relationship with China is highly ambivalent, since they are rivals for world revolutionary leadership, and of little moment compared to her close dependence upon the USSR. The *sine qua non* of respectability for African countries, it has been said, is to expel the Chinese ambassador.

In South-east Asia, China suffered her most serious setback abroad when the Indonesia Communist Party was wiped out. For many years this communist party had vacillated between Russian and Chinese styles of revolution, mixed with a dash of opportunistic flirtation with nationalist militarists. In the end they opted for a singularly disastrous strategy: that of reaching power via the winning-over of nationalist politicians and army leaders at the top, as against either a Chinese-style, militant peasant-based strategy, or a Russian-style proletarian, city-based strategy. The new policy combined Russian emphasis on coexistence and cooperation with 'progressive', 'national democratic' bourgeois elements (Soekarno's nationalist Partai Nasional Indonesia) with a Chinese emphasis on winning control of a segment of the army. The right wing played this game much better than the left: among the several hundred thousand dead was the architect of this policy, D.N. Aidit, the secretary-general of the party.

Yet the crucial confrontation in Asia, that in Vietnam, has been a moral victory for communism. It is already reflected (though it is only one part of the whole explanation), in the astounding electoral successes of the revolutionary communist movement in India: the Communist Party of India (Marxist-Leninist), as well as in the growth of the Naxalites. In a situation where the orthodox political parties are increasingly unable to provide stable governments at both national and state levels, where Congress itself is split into two, the ability of parties as small as the CPI (Marxist), estimated to have 76,000 members in 1968, to secure as many as 80 out of 280 seats in the West Bengal election of 1969 recalls the similar capacity of an equally small revolutionary party, numbering less than 100,000, to take over in Russia, a country of over 140 million people, in November 1917.

The belief is widely held, of course, that China will become less revolutionary and intransigent as she becomes richer. A similar theory of the inevitable 'convergence' of US and Soviet society, dictated by the logic of

India's rural population explosion has prevented per capita income from rising much since independence; in many areas monsoon failure means famine

Peasant demonstration in Uruguay where uneven living standards between town and country bring conflict

industrialism (so that the two societies will become more and more alike), has been sceptically received on theoretical as well as empirical grounds. Some, however, do point to the increasing evidence for the emergence of new patterns of class-stratification in the USSR and in other Eastern European countries, once the initial period of the breaking-up of the old bourgeois classes has been completed. However, the undoubted diminution of Soviet revolutionism abroad has been much more attributable to the logic of the bomb than to the logic of industrialism.

It would be singularly rash to assume that the Chinese revolution will follow the course of earlier ones, whatever happens in Eastern Europe or Cuba. No other country has, in modern times, ever unleashed movements like the 'commune' movement or the 'cultural revolution' in an effort to break traditional and new tendencies towards bureaucracy and privilege; nor does history provide examples of the rise of a giant power with a still overwhelmingly peasant society, albeit backed now by highly developed modern industry – even to nuclear and science-backed industry – and fused by a highly centralized party and army structure, which seeks to make its impact primarily via revolutionizing the 'world's countryside'.

Urbanism without industrialism

The appeal of this type of communism might appear to be less relevant outside agrarian Asia. In Latin America, for example, fifty-seven per cent of the population of Argentina, Uruguay and Chile lives in urban places of 20,000 or more people, and twenty-nine per cent of the remainder of Latin America. On the other hand, the great mass of humanity still lives in Asia, in China, India and Indonesia. China is 86·7 per cent rural. India is still overwhelmingly a village society: half of her total population and 67·5 per cent of her rural population live in communities of 999 inhabitants or less. About a quarter of these rural households own no land at all, and another quarter less than one acre.

Maoism still has great potential in agrarian societies as poor as these. But there is nothing, either, to prevent Maoism being reworked so that its

In Africa, Asia and Latin America cities grow rapidly but do not industrialize at the same rate: (*top*) Nairobi – a legacy of colonial planning, (*above*) Brazilian *favelas*, shanty-towns for country immigrants

Below Scene in Calcutta

militancy becomes more relevant to urban conditions. Such a task is unlikely to be accomplished by the present generation of Maoists, whose major practice is a mechanistic repetition of fixed formulae which is an effective guarantee that their readiness to plunge into revolutionary action will be ineffective.

In the West, urbanism and industrialism grew up together. In Africa, Asia and Latin America today, cities and towns are growing at very rapid rates, but they are not industrializing at the same rates. There is a new world vocabulary of local names (*bidonvilles*, shanty-towns, *favelas*, *ranchos*, *bustees*) for similar habitations, made out of packing-cases, corrugated iron or sun-dried brick in encampments, usually illegal, often on seized land, which house the ever-swelling immigration from the countryside. They are not necessarily permanent features of the landscape: in cities as different as Casablanca and Johannesburg they have been swept away, if not always by the most liberal or humane of methods. Nor, where they do persist, are they 'disorganized' populations. Usually, they are articulated to wider national life: to religious, political and ethnic organizations, by ties of patronage, legitimate or criminal, which provide some, however ineffective, palliatives and – more often and more importantly – hope in the face of an abundance of personal and common problems. At present, the wider social frameworks within which the shanty-dwellers are incorporated are largely conservative: there seem to be no grounds for assuming that this will inevitably continue to be the case. More likely, a new equation for the analysis of radicalism may be needed: one which includes the two familiar terms 'urban proletariat' and 'peasant', but which further adds the new term 'urban underclass' (a better term than the misleading and pejorative 'lumpenproletariat', with its connotations of demoralization and criminality).

This 'underclass' is not, of course, unemployed all the time otherwise it would be unlikely to survive at all. Research has shown that much of the shanty-town population does work – as many as sixty to seventy per cent are in stable employment in Latin American shanty-towns – even if poorly rewarded: others are highly insecure, shifting from occupation to occupation, usually combining a mixture of petty trading and micro-enterprise with the sale of one's labour, and often with thieving as a way of life, battening on one's kin or being exploited by the latter as cheap labour. In Latin America at least, Mangin has shown that the shanty-town populations are mainly literate, that over time they invest in housing improvements (replacing reed-mats by brick houses), establish businesses, develop community services, etc. Similar communities have persisted over decades in India. There is not much community solidarity or organized social life, but the main needs of the residents, given their present level of wants, are met. But their wants are constantly expanding: there is a very real 'revolution of rising expectations'. Inevitably, there are many variations and phases in this process: shanty-town development follows different patterns in different parts of the world, in accordance with different economic, cultural and other factors. They no more develop according to a single universal pattern than more familiar towns and cities have done, and need much more study than they have received, for they are unlikely to fit either existing models of the underdeveloped world or existing notions of urban life.

'Rich men's clubs' and 'proletarian' nations

There is much we do not know, whether it be the significance of this urban implosion, or the implications of the communications revolution. Hence our capacity to estimate the future is not very great. But we can already see that the shrinkage of space and time have internationalized and speeded up both the processes of repression and revolution. In that sense 'the medium is the message': the very existence of radio transforms our lives. Yet the ultimate factor is still the nature of the message – and which message gets through.

The internationalization of communications, and the growth of *world* politics, means that in future it can never be the case again that a revolution can occur in Mexico that does not have an immediate impact right across the globe. By the time of the early 1960s, the explanation of the peaceful

World population
1968

Per capita income
throughout the world
1968

Europe

Latin America

North America

Soviet Union

Africa

Asia

Oceania

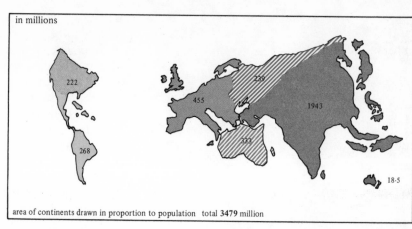

in millions

222

239

455

1943

333

18·5

area of continents drawn in proportion to population total **3479** million

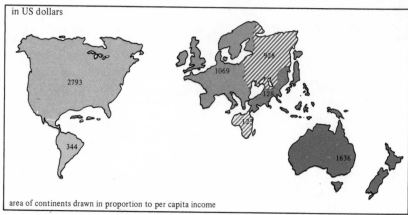

in US dollars

2793

926

1069

128

344

1636

area of continents drawn in proportion to per capita income

In Latin America poverty means the death of children: a babies' coffin shop in the capital of Colombia, Bogotá

hand-over of power in Franco-British black Africa had to be sought in other parts of the globe, where debilitating human and economic loss of blood by Britain and France had occurred, in France's case in a last-ditch attempt to maintain colonial control over Indo-China and Algeria, and in Britain's in the Malaya and Mau Mau campaigns. These experiences pointed to one incontrovertible conclusion: that it would be inadvisable to repeat the experience of Indonesia or Algeria, where large-scale struggle had gone on for years, ending in one case in straight defeat, and in the other in patent inability to repress the rebellion. Better, then, leave as a benefactor rather than risk being defeated or embroiled in protracted counter-revolution.

The handing-over of independence by no means necessarily led to successful modernization. Some countries have achieved quite striking results in certain sectors of the economy. Thus Kenya's post-independence agricultural production went up by forty-five per cent per annum between 1954 and 1964, three-quarters of it from small farms (while the population grew by three per cent per annum). The development of the Ivory Coast's exports, or the measure of success attained in land-reform programmes in the Philippines or Taiwan, have been substantial. Indeed, the greatest wealth per capita in the modern world is to be found in an 'underdeveloped' country, Kuwait. And a country, which although independent is still 'colonial' in its social pattern, South Africa, has achieved a notable degree of industrialization. Of course, Kuwait is wealthy without being industrialized; South Africa's industrialization is still mainly in the sphere of extractive industry. Countries like Brazil, with a more substantial industrial development round São Paulo, still contain a latifundia type of agriculture and areas, like the North-east, where rural poverty is the norm. Nor is there enough urban industry to absorb the immigrant population into productive employment.

Even those countries which have introduced sizeable and effective programmes of land reform have been hard put to settle an ever-increasing number of landless. Indeed, it has been the very success of the middle peasantry which has generated the twin problems of a growing landless population in the countryside, made up of pocket-handkerchief peasants

56

Birth-control poster
in Tamil

who have lost their land or given up the effort to live on the verge of subsistence, and preferred instead to migrate to the towns in the hope of a
better life. The development of a class of rich farmers also sharpens social
oppositions in the countryside itself. Moreover, the national statistics often
cited as indicating that a few Third World countries are approaching the
income standards of the more backward countries of Europe, such as
Portugal, are, like most national statistics of this kind, averages based on
the mixing together of the incomes of the few extremely rich, the middling
and the vast mass of the poor.

Where production increases have been achieved, they have usually been
negated by changes in world prices. Thus Ghana doubled cocoa production
during Nkrumah's regime, during which time the price fell by half. But in
many parts of the world, production has not increased at an adequate rate,
whether we are considering export-cash-crops required to bring in foreign
earnings or the volume of food production required to feed the population.
In India, for example, there were 13·53 ounces of foodgrains available per
person per day in 1952, and still only 14·70 ounces in 1969. Improved productivity in agriculture is quite compatible with 'progressive stagnation':
'involution'. Geertz has shown that over hundreds of years of colonial rule
in Java, there was constant improvement in the techniques and yields in
irrigation rice-cultivation. Yet the outcome of all this innovation was to
maintain a greatly increased population at virtually the same levels of
consumption.

Technical improvements in agriculture, whether secular improvements or
dramatic breakthroughs, do not solve the elemental man/land or man/food-
supply problems. The current hopes for a 'green revolution' as the result of
new strains of high-yielding crops, still leave such problems to be solved, for
if famines can be overcome, problems of distribution and inequality remain.
Moreover, in an era when new knowledge and dreams about what is possible reach the village via the school or the radio; when, in the towns, the
rich can be seen to be living lives of unbelievable luxury in the midst of a
sea of slums; when there is widespread propaganda about countries where
such conditions do not exist, any gains that a poor country may make are
more than outmatched by the new wants that are generated daily.

Whatever the positive achievements of the poor countries, they are
increasingly losing in the attempt to catch up with the advanced countries.
Vis-à-vis the very richest countries, even the combined resources of such rich
countries as those of Western Europe, taken together, prove inadequate, as
the space race has dramatically demonstrated. We often forget, too, that
General Motors spends more than the Japanese government, Ford more
than the French, ICI more than the Norwegian – and the Pentagon more than
the British. For the poorer countries, population growth, the steady widening of the two blades of the 'scissors' of the prices for manufactured goods
on the one hand as against the prices for raw materials on the other, the
growing technological gap as the wealthy countries move into the era of
cybernetics, electronics, nuclear energy and man-made raw materials, mean
that the highest rates of return on capital and in consequence the greatest
volume of investment, now occur not in the countries which Lenin described
as the source of 'super-profits' – the colonial and backward countries – but
in those countries which make up the 'rich men's club'.

The classic way of modernizing fast for poor countries in this century has
been to go communist. Indeed, the meaning of communism in our time so
far has been development, for the only countries to have gone communist
have been backward countries, and they have been the only backward
countries which have successfully modernized. In contrast, communism in
advanced societies has been remarkably unsuccessful; even where it has
produced a large mass movement, it has become bedded down within
capitalism, as the French Communist Party so graphically demonstrated in
1968, and also, in more parliamentary form, in the postwar electoral
gradualism of the Italian Communist Party.

Given continued prosperity in the West, there seems no reason to assume
that an increasingly inwards-turning First World is likely to produce either

World population growth

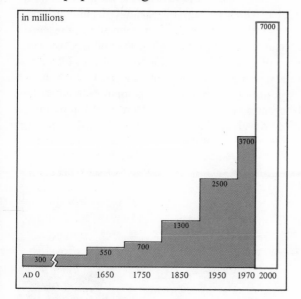

An operating theatre on Bombay Central Station:
vasectomy is worth one pound in cash to each patient

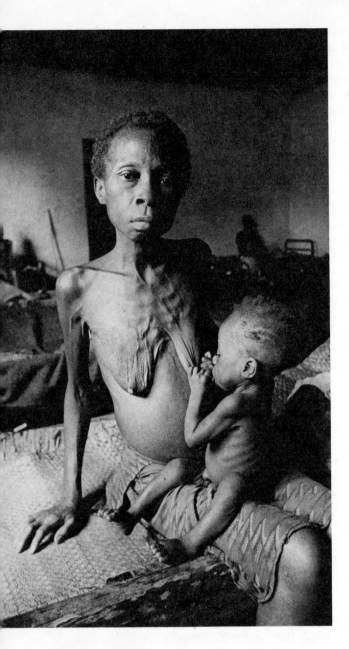

Millions were brought to the verge of starvation during the Biafran War

Right An early comment on the distance between the 'haves' and 'have-nots' by Low in the London *Evening Standard* (1946)

a sizeable internal communist challenge, or, if it does, that it cannot continue to be contained. But this proposition rests upon several assumptions: firstly, that the economies of the Western countries will continue to flourish unscathed if the economy of the Third World begins to disintegrate; secondly, that communism in the West will not change into or become superseded by a more revolutionary challenge in such an event; thirdly, that the West need not become politically involved in trying to contain revolutionary change in the Third World. Despite the increasing technological distance between rich and poor, and the higher returns on capital invested in the rich countries (including Japan, South Africa and Australia), the developed countries still need markets and certainly some crucial raw materials, notably oil. And 'super-profits' are still made from such strategic commodities, as well as some much less strategic ones. In any case, the history of the postwar period suggests that ideologies develop a life of their own, and the ideology of anti-communism has lodged so deeply in the minds of so many Americans, particularly among political élites, that the likelihood of the United States passively contemplating the spectacle of countries in the Third World quitting the capitalist sphere of influence is slight: nor does the recent experience of, say, the Dominican Republic or Vietnam lend it much credibility.

The problems facing countries smaller than Russia or China which seek to industrialize is particularly important, because even if a small country decides to modernize the communist way, it will lack the massive natural resources and resources of population that the USSR or China were able to draw upon both in order to build modern industry (by milking the peasantry) and in order to generate an enormous internal market.

Some development, and even industrialization, have occurred in smaller communist countries, notably North Korea, which had the advantage of an existing industrial base, and hence was more favourable ground than, say, monocultural agrarian Cuba, which remains obdurately dependent upon sugar, unable internally to overcome the organization problems presented by this dominant crop-specialization, and dependent in consequence upon those who buy it. This kind of qualified independence seems an inevitable fate for future revolutionary powers, as it was in Eastern Europe in the Stalin era, when gross exploitation via market prices manipulated by the USSR took place. Such legacies of history and culture profoundly affect each country's trajectory of development or non-development, whatever their economic system and reigning institutionalized ideology, to an extent

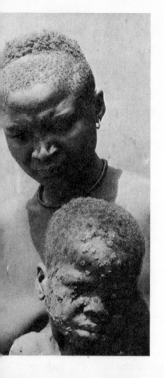

Three diseases the UN World Health Organization is bringing under control: (*left*) yaws, which can be cured by a single injection of penicillin; (*below*) leprosy, for which sulfone drugs, discovered in 1943, are highly effective; and (*bottom*) tuberculosis – more than 150 million vaccinations have been made in sixty-one countries

not always allowed for in theoretical models of development which assume that development must always conform to a single pattern. A very different disease blights those explanatory models which take as their framework of analysis the country or nation-state, and fail to see it as a member of a whole set of poor countries which share a common life-situation *vis-à-vis* a second set of developed countries, which latter collectively control the opportunities and life-chances of the poorer ones. Indeed, it has been argued by some Marxists that the prosperity of the developed countries still depends on there being underdeveloped countries elsewhere which they exploit.

The nation-state remains a key unit of action, but in its turn is limited in autonomy by its membership of higher-level, more inclusive economic and political and cultural groupings (blocs, economic trading areas, etc.) and by the operation of the market (terms of trade, tariff agreements, etc.). Plainly, only giant nations can hope to solve their own problems within such a context, and then only at enormous cost and with great difficulty. Since it seems highly unlikely that any serious collective world-level action will be taken to alter the world market system or the system of world rival political blocs, small countries are faced with the relative (and sometimes absolute) deterioration of their situation, with degeneration instead of stagnation: they are not merely in a condition of being 'underdeveloped', but are changing for the worse, '*underdeveloping*'.

But some models of underdevelopment carry the notion of the 'holistic' nature of the world economy to extremes, assuming that change in the total world social and economic system must occur before the development of the backward world can seriously commence. In one sense this may be right, but it is too deterministic a model, for general change is unlikely to come about except as a result of particular challenges to particular governments. Moreover, history suggests that decisive economic modernization is likely to occur as a result of radical political change (including 'conservative-radical' changes in the Japanese and German cases), rather than as a result of the direct restructuring of purely economic arrangements. Such changes have occurred on a world scale only as a result of world wars. But they have still taken place within the boundaries of the nation-state, the widest unit which normally acts politically. Hence the centrality of nationalism in both nineteenth-century Europe and the twentieth-century Third World as a motor of modernization.

If the notion of total system-change at world level is too apocalyptic to be useful, the opposite kind of model is all too prevalent. This is the assumption that national cultures are not wholes at all, but merely assemblages of items; bits and pieces can therefore be detached, lent or borrowed, and bought and sold. The receiving country can then acquire cultural elements from other 'diffusing' countries. The problem of development then simply becomes one of ensuring that requisite amounts of the needed item are diffused. Normally, this kind of theory assumes that the main obstacle to this process of diffusion is something called 'traditionalism'.

The difficulty with this model is that traditionalism scarcely exists in underdeveloped countries today, certainly with regard to political authority structures, for most countries are ruled by quite untraditional colonels or generals, or by mass parties led by 'charismatic' leaders who do not claim (indeed commonly scorn) any authority of a traditional or even of a formal constitutional kind. In economic terms, again, the great bulk of humankind have long been involved in the world market as producers of cash-crops, as wage-workers, or as consumers. Education and modern communications ensure the steady intrusion of new social practices ranging from changed patterns of marriage to the modernization or elimination of religion.

More real barriers to diffusion are to be found in the resistance of entrenched interests, both old and new, at home and abroad, to the diffusion of those things which will compete with their own sources of wealth and privilege. They have no universal aversion to diffusion in general; the resistance is differential. The one crucial cultural complex that does not get diffused successfully is modern factory industry (extractive industries, which supply raw materials to foreign industrialized countries, metal ores,

Schoolgirl in Swaziland

World literacy 1968

% illiterate population over 15 years

Region	%
North America	2
Latin America	34
Europe	5
Soviet Union	2
Africa	82
Asia	54
Oceania	1

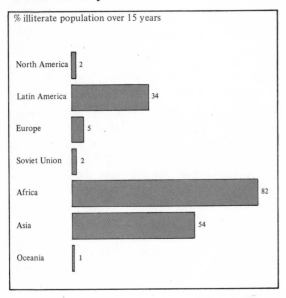

In the mountain villages of the Andes, girls are beginning to receive the same education as boys

oil, etc., do expand). This is not, of course, solely a function of deliberate restriction in every case, for it is singularly difficult for any poor country to construct a heavy industrial base with a tiny internal market and limited local demand for, say, steel or coal. The limited internal consumer market, again, and the superior prices of advanced suppliers, put them at a disadvantage as producers even of light consumer goods. To create larger markets requires political 'common market' arrangements which, in the nature of things, are difficult to bring about, since many small countries are precariously dependent on maintaining established markets in the advanced countries.

A second type of theory emphasizes shortfalls in capital investment rather than traditionalism as the key obstacle to development. The trouble with this model is that there has indeed been lots of investment in underdeveloped countries, but not development of the right kind, generating a diversified and industrialized economy capable of competing effectively on the world market (as small industrial countries like the Netherlands and the UK do – or even small primarily agricultural countries like New Zealand or Denmark). As for the volume of capital, the overall pattern is one of outflow *from* the underdeveloped countries *to* the richer ones (where corporations also raise a great deal of the capital they use to develop branches of their firms from local sources). Such outflows of capital have been crucial resources for the developed countries at times. Thus Britain financed much of her immediate postwar recovery from colonial sterling balances held in London, the income from rubber and oil being specially important. Some economists believe, however, that the colonial game overall, and certainly for long periods of time, was not worth the candle, and that the costs of holding down and administering empires consumed resources which would have been put to better economic use if invested at home. Today, many argue, the periodic crises which Britain undergoes in respect of her balance of payments could be wiped out if overseas military expenditure were eliminated. The present pattern is moving in the opposite direction.

The outflow from the underdeveloped countries is not simply an economic or financial one: it is also a human haemorrhage, commonly labelled the 'brain drain', in which the professional, skilled people from poor countries go to the USA or to Europe, or go to acquire skills and stay once they have qualified. Thus it has been claimed that there are more American-trained Iranian doctors practising in New York City than in the whole of Iran. Certainly, the global figures reveal an unmistakable pattern: 570,595 professional, technical and kindred workers entered the USA between 1952 and 1956 from underdeveloped countries.

Conclusion

Models which attempt to explain the causes of underdevelopment (and hence, by implication, the cure for this condition) in terms of the diffusion or non-diffusion of particular 'traits' or elements differ widely in the particular elements they identify as being the crucial ones. Some of them emphasize that particular kinds of *values* are the key requirement – attitudes to work, ideas about equality and achievement, the development of specialization and so forth. If specialization in theorizing about development was what was needed, there would be no poor countries left. But a little scepticism is in order when we find that engineers claim that what is needed is technology or technological expertise; teachers that what is needed is literacy, high general levels of skill, or an educated, thinking population; administrators, an adequate supply of trained civil servants; and so on. What they rarely admit is that all these things are needed, and that to be an underdeveloped country means to lack all of them together, not any particular one, so that if development is to come about, it needs to overcome shortcomings in the supply of capital *and* skilled administrators, of literacy *and* machinery, doctors *and* technicians simultaneously, if particular and general advance is to be achieved. In a phrase, social planning: the coordination of the separate elements of development.

Of course, this did not happen in nineteenth-century industrialization.

Havana University needs more agricultural experts;
the aim is 40,000 for Cuba by 1974

Below In Haiti WHO centres for malnourished children
give food and education in nutrition
Bottom Family planning in Jamaica; a WHO official
explains the use of the loop

Then, market competition allowed the most efficient or ruthless units to flourish and win out over less equipped competitors. This type of development is usually unacceptable to today's ruling élites in developing countries, who usually wish to keep economic power as effectively in their hands as their monopoly of political power, who are affected by the examples of socialist and communist planning, and for whom, in any case, only the state can provide capital on the scale required.

With the increased scale of operation characteristic of modern industry and the volume of capital required for rapid development on a large scale, plus the concomitant need to mobilize people, the state, not the small entrepreneur or even the more substantial 'middle classes', becomes the decisive agent. The middle classes are unlikely to play the role they played in Europe or in the USA. They are too weak and too much of a dependent variable within a pattern of overseas-controlled import/export trade to be able to act successfully as the generators of industrial development or of agricultural modernization. With state support, however, peasant agriculture, taken collectively, can make striking developments, as when the state provides technical assistance (seed-provision services, fertilizer and spraying programmes, the use of tractors and machinery on consolidated blocks or as centralized services to smallholders, etc.), or in the form of credit and marketing facilities via cooperatives, price-stabilization schemes, marketing boards, long-term trade agreements and the like.

Such successes, however, have been far too limited to alter the global pattern of a continually widening gap between the haves and the have-nots. Undoubtedly, more and more of them will be inclined to opt for radical solutions to their problems. Undoubtedly, this will evoke repressive responses from the powers that compete for control of the world.

In the 1940s and 1950s, the danger of the Third World War, a war between the USSR and the capitalist West, was the universal nightmare. In the 1960s the danger of what I term the Fourth World War began to look much more serious. It might not begin over the issue of communism at all, but start in the form of radical nationalisms of a type unacceptable to the Western powers. Variants of this, from Arbenz's Guatemala to Mossadeq's Iran or Nasser's Egypt and Bosch's Dominican Republic have already been dangerous enough flashpoints. Conflicts between and within Third World countries themselves are likely to increase also as their desperation grows. One outcome has been an enormous expenditure on armaments, even on the part of the underdeveloped countries themselves, a factor which obviously steps up the danger of military conflict, and which further impedes these countries in their development efforts.

At the end of 1970 the military expenditure of the major powers was about twenty-five times as great as the total amount of official aid. The ultimate possibility of the Fourth World War must put at a discount any theory which assumes the inevitability of progress. Neither can we assume the inevitability of revolution, even if development is frustrated, for revolutions are difficult to achieve, and chaos or stagnation, in 'broken-backed states' racked by famine, rebellion and instability, are quite conceivable. Conversely, it is not beyond the wit of man to begin to relieve the lot of the world's poor. A mere change in world prices, without any technological transformation, would accomplish much quite speedily. Nor is it inconceivable that a Russo-American *détente* that moved from mere 'coexistence' to positive cooperation to tackle world backwardness (and in the process, the winding-down of the arms race) might make the competition between past varieties of communism and capitalism gradually become a thing of the past, such as past conflicts between Islam and Christianity, or Protestantism and Catholicism have become. But at present, the chances look slim indeed. The population of the world has taken the entire history of humanity to reach its present 3·15 billion; it will double again by the year 2000. If it does not rapidly solve its major problems – those of economic development and the elimination of war – human civilization is unlikely to survive to the year 2000. If it does, there will be the problems of 3 billion new people in the world to cope with.

Richard N. Cooper

The Conception of a World Economy

With occasional setbacks, the world economy progressed rapidly in the late nineteenth and early twentieth centuries. Industrialization proceeded, foreign trade grew, international specialization increased, capital flowed to areas of relative scarcity and incomes rose. All this was shattered by the Great Depression of the 1930s. World trade spiralled downward, capital fled homeward, incomes plummeted. The decline in world trade was due partly to the drop in incomes, but partly also to the erection by most nations of stiff barriers to trade, in a misguided effort to divert home demand from foreign goods in order to stimulate domestic production and employment.

Restricting imports may be narrowly defensible for a single country acting alone in an otherwise buoyant world economy, but it is self-defeating when all countries are behaving in the same way. Each country may succeed in diverting demand inward, but the actions of others reduce its exports; the net effect is no increase in home demand, but rather a reduction in the gains from international specialization. Worse still, such actions foster xenophobic and chauvinistic sentiments, rarely far below the surface, and they therefore have implications ranging beyond the international division of labour. For once several nations embark on this course, others in self-defence must follow – if not by imposing higher tariffs, then by depreciation of their currencies or other expedients.

The 1930s saw most of them. The great crash brought with it, and was in turn reinforced by, sharp increases in tariffs, competitive depreciation of currencies, imposition of quantitative restrictions on imports, blocked currencies, resort to state trading and increasing discrimination among trading countries. The world economy as an integrated market for goods and capital collapsed. The period saw the highest tariffs in American history, the abandonment by Britain of nearly a century of free trade, the formation of a discriminatory trading area among members of the British Commonwealth, brought about largely by increases in tariffs on non-members, and the adoption by Germany of import quotas and blocked currencies to discriminate among its trading partners in Eastern Europe and Latin America.

The economic collapse of the 1930s was one of the causes of the Second World War. The most compelling popular appeal by Adolf Hitler, it should be recalled, was his promise to put the unemployed to work, to restore production in the German economy which, in terms of unemployment, was hardest hit of all countries. The depression in Germany, via the fall in exports and the massive withdrawal of foreign funds on which Germany had come to depend so heavily in the 1920s, could be plausibly linked with the economic crisis in the United States and the financial crisis in Britain. A persuasive case in conjectural history can be made that, if the Great Depression and the associated beggar-thy-neighbour policies had been avoided, Hitler would not have come to power and the Second World War would not have occurred. So at any rate it seemed to the American and British officials who, soon after America's entry into the war in 1941, were charged with designing a viable and durable world economy for the postwar era.

The disastrous experience of the 1930s provided the agenda for reform. Led on the American side by Secretary of State Cordell Hull, Secretary of Treasury Henry Morgenthau Jr, and their able assistants Dean Acheson and Harry Dexter White, and guided intellectually on the British side by John Maynard Keynes and James Meade, the American and British

A GATT meeting in Geneva; from 1947 GATT provided a world forum for tariff negotiation and the resolution of trade disputes

63

Lord Halifax puts the British signature to the Bretton Woods Agreement, which established the postwar World Bank and International Monetary Fund

Below The GATT Kennedy Round talks of 1964-7 brought average tariff levels on industrial goods in major countries down to under ten per cent

Use of IMF by main members 1947-70

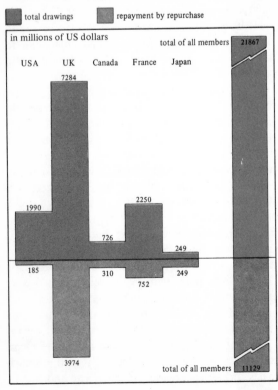

officials hammered out grand designs for the postwar period, first separately, then in collaboration. While there were important differences between the American and British planners, on which more will be said below, they shared a conception of the world economy in which interferences to trade were held to a minimum, access to markets was available to all on roughly equal terms and restrictive national policies were severely limited by international rules and were subject to international consultation. Above all they desired to avoid the economically destructive actions and politically damaging recriminations of the 1930s. In short, they desired to bring international commercial and financial relations under some sort of rule of law.

The institutional structure expected to emerge from this collaboration was a three-pronged one, involving an International Monetary Fund to oversee matters relating to exchange rates and national balance-of-payments positions; an International Trade Organization to oversee commercial policy and trading relationships among countries; and an International Bank for Reconstruction and Development to facilitate the flow of long-term capital to the nations badly damaged by the war and to the poor but potentially progressive nations of the world. These organizations were part of the broader movement to institutionalize international relations that resulted in the creation of the United Nations and a host of other specialized international organizations. Of the three economic institutions only the International Monetary Fund (IMF) and the International Bank for Reconstruction and Development (IBRD, or World Bank as it came generally to be called) were actually created. The International Trade Organization (ITO) faltered on national misunderstandings, domestic politics, gradual dissipation of the cooperative spirit that had developed during the war and, not least, sharply divergent conceptions of the national and international interest. It was replaced in function by the more limited General Agreement on Tariffs and Trade (GATT).

The principal points of difference between the American and British planners concerned the degree of autonomy that nations should enjoy in framing and executing their domestic economic policies, the extent to which quantitative restrictions on imports should be retained and the extent to which discriminatory (preferential) trading arrangements among nations should be tolerated.

The first of these issues found ambivalence on both sides. Britain's Labour Party wanted the scope to build a socialist society in the postwar period, and they feared American criticism and, through international organizations, interference with this objective. For this reason, they wanted to confine international rules and supervision as narrowly as possible to achieve the broadly agreed international objectives. In addition, Britain as a whole was committed to the maintenance of full employment, and British officials wanted to be free to pursue that objective without hindrance from the international system, such as had occurred in the interwar period. On the other hand, they recognized that a viable world economy along the lines desired would function only if other major countries, and the United States in particular, maintained conditions of full employment as well, and they pushed hard for the United States to commit itself in international agreement to this objective.

For their part, the American planners fully agreed that maintenance of full employment was a necessary condition for the world economy they had in mind, but they doubted the enforceability of any international commitment in this area. Moreover, they were reluctant to undertake any specific commitment to full employment because important segments of the American public were suspicious of 'Keynesian' measures to maintain full employment – through the active manipulation of tax and expenditure levels to stabilize the economy – and they feared that such a commitment might jeopardize public (and in particular Congressional) acceptance of the rest of the plans. British scepticism regarding the depth of American commitment to full employment in turn reinforced British determination to keep their options open, especially with respect to the use of quantitative restrictions (QRs) and the retention of the Imperial Preference System. In

World Bank loans for postwar European reconstruction: (*left*) hot steel rolling mill at Denain, part of a $250,000,000 loan to France; (*right*) a section of the coastal Adriatic Highway in Yugoslavia, which in 1963 borrowed about $35,000,000 to open the country to Western European traffic

Main sources of aid to underdeveloped countries

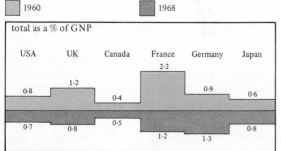

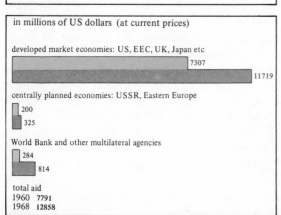

the end these differences were compromised in various ways, largely verbal, and the employment issue was ultimately resolved by its failure to materialize as a major problem.

A second issue of contention, related to disagreement on the employment question, was the extent to which QRs should be tolerated or encouraged in the postwar world. Revulsion against QRs was based partly on their association with Nazi Germany, which had used them extensively and exploitatively before the war, but it also reflected the predilection of Anglo-Saxon economics for a free market. Quotas on imports interfered with the flow of trade more than did tariffs, since quotas could not be surmounted no matter how competitive the import products were. For this reason too they were more effective than tariffs in protecting domestic monopolies, a fact that also counted against them. The majority of British planners shared the distaste for quotas and other QRs, but they feared that Britain might have to use them in an emergency, especially if there were a deep postwar depression in the United States. Americans worried about quotas in addition because they were difficult in practice to apply on a non-discriminatory basis; it is in the nature of operative quotas that the desired entry to a market exceeds what is to be allowed in, so some more or less arbitrary selection among would-be entrants is required. In the end the differences over QRs were resolved by prohibiting their use in international trade except when a country was in acute balance-of-payments difficulties, and then they were to be used on a basis that did not discriminate among countries and was subject to periodic international review.

Third, the United States took strong exception to the Imperial Preference System as prejudicial to American exports and politically undesirable for introducing trade privileges into foreign affairs. (The Imperial Preference System established preferential tariff rates among members of the British Commonwealth following the Ottawa Agreement of 1932, partly to mitigate the blow of Britain's abandonment of virtually free trade.) Cordell Hull, especially, was vehement on the subject, and to obtain British agreement to abolish this system after the war became a major objective of American policy. On their side, British officials were concerned with the extraordinarily high level of American tariffs (enacted as the Hawley-Smoot Tariff in 1930, an all-time high in American history), and they agreed to abolish Imperial Preference only reluctantly and guardedly in exchange for reductions in American tariffs. After the war, however, strong domestic support developed in Britain for the retention of this system; the issue was never successfully resolved, and the resulting impasse was one of the two issues on which the charter for an International Trade Organization finally failed to achieve ratification in the American Senate. The second issue was the insistence by many of the poor countries that they retain their complete

Top General Marshall in Moscow, 1947, with John
Foster Dulles (right); the Plan to bolster the European
economy against Russian subversion resulted in some
$16 billion worth of aid
Above An American view of Marshall Aid

Below Marshall Plan signatures on 17 March 1948
including those of Bevin and Bidault

freedom of action in the field of commercial policy, regardless of the new
trading rules, in the supposed interests of economic development.

The compromise agreements that were finally reached were reflected in
two international undertakings of considerable importance: the Bretton
Woods Agreement (named after the town in New Hampshire where the
final conference was held) establishing the IMF and the IBRD, signed in 1944;
and GATT, signed in Geneva in 1947. These agreements together provide
the basic legal framework in which postwar world trade and financial
relations have taken place.

The Bretton Woods Agreement set down the rules for international
financial intercourse. Each country was obliged to fix the value of its currency in terms of gold and permit it to be used freely within small margins
around this 'par value' for payment for foreign goods and services. In technical terms, currencies were to be fully convertible for current (as distinguished from capital) transactions. Purchases of foreign securities were not
treated equally with purchases of foreign goods or services, for the experience of the 1930s had taught that international capital movements could be
highly disruptive of national prosperity and might therefore have to be kept
under control.

It was recognized that with fixed exchange rates, currency convertibility
and national economic policies to preserve full employment, countries
would from time to time run into balance-of-payments difficulties. Temporary deficits were to be financed out of international reserves, traditionally monetary gold, but the IMF was created with the twofold purpose of
policing the new rules and of providing a source of funds to help member
countries finance deficits. Each country was entitled to borrow from the
IMF up to a stipulated amount, related to its quota, which also determined
its financial subscription to the Fund and its voting rights in the Fund's
decisions. The scheme that actually emerged, however, provided for rather
more national autonomy and rather less in financial resources than the
preliminary proposals out of which it grew, so the IMF has from time to time
been faced with the possibility of having too few resources to carry out its
original design. As a result, it has had to be somewhat stricter in its lending
operations than was originally envisaged.

When a payments imbalance was clearly not temporary – when a country
was confronted with a 'fundamental disequilibrium' in the undefined terms
of the Agreement – then the country concerned was to change the par value
of its currency by revaluing or devaluing it in terms of other currencies, as
the occasion required. If a country in persistent surplus refused to revalue,
its currency might be declared 'scarce' and other countries would then be
permitted to discriminate against the offending country in their international
transactions.

The basic framework prevailed throughout the postwar period, although
the scarce currency clause was never invoked, and most countries took many
years, under 'transitional' provisions, to accept in full the obligations of the
Agreement. The IMF started operations in 1947 in Washington with
forty-four members; by 1970 it had 116 members.

The Bretton Woods Agreement also established the World Bank (IBRD),
whose task it was to provide long-term debt capital to needy countries.
Institutionalized lending was thought to be necessary, especially to developing countries, because their capital requirements far exceeded what the
barely revived postwar capital markets could handle, and more importantly
because extensive defaults on foreign bonds in the 1930s, especially the bonds
of many less developed (but also a number of European) countries had left
the residents of the major capital-exporting countries extremely distrustful
of foreign securities. The World Bank was expected to bridge this gap between need and availability both by direct lending to needy countries out of
its own resources, which comprised the paid-in portion of subscriptions of
member countries, and by borrowing in its own name on the various capital
markets, for which the uncalled portion of the subscriptions served as a
guarantee fund, and then re-lending the proceeds. Acceptance of the obligations of the Bretton Woods Agreement, as evidenced by membership in the

Marshall Plan funds financed agricultural mechanization in Turkey, which was to become an important NATO base

A German poster offers an open road to Marshall Aid

IMF, is a condition for borrowing from the World Bank, which by 1970 also had 116 members. Bank lending activity was low in the early years of operation, when it was preoccupied with establishing a high credit rating in private capital markets, which objective was thought to require conservative lending practices. In the late sixties, however, the World Bank relaxed somewhat its stringent conditions on the projects for which it would lend, and in 1970 the scale of new lending exceeded $2,000 million a year.

GATT set down the rules governing international trade. It was only an interim agreement, pending the completion and entry into force of a world trade charter establishing the International Trade Organization (ITO). But since the charter failed in ratification, GATT remained the operative instrument throughout the subsequent period. GATT has five principal guidelines to trading relations among its adherents, or 'contracting parties' as they are technically called. First, it provides that each country must treat its trading partners equally in the application of tariffs and other trade regulations – the 'most-favoured-nation' clause of traditional trade treaties. A major exception to the equal-treatment provision is made for the creation of free trade areas or customs unions, in which a group of nations agrees to eliminate duties and other restraints to (virtually) all trade among themselves, while retaining tariffs and other restrictions on imports from other countries.

Second, the adherents are to endeavour, on a reciprocal basis, to reduce tariffs. Third, there are a number of proscriptions regarding trade policy, the most important of which is that countries should not impose quantitative restrictions on imports, except when required for balance-of-payments reasons, and then only under international surveillance. Fourth, adherents agree to subject changes in trade policy which affect other countries to a process of international consultation to be sure that their interests at least get a hearing. Finally, when the rules have been violated and the trading interests of one or more adherents have been damaged, provision is made for compensation or, in extreme cases, for controlled retaliation, designed to limit the damage.

GATT fell short of the proposed trade charter for the ITO in that it did not cover domestic employment, international investment and the special trade problems of the less developed countries; and it provided for no permanent organization, analogous to the IMF in the financial area, to oversee commercial relations. Finally, in a number of respects it did not require adherents to bring their existing policies into conformity with the new rules, only to apply them to future policies. In particular, it did not require the dismantlement of the Imperial Preference System, since that antedated GATT.

GATT went into effect in 1947 with twenty-three 'contracting parties', a number that grew to eighty in the subsequent two decades. While it technically involved no organization, a small secretariat was established in Geneva under the financial auspices of the Economic and Social Council of the United Nations (which technically is also the parent body for the IMF and the IBRD, although the relationship is *pro forma*), and contracting nations established permanent representatives there to discuss issues of trade policy and practice on a continuing basis. GATT provides a forum for periodic tariff negotiations as well as for resolution of trade disputes.

The conception of the world economy that emerged from the Second World War, in summary, was one that was universal in scope, providing equal treatment to all nations; legal in form, providing for the creation of new international institutions to facilitate and police adherence to the rules and to help resolve disputes among nations; and economic in content, in that it focused rather narrowly on the economic relations among nations, on the assumption that good economics makes good politics, or at least in the negative conviction that bad economics is likely to lead to bad political relations among countries. The basic principle was that a rule of law had to be introduced among nations, in the dual sense of providing codes of internationally acceptable behaviour by nations and of providing for the orderly and reasoned resolution of disputes. The scheme that emerged fell far short of US Secretary of Treasury Morgenthau's dream of bringing President

Foundation of the Common Market, 9 May 1950: the French foreign minister Robert Schuman announces detailed plans for a coal and steel community

Below French cartoon, June 1962, on British exclusion from the Market. 'We don't want fatty Commonwealth,' says de Gaulle, alarmed that Europe's resources would be drained.
Bottom EFTA as the poor man's answer to the Common Market (British cartoonist David Low); EFTA was created in 1959 and tariffs were removed by 1968

"LOOK WHAT I MADE OUT OF THE SPARE WHEEL"

Roosevelt's New Deal to the rest of the world; but it also contrasted sharply with the prewar regime in which governments pursued foreign economic policy in a framework determined largely by strictly national conceptions of national welfare and implemented unilaterally or through bilateral treaties between nations.

Evolution of the structure of the world economy, 1947-70

These universalistic plans, laid down in the mid-forties, were derailed by unanticipated delays in the reconstruction of Europe and by the dissolution of wartime cooperation among the Allies into the tensions of the cold war, the latter development leading to the decision to rearm Germany and the attendant need to embed a resurgent Germany in a framework politically acceptable to the rest of Western Europe.

The result, in contrast to the world economy envisaged in 1945, was a heavy *regional* emphasis on Western Europe, which emphasis in turn took two forms, one encompassing the whole of non-communist Europe, the other concentrating on a smaller core of countries in Western Europe. The emphasis on all of non-communist Europe arose from the widespread destruction of the war and the general need for recovery, combined with the perceived threat of subversion or invasion by Russia. The American response to these two needs was the Marshall Plan, under which some $16 billion in grant aid was extended to Europe for economic recovery, and sponsorship of the North Atlantic Treaty Organization (NATO) for the military defence of Western Europe. The Marshall Aid programme led to the creation of the Organization for European Economic Cooperation (OEEC) to coordinate recovery plans among the European countries, to allocate American aid and to facilitate and guide mutual aid within Europe.

One concrete and highly successful manifestation of mutual European cooperation was the creation in 1950 of the European Payments Union (EPU), which in effect permitted the currencies of European countries to become fully convertible for transactions within Europe (capital movements were still subject to control, however) while permitting discrimination against payments to the United States, Canada and other 'hard' currency countries. The need for this European-wide convertibility arose because defensive currency restrictions by each European country, by inhibiting payments to other European countries despite their need for foreign exchange earnings, was impeding the recovery of all. In effect, the EPU was a functional substitute for use of the scarce currency clause (described above), which the IMF never invoked. The United States accepted the discrimination against it – though not without domestic objection – for the sake of European recovery.

A second manifestation of intra-European cooperation was the Code of Liberalization, also adopted in 1950, which led to step-by-step removal of import quotas on trade within Europe, at a pace which was governed from country to country by balance-of-payments strength, but with all countries committed to achieving target levels of liberalization of imports. Later this liberalization was also extended to goods from the United States and other 'dollar area' countries. Again this discrimination violated GATT (although the use of quotas for balance-of-payments reasons did not), but again the United States put European recovery above adherence to the international rules. By 1961 all European quotas on industrial goods were virtually eliminated, the EPU had passed out of existence, and the OEEC was transformed into a new and enlarged organization, the Organization for Economic Cooperation and Development (OECD).

Emphasis on a smaller core of West European countries arose particularly from the need to provide a politically acceptable framework for the recovery and rearmament of Germany. It therefore had a more explicitly political cast than did the looser economic cooperation among all European countries, even when it took an economic form. Some Europeans hoped also that a politically united Europe could preserve the influence and protect the vital interests of a Europe that was now wedged between two continental superpowers, the USA and the USSR. The United States strongly supported the

Above Rome, 25 March
1957: the signature of
the Rome treaties which set
up the Common Market and
Euratom. Among those
signing: Spaak (extreme
left), Adenauer and
Hallstein (centre)

Left Early in 1953 the
joint community in coal and
steel became effective. It was
celebrated by an iron-ore
train which crossed
the Franco-Luxembourg
border on 10 February

Krokodil and the capitalists (January 1952):
(left to right) Krupp, Rothschild, Lady Astor, Dupont,
Rockefeller, Ford and Harriman. The ancestral portraits
are of Krupp, Morgan, Rockefeller and Ford

Conservative slogan for the 1964 election; but Britain
was no longer booming and the new Labour government
was forced to borrow heavily from the IMF

Keep Britain BOOMING
Vote CONSERVATIVE

move towards political union within Europe as an additional counterweight
to the expansion of Soviet Russia, to relieve some of the economic and
defence burden borne by the United States and, not least, to reduce the
internecine European squabbling that had historically erupted into war all
too often, with increasingly devastating effect. On the basis of these essentially political motives, the European Coal and Steel Community (ECSC)
encompassing Belgium, France, West Germany, Italy, Luxembourg and the
Netherlands was formed in 1951, followed by the abortive European
Defence Community (rejected by the French Parliament) in 1954, and the
European Economic Community (EEC) in 1957.

On the Second World War assumption that steel provides the basis for
a modern war machine, the ECSC attempted to provide a supranational
framework for the surveillance and supervision of a resurgent German steel
industry. It provided not only for free trade in coal, iron and steel through
the removal of duties and quotas, but also for the regulation of competition
in those industries and the partial harmonization of other features of the
economic environment that affect trade flows, such as transport rates. The
EEC went much further and provided for complete free trade among the six
member countries in all commodities, for a common trade policy with
respect to the rest of the world, for the gradual elimination of impediments
to the movement of capital and labour within the Community and for the
harmonization of policies affecting costs, competition and the general course
of national economic development. The EEC completed its customs union
(entailing duty-free trade within the Community and a common external
tariff on imports from outside the Community) by 1969, ahead of the
schedule originally envisaged in the Rome Treaty establishing the EEC
in 1957.

Because of its conflict with the equal treatment provisions, the ECSC
required, and got, a waiver of that condition under GATT. The EEC was a
customs union, so it required no waiver in principle. However, several
countries claimed that the Community's common external tariff restricted
trade with outsiders more than did the pre-existing tariffs of the member
countries, a violation of GATT undertakings that would have required compensation. The EEC denied this claim, and the issue was never formally
resolved, although certain downward adjustments in the common tariff were
made unilaterally by the EEC.

One of the major problems faced by the European Community, and one
that created much contention with non-members, was trade in agricultural
products. Because of extensive government support to agriculture in most
countries, simple removal of tariffs would be inadequate to ensure fair and
free competition. A common agricultural policy was required, and its
formation caused several of the most severe crises faced by the EEC. The
scheme finally agreed upon tended to settle internal differences at the
expense of non-members, for it entailed the establishment of rather high
agricultural support prices for many commodities, combined, on the one
hand, with variable levies to prevent the price of duty-paid imports from
falling much below the support prices, regardless of costs in the exporting
countries, and, on the other hand, with government-financed subsidies to
exports to dispose in world markets of the production surpluses that
inevitably resulted from high support prices in the absence of production
controls. Thus the Community became increasingly self-sufficient in a
number of agricultural products during the late sixties, and the decline in
its imports and enlargement of its exports of agricultural products became a
growing source of trade tension with other agricultural exporting countries,
notably the United States.

A third contentious feature of the EEC was its arrangement for the former
colonies of France, Belgium and, to a minor degree, the Netherlands. These
had had special trading arrangements with the metropolitan countries
before the formation of the EEC, and France, in particular, insisted that these
or similar arrangements be continued, even though the colonies (situated
largely in West and Central Africa) had in all cases become independent
countries by 1960. The problem within the Community was resolved by

granting Community-wide preferential treatment to the goods from those countries, and in turn EEC products received preferential treatment over other imports into the 'associated overseas countries', as they came to be called. These arrangements were in clear violation of GATT, although there was no formal ruling to that effect. They did, however, damage the trading interests of a number of other countries, and partly to mitigate these the EEC made a number of new preferential trading arrangements during the late sixties with countries in and around the Mediterranean.

The ambitions of the founders of the EEC went well beyond the formation of a customs union and looked ultimately to political unification. Although this objective was not universally shared within the Community (it was notably rejected by General de Gaulle and his followers in France), the Community took a number of tentative steps toward the coordination and even harmonization of other aspects of economic policy, including monetary and fiscal policies for economic stabilization, regional policies to help the economically depressed areas of member countries, tax policies and industrial policies. In 1970 a modest step was taken towards the harmonization of exchange rate policies, looking towards the day of full monetary integration. An interesting experiment in government support for adjustment to economic change was the Social Fund established to help firms and workers that were hurt by tariff reductions within the Community to find new modes of employment or respond successfully to the new competition. The experiment is interesting in that the Social Fund went virtually unused, demonstrating that in an environment of strong total demand the dislocations were substantially less than had been projected when the Community was formed and that such dislocations as did occur could be accommodated easily without special provisions.

Britain was invited to join the discussions leading first to the formation of the ECSC and later to the formation of the EEC, but participated only perfunctorily. Anxious about the consequences for intra-European trade of the formation of the EEC, Britain proposed in the mid-fifties the establishment of a free trade area in industrial goods for all of Europe, but France, with strong interest in widening agricultural trade, rejected the idea and the EEC declined to cooperate. Subsequently, in 1959, seven nations (Austria, Denmark, Norway, Portugal, Sweden, Switzerland and the United Kingdom) formed the European Free Trade Association (EFTA) under which tariffs and other artificial impediments to trade in industrial goods were to be eliminated among member countries. Unlike the members of the EEC, however, each member of EFTA was free to pursue an independent commercial policy with regard to non-members, and no attempt was made to harmonize policies, commercial or otherwise, although over the course of time the nations found it convenient to cooperate in a number of areas not strictly

After 1953 markets expanded and world trade grew at the rate of eight per cent a year: (*top*) Krupp factory in action again in Essen (1961); (*above*) West German cartoon (1957) caricatures Erhard and his golden calf, the economic miracle

Right Tokyo Stock Exchange; Japanese output grew at nearly ten per cent per year, an unprecedented rate

Rates of exchange against US dollar

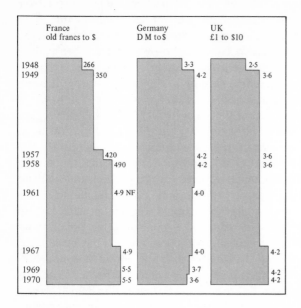

	France old francs to $	Germany D M to $	UK £1 to $10
1948	266	3·3	2·5
1949	350	4·2	3·6
1957	420	4·2	3·6
1958	490	4·2	3·6
1961	4·9 NF	4·0	
1967	4·9	4·0	4·2
1969	5·5	3·7	4·2
1970	5·5	3·6	4·2

Above Russian cartoon following the 1949 European devaluations: a bloated Uncle Sam takes his slice of each cake; (*below*) the New York Stock Exchange – after the war the US became the world's major foreign investor and took a large stake in European industries

required by the Stockholm Convention which established EFTA. Tariffs within EFTA were eliminated by 1968. In the meantime, Britain, joined by Denmark, Ireland and Norway, applied in 1961 for full membership in the EEC (the Rome Treaty had allowed for any *European* country later to join the Community as a full member). They applied again in 1967, after General de Gaulle had pointedly rejected Britain's first application in early 1963. Discussions of these applications were stalled in the late sixties but resumed in 1970, leaving the shape of Europe still to be determined in the 1970s.

While institutional progress was being made among a small group of countries within the EEC, economic cooperation was also continuing on a broader scale, with the formation, in 1961, of the Organization for Economic Cooperation and Development (OECD), an outgrowth of the old OEEC with membership extended to Canada and the United States and, in 1964, to Japan. The OECD became the major forum of non-communist industrial countries to exchange information about, analyze, and discuss actual and prospective economic developments and policies. Although it was not a decision-taking organization, its terms of reference were broader than those of the IMF or GATT, so it could take up issues such as maritime policies, tourism and capital movements which were not well covered in other organizations. It also provided a forum for discussing, in an informal and non-directive fashion, the coordination of national economic policies for stabilization and growth and the coordination of foreign aid and other policies towards less developed countries.

In the meantime, the less developed countries, impatient with the domination by the industrial countries of the IMF, the IBRD, and GATT, reacted by urging the creation of an international agency responsive especially to their own economic needs, not merely on questions of tariffs or capital assistance, but on the whole range of economic policies. The first meeting of the resulting United Nations Conference on Trade and Development (UNCTAD) was held in Geneva in 1964; it was the largest international conference ever held, with 120 countries represented by over 2,000 delegates. It established, often in spite of the objections of the major countries and especially the United States, an agenda for action by the industrial countries, and met again in New Delhi in 1968 to review the progress. Many of the proposals were thoroughly aired and dropped as either impracticable or politically unfeasible. But the IMF did relax its lending criteria to help cover fluctuations in export earnings, and by 1970 most of the industrial countries had agreed in principle to give preference in their tariff policies to the manufactured products of less developed countries as against those of other developed countries, and were discussing the most convenient way to do

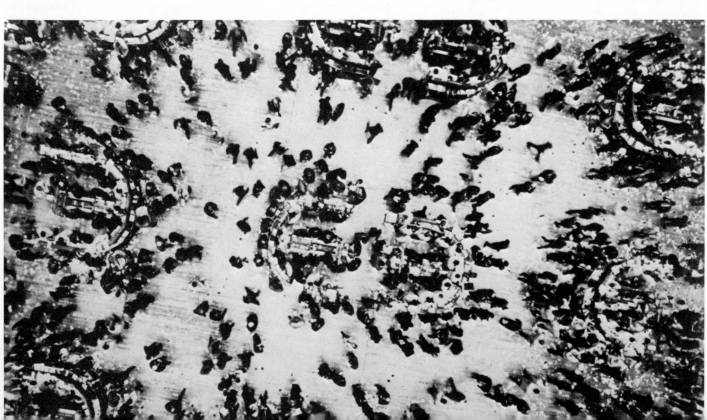

A Russian view of the dollar: 'A Surprise in Bed'

Another Russian comment on the dollar: 'The Devil's Wheel' (between the Bank and the Stock Exchange)

this. If implemented this move would mark a further break with the principle of equal treatment.

While these formal, institutional arrangements in the world economy were occurring, other less formal but equally important developments took place. The most significant of these was the emergence of the US dollar as an international currency. It was expected that the balance-of-payments position of the United States would be exceptionally strong after the Second World War, but it was not anticipated that the dollar would come to be widely held by other countries as international reserves, to the point at which in 1960 $11 billion were held by central banks and governments, amounting to nearly one-fifth of international reserves. The pound sterling, which had come to be held as international reserves before the First World War, remained quantitatively important but was eclipsed by the dollar in providing additions to world reserves, since foreign official holdings of sterling did not grow after their large build-up during the Second World War. Widespread use of the dollar as an international currency gave rise to some anxiety in the 1960s, since the dollars made available to the rest of the world (through the payments deficits of the United States) were not well keyed to the liquidity requirements of the world economy.

A second important development, related to the growing use of the dollar as a reserve currency, was the emergence in the late 1950s and rapid growth throughout the 1960s of the 'eurodollar' market, an international market in short-term financial claims outside the United States but denominated in dollars. London was the centre of the eurodollar market, but financial centres throughout Europe and in Canada dealt heavily in these claims. Their significance is that they provided a place to lend and borrow funds outside the monetary system of any national economy. At the same time, because of the ease of dealing in them, eurodollars provided a link with most national money markets. By 1970 the eurodollar market exceeded $50 billion in size, and was thus larger than the domestic money supply of any country except the United States.

A parallel development, but somewhat later and in much smaller magnitude, was the emergence of an international bond market, again (because the bonds were denominated in dollars or some other 'foreign' currency) outside the regulatory provisions of the major European countries. Both markets represented powerful integrative forces, since by providing alternative investments for investors and alternative sources of funds for borrowers they tended to link national money and capital markets indirectly, even when there was no direct link between them. As a result, most countries found it increasingly difficult during the 1960s to pursue autonomous monetary policies. On more than one occasion countries had to abandon attempts to use monetary policy to stabilize the domestic economy because, for example, any tightening of monetary conditions in order to dampen inflationary pressures would simply attract short-term and even long-term funds from abroad, thereby undercutting the objective of the national monetary authorities to discourage spending by reducing the availability of funds. On other occasions countries took deliberate action to break the link between foreign and domestic money markets, for example by prohibiting the payment of interest on deposits by foreigners, in order to preserve some degree of national monetary autonomy.

A third development of great potential importance was the rapid growth, after the mid-fifties, of foreign business investment. The phenomenon was widespread, but in volume the most important component was American business investment abroad, which grew from $12 billion in 1950 to over $70 billion in 1970, of which about $22 billion was in Europe. Although this last still accounted for only a small proportion of total business investment in Europe, the growth was sufficiently rapid to cause considerable alarm in some circles about preserving European independence from control by Americans. Even this concern was characterized by a certain ambivalence, however, since it was recognized that American firms brought with them new technology and new management techniques, both of which helped to raise European incomes. But the growing importance of the multinational

World exports 1953-69

USA and Canada · EEC · EFTA · Japan · Underdeveloped countries · Eastern bloc

export figures include inter-group trade

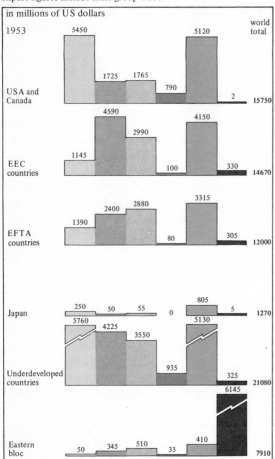

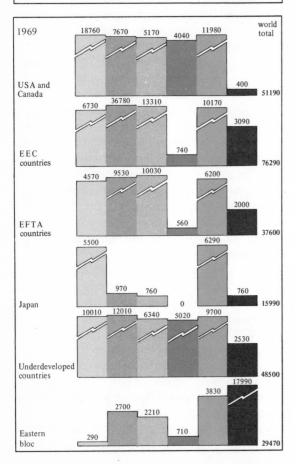

corporation, like the emergence of the eurodollar and the eurobond markets, posed new challenges to national autonomy in the area of economic policy.

Performance of the world economy

Let us turn now from structure to performance. By historical standards, the performance of the world economy from 1945 to 1970 must be rated an outstanding success. The first several years were dominated by recovery from the Second World War, so rapid growth in output and trade can be discounted. But from 1953, widely accepted as postdating the recovery, world trade grew at the extraordinary rate of over eight per cent a year, a rate without historical precedent over such a long period of time. The reasons for this rapid growth are manifold, but foremost among them is the fact that governments gained control over the business cycle, which in the past had periodically sent economies into deep depression. While ups and downs in business activity persisted in the postwar era, they were much muted. Full employment generally prevailed throughout the period, especially in Europe. In Britain, for example, the rate of unemployment rarely rose above two and a half per cent of the labour force, compared with an average above ten per cent in the generally prosperous 1920s. The widely anticipated and feared postwar depression in the United States did not materialize until 1949, and then it was mild compared both to the past and to expectations. Speaking broadly, the governments of the industrial countries were committed to the maintenance of full employment and they generally found the means to achieve it. This was of great importance for the world economy, since it meant that all markets were expanding, providing conditions under which adjustment to economic change is far easier than when markets are stagnant.

In addition to maintaining full employment, the industrial countries also managed to expand their productive capacity at a rate that was rapid by historical standards. As a group their total real output grew by 4·4 per cent a year over the period 1953-68, with a range from 2·9 per cent for Britain to 9·8 per cent for Japan. The growth in output, moreover, was generally such as to reduce the relative inequality among industrial countries, since countries with the highest per capita incomes in the early part of the period – the United States, Canada, Switzerland and Britain – grew less than average, while countries with relatively low per capita incomes – Japan, Greece, Spain, Italy, Austria – tended to grow more rapidly than the average.

Contrary to widespread impression, the less developed countries also grew rapidly during the fifties and sixties, and indeed taken as a group they grew more rapidly than did the industrial countries, nearly five per cent a year as against under four and a half per cent a year. Growth in the less developed countries in the sixties in fact exceeded the five per cent target of the United Nations 'Development Decade', initially thought to have been barely achievable. Because of a growth in population of over two per cent a year, however, growth in per capita incomes in the less developed countries, although still at a rate without historical precedent lagged behind those in the industrial countries and the relative (as well as absolute) levels of per capita income diverged between the two groups.

Economic growth and control of the business cycle were the most important influences on trade, but a reduction in tariffs and other barriers to trade also contributed to the rapid growth in trade. In addition to trade liberalization (the removal of quotas) under the OEEC, six major multilateral tariff negotiations were undertaken under the auspices of GATT, in 1947, 1948, 1950-1, 1956, 1961-2 and 1964-7, the last being known as the Kennedy Round because it followed a trade initiative by President Kennedy of the United States in response to the formation of the EEC. The Kennedy Round was distinguished by extensive across-the-board tariff reductions, breaking with the previous practice of selectively negotiated reductions, by over one-third on industrial goods, bringing average tariff levels in the major countries to under ten per cent on manufactured goods. The reductions in the Kennedy Round, like those in earlier negotiations, were extended to all other adherents of GATT under the equal treatment clause, even those (largely less developed countries) that did not agree to reduce their own

British meat imports; by 1970 world tariffs in general were lower than ever before, but more world trade was subject to preferential arrangements in spite of paper commitment to the contrary

tariffs during the negotiations. In addition, the discriminatory tariff reductions within the EEC and EFTA also greatly stimulated trade in the sixties within those areas. A fourth factor contributing to the growth of trade was the improvement in international transportation and communication, resulting both in reduced costs (relative to the value of goods shipped) and in increased reliability. The same factors have also greatly increased international travel, which at eleven per cent a year grew even more rapidly than international trade.

On the financial side, the IMF remained very conservative during its early years of existence, to the point that it felt obliged to protest in 1953 that some of its members were under the impression that its funds were not available for use. From the mid-fifties, however, the Fund gained momentum, and its crowning achievement came in 1970 when a new man-made form of international money, technically and somewhat obscurely called Special Drawing Rights (SDRs), was created under IMF auspices. The problem was that gold, the traditional form in which countries held their international reserves after 1870, was becoming available in quantities too small to satisfy the reserve needs of a rapidly growing world economy. As noted above, the US dollar provided additional reserves to supplement gold, but reliance on the dollar also had its weaknesses.

In the first place, the US balance-of-payments deficit, which was the source of additional dollars for the rest of the world, was not keyed to the requirements of international reserves. Second, the use of a national currency for international reserves seemed to give that country an international printing press, leaving it under no apparent restraint in its international spending. Many observers felt that the process of reserve creation should be made subject to international supervision (the same argument applied to new gold production, which also was not keyed to reserve requirements), and the solution was to create SDRs, more aptly called 'paper gold', to be created according to international decision, allocated to countries according to a fixed formula, and used, like monetary gold, to settle debts between the central banks and governments of the world. Three and a half billion dollars worth of SDRs were created and distributed for the first time in January 1970. In principle, this represents a solution to the problem of international liquidity that had preoccupied monetary officials during the sixties.

Increased growth and stability

An overview of the performance of the world economy 1945-70 would suggest, then, that it did well in a number of dimensions. There was more economic growth and greater economic stability than in the past. There was some tendency to reduce international inequality in relative terms, although rapid growth in population in some less developed countries resulted in an increase in inequality for them. There was not even much inflation after the immediate postwar adjustment – prices of goods moving

Preferential trading areas

- EEC and associates (Greece and Turkey)
- EFTA
- Central American Common Market
- LAFTA
- COMECON-CMEA
- Sterling Area
- East African Community
- Conseil de l'Entente

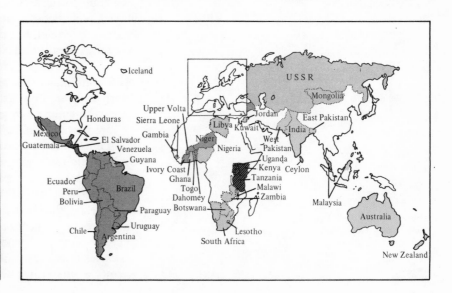

International liquidity at end of 1960 and mid-1970

1960　　1970

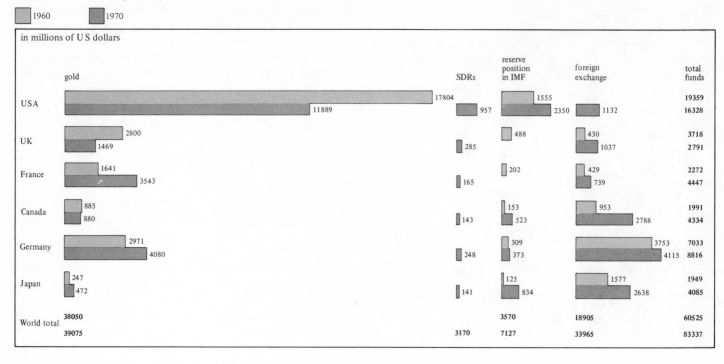

in millions of US dollars

	gold	SDRs	reserve position in IMF	foreign exchange	total funds
USA (1960)	17804		1555		19359
USA (1970)	11889	957	2350	1132	16328
UK (1960)	2800		488	430	3718
UK (1970)	1469	285		1037	2791
France (1960)	1641		202	429	2272
France (1970)	3543	165		739	4447
Canada (1960)	885		153	953	1991
Canada (1970)	880	143	523	2788	4334
Germany (1960)	2971		309	3753	7033
Germany (1970)	4080	248	373	4115	8816
Japan (1960)	247		125	1577	1949
Japan (1970)	472	141	834	2638	4085
World total (1960)	38050		3570	18905	60525
World total (1970)	39075	3170	7127	33965	83337

Balance of payments in current account 1950-68

1950　　1968

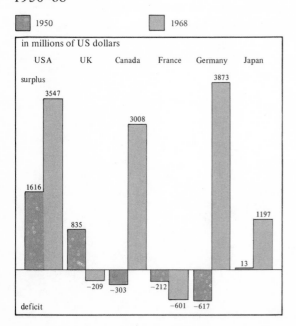

in millions of US dollars

	USA	UK	Canada	France	Germany	Japan
surplus 1950	1616	835				13
surplus 1968	3547		3008		3873	1197
deficit 1950			−209	−303	−617	
deficit 1968				−212	−601	

in international trade increased by less than one per cent a year – when account is taken of the fact that increases in the consumer price index, so visible in most countries, are in large part a reflection of the rapid economic growth, since the price of labour (for services) enters heavily into such indexes, and the price of labour is also the income of labourers. None the less world inflation did accelerate markedly in the last few years of the sixties.

By 1970 a true 'world economy' was probably closer to reality than ever before. Trade flourished and capital, although subject to restrictions, moved in unprecedented volume. More to the point, movement of both goods and capital impinged heavily on domestic economies, and the sensitivity of international transactions to domestic economic developments tied the economies of the industrial countries more closely together than ever before. For example, because of the eurodollar and eurobond markets countries find great difficulty in pursuing monetary policies aimed at damping booms or stimulating demand, unless by chance or by design they are in phase with other countries.

One of the ironies of the world economy in 1970 was that, despite a commitment on paper to non-discrimination in international trade, probably a higher proportion of world trade was subject to preferential tariff arrangements than at any previous time, excepting only the special arrangements prevailing during and immediately following the Second World War. The biggest preferential groups were the EEC, EFTA and the Commonwealth Preference System, but there were also a host of other arrangements, e.g. between Australia and New Zealand and for automobiles between Canada and the United States, most of them new. But it was probably also true that tariffs of the major trading nations on industrial goods were lower than ever before. In sharp contrast, temperate agricultural products were traded in markets fragmented by nationalistic policies.

Moreover, the trade of the less developed countries, which accounted for about one-fifth of the world total, fell outside some of these generalizations. Under the most-favoured-nation clause, exports of less developed countries were subject to the same low duties that, at the end of the period, burdened trade among industrial countries. But their exports faced two special difficulties. First, the tariff structure of most industrial countries was of such a character that it encouraged the location of processing industries at home, so that even simple processes, such as oil-seed crushing, were done in the industrial importing rather than the non-industrial exporting countries. Second, whenever less developed countries were successful in the export of finished manufactures, as with some lines of cotton textiles, industrial countries either imposed import restraints or threatened to, thus impeding the process of efficient industrialization in the poor countries.

For their part, most less developed countries, far from following a more liberal trade policy during the fifties and sixties, increasingly raised barriers to imports, sometimes to truly extraordinary heights. Tariffs of 300 per cent were not uncommon in many countries. Under the name of development, most such countries – there were notable exceptions – pursued a strategy of 'import substitution', whereby the domestic production of goods formerly imported was encouraged under conditions of extreme protection from import competition, often leading to very high costs of production relative to those prevailing elsewhere. Aware of the high costs involved in producing a wide range of industrial goods in what are frequently very small markets, a number of less developed countries attempted to form partial or complete free trade areas among themselves, to enlarge the market, among which the most successful were the Central American Common Market and the East African Customs Union.

Finally, the 'world economy' for practical purposes excluded the communist countries, despite major efforts in the early years after the war to include Russia in the IMF and the ITO. Trade with the communist countries took place, and in fact grew about as rapidly as world trade overall in the sixties, but it was subject to special arrangements and was continually plagued by currency problems. For these reasons, and because firms in

South African gold reserves in the vaults at Pretoria; each ingot is worth £5,000 ($12,000)

Right Cartoonist's guide to the US financial system

GNP at 1963 prices

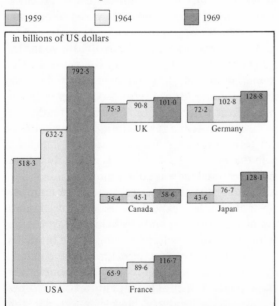

in billions of US dollars

1959 1964 1969

USA: 518·3, 632·2, 792·5
UK: 75·3, 90·8, 101·0
Germany: 72·2, 102·8, 128·8
Canada: 35·4, 45·1, 58·6
Japan: 43·6, 76·7, 128·1
France: 65·9, 89·6, 116·7

In London the crowds of a pre-television era watch ministers on their way to Parliament for the debate on the fall of the pound (1949). Britain's financial state after the war was desperate, the road to recovery painfully slow and uncertain

Harold Wilson tries to patch up the pound: a *Guardian* comment (1969) on Britain's foreign debts

communist countries were not generally free to trade or borrow as they wished, transactions of the rest of the world with the communist countries remained of relatively minor importance.

Unfinished business

At the close of the period under consideration, several problems seemed likely to dominate international economic policy in the 1970s. The first was the mechanism by which countries correct imbalances in their international payments. Under the Bretton Woods Agreement a distinction was drawn between temporary and fundamental imbalances, the former to be financed by drawing on international reserves, the latter to be corrected by discrete changes in a country's exchange rate, up or down as the occasion required. This mechanism was used frequently after the formation of the IMF, mostly by less developed countries, but also by a number of major countries. Most of the currencies of the world were devalued against the dollar in 1949, a part of the postwar readjustment. Subsequently, among the major trading countries France devalued its franc in 1957, 1958 and 1969; Britain devalued the pound in 1967; Germany revalued the mark in 1961 and again in 1969; the Netherlands revalued the guilder in 1961; and Canada devalued its dollar in 1962 and revalued it in 1970.

Despite frequent use, the mechanism revealed various imperfections. There was always considerable uncertainty about whether a given imbalance was merely temporary or whether it would prove fundamental, and during this period a test of will often developed between those who thought the exchange parity should be changed – and moved considerable sums of money across the exchange markets in anticipation of such a change – and the governmental authorities who were reluctant to admit the need for a change. Considerations of national or political prestige frequently clouded the decision whether or not to change a parity. As time went on and the international mobility of capital increased, the sums involved in speculation for or against a currency became quite enormous (in anticipation of a revaluation of the mark $4,000 million moved into Germany in a single month in 1969, an amount equivalent to nearly one-fifth of the total German money supply), and when changes in parities did occur large losses were incurred by the national authorities as a result. Despite an impressive array of agreements among central banks to provide short-term financial support to one another in periods of heavy currency speculation, the large movements of funds greatly disturbed both foreign exchange markets and internal financial markets and complicated the processes of normal foreign trade and other international and even internal transactions.

By 1970, therefore, governments were exploring possible modifications in the mechanism of adjustment to payments imbalances, searching for ways to introduce somewhat greater flexibility into the movement of exchange rates while still retaining the supposed advantages of a system of basically fixed rates. But disagreements over the appropriate changes continued.

A second issue concerned the export prospects and possibilities of the less developed countries. These countries required growing sources of foreign exchange in order to buy materials and capital equipment essential to their development. Foreign assistance in the form of grants or loans in the required amounts was neither desirable nor politically possible. Traditional exports of tropical foodstuffs, beverages and raw materials would continue to be their major source of foreign earnings for some time to come, but demand for these products in the industrial countries was not likely to grow rapidly enough to provide the required increase in earnings.

The logic of this situation suggested that the less developed countries would have to increase substantially their exports of manufactured goods or else settle for rates of economic growth substantially below the aspirations of their leaders and below the rates of growth prevailing in the industrial countries. The difficulty was that the manufactures that these countries could export competitively were those requiring for production relatively large amounts of low-skill labour, goods such as low-quality textiles, clothes, shoes and other leather goods, wood products, bicycles and other light

The inevitable French devaluation of 1969, long resisted
by de Gaulle for reasons of national pride

Below Russian cartoon (1969), 'A New Serious Patient'
Bottom 'To new shores?' A German cartoon (1969) shows
an unsteady international monetary system hopping
from one crisis to another

manufactures. These goods, in turn, competed directly with the relatively
low-skill, often non-progressive industries of the industrial countries, so
that adjustment to import competition was especially difficult and such
imports encountered political resistance.

In fact the exports of light manufactures by the less developed countries
grew very rapidly during the fifties and sixties, twice as rapidly as world trade
in general, but from a low starting-point. Resistance to these growing
imports into the industrial countries led in 1962 to the signing of the Long-
term Cotton Textile Agreement, under which exporting countries agreed
to restrain the rate of growth of their exports of cotton textiles when requested to do so, and, failing that, importing countries were permitted to
impose restrictions, GATT notwithstanding. In 1970 an attempt was made by
the United States to extend this agreement to woollen and synthetic textiles,
and protectionist pressures also mounted over shoes and other products.

At the same time, several proposals for granting tariff preferences to the
manufactures of less developed countries, arising out of the earlier UNCTAD
sessions, were under serious consideration, and the major industrial countries were committed in principle to granting some form of such preferences.
There was some indication, however, that these proposals were in the nature
of political gestures rather than being addressed to the fundamental need
for assuring ready access to the major markets of the world and at the same
time taking steps to ease any burden of adjustment falling on domestic
segments of the labour force and domestic firms. The preferential tariff proposals were hedged with exceptions and escape clauses and they failed to
insure against nullification through side-agreements concerning restraint in
export growth. This too would be a major issue in the 1970s.

A third, less immediately pressing but ultimately no less important issue
concerned the national response to growing economic interdependence
among the industrial countries themselves. High mobility of capital and
even of labour (especially skilled labour, leading to 'brain drains') erodes
national autonomy in determining and successfully carrying out national
economic and social objectives. The influence of monetary policy over the
course of the domestic economy is sharply curtailed, for instance, if attempts
to tighten money simply result in inflows of funds from abroad to make up
the difference, and attempts to ease domestic monetary conditions instead
stimulate an outflow of funds. Similarly, the increasing mobility of business
establishments can inhibit the use of high business taxes, for such taxes will
discourage the location of firms in a high-tax country when they have
alternative places to locate and when, with the relatively low tariffs and other
barriers to trade prevailing at the end of the sixties, they can none the less
enjoy selling in the market of the high-tax country. In addition, the fact that
a rapidly increasing share of *inter*national trade is *intra*-firm trade provides
companies with an opportunity, by manipulating the prices at which goods
and services are sold between different parts of the same firm, to minimize
their total tax payments by shifting profits to those parts of the firm that are
in countries with relatively low taxes on profits. The growth of the multi-
national firm also complicates the task of those countries that desire to
pursue a policy of preserving competition from imports, since the takeover
of existing foreign firms reduces potential competition, and the difficulties
of detecting market collusion increase with the range of legitimate business
activity outside the country. Even redistributive taxation for social reasons
can be inhibited by the growing mobility of individuals, especially the highly
skilled individual, who can find employment opportunities in culturally
familiar surroundings abroad if he feels too hard pressed at home.

If the increasing movement towards one world economy that was evident
in the sixties especially among the industrial countries continues, it will
render the nation-state obsolete in the realm of economic policy. It suggests
the need to extend the jurisdiction of government to encompass the enlarged range of mobility for firms, funds and persons. In the 1970s new
forms of inter-governmental cooperation and collaboration will have to be
worked out if the tendencies towards world economy are not to be reversed
through nationalistic attempts to retain control.

Consumer society to come:
an Argentinian couple
riveted by a television
set in a Buenos Aires
store window

Lucy Webster

Problems of Prosperity

During the twenty-five years 1945-70, almost every country in the world was dominated by its own striving for material prosperity. None the less, the prosperity that was attained was only partial, nor did it prove to be as satisfying as had been expected. 'Partial prosperity', 'relative prosperity', 'minority prosperity': these terms describe the facts. These terms also indicate a large part of the problem: prosperity was not normal. In a few societies it was normal to be well off, and unusual to be really poor; but in the world as a whole the opposite was true. Some of the problems of the period arose from the uneven distribution of prosperity, and other problems arose from a limited and unbalanced perception of the concept of prosperity as a goal.

The quarter of a century after the Second World War was shaped by three predominant concerns which followed each other in overlapping waves. The first concern was to *create* prosperity, the second was to *spread* it, and the third was to *question* its value.

At the end of the Second World War most countries viewed the immediate future as a tunnel of tribulation with some degree of brightness opening out at the end. In Western Europe the trials of reconstruction did in fact lead to real prosperity for many peoples and by 1958 the average per capita income was about $1,000 a year. In the pre-industrial countries of Africa and Asia hopes were very high; it was widely felt that prosperity would flow naturally from political independence. But in fact by 1958 per capita income in East and South-east Asia, excluding Japan, was about $90 a year and that in Africa was about $110.

Thus the goal – prosperity and an expanding gross national product – which had seemed natural and attainable in the late forties looked more difficult ten years later and this goal was also seen to be more complicated. In pre-industrial countries the prior conditions of prosperity would need to be sought first. Moreover, in the late fifties and early sixties even the most affluent societies began to notice internal pockets of poverty which persisted and did not shrink away into the surrounding affluence: the hidden poor were discovered. Within countries and between countries acceptable levels of productivity had not led automatically to acceptable patterns of distribution. This fact, although only reluctantly admitted, did lead to a slight shift in emphasis: simply to create prosperity was not an adequate goal, prosperity had to be generated where it was needed.

Throughout the 1960s the affluent corners of the world experienced crises which made many people question the earlier assumption that creating and spreading prosperity was a valid goal in any form. The urban crisis, the technological/automation crisis, the alienation/participation crisis, the drug crisis, the student crisis, the environment crisis, combined to shake the faith of many. While each of these and other related problems were seen as critical only by a minority, the cumulative effect was great. The need to preserve an environment for living presented the most basic challenge to the age-old cult of productivity and consumption. Many came to perceive what the few had noted first: earth with its air and water is a finite system which cannot be continually exploited with profligate abandon, and even if it could be, there might be better goals in life for man.

The geography of affluence

In the twenty-five years after the Second World War the global map of affluence did not change greatly. This is shown on the diagram which

81

Balance of rich and poor 1950-66

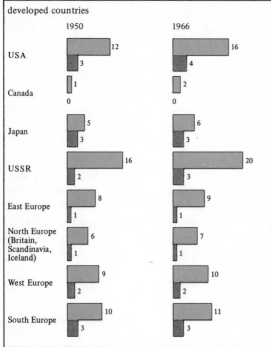

rich ▪️ poor

proportion of population in each category in tens of millions

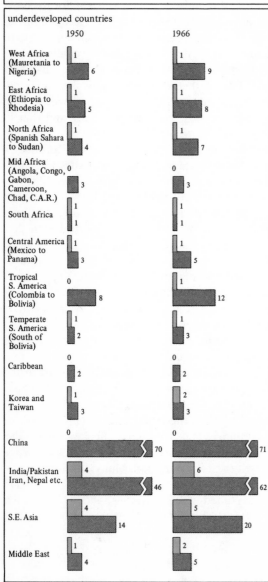

indicates the balance of rich and poor in 1950 and 1966. People who are considered poor are shown as grey, and people viewed as rich as green. The terms 'rich' and 'poor' do not relate to any absolute level of income, but reflect local definitions and perceptions for each country. Thus the 'poor' in the United States are the people officially defined as poor in the US context, and the 'rich' in India are the people perceived as prosperous in that context. These local definitions correspond to educated everyday speech in which people anywhere in the world might refer to a poor American, or a rich Filipino.

Two points stand out most clearly from the diagram. Firstly, it shows that time has worked but minor changes. Secondly, the diagram is much more grey than green. In the twenty-five years after the Second World War many more people were troubled by the lack of prosperity than by its excesses.

Throughout this entire period hundreds and hundreds of millions of people experienced no appreciable improvement in their standard of living: the norm remained less than $200 per year per person throughout country after country in the pre-industrial parts of the world. In such countries information *about* affluence spread very effectively through films and radio, through magazines and literacy and education, and later through television, but affluence itself did not spread, at least not enough to be noticed. The idea that the poor are getting poorer was not really true – except in a few countries. However, the fact that the poor countries became richer so very slowly, and by so little that most people could see no change, was one of the greatest problems of the period. In several respects it became one of the problems of prosperity. For the rich did become richer, significantly richer, and thus the contrast grew. For the first time in history the contrast between rich and poor became both clear and unpalatable to hundreds of millions of poor people throughout the world. The explosion in information and communications provided knowledge and images of prosperity, while the general spread of egalitarian ideas provided hope and rising expectations.

In most pre-industrial countries prosperity was experienced only by a small but growing minority. The professional and commercial and official middle classes grew. These groups expanded to absorb a large share of their countries' growing wealth. Thus a relatively affluent sub-culture developed whose members experienced many of the same internal problems of prosperity as did the affluent groups in richer countries. On the other hand, these middle-class groups in poor countries did not expand as fast or as far as the expectations of the growing numbers of educated and partially educated people. Thus a new sub-middle class was created which experienced the problems of being outside the affluent society with particular acuity. This class, consisting largely of unemployed and under-employed white-collar workers, epitomized the frustrations of seeing and expecting affluence without having it.

Relative poverty

How many people are prosperous in the prosperous countries is a moot point. For many years it was felt that if everyone worked for a bigger cake for all, all the people would come to have enough. And thus it was assumed that prosperity would automatically draw people out of the pockets of poverty. But by 1960 it was noted in a number of countries that the poor were still there and, what was worse, the evidence suggested that it was endemic to the system that certain groups would remain outside the aura of growing prosperity.

This was most clear in the richest country, with its maximum technological change and minimum social services. In the United States during the very years of greatest economic growth and lowest national unemployment, about a quarter of the families in many cities were living on 'sub-employment' incomes near or below the official poverty line. While large corporations and the people with the skills to work in these prospered, a second-class economy languished. In fact, technological progress increased the size of this second-class economy. In factories, and especially on farms, machines replaced unskilled people and forced them into the ranks of welfare families and into sub-employment with part-time or casual jobs in small non-union factories, restaurants and garages. In the early 1960s twenty per cent of Americans lived in families which were officially classified as below the poverty line.

Similar pockets of poverty tended to persist in almost all Western European countries, although the more extensive welfare systems limited the extent of the poverty and cushioned some aspects of its cruelty. Gradually it was recognized that one of the serious problems of prosperity was that affluence did not automatically spread to fill in the depressions of need, but often piled up where least needed. While the welfare systems of most industrial societies mitigated this tendency, they did not reverse it.

Relative affluence

If affluence began where poverty ended, one could rightly say that the people in the relatively prosperous countries were actually prosperous – even if a fifth of them did live in poverty. But affluence did not begin where poverty ended. This became clear in the late sixties. In Britain most notably, but in other countries as well, group after group of solid workers in respected skilled jobs went on strike for the wages and the status and the recognition which might hopefully shift them from the outside to the inside of the consumer affluent society. In France in 1968 one element that made the events of May something more than a student demonstration was the fact that many workers saw in the supermarket, gadget-orientated ethos around them much that they could both envy and despise. The frustrations and the back-to-the-wall feelings of the white manual workers in the United States were largely expressed in right-wing gestures: support for George Wallace, patriotic protests against students and other Vietnam War protesters, fear of black neighbours, and a fence round the house. While relatively egalitarian countries such as the Scandinavian countries did not develop outsider groups to any such extent, the norm of the sixties was some form of middle-majority alienation in most prosperous countries – in the Netherlands, Germany and Japan as well as in the countries already mentioned.

Differences existed between these groups in the different countries, but the point here is their similarity. Through the late fifties and the sixties, in country after country where everyone had heard of the affluent society, group after group came to see themselves as outsiders. These groups and these people were not the poor who had really fallen outside the economy and the society of their nations; these were people who were by any objective standard the real backbone of their nations, but they felt that this objective truth was not recognized by others and thus they could not believe in it themselves and felt alienated.

The magic credit card: British cartoon

Advertising in the Eastern bloc: (*below*) a Russian hoarding proclaims the virtues of government coffee; (*right*) a station poster invokes Parisian glamour

Commuters at a London tube station during a partial strike, October 1969: crowded and slow, but still painless compared to Tokyo or New York

Automobile production line: the car became a symbol of affluence in the sixties throughout the Western world

Perhaps the affluent society was by definition something which few people could feel they were part of. If belonging meant being rewarded with enough money to acquire most of the goods which the glossy images of affluence extolled, then few people would feel adequately rewarded. And since the ethos and standards of the time were largely material, not to be rewarded was almost the same as not being recognized.

In fact more people were better rewarded with the material goods of life than ever before in history. The quarter of a century following the Second World War was marked by a dramatic expansion in the numbers of people who came to own a whole range of consumer products. In the prosperous countries there were enough of some products for practically every family to have one. Even poor people had television sets, and the middle-majority man who protested at being outside the affluent society was likely to have a car as well. Evidently this was not enough if one still felt one needed more – and that other people had more. The needs felt here were partly a question of one's self-image relative to one's image of the good life, and partly they were valid physical and objective needs. There was a tendency for new possessions to generate the need for additional new possessions – a washing-machine requires a dryer, a car needs a garage, a house out of town requires a car and a plethora of other equipment, and so forth. Thus the prosperity of the fifties and sixties tended to create a sense of not having quite made it.

The diagram at the beginning of this article indicates the official view of adequacy and poverty in each country and reflects the views which people held of other people's prosperity. But in fact many people who looked prosperous did not feel it. Thus the diagram of affluence, grey and unprosperous as it is, is if anything too optimistic. In many of the most prosperous countries the particular images held of an affluent consumer society were widely felt to be part of a style of life which was out of reach. A map showing only the people who considered *themselves* prosperous might include only the economic top two-fifths of the people in the prosperous countries. But how people view themselves is a question of social and individual expectations as well as a question of economics. As the 1960s ended it became clear that some and perhaps many of the problems of prosperity were problems of misplaced expectations and invalid goals.

Questions and antitheses

The cult of productivity and consumption has its roots deep in Western culture – in the Industrial Revolution, in the Protestant ethic, in various forms of religious and economic imperialism. And perhaps its greatest triumph was the hundred years of industrial expansion in North America up to 1960. Frontier habits combined with unprecedented material assets to generate a hundred-year orgy of creative exploitation. There was enormous faith in progress, development, initiative and work. In the 1960s the validity of this faith was questioned. In discussing the questions which were raised, it should be borne in mind that during the very period of questioning a new 'technotronic', 'post-industrial' cult of expansion and productivity began to emerge.

If the long-respected cult of productivity was the original thesis of the quarter of a century following the Second World War, the themes of antithesis which arose during the 1960s were less unified. In fact there was a continuum of reactions against the thesis that productivity equals prosperity and freedom for all. At one end of this continuum were reactions against too little prosperity and its unequal distribution. At the other end were reactions against too much misshapen prosperity. And between were many reactions which took more or less account of both sets of facts. For example, the US blue-collar workers who demonstrated against black integration and other liberal efforts, were reacting against not having a large enough share in prosperity, but they did not question the basic goals of the affluent society. At the other extreme were the Dutch youths who formed the Provos movement: they hardly cared about quantity or shares, but only about the quality of life and its goals. Groups between on the continuum included the French workers who joined the 1968 student protests: they questioned the apparently empty Americanized goals around them, but they did so especially because the share of the new affluence which came to them was particularly inadequate and shoddy.

Student protest movements arose as a response to both sets of facts. Through both the fifties and sixties there was a strong desire among young people and students in the affluent countries to identify with the problems and with some of the more radical politics of Third World pre-industrial countries. The young people who went to these countries in Peace Corps and Voluntary Service programmes and those who campaigned at home for movements such as Oxfam were impressed with the quantitative failure of the system, and often they were moderately optimistic: they felt that quantitative changes and shifts could make the system work.

Later, Third World First supporters and the admirers of Mao Tse-tung and Che Guevara were more pessimistic. While still responding to the failure of the system to deal with quantitative problems, they declared that any step-by-step changes would be useless. By the end of the sixties total change was demanded. It was demanded because the existing system did not work: it did not provide enough for enough people. Total change was also demanded because even if the system could be made to work it wouldn't be any good. Towards the end of the sixties the students who shouted that the system was hopeless were joined by those who quietly feared that present world trends in exploitation and pollution could soon destroy the ecology of earth, and might even sooner create an intolerable environment for man.

The issues for student protest were real issues. And the perception of what was wrong was often valid. However, most radical student and youth movements did not have any meaningful programme for solving problems either in the short run or even 'come the revolution'. The new world demanded was not clearly defined; there was no Utopian goal-defining wing of the

A Russian cartoon (1959) captioned: 'SOS . . . Spare Our Souls'

Above Coca Cola makes the *Time* magazine cover

Right Times Square, New York, hub of a city: a long exposure picture on a rainy night

Right The other America: in the early sixties as much as twenty per cent of the population lived in families officially classified as below the poverty line

A religious organization distributes meal tickets to the poor (1961)

revolutionary student movement. Nor was there often much empathy between the main stream of the movement and those groups which did from time to time define themselves by working for immediate goals in the politics and policies of every day. Thus it was clear what students in revolt were against but less clear what they were for. This fact led to an underestimation of the seriousness of the movement. To talk of boutique communists as in France was in fact delightfully descriptive, but also unjustifiably disparaging. The central themes of student revolt were felt and understood in the beliefs and attitudes of a wide segment of young people, even though they were not articulated in programmatic terms which older people could understand. The young people nurtured on television images and schooled in the arts of flexible lateral thought could not express their thoughts in words but tended to refer to them in gestures or slogans, and this was possible even internationally *because* there were core questions and attitudes which were widely understood.

The core questions which youth raised related to problems both in the university and in society. University problems generated the widest consensus not only because they were most immediately to hand, but also because it was here that student expectations of fairness and human liberties were most clearly violated. Students did not need to believe in or identify with the class struggle to feel imposed upon – they just needed to believe the liberal tenets of Locke and Mill. Prosperity led to an enormous growth in student populations and this led to pressure on living accommodation, classroom space, teaching facilities and faculty time. Especially in the larger universities, there was little student-faculty dialogue, and professors were remote and preoccupied. There was little sense of being in a community of scholars, but rather a sense of being processed by syllabuses, schedules and computers.

Students questioned whether the university was not primarily an instrument to condition them for the existing society which they disliked. The problems of crowding and impersonal bureaucracy were worst in countries such as France and Germany where any student of a certain standard could enter university. Questions about values and the lack of critical judgement in the university were most pressing in countries such as the United States and Britain where the search for relevance of university work to the world outside led to practices which seemed to prove the manipulative intent of the university. Courses were designed for their relevance to industry, university/industry exchanges were encouraged, and large segments of academic research budgets were dependent upon space research and military projects.

The questions which students raised were raised widely and felt widely. However, the Marxist, Maoist and Marcusian answers which the most vocal students tended to bring to these questions were believed less widely; there was no common youth ideology, but rather a common style, mood and attitude. This led to extraordinary solidarity: the generation gap's inter-generation discord was matched by intra-generation accord which produced a band-wagon effect. When a group of youth leaders took a position, it did not matter precisely what they said or what they demanded, providing they spoke to the attitudes and the questions of common concern.

Beyond the universities many groups shared with students their questions and their doubts about prosperity. There were doubts about the pace of technological change and about the direction of change. Other doubts concerned the tendency of consensus politics in many countries to provide few levers for the social control of trends.

Change and the crisis of identity

The pace of technological change threatened people's status and roles more than it threatened their jobs. In the United States unskilled industrial and agricultural workers did in fact lose jobs to join a displaced urban proletariat. But in Western Europe and Japan change was gentler so that the people who did move from farm to city and from unskilled jobs to other jobs were not so much pushed out as lured on. This difference was not due to any greater poverty in American life, but to its greater costs: the perceived minimum living standards were so high that all sorts of machines became cheaper than men. In other prosperous countries unemployment tended to be concentrated in certain regions and certain industries; and general technological unemployment was more a fear than a fact. It was not only feared by unskilled workers, but also by skilled workers and by white-collar workers as sophisticated machines including computers were developed with the capacity to replace many jobs. In spite of this capacity there was in fact little beyond a gradual orderly displacement of man by machines. None the less, the threat was there. The future might well be worse and in any case, to be unfavourably compared with a machine did not increase human dignity.

The threat of automation was part of the crisis of identity which marked the late fifties and the sixties. Once the prosperous countries had fought their war, won their reconstruction, and even won some *Wirtschaftswunder*, the fascination of productivity and building and working machines decreased. If machines could not only do what man could do but do it better, what was the value of man? Increasing automation led to increasing specialization and the fragmentation of tasks so that the operator could not have the same sense of achievement as the craftsman had. As the sophistication of machines increased, pride in controlling the beast might too have increased, but with specialization the opposite was usually true. And often a worker

Top Hobo at an Indiana station, between trains
Above A tramp in Paris

At Milan Station, 1962, the poor bed down on sacks and newspapers; the city offered little hope for unskilled immigrants from the underdeveloped south

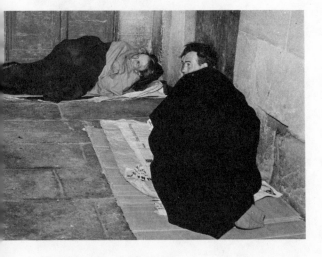

Time magazine cover: in the late sixties the middle classes in the United States felt their material prosperity and way of life threatened by the breakdown of law and order

could ask whether he was running his machine or whether it was running him. Society could ask the same question about all of its machines.

Technology had its own direction as well as its own momentum. In the production of consumer goods, in the growth, in the sprawl and the crawl of cities, in space research and military expenditure, the *main* priorities selected themselves; people were not in control.

Technology and choice

In selecting consumer goods and services the number of choices available to people was enormous, but the range was essentially limited to goods which had proved profitable within the market economy. People had a vast choice of type of car, but could not choose adequate public transport in lieu of a car. People could choose any number of items for the home, but if they wanted a neighbourhood play area for children, scarcity value dictated a completely different level of expenditure – either in high prices near other amenities, or in travel time and costs elsewhere. There were ample means to make minor choices, but few means to determine major priorities. The quality of life was not determined by people, but by invisible, mindless market mechanisms.

This invisible hand tended to give each family a patch of grass and a few trees so that no one had fields and woods to share and enjoy. The market mechanisms tended to proliferate individual houses, built at the edge of the countryside, destroying the countryside as they spread. The sub-urban sprawl of mean houses with mean gardens which had enveloped British cities during the 1930s began to appear in some parts of continental European cities; and Japan developed its own subtopia of crowded houses packed together without plan.

Throughout Western Europe, the market economy spread houses thinly and expensively across the land to meet the market demand of the rich, and the bits of land left over were used for subsidized homes for the poor. The pressure of people on land was immense. The jobs and the excitement of the megalopolis drew people in like a magnet, forming giant urban regions. Western Holland became one vast city region, as did other wide areas – around London, around Frankfurt and Mainz, and around Düsseldorf and Cologne. While suburban sprawl was mainly a feature of Northern Europe, during the fifties and sixties traditionally enclosed cities such as Paris and Brussels and Milan also spread outwards, not only in high-rise suburbs, but even to include some lower-density housing. As European cities spread outwards they did not leave a vacuum in the centre as North American cities had done. Centuries of thoughtful development was preserved with pride not only by the city councils, but especially by the lavish attentions of the rich. But in North America where space seemed vast and waste was normal the greatest problem of the cities was their discarded centres. Abandoned

The counter-revolution; construction workers bring out the Stars and Stripes in lower Broadway for Nixon and a patriotic war in Vietnam (1969)

nous sommes le pouvoir

'We are the power': the May 1968 student rebellion also brought one of France's largest industrial strikes involving nearly 10 million workers, whose demands were financial rather than ideological. According to Marcusian theory students in the West have taken over the disruptive role forecast by Marx for the proletariat

Striking miners outside union headquarters in London. As in the US, the exhaustion of coal-seams and advent of new forms of power brought low wages, unemployment and strikes among miners at the end of the sixties

Working population involved in industrial disputes

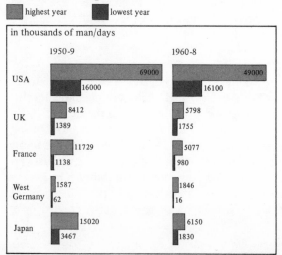

	highest year		lowest year	

in thousands of man/days

	1950-9		1960-8	
USA	69000		49000	
	16000		16100	
UK	8412		5798	
	1389		1755	
France	11729		5077	
	1138		980	
West Germany	1587		1846	
	62		16	
Japan	15020		6150	
	3467		1830	

first by the middle classes and then by business and commerce which followed the people to the suburbs, the central cities were left in poverty to cope with all the problems of the poor.

Considering the pressure on land, some of the architects and planners did surprisingly well. In the Netherlands as the western 'Randstad' city region encroached upon the older villages around Utrecht, woods and heath were left free from development for walking and cycling. In Britain and Germany new clusters of houses often succeeded in making aesthetic and social sub-communities while at the same time making good use of building land so other land was free. Throughout Europe apartment blocks varied greatly in their livability, and good people-orientated architecture and planning was critical in making the growing urban, sub-urban megalopolises human. Low-rise blocks in Holland, Switzerland and Germany were often positioned to suit and complement their setting and also to create pleasant community areas between or near the blocks. High-rise blocks were less successful, in spite of the brave and thorough theory on which this development was based. In Italy especially, and sometimes in France, the high blocks which actually dominated the scene were often positioned with no relevance to the scale or the texture or the shape of the space in which they stood: where outdoors could a child go? Even the most carefully planned clusters of high-rise blocks at the edges of London and Paris looked somewhat bleak and out of scale with the trees and lawns below, and the people who were expected to live in them were almost never happy. None the less, as the sixties ended planners had an increasingly accurate awareness of human needs; the problem was to keep up with the growing pressure of people. Since this would require more investment in housing, as well as increasingly intelligent investment, the question arose: could more people be given more choices? Could private spending be deflected from gadgets and machines to homes and parks? Could people control the context in which market mechanisms would work, so that these mechanisms would work for people?

The housing that was built in the prosperous world in the sixties might have been truly human with something of the order of twenty-five per cent additional investment, and this offered hope for the future. However, the transport facilities generated round London or Paris or Milan or Tokyo during the sixties would have needed a completely different order of additional investment (say 250 per cent) to have become truly human. The pressure of cars upon roads and the pressure of roads upon land in urban areas was so great that *laissez-faire* drift-and-response solutions were clearly inadequate. The acres and acres of freeways and highways of Los Angeles showed that that kind of problem-solving provided no solution at all. None the less, for all the radical solutions mooted (moving pavements, coin-operated cars, monorails), the number carried out was very small. San Francisco built a rapid transit system, and the Tokyo-Yokohama-Osaka region developed super-speed trains. A few cities created pedestrian precinct centres, and many cities had pedestrian shopping areas. While such partial programmes were groping in the right direction, they were so far from any adequate solutions that it was impossible to see across the gap.

Certain planning principles were found to ease congestion and could even be applied in a way which also improved the quality of life. The basic principle was to separate different types of traffic flow except at planned interchange points: separating people from vehicles, major routes from local ones, etc. While this principle was only an idea in inward-orientated cities such as London, it was actually used (not always deliberately) in wider, more decentralized city regions. It made life in Los Angeles almost tolerable – in spite of other hopeless factors; and it made the Amsterdam-Rotterdam-Utrecht urban triangle positively pleasant, although it was as densely populated as almost any place on earth.

In twenty or thirty years of rapid growth the roads of Los Angeles County gradually developed a distinctive pattern which was not quite so hopeless to live in as an observer might have thought. The roads formed a three-tier system: freeways, highways and main streets, and residential streets. The

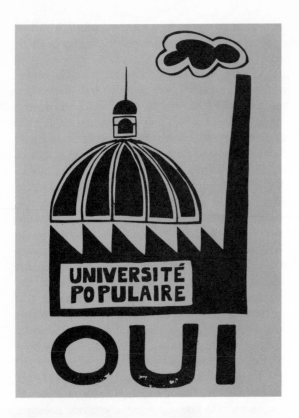

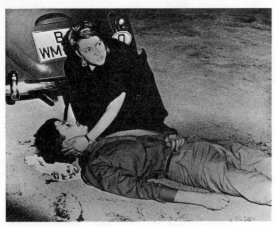

Top 'People's University – yes!' A May 1968 poster in Paris protests against low rates of entry for the working classes and a university system geared to academics rather than the people
West Berlin student revolt: (*above*) a twenty-six-year-old student, Benno Ohnesorg, killed by a police bullet; (*below*) water hoses used against the barricades

limited interchange points between freeways and the older generation of highways kept these two flows of traffic separate; the timing of traffic-lights and the positioning of 'stop' street-signs kept the residential streets free of most main street-highway traffic. The system worked: it assured movement and a certain degree of relative quiet. It lessened the bad effects of the two greatest problems of Los Angeles transport: that there was no transport except cars and a very few buses, and that consequently the land was paved with roads – too much cement and tarmac for people.

The city built for cars had almost no public transport. A Los Angeles family was likely to feel poor and might also *be* poor if it did not have two cars. In the skilled working class there was tremendous pressure on a family to have more money and more mobility, and a second car was likely to be a key to both these goals – with it the wife could work and the children could do extra things like Scouts or music lessons. Without a second car such extra activities seemed just that bit too difficult to do, with long walks and long waits for poor buses. In the unskilled working class which included many blacks the lack of public transport often made two jobs in the family extremely difficult, and sometimes even prevented the main potential bread-winner from bothering to spend several hours and several bus changes getting to a labour exchange or other place where he could apply for work. Almost everyone who had not slipped out of the economy and given up needed a car; and therefore most people had cars; so the land was paved with roads and there was no effective demand for alternative transport; so there was no alternative transport and everyone needed cars; and so forth. The poverty of alternatives produced a poverty of opportunity and the cost to the individual family of escaping this poverty was very high.

During the fifties and sixties traffic management in Los Angeles did tend to solve traffic problems, but the human problems of the car culture were not even tackled. But the questions which needed to be faced were at last raised. Could the projected growth in numbers of cars be handled by projecting and expanding current road construction and road-use programmes into the future? If not, what would be the alternative? Could some form of public transportation be created which would be sufficiently convenient to wean people from cars – at least some of the people some of the time? Could people be given a real choice not to use a car?

In the Amsterdam-Rotterdam-Utrecht triangle people had real choices. Here the principle of separate traffic flow for different functions was integrated with a multi-vehicle system which provided a rich array of interchangeable choices. Whether a family had no car, or one car, or two, it had choices. Trains which were frequently modernized and which criss-crossed the country in a close network, were used for longer distances. Motorways with coaches and cars were used for other lesser routes; in addition there were local buses and trams with their own relatively local routes; there were bicycles on bicycle paths; and finally pedestrians. Each had its own system so a person could drive or cycle for days, or travel anywhere by train, hardly noting the other systems. Alternatively a person could travel a short way by tram or cycle, go on a train, or on a coach, take his cycle on the train, or not, hire a car at the end, etc., etc. The combinations and permutations were vast, offering great flexibility and great choice. The very density of population in western Holland made these multiple complementary alternatives economically viable.

Process, change and consensus

While pure *laissez-faire* drift-and-response policies were inadequate, as indicated by the situation in Los Angeles, the Dutch example indicates that organic response-and-drift policies did work. At least in the field of transportation it was possible to create a context in which market mechanisms worked to generate a rich range of choices for everyone. Which is not to say that the Provos were wrong. Radical thought and dramatic gestures were needed to break the cycle of contented bourgeois inevitability. The Provos became part of the process of challenge, response and drift. They pointed out the challenge and helped to generate a response which created or at

least helped to develop a relatively adequate context for this drift.

Most radical groups, including the New Left and most students in revolt, did not speak of themselves as part of a continuing process. They said that the present could not be redeemed and that synthesis was not the object. Some said the object was destruction, and others that antithesis would be enough. But such statements could not mean the same in 1956 and 1968 as they had meant in 1905 or 1917. In the fifties and sixties most people knew that real change would be more difficult than revolution, but that degrees of change are inevitable. Thus, whether the radicals liked it or not, their ideas would be absorbed.

Throughout the world the public language of change and revolution was stale, inaccurate and unnecessarily divisive. None the less, in relatively articulate circles in the relatively prosperous countries some synthesizing terms and concepts had begun to emerge. It was widely believed in the Establishment and the anti-Establishment that consensus politics led to undue inertia. And the varied ways of perceiving inertia divided people into political categories and gave them a common language of discourse. To those on the right the stability of society was natural and desirable, to the far left inertia was a deliberate plot by those at the top to stay there. Most people in between felt that inertia was a form of homeostasis which was natural, but at least somewhat undesirable, and they were concerned with the mechanisms and the problems of shifting from one equilibrium system to a new one.

Above Campus war: 'Pigs [police] Shoot to Kill', warns the Berkeley student magazine
Below Helmeted militant Japanese students (*zengakuren*) demonstrate against the 1969 visit of the USS *Enterprise*, bound for Vietnam

Regardless of how change was perceived, it was clear that the tendency to consensus politics made it slow and smooth. This was particularly irritating to those who wanted not only the substance of change but also the sense of motion and the fun of participation. Perhaps the most alienating type of consensus politics to those outside the consensus was the relatively tight majority coalition which left a large minority unrepresented. Although this type of coalition existed in a socialist form especially in Scandinavia, it was most notable in the conservative form it took in Japan.

In Japan in 1955 the Liberal Party and the Democratic Party formed a conservative alliance in the Liberal Democratic Party, and from then onwards there was no effective opposition. The Socialist Party which was next in size never controlled much more than a third of the seats in the Diet. The Liberal coalition not only represented the nation's political establishment but also its economic and its social establishment, and with the aid of various occupational and interest groups it reached deep into almost all of the most respected segments of Japanese life. Because the coalition and its quasi-supportive bodies were effective in forging a consensus, and the channels for building an alternative consensus tended to wither, the resulting frustration in the anti-Establishment was even greater and certainly it was deeper than the occasional outburst of student and worker violence would have necessarily indicated.

The consensus politics of some other countries was more broadly based and less rigid. In Western Germany, the coalition which emerged subsumed something more than a right- or left-based majority, and it spanned a wide

In the mid-sixties legislation began against air pollution (but in Japan industrial pressure groups proved too strong): (*above*) Britain: the north-east; (*below*) smog over Los Angeles, caused by unburned hydrocarbons from exhaust gases and oil refineries

Canal pollution near Groningen, Holland

The oil tanker *Torrey Canyon* blazes in the English Channel; the danger of oil pollution on a vast scale was averted by bombing raids on the cargo

range across the political and the social spectrum. In the United States there was of course no prospect of actual coalition, but it could be said, and often was, that the two parties were much alike on major issues.

In the German Federal Republic the similarities between the Christian Democrats and the Social Democrats became so great that these long-standing opponents came together in coalition. Many socialists felt betrayed. The betrayal of the left within the centre-left party helped to precipitate the student protest movements of the sixties. But in Germany the students had but small support from others: coalition governments were not a cause of bourgeois contentment, but just a symptom; and many workers were, at least psychologically, part of the bourgeoisie. In Germany the great problem of prosperity was that prosperity reinforced the selfish family-only orientation of those who were successful. The coalition was a pact of the contented majority to continue in comfortable safety. The need for safety after shock was natural; and, objectively, German society was hardly more indifferent or cruel to its weak and sick and poor than were most other societies. Still, the mass of solid citizenry was somehow more solid and also more insecure than in many countries; more people in all sorts of jobs worked harder and felt they had earned the right to relax with the good things of life and to try and forget the past. It is not surprising that youth, looking across a generation at this solid mass of virtue, doubted its sensitivity and its fervour. Not all who doubted felt alienated, but for those who did, it made little impression that Willy Brandt was in fact an imaginative man with generous and daring policies whom youth might well have helped.

In the United States successive governments failed to respond adequately to various demands of the public. The silent majority was cited as giving support to policies which the more vocal segments of the public clearly did not support. While people called for an end to American involvement in Vietnam, the Johnson administration and subsequently the Nixon administration continued American involvement. While people questioned the expenditure of money on space research and on the military stockpiling of thermonuclear weapons, and asked for social programmes instead, successive governments continued old policies, or else shifted them so slowly that the impatient observer could hardly notice. It is not clear that any silent majority did in fact support any of these policies to the extent that they would not have preferred various more creative options – had they been presented with any real options. However, the options that were suggested were clouded round by attitudes and a style that was clearly not supported by the silent majority. The silent majority did not buy the liberal attitudes as they perceived them in the frenzy of an escalating debate. Even less did they accept the attitudes and the style of students and the left who were engaged in confrontation politics.

The theory of confrontation politics was to drive wedges into the stagnant social order, force the soft liberal centre to take sides, extend consciousness of the need for revolution and confidence in its possibility, while waiting for a chance to precipitate the revolutionary apocalypse. One of the most serious faults in this theory was that it made it too easy to believe that the symbolic symptomatic behaviour of a protest march or demonstration was a real event in history: that the happenings of confrontation politics constituted some genuine, relevant form of social surgery. In fact a demonstration could be no more than a quasi-event in history which, to be consummated, needed a response. The American response to most of the protest actions of the fifties and the sixties was the consolidation of the stance of the silent majority. Thus while it was unclear how firmly the silent majority supported the actual policies of the Johnson and the Nixon administrations, it was very clear that the majority opposed the advocates of confrontation politics. Opinion polls showed that a clear majority of Americans approved of Mayor Daley's treatment of the Chicago demonstrators during the 1968 election campaign. However, the protests against American involvement in Vietnam, and against some of the other stock policies of successive US administrations, was much more broadly based than most demonstrations

Open road, Berkeley, California; motorways, decentralized towns and a suburban landscape ever nearer the futurologist's vision of San-An

indicated. This fact was lost on the silent majority. And the administration could therefore sometimes pretend that protest only came from intellectuals and leftists and left-liberals and rabble. This excuse for inaction accounted for considerable delay in the shifting of policies, and was the main historical effect of the politics of confrontation.

The consensus reflected in the coalitions in Japan and Western Germany had a parallel in the unchanging policies of successive United States government administrations. Lured by the perceived inevitability and the challenge of competing with communism, US policy had dug itself into certain ruts from 1949 into the 1960s. The commitment to Vietnam, to an expanding arms race, and to space exploration, while not of course comparable in many respects, were all natural parts of this unchanging stance. Each administration found it difficult to respond quickly when people objected to some of these policies; but gradually there was a response: space budgets were cut and troops were withdrawn from Vietnam. While failing to respond quickly, it was necessary to have some degree of consensus supporting existing policies. And since most of the people most of the time live in a state of relative political passivity, it was possible to say there was a majority who had been silent on the issues of protest. This majority would not, by definition, become very articulate on the issues, but it could be goaded into comment on the supercilious attitudes of the vocal minority. And nothing could have been more effective as such a goad than the demonstrations of the students and the left.

Stability and mechanisms of change

Changing gear takes a long time in the modern technocratic state. Policy tends to be the cumulative effect of small incremental changes. The prosperous technocratic states of the post Second World War period were especially stable – for one thing there were so many people with a stake in preserving the *status quo*. And yet these nations had many problems and there was a great deal of discontent. The political protest and questioning of the 1960s can be seen as an array of responses to these facts.

On the one hand it was asked what was wrong with the mechanisms for social change. Was parliamentary democracy an adequate handle for control of the increasingly specialized technocratic executive of government?

The rise of the automobile industry

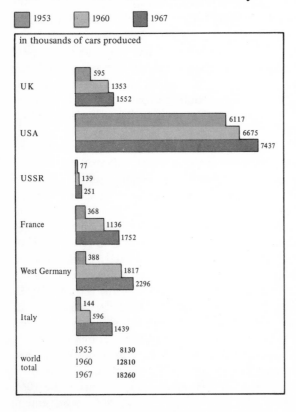

■ 1953   □ 1960   ■ 1967

in thousands of cars produced

	1953	1960	1967
UK	595	1353	1552
USA	6117	6675	7437
USSR	77	139	251
France	368	1136	1752
West Germany	388	1817	2296
Italy	144	596	1439

world total	1953	8130
	1960	12810
	1967	18260

Right Parking in the USA: one of the many problems created by the rise of the motor car

Californian debris of the sixties; little effort has been made in the Western world to dispose of unwanted cars

The other side of the Statue of Liberty

Were periodic elections an adequate means for the citizen to influence legislation? Were there other means implicit in the system which needed more use, or should new mechanisms be developed?

In other circles it was asked whether a completely different kind of democracy was not needed: not parliamentary democracy, but direct participatory democracy.

The concept of participatory democracy was in no sense the property of the groups in the vanguard of protest during the 1960s. It had roots in the writings of Proudhon and Bakunin, and in the philosophy of the syndicalist movements of the nineteenth and early twentieth centuries. In the post Second World War period, the vanguard talk of direct democracy was preceded and accompanied by facts and discussion which spanned the political spectrum and encompassed direct participation in the management of industry as well as direct political participation. In Yugoslavia, and to some extent in Israel and certain Arab and East African states, all sorts of economic enterprises, and a smaller range of political and cultural institutions, were run by direct participation. Then there were the continually new experiments in China and Cuba. In Eastern Europe a whole range of participatory mechanisms were discussed and some were tried – most notably in Czechoslovakia in the first eight months of 1968, but elsewhere too, more quietly. Even in the predominantly capitalist economies of Western Europe, industrial democracy was discussed fully and tried partially; and fresh approaches to political participation were also discussed.

Direct democracy had many appeals – especially to the youth of the prosperous world of the 1960s. It offered immediacy and an almost religious form of non-mechanistic purity. It offered concrete samplings of a type of communist Utopia which could be obtained in the here and now without intervening mediating stages. It rejected the rationalist historical doctrine of Marxist-Leninist theory, that a compromised and compromising stage of history, socialism, would lead to another and different Utopian stage, communism. There was in fact no rational historical evidence that this long-established theory would prove true: that socialism with its industrialization, increased productive capacity, and many uncommunist features such as use of the profit motive, was leading to or ever would lead to communism. Moreover, it was part of the religious mood of youth to believe in the eternal now, to say that what a nation lives it becomes, and that means can only generate ends which are consistent with the means. To young people who believed in *living* the alternative society, stage-by-stage historical determinism looked manipulative and false.

Direct democracy also appeared to offer an alternative to the complexity of the bureaucratic technocratic state. In the alternative society envisaged by an important segment of the youth protest movement of the 1960s there would be direct participation in decisions and work in each institution of society. The individual would be free to express his will directly without bureaucratic constraints. To envisage and work for this Utopian future gave young people an excuse for not tackling the complexities of the existing technocratic society. And was it not clearly futile to work for change within the system? The socialism of the Marxist-Leninist socialist state was harshly programmatic and degrading, but did not lead to any truly human goal. Likewise the liberalism and the democratic socialism of the prosperous industrial states were full of talk and plans and programmes which led to very little result relative to any truly adequate human goals. The bureaucratic state in all its forms throughout the world was too stable to be greatly or quickly moved. And in the eyes of youth, and of many others who opted out more quietly, all the theories and the mechanisms of political change were too complicated, and also completely inadequate. The questions mentioned earlier about the control and use of parliamentary democracy were questions raised by people who understood programmatic linear thought; to many young people such questions about mechanistic refinements on a hopelessly mechanistic system, were trivial questions.

The more radical advocates of direct democracy also believed in direct action. Many kinds of direct action were tried. Some were appropriate to

95

their objectives and to the response expected, but many were not. The confrontation politics of protest groups in the United States were not usually relevant to the aims of the protest, nor to the surrounding climate of opinions and possibilities and, consequently, were often counter-productive. On the other hand, some types of direct action did work. In the Netherlands not only the Provos, but also a number of other radical political and religious groups used confrontation politics to make real changes in public attitudes and public policy. Their actions were revolutionary in the sense of turning upside down many preconceived ideas, but they did not cause revulsion, nor were their actions revolting irrelevantly against the system. Their actions worked by transformation: by transforming and converting old attitudes and old policies to new ones.

The modern technocratic state required specialization. It proliferated compartments for different styles of life, for different types of knowledge and for different kinds of work. This specialization contributed to both the stability and the inadequacy of 'the system'. Specialization by job was epitomized in professionalism. Each profession created its own elaborate system of self-censorship. A person who had earned the compliment that he was 'professional' in his work, knew and followed not only the technical code of his profession, but also its code of values. Since these group values were partly based on principles of group survival they were of limited validity and tended to limit the sensitivity of people within the group to values outside.

The increased fragmentation of society into groups in the modern technocratic state led to an increase in self-justifying forms of thought and behaviour which were not properly responsive to wider needs. Thus one of the problems of prosperity was a fragmentation of values. In the post Second World War period many old values and old assumptions had been dropped; and a clear map of new values had not yet emerged. Many of the discarded values had been based on hierarchical relationships between man and man, and between man and God. The groping after new values in the 1950s and 1960s indicated that the new relationships would be more fluid and more egalitarian; it also indicated that because of this fluidity it would take some time for the new values to fill an adequately integrating role. None the less, many of the emerging goals and hopes were more universal than ever before in history, and thus potentially integrating on an unprecedented scale.

'Little boxes': (*top*) wooden houses in the Honmura Mita district in Tokyo; (*above*) British suburban sprawl in Kent

Below In Los Angeles the separate traffic-flow systems of the fifties and sixties made life more livable for people with cars

Expectations and possible goals

While the 'love generation' of the youth of the 1960s called for direct inter-personal relations before structures and mechanisms, society in the prosperous technological countries had developed two exceptionally efficient institutions for loneliness: the isolated individual family, and the large corporation. And as youth began to say that preservation was more important than production, it was noted that these two institutions generated more consumption, waste and pollution than was justified by the rather doubtful quality of life resulting.

The development of suburban housing in the 1950s and 1960s made the single small family more isolated than ever before. As a family moved into a suburban-type house it lost contact with the cosier neighbours of more crowded housing, and also with members of the wider multi-generational family. It became independent – earning its income without interaction with family or friends, and, above all, spending its income as a small, self-sufficient economic unit. Each home was a man's castle; each household had to execute within itself all the functions of consumption, maintenance, repairs and entertainment which a bustling community had filled in the medieval castle. Not surprisingly this led to loneliness and a sense of isolation. It also necessitated a great deal of assistance from machines using up limited metal resources and fed by limited power resources. It led to pre-packaged labour-saving food in packages which had generated pollution in their production, and would generate more pollution when discarded.

The individual family unit of economic consumption required a certain minimum level of expenditure to be viable. And in so far as this minimum was higher in North America than Europe, this was partly a reflection of the fact that American homes were more isolated than those in Europe: with no effective local public transport, with larger distances between houses and between houses and towns, and with fewer housewives working for each other and for local businesses as babysitters, cleaners, shop assistants, clerks, etc. In America in the early 1960s the minimum cost of running a suburban-type four- or five-person household with all the expected and normal mechanical conveniences was about $5,000 (the official poverty line at that time was $3,000). In Europe at the same date about half to two-thirds of this sum was needed, depending on the country, to run the minimum single-family home and household with its expected normal mechanical aids. The high cost of paying for even the minimum expected norms of family life put particular pressure on people who were just barely able to make it. And the families which didn't make it were often better off since they lived in less splendid isolation or partly on state assistance and thus had more discretionary spending power.

The demand for washing-machines and cars and convenience foods was not created by the companies that made the products nor by their advertising agents. The products were genuinely wanted. And most products were actually needed. They were needed either because of the physical requirements of the independent family home, or they were needed because of its psychological isolation.

While the manufacturing corporation did not create needs, it did attempt to fill them. It thereby contributed to a process of exploitation, consumption and pollution which was excessive, but also natural. The business of manufacturing *is* the conversion of resources into products at minimum costs. This necessitated the exploitation of resources without regard to the interests of future generations. As many costs as possible tended to be passed off as external costs to be payed by the community, either by having it clean up the land and the waters polluted by waste materials, or by living with the polluted rivers, lakes, seas, land and air.

One of the questions of the 1960s was how to internalize the social costs of pollution. Much more, and more effective, legislation would certainly be needed. Much of this would need to be international in scope. Since laws which simply prohibit are imprecise regulators and difficult to enforce, a system of charges for pollution would also be needed. While it might be

Practical housing often means social fragmentation: French tower block

Danish flats on the outskirts of Copenhagen, for families with children only

made illegal to produce cars emitting more than a precise amount of exhaust fumes, it need not be illegal to treat logs for paper-milling with mercury; but there would be a charge for each degree of mercury contamination of rivers and lakes. Payment for the discharge of industrial effluent has helped maintain a relatively acceptable state of equilibrium in the Ruhr Valley during most of the period since 1913. Such a pricing system helps to ensure that industry and its customers pay the actual cost of the products. In the Ruhr, the income from these payments have been used on projects such as waste-treatment and the oxidation of lakes.

Paper made with less mercury pollution, and cars made to produce less exhaust fumes, would cost the consumer more. If the costs of goods are increased, what becomes of the people who already live in some degree of poverty? A partial answer to this question has been suggested by the irony of the 1960s: the richest society did not provide the richest life. The car culture of North America *did* lead to marginally lower unit costs of cars and other consumer durables, but at the same time it led to a style of life and of expectations which made the total normal cost of living much higher in North America than elsewhere. This in turn made manpower more expensive than machines and was one cause of the chronic unemployment which became a feature of the late 1960s, even in a period of serious inflation. Maximizing productivity did not maximize the quality of life.

A richer life style was found in countries where the individual family did not have to be self-sufficient and own and supply absolutely everything for itself. One of the themes of the protest movements of the 1960s was that a still richer style of life could follow from more human contact and interaction. This was also one theme of the emerging post-industrial corporation. While the large corporation typical of the more immediate post Second World War period was almost entirely orientated towards maximum productivity and profitability, the later super-corporations began to be at least marginally aware of some wider social values. This awareness included concern for their use of employees, and for the use of resources in a way which was not simply exploitative for short-term profitability. While the large industrial corporation had been hierarchical, to be efficient in relation to simple goals, the more complex goals of the post-industrial giant corporation required more flexible and more imaginative interaction between people. For those who could make a contribution in an organization with complex goals and relationships, the post-industrial corporation provided a rich working experience. But this experience was the privilege of a minority.

As the 1960s ended questions were raised as to how more people could live fully and productively in a way that would be of true value. There was a series of contradictions. Society might run out of things to do: production could be centralized, machines and computers could progressively replace both blue-collar and white-collar workers, and ecological requirements would gradually need to restrain production. Vast productive capacity

Pierre Jeanneret, Le Corbusier's cousin, with the plan of Chandigarh, the new capital of the Punjab, designed with health and tranquillity in mind

Brasilia, the extravagant new capital of Brazil, where the government has been sited since 1960: it was planned to avoid overcrowding – some would say over-successfully

The Tokyo-Osaka line built in the early sixties is one of the fastest in the world; the Bullet express reaches speeds of 120 m.p.h.

Patterns of the future: (*top*) Montreal complex with suspended connecting pedestrian streets; (*above*) A Buckminster Fuller floating community; each triangular unit would contain shops, schools, homes and all facilities for 5,000 people. It would be anchored on the waterfront of an existing city

existed while people were hungry and in need. Clearly market mechanisms did not work adequately; yet there was little evidence that centralized planning would work any better and people had no taste for bureaucracy.

However, ideas had been raised which, if taken seriously, could turn these anomalies upside down. It was suggested that the goal of life is not production nor consumption, but the experience of living and the joy of the process. It was suggested that total costs must include social costs to the environment and to future generations, and that a total equation would have to be a world equation. It was suggested that many traditional institutions, patterns and philosophies irreverently exploited people and resources but did not recognize the full range of human potential.

A decrease in exploitation was a feature of the period, but this trend was somewhat obscured and even slowed down by the noise of impatience – by women calling for 'liberation', by the Welsh and Basque demanding more autonomy, and by the charge of 'neo-colonialism' – that rich countries were still exploiting poor ones. The term 'neo-colonialism' was an especially great impediment to understanding and to corrective action. Since most post-colonial exploitation was not intentional, the exploiter did not perceive that anything relevant to him was being said, and since the term implied a one-sided relationship which only the exploiter could correct, paralysis resulted.

In fact, one of the great developments of the period was that there were no longer any truly one-sided relationships. There were many asymmetrical relationships, but very few in which the weaker party did not have considerable power and consequent responsibility. Even client states of the Soviet Union or the United States could have considerable leverage when their power was used with care. Certainly the new states of Africa and Asia had freedom of choice to stand alone or to exploit the stronger investor states, or even to be exploited to serve a short-term advantage.

The poor and the weak had acquired new power and new responsibility. Trade Union power was achieved not only by competing for existing rewards, but also by productivity agreements to generate new rewards. Women could create new jobs at the places and the times that suited them. Black and other minority groups could generate and command their own banks and businesses. Developing countries could decide to export primary products on terms which allowed for the creation of local industry and local modern employment. Going against the grain of established, more exploitative, relationships created real change. Where paternalism had failed, the new relationships initiated from below began to succeed.

The protest movements of the 1960s were to a great extent reactions against the protective paternalism of prosperity. They were an irritated immature response, and fed upon the society they rejected, but the protest contained seeds of transformation. It would not be possible or even desirable to dampen down the twentieth century's energy for productivity, but more participation by more people could generate work where it was needed to use fallow resources without misusing the environment.

Fernando Henriques

Race and Racialism

What can be regarded as the tyranny of colour springs out of the doctrine of racism. Nearly thirty years ago Ruth Benedict defined this as '. . . the dogma that one ethnic group is condemned by nature to congenital inferiority and another group is destined to congenital superiority.' Racialism is this doctrine in action. The classical expression is that of the simple, tribal group which, in relative isolation, comes to depend on xenophobia and on exclusivity for its survival. At a later stage in the history of man the rise of empire leads to the conquest and subjugation of alien peoples. Racialism thus becomes a tool by which the dominant group maintains its power.

It is, however, a confusing term. All societies in history, from tribes or villages to larger groupings, have to some extent derived their sense of identity from a conviction that they were not as other people. They have tended to feel that they were set apart, especially favoured by the gods, and that others – strangers, outsiders, 'foreign devils' in the term applied by the Chinese to those beyond their frontiers – were inferior. One American Indian tribe referred to itself as the Human Beings: all others, by definition, were subhuman or even non-human. The enslavement of one human species by another, still clandestinely practised here and there in remote corners of the world in 1970, is also almost as old as recorded history.

What made these ingrained human tendencies seem intolerable was their elevation during the empire-building of the nineteenth and early twentieth centuries into an ideology of white supremacy – particularly evident in the so-called 'Anglo-Saxon' countries of northern Europe and North America. At the height of their technological and military power these countries were able to seize control of vast areas of the non-white world, and from the ease of their conquest and the palpable discrepancy between their own power and that of the subject peoples drew confirming assurance of an innate differentiation between race and race. The doctrine was qualified, it is true, by the theory that the imperial nations had a duty, a mission, to 'civilize' the subject races. This implied that when they had been 'raised' sufficiently they might achieve independence. It is true too that the doctrine, either in theory or in actuality, was never unanimously accepted in Europe and the United States. It ran counter to humanitarian sentiment and to radical ideology, so that the twentieth-century leaders of non-white movements for independence were able to draw upon an arsenal of white protest to reinforce their own burning sense of injustice. If racism in its modern form was a white invention, so – one might maintain – were the contrary principles of the brotherhood of man, even if for long periods these were more honoured in the breach than in the observance.

Whatever the theory of imperialism, the reality of effective subjugation was drastically altered by the Second World War. The old empires of Britain, France, Belgium, the Netherlands and (to a lesser degree) Portugal were shaken to their foundations. The aftermath of war created a complex situation in which fatigue, political rebellion, a changing world economy and revived notions of fundamental human rights all combined to hasten the dissolution of the existing order. The internal affairs of multi-racial societies, notably the United States, were affected by the same world developments. Assumptions of superiority, of an ordained hierarchy of races, were challenged on every side.

Of the forty-nine states which signed the original charter of the United Nations in San Francisco in 1945, only two – Ethiopia and Liberia – represented the black nations of Africa. Other non-white peoples were likewise

Black prisoner in a Chicago jail; the sixties brought new intensity to bitter American race issues

Above Black and white on a Cape Town footbridge

Right 'Separate development' for blacks in Johannesburg

Composition of working population in South Africa

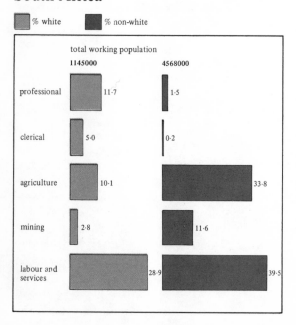

conspicuous by their absence. By 1970 the Afro-Asian bloc at the United Nations constituted a majority. The change was remarkable. The creation of independent states out of former colonial areas profoundly influenced the relationship between European and non-European. The European had to shed ideas of inherent superiority. The non-European had to learn that political independence did not automatically bring economic freedom, and that the oppressor was not invariably white. The process was for both parties instructive and sometimes traumatic. As so often in human affairs the real gains made – astounding in view of the attitudes of the previous century – were accompanied, perhaps outpaced, by rising expectations. Euphoria was swiftly succeeded by disillusionment, and by new resentments and demands. By the sixties the apparent waning of white power was overlaid with a world-wide proclamation of black power. Accusations of white racialism – and suggestions that the slogans of black power exhibited a form of 'reverse racialism' – were more common in the post-colonial era than during it.

Thus, there were *coups d'état*, jailings of defeated rivals, tribal and regional clashes, and even (as in the former Belgian Congo and in Nigeria) civil wars – though none of the upheavals in Africa approached the scale of the Muslim-Hindu encounter in the India of the late forties, or of Indonesia at a subsequent period. It should be stressed that, except in Kenya, the unscrambling of empire in Africa produced no cases of violence against whites. Europeans killed in the Congo were victims of what was regarded as white intervention. Another obvious point is that the new African nations were artefacts of imperial policy. Their frontiers had often been arbitrarily drawn, so as to enclose peoples of diverse cultures and language.

A further source of racial antagonism, after independence, came with the natural desire of the indigenous population to 'Africanize' government service. This entailed not only the gradual exclusion of white officials but also of certain non-whites. In many former British colonies, such as Kenya, Tanzania and Zambia, Indian immigration had been encouraged and thriving Asian communities had come into being. In the sixties some African governments began through various measures such as the withholding of licences to force the Asians out of the economic life of their adopted countries. Their plight was lamentable. Many were holders of British passports; but the British, alarmed by the growth of non-white immigrant settlement, refused admission except under a tightly controlled permit system.

Considerably more inflammatory, however, was the resistance to decolonization in the settler countries of Africa. The French *colons* withdrew from Algeria only after a savage and protracted war for liberation. Resistance was more stubborn and far more successful in South Africa and

Africans burning the pass books compulsory in towns

Right Sharpeville, 21 March 1960: police machine-gunned Africans at a protest demonstration against the pass laws; 67 people were killed and 186 wounded, most of them shot in the back

British *Daily Mail* cartoon following the conviction for treason of Nelson Mandela and six other members of the African National Congress Party, a non-extremist group. Mandela had led an underground resistance campaign of non-cooperation in apartheid

– encouraged by the South African example – in Rhodesia. The Portuguese also hung on defiantly to their African colonies of Angola and Mozambique, after they had lost Goa, Daman and Diu to India in 1961. Despite guerrilla activities white settlement continued: there were 200,000 Portuguese in Angola by 1960. The Portuguese defended themselves by insisting that their Angolese involvement dated as far back as 1575, and that their African territories were (as with Algeria in French eyes) not colonies but parts of a comprehensive system, legally on a par with the mother country. At least their case, if anachronistic, did not go against the grain of contemporary history, which could not be said of Rhodesia or of the creation of apartheid in South Africa.

The scene then was immensely complex and confused. Events were open to widely and wildly different interpretation, according to the viewpoint of the observer. They were given world publicity, and the rhetoric and tactics of one country were at once made known elsewhere. Much of the impetus in this respect was provided by the growth of black militance (which in turn stimulated intransigence among American Indians, Mexicans and Puerto Ricans, not to mention white women) in the United States. By the same token the attention of the world focused upon the 'backlash' obstinacy of the white regime in South Africa, though of course the two societies were far from similar in their ultimate goals. Complaints of racial discrimination, for instance against the Tartars in the Soviet Union, could be levelled against many nations in the modern world. A short article can only deal with a few significant situations. Because of the fascination that affairs in the United States and in South Africa have held for the postwar world, we single them out for relatively full treatment.

The United States

The black Americans who returned in 1945 and 1946 to the United States had ostensibly been engaged in a war for democracy, but they had fought that war under segregated conditions. It was not until 26 July 1948 that President Truman issued Executive Order 9981, which began the genuine integration of the armed forces. On 1 October of that year the California Supreme Court declared that the state statute prohibiting racial inter-marriage violated the US Constitution. Both events were milestones in the great struggle of negro Americans to achieve equality before the law with whites. But the returning black veterans were faced with the paradox that, having assisted in the overthrow of Hitler, they came back to their own country to conditions they deemed not totally dissimilar from those which the Jews had suffered under Hitler. Certainly gas chambers did not exist, yet a substantial minority of the states forbade marriage between Caucasian and non-Caucasian. The latter in the USA were standard, accepted terms

Southern Rhodesia joined South Africa and Portuguese Africa as bastions of white supremacy in November 1965, when the prime minister Ian Smith declared unilateral independence from Britain (Vicky cartoon)

Washing day in Bulawayo; in Rhodesia the African majority consists of ninety-four per cent of the population

Freedom fighters in Rhodesia, 1970

by which whites were distinguished from non-whites. There were no forced labour camps, but black people were 'the last to be hired and the first to be fired'.

The period of the cold war helped to distract many white Americans from the problem in their midst. The decade from 1945 onwards was characterized by riots engendered by attempts at integration of housing, such as that at Trumbull Park in Chicago on 4 August 1953, and by various government efforts to combat discrimination, exemplified by the Truman committee appointed in December 1951 to supervise non-discrimination in government contracts. The outsider might have thought that quiet progress was being made. His view was encouraged by the Tuskegee Institute's statement in 1952 that that year was the first for several decades in which no lynchings of negroes had been reported.

It is only towards the middle of the fifties that two extremely important events occurred.

On 17 May 1954 the Supreme Court of the United States in its ruling in the case of Brown *v*. Board of Education of Topeka, prohibited racial segregation in the public schools' system of the country. In its judgement the Court stated that separation in schools deprived the black minority of equal educational opportunities. It was a decision which set the course for the fight which was still continuing, albeit half-heartedly, under the administration of President Nixon, to integrate the schools. In 1896 another famous decision had been made by the Court in the case of Plessy *v*. Ferguson. This judgement sustained a Louisiana statute requiring separate accommodation for negroes and whites in railway trains. This was the beginning of the famous 'separate but equal' doctrine. In delivering its judgement the Court stated: 'Legislation is powerless to eradicate racial instincts or to abolish instincts based upon physical differences. . . . If one race is inferior to the other socially, the Constitution of the United States cannot put them on the same plane. . . .' This decision was the fount of a whole spate of segregation laws in the succeeding years. Why should it have taken nearly sixty years for the full reversal of the decision of 1896?

The answer is possibly twofold. The existence of slavery in the USA created a racist society. Reference to the social and political literature of the South both *ante-* and *post-bellum* is more than sufficient evidence of that contention. In a *national* sample of white Americans in 1942 only forty-two per cent believed negroes to be as intelligent as whites. By 1956 a similar sample showed that the percentage had risen to seventy-eight. At the end of 1970 four out of five white Americans believed negroes to have an intelligence similar to their own. There has been some improvement but it still means that a fifth of the white population – something of the order of 30 million people – considered negroes inherently inferior to themselves. The persistence of anti-miscegenation state statutes, which were still in force in 1970 in as many as fourteen states, is proof of profound racial antipathy.

It is true to say that there were distinct changes in the attitudes of whites towards negroes. As a result economic and educational opportunities opened up for a minority of black Americans promoted by a mass of civil rights legislation. But this did not change the basic pattern of denial experienced by the ghetto. Improvement took place even in the ghetto but it was far exceeded by rising expectations. The situation was complicated by considerations of class. For a majority of white Americans the stereotype of the negro was one associated with low economic status. Poverty was the hallmark of those who had failed in American society and so identified those who were inherently inferior.

Leaving aside the substantial minority who believed in the racial inferiority of the negro, recent studies have suggested that the white view of the negro is that his low status is mainly due to the negro himself, and not to the constraints imposed by the American social structure. The negro could do more for himself, why doesn't he? The implication is because of his inferiority. How do you set out to better yourself if you are young and black and living in the ghetto in the United States today? The attitude is similar to that of the successful European immigrant in New York who said to the

Above Tanzanians and Mozambicans march through the streets of Dar-es-Salaam on the anniversary of guerrilla war in Mozambique. The Portuguese were the first colonials to arrive in Africa and intend to be the last to leave. Troops were sent to Angola, where rebellion broke out in March 1961, and to Mozambique and Portuguese Guinea two years later; the strain on the Portuguese economy is considerable
Below Education for freedom in Angola: children play at arms drill in guerilla-held territory

author – 'Anyone who is poor in this country today, that is entirely his own fault.' Neither the black ghetto nor the underprivileged white poor necessarily agree.

The second part of the answer is constitutional. The Founding Fathers of the United States Constitution in their wisdom were concerned to limit the powers of federal government. To this end a sharp distinction was made between matters which were the concern of the individual states and those of the central government. Many areas, such as schooling, transport and marriage were reserved to the states, and these are precisely the areas in which discrimination was exercised to the detriment of the negro. Unless it could be shown to the satisfaction of the Supreme Court, the interpreters of the Constitution, that domestic legislation of the states was repugnant to the Constitution, little could be done to alleviate the social injustice inflicted on the negro. For the previous fifteen years the Court had been striking down various discriminatory statutes and practices, for example those providing separate law schools for negroes in some Southern states. But the Court could not go faster than public opinion, or at least not much faster. The interpretation of the law was influenced by the prevailing social atmosphere. After all, the Constitution of the United States in 1954 was almost identical with that of 1896. The fact that judges in the later year held an entirely different view from that of their predecessors was not due to a change in the law, but to a change in the climate of opinion in the United States.

The Brown decision on school integration provoked a long battle under four presidents which at the end of 1970 was still in progress. The Deep South girded its loins for the fight. In some areas attempts failed. In others in the late sixties some success at thwarting the intention of federal authority was achieved. It might be that the Nixon administration with relation to schools' integration was moving into the phase of what Daniel Moynihan called 'benign neglect'.

The integration of schooling in the United States is not to be seen only in terms of removing a gross social injustice suffered by the negro but also as striking at the actual heart of racist thought and behaviour in that country. For white and black to be schooled together is to begin to remove the racist antipathy so frequently engendered by parents. Adults are aware of this, and apparently are prepared to fight the issue by any means which come to hand. A recent example was that of George C. Wallace's campaign in Alabama for the governorship in which posters were used showing a white girl surrounded by black boys at a school.

Interestingly enough, it was not a black veteran who triggered off an event which seized the imagination of the world – the Montgomery bus boycott – but a tired, black, middle-aged woman – Mrs Rosa Parks.

Her action on 1 December 1955 in refusing to sit in the section of a bus reserved for coloured people precipitated a series of non-violent campaigns for the recognition of the civil rights of the negro. It also brought on the national stage a man who was to become the embodiment of the black man's struggle for equality – Martin Luther King. For a year the negro community of Montgomery, Alabama, organized their own transport and boycotted the buses. Victory was achieved when the Supreme Court, on 13 November 1956, declared that Alabama's transport segregation laws were unconstitutional.

The significance of the Montgomery bus boycott cannot be overestimated. It acted on the imagination of young people both black and white in the United States. For probably the first time in their history white youth began to believe that the struggle of the negro was its own struggle. Two organizations, CORE (Congress for Racial Equality), and SNCC (Student Non-violent Coordinating Committee), were to be involved in a series of events which brought home to the citizens of the USA the seriousness of the racial problem which confronted them. CORE, which was founded in 1942, had attempted to apply the Gandhian philosophy of non-violence to the domestic racial situation. SNCC, created in 1960, had similar ideals. Both engaged in dramatic action in what became known as 'Freedom Rides'.

These were bus rides undertaken mainly by students of both races to demonstrate whether inter-state transportation was in truth integrated.

The first Freedom Ride started from Washington, DC, in April 1961. The route chosen was through Virginia, the Carolinas, Georgia, Alabama to New Orleans. Seven negroes and six whites volunteered for this journey. What ensued was predictable. In Anniston, Alabama, mobs set the bus on fire, and the riders were severely beaten. Drivers refused to continue the journey. Further rides followed which were protected by federal marshals. Reaction from the federal government was comparatively swift. By September the Inter-state Commerce Commission had ruled that passengers travelling from state to state were to be seated irrespective of colour, and that desegregated terminals must be provided for them.

It is difficult to convey the depth of the feeling of racial hostility against the negro which characterized the Deep South of the United States between 1945 and 1970. The case of the admission of James Meredith to the University of Mississippi can be taken as some indication of these feelings.

In 1960 Meredith, a staff sergeant in the USAF, had returned to his home state, Mississippi. In January 1961 he sought registration as a student at the University of Mississippi. Inevitably he was rejected. Meredith then embarked on sixteen months of litigation to have his application accepted. Eventually, the Federal Court ordered the University to admit him. This was the beginning of a whole series of actions which turned the University almost into a battlefield. The reaction of the governor of the state, Ross Barnett, was to publish a proclamation:

... that the arrest or attempts to arrest, or the fining or the attempts to fine, of any state official in the performance of his official duties, by any representative of the federal government, is illegal, and such representative or representatives of the federal government are to be summarily arrested and jailed.

The latter is a perfect example of the use of the doctrine of states rights in order to uphold racial supremacy.

The Federal Court had issued its instructions on 24 September 1962. On the twenty-eighth, when Meredith attempted to register, both the governor and his lieutenant in person prevented him from entering the University registry. Three days later the Federal Court of Appeals ordered the governor

Mau Mau suspects; the one major armed clash between the British and Africans that accompanied the dismantling of empire took place in Kenya. Between 1952 and 1955 over 10,000 people were killed in fighting with the Mau Mau

Africans aided by white mercenaries fought over the Congo's mineral wealth when the Belgians withdrew in 1960: (below) Katangese rebels arrest suspected Congolese government supporters in Stanleyville

Biafra: old tribal enmities between Ibos and Hausas were emphasized by colonial boundaries and led to secession from Nigeria on 30 May 1967 and war

Distribution of ethnic groups in Nigeria 1963

in thousands	
total	55558
Hausa	11321
Ibo	9246
Fulani	4780
Kanuri	2259
Ibibio	2006
Tiu	1394
Ijaw	1089
Edo	955
27 other groups	2088

to pay a fine of $10,000 a day unless by 2 October he complied with the order made. By this time President Kennedy was actively involved, and was in constant communication with Barnett. The president, by midnight on 1 October, had stated that the governor and those associated with him were 'willingly obstructing the enforcement of Federal Court orders . . .'. He then authorized the calling up of 11,000 men of the Mississippi National Guard into the service of the United States. Kennedy appeared on television to inform the nation of the action he had taken. In the course of his address he stated:

I deeply regret the fact that any action by the Executive Branch was necessary in this case, but all other avenues and alternatives, including persuasion and conciliation, had been tried and exhausted. Had the police powers of Mississippi been used to support the orders of the Court, instead of deliberately and unlawfully blocking them . . . a peaceable and sensible solution would have been possible without any federal intervention . . .

Rioting had already broken out before the president's address to the nation. The arsenal at the disposal of citizens and students was formidable. It included petrol bombs, firearms, bricks, stones and iron bars. Their target was the 400 United States marshals and a small number of National Guardsmen, who defended themselves with tear gas. As the battle raged regular army troops came to the assistance of the marshals. By dawn on 2 October the last rioters were cleared from the University. At 8.35 that morning Meredith, accompanied by Chief United States Marshal McShane, was enrolled at the University registry.

This had been achieved at the cost of 375 injured and two dead, one of

Singapore riots in 1964: Malays feel economic and racial resentment against the Chinese, whose immigration was encouraged during the colonial period and who dominate the civil service

In Guyana both Africans and Indians were brought in under colonial rule; self-government brought rioting between the communities and over one hundred people were killed in the 1964 racial clashes. By 1970 economic tensions had lessened considerably

whom was the correspondent of Agence France Presse, Paul Guihard. In subsequent weeks no less than 15,000 federal troops and 600 US marshals were in and around the campus of the University to ensure the safe presence of James Meredith.

The effect on world opinion of the 'Battle of Ole Mis' was twofold. On the one hand it demonstrated the persistent hostility of the South to the granting of equality to the negro, and on the other hand it showed that in the cause of social justice the government of the United States was prepared to go to extreme lengths for the sake of a single individual. Meredith stayed his course and graduated in political science.

Non-violent cooperation to achieve social equality for the negro and federal intervention to promote integration, as in the case of Little Rock in Arkansas and Ole Mis, were two aspects of the racial situation in the United States. But there was a third – the use of violence, which grew with a switch from peaceful protest to vehement militance.

Between 1963 and 1967 in a large number of cities and towns which possessed a negro population there were open clashes between white and black accompanied by rioting and arson. The destruction that ensued amounted to many millions of dollars. The pattern of these disturbances as they spread across the nation became familiar. The arrest of a negro youth on a real or imagined charge, the shooting of a negro suspect by a white policeman, a rumour that a negro was being brutally treated while under interrogation by the police were typical incidents which precipitated days of violence and rioting. Sometimes variants occurred as in the case of the bombing of a negro church in Birmingham, Alabama, in 1963. Generally the confrontation was between negroes and a predominantly white police force, but there were incidents when a white mob engaged a black one with whatever weapons were to hand.

It is not easy to discover all the relevant factors which produced those years of violence. The stock white answers produced varied from the negro's failure to participate in the melting-pot process to the black man's instinctive resort to criminal action unless firmly controlled. The negro was not the creator of the American ghetto but he is its most permanent resident. European immigrants sojourned for a time in ghetto-like conditions in most cities of the United States. But for the emancipated negro who began to move North after the Civil War it became the ordained way of life.

The violence of the American cities in the later sixties could have been said to be spontaneous and unorganized. But there were movements which utilized the changing mood of the negro to create organizations which were in opposition to the white society in which they had their being. They revealed two quite contrary characteristics – the endeavour to look towards and to seek the redemption of black people in a quasi-religious way and the attempt to create a militant organization which would confront the white power structure and force it to come to terms with the negro. The first was typified by the Black Muslims, founded in Detroit in 1930 by Wali Farad, reputedly an orthodox Muslim from Mecca, and led by Elijah Muhammed (born Elijah Poole) from 1934 onwards. In 1963 Malcolm X, a former colleague of Muhammed, broke away to form the Organization of Afro-American Unity. Malcolm X was assassinated in 1965.

The Muslim's creed with relation to white people is simple. 'Never be the aggressor. Never look for trouble; but if any man molest you, may Allah bless you.' They have built up an organization which includes mosques, schools and businesses. It is rare for them to cooperate with other black groups. They would like to see the establishment of a separate black state inside America. The emphasis is on the religious unity of Islam which makes no distinction of colour. On the other hand the Organization of Afro-American Unity was essentially non-sectarian and set out to attract the intellectual negro who did not believe in racial integration. Both can be regarded as movements coming into being as a result of the black individual's predicament in a white racist society. They were attempts at assertion. Their following was mainly among the black militant youth of the ghettoes.

The second is best represented by the Black Power movements of which

In 1967-8 Asians in Nairobi with British passports
shut up shop and left Kenya in their thousands as a result
of the extreme policies of Africanization that followed
independence (as in Zambia and Tanzania)

In February 1968 the future of many Kenyan Asians with
British citizenship was threatened by the Commonwealth
Immigrants Act, which restricted their right of entry
into Britain

the most famous example is that of the Black Panthers. Their birthplace was
Alabama. In March 1966 the Lowndes County Freedom Organization in the
state of Alabama was formed in order to get black candidates adopted in
local elections. The symbol adopted by the organization was that of a black
panther. From 1966 onwards branches of the Black Panthers proliferated
all over the United States. Their aim was the organization of the black
people of America in such a way that they could challenge the white power
structure. The argument would be that wherever there are sufficient numbers of negroes they should endeavour to achieve political control. In the
late sixties they were probably regarded as the most serious militant threat
to organized law and order in the USA.

For the first time in these years the negro struggle in the United States
took on an overt, violent form. This was reflected, not only in the actions of
the Panthers, but in their semi-guerrilla clothing and the virulence of their
manifestos which demanded 'death to the pigs' – that is the white police.
At the same time they appeared to be willing to cooperate with some
sympathetic whites. By the end of the sixties the Panther movement was
virtually destroyed through the combined efforts of the FBI and the police.
Most of their leaders were either killed, imprisoned or driven into exile.
Nevertheless, their hold on the imagination of the negro masses persisted
as martyred symbols of their race.

It is possible that the Panthers' mantle of violence fell on the Weathermen
– young white radicals whose tactics were to destroy public buildings by
planting bombs. There were signs, however, by the end of 1970 that overt
violence and militancy by both black and white was beginning to disappear.

It is important to appreciate that the phrase used was Black Power not
Negro Power. The usage of Black to denote a person of African descent as
opposed to the former usage of Negro, Afro-American and Negro-American
is of considerable significance. It was undoubtedly connected with the
emergence of independent black states in Africa. At the end of 1970 the
affinity with that continent was perhaps still only on the emotional level, but
it was being given a more real dimension as was evinced by the growth of
Black Studies programmes in colleges and universities. The use of Black
would seem to indicate an emphasis on separation from the white society
which the negro inhabits. Extremists even suggested that a black state within
a state should be created in America. Clearly this was not a viable notion.
But insistence on separateness had, as some black leaders said, an important function in creating self-respect among a people who had been for
so long denied this elementary need. One can see that militancy and separateness were beginning to have an effect on the image of the negro possessed
by whites in America.

Such movements represented a dramatic change in the attitude of the
negro towards the white. For the first time the black man was forcing the
pace in the predominantly white society. The 'racist' Panthers were a
response to white racism. They were calling on black people to cease sub-
mission and to engage in a kind of warfare until their demands were met.
There is little question that the oratory of individuals like Stokely
Carmichael – like so many black leaders in the United States of West Indian
origin – Eldridge Cleaver and Rap Brown set alight the imagination of the
black masses. But it must be remembered that Black Power was, and is,
not a monolithic movement in the sense of the Communist Party of the
Soviet Union. It is a philosophy which is expressed in a variety of ways
according to the context in which the black person finds himself. For
example, its advent in the English-speaking Caribbean in the last years of
the sixties saw the expression of ideas very far removed from those used in
the American context. The American negro might believe that the white
power structure would only yield when convinced of the intransigence and
militancy of the negro. In Barbados Black Power extremists spoke of
achieving power through the normal democratic process.

It might be said that the negro in his history in the USA has had the
choice of assimilation or separateness. In the period from the Civil War until
the 1960s the emphasis for both negroes and white liberals was upon

Right Seven hundred West Indians on the No. 8 platform at Paddington Station, 1959; large-scale coloured immigration to Britain caused by desperate poverty began in 1948 and by 1970 the coloured population amounted to two per cent

Above Protest march at the restrictive 1968 Commonwealth Immigrants Act

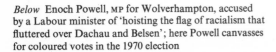

Below Enoch Powell, MP for Wolverhampton, accused by a Labour minister of 'hoisting the flag of racialism that fluttered over Dachau and Belsen'; here Powell canvasses for coloured votes in the 1970 election

assimilation. The phrase 'Black is beautiful', Afro hair styles and the general concern for things African on the part of the black Americans during the sixties indicated that separateness was the new doctrine. The change produced new problems. The older generation of negroes, characterized by the young as 'Uncle Toms', still wished for assimilation. More important, the demand for separateness called in question the whole struggle for equality through integration. It represented an assertion by negroes of the old Southern doctrine of 'separate but equal'. This must be understood as a reaction on the part of negro youth to the slowness which has marked his progress from inferiority. The political and social implications of this change cannot yet be assessed. It is possible that the value for the negro is in the creation of an authenticity which is necessary if he is to survive.

The most remarkable event in race relations in the United States between 1945 and 1970 was the philosophy, thought and action which can be subsumed under Black Power. The most articulate exponent was undoubtedly Eldridge Cleaver. He put into words the anger and frustration of generations of black people in his country. A self-confessed rapist of white women, he was capable of analyzing his actions in terms of the predicament in which the negro exists in the United States. His writings forced white liberals to realize their burden of guilt, and made black people aware that their apparent inferiority was a device of their former white masters to perpetuate their own superiority.

The United States may, in the unfortunate though well-intentioned phrase of Daniel Moynihan, move into an era of benign neglect as regards its racial problems and concentrate instead on economic or environmental problems, but its destiny will be decided by the success of its struggle to achieve racial equality. To that it is committed.

Africa

In the part of Africa which still by 1970 experienced white domination no committal to equality had been made. Two main areas – the Republic of South Africa, and Angola and Mozambique under Portuguese control – exemplify the determination of the European to continue in his traditional colonizing role.

Between 1945 and 1970 South Africa's nationalist governments were determined to ensure that she remained a bastion of white supremacy. The course was set by the victory of the Nationalist Party in the election of 1948. Its campaign was based on the implementation of the policy of apartheid. The word itself was first used publicly by Dr Malan in the South African Parliament in January 1944: 'To ensure the safety of the white race and of Christian civilization by the honest maintenance of the principles of apartheid and guardianship.' The white South African persuaded himself that it was his historic duty to maintain the supremacy and superiority of the whites against people of colour. The means at his disposal in the past were those in common use by all colonial governments. In the decades after the war those means became infinitely more powerful. The anachronism in the South African situation was that, whereas the former great European colonial powers of the world had in the main abdicated from their role of guardian of the 'native' peoples they had conquered, the Republic felt that this duty was even more important in 1970.

Some notion of the surveillance and harassment to which the African population is subjected may be gleaned from statistics. In 1957, 1,021,190 Bantu were convicted of crimes. Over half these offences were concerned with infringements of the notorious 'pass' and liquor laws. It has been estimated that '. . . one African adult man out of three is arrested and convicted of an offence each year. . . .' As a result of demonstration against the 'pass' laws more than 2,000 African women were imprisoned for a week in Johannesburg in October 1958. From the government's point of view such activities served to impress the Africans with their power and authority. They also gave notice to the world of South Africa's police state philosophy.

Successful economic exploitation was not a sufficient justification for the European's rejection of the African. Other means had to be found in order to demonstrate the righteousness of the cause. One of the bulwarks of the Afrikaaner in his struggle to establish himself in his southern kingdom was the Dutch Reformed Church. Of all the Christian denominations in South Africa it was the only one which actually supported the separation of the races. It became increasingly difficult to use scriptural authority to support actions which were patently un-Christian. It was possible for the Synod of the Dutch Reformed Church in April 1963 to support the notion that separation of individual churches made for a more efficient ministry – whites would more efficiently achieve the kingdom of God if they were segregated from blacks. The previous year it had expelled a member for supporting racial integration: Professor A.S. Geyser, a minister of the Church and professor of theology at the University of Pretoria, was charged with heresy and deposed from his appointments on the grounds of his opposition to racial segregation. In the following year Geyser carried his appeal to the Supreme Court. Very wisely the Church took the decision, before the Court pronounced, to reinstate him. The dilemma which ought to face the Dutch Reformed Church is obvious – if the New Testament is taken as the basis of Christianity the theological gymnastics demanded to support apartheid are becoming increasingly impossible to perform.

The flood of segregationalist legislation initiated by the nationalist government of 1948 continued. The Group Areas Act of 1950 was a major example of such legislation. The Act gave powers to the government '. . . to make provision for the establishment of Group Areas, that is, separate areas for the different racial groups, by compulsion if necessary. . . .' Compulsion was certainly used and imposed incalculable hardship on black and coloured people. Designation of an area in which different ethnic groups were living as a white area meant the enforced removal of all not classified as Caucasian.

The most notorious enactments were concerned with restrictive measures designed to keep the racial *status quo* in being. The Communist Party in 1950 was effectively banned by special legislation. Ten years later the Unlawful Organizations Act banned all African and Indian political associations. The Suppression of Communism Act of 1950 gave the minister of justice power to ban anyone who was suspected of promoting any one of the aims of communism. There was neither trial nor any right of appeal on the part of the individual. In practice this meant that anyone who

After the war in Algeria (1954-62), thousands of Algerian immigrants to France were treated as pariahs; they made shacks out of packing-cases and corrugated iron

Indonesian immigrants to Holland after Indonesia achieved independence tended to settle into mutual acceptance with the Dutch

Top In America riots and looting followed the assassination
of Martin Luther King, the moderate negro leader,
on 4 April 1968 in Memphis, Tennessee; for many it meant
that white violence must be repaid in kind
Above The King funeral brought scenes of hysteria

Negroes march to the Capitol in an anti-poverty
demonstration; black people had little share in postwar
American economic growth

declared himself in favour of racial equality – one of the aims of the CP –
could be banned. Banning as interpreted meant confinement to the district
in which the individual resided and/or house arrest. For anyone to quote
such a person's opinions was an offence.

The General Law Amendment Act of 1963 and the Criminal Procedure
Amendment Act of 1965 gave immense power to the police and the attorney-
general respectively. The former empowered the police to arrest without a
warrant anyone suspected of a political offence. The individual could be
detained for a ninety-day period. At its expiration he could be detained for a
further ninety days. There were some cases in which the period was extended
three times. The Act of 1965 gave the attorney-general discretion to detain
any person he regarded as a material witness in any criminal proceedings
either to protect him from intimidation, or to prevent his absconding. It is
easy to see how such powers could be used to coerce unwilling witnesses.

The reality of such legislation was made apparent to the world in the
treason trial of 1956. In December of that year 156 opponents of apartheid
were arrested. Ninety-one were committed for trial. The case dragged on
until March 1961 when all were acquitted. Many were well-known white
liberals in addition to Africans. Although the defendants were technically
acquitted many of them had been ruined in the process. In 1963 a number of
people were arrested under the 'ninety-day law' and subsequently brought
to trial and convicted. The same pattern recurred in 1964. The most outstanding trial of that year was that of the leaders of the banned African
National Congress including Nelson Mandela and Walter Sisulu. Of the
eight brought to trial only one was acquitted. The rest were sentenced to
life imprisonment.

By 1970 most foreign observers and South African liberals were convinced that a police state dedicated to white supremacy had come into
being in that country. The price to the nation of the secret services was now
5·3 million rands a year. The General Law Amendment Act of 1969,
which was totally opposed by the legal profession and the greater part of the
press, gave powers to any minister to suppress evidence before a court if, in
his opinion, this would be against the interests of the state. It also made it
an offence to publicize any matter which was currently being dealt with by
the Bureau of State Security. In the same year the Black Sash Organization
– an anti-apartheid white women's movement – reported that nearly 500
individuals were the subject of banning orders. In the year 1967-8, 13,792
whites, 561,405 Bantu, 77,374 coloureds and 2,325 Asians were admitted
to prison.

While there had been numerous incidents and acts of suppression by the
government in the preceding years, it was not until the Sharpeville Massacre
on 21 March 1960 that the world became aware of the deterioration of the
situation in South Africa. On that day in the township of Sharpeville, about
forty miles from Johannesburg, a crowd of Africans gathered outside the
police station to protest against the pass laws. The reaction of the police was
to fire indiscriminately into the crowd. Sixty-seven persons were killed and
186 wounded. Of the latter 155 were shot in the back while running away.
World opinion reacted violently. But, as in the case of Prime Minister
Harold Macmillan's 'wind of change' speech to the South African Parliament in the month before, the official response was predictable. 'White
South Africa is now standing with its back to the wall. For the maintenance
of its traditional colour policy of separation between white and non-white,
it can count on no support from outside. It stands alone like a Blood River
laager . . .' (*Die Volksblad*, 10 February 1960)

In its anxiety to preserve racial purity South Africa has invaded the most
private rights of the individual. This has been exemplified in the laws prohibiting, not only marriage, but any carnal acts between European and non-
European. Before the last war in 1927 the Hertzog government had passed
an Immorality Act which penalized sexual relations between Africans and
Europeans. This was extended, by further Acts in 1949 and 1950, to such
relations between Europeans and coloureds. As the then minister of finance,
Dr T.E.Dönges put it: it was not concerned with sexual immorality but

Right A child in Harlem: the American ghetto remains, and the negro is its most permanent resident

Negroes in the Deep South

'to try to preserve some sort of apartheid in what one may call prostitution . . .' Not even the most diehard white Southerner in the United States had ever voiced such an opinion, although as a matter of fact Dönges in his speech in support of the Bill quoted the anti-miscegenation laws of the USA which at that time obtained in some thirty states.

South Africa withdrew from membership of specialized UN organizations such as UNESCO (1956) and FAO (1964) and ILO (1964), and was suspended from the Economic Commission for Africa in 1963. Britain as a member state of the United Nations reluctantly accepted this fact. No one could suggest that successive British governments took the lead in speaking out on what was in essence a moral problem. To deny equality in the proper sense to a whole category of human beings is a moral affront. The argument in Britain during the period under review was concerned with morality on the one hand and self-interest on the other. Trade between Britain and South Africa amounted to many millions of pounds a year. The lobby which emphasized that apartheid was a matter for South Africa alone to decide was extremely powerful. Thus up to 1970 efforts to achieve a boycott of South African goods always failed. But the problem remained. The advent of a Tory government pledged to re-think the question of the resumption of the sale of arms to South Africa revived the whole issue in the public mind. Supporters of the Republic maintained that if Britain were to cut her trade ties with South Africa, France, Germany and the USA would be more than ready to fill the vacuum. This might be so but the moral imperative still remained. Could Britain as a nation devoted to the principles of democracy give economic and quasi-military support to a regime which openly suppressed the majority of its population?

In 1957 Eisenhower sent in troops to Little Rock, Arkansas, to enforce integration in a high school; but progress in the Deep South has been slow since then

The American negro since 1965

negro population

- less than 1%
- over 1%
- over 5%
- over 10%
- over 25%
- over 50%
- ▲ cities with over 200 000 negro inhabitants

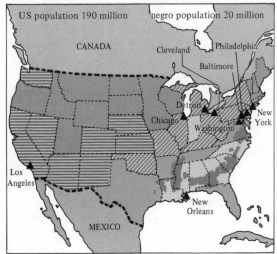

The negro revolt 1965-7

- ◉ Negro riots 1965
- ◯ Negro riots 1966
- ● Negro riots 1967
- † Deaths

The decades after the war also showed another side of racial attitudes in Africa. The confrontation between white and black, whether in South Africa, Angola or Rhodesia, posed the entire problem of the future of the European in the continent. But there was another, equally important problem. The carving up of Africa in the nineteenth century by the great colonial powers almost entirely ignored linguistic and tribal boundaries. It was a matter of political convenience where frontiers ran. Extraordinary anomalies were created such as a Gold Coast chieftain having seventy-five per cent of his adherents in French territory. The policy of the British colonial government up to the time of Nigeria's independence in 1960 was to ensure that the rule of law was maintained. No efforts were made to create anything approaching a nation. The traditional enmity of Hausa and Ibo persisted as part of the system. It is against this background that the tragic events of the late sixties in Nigeria must be understood.

The Ibo leader, General Ironsi, led the coup of January 1966 in which most of the outstanding northern leaders were killed. Ojukwu, the inspirer of the ill-fated Biafran nation, cast himself in the role of the pre-1914 Serbian nationalists. Chauvinism is seldom lacking in the world of politics. That Africans exhibit this characteristic should not be a matter of surprise. The black population of Africa has suffered the exploitation of the European for a long period. The experience, however, has not produced a conglomeration of altruists and martyrs but ordinary political men. Their memories are as short or as long as those of their white contemporaries in Northern Ireland.

In its first years of independence as a nation Nigeria had preserved a semblance of unity. In the case of the former Belgian Congo (Congo-Kinshasa) divisive forces hardly waited upon the declaration of independence. The new state was proclaimed on 30 June 1960. On 11 July Moïse Tshombe proclaimed the secession of Katanga from the new state. For nearly five years the world watched as black Africans aided by white mercenaries and European economic interests – the mineral wealth of the Congo in cobalt, zinc and copper is significant – fought each other. The internecine conflict produced its inevitable toll of massacre, famine and rape. The decision of the Security Council of the UN to intervene with an international peace-keeping force was regarded as a major test for that organization. Unfortunately, the function of this force was never clearly decided. Events such as the murder of Patrice Lumumba in January 1961 did much to destroy faith in the efficacy of the UN as an effective political force.

The history of both the Congo and Nigeria in the 1960s demonstrate that the European has to a great extent failed in his ultimate political role – to provide stability after his withdrawal. It also shows that the unity of colour may be a function of white domination, and that black Africans are as much a prey to the pressures of political life as their former white masters.

Guyana and Malaysia

This type of internecine conflict was by no means confined to Africa. In the sixties Guyana erupted into armed conflict between those of African descent and East Indians. The latter, in the nineteenth-century colonial period, had been brought in as indentured labour after the emancipation of the negro slaves, to work on the sugar estates. Hostility was engendered from the inception of this immigration. Negroes regarded the East Indians as blacklegs who enabled their former masters to perpetuate quasi-servile conditions of labour. In the aftermath of the colonial situation, to economic and social insecurity was added the fear that the increasing birthrate of the East Indians would mean the negroes' permanent relegation to the status of a minority. The movement for independence had produced a monolithic party. This unity was disrupted, ostensibly on ideological grounds, in reality because of insecurity. By 1970 more and more accommodation was being achieved between the ethnic groups as Guyanese economic conditions improved.

Ethnic tensions in Malaysia appear to be both different from and similar to those of Guyana. Throughout the British colonial dispensation the

The Ku Klux Klan: negro moves to militancy for social justice in the sixties brought out the white racists again

'Nazis' in protest against housing for negroes in Chicago

immigration of Indians and Chinese was encouraged by the government. The reason was the apparent refusal of Malays to assist in the exploitation of their country. The independent government of 1970 claimed that no effort was made to integrate these communities into the mainstream of Malay life and culture. What has been called a pluralistic society grew up, that is a society in which the different ethnic groups maintain a kind of ethnic autonomy, and relationships between them are confined largely to those of an economic nature. If to this legacy is added the long struggle, from 1948 onwards, against the Chinese-dominated Malayan Communist Party, it is clear that the attempt to create a Malayan nation was beset with difficulties.

The indigenous Malay has always felt resentment against both Chinese and Indian. He was economically disadvantaged as compared with them. By 1968 he was aware that the civil service of his country was dominated by non-Malays. From 1957 until 1969 a number of minor confrontations had taken place between Malays and Chinese. On 13 May 1969, however, the most serious outbreak occurred. This involved all ethnic groups. In the following six weeks nearly 200 people were killed, 439 injured and over 9,000 arrested.

No longer a colony, Malaya faced the task of building a nation out of diverse ethnic components, as did Guyana. If religion is substituted for race it was the same intractable problem which confronted the Roman Catholic and Protestant people of Ulster.

The immigrant situation in Europe

The Dutch, consequent upon their withdrawal from Indonesia, encountered a special problem. Throughout the colonial period they had entered into sexual unions with the indigenous peoples. The resulting progeny had adhered to Dutch ways. These Indos, as they are popularly known, at the time of the independence of Indonesia were given the option of acquiring citizenship in the new state, or of becoming Dutch subjects and migrating to Holland. Over 300,000 chose this course. Holland, one of the most densely populated areas in the world, was faced with the social and physical accommodation of thousands of people of a different ethnic origin. To their credit the Dutch people took special measures to facilitate the incorporation of the Indos into the life of the Netherlands, for example, the setting aside of a quota of all new housing for immigrants.

In the Caribbean the special status of the Netherlands Indies in relation to Holland which emerged after the war encouraged the migration of coloured West Indians from Surinam to Holland. The evidence suggests that their absorption into the society was far less successful than in the case of the Indos. Reasons for this are not easily discoverable. It is possible that the Indos' deliberate choice of the Dutch way of life, together with feelings of guilt and responsibility for their existence, may have determined the Dutch attitude of acceptance. Such considerations would appear to have been absent in the case of the Surinamese.

The migration to France of coloured peoples since the war has been of a different order. The largest category of immigrants was that of Algerians and the Algerian War of 1954-62 created acute division within France. Great hostility was generated against North Africans, and to be Algerian in France was to be regarded as a pariah. Migration from black Africa consisted mainly of members of élitist groups from French Africa, and the lowest category of unskilled workers. The latter group, not intending to settle permanently, has created a way of life insulated from the mainstream of French life. In the case of coloured West Indians their appearance in the metropolitan country is determined largely by the fact that postwar development turned France's Caribbean colonies into integral departments of France. As French citizens the people of the Antilles have the right to come and go as they please.

The presence of such immigrant groups has begun to destroy the myth of French colour-blindness. Some observers maintain that France has become a racist society. But the situation is confused. On the one hand complete

Black is beautiful

Black changed its meaning in the late sixties in America, and came to stand for pride in African descent and culture, for identity and separateness from white tradition. Emotional affinity with the new independent African nations grew, and Black Studies programmes were instituted in colleges and universities. Violence increasingly became a feature of the Black Power movements which began in 1965, and the response among many white Americans was all too often one of fear and hatred.

Above Linocut by African artist, Jacob Afolabi 1964

Right Festival of the negro arts in Dakar, Senegal

Above right The wall of a 'Black Power' house in Chicago's negro ghetto is decorated with jazz musicians, including Charlie Parker (top left). Many American negroes are becoming increasingly convinced that 'soul' music is their outstanding contribution to world culture

Above Marsha Hunt, successful actress and singer; star of the rock-musical *Hair*

For some, black was beautiful for business: models, photographers, wigmakers, bookshops (*right*) among others

Right Black Panthers aimed to organize blacks to challenge the white power structure and take control. The movement began in Alabama, March 1966, when the Lowndes County Freedom Organization was formed to get black candidates adopted in local elections

UN forces moved in to Cyprus in 1964 when growing pressure for union with Greece led to further clashes between Greek and Turkish Cypriots. Cyprus brought Greece and Turkey to the verge of war; by 1970 the dispute was quiescent and unresolved

'Long live the Basques.' Hunted by the police, Basque Nationalists pursued their hopeless struggle for independence and waited for Franco's death

acceptance of the French ethos by members of the black élite creates social acceptance. A black West Indian, Gaston Monnerville, became president of the French Senate. On the other hand the black worker from Senegal may be made aware of his colour daily, and of his inferiority, in the streets of Paris. The evidence suggests that there may well be intellectual accommodation of the non-European, but that social equality is denied.

Britain's history of large-scale coloured immigration goes back to 1948, with the arrival of the *Empire Windrush* from Kingston, Jamaica, with over two hundred migrants. Britain had become used to the presence of coloured people in the armed forces of both the UK and USA. Servicemen returning to the Caribbean brought information concerning the 'mother country'. The desperate economic and demographic situation in the West Indies precipitated the flow of people which was still continuing in 1970. The economic motivation for immigration applies equally in the case of Indian and Pakistani migrants. It has been estimated that the coloured population of Britain in 1969-70 was of the order of over a million, that is about two per cent of the total.

Up to 1962 no restrictions were placed upon entry into Britain. In that year the first Commonwealth Immigrants Act was passed. The so-called race riots in 1958 in Nottingham and Notting Hill Gate in London may have precipitated this action. Entry is now virtually restricted to those in possession of a work voucher issued by the Ministry of Labour to bona fide students, and to dependants of those already in the UK. The incidents in Nottingham and London brought home to people that there was strong latent hostility against non-Europeans within the society. Britain discovered that in fact she was potentially a racist society.

Restriction was followed by the Race Relations Act of 1965 which made discrimination in public places unlawful, and set up the Race Relations Board to consider complaints concerning discrimination. The most significant departure, however, was the Commonwealth Immigrants Act of 1968. This Act restricted the right of entry to Britain of Kenyan Asians. Under the British dispensation large numbers of Asians had migrated to Central and East African colonies. After independence these countries (Kenya, Tanzania and Zambia) embarked on policies of Africanization. Asians were given the opportunity of becoming nationals of these states. Many, secure in their possession of reputedly valid British passports, declined to do so. Further legislation deprived them of their means of livelihood. They wished to emigrate to Britain. Agitation in the UK had been mounting against continued immigration and in February 1968 the government gave way to public pressure and passed the Act.

From the observer's point of view Britain's equivocal attitude over Rhodesia, the refusal to recognize the validity of passports legally granted and the new government's endeavour in 1970 to reopen the issue of sale of arms to South Africa all demonstrated an admission that principles can be dispensed with in the face of popular opinion and economic self-interest.

The most significant event with relation to racial attitudes in Britain was the advent to prominence in the late sixties of Mr Enoch Powell. He maintained that coloured immigration was striking at the heart of what he took to be essentially English. The presence of immigrants could only serve to destroy the great heritage which Britain possessed. If immigration continued, so his argument ran, the inevitable outcome would be bloodshed and naked conflict. His solution was the creation of a Ministry of Repatriation the business of which would be to encourage and assist the repatriation of coloured immigrants back to their place of origin. That many had been born in Britain, and knew no other country did not appear to have entered his thinking.

It would be wrong to assume that racial hostility did not exist in Britain – it was there before Mr Powell – but it could be said that it was not of the same inherent order and kind that exists in South Africa. It had been created by the influx of immigrants to areas in which there was a demand for their labour. The fact that these same areas were also those in which the demand for housing was most acute for both the host and immigrant

Top Flemish posters demand freedom of religion and Brussels for the Flemish; despite legislation, clashes continued in Belgium between Flemings and the French-speaking Walloons

Above The *Québec libre* sign is removed from a roadway; in 1970 extremists of the French separatist movement in Canada tested the nerve of the Trudeau regime by kidnapping a British diplomat, James Cross, and murdering another hostage, Pierre Laporte, minister of labour in the Quebec government

populations generated a conflict-type situation. Xenophobia may be a characteristic of the English. It can, however, only be precipitated into violence if there is a real or imagined competition for the essentials of life with a group which wears its identity like a banner.

Conclusions

Looking back on the twenty-five years between 1945 and 1970 certain patterns can be distinguished. The false dawn of the years immediately after 1945, the dawn of which Wendell Willkie and his *One World* (1943) was the prophet, never fulfilled its promise of world unity. The dissolution of empire and the advent of new states in Africa and Asia did not lessen the tension between white and black, between European and non-European. The paradox is not too difficult to explain – independence was at times only won through bloodshed as in Indo-China and Algeria, and there remained great areas of racialism, such as the USA and South Africa, for which there was to be no foreseeable solution.

Fear of renewed economic exploitation by the European had forced the emergence of the Afro-Asian bloc at the United Nations. At the continental level the same fear led to the formation of the Organization of African Unity. Such actions were not merely informed by fear – there was a powerful philosophical and emotional component. The coloured people of the world had suffered subjugation and degradation from the European up to that time. Frantz Fanon of Martinique could write in 1952 that it was the whites who were the murderers and destroyers in history. The black victim must by definition be superior to his oppressor. The danger is that the very human vices of the non-European will be obscured. Curiously enough it is the white liberal who was most easily seduced by the notion of the all-pervading superiority of the black. On the other hand black leaders in the United States have publicly expressed their gratitude to whites for giving the negro the nobility of suffering. That is to say, whites have made them realize themselves through suffering. In part this is irony. In part a statement of the truth.

The case of the New World negro is different from that of the African. The latter demanded his freedom from European domination. With only three major exceptions – South Africa, Rhodesia and Portuguese Africa – he has obtained it. In the Americas the man of colour whether politically free, as in parts of the Caribbean, or living as a minority in a white society, as in the USA and Brazil, has suffered both domination and cultural deprivation. The 'middle passage' for the African going as a slave to the New World symbolizes the destruction of his culture. Thus it is not surprising that *négritude* stems out of the Caribbean. The Martinican Aimé Césaire, in lamenting the lost roots of his homeland, Africa, is expressing the same emotion as the negro ghetto boy bent over his Swahili grammar. *Négritude* springs out of the colonial situation of the negro. It is a philosophy of deprivation – of a desire for the culturally deprived African to assert his authenticity and identity as distinct from the European. Rejection by the white has led to a reaffirmation of that which is black.

Pan-Africanism, an idea which goes back to the beginning of the century, is not a political reality. African states are not united among themselves – Malawi courts South Africa and condemns the movement for black freedom in South Africa. Pan-Arabism has had a chimerical quality. Pan-Slavism in Europe was fragmented by nationalism. Neither religion nor race necessarily provides a secure foundation for unity.

But the history of these twenty-five years contains a most serious warning. It is possible that if continued reluctance on the part of the white peoples of the world to give equality and self-respect to the non-European persists, the world may see a total confrontation of black against white. In the rhetoric of the non-white world, as characterized by Frantz Fanon, the white man is a devil. So long as apartheid and other manifestations of white supremacy remain, such rhetoric will gain followers. There could be a terrible explosion of racial conflict if white societies persist in the belief that God has willed them to rule over lesser breeds.

George Melly
Mass Pleasures

What are mass pleasures? Those leisure activities or pursuits, whether participatory or non-participatory, which involve a majority of people at national, international or world level.

As a general definition this would do, only, in that my brief is to describe the mass pleasures of a particular period, it is necessary to go further. What then, if anything, distinguishes the mass pleasures of the last twenty-five years from earlier periods?

Most noticeable is the fact that very few of them are now the result of direct visual or auditory contact between the source of pleasure and its audience. In most cases the pleasure is filtered through some kind of reproducing device *en route*. This in itself is not new. From the beginning of the century the radio, the gramophone record and the cinema have played an increasing part in purveying mass pleasures, yet it is the rise of television, in itself exactly contained within the period under review, which has confirmed and intensified the process. The reason for this lies in television's ability to transmit events as they are taking place, thereby effecting a total suspension of disbelief while simultaneously destroying the need to exercise the imaginative faculties. The earlier media were unable to do this. Radio could broadcast the sound of an event but the mind's eye had to create a suitable image. The film could manage to simulate sound and image, but the spectator was aware of a time-lag. Television can let us see and hear an event as it is taking place, and the fact it both can and increasingly does use film is immaterial. Psychologically it seems more 'real' than the earlier media. For many people it seems more real than reality itself.

For this reason, as much as for its rapid, world-wide spread and growth, I shall be putting television at the centre of my argument, discussing also the way in which it has changed and modified earlier mass pleasures, directly in the case of radio, spectator sports and the cinema, indirectly in such areas as holidays, eating habits, fashion and even sexual mores. I shall also try and demonstrate how the nature of television has affected the relation between the purveyors of mass culture and their audience, a point of view expressed by Edgar Morin when he wrote that 'the mass media are disappearing as such, to be no more than universal middle men in production-creation-consumption relationships' (Edgar Morin, *New Trends in the Study of Mass Communications*, Centre for Contemporary Cultural Studies, Birmingham University, 1968).

Yet before launching into this formidable programme (and given the space I can hope to do little more than sketch in the contours) it's important to examine certain prejudices which anyone reading this book may hold, and which I know cloud my own objectivity. In particular, I would draw attention to the blurred semantic associations of the word 'mass'.

Up until the Second World War 'the masses' was an acceptable and positive expression much favoured by the intellectual left, but for a variety of reasons this is no longer the case. Even among Marxists the word 'people', or 'the people', or 'working people' has replaced the collective noun; 'popular' or, in context, 'folk', or, in relation to the young, 'pop' the adjectival form. For intellectuals, on whatever level, the word 'mass' suggests today a mindless hydra sucking contentedly at the vast udders of cynical manipulatory interests. As to why this semantic change should have come about, I have no cut and dried theory. Possibly J.B. Priestley's invention of the hold-all term 'admass' had something to do with it, but it's my belief that we find words to express concepts rather than the other way round.

Der Spiegel attacks the conservative Axel Springer group's near monopoly of the press and other news media in West Germany; this was one of the main issues in the West German student demonstrations of the late sixties

In Great Britain and other Western countries newspapers and magazines were hard hit by television which brought faster and more easily digested news programmes; the end of the period saw a growing number of mergers and closures

Rightly or wrongly, many intellectuals believe in a world-wide conspiracy to destroy individualism for either commercial or political reasons, and the word 'mass' has come to imply the passive victim of this conspiracy.

As is usually the case, a golden age or Utopia has been set up as an imaginary alternative. Using writers like George Orwell or Richard Hoggart as cultural sources, those dismayed by present trends offer a nostalgic picture of pre-media working-class culture, stressing its regional diversity and local relevance. Parallel to this runs a tendency to fasten gratefully on any aspect of working-class culture which retains its regional identity; to praise black bread in order to denigrate white sliced loaves; to admire Spanish flamenco or primitive negro blues, the better to dismiss the main body of popular music.

Finally, within what we might call the conservative wing of concerned intellectual opposition to present-day mass culture, there is the belief that if only something 'better' were on offer people, as a whole, would soon learn to prefer it. Any proof of this is eagerly seized on: queues outside the cinema for *Tom Jones* or *Easy Rider*, the popularity on British television of *Steptoe and Son* or *Cathy Come Home*, and so on. What is ignored is that such artefacts, while certainly possessing qualities which satisfy intellectuals, operate equally effectively on other levels and may in consequence owe their popular success to factors which, from an intellectual point of view, are irrelevant. Later in this essay I shall try and look at both television and cinema in relation to this idea.

An alternative attack comes from those whose mistrust of the mass media springs, not from their effect on popular culture, but from their power to sabotage high culture. This attitude is presented at its most cogent by the American critic Dwight MacDonald in his bad-tempered but closely argued essay 'Masscult and Midcult' (1961). It is his contention that the masses as such are irredeemable; that the cultural tradition is dependent on a small if world-wide élite; and that it is not the cretinizing effect of the mass media which matters, but their attempts to turn their audiences into middle-brows – thus confusing and muddying the two streams.

In contrast to these two arguments there is a third intellectual reaction to postwar developments in mass culture which, despite its semantic rejection of the word 'mass', would seem to defend it without qualifications. What has become known as the 'pop' approach relies on embracing enthusiastically

exactly those aspects of mass culture which most appal the traditionalists: mass-produced and disposable objects, consumer goods, television commercials and so on, but it's necessary to emphasize that the bets are hedged, the choice selective. The pop intellectual defends his identity through a certain irony, using such devices as 'camp' or 'kitsch' to allow of retreat. To listen to pop-minded intellectuals discussing a football match is a very different experience from listening to working-class fans doing the same thing. The intellectuals may know as much about the game but will tend, however hard they try to suppress their inclination, to make cultural cross-references. Even those intellectuals most committed to the support of recent mass cultures make their commitment through a traditional cultural grid.

If I have appeared harsh in describing the three principal Western intellectual positions *vis-à-vis* mass culture, it is not because I feel myself free of them. There is no doubt in my mind that the technological developments of the last twenty-five years, particularly television, have helped and continue to help destroy or dilute a great deal of value in local, regional and high culture, and have placed the manipulators or would-be manipulators in a position of unprecedented power. Yet to remain blind to the beauty, glamour and convenience of some of the artefacts of our civilization is absurd. The pop tenet, that it is time for the intellectual to leave the ivory tower, is something I find immensely sympathetic. The danger is that, in his determination to enjoy what is available without prejudice, the pop intellectual may find himself working in the interests of those who see leisure, affluence and technological plenitude as the weapons of a new tyranny. There is no one who demonstrates this trap more clearly than the pop Machiavelli, Professor Marshall McLuhan.

As Jonathan Miller has shown (*McLuhan*, 1971), for all McLuhan's whizz-kid surface his thinking is basically reactionary and élitist, not in the cultural sense like MacDonald, but politically and socially. His early enthusiasm was reserved for writers like G.K. Chesterton, and later he subscribed to the theories of the US Southern States Agrarians. Beneath his advertising slogans in favour of modernity is the belief that the destruction of the written word, the media of individualism, could lead again to world rule by a small educated élite. Those dazzling half-truths, 'the global electronic village' and so on, conceal the hope that technology will enable us to return to the hierarchic structure of pre-Renaissance Europe on a world-wide scale. His enthusiasm for television, for example, is based on the fact that he sees it as a priest in the pulpit feeding certainties to an unlettered congregation. In his earlier books, *The Gutenberg Galaxy* (1962) in particular, despite (or perhaps because of) his approach, he threw out many original and penetrating insights into the effects of the new media, but he has become increasingly the victim of his own myth; a dotty guru at the service of the cretinizers, and it is no wonder that Madison Avenue treats him with such reverence.

Yet as I intend to describe later, the West has already recruited a resistance, and, although in the main confined to one group – the young – its adherents exist on a large enough scale to justify inclusion in our context. Unlike their parents or grandparents, most of whom, having experienced war or depression at first hand, were prepared to accept conformity in exchange for affluence, many hundreds of thousands of young people have already rejected the consumer society and, however confusedly, are searching for a way out. In their pleasures, they are prepared and indeed demand to use those elements of technology which can serve them (tape recorders, hi-fi equipment, motor bikes, films, etc.); but they seem determined to do so without paying the price demanded by McLuhan's masters. Indeed this combination of deliberate simplicity, not to say squalor, and free access to the playthings of technology suggests a rather McLuhanesque name for them – the electronic gipsies.

To date I have sketched in only the Western background against which mass pleasures have changed and grown over the last quarter of a century: an increasingly well-stocked toy-shop in which traditional toys have been largely superseded by gadgets of ever-increasing ingenuity, but at the cost

In the West the Pop Art movement rocketed the comic book heroes into new cultural worlds: (*below*) Captain Marvel; (*bottom*) in the East and particularly in China, comics remained politically relevant

perhaps of some atrophying of the recipient's imaginative faculties.

In the Eastern bloc the situation is radically different. Here pleasure is in no way linked to increased consumption or the accumulation of possessions. The media are at the service, not of envy-buying, but of the preservation of the political *status quo*.

Technological competition may exist on a national basis – Russia's space programme versus America's, for example; but the nineteenth-century notions of thrift and plain living as virtues still persist in the private sector. In the West, the proofs of prosperity – two cars, a new washing machine, colour television – are not simply a source of pleasure to their owner, but a patriotic duty as well: a proof that 'Free Enterprise' works. To the communist citizen, to lust after private affluence is a vice, and in consequence their rebellious young (I am not, of course, referring to those revolutionaries who fight for intellectual freedom) yearn above all for those very symbols of material affluence which their Western contemporaries are in the process of rejecting.

There is, however, one area where the pleasures of the two peoples overlap, and that is sport: particularly at its apex, international sport. This passion is not only tolerated but encouraged by both systems, because it can be so easily harnessed to ideology. To win is a proof of the superiority of the political system under which the victors live; to lose, an additional reason for hating the opposition.

In this field too the mass media have played their part in totally changing the meaning and impact of the contests. Through these devices, events which in the comparatively recent past could exercise their full emotive effect only on those actually present, may be seen simultaneously by whole nations. Furthermore, through commentary and selective transmission, an apparently objective account may in fact offer a highly subjective picture. I don't believe in McLuhan's epigrammatic dictum that 'the medium is the message', but have no doubt that the medium can distort the message.

For a true pessimist, the Western world may be seen as moving towards the fulfilment of Aldous Huxley's vision in *Brave New World*, the Eastern bloc as doing its best to meet Orwell's dateline. Both court the underdeveloped 'Third World': the West with the plastic beads of affluence, the East with the repressive bible of political stability.

Meanwhile, under licence, the masses enjoy themselves as best they can; and if in this essay I concentrate more on the Western sector this is not only because the facts are available, but also because mass pleasures here, geared to the needs of a society based on consumption and obsolescence, have changed much more radically.

One thing remains before examining specific instances, and that is to define what qualifies a member of the masses. I suppose that the broadest distinguishing characteristic is an inability to escape from the limits of an education which, whether by design or not, has extended no further than instruction in the skills necessary to earn a living. A member of the 'mass' in this sense, tends to be unable to make value judgements, still less comparative judgements, and is likely to see life as a series of unrelated experiences, pleasurable or otherwise, and to think in clichés: a great advantage to the authorities. So defined, the masses are the 'gammas' of Huxley's world, the 'proles' of Orwell's.

As an optimist I believe, although sometimes with difficulty, that the human spirit is finally resistant to such classification. In the past it has always been misery which has led to opposition and revolt. There are signs today, in Western society at any rate, that the next upsurge of individualism may be brought about in rejection of forcible feeding.

Television

In 1925 John Baird, usually accepted as the inventor of television, successfully transmitted the recognizable image of a ventriloquist's dummy called 'Bill' from one room to another. In 1931 the USSR began regular transmissions (but for whom?). In 1936 the BBC followed suit and continued up until the war. Nevertheless, as an effective medium, the history of television

Top Early American TV; but the luxury soon became a necessity. UNESCO figures show that by 1967, North Americans had 285 sets per 1,000 people
Above In Kuwait, oil brought wealth and a correspondingly high number of TV sets

Below President Johnson in the White House watches an early *Saturn* launching

The Bluebell girls: in spite of strict moral taboos, TV won over the admass audience from the cinemas
Above right BBC interview with Martin Luther King; the public service channel was later to join the commercial companies in the race for viewing figures

Gerald Scarfe's vision of the TV consumer society

is postwar, and indeed it is the only instrument of modern mass pleasure which is virtually enclosed by the period under discussion.

On one level (and with the exception of South Africa which, possibly due to the insurmountable difficulty of establishing a channel visible to whites only, has until 1970 forbidden television to all) the number of sets per head of population can be seen as a useful gauge in judging a nation's material prosperity. But more central to the argument is my belief that during the twenty-five years under consideration the medium radically affected our notions of reality. In most households in successful industrial countries, the television set has become an additional member of the family circle, replacing not only the Bible and the piano of the nineteenth century, but elbowing the prewar 'wireless' set into a subsidiary position.

As to the speed with which the box has conquered, according to UNESCO's figures, in the year 1953 there were 31·4 million receiving sets in the world, that is 12 sets for 1,000 people. By 1967 there were 214 million sets, that is 63 sets for 1,000.

Predictably, the sets were unevenly distributed. Even in 1953 the USA and Canada could show 122 sets per 1,000 as against Europe's 8 and the USSR's 1. By 1967 North America had reached 285 sets per 1,000, a sizeable increase certainly but nothing compared with Europe's jump to 159 sets, while even the USSR had moved from 1 set per 1,000 to 96 sets. Superficially more surprising, until we remember that it includes Japan, a highly successful industrial country, Asia had progressed from 0 sets per 1,000 to 12. Africa, on the other hand, although starting even, had reached only 2·3 sets per 1,000 by the end of the same period.

No surprises then; in successful industrial societies, the number of sets per head increases faster than in poor or emergent societies; in capitalist societies faster than communist societies; those countries directly affected by the war took longer to get under way than those unoccupied or never bombed. It must be obvious, too, that eventually a saturation point will be reached, affected only by slumps, booms, the replacement of outworn sets, or technical innovations such as larger screens or the introduction of colour.

Before leaving the multiplication and distribution of television sets during the last twenty-five years in order to consider what to me seems the more important, if parallel, theme of the change in what they actually transmit, it is relevant to indicate the shift in the social and economic class of their owners; for in the Western bloc at any rate the emphasis has moved significantly, while in the Eastern bloc too the increase in the number of sets in the USSR indicates that ownership is no longer confined to the higher echelons of the party bureaucracy but is spreading downwards and outwards: a process I imagine to be limited only by economic factors since, given the medium's effectiveness as an instrument of propaganda, there is no ideological reason why it should not become as widespread in the communist world as in the West, although naturally its message would be different.

125

Right Dracula revamped for the cinema kept his hundred-year hold on the public

A timid and early starter in 'permissive' themes: *Tea and Sympathy*, with Deborah Kerr

The decline of the cinema and rise of television 1955-68

| | 1955 | | 1968 |

	cinema attendance in millions		television sets in use in thousands	
USA	2400	1301	36180	82200
UK	1182	237	4624	15419
USSR	2506	4715	1170	26800
France	421	216	225	9252
West Germany	767	192	200	14958
Italy	775	567	130	8099

As to the West, we have access to precise information as to the social broadening of television ownership, and here perhaps Britain, still the most rigidly structured country in the class sense, offers the most clear-cut example. According to W. A. Belson (*The Impact of Television*, 1967) in 1947 forty-eight per cent of the admittedly small number of sets in the British Isles were owned by the top twelve per cent of the population in economic terms, while only twenty-five per cent were owned by that sixty-eight per cent of the population usually described as working class. By 1955, however, only fourteen per cent of the sets were owned by the top income group, while sixty-two per cent were owned by the working class.

Superficially, all this seems to prove is that there were more sets, that they had become cheaper, and that therefore a higher proportion were owned by the less wealthy; but there are other factors to show that, while this entered into it, the medium itself was changing in such a way as to direct its main appeal at a mass audience. To quote J. G. Blumer and J. Madge (*Citizenship and Television*, PEP report, 1967) by 1966 the average number of evening hours of television watched per week by the upper-middle classes in Britain was 10·1, the lower-middle classes watched 12·0, while the working classes watched 13·9 hours.

Here again, other reasons can be produced to explain this difference. The lower- middle and working classes, having less money, are naturally attracted to a form of entertainment which, after a fairly heavy initial outlay, is extremely cheap. Then, too, the upper-middle classes have traditionally other resources: visits to the theatre, the holding of dinner-parties, eating out, etc. which, for social and economic reasons, are not part of the less prosperous classes' pattern. Yet despite, or indeed because of this, it is obvious that those who put out television programmes, knowing that the greater part of their audience are working class, will slant what they offer to their presumed tastes and needs. On the whole, and given certain exceptions (mostly of local significance), television in Britain, as well as in the United States and the rest of the Western world, has now become effectively a mass pleasure.

To prove that is a simple matter of quoting statistics, but now I must face the more complex subject of what appears on those screens once they're switched on. In any essay of this length it is impossible to cover the development of television in every country in the world over a quarter of a century, so I propose to define the three major systems of television and then choose three countries, most typical of each system, to examine more closely. In a recent broadcast Professor Hoggart summed up these systems as 'the authoritarian', 'the commercial' and 'the piebald'.

126

Two hit films of the sixties: Sam Peckinpah's *The Wild Bunch* (*top*), a bloody and stylishly directed western; (*below*) Julie Andrews in *The Sound of Music*, a schmalzy musical and the biggest grosser of all time
Bottom The Battle of Borodino from the Russian production of *War and Peace*

The authoritarian system, of which I suppose Russia to be most typical, is the easiest to assess because it has changed so little, except technically, since it began. Television in Russia has a simple function. To quote Gayle Durham Hollander ('Developments in Soviet Radio and Television News Reporting' *Public Opinion Quarterly*, 31, 1967): 'All mass media are still viewed as means of socializing the Soviet Citizen, they are instruments of indoctrination in communist values and ideology as interpreted by the Party leadership at any given time.'

There is in fact very little to say about authoritarian television. Such culture and light entertainment as it offers tends to be traditional, wholesome and rather stodgy. Experimental modernism, the Western obsession with loss of personal identity, or even mild satire are obviously taboo. The ambivalence is perhaps best described in the wistful words of Peter Sellers' communist shop steward in the film *I'm All Right Jack* – 'Fields of corn and ballet in the evening.'

The commercial system on the other hand has altered considerably over the period, and certainly for the worse. Here the United States provide the leading example. In the US a programme is sold direct to a sponsor who, in exchange for advertising their product, puts up the money. It follows, therefore, that the pilot programmes are tailor-made to appeal to the tastes and prejudices of the heads of corporations, not usually the most adventurous of men, and that if subsequently any programme shows signs of developing in such a way as to offend their sensibilities, its sponsorship is withdrawn and, cut off from its financial backing, the programme collapses.

The natural effect is to ensure that nothing controversial, disturbing, critical of the *status quo*, stands much chance on television in the United States except on the few educative channels. People buy when they feel secure, when they believe themselves to live in the best of all possible worlds. Basically, American television offers an image of the American family both homely and acquisitive, undisturbed by doubts, the moving equivalent of those *Saturday Evening Post* covers which performed the same reassuring function between and after the wars.

The problem is complicated by the fact that American society consists of so many groups, racial, ethnic, religious and regional, all with their own sensitive areas and prejudices. It follows that, as all these, except for dropouts and the very poor, represent potential buyers and that none must be offended, tensions, differences, strong opinions – in effect, all reference to life as it is lived, outside news coverage – must be either suppressed or shown only in the most superficial and easily resolved way. Furthermore, since a

large area of America is extremely puritanical in the sexual field, a positively mid-Victorian propriety rules which yet again, in a society which in many areas is putting traditional moral standards to an even somewhat excessive test, helps to distance 'television land' from any reality.

Sometimes, of course, there is what superficially might appear to represent an advance. An obvious example is the treatment of negroes on the small screen. Yet here too a little thought will show that the reason 'Amos 'n Andy' have shuffled off-screen to be replaced by coloured doctors, cops and young coffee-coloured middle-class mums is because the negro population is advancing on two fronts, economically and politically. In relation to the first, they represent increasingly a buyers' market and are therefore to be flattered rather than laughed at. As to the second, it is in the interest of capitalism to make as many as possible feel that they have a stake in society; the absolutely mathematical distribution precision with which one coloured actor per so many whites is introduced into so many programmes is as insulting as, if slightly more subtle than, the lazy, head-scratching, eye-rolling negro stereotypes of yesteryear.

The depressing thing about conveyor-belt television is that it soon alienates anyone with ideas or talent, and that from a medium which has demonstrated its potential as creatively valid. In the early days of American television, before they'd 'ironed out the wrinkles', there was room for the creative artist, particularly in the field of the one-shot play. Almost all pessimistic discussions on the subject pay lip service to Paddy Chayensky's

Children on holiday at Disneyland near Los Angeles

Caribbean sun worshippers; medical warnings of faster ageing skin and increased risk of skin cancer were mainly ignored, as winter suntans joined other status symbols

Mallorca souvenir shop; package tours brought the sun within the reach and pocket of most people in Britain and the US, and a man who set out modestly to provide decent holidays might find himself with a business gold-mine on his hands

Monaco harbour, a traditional playground of the rich which lived on as a popular holiday spot

Tourism in Europe 1968

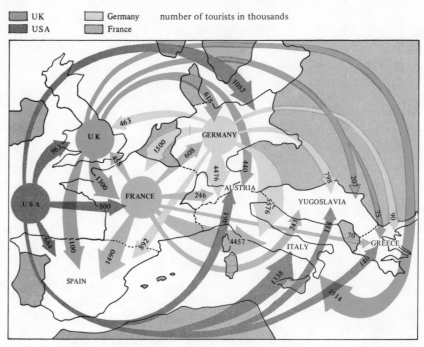

Marty, but with good reason. Now there are virtually no single plays: they don't hook viewers like serials, they don't create a captive audience to be bombarded weekly by the sponsors' product. Serials are written by committees, obeying the dictates of computers and experts in market research.

Yet, in that American television began as the handmaiden of advertising, its progress, however saddening, was more or less predictable. More complex, in a way more illustrative of the way in which mass pleasures are open to exploitation against the true interests of those they cater for, has been the history of television under what Richard Hoggart calls 'the piebald system'. Here, in that it now accommodates both the commercial system (although in a modified version compared with the United States) and the non-commercial system, Great Britain is an obvious choice to examine.

When British television reopened in 1946 it was still part of the British Broadcasting Corporation, and considered as little more than a novelty. By the end of the forties however, television, while still ignored by intellectuals, was becoming a mass obsession and in consequence of great interest to those who saw it as a potential advertising medium. In 1954, through pressure and a certain amount of luck, they had their way, and an alternative commercial channel was introduced. Furthermore, the masses took for granted that this was their channel. In most working-class and lower-middle-class households the switch was never changed.

For a time this had no effect on the quality of BBC television. On the contrary the hiving-off of the less intelligent viewers made it feel free to raise its sights. Throughout the second half of the fifties and most of the sixties British non-commercial television was the most exciting in the world. Furthermore, the BBC began to win back the more intelligent members of the mass audience in increasing numbers and there was hope, for a time, that a genuine popular medium of true value might evolve if only the balance held.

It was not held. Various mishaps and accidents – the overspending on colour installation, a prime minister's belief that the BBC was politically biased, his appointment of a powerful but cautious chairman, the government's refusal to raise licence fees to meet rising costs – forced the BBC into direct competition with its commercial rival. There are still admirable programmes, but the general feel is that pressure is being brought to bear to lower standards and that viewing figures are becoming the main criterion.

What is impossible to decide is whether the series of coincidences and collision of personalities are responsible for this state of affairs or if, on the contrary, they are no more than outward signs of the impossibility of

East End pub, London in the fifties. By the 1960s, no
longer a male preserve, nor a refuge from TV

Germans in expansive mood at the Hofbrauhaus in Munich

developing a disinterested medium in a society geared for profit and where, furthermore, politicians tend to think of television as invented for their own especial benefit.

Before leaving television for the other mass pleasures, most of which it has promoted or transformed, there are a few general points to make in relation to the medium *per se*, among which its omnipresence seems to me the most important.

In the beginning it was confined to a few hours a day, a special treat. Increasingly over the last decade it has extended itself (in America it runs almost round the clock) and in many households there is a feeling that if it's not on something is missing. This tends to reduce communication between members of a family so conditioned to a minimum, yet at the same time attention to what is on the box is only spasmodic. A kind of half-cocked reality seeps into the living-room in which reality and fantasy, corpses and washing-up powder, ballroom-dancers and assassinations are jumbled together as in a dream.

To go to a working-class pub these days is no escape. There too the telly is on, usually high up, and by 1970, often in colour. The effect is not unlike that produced on me by the pervasive presence of the Cross in Catholic countries. A humble crucifix at home (the black and white screen in the corner of the living-room) while in the local church (pub) is a larger, more elaborate version of the same holy image (a big colour set). Even *en route* the pale glow through most of the living-room windows show that the families are at worship, while in the electrical shop in the high street row upon row of sets at various sizes and prices repeat the same holy images, performing silently for the benefit of passers-by.

However good or bad the programmes, the pervasiveness of the medium is surely helping to destroy the sense of reality for many people, becoming indeed more real *than* reality. A few years ago I appeared for several weeks on the same programme, a 'talking-head' or discussion show, and noticed that in a local pub, where I had gone in for a drink most days for almost a year, I became an object of near-reverence. Then, when I no longer appeared, my aura began to fade again. Slowly I found that I was becoming anonymous.

130

Betting shops for horse-racing proved a booming business
in the England of the sixties
Right 'Night after night watching the wheel go round . . .
      Hey Las Vegas! The devil gave us to you
      One of these days
      I'm gonna burn you down' (1970 pop song)

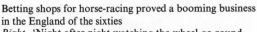

A Japanese *Pachinko* parlour: household goods for prizes

Radio

The ubiquity of television has affected other mass pleasures, and none more
than radio. Here too Great Britain provides the most useful model for yet
again its radio is following America's lead and a form of slow but apparently inevitable emasculation is taking place in the name of streamlining
and 'demand'.

Even before the war British radio offered a great deal of material on
several channels but as, unlike television, it involved only one of the senses,
the ear, it was less absorbing and at the same time, by forcing the inner eye
to match image to words, less conducive to passivity. Plays and comedy
shows were listened to consciously and in those days it was the principle on
each channel to broadcast a variety of programmes, not only playing the
changes in speech and music, but of varying lengths and requiring a change
of response. The growth of television as the principal home pleasure
gradually changed this. The old wireless set with its fretwork front and look
of solid authority was replaced by the transistor, a means to carry noise
about with you: an extension of the growing need to distort reality.

What was disappearing was the possibility of choice in pursuit of pleasure. At the beginning of the period most available mass pleasures required
some effort. To go to the pictures, the music-hall, a race meeting or the
greyhound track all involved getting from point A to point B. To play a 78
rpm gramophone record meant, in many cases, winding up the machine,
changing the needle and, as only three and a half minutes of music was
involved, listening consciously. Even the wireless, in that the programmes
were not all of a piece, meant that anything that really bored the listener
tended to drive him to switch off. But because the visual image is always
more seductive and difficult programmes are increasingly confined to the
late hours, television is harder to turn off, and against this competition
radio has tended to reduce its thoughtful output in order to offer an
extended, almost abstract pattern.

Well after the war and even during the ascendancy of television, the radio
in Britain continued to provide considerable choice. Admittedly the immediate postwar creation of three channels aimed at different audiences

could be criticized as confirming a compartmentalized culture, but for the next twenty years there was plenty of variety in both length and content. Then, in 1967, the whole pattern was changed. A wavelength devoted entirely to pop music was introduced (basing itself ironically enough on the recently suppressed pirate radio stations), and the other three channels were streamed to provide light music, news and current affairs, and serious music respectively. What remained of the Third Programme, Britain's unique contribution to the idea of radio as an educative force, was reduced to the role of bridging the interval gaps between the acts of an opera. The music programme itself, admirable in its choice of classical and modern music, provided by its very continuity an invitation not to listen, but to let the music wash over the mind at an unconscious level.

The old form of British radio may have implied educational disparity but it was based throughout on variety in both treatment and length. The new provides aural wallpaper in four patterns. It is there to colour reality, to fill in the long waits in traffic jams. As in the case of television there are still good programmes, but the tendency, as a notorious document 'Broadcasting in the Seventies' explained, is to treat radio 'less as a medium for family entertainment, more as a continuous supplier of music and information'.

Cinema

Whereas radio has remained a mass pleasure by becoming mobile, while at the same time conceding pride of place to television, the cinema, greatest of all mass pleasures between the wars, has been unable to retain its parity. During the fifties and sixties it staggered on from crisis to crisis. By 1970 the industry had no idea what to do to survive.

On a simple level this can be explained away on the grounds that once you have a television set there's no longer any need to 'go to the pictures' because the pictures come to you. This is true in part, but it is not enough to account for everything. For a start there is a great difference between the two medias; enough of a difference, one would have imagined, to make a visit to the cinema worth pursuing. The cinema screen is enormous, the television screen is small. Film can show events like the retreat from Moscow convincingly. On television a cocktail party has to be carefully directed if it's not to look confusing. More important still, the act of watching a film is very different. You sit among a mass of strangers in the dark instead of in the company of your own family in your own living-room, and it is perhaps here that the clue may be.

The dominant tendency of the last twenty-five years, in the West at any rate, has been away from communal experience. Economic progress and the continuous pressure towards individual consumption have led towards 'the nuclear family': father, mother and two children in a small house or flat and away from the extended family and life drawn from a localized area with its own flavour. Television fits into this pattern, cinema does not.

It is also relevant that what audience there is for cinema has become much younger. On a psychological level this is not difficult to explain. Adolescence is the time when the desire to break with the family is strongest and the need for tribal activity at its most intense. Nevertheless, the attempts by the industry to cash in on this specialized market is fraught with difficulties in that the product must reflect the aspirations and convictions of a generation which is constant only in its inconstancy.

The film industry was geared, until television drew off its solid once-a-week family audience, to supplying a steady demand. If a genre was successful it was imitated: gangster film begat gangster film, musical begat musical. During the sixties this began to fail, yet the middle-aged moguls, many of them absurdly dressed in the fashions of the young, still did their best to apply the same rules. They waited until some maverick film hit the jackpot and then rushed in to turn out carbon copies. They couldn't succeed because they seemed blind to the fact that the original artefact caught on because its creators were ahead of their time and so had this film ready at exactly the right psychological moment, whereas they, by the very time it takes to make a film, were certain to be out of date.

Football, one of the sports helped by TV to grow in popularity: Newcastle fans invade the pitch after a winning goal

Pelé, the Brazilian inside forward, manages to get the ball away before the tackle

Brazil – World Cup champions in 1970 for the third time; Pelé holds up the Jules Rimet trophy, which the Brazilians had won outright

132

During the fifties and sixties sportsmen became professional heroes; ruthless training methods, world travel and commercial exploitation took over from gentlemanly competition: the American golfer Jack Nicklaus

The other main weapon in the cinema's depleted armoury is sex. Within the last five years it has become possible to show in a public cinema sexual activities which, at the beginning of our period, would have provoked prosecution if raided during a private screening to half a dozen timber merchants. Typically this new problem sprang originally from the struggle of serious film-makers to assert their right to show sex where it was important in relation to their subject-matter. As a result, during the later fifties and early sixties, the public queued to see several extremely good films but, equally predictably, there were others who soon realized there was no need for the films to be good. In America in particular, where television is almost absurdly puritanical, the sex film is becoming omnipresent. It is, however, eventually self-defeating because, in all but the most specialized voyeuristic terms, it must eventually become commonplace. As a spectator sport pornography needs the added aphrodisiacs of illegality and secrecy. Without them it must eventually fail to draw the crowds and especially as the young – tomorrow's audience, if there is to be one – are already unimpressed by pornography except as a weapon with which they can tease authority and their elders.

Nevertheless, in the meantime a large proportion of the audience for non-specifically sexual films has been lost, which means less non-specifically sexual films can be made and, final irony, those serious film-makers who fought for greater freedom are now pressured to include sexual episodes in films where they are totally irrelevant.

Yet, while cinema faces ruin, it is still employing a great deal of genuine talent, much of it weaned from television. This is because it offers so much wider a canvas and, still, more material rewards. As a result the last twenty-five years has drawn much of its style from this dying lion although, in most cases, at one remove. Television is the principal hyena here. Greedy and always hungry, it rushes in ever more boldly to steal from between the cinema's toothless jaws. To take one example, the frozen shot, now a cliché not only of TV features but of commercial advertising films as well, appeared originally, as far as I can check, as the end shot of Truffaut's *400 Blows* (*Quatre Cent Coups*), a New Wave French film. It is in fact through the medium of television that many *avant-garde* ideas, at one time inaccessible to a mass audience, rapidly filter through to become stylistic clichés. Visually there has never been a world so sophisticated in its ability to 'read' new styles. Unfortunately, this ability is related to a comparative lack of informative content.

Below Cassius Clay (Muhammad Ali), the black champion with lightning reflexes
Right Opening of the 1968 Mexican Olympics

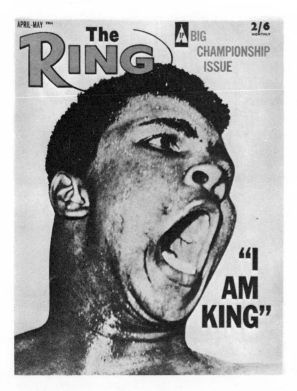

Top Elvis Presley, rock hero of the fifties, in an African setting
Above Jiving, the dance style of the young in the forties and fifties, at a Paris rock festival

Woodstock: one of the mass pop festivals of the late sixties; the passwords were peace and love

To show this process here in any detail is impossible but there is a case available which demonstrates my thesis – the James Bond myth. Ian Fleming's James Bond novels, written during the fifties and early sixties, were basically an upper-middle-class fantasy, updated to make room for our sexually permissive attitudes, given verisimilitude by a great deal of technical information, but otherwise not far removed from 'Sapper' and the other creators of 'club-room' heroes.

When it came to turn the novels into films a subtle change took place. Bond was socially down-graded, his world was simplified to become a comic-strip version of the original – the 'one mighty bound' imagery made credible through brilliant filming and editing. The Bond films imposed a life-style, luxurious yet dangerous, which has filtered through the rest of the media to alter almost every existing mass pleasure. The motels, steak-houses, hire-purchase, chain tailors, Mediterranean package tours, all owe their flavour to Bond and his imitators. Television commercials too, if the products are sophisticated, are his descendants.

The Bond cycle and its derivatives were the last consistent block-busters. The cinema still has influence (all over the Western world the 'Easy Riders' zoom through the city streets), but in numerical and commercial terms it hardly qualifies as a mass pleasure except in underdeveloped countries, whereas in 1945 it stood at the top of the list. In Britain for example, according to JICNARS (Joint Industry Committee for National Readership Survey) between February and June 1968 only five per cent of the population went to the cinema regularly while forty-six per cent never went at all, and there is no reason to believe that this trend has been reversed or even held since then. The odd film still hits the jackpot. For the industry, however, making films is no longer a question of supply and demand but a form of gambling and with no fixed odds. How is it possible to explain, let alone predict, why a musical like *The Sound of Music* plays to full houses year after year, when others, which have apparently been equally tailored for the same market, flop disastrously?

The tragedy of the cinema in the West is that it has become in the main an élitist or at any rate specialized pleasure. Of course, even at the beginning of our period, when it was a real mass pleasure, a great deal of its output was nonsense, but the existence of a regular audience made it possible for some film-makers to experiment without committing economic suicide. Today the cost of producing even a comparatively modest feature film implies a mass audience and, except for the occasional arbitrary success, there just isn't one.

In the Eastern bloc, at any rate in Russia and the more rigid satellites, the situation has been different if hardly more encouraging. Because of the comparative rarity of television the cinema has remained a mass pleasure but, during the period under review, the larger proportion of the output has been pretty stolid. The cinema, Lenin's baby, has remained at the service of the state, capable of producing a few magnificent if rather ponderous epics like the version of *War and Peace*, or an unexpected masterpiece like the film version of Chekov's *Lady with a Dog*, but in the main the revolutionary excitement of the early cinema has evaporated and, as television spreads, so, I believe, the cinema will follow the West into decline.

In the more flexible satellites like Hungary, Czechoslovakia or Poland, it's been a different story. There the *avant-garde*, taking advantage of the least thaw, have produced several remarkable movies, but it is unlikely that many of them reach a mass audience in their countries of origin. When they're shown in the West it's in art houses and to intellectuals.

Travel

I mentioned earlier that, among many other mass pleasures, foreign travel owes much of its rapid growth to the Bond syndrome. Naturally it's not the whole story. More and cheaper air travel, blockbookings and more widespread affluence have made it feasible; but even so it was necessary to find a way to break down the resistance of the masses to untried experience and here the Bond syndrome has provided the key.

One of the last recording sessions with all four Beatles together, *Let it Be*; also in view – Yoko Ono and Paul McCartney's stepdaughter, Heather. By 1970, in Paul's words: 'The party's over but no one wants to admit it'

Sleeve for one of the Beatles' many successes

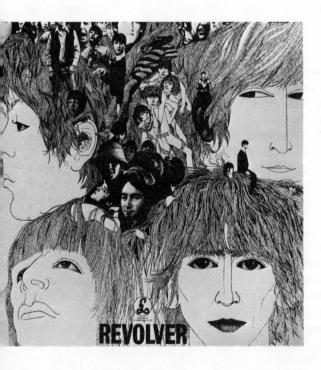

The old conservatism was based on fear of social gaucherie; the cover-story was that those who subscribed to it were 'ordinary folk'. This has been overcome by making sure that there would be nothing unexpected to face. The menus would be large in size but translated into several languages and full of phrases like 'may we suggest', the price all-in including service. Yet – except where mismanagement or inexperience leads to failure – the vacation holds out the same promise of luxury in the Bond-Martini ad mould.

The large standardized hotels springing up along the coasts of Europe are the result of this revolution. The life of the country outside is a picturesque bonus, to be visited but in no way infiltrated. At its most crude, and I quote a recent travel ad, what mass tourism offers apart from standardized luxury is 'sun, sea and sand'. It's easy to sneer at the lack of curiosity, the prevalence of chips with everything, the purchase of trashy souvenirs. The rich retreat from their traditional playgrounds to those further away and deliberately priced out of mass range. The intellectuals nose out 'the unspoilt little bistro' where there's still plenty of garlic in the salad dressing. Sentimentalists of the old popular culture deplore the disappearance of the traditional working-class holiday. Yet, basically what most pre-package-tour holiday-makers were after was 'sun, sea and sand'. What they regret is the disappearance of exclusivity, of cachet. Most people have boring monotonous jobs. To grudge them the excitement of going abroad is mean-minded and at the same time useless, yet, if they do go abroad, standardized architecture and an acceptable mass cuisine are now inevitable.

As to who make up the bulk of the new tourists, they are mostly between twenty-five and forty and in the middle income bracket. At one time this would have excluded them as representatives of the masses, but no longer. In prosperous countries workers frequently earn more than those in white-collar jobs or even in the professions.

Over the last fifteen years international tourism has been expanding at the rate of about twelve per cent a year. True, it is from the more prosperous countries that most of the tourists are drawn. According to Michael Peters (*International Tourism*, Hutchinson, 1969) eighty per cent of tourist expenditure was drawn from twelve countries: USA, West Germany, UK, France, Canada, Belgium, Netherlands, Italy, Switzerland, Sweden,

Denmark and Austria. In recent years the growing number of Japanese tourists especially in the United States, is indicative not only of their identification with Western civilization but also of their expanding economy.

As yet a high proportion of tourism is between these countries but, more significant in my view, is the rapid development of amenities in those poorer countries which can guarantee sun. The North African coast, Spain and Portugal are typical while, for many Americans, the Caribbean offers the same facilities.

We must, as I've already suggested, guard against confusing the decay of privilege with fake moral criticism of the expanding field of mass pleasures. Nevertheless, it's hypocritical not to recognize that the imposition of an international standard of affluent fantasy may be instrumental in destroying the savour of indigenous cultural life.

As Michael Peters points out, tourism is only a part of 'the leisure industries'. It reflects the trend towards an amalgam into which cars, clothes, television programmes, places of entertainment, even sexual ideals are melted down to form a world-wide, interchangeable currency of pleasure. To take a concrete example, the British 'pub', that predominantly nineteenth-century temple of engraved glass, carved mahogany and warm beer, is being systematically gutted and transformed into a luxury cocktail lounge complete with canned music. There are gains in hygiene, more food available, rooms set aside for children and so on, but the price is the sacrifice of a localized institution with its roots in local social history.

At the same time the new universality recognizes in the masses some vestiges of hunger for the past; a hunger it satisfies by an illusory solution. The device is to give mass-produced chemically balanced cakes and bread names suggestive of home-baking, to decorate hotel lobbies in a pantomime version of the country's native architecture, to display copies of eighteenth-century prints in modern bars, to describe food on the menus of restaurant chains as 'farmhouse fresh' or 'prepared from the traditional recipe subtly adjusted to the modern palate'. Presumably this Disneyland-like nod in the direction of the past will continue but on any real level there is little doubt that, with the spread of affluence in the West, local differences will disappear; a state already foreshadowed by the interchangeable airports of our cities – those cathedrals of our time.

Sport

Sport, the remaining major mass pleasure to be examined, seems at first sight less affected by the general drift towards universality. For one thing, some sports are confined to a single country or group of countries. For another, sport is played across ideological boundaries much more generally than other mass pleasures. Conversely, the meaning of sport differs from place to place. For Brazil for example, a relatively poor country under an authoritarian government, success at football is seen as a proof of virility and acts at the same time as a safety-valve for frustration; a fact fully appreciated by the authorities. For Britain on the other hand, to regain its international supremacy in this sport is more a question of damaged pride, dating back to the early fifties when the country which had taught the game to the world was almost consistently beaten on its home ground by the professionalism of foreign teams.

In this sentence lies the crux of the matter. Over the twenty-five years under review spectator sport has become predominantly professional. For a few years after the war there was still room for the individual of genius, for inspired amateurism. The sportsmen are paid high wages, drive big cars, marry fashion models. The old close identification between spectator and player is broken and yet the player is still a symbol of the possibilities open to a number of the masses given the requisite talent. A symbol, but a frustrating one. Worship can turn to hate in the course of a single game. The increase of violence both among players and spectators is a proof that some kind of unresolved tension has arisen. In my view it's based on a sense of loss.

It's significant how much, in the West at any rate, the image of the

Hell's Angels, ton-ups, rockers and easy riders: the motor bike became stock-in-trade for young aggression and rebellion

James Dean, star of *Rebel Without A Cause* and *East of Eden*: inarticulate, hesitant, highly emotional, he attracted massive identification from his fans. He was killed in a car crash in 1955 at the age of twenty-four

athlete has changed. He approximates much more closely to the pop star; an observation reinforced by the fact that one of the more prominent of the younger Spanish bull-fighters was nicknamed 'El Beatle' and one of the most brilliant British footballers, Georgie Best, became a pin-up, less on the walls of teenage boys (as was the case with Best's pale nobbly forerunners), than of their sisters.

Of course local loyalty still exists but it is conferred mainly upon those teams or athletes that aspire to national or international supremacy. The old spirit of grumbling semi-humorous loyalty towards the home team whatever its failings is dying away. Television can bring world-class sport of every kind into every home. It is perhaps significant that the sportsman who has gained most as a charismatic symbol since the war should be the international racing-motorist; his life a mixture of jet-travel, great hotels, expensive technological equipment and enormous risk.

Yet it would be a mistake not to stress yet again that this 'pop' view of sport is confined, like pop culture in general, to the West, and the same applies to such side-issues as the open commercial exploitation of the great international events. On the other hand the central meaning of such manifestations as the World Cup or the Olympic Games is common to both ideologies. Sport is a useful way of fanning nationalist or idealist fervour at comparatively little cost. The East may stress the puritanical approach, the West the razzle-dazzle, but both use sport as a way of boosting national or ideological morale.

A final trend that has developed during our period is the decline of sports confined to one or comparatively few countries in favour of those with the widest international appeal. Cricket for example, a game more or less confined to Britain and its former colonies and dependents, is losing its grip. On the other hand golf and tennis tournaments (both incidentally eminently televisual) have become more and more prominent.

Very broadly the history of mass pleasures over the last twenty-five years may be summed up like this:
In the Eastern bloc: very little change except for the slow spread of television; all the media are tested with ideological Geiger-counters, a practice inducing conservation and conformism in both content and means of expression.
In the West: the change has been rapid and far-reaching; the emergence of America as a superpower and provider of goodies has undermined the already shaky indigenous cultures of Europe and built up in their place a series of identical pleasure-markets 'as advertised on TV'.

Mass pleasures are becoming more and more a cut-price version of the old élitist pleasures but at the expense of the old élitist advantages both practical and prestigious: huge night-clubs (the essence of the night-club was its intimacy) where those with tables at the back see the star as a tiny heavily amplified figure; cars for almost everybody, which in the end means

A twenty-five-year-old drug addict injects a shot of heroin in Piccadilly Circus, London

Below Mealtime in a commune: for some, the solution to modern society was rejection of its values
Right Hair: the revolutionary love-rock musical that swept the world in 1970

By 1970 sexual censorship of people, plays, films or novels seemed a thing of the past in Britain and the US

Below Striptease; but many of the young were becoming indifferent to voyeurism and pornography
Bottom Scene from a Japanese play, *Vultures*

taking much longer to get anywhere; broiler pornography on every book-stall – Walter Mitty as De Sade; the spoliation of areas considered to be beautiful by the building of thousands of ill-planned houses or bungalows for the benefit of those who want to live somewhere beautiful, etc.

This last paragraph reads like a typical romantic conservative complaint, but my reasons for writing it are different. Not only would it be impossible to return to the romantic conservative ideal – the great eighteenth-century house and the pretty village of damp dark little cottages at the gates – but even if it were, it would be against my whole thesis. Pleasure is the right of everybody, and it looks as though, with the move towards computerized industry and the use of atomic power, there will be more and more time to pursue it. The real worry is not that there may be too much pleasure, but that the machinery for providing it is in the hands of those who think solely of profit and whose aim is to impose *as pleasure* what is in reality most convenient and profitable to them. It could be said that this has always been the case but the trouble now is that the pleasure-sellers have much more powerful weapons of persuasion. The whole mass media for example is falling into their hands; and through these media they are able to offer a constant glamorized ideal image of a persuasive gloss and covering both reality and fantasy.

Pop culture

There is, however, as I suggested at the beginning, growing opposition and now, at the end, it's time to consider this underground. Until recently, opposition to the corruption of mass taste, the imposition of standards and limits to mass pleasure, was for the most part the self-imposed task of the middle classes. In liberal-minded times, or in the case of those middle-class reformers whose sympathies were on the left, this usually took an educative rather than a repressive form. In more rigid periods, or when the reformer was of an authoritative cast of mind, they resorted to the law as a means of curbing or preventing excess.

In the realm of mass pleasure neither school has ever achieved much success (in practical reforms both have won many necessary battles). The authoritarians may have closed brothels, banned off-the-course betting, limited or prohibited the drinking of alcohol, and prosecuted the vendors of vulgar or erotic imagery, but prostitution, betting, boozing and laughing or leering at sex continued in other, possibly illegal forms. The educational reformists may have persuaded the middle classes to aim at simplicity in the decoration of their sitting-rooms or object to white entertainers blacking-up to caricature negro mannerisms, but the furniture-shops in working-class areas have remained as garish and tasteless as before and racialist humour as prevalent in private if not in public.

This failure has been based on a different standard of mores. The middle-class life in warm comfortable houses, surrounded by books and objects, was and is in itself mildly if continuously pleasurable. Until recently, and in many cases still, working-class life was not in itself pleasurable, and as a result active pleasure tended to seem like a form of revolt rather than extension of cultural interests into the public field.

After the Second World War in the Western bloc, this began to change. A higher proportion of people moved, if not into the middle classes in the old sense, at least into a comparable material sphere and this has led, as we've seen, to a more passive attitude towards pleasure. In place of the orgiastic release implied in earlier forms of entertainment, that lack of thrift or caution in their pursuit about which Richard Hoggart is so perceptively sympathetic, a more cautious and controlled use of 'leisure' is taking over. The emphasis is on possession or demonstrable expenditure. The drift is away from regional or national differences and towards an inter-changeable mass culture of a bland, rather flavourless consistency.

There are still areas open to the activities of the reformists both educative and authoritarian. The former are hamstrung, however, by the incompre-hension of those who, given what they want, are told that they don't really want it, or at any rate wouldn't if they were given something else. The latter

Top The world's first sex and pornography trade fair in Copenhagen 1969; throughout Western Europe specialized sex shops were making their appearance in ordinary shopping areas (*above*)

Below 1970 advertisement: sex, youth, beauty, wealth, alcohol – a dream package without problems or hangover

tend to concentrate on sexuality, but their weakness is that in the main sexual permissiveness has if anything lowered the sexual climate. There's a lot more sexuality in evidence, but a lot less pressure and prurience.

At the beginning of our period both species of reformer were still in evidence with the reformists in the ascendant. The English writer, Michael Frayn, called them 'the herbivores' and Britain under the immediate post-war Labour government was perhaps their ideal pasture. They believed in 'good design' and 'fun'. They had it their own way for a time because Frayn's 'carnivores', those who feed on the masses, took a few years to get things organized, and besides there was not, in those days, enough money around to buy the goods and pleasures proper to a consumers' society, nor indeed the raw materials or machinery to manufacture them.

By the middle fifties, however, 'affluence' had become a reality. The older mass pleasures were dying or becoming modified in the ways I have suggested and it began to look as if the 'carnivores' were to have it all their own way. The challenge came, however, not from the 'herbivores' (in Britain the efforts of a young working-class playwright, Arnold Wesker, to bring 'culture and fun' to the masses met with a marked lack of success), but from a new quarter; the performers of pop music, and their allies, the pop-minded intellectuals. Throughout the last fifteen years the various phases of the pop revolution have offered the most consistent opposition to the general drift towards bland uniformity in the field of mass pleasures and yet, in terms of numbers on a world-wide scale, pop, whether considered as a life-style or a means of expression, is big enough to qualify as a mass pleasure.

What inhibits any detailed consideration of its effect here is the rapid and constant changes it has been through. In its early days, 1955-60, it tended to embrace the artefacts of civilization; to elevate its gadgetry into art on the intellectual wing, to admire it for its own sake at the more primitive end of the scale. Intense dandyism in the early sixties gave way to deliberate slovenliness, albeit highly stylized, in the following five years. Apolitical hedonism moved towards a generalized revolutionary bias, and so on.

Nevertheless, pop has always been (and remains) in opposition. Its volte-faces and contradictions are to do with evading the embrace of a society who recognize in it, and have indeed drawn from it, enormous financial rewards. This is the paradox of pop culture and, perhaps, its weakness. It lacks a set of constant standards which can be used to face mid-cult head on. Pop is always on the run. Its moments of revolt are effective in context but destroyed by time. It's also predominantly a youth culture, as exclusive in this condition as any other closed society. Most of its adherents use it to express their adolescent revolt, and then move on or indeed back into the even orderly world where happiness is a new car outside the mortaged house.

Yet there is a movement within pop culture which may, in time, help to reanimate mass pleasures and that is the way that the centre has shifted from a basically uneducated lumpenproletariat (early rock and roll) towards the ever-growing and, in the traditional sense, classless body of students (heavy rock). This may mean no more than a new élitist culture; there are indeed signs of this in a certain pretension that has crept into pop culture during the last five years. But, given the spread of higher education in the West, given the turnover in the student body (a disadvantage when considered in relation to the possibility of pop culture putting down roots; an advantage in helping pop culture to avoid becoming simply an extension of the main body of culture and thereby losing its influence on popular culture altogether), there is some hope that pop, if it can survive, may keep the debate open.

At the time of writing (autumn, 1970) pop culture with its diverse artefacts, records, happenings, underground cinema, posters, etc. is still the only opposition on a mass scale to vegetative passive mass pleasure. For all its aggression, uniformity of non-conformity, arrogance and reliance on soft drugs, it remains alive. It is nearer to the music-hall, the early cinema, the Elizabethan theatre than to the star-spectacular or the long crawl to a lay-by for a picnic meal flavoured by the exhaust-pipes of fellow motorists.

Jackson Pollock: *No. 6* (1949)

Ronald Hayman

The Arts: Reductionism and Pluralism

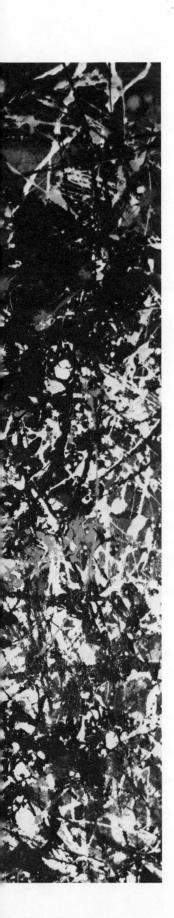

Pavese said that literature was one defence against the attacks of life and silence was the other. 'But we must choose that silence for ourselves, not have it imposed on us, not even by death. . . . Those who by their very nature can suffer completely, utterly, have an advantage. This is how we can disarm the power of suffering, make it our own creation, our own choice, submit to it. A justification for suicide.' He wrote this in a diary of 1938 and killed himself in 1950. Virginia Woolf killed herself in 1941, Sylvia Plath in 1963 and Mark Rothko in 1970. But suicide is not the only way of giving up the attempt to communicate. E. M. Forster, who did not die until 1970, published his last novel in 1924. T. S. Eliot, who lived till 1965, wrote no poetry after *Four Quartets* (1935-42), only a few very minor poems and three verse plays, each worse and less poetic than its predecessor. Marcel Duchamp turned from art to chess, but according to Ottavio Paz his inactivity has been as fruitful for the twentieth century as Picasso's incessant activity. 'Our time is one which affirms itself only by negating itself and which negates itself only to invent and transcend itself.'

Silence and Mallarmé

Even for the artists who have not chosen absolute silence, silence has become a constant possibility, a negative to use positively. Duchamp wanted modern art to return to the direction which had been indicated by Mallarmé, and to an important extent this has happened. The spaces between clusters of signs and sounds have become more important than ever before in the history of art. Pierre Boulez's Third Piano Sonata (1957) which he described as 'symmetrical and mobile distribution around a central constellation' is based on his study of Mallarmé's *Un Coup de dés*. Not only can the five movements be played in any order, but the sections in each one of them are completely interchangeable, so that all the decisions about beginning, middle and end have to be made by the performer. *Le Marteau sans maître* (1954) was written in a similar way without any sense of temporal progression and *Pli selon pli* (1960) made use of words which Mallarmé had already bled completely of meaning. Boulez has made a thorough practical exploration of Mallarmé's belief that instrumental music is necessarily incomplete, that it must tend towards song, 'that Music and Literature are each an alternative force – here tending towards the darkness, there glittering with certainty – of a phenomenon, the only one, as I have called it, the Idea'. The aleatory or chance element (Boulez's word) which has come to be so important in so much music, painting, sculpture, writing and acting in the postwar period can be traced back to Mallarmé's use of chance to keep tabs on the Absolute. As in a mobile, the component parts of *Un Coup de dés* are, in effect, constantly changing in their relationships with one another. The poem remains open-ended, refusing to be pinned down to a definitive interpretation. As Roland Barthes has put it in his work *Writing Degree Zero*:

Mallarmé's typographical agraphia seek to create around rarefied words an empty zone in which speech, liberated from its guilty social overtones, may, by some happy contrivance, no longer reverberate. The word . . . is then freed from responsibility in relation to all possible context; it appears in one brief act, which, being devoid of reflections, declares its solitude, and therefore its innocence. This art has the very structure of suicide: in it, silence is a homogeneous poetic time which traps the word between two layers and sets it off less as a fragment of a cryptogram than as a light, a void, a murder, a freedom.

141

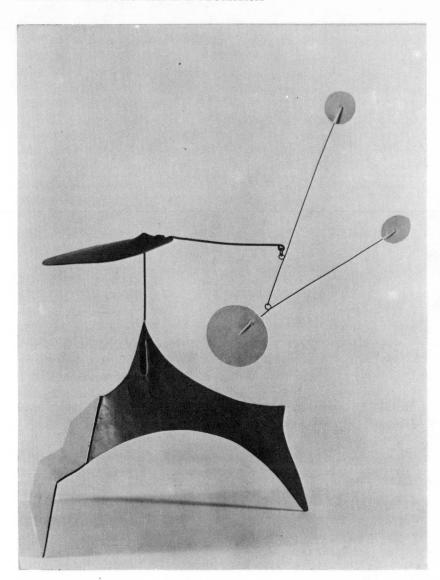

Right Alexander Calder: *Skeletal Base* (metal; 1959)

Below Billie Whitelaw, Robert Stephens and Rosemary Harris in George Devine's 1964 production of Beckett's *Play* at the National Theatre, London

Via negative

Though it does not have to end in suicide either for the artist or the art, the *via negativa* has undoubtedly been one of the main roads since the war. In André Gide's *Les Faux-Monnayeurs* (1925) the novelist-hero was hostile to naturalism but still wanted to cram everything into his novel. James Joyce, his appetite perhaps whetted by failing eyesight, compulsively crowded as much living material as he could get out of twenty-four hours of Dublin life into *Ulysses* (1922). Jorge Luis Borges's response to the stimulus of failing sight was the opposite. 'Why take 500 pages to develop an idea whose oral demonstration fits into a few minutes?' His reading, earlier, was voracious but his writing always most abstemious. His fiction consists of short stories, highly original in the way they combine directness with obliqueness in their rendering of ideas. They have mostly resembled fastidious and erudite foot-notes to the *mélange* inside his head of the literature he knows and the literature he has imagined but disdained to transcribe. They are – to combine two of his favourite images – like a labyrinth of mirrors. Their brilliant surfaces are reflections on the fact of fiction and the uncertainty of reality.

The imagination of Samuel Beckett (who was Joyce's compatriot and friend but never as is commonly believed his secretary) was also conditioned first by the fear and later by the reality of failing eyesight as he explored different styles of negation. His plays effectively widened the frontiers of theatrical feasibility by austerely rejecting ninety-five per cent of the opportunities that the medium offered. The progressive exclusion of movement and external action was a disadvantage in the later plays but an advantage in *Waiting for Godot* and *Krapp's Last Tape*, as in the novels he

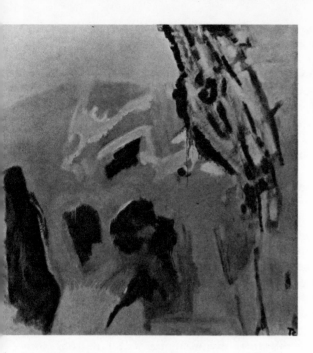

Pierre Tal Coat: *Pathway at the Bottom of the Valley* (1956)

Bram van Velde: *Painting* (1960)

wrote in the fifties, dedicated, like the paintings of Tal Coat in his 1949 description of them, to 'the expression that there is nothing to express, nothing with which to express, nothing from which to express, no power to express, no desire to express, together with the obligation to express'. Bram van Velde's paintings he saw as belonging to a new order because of their unapologetic inexpressiveness. He was 'the first whose painting is bereft, rid if you prefer, of occasion in every shape and form, ideal as well as material, and the first whose hands have not been tied by the certitude that expression is an impossible act'. Or as van Velde had formulated it himself in 1948, 'What I want to express is too strange, too violent for me to hold it in a word or a thought; it has to come out somehow and so I paint.'

The concern with releasing rather than expressing violence and the willing abandonment of conscious control over the results of the act of creation suggest an affinity with the American action painters, who were only concerned with 'reality' in so far as it entered into the process of applying paint to canvas. Working without preliminary sketches and as far as possible without preconceptions, Jackson Pollock used to stretch his canvas on the floor or the wall, latterly dispensing altogether with brushwork and using his fingers to drip the paint on, wanting to feel that he himself was part of the painting. He used sand and broken glass to thicken his impasto, attacking the surface with a stick, a trowel or a knife, and superimposing layer upon layer of paint. While he was at work, he said, he had no idea of what he was doing. 'The painting has a life of its own. I try to let it come through.'

There is an exact analogy to this in the recoil of the American Black Mountain poets against any use of the will to impose order on a poem. Charles Olson's *Projective Verse* is a manifesto for 'field composition' by which the poet 'can go by no track other than the one the poem under hand declares, for itself'. Old ideas of rhythm and metre were to be jettisoned. The spoken phrase had to become the only measure; the syllable became the unit. There could be no question of development. One perception should lead immediately to the next. Observation should not be allowed 'to sap the going energy of the content towards its form'. Robert Creeley, too, asserted that '"subject" is at best a material for the poem and that poems finally derive from some deeper complex of activity'. This approach was partly foreshadowed by the old belief in inspiration, by W.B.Yeats's interest in automatic writing, by Paul Valéry's insistence that the poet is discovering the form of his lyric instant by instant, and by Hart Crane's refusal to understand his poems until after they were written. But (except for being anticipated by Mallarmé) Olson's exploitation of the typewriter was new. With the precision of spacing it offered, he saw it as providing the poet with an equivalent of musical staves and bars. And when he sat down to work straight on to the machine, hanging his syllables on the blankness of the paper, he did not believe in revising.

Prewar art had already repudiated the function of holding a mirror up to nature, though not as decisively as postwar art. As Gottfried Benn said, the Expressionist distortions of reality were necessary because reality was a capitalist concept: 'It meant selected "slices of life", industrial products, mortgages, etc. Reality was a synonym for Darwinism, international steeplechases and all that stemmed from privilege.' Far better not to reproduce it but 'to cultivate a sort of secret intoxication'. Scientific progress, which was revealing the *perpetuum mobile* of Nature, simultaneously pointed to the impossibility of pinning it down in a landscape or a still-life. The painter's function was changing rapidly. Instead of depicting what he saw, he had to create what he could not see, invent new pictorial facts. Shakespeare had already said that the imagination could body forth 'the forms of things unknown' but Paul Klee wanted to paint as if Europe had never existed and Georges Braque said he did not believe in things, only in the relationships between them. Kasimir Malevich spoke of 'a feeling of the absence of the object' and Surrealism thrived on abstraction.

Meanwhile, Nature was disappearing from literature. The nineteenth-century novel was full of leisurely landscape painting, and for Marcel

Marcel Dalio and Mila Parély in Jean Renoir's
La Règle du Jeu (1939)

Max von Sydow and Bengt Ekerot in Ingmar Bergman's
The Seventh Seal (1956)

Proust it was essential to describe the hawthorns. D. H. Lawrence's descriptions of non-industrial scenery are integral to his criticism of industrialism and there are lengthy passages in late novels like *Kangaroo* (1923) and *The Plumed Serpent* (1926) which might have come straight out of his travel books. In the Russian novel the landscape still lives: Boris Pasternak painted it lovingly, but in the less leisurely Western novel it is almost as if the sun in Albert Camus's *L'Étranger* (1942), which helped to drive the hero into a pointless act of killing, also had the effect of drying up all the natural greenery. The vast majority of postwar novelists have made less use of natural scenery than film directors have done. Not that Jean Renoir, Bresson, Antonioni, Satyajit Ray, Bergman or Truffaut could have involved cinema audiences in natural life as deeply as Wordsworth or Hardy, but they have used it as very much more than a background for the action that happened to take place in the open air. In a film, of course, the danger of slowing down the story is incomparably smaller. A single shot can show detail it would take pages to describe and the audience is left free to register it only incidentally. More important, the contemporary reader has been conditioned by film and television to assimilate narrative information so rapidly that he cannot be expected to tolerate the interruption of action for description as a Victorian reader would.

But there is more than this to the disappearance of Nature from most forms of contemporary art. The art of any period not only reflects what people see, it teaches them what to look for, and the hostility of artists to an environment which seems to be growing increasingly artificial has had the effect, broadly speaking, of stopping them from encouraging their public to look outwards. Since Gerard Manley Hopkins, hardly any of our poets have developed a keen eye for natural scenery and what Olson had to say about the poet's relationship to Nature was that he served it best by staying

Monica Vitti and Richard Harris in Antonioni's
The Red Desert (1964)

inside himself. 'If he is contained within his own nature as he is participant in the larger force, he will be able to listen, and his hearing through himself will give him secrets objects share.' An optimism which has not been justified by the actual poetry.

For Alain Robbe-Grillet, the dismissal of Nature from the novel was essential because 'the idea of a nature inevitably leads to one which is common to all things, which means *superior*'. Phrases like 'capricious weather', 'majestic mountains', 'heart of the forest', 'village crouching in the hollow of a valley' are anthropomorphic images which imply a relationship between the universe and the people who inhabit it. 'Man looks at the world,' he insisted, 'but the world does not look back at him.' He castigated Jean-Paul Sartre for establishing 'visceral relationships' with the world in *La Nausée* (1938) and scrupulously avoided the pathetic fallacy in his own novels. Obsessively descriptive, they tallied exactly with what he wrote about the modern novel in general. Description, he said, does not begin by giving the reader an overall picture.

It seems to spring from a minute and unimportant detail, which is more like a geometrical point . . . from which it invents lines, planes, and a whole architecture, and our impression that these are being invented in the course of the description is reinforced by the fact that it suddenly contradicts itself, repeats itself, thinks better of it, branches off in a different direction, etc. . . . . The lines of the drawing . . . contradict each other until the very construction of the image renders it more and more uncertain . . . in the end it has become a twofold movement of getting created and getting stuck.

Different though they are, there is a similar ambiguity in Beckett's novels about the reality of the objects and events described, while the very precision of the formal description has the effect of adding to the uncertainty. Is something happening, or nothing, or Nothing? Compulsively soliloquizing about a painful movement through space, which corresponds with the narrator's pained progress through his soliloquy, the heroes of his fifties novels had to dig the ground from under their own feet to build a footway into the void. The landscape of mud was a mental construct and the crawling an image of cerebration. *Imagination Dead Imagine* (1965) and *Lessness* (1970) slid considerably further down the asymptote from speech into silence. Both were more like prose poems than novels, desiccated statements about desiccation, devoid of development.

If we are currently progressing towards a novel without progression, Camus's *L'Étranger* may emerge as having been a major turning-point. The lack of connection in it between Meursault's involvement in the killing and his candid indifference about emotional relationships may have looked like one of its principal weaknesses but in fact this was only a secondary result of the complete absence of causality. *Post hoc* was not allowed to imply *propter hoc*. As Sartre pointed out, Camus had deliberately suppressed all causal links between the sentences. The events themselves were normal enough but the inconsequent narrative made the sequence look absurd. It was a style which derived partly from Ernest Hemingway's flatness of statement and partly from John Dos Passos's more socially orientated newspaperish factuality. This is what Barthes has called 'the zero degree' of writing, 'a style of absence which is almost an ideal absence of style; writing is then reduced to a sort of negative mood in which the social or mythical characters of a language are abolished in favour of a neutral and inert state of form'. Hemingway claimed to have achieved 'a certain clarification of the language' and the apparent withdrawal of the writer from his material has sometimes worked advantageously. But, as George Steiner complained, the method is based on a narrow conception of the resources of literacy. 'Imagine trying to translate the consciousness of Raskolnikov into the language of *The Killers*.'

Degrees of reductionism

Of course there is more than one *via negativa* and of the various paths that lead away from the direct imitation of external reality, some are more reductive than others. Painting seems to be able to survive more easily than sculpture without even a vestige of the figurative element and the abstract

145

Naum Gabo: *Construction in Space* (bronze; 1961)

Below Antoine Pevsner: *Maquette of a Monument Symbolizing the Liberation of the Spirit* (bronze; 1952)
Bottom Joan Miró: *Man and Woman* (wrought iron, ceramic and wood; 1956-61)

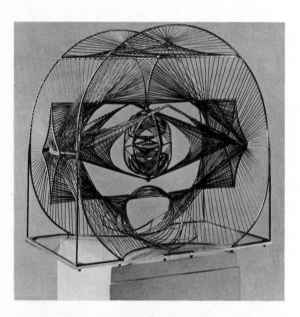

sculptors who grew up into the rarefied postwar atmosphere in which abstraction was taken very much for granted did not produce such interesting work as older sculptors like Jean Arp and Constantin Brancusi, Naum Gabo, Antoine Pevsner, Joan Miró and László Moholy-Nagy, who grew up in a more representational *ambiance*, to develop more gradually and empirically towards partially or completely discarding the figurative element. Both by practice and precept Brancusi encouraged the sculptor to be more concerned with his materials. 'It is while carving stone that you discover the spirit of your material and the properties peculiar to it. Your hand thinks and follows the thoughts of the material.' But while this attitude has an obvious affinity with that of Jackson Pollock, the dictum provides diminishing returns when applied to a material like metal on which the sculptor can impose his will far more completely. And in much postwar work there has been concern for the material, unaccompanied by any strong desire to do anything with it. When Barry Flanagan, for instance, used commonplace materials like rope, cloth and sand, it seemed more out of a wish to protest against the exclusion of these from traditional sculpture than out of a wish to *make* anything.

In painting, though there has been a good deal of extremism in postwar abstraction, it is a mistake to assume that it had gone further than in the first half of the century. Even Robert Rauschenberg's big all-black and all-white canvases of 1953, Lucio Fontana's all-white paintings of 1956 and Yves Klein's all-blue paintings of 1957 had Malevich and Rodzhenko as their precursors. In 1913 Malevich produced a black square on a white background, followed five years later by a white square containing another. The same year saw Rodzhenko's black upon black, followed by a panel covered evenly with bright purple. I suppose it could be argued that Rauschenberg was revealing a new horizon of negativity when he exhibited a blank space from which he had rubbed out a De Kooning drawing or that Klein was when he held an exhibition of bare walls. People actually paid money for imaginary paintings. But if Harold Rosenberg is right to argue (as he does in *The Tradition of the New*) that the test of a new painting's seriousness is 'the degree to which the act on the canvas is an extension of the artist's total effort to make over his experience', it would be interesting to know just what kind of an encounter with nothingness Rauschenberg and Klein were trying to make over. The Pop Art which derives from an all-out effort to avoid significant content is open to the same criticism. Not all negation helps the age to invent and transcend itself. In Duchamp's rebellion against retinal art, his assault against 'the possibility of recognizing any two things as being like each other', he produced ready-mades which were effectively non-significant except for the criticism they implied of the art that aimed at significance. But, as he said, 'anything can become very beautiful if the gesture is repeated often enough; this is why the number of my ready-mades is very limited'. An implicit warning Pop Art has ignored.

One of the factors that have made reductionism necessary has been the sheer profusion of postwar art. Never has there been such a quantity of people calling themselves artists and engaging not only in painting, writing, theatre, music and sculpture but in a whole range of related activities which have made it harder than ever before to determine the frontier between what is art and what is not. In England the New Activities Committee set up by the Arts Council to investigate the question of subsidizing new art forms found it hard to decide which experiments ought to be taken seriously as art. They were faced with a barrage of requests for money, including one from a committee which urged that a certain Mr Pennington should be subsidized to fire cap pistols at the American Embassy. Many of the varieties of social protest and experiments in life-style which they encountered did seem to deserve support but without qualifying as art.

At the same time, the audience for the arts expanded with extraordinary speed, producing new demands and new kinds of demand. According to one theory, human consciousness had been itself expanded in such a way that people needed the arts to supply them with symbolic images which would

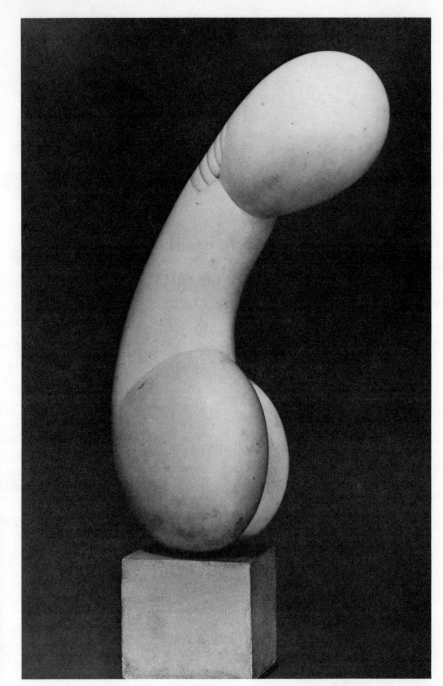

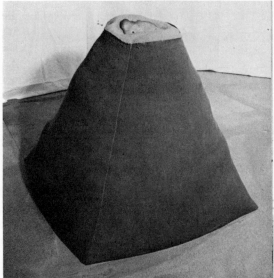

Barry Flanagan: *al casb 4'67* (1967)

Right Brancusi: *Princess X* (white marble and stone; 1916)

help them to adjust to the new electronic environment, in the same way that tribal and religious images in primitive societies helped men to feel at one with their environment. The mass media, though valuable patrons of the arts and valuable in offering instant communication with an audience of millions, have patronized only the kind of art that could be communicated instantly, and then devoured it. Of the thousands of television plays created, only a handful have had any life beyond a single transmission.

Apart from the final suicide, how did an artist like Rothko respond to an artistic climate like this? A Russian who lived in the United States from the age of ten, he was in his early forties when after the war New York was displacing Paris as the centre of international art. He was then painting landscapes suffused with fog; from the beginning of the fifties onwards he avoided all reference to specific objects and Michel Butor is probably right to see his art as 'an answer to a crowded city. . . . The dross of abundance contaminates everything. . . . We must introduce an empty space, a blank page, where the mind can find the repose necessary to its activity.' In the soft-edged rectangles of beautifully uneven colour there is no space for any sign of dissension, external or internal. Silently, eloquently, tastefully, they adumbrate the painter's absence.

147

Right Mark Rothko: *Red-Brown, Black, Green, Red* (1962)

Below Josef Albers: *Departing in Yellow* (1964)

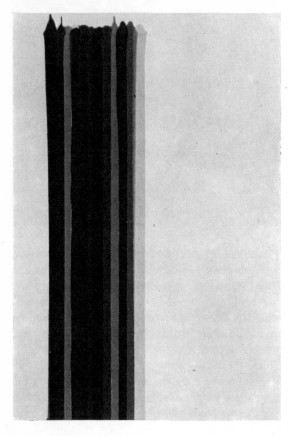

Morris Louis: *None* (1961)

Though Rothko had his imitators, none of whom could rival his finesse, his soft-edged style had less influence on the period than the old hard-edged abstractionism which led straight into Post-Painterly Abstraction. Josef Albers, who settled in America when the Bauhaus closed in 1933, first of all teaching at Black Mountain College, worked primarily with geometric shapes and hard edges, though the edges of the Post-Painterly Abstractionists were not always hard. Morris Louis, one of the originators of the movement, made a feature of applying pigment so thickly to unsized canvas that the texture of the paint-soaked fabric became integral to the painting, though the word 'painting' is almost a misnomer for this method of staining the canvas. He used acrylic paint and the colours seemed to manifest themselves independently of ideas of shape or form. Often he left large areas of canvas untouched. In the introduction to a catalogue of a retrospective exhibition after his death in 1962, Michael Fried said that Louis had opened up the picture-plane 'more radically than ever, as though seeing the first marking we are for the first time shown the void. The dazzling blankness of the untouched canvas at once repulses and engulfs the eye, like an infinite abyss.'

The austerely reductive vein which predominated in Ad Reinhardt's work from 1951 until his death in 1967 also led towards a Beckett-like apprehension of the Nothing than which nothing is more real. He said that the great qualities of Asian art were monotony, detachment, inaction and dignity, and in 1957 he drew up 'Twelve Rules for a New Academy' – 'No texture, no accidents or automatism, no brushwork or calligraphy, no sketching or drawing, no forms, no design, no colour'. In the final phase of his work, the colours are so dark and so close-valued that you have to study the canvas carefully to see that it is not black all over. Many of his paintings were damaged in exhibitions because the viewers, unable to see anything, instinctively put out their hands, like blind men, to touch.

Though the Op and Kinetic art of painters like Victor Vasarely and Bridget Riley, the Structuralism of Frank Stella, the Concrete painting of Max Bill, the essays in flat colour and geometric shapes of painters like Auguste Herbin and Richard Mortensen were vastly different in the impact they made, they were similar in their emphasis on abnegation. The influence

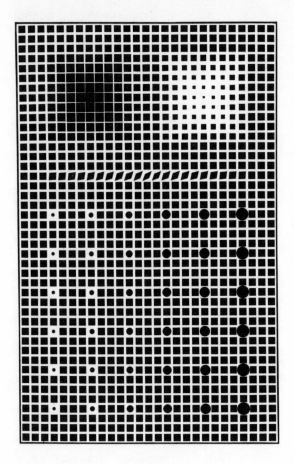

Victor Vasarely: *Supernovae* (1959-61)

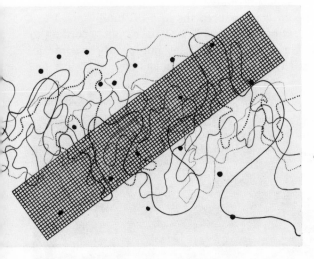

Part of John Cage's score for *Fontana Mix* (1958)

that overshadowed them all, of course, was Mondrian, with his insistence that the reality represented by geometrical painting had to be a constant reality, untouched by personal emotion. He had seen the possibility of a plastic art based purely on relations and the best of his own work, as Pierre Francastel has said, succeeded in organizing the space around it. 'Its linear but non-symmetrical forms lead the spectator to geometrize (and activate) this space. Here we have a sort of extension of the genetic values of lines and surfaces.' But if we apply this test to his later work, which is repetitive, or to the postwar abstract art which followed in his wake, emulating his simplicity without going through the processes of distillation by which he achieved it, the results are mostly disappointing.

Reductionism in *avant-garde* music has been different, though the conditioning of the contemporary audience to absorb information quickly in any medium naturally has its consequences. Predictability was an important factor in classical music, which abounded in leisurely development and multiple repetition. Development, as Webern pointed out, is a form of repetition and there has been relatively little of either in postwar *avant-garde* music. Constantly changing rhythms, as in *Le Marteau sans maître*, have militated against them and generally the composer has been dealing out musical information very quickly, often giving the audience more than it can take in.

The traditional artist believed in natural laws. For Goethe colour was natural law as related to the sense of sight and for Webern music was natural law as related to the sense of hearing. He saw the Schoenbergian tone-row as more natural than a scale based on only seven of the twelve notes. But postwar music has reflected the general scepticism about one-to-one relationships between cause and effect, while extremists have been hostile to any form of purposefulness. For Karlheinz Stockhausen the structure of the piece was not 'a sequence of development in time' but 'a directionless time-field in which the individual groups have no particular direction in time'. Edgard Varèse, who started his experiments in the twenties, was the first composer to see that if the chord was freed from dependence on everything that comes before or after it as part of a development, the next step was to think in terms of individual sounds. So, dispensing with harmony, he wrote a non-linear music of contrasting tones, timbres and rhythms, taking rock-formation as a model for the relationships between his note-clusters. 'I was not influenced', he said, 'by composers as much as by natural objects and physical phenomena. As a child I was tremendously impressed by the qualities and character of the granite I found in Burgundy.'

It is in music, the least representational of the arts, that conscious imitation of Nature has been most important for the postwar *avant-garde*. Olivier Messiaen, too, became less abstract as he developed. Influenced by Debussy, he had the same belief that he could hear 'the mysterious accord that exists between Nature and the human imagination' and the same desire to reproduce it. *Le Reveil des oiseaux* (1953) was the first of the series of works in which the close attention he paid to bird-song was the main stimulus to his musical creativity and no postwar painter or poet has drawn on Nature as he does in his *Chronochromie* (1960). 'Nature is the supreme resource,' he said, 'an inexhaustible treasure-house of sounds, colours, forms and rhythms, and the unequalled model for total development and perpetual variation.' Not that there was any thematic development of the old sort in the work. The self-abnegation was as complete as was demanded by John Cage, who said 'the composer should clear his mind of music and set about discovering means to let sounds be themselves rather than vehicles for man-made theories or expressions of human sentiments'. For Cage, Varèse had not gone far enough in this direction. 'Rather than dealing with sounds as sounds, he deals with them as Varèse.'

To Cage, who was deeply influenced by Oriental philosophy, 'all of nature is a multiplicity of things, each one of which is at the centre of the universe'. Sounds exist in their own right, independently of human perceptions, and all sounds are equally valid. Recently listening to a record of a

The Merce Cunningham dance company in *Variations V*, music by John Cage (22 November 1966)

string quartet he had written in the forties, when he heard in the background the noise of traffic and insects he regretted not having written those sounds into the music. There should be no barrier between art and life: 'Theatre takes place all the time wherever one is and art simply facilitates persuading one that this is the case.' The work he did with Rauschenberg for Merce Cunningham's dance company in 1953-4 was, therefore, based on random events. Since art implies selection, the selection itself must be randomized in order to make it independent of the composer's will. Cage used dice and the *I Ching*, at first throwing coins and later having the process computerized. William Burroughs's use of cut-up techniques in his fiction was aimed at producing a similar randomization. In Cage's later works there was no notation, only hints for improvisation: the *Aria for Cathy Berberian* (1958) was written out in the form of a series of coloured curves, like graphs, accompanied by a text using nonsense syllables and phrases in five languages. The generation of composers that grew up after Cage had no training in traditional harmony. Earle Brown said that he owed more to Jackson Pollock and Alexander Calder than to any musician.

Cage started using aleatory methods in 1951. Critical of him as Boulez was, he was profoundly influenced, though the influence was mainly filtered through Stockhausen, whose *Klavierstuck XI* (1956) was, structurally at least, the model for his crucial Third Piano Sonata (1957). Both Boulez and Stockhausen had been pupils of Messiaen, who had introduced them to the complex rhythms of Indian *ragas* and *talas*. Boulez was also exposed to the influence of Japanese temple music and Balinese music. The gamalan orchestra of xylophones, vibraphone, celeste, harps, piano and bells which he used together with normal orchestral instruments in *Pli selon pli* derived from the Javanese and Balinese bands of pitched and unpitched percussion instruments. Part of the composition, as in so many of his works, was left open to improvisation.

The self-abnegation of the composer has often tended to drive modern music in the direction of mathematics. Boulez was trained as a mathematician and Stockhausen as a mathematical engineer. Varèse had scientific training and thought of becoming a mathematical engineer, while Xenakis was an architect who worked for twelve years as an assistant to Le Corbusier. With minds like these at work and with the growing influence that polyrhythmic Oriental music has exerted on Occidental composers, the drift towards electronic music can partly be explained through the possibility it offers of precision in complex time relationships. Some of Stockhausen's rhythms, for instance, would have been beyond human performers. In 1955 Ernst Krenek introduced the idea of 'totally pre-determined music', every element of which was to be worked out according to a pre-selected series. As Nature has been edging into *avant-garde* music, human nature has been partly edged out. The human voice, of course, has

Below Ryszard Cieslak in Grotowski's production of *The Constant Prince*

Right Madge Ryan in William Gaskill's production of *Mother Courage* at the National Theatre (1965)

David Warner in the Royal Shakespeare Company's production of *Henry IV* – part of the *Wars of the Roses* trilogy

Jean-Paul Belmondo in Jean-Luc Godard's *Pierrot le Fou*

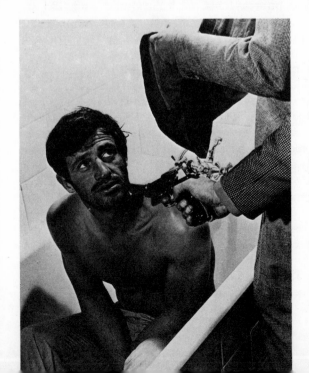

continued to be very important but, as if to honour Mallarmé's ghost, Luigi Nono has dismembered the poems he has used as texts to make them incomprehensible.

Reductionism in the theatre emerged in its purest form in Poland through Jerzy Grotowski's work. Ascetically he renounced all the inessentials of theatrical communication – scenery, changes of lighting, sound effects and the theatre building itself. The only essential, he discovered, was a living relationship between actors and audience. By stripping everything else away, he concentrated attention on the expressive power of the actor's body, but this had the effect of rendering personality less important, not more so. In *The Constant Prince* the effects Ryszard Cieslak achieved with his voice and body were extraordinarily forceful, but they seemed to have nothing to do with him as an individual. At the same time the words had less importance than they have traditionally in the theatre.

Grotowski's influence became very considerable in the sixties, mainly via Peter Brook, but by far the most important influence on the period was Bertolt Brecht, also in many ways a reductionist. He had even more effect as a director than as a playwright. His production style was based almost entirely on theories he had worked out in the thirties and forties. His emphasis on the historical aspects of a production, treating even contemporary plays as documents bearing on social, political and economic conditions, led to an extremely solid realism and a widening of focus from the hero in the centre to take in the minor characters on the fringe. The hero became less heroic, more a representative of the group than someone who stood out from it by virtue of exceptional qualities. The 'alienation effects' contributed to a stylization that balanced the realism by reminding the audience that it was inside a theatre watching a play, not witnessing life actually being lived out in front of it. Since Brecht thought of art as an instrument for effecting social change, it is ironical that he should have had so much more influence as a stylist than as a propagandist. As a didactic demonstration of the stupidities of war, *Mother Courage* was ineffective both when it was written (1939) and when produced by Brecht's Berliner Ensemble (1949). But the production was immensely successful. After the appearance of the Berliner Ensemble at the Paris International Festival (1954) and in London (1955) the Brechtian style began to affect directors, actors, designers and playwrights all over the world. In England John Osborne's plays *The Entertainer* (1957) and *Luther* (1961) and the Royal Shakespeare Company's production of *The Wars of the Roses* (a condensation of Shakespeare's *Henry IV Parts 1 and 2* and *Henry V*) were three creations which would have taken a totally different form but for the Brechtian example. It was also mainly thanks to Brecht that it became unnecessary for actors, costumes or settings to be glamorous. The *verismo* which Italian directors like Rosselini and De Sica had brought to the screen immediately after the war did not spread to the stage until the middle fifties.

There has also been a strong tendency in the theatre to devalue preconceptions, to lean on the inspiration of the moment, to admit the element of chance. After the war, structure came more and more to be regarded as something to be evolved organically, if at all, rather than to be imposed, and this affected acting, direction and writing. 'Well-made play' became a term of abuse. Stanislavsky had believed that all a character's objectives should tend in the same direction, conscious intentions harmonizing both with unconscious motives and with external behaviour. Partly because it became harder to believe in these harmonies, a more democratic way of working emerged in which directors imposed less on actors, allowing them to build up their performances more in terms of what felt right for the individual moment. The tradition by which the director would map out moves and motives ahead of the first rehearsal largely withered away to make room for a more empirical approach, with frequent recourse to improvisation. Though it has been frequently less visible in the theatre than it has in the cinema: Jean-Luc Godard shot *Pierrot le Fou* (1965) without a script and described *La Chinoise* (1967) as 'un film en train de se faire'.

151

Above Peter and Alison Smithson: Hunstanton Secondary Modern School, Norfolk (1950-4)

Left Louis Kahn: Richards Medical Research Building, Pennsylvania University, Philadelphia (1957-61)

Below Le Corbusier: Unité d'Habitation, Marseilles (1946-52)

Pluralistic architecture

In spite of Mies van der Rohe's formula 'less is more' and Buckminster Fuller's talk of an architecture 'evolving towards invisibility', the closest architectural approximation to reductionism was the movement – if it was a movement, and like most 'movements' it was largely the invention of the press – known as the New Brutalism. When Alison and Peter Smithson followed their secondary modern school at Hunstanton (1950-4) with a project for Sheffield University extension (1955), Reyner Banham hailed it as 'the furthest development of New Brutalist architecture towards the completely aformal, anti-geometric yet systematic compositional methods exemplified in painting by Pollock and Burri'. The design was more aggressively unpicturesque than Hunstanton, less rectangular, and based on the same refusal to disguise the materials with whitewash and patent glazing. Concrete would be visible as concrete, brick and steel as brick and steel. But far from having a new and random aesthetic, the Smithsons derived most of their ideas from Mies, Corbusier and the Bauhaus. There was nothing new in their obsession with exposing the actual nature of the materials and the techniques of assembling them or in their attempt 'to establish a unity between the built form and the men using it'. Nor did any of their designs go as far as Alison Smithson's 1953 project for a house with its interior structure completely exposed, with no finish either inside or outside. In the Sheffield project Banham praised the display of pipes and ducts and he claimed the art gallery Louis Kahn had just finished at Yale (1952-4) as another example of New Brutalism, though it lacked the apparently random shaping of the Sheffield project. Some of Kahn's later work like the Richards Medical Research Building (1957-61) is more brutally unpicturesque and Alvar Aalto's church at Vuoksenniska makes a strikingly non-stylish use of accidental features, but there is no lack of design.

'Anti-design' in any case is not feasible in the same sense as anti-art. Rebellion against tradition is feasible enough but in fact there has still been no effective rebellion against the International Style, which was at its peak in the late twenties and early thirties. Of course it has not survived in its pure form and there have been successive waves of reaction against it. After the war it was attacked as too functional and there was a resurgence of interest in the picturesque, only to be followed by a revival of the style in the early fifties when the public's attitude to modernist architecture changed. The hostility melted away and suddenly it became fashionable. Eero Saarinen became a culture hero. But the new consistency in the language of international architecture was a precarious one which had disappeared well before the end of the decade.

It was impossible for the International Style to recover its original momentum and logic. Its heroic impetus depended on a conjunction of social, moral and aesthetic motives. Le Corbusier, Frank Lloyd Wright,

Above Eero Saarinen:
TWA Terminal,
Kennedy Airport,
New York (1956-62)
Left Skidmore, Owings
and Merrill: Lever House,
New York (1951-2)

Below Frank Lloyd Wright:
Marin Civic Centre,
California (1959-61)

Mies and Gropius were all idealists concerned with the restructuring of society: their architecture was a means which only became an end in itself when the original end turned out to be Utopian. The ideal cities they projected were intended as prototypes for a reformed society, but even Le Corbusier had little effect on the social planning of the period. His Unité d'Habitation at Marseilles (1946-52) did not lead to any series of similar experiments in containing a community in a single building, and apart from Chandigarh (1950-62) he was almost completely deprived of state commissions. The disintegration of the Congrès Internationaux d'Architecture Moderne and of Team Ten, the group formed to take over from it as an international forum, showed that architects had little interest in keeping a lingua franca alive.

In the absence of any forceful new style, the keynotes of the postwar period have been pluralism and eclecticism. Architects have been less concerned to influence styles of living in the future than to ponder the past, consciously borrowing some ideas while allowing others to seep in unnoticed. Le Corbusier, who went on developing to the end of his life, was as much of an innovator as any other architect. Frank Lloyd Wright also enjoyed a vigorous creativity in his old age and Mies, who may have been profoundly affected by Mondrian, was the main apostle of the clear-cut simplifying rectangularity which dictated the shape of so many postwar buildings in New York. Lever House (1951-2) designed by Gordon Bunshaft of Skidmore, Owings and Merrill, set the major commercial trend for the fifties with its anonymous glassy squareness. Saarinen, a dominant figure until his death in 1961, was less consistent, less committed and more eclectic than Mies, Le Corbusier and Wright, and had little in common with contemporaries like Pier Luigi Nervi and Marcel Breuer.

The sixties were even more pluralistic than the fifties, and no less eclectic. Late though he matured, the American Paul Rudolph was to emerge as one of the important stylists of the decade, but mainly because he assimilated the influences of Mies and Le Corbusier on a profounder level than most of his contemporaries. As John Jacobus has pointed out, the cartwheel idea which is basic to his Art and Architecture Building at Yale (1959-63) is derived from Frank Lloyd Wright and the façade bears a striking resemblance to Wright's Larkin Building (1904). Nevertheless, the imposing lengths of scored concrete are given a striking and satisfying relationship to the carefully proportioned windows.

Right Paul Rudolph: Art and Architecture School, Yale University, Connecticut (1959-63)

Below Pier Luigi Nervi: Exhibition Hall, Turin (1948-9)
Bottom Mies van der Rohe and Philip Johnson: Seagram Building, New York (1955-8)

Pluralism and eclecticism

Not that the other arts have been innocent of pluralism and eclecticism. Extremist experimentalism has existed in all of them alongside staunch traditionalism, and some of the best work of the postwar period has been done in conventional modes. Boulez made the pronouncement that 'Anyone who has not felt . . . the necessity of the twelve-tone language is *superfluous.* For everything he writes will fall short of the imperatives of our time.' But Shostakovich, Britten and Stravinsky have hardly ever felt the necessity for it. In sculpture Henry Moore has never abandoned traditional materials, anthropocentric subjects or his aspiration towards monumentality. Robert Lowell is formally a conservative and so are Solzhenitsyn and Saul Bellow. Whether we are discussing art or music, poetry or the novel, no generalization can be made about any of them except in terms of pluralism. 'Since the war all the arts have been pluralistic' is a safe statement.

Consider the novel and the impossibility of talking about *the* novel. Tolstoy, Zola, Gottfried Keller, Henry James and Hardy had far more in common than Solzhenitsyn, Robbe-Grillet, Günter Grass, Saul Bellow and Iris Murdoch. Not that the differences that matter are mainly national. Bellow, Mailer, Styron and Barth in the United States are as dissimilar as Iris Murdoch, William Golding and Angus Wilson in Great Britain.

Nor do I mean to imply that no useful statements can be made about the changes of the twenty-five years in question. The social realism, the political commitment and the ontological seriousness which were so typical of the years immediately after the war conspicuously failed to survive in the Western novel (and survived only in a very different form in the iron curtain novel). George Orwell and Camus turned out not to be primarily novelists; Sartre and André Malraux abandoned the novel; while Mailer and Günter Grass both became involved in political action, Mailer annexing more and more non-fictional areas into his writing. The aggressive provincialism of Kingsley Amis, John Wain and John Braine was taken with surprising seriousness overseas and a writer like John Barth, who once said he did not know very much about reality, is characteristic of one of the moods prevailing at the end of the sixties.

Generally the endemic scepticism about the factuality of facts and about one-to-one relationships between cause and effect have driven the novel away from seriousness and realism. Allegory and comedy have emerged as two of the dominant modes. Georg Lukács's thesis is that modernist literature is basically allegorical and though it is misleading to bracket Kafka with Joyce, Beckett, Moravia and so many other dissimilar writers, it is true that Kafka had more influence on postwar fiction than he is usually credited with, and for a wide variety of novelists, including Beckett, Camus and William Golding (as for playwrights like Ionesco, Pinter, Genêt, Arrabal, Frisch, Dürrenmatt and Albee), allegory has provided a means of

154

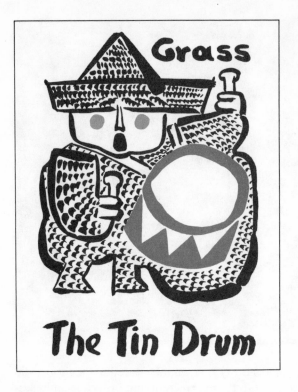

Günter Grass's own cover design for *The Tin Drum* (1959)

Michael Gough as Hugo in Peter Glenville's production at the Lyric, Hammersmith, of *Crime Passionel*, an English version of Sartre's 1947 play *Les Mains Sales*

underpinning fantasy with statements about the human condition. Science fiction too has often bordered on allegory and so – in a different way – have the myth-like stories of childhood innocence corroded by adult society in the fiction of Carson McCullers, J.D.Salinger and James Purdy.

At the same time narrative has shied away from the god's-eye viewpoint and madness has provided a useful refuge from the responsibilities of a square-on confrontation with the mixture of pressures and impressions that make up external reality. 'Granted: I'm the inmate of a mental hospital' is the tone-setting opening phrase of *The Tin Drum* (1959), while Bellow's *Herzog* starts off his narrative by saying 'If I am out of my mind, it's all right with me.' And these are two of the most committed and conscientious novels to be written since the war: the mad persona provided a means of simultaneously reflecting and filtering the disorderly material thrown up by the period. Vladimir Nabokov, a more eccentric connoisseur of insanity, dealt in *Pale Fire* (1962) with a mad poet seen through the eyes of a mad critic and prefaced *Lolita* (1955) with an introduction by an imaginary Ph.D. who proclaims the narrator of what follows to be a maniac.

Comedy in postwar fiction has taken a huge variety of different forms. The mordant satire of Angus Wilson's early short stories has nothing but class consciousness in common with the boisterous jocularity of Kingsley Amis. Nabokov's elaborate parody in *Pale Fire* does have something in common with Thomas Pynchon's parodistic exploitation of the conventional novel's conventions and John Barth's intricate burlesque of history in *The Sot-Weed Factor* (1960). But the common denominator is self-consciousness about the form raised to such a high power that parody is the only way of turning a negative into a positive.

In playwriting too, while naturalism has gone on thriving alongside experiment, one of the trends has been a shift away from the seriousness of the late forties to comedy. Even if some of it is slanted very pessimistically, it creates a quite different mood from that of the late forties, when Freud and existentialism were two of the dominant influences. What was new in plays like Tennessee Williams's *A Streetcar Named Desire* (1947) and Arthur Miller's *Death of a Salesman* (1948) was their daring dovetailing of interior and exterior realities, as in a Picasso painting where views from different angles are forced into the same composition. Miller's play represented a thoughtful and craftsmanlike effort to construct a social tragedy round a salesman-Everyman, but the necessity he felt of making the lady protest so hard that attention must be paid to such a man indicated that the framework of the play was not strong enough to give its hero the Lear-like resonance he needed. None of the other efforts to build a new heroic drama round the figure of the Common Man were any more successful. One index of the distance travelled since 1947 when Sartre wrote *Les Mains Sales* is the datedness of his attempts to endow both the communist leader and the young killer with a heroic aura. We still have our heroes, of course, despite the anti-heroic wave of Brechtian influence, but now it is easier for them to flourish on lower cultural levels – as in cartoon strips and television serials.

The belief which was cultivated at the end of the forties in the possibility of a renaissance of poetic drama depended partly on a shaky survival of heroic values. Christopher Fry's 1948 play *The Lady's Not for Burning* enjoyed a considerable vogue but the world-weary bitterness Fry intended melted into bitter-sweetness in the production that was so successful in England and the United States and the fault was partly in the writing: the undertones were lost under the romantic emotions and the effervescent self-consciousness of the language. In *Saint's Day* (1951) and *Marching Song* (1954), though both plays failed commercially, John Whiting achieved in prose what neither Fry nor Eliot could achieve in verse, at the same time as getting closer to tragedy than Arthur Miller had.

The poetry that theatre needed at this time was of a very different sort. The label 'Theatre of the Absurd' is misleading because it suggests Ionesco, Genêt, Beckett, Pinter, Adamov, Albee, Arrabal and Frisch were all theatrical advocates of Camus's formulation of absurdity in *Le Mythe de*

Jocelyn Herbert's design for Tony Richardson's 1957 production of Ionesco's *The Chairs* at the Royal Court Theatre, London

Jann Haworth: *Maid* (nylon, kapok, stocking; 1966)

Jim Dine: *All In One Lycra Plus Attachments* (1965)

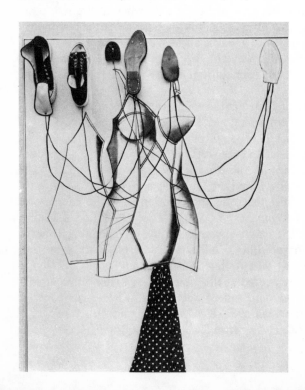

Sisyphe (1942). The kind of absurdity Ionesco introduced to the theatre did not have all that much to do with the proposition that life is a meaningless Sisyphean treadmill. His plays started out from a realization of the comic potential of inconsequential dialogue which could be manufactured by copying sentences almost at random out of a French-English phrasebook. His theorizing about the meaninglessness of contemporary existence had very little to do with his discovery of the dramatic poetry of banality or with the freedom he allowed himself in his visual exploitation of stage space. He was the first writer to make Surrealism theatrically viable.

By repudiating structural and syntactical logic, he opened the theatre's doors to a poetry that had nothing to do with verse. In *La Leçon* (1951) language became a thing, substantial enough for the teacher to kill his pupil with it. In *Les Chaises* (also 1951) the mad old couple filled the stage with empty chairs representing the guests they had invited to hear the speech which would sum up their lives. Instead of having to go on depending on character, situation and developing relationships, the dramatist could give free vent to his imagination, translate his fantasies bodily into stage pictures. Sprinkled into theatrical dialogue, the seeds of private preoccupations could grow into luxuriant allegories.

As in the novel, the anti-psychological tendency encouraged a large-scale exploitation of madness, not by explaining it but by taking it for granted, as in playwrights as diverse as Genêt and David Storey; while the new freedom to explore the possibility of creating interesting visual effects in the stage space without being limited by the logic of a developing plot encouraged the theatre to occupy the territory Artaud had discovered in the twenties and thirties. If the words had a diminished importance in Grotowski's productions, they were of still less value in the Happenings which represented an invasion of theatrical three-dimensionality by painters like Allan Kaprow, Jim Dine, Claes Oldenburg and George Brecht. Kaprow, who was a painter until 1957 and had been a student of John Cage's, said that Happenings were what his paintings had become.

Meanwhile, without creating Happenings, other painters were bursting from two dimensions into three. In 1930 Aragon had predicted a time when painters would discard brushwork and develop collage techniques. This has happened, and collage has given birth to assemblage. Robert Rauschenberg, Jasper Johns and Jim Dine produced painted canvases with three-dimensional objects attached to them, as in Dine's *All In One Lycra Plus Attachments* (1965), and with the blurring of the division between painting and sculpture, three-dimensional structures have been created either out of pre-existent objects or parodying pre-existent objects, like Oldenburg's *Soft*

Claes Oldenburg:
Soft Washstand (vinyl
plexiglas and
kapok; 1965)

Below Robert
Rauschenberg: *Wall Street*
(1961)

Bottom Jasper Johns:
Painted Bronze (1960)

Bottom right
Richard Hamilton: *Just
what is it that makes today's
homes so different?* (1956)

Washstand (1965). Jann Haworth's *Maid* (1966) was neither a doll nor a sculpture.

Disappointingly this new freedom, which ought to have been invigorating, was negative in its effects. Even a big talent like Jasper Johns's did not develop as it might have done in a more critical climate. His early work was arresting, probably, as Leo Steinberg suggested, because of the mute statement it was making about dereliction. Those targets were never going to be shot at, the flags never hoisted. The numbers and letters would never be used. Where three-dimensional effects were needed, he made plaster-casts; otherwise everything was flat, expressionless, except in so far as it expressed a mood.

But the new public demand for art, which ought, like the new freedom, to have exerted a healthy influence, has in fact been damaging. A market in which high prices are paid for second-rate works of art by fashionable artists encourages first-rate artists to become fashionable second-raters. Johns was once asked whether his painted bronze beer cans (1960) represented a social attitude to beer cans or to art. What prompted them in fact was a remark of De Kooning, who called the art dealer Leo Castelli a son of a bitch who could sell two beer cans if you gave them to him. And when Johns sculpted two beer cans and gave them to him, he sold them.

In theory the new artists have been using new materials to put new audiences in closer touch with their environment. The Pop artists' concern with the symbols of admass society like Coca-Cola bottles, comic strips, advertisements, film stars, machinery and machine products is often said to be satirical. It is also said that Pop Art is anti-illusionist because it shows up the spuriousness of the illusions it illustrates. In fact the artists have often been bemused into reflecting the spurious glamour of their subject-matter. The uncritical climate has made the artists themselves uncritical. There was unconscious but revealing irony in Oldenburg's statement: 'I am for an art that embroils itself with the everyday crap and still comes out on top.'

One of the most depressing aspects was the conformism that grew up between the artists who blithely imagined they had joined a non-conformist collective. Another was the contentment with creating works of art that were *about* technical devices instead of inventing or improving technical

David Hockney: *The First Marriage* (1962)

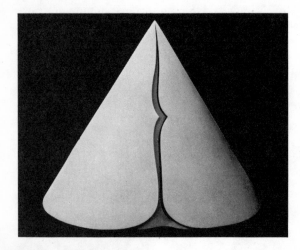

Philip King: *Rosebud* (plastic; 1962)

Giacometti:
Man Pointing
(bronze; 1947)

devices to make statements about something else. Much of David Hockney's work, as he said himself, falls into this category. A third was the emergence of a new attitude which makes the work of art unimportant compared with the activity of creating it. 'Whatever I'm doing at the moment', said Eduardo Paolozzi, 'is the important thing.' It is easy enough to see how this attitude developed out of Jackson Pollock's, but it is negative in a way which cannot but have a debasing effect on the art.

The cult of assemblage was probably one symptom of a growing reluctance either to make or to depict, a reductionist tendency which limits the artist's function to establishing or demonstrating new relationships between pre-existent objects or materials or making casual geometric gestures in two or three dimensions. All too often the impact and interest of the demonstration or gesture were far too slight to justify either the effort that had gone into making it or the effort of going to a gallery to look at it. Philip King's sculptures, for instance, take up a good deal of space to work out very simple ideas, and the existence of the new structure does nothing to modify the space around it. It is only in a highly pluralistic culture that such work could be awarded prizes and serious attention at the same time as sculptors like Giacometti and Henry Moore have gone on developing. The word 'sculpture' is put under a strain to embrace the two kinds of product.

At the same time 'poetry' is a word which has to stretch from Ezra Pound to the 'Pop' poets who write mainly for the sake of performing their own work at public readings. In 1965 6,000 people packed into the Albert Hall in London for 'Poetry International' and some of the Pop poets developed almost the same kind of fan following as Pop singers. Basically, this is an anti-literary movement, which started in the United States and became dangerous when Allen Ginsberg began to assume the role of a religious leader. His own poetry deteriorated as his popularity soared and he was taken seriously when he claimed that he was capable of 'reducing the bomb to insignificance because the poem is greater than the bomb'. Some poetry readings take on the quality of a religious meeting: the audience feels a sense of community and the poet-priest feels a sense of power, though this does not always induce delusions of grandeur.

Of course the reaction against tradition which made this sub-poetry possible has also produced a number of healthy consequences, of which the most important is the flowering of poetry in the United States both before and since the war. Both T.S.Eliot and Ezra Pound left America to steep themselves in the European tradition and of course they were right because all they were leaving behind was Whitman. But a poet growing up into the fifties or sixties and wanting to live in the thick of a vigorous poetic tradition would have done better to leave Europe for the States (as Denise Levertov and Thom Gunn did). America had not quite seen the *risorgimento* Pound had predicted, big enough 'to make the Italian Renaissance look like a tempest in a tea-pot' but, thanks partly to the mighty influence he was wielding from his self-imposed exile, it has had Wallace Stevens, William Carlos Williams, Marianne Moore, Hart Crane, E.E.Cummings, John Crowe Ransom, Allen Tate, Richard Eberhart, Theodore Roethke, Elizabeth Bishop, Robert Duncan, Randall Jarrell, Robert Penn Warren, John Berryman, Robert Lowell, Howard Nemerov and Gary Snyder. Except for Hart Crane, who killed himself in 1932, all these have enlivened the postwar scene. The tradition they were writing in certainly has its roots in Whitman and the nineteenth century but it only surfaced in the twentieth, and England's eclipse has only been obvious since the war. Britain produced a few important poets like Ted Hughes and Charles Tomlinson but the general drift of the fifties was towards a complacent provincialism (as with Philip Larkin) and there was little revitalization in the sixties. There has been much more liveliness in Russia, communist Europe and Latin America with poets like Vosnezensky, Zbigniew Herbert, Miroslav Holub, Neruda and Paz.

There's no gauging the effect communist state pressure has had on literature; even music has been profoundly affected. Until 1937 Shostakovich was an experimentalist but after his work was attacked for its negativistic

Top Henry Moore: *Two-piece Reclining Figure* (1960)

Above Francis Bacon: *Head Surrounded by Sides of Beef* (1954)

rejection of simplicity and realism, he contritely reverted to melody, tonality and romantic emotionalism. In 1948 Zhdanov attacked him and Prokofiev for formalism and for departing from classical and folk-idioms. A month later Prokofiev publicly confessed he had been 'guilty of atonalism'. He never returned to it and neither did Shostakovich until the end of the sixties in his Twelfth String Quartet, which intermittently uses the Schoenbergian tone-row and it is modelled, as Hans Keller pointed out, on Schoenberg's pre-atonal First Chamber Symphony.

Of course the pluralism of postwar music is not primarily due to political factors. The commissars have nothing to do with the inspiration Stravinsky and Britten have found in folk-tunes or with their melody and tonality. Eclecticism is much more permissible today than in the prewar culture when more stress was laid on originality and self-expression. As Leonard Meyer said:

If a work of art is an impersonal construct, and creation a kind of problem-solving, then experiments with mixtures of means and materials, either within or between works, need not constitute an imperfection. On the contrary, the skilful and elegant combinations of disparate styles (or of ideas borrowed from different works and different composers) within a single work may become a challenging and attractive problem.

Britten, Stravinsky, Henze, Lowell and John Barth are all eclectic in this sense, and so, on a lower level, is Pop Art.

Not that there are only two cultural levels: there are dozens. That is why Harold Rosenberg said 'Modern Art does not have to be actually new. It only has to be new to somebody.' Rather than thinking in terms of an élite and a mass audience, we should picture a series of concentric circles, the smaller of which will get smaller as the bigger grow bigger, for the democratization of education which increases the demand for the arts inevitably produces a loss of quality at the top of the teaching pyramid. But even the smallest circle will never shrink to nothing, and there will always be degrees of élitism because there will always be some people who are able and willing to make more effort of concentration than others. Reading a difficult poem or looking at a difficult picture is a generically different activity from listening to Pop poetry or looking at Pop Art. But so long as the circles remain roughly concentric and influence continues to move outwards as well as inwards from one to the next, there will be no reason to believe the pessimists who say that art, as we know it now, is an individual-istic activity which cannot survive in a collective society. Certainly the literature that is not written for performance is currently at a disadvantage over the art designed for public consumption. But even the pessimists do not seem to believe that all the books, paintings, sculpture and music now in existence will be destroyed, and so long as they exist they cannot but be an influence on the art of the future. There will be no discontinuity, only development of the same sort we have already experienced, and if the same pluralism continues, much of the art of 1970-2000 will be rather like much of the art of 1945-70.

Jasper Johns: *0 – 9* (encaustic on newspaper on canvas; 1958-9)

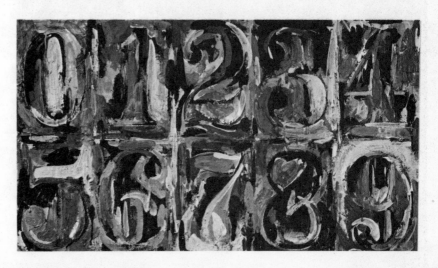

The first men on the moon:
Aldrin descends the ladder
of the lunar module to join
Armstrong on the moon's
surface, where they spent
twenty-one hours in
July 1969

John Maddox

The World of Science

The end of the Second World War was an auspicious time for scientists and especially for the physicists, the chemists and the engineers. In 1945 it was clear that the Allied victory had rested to a large extent on the development of new weapons systems of which the nuclear weapons exploded over Hiroshima and Nagasaki were merely the most conspicuous. Both in the West and in Germany, radar had become one of the essential tools in the battle by ground forces against aircraft, and it was obvious that the potentialities of radar systems both in the defence against air attack and in telecommunications were still largely to be exploited. The preoccupation during the war with air defence also led to the construction of machines for predicting the movement of aircraft and for training anti-aircraft guns against likely targets; it was already clear that from these developments would spring what Dr Norbert Wiener called the cybernetic machines.

Elsewhere, too, the scientists' star had risen high. Jet engines had made it possible for Western aircraft to establish an early supremacy over their rivals, both from Germany and from Japan, with the result that everybody could see the potential benefits for air transport. But the Second World War was also a time during which biologists as well as the physical scientists made reputations for themselves and in the process learned methods of work so different from the familiar ways of the relatively amateur decades before the war that it may fairly be said that the conduct of the scientific enterprise had matured.

The development of the antibiotic penicillin is the classic story. The material, of course, had been available since the early thirties, after Sir Alexander Fleming had almost by accident discovered the mould of penicillin and recognized that it could secrete a chemical which could inhibit the growth of some bacteria. During the war the task was to turn this academic discovery into a practical method of combating infectious disease, which in turn amounted to an attempt to grow large quantities of the penicillin mould and to isolate the chemicals which were secreted. The biologists, chemists and chemical engineers involved with this problem found themselves a part of a large and complicated team devoted to a whole sequence of separate problems to be solved before penicillin could be manufactured on a large scale and then used in practice against disease. This bringing together of different disciplines for the solution of an important problem amounted to a break with the tradition of prewar science.

The Second World War thus made modern science technically mature. Indeed, the outstanding characteristic of military developments during the Second World War was predominantly the way in which goals were first defined in the abstract and then tackled by teams – sometimes armies – of scientists. This, for example, is what happened with the development of nuclear weapons. The first step, by 1938, was the recognition that it should be feasible to set up within a mass of fissile uranium a self-sustaining chain reaction in which disintegrating atomic nuclei would release atomic particles capable of stimulating the fission of other nuclei. Once it had been recognized that such a chain reaction could make a nuclear explosion, it was simply necessary to find a way of extracting from natural uranium a sufficient quantity of fissile uranium (seven parts in a thousand of the natural material) or of manufacturing some other material with characteristics similar to those of fissile uranium. It was easy enough, in the early forties, to map out several possible routes to these objectives. The novelty of the Manhattan Project in the United States was not merely the gigantic

Expenditure on research and development 1965

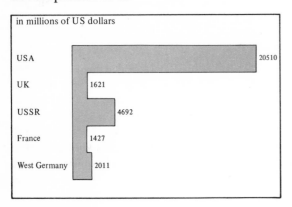

in millions of US dollars

USA	20510
UK	1621
USSR	4692
France	1427
West Germany	2011

Growth of scientific books published 1954-68

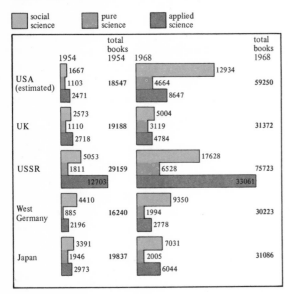

social science   pure science   applied science

	1954	total books 1954	1968	total books 1968
USA (estimated)	1667 / 1103 / 2471	18547	12934 / 4664 / 8647	59250
UK	2573 / 1110 / 2718	19188	5004 / 3119 / 4784	31372
USSR	5053 / 1811 / 12703	29159	17628 / 6528 / 33061	75723
West Germany	4410 / 885 / 2196	16240	9350 / 1994 / 2778	30223
Japan	3391 / 1946 / 2973	19837	7031 / 2005 / 6044	31086

scale (for those times) on which the operation was conducted but also the highly coordinated fashion in which several fundamental-research laboratories and several industrial-development plants were harnessed to the common goal. The explosion of the first nuclear weapon in 1945 was one of the first fruits of the belief that grew up during the war that in the attainment of objectives which have been shown theoretically to be feasible, it is merely necessary to deploy enough men, enough money and enough resources.

It is inevitable that the sense of achievement which the Second World War created among the physical scientists should have left its mark on science and technology in the forties and the early fifties. Some of the more important consequences were in scientific education and in the way university departments grew rapidly and increased enormously their involvement in scientific research. But this was also a period in which scientists and their well-wishers were quick to point out how much more profit there would be in industry, and how much more rapid would be productive innovations, if only larger numbers of people with technical or scientific backgrounds were hard at work at industrial research. In the United States this view was quickly adopted, at least by several of the larger companies, with the result that the foundations were laid for some of the great technical enterprises which have now become some of the largest corporations in the world. This, for example, is the period during which the IBM Corporation set up as a very large employer of qualified scientists and technologists. Outside the United States, the lesson was understood but not as quickly learned, and even in the mid-fifties, economists in Britain were still wringing their hands over the pitifully small numbers of scientists then employed in basic industries such as shipbuilding, textiles and steel.

The ascendancy of the physicists in the years immediately after the war was inevitably accompanied by something of a backlash. The physicists themselves had been the first to contribute to this, often in the spirit of the late Dr Robert Oppenheimer's remark on witnessing the first nuclear explosion in the Alamogordo Desert in May 1945 that 'the physicists have known guilt'. In Britain and in the United States groups of physicists who had been intimately concerned with military developments during the war found themselves setting up associations to draw attention to the social problems created by the arrival of nuclear weapons. Ever since, the journal founded by the American group, the *Bulletin of the Atomic Scientists*, has been a vigorous and articulate and sometimes influential critic of the thoughtless use of the mature methods of applied science developed during the Second World War. It is not unreasonable to see in these beginnings the origins of the more clamant but often less level-headed protests at the role of science in modern society which have more recently been made public. In short, the Second World War was a time when the application of science was made into a mature and powerful means of transforming society, and when people of all kinds began to wonder what limitations there must be on such a force.

Nuclear growth for war and peace

As during the Second World War so afterwards, the dilemma of the social relations of science are most vividly illustrated by the case of nuclear energy. To begin with, it was plain that the rudimentary weapons of the Second World War could be rapidly improved in every technical sense. The result was that by the late forties the United States was equipped with a powerful and diverse armoury of nuclear weapons and that the Soviet Union was also able to make nuclear weapons for itself. The speed with which this supposedly secret knowledge had spread outside the United States, helped though it may have been by espionage as well as by the publication of the official United States report on the subject (the Smythe Report), was at the time a surprise but is now, with hindsight, merely one of the most striking examples of the simple rule that where the application of known scientific principles is concerned, and where goals are specified in advance, there are no secrets but only time-lags. The fact that both the Soviet Union and the United States were quickly able to make thermo-

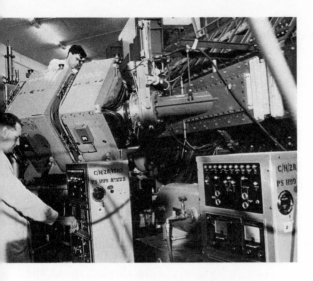

The Nimrod injector at the Rutherford High Energy Laboratory in Berkshire: since the war proton-accelerating machines have been used to study the relationships between fundamental particles – some stable for very short periods only – and to create new ones in the laboratory

Penicillin: the Beecham Research Laboratories Plant in Sussex. Although known since the thirties, penicillin was not medically developed until the war years

nuclear bombs as well as fission bombs – by the mid-fifties, both had taken this step to increase a thousandfold the explosive power of weapons like those exploded at Hiroshima – is another illustration of the same principle.

In passing, it remains something of a puzzle that the number of nuclear powers twenty-five years later was only five. Britain assumed almost without question in the years after the war that the manufacture of nuclear explosives would be essential, and persevered with the enterprise even though the United States Atomic Energy Act of 1946 isolated the United Kingdom from the research programme then under way at the wartime laboratories of the Manhattan Project. The fourth nuclear power, France, was persuaded in the same direction by political rather than by technical considerations, and it remains doubtful whether French nuclear weapons play a useful part either in the defence of France or in the wider defence of Western Europe as a whole. Political considerations also account for the fact that mainland China has developed nuclear weapons when other countries which could have taken this step sooner – Canada and Sweden are two obvious examples – have deliberately refrained from making nuclear weapons. In short, the spread of nuclear weapons since the Second World War has been less extensive than it might have been. Moreover, the strictly military applications of nuclear energy have also been somewhat detached from other kinds of scientific and technical activity – in this sense, the peaceful applications or potential applications have been more important than the military ones.

That said, it is remarkable that the best part of a decade should have gone by after the ending of the Second World War before the peaceful application of nuclear fission attracted money and effort on a scale likely to ensure success. By the mid-fifties, however, the Atomic Energy Commission in the United States had built half a dozen experimental reactors to serve as models for later nuclear reactors in which such large amounts of power would be released that steam-turbines for central power-stations could be kept supplied. In Britain, the pace of peaceful development was almost as rapid and, by the end of 1955, the British government – faced with what seemed to be a chronic shortage of coal, the country's traditional fuel – had embarked on a deliberate and substantial programme for the building of nuclear power-stations.

The record of the development of this new industry since the mid-fifties is a splendid illustration both of the power and of the limitations of the techniques of technical development evolved during the Second World War. As it happens, there has been no radically new addition to the knowledge of nuclear fission since 1945. In spite of a host of refinements of understanding, the basic principle remains that the atomic nuclei of some atoms (of which uranium atoms are the most familiar) can be made inherently unstable by the atomic particles called neutrons and therefore made to split into two fragments with the release of energy and more neutrons. Thus the efficient design of nuclear power-stations is not a scientific problem but a technical one. How can it be arranged that the chain reaction which a nuclear weapon develops explosively is controlled and predictable? How can it be arranged that the fullest use is made of the atomic particles flung off during the fission of a uranium atomic nucleus, so that the chain reaction is not merely controlled but also as efficient? And how, above all, can the necessary machinery be built in such a way that the cost of servicing the installation does not exceed the cost of making electricity by conventional methods?

These have been the preoccupations of nuclear engineers in the past few years. It remains a simple truth that the economic objective of how to make a commercially competitive nuclear power-station is harder to attain than the strictly technical objective of arranging that fissile uranium should release energy in a controlled fashion. To be sure, this should have been anticipated, if only because the first problem includes the second. Nevertheless, nuclear engineers have lost a great deal of respect in the past decade because of their immoderate claims for new types of nuclear reactors which, at the time, were offered as means of producing nuclear power at competitive prices before anybody could have defined with sufficient accuracy

After the explosion of the first atomic bomb in New Mexico in 1945: scientists (including Robert Oppenheimer, third from left) measure sand radioactivity

Britain's nuclear power-stations at Calder Hall (*below*) and Chapelcross, Dumfriesshire (*bottom*), where a technician checks the apparatus for detecting a leak on any of the 1,696 channels of the reactor

the costs of comparatively unimportant items of machinery in the process upon which the commercial competitiveness of these plans would eventually depend. In short, if nuclear weapons put the physicists into the ascendancy in the years immediately after the war, the vicissitudes of the development of nuclear power-stations have served as well as anything to show that where non-technical considerations supervene, technical arguments may be misleading.

That said, it must be taken as a great gain of the years 1945-70 that the development of nuclear power-stations finally removed the threat that there might eventually be a physical shortage of fuel. Since the war, the consumption of coal and oil has grown rapidly in countries of all kinds, chiefly with the spread of industrialization. The known reserves of coal in the earth's crust are probably sufficient to last for several tens of thousands of years at the present rate of consumption, but the pace of growth in industry is considerably foreshortening this complacent picture and, in any case, much of the world's reserves of coal could be mined only at exceedingly high cost. With petroleum, so far, it seems to have been possible to keep on finding new reserves at much the speed with which crude oil is extracted from the ground, but nobody can be sure when this happy balance will cease to be the case (and known reserves are likely to be sufficient for only thirty-five years or thereabouts). Luckily, however, the full exploitation of the uranium accessible in the earth's crust would add an amount of energy comparable with that locked up in the known reserves of coal. Thorium, another potentially fissile material, is an even larger potential source of energy. And finally there is the prospect that when all these sources of energy have been consumed, it will be possible to build machinery for extracting energy from hydrogen on exactly the same principle on which thermonuclear weapons are constructed but with control. In short, for all their limitations, the nuclear physicists and engineers have liberated national economies from an important source of anxiety. The promise remains, even if practice is less than perfect.

The discovery of DNA

The scientific foundations for the nuclear energy industry lie in the academic research carried out in the early thirties by the Italian physicist Fermi and by scattered groups of European scientists, in Germany, Denmark and France. Although nuclear energy is now a branch of technology, it is a sign of the transformation of the modern world brought about by the continued deepening of scientific understanding. In this sense, the most striking development of all the achievements of science since the war is probably the development of what is now called molecular biology – the explanation of biological processes in terms of entirely understandable interactions between molecules and which is therefore comparable with the explanation provided in the first half of the nineteenth century of the behaviour of physical materials in terms of the interaction between atoms. Molecular biology, in short, has made biology understood in strictly mechanistic terms.

How has this come about? In the years immediately before the war, there was mild interest in explanations of some then inexplicable biological phenomena. One puzzle, for example, seemed to be the regularity with which small chemical entities or molecules are strung together so as to form much longer molecules in naturally occurring materials such as silk, hair and wool. In the thirties these materials were recognized as proteins and thus as being chemically similar to materials such as insulin which can rid a diabetic of the symptoms of his disease and, even more important, the enzymes which were being recognized in the thirties as essential catalysts of chemical change in all kinds of living things. In the event, however, the analytical techniques then available, in physics and chemistry, were sufficient only to suggest that proteins would turn out to be important in the understanding of biological processes. They were insufficient to throw light on the way in which protein molecules are put together and the way in which they may be manufactured in living tissues.

Much of the recent progress in the molecular explanation of biology has been made possible either by experimental techniques developed during the war or by such developments as the availability of radioactive isotopes. For several reasons, however, it became clear towards the end of the fifties that the importance of protein substances in living things, great though it may be, is less than that of some previously badly characterized materials known as nucleic acids. The latter, after all, were the invariable components of genetic material found in most kinds of living tissues and embodied, for example, in chromosomes. This is why the interest of those seeking a molecular explanation of living things turned first of all to a search for a description in molecular terms of nucleic acids. The foundations of what may now be called molecular biology date from the appearance in 1952 of an explanation by Dr F.H.C.Crick and Dr J.D.Watson of how molecules of nucleic acids could serve as repositories both for the information passed on from one cell to its progeny in the course of biological development and also for information of the kind needed to distinguish one kind of cell from another – a mouse cell from a human cell or a liver cell from a kidney cell, for example.

The publication of the article by Watson and Crick radically transformed the scientific view of living processes. Molecules of nucleic acids are, like protein molecules, long strings of smaller chemical entities. The essence of the new doctrine of molecular biology is that the kind of nucleic acid molecules found in the genetically significant parts of living things (and called DNA) can in the right chemical environment be replicated exactly in their own image. In fact, these molecules consist of pairs of nucleic acid strings twisted together, each fitting to the other as a hand fits to a glove. When a single cell divides so as to produce two offspring, each string in the pair serves as a kind of template for the modelling of another string-like molecule identical with its partner. The process by means of which this spiral structure serves as a prescription for the regular conduct of chemical operations within the living cell is still only partly understood. From this point of view, mouse cells differ from human cells in the kind of DNA which they contain. Then, in either human beings or in mice, liver cells differ from kidney cells in that different parts of a common genetic inheritance are able to be effective.

The consequences of these simple relationships for the organization of living things now extend throughout biology. It turns out, for example, that the protein molecules which play crucial roles at the biochemical level in living things are themselves manufactured in parts of cells remote from the genetic DNA. How then are they assembled in the proper way? The genetic specification for, say, the protein haemoglobin which carries oxygen round the blood-stream is embodied in the genetic DNA in every cell, but in those cells which manufacture haemoglobin, the genetic instructions are transferred first of all to a smaller molecule of another nucleic acid called RNA, and this in turn puts its stamp on the protein molecule as it is in turn assembled from smaller entities. Not the least of the consequences of this development is the way in which the interaction between nucleic acids and protein molecules has provided an explanation and sometimes a remedy for inherited genetic diseases caused by the deficiency of some protein molecule – phenylketonuria (the inheritance of which leads quickly to mental defects at about one year) is such a case. Haemophilia may in due course be another in which a remedy or at least a palliative may be based on the understanding provided by molecular biology.

More far-reaching implications of the discovery concern the process of development and indeed the nature of life itself. In the growth of an embryo – a human embryo, for example – there is a regular sequence of events by means of which different parts of the developing body reach functional competence in a well-defined and regular sequence. How is it that, with mammalian reproduction, a single pair of cells uniting at fertilization can give rise to such a well-determined sequence of events? It is now clear that the genetic DNA contains not merely the information necessary to characterize a liver cell or a kidney cell but also a prescription for allowing one stage of development to succeed another in the appropriate order.

Hungarian experiment in the use of radiation to preserve food: unimpaired irradiated wheat (left), untreated and unusable wheat (right)

Technique for locating tumours with the aid of radioactive elements in the body (Massachussetts General Hospital)

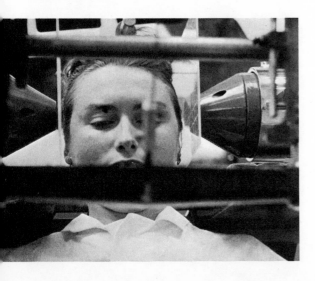

Mount Palomar Observatory: during the late forties astronomers using the 200-inch telescope came to realize the size of the universe and that a typical galaxy might consist of some 100 thousand million stars in various stages of evolution

But where does this characteristic pattern of development come from? There is now sufficient evidence within molecular biology itself to show how one pattern of development may evolve from another by methods which are entirely understandable in terms of how different protein molecules or different nucleic acid molecules link together in different circumstances. In short, molecular biology provides a framework for explaining the evolution of different forms of life even if, as yet, it provides no definite description of how familiar living forms may have differentiated, some 3,000 million years ago, from strictly inanimate forms of matter.

The same body of understanding about the relationships between nucleic acids and proteins in living things has also helped to provide a new understanding of entities such as viruses, which are now recognized to be biological devices for subverting the normal working of a living cell by the importation of a piece of foreign nucleic acid laden with subversive chemical instructions. The same development has also created a host of new problems in, for example, the understanding of cancer. At least some forms of the disease are now known to be characterized by the incorporation of foreign genetic material, possibly in virus form, into the hereditary nucleic acid. It does not follow from this that some forms of cancer are infectious, like measles – the viruses may be more effective as methods of transmitting cancer from one part of the body to another. But in due course these developments are certain to throw a penetrating light not merely on the detailed understanding of living things but on far-reaching questions such as the circumstances in which living things as such may first have developed.

So does it follow from this that molecular biology has made it possible for people to tinker with the genetic constitution of living things, either at random or deliberately? First of all, the development of molecular biology has made it much easier to appreciate the role which seems to be played by exceedingly small amounts of certain chemicals in the causation of cancer or of other perversions of normal life. For example, some chemicals are now known to cause cancer by interfering with the replication of DNA. In due course it will also no doubt be possible to account for the way in which drugs such as thalidomide interfere with the normal development of human embryos, possibly by interfering with built-in sequences of development embodied in inherited DNA. All this is what might be called 'accidental' genetic engineering – what of the prospects of bringing about deliberately

Radio telescope at Arecibo, Puerto Rico, used to help map the surface of Venus; radio astronomy developed from wartime techniques and during the fifties scientists began to keep track of radio waves from distant parts of the universe

A million suns probably with solar systems of their own: 'Messier 13' in the constellation Hercules within our own Milky Way system, and a near neighbour at about 22,000 light years

Galaxy in the constellation Cygnus: the spiral mist is about 2 million light years away. Around the yellow core of older, cooler stars are grouped spirals of young, blue, hotter ones

chosen changes in the genetic constitution of animals or plants by external chemical interference? This is a prospect which in the past few years has caused all kinds of anxieties and has raised a host of entirely proper questions about the circumstances in which it may eventually be possible for molecular biologists to ring the changes on naturally occurring living forms.

The most obvious use for molecular biology in the treatment of human conditions is in the treatment of deficiency diseases such as haemophilia which exist because of genetic impairments, but there is at present no obvious way of doing this. The first thing to be said is that there is at present no assurance that molecular biology as at present developed will ever be able to make the precise changes in the chemical constitution of DNA molecules that would be necessary to turn an organism with one characteristic into the same organism with a different characteristic. Tinkering with DNA will not change the colour of a person's hair, for example. It is possible that the application of molecular biology may in some circumstances help to select animals for stock-breeding more accurately than in present practice, but even that is a long way off. Third, it is more than likely that the deliberate application of molecular biology will provide the foundations for a new kind of chemical industry for the manufacture of biological chemicals. But there is no doubt at all that by changing the way in which people regard and can now describe living processes, molecular biology has brought about a revolution throughout this field of science the results of which cannot yet be known.

Studying the universe

The progress of science is perhaps best measured by the extent to which it helps to explain the origin of familiar things, implying a deeper understanding of the natural world. The way in which understanding of the physical universe has been transformed in the past few decades is as remarkable as anything that has happened in molecular biology.

In the late forties, astronomers were able for the first time to enjoy the benefits of the 200-inch telescope on Palomar Mountain, which had been started in the mid-thirties but which was completed only during the war. The first results of this development were that astronomers were quickly able to appreciate that the scale of the universe was even greater than had previously been thought. The recent history of observational astronomy seems in many ways to have been a progressive lengthening of the scale on which the universe must be considered. In the late forties it was apparent that there were even more nebulae consisting of clusters of stars outside the Galaxy than had previously been thought, that these distant galaxies were even more massive than had previously been suspected and that their distances were greater. This is the point at which astronomers began with some awe to acknowledge that a typical galaxy, of which the Milky Way seems to be quite representative, may contain as many as 100,000 million stars in various stages of evolution.

More detailed observation revealed several other important characteristics of the visible sky. First, there seems to be no physical property to distinguish the near-by galaxies from those at greater distances, which in turn suggested that if only it were possible to observe the universe not from this galaxy but, say, from one a thousand light years away, the universe would look very much the same as it does from the earth.

Second, within galaxies, similar processes seem to be at work. One striking observation with the new postwar telescopes, for example, was that several near-by galaxies are close enough for astronomers to detect occasions when a whole star explodes – the phenomena known as supernovae. These are now recognized to have occurred within the Milky Way on several occasions in the past thousand years, and the glowing cloud of gas which forms the Crab nebula is indeed the remnant of such a supernova dating from nearly a thousand years ago. The same technical development led to the discovery that near-by galaxies contain a diversity of types of stars similar in every way to that observed within the Milky Way – some large red stars, some apparently small hot white stars, some with large

Dr Watson and Dr Crick (right),
1962 Nobel prize-winners
for medicine, discoverers of
the molecular structure of DNA
(model in background)

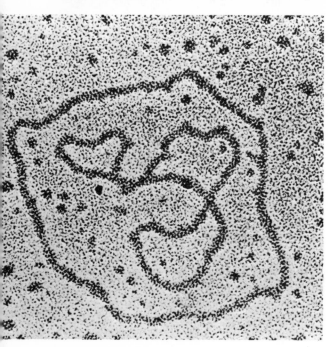

Above A DNA virus in a living cell

Below Fibres and knobs (magnified 5,000 times) from
the nerve tissue of a marine snail's abdomen; they are
believed to pass nerve impulses between cells

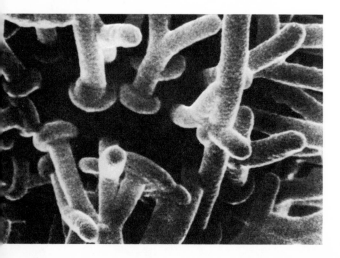

amounts of metal in their atmospheres and some apparently free from metal atoms.

The first consequence was the emergence of the philosophical position that the universe is indeed a uniform place within which the proverbial space-traveller would be hard pressed to find really distinctive landmarks. To be sure, some galaxies may be older than others but old galaxies and new galaxies seem to be mixed up at random. And, of course, distant galaxies seem different from those lying comparatively close, but only because the light from distant galaxies has to travel a great distance and is, therefore, representative of a distant and rapidly receding part of the universe. This is probably why the light is redder in colour than it would otherwise be.

One tangible expression of the view that if it were possible to see the universe from outside, one region would look very much like any other, was the theory put forward in the late forties by Professor Fred Hoyle of Cambridge University and his associates Herman Bondi and Thomas Gold that the universe is not a fixed aggregation of matter but rather a region in which matter is continually being created as the visible objects – galaxies and the like – continually recede from each other. This doctrine is of course an assault on the more traditional view that the expanding universe was once, at the beginning of time so to speak, a comparatively tight concentration of a very large amount of matter in a small space. This theory and that which holds that the universe has been continually re-created have been at the centre of cosmological speculation ever since the early fifties. Over the years, evidence has accumulated to suggest that the continuous-creation theory leaves much to be desired, but only the bravest spirits would suggest that the issue is now settled – too little is understood about some of the more spectacular phenomena now recognized in distant parts of the universe for this to be the case.

The conflicts which have accumulated in cosmology are now so sharp that they will only be resolved by some radical change in the way in which cosmologists and physicists regard the natural world. A great deal of the progress – if that is the right word – in the twenty-five years since the war has been made possible by the development of new instruments and new techniques for the observation of distant objects in the universe.

The chief innovation is the development of radio-astronomy, a technique born of the devices developed during the Second World War for the detection of electromagnetic waves or radio waves from great distances and for the radar observation of distant objects such as aircraft. Quite early on, by the early fifties, these techniques were being used for the detection of radio signals emitted unexpectedly from distant objects in the universe. At the same time, ways were developed for bouncing radio signals from some of the near-by objects in the universe – the moon, the planets and the like. Over the years, there has grown up an entirely new discipline based on these techniques. For one thing, it is now possible to track the movement of objects in the solar system – not merely the planets but also, for example, the artificial space vehicles that are launched by the Russians and Americans. Radio-astronomy has also thrown a great deal of light on the construction of the Galaxy. In the past few years, in particular, it has been possible to pick out clouds of gas that consist not merely of hydrogen – the most common constituent of the Galaxy – but also of exceedingly sophisticated chemical molecules including such things as formaldehyde, hydrozine and ammonia. The mapping of these clouds of gas has helped enormously to simplify the understanding of how the stars of which the Galaxy is made may have evolved. Then, radio-astronomy has also made possible the exploration of the more distant parts of the universe. One of the chief discoveries has been that some but not all of the very distant galaxies, many of them beyond the range of optical observation, emit copious amounts of radio energy. Some of these are the so-called 'quasi-stellar' objects, the objects in the sky so far away that the light from them is reddened to an extraordinary degree but which nevertheless are so small that their size cannot be measured by the most refined techniques.

Two decades of radio-astronomy have shown first of all that the emission

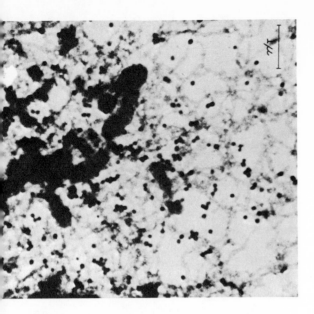

Cells in a tumour: by 1970 some forms of cancer were known to be characterized by foreign genetic material incorporated (possibly in virus form) into the hereditary nucleic acid

Dr Christiaan Barnard, the South African surgeon who performed the first heart transplant with a human donor on 3 December 1967; a year later initial optimism was dampened by the low survival rates

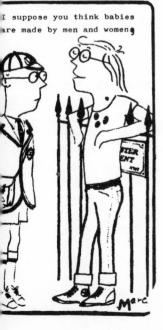

A *Times* cartoon by Marc on test-tube babies

of radio waves from objects in the heavens may be a more common phenomenon than had previously been suspected, and there has been a great deal of progress in understanding of how the movement of electrified particles, and particularly electrons, through the magnetic fields which seem to exist within galaxies such as the Milky Way could account for some of the radio emissions now being detected. But it is also equally clear that the emission of very large amounts of radio energy from the very distant galaxies cannot be explained without some missing piece in the jigsaw-puzzle. The chances are that what is going on represents a phenomenon intimately associated with the dense aggregation of matter into nebulae which are in some sense or another unstable. The emission of these very large amounts of radio energy may indeed represent occasions on which matter is actually being made to disappear.

The optical astronomers have also helped to sharpen some of the outstanding dilemmas in cosmology. In the past few years, for example, there has been spectacular progress in the extension of the region of the electromagnetic spectrum within which astronomical observations can be made. The search for infra-red radiation from stars and even from distant galaxies has been particularly important, and has been made possible by the development of balloons to carry infra-red telescopes above a large part of the atmosphere and also by the development of instruments which could be sited on high mountains and which are sensitive enough not to be grossly disturbed by carbon dioxide and water vapour in the atmosphere. More recently there has been the development of infra-red satellites which can circle the earth and make generous records of the amount of infra-red radiation which it emits. In the years ahead, these devices will clearly yield richly, but already it is plain that they support the subversive character of much of the information already gathered by the radio-astronomers.

The coming of rockets and satellites has also made it possible for astronomers to observe regions of the spectrum lying on the short wavelength side of what the classical optical astronomers have been able to observe – ultra-violet light, x-rays and even the exceedingly short wavelength and highly energetic x-rays called gamma rays. Here again, it seems, the universe is very much more active than people were first inclined to believe. It seems inevitable that the new observations in the ultra-violet and x-ray regions of the spectrum will help, first of all, further to confuse the present concept of how the universe is constructed and then, finally, may provide some of the clues with which a proper understanding can be constructed.

If, however, the results of the years 1945-70 have been to overturn a great many accepted views in cosmology without replacing them by views which can more readily be accepted, it is only fair to say that in the same period there has been deepening understanding of some of the more familiar processes which can be observed to occur in the comparatively near parts of the universe. Not the least of these is the close understanding which has now been generated of how ordinary stars evolve in the course of time. Even at the end of the Second World War there was almost complete confusion on this point. By that time, of course, astronomers had been able to identify several different types of stars in the neighbouring regions of the galaxy to which we belong. Some were small and hot – sometimes so hot that they seemed blue in appearance. Others were large and red, still others were small, intensely white but comparatively cold.

Why should there be such a variation in the different kinds of stars easily to be seen and how were they related to each other in evolutionary terms? Not until after the war did it become clear that the first step in the formation of a star, usually from a cloud of gas sometimes mixed with the debris of old exploded stars, is the aggregation together of a cloud of material which is, to begin with, large, diffuse, but hot in the middle. At the first stages of its evolution, this protostar is able to keep much of its energy because the outer cool layers of gas absorb the heat from the inside and prevent it from becoming hot. As time goes on, gravity pulls the matter of the star together so that eventually it becomes a hot, white, new star – and now it is possible to identify new regions in the Galaxy in which there seem to be clouds of gas

The 'continental drift' theory

If the continents are fitted together, like a gigantic jigsaw-puzzle, along the 2,000-metre contour of the continental shelf, the fit is too good to be coincidental. It is thought that the Americas, Europe and Africa could once have been one great land mass, which slowly tore apart.

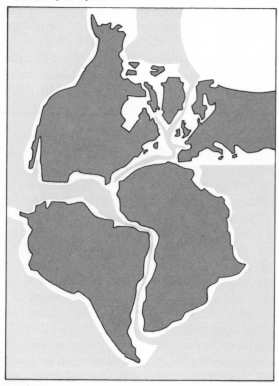

Left Scientists at Houston, Texas, note seismic data

Below Birth of an island in November 1963, south of Iceland; the area is about two square miles. Earthquake and volcanic activity along the faults in the earth's crust were linked in the sixties with the theory of continental drift

and dust, mostly hydrogen, embedded in which are clusters of new stars. Eventually, these new stars consume much of the hydrogen fuel which gives them energy and become less hot. The sun is at a comparatively early stage in its evolution but is already well past the point of extreme youth in which the star is more like a cloud of gas with heat in the middle than the compact object we can see in the sky each day. At a later stage in its evolution, the star becomes larger, because by then it has used up much of its hydrogen fuel and has to rely on other sources of nuclear energy, mostly helium and such materials. The red giant stars they are called – the prominent star Betelgeuse in the night sky is such a one. But the next stage is when all the fuel, hydrogen as well as helium, is exhausted. Then the star no longer has internal sources of energy with which to support its bulk and the outside collapses into a compact star.

One of several things may then happen. Either the star will be so small that it remains small and compact, comparatively invisible in the Galaxy, or it will be large enough for some catastrophic event to take place. Either there will be oscillations in which spurts of energy and matter are thrown off or, possibly, there will be a gigantic explosion in which the star as a whole will be destroyed, leaving perhaps only a small invisible remnant.

It has recently become plain that some of the most startling objects in the sky – the Crab nebula is perhaps the most conspicuous – are remnants of such exploded stars. It has also become clear that the strange stars which appear to send out a little burst of radio energy every now and again – the pulsating stars as they are called – are the terminal stages in the evolution of a star. One way and another, then, observational astronomy in the past few years has made clear the chain of evolutionary relationships between the different kinds of stars. It is striking how much of this work has been made possible by purely theoretical calculations of the ways in which stars of one kind or another should behave.

It is also remarkable how in the past few years the same theoretical astronomers, starting from their concern for the way in which different kinds of stars are related to each other, have been able to account for the way in which the natural elements – materials like iron and uranium – have been formed during the process of the evolution of stars. To begin with, all stars were made of hydrogen. The largest stars consume thermonuclear fuel which keeps them burning more quickly than the others and so they rapidly turn hydrogen first into helium, then into carbon, then into oxygen and then into still heavier elements. Eventually, the argument goes, these rapidly burning stars, usually the largest of them, explode and scatter the elements which they have created about the neighbouring regions of the galaxy. These materials are in turn incorporated in the substance of stars forming later stages in the evolution of a galaxy. The result is that the materials such as iron, aluminium and even oxygen which are familiar ingredients of ordinary life are themselves the fossilized debris of earlier exploded stars.

The changing face of physics

In much the same way as in astronomy, the high-energy physicists who have been principally concerned since the war with the development of techniques for understanding the relationships between different particles of matter – the so-called fundamental particles – have thrown light on a great many previous puzzles and have created problems which are at present well beyond the framework of what is now understood. At the end of the Second World War, the question of how matter is composed of smaller particles seemed almost within sight of a solution.

At the beginning of the century, Sir J.J. Thomson and Sir Ernest Rutherford between them had demonstrated first the existence of electrons and then the way in which atoms were put together from electrons in the heavier atomic particles known as protons and neutrons. By the early thirties, indeed, Sir James Chadwick had demonstrated the existence of neutrons and it had also been shown that there exist particles which are similar to electrons in every respect except that their electric charge is positive and not

Dr Louis Leakey: excavations in southern East Africa revealed skeleton fragments from creatures similar to apes and man, which seem to have been unsuccessful attempts at human evolution

Pieces of skull which helped change scholars' views of the time-scale of man's evolution: two and a half million years rather than the quarter of a million previously accepted

negative. In the late thirties, however, this simple catalogue of the basic particles had been made untidy by the discovery that cosmic rays – the particles which seem to reach the earth from distant parts of the Galaxy or even of the universe – contain particles apparently somewhere in between electrons and positrons in their mass. Specifically, these mesotrons as they were called were thought to be something like 200 times heavier than an electron and therefore something like one-ninth the mass of a proton. Not until after the war, when the physicists were able to get back to work, did it become clear that the mesotrons do indeed exist and that their existence poses all kinds of problems about the nature of the fundamental particles of which matter is constructed.

The first discovery was made possible by two technical developments – balloons which could fly to great height in the atmosphere and photographic plates which were sensitive enough to the passage of individual atomic particles for a track to be left behind in the emulsion. Both these developments were by the late Professor C. F. Powell from the University of Bristol. Quickly, however, it became plain that there was not one kind of mesotron but two, and these were called respectively the mu-mesons and the pi-mesons. But then it turned out that the mu-meson was in some peculiar way similar to the electron but just happened to be more than 200 times heavier. Its great mass and therefore the energy with which mu-mesons normally occurred in cosmic rays implied that mu-mesons could travel for very large distances through the atmosphere and through the rocks in the surface of the earth, so that one of the most convenient ways of detecting them was to carry apparatus to the bottom of a mine-shaft or even into an underground railway-tunnel.

The discovery of the pi-mesons was also important, chiefly because it opened the way to the discovery of a great many other apparently free-living particles of matter, each of them no larger than the nucleus of a hydrogen atom – a single proton – and each of them related to the others in a way which is not completely understood. The first discoveries of these quite unexpected particles came in the late forties, again in studies of cosmic rays, when it turned out that the meson particles were each of them two or three times heavier than an electron. There were also some particles which were 1,000 times heavier than an electron or even heavier, although only just heavier than a proton.

Since that time, a great many other heavy particles, as they are called, have been discovered, not merely in cosmic rays but also in the streams of electrons or protons which can be manufactured by the machines for accelerating particles to very high energies – machines such as those built immediately after the war at Berkeley in California and at Brookhaven, also in the United States and, more recently on a still larger scale in Geneva and Serpukhov in Siberia. One way and another, these machines have made it possible to create in the laboratory the particles which previously were not supposed to exist at all. The same work has shown how it is possible to turn one kind of atomic particle into another, apparently with ease, given the resources of a large accelerating machine.

All kinds of questions stem from fifteen years of work in this field. First, there are problems of simply understanding the relationships between the host of particles, most of them stable only for small fractions of a second. Then there are problems of understanding the relationships between these particles and, say, the more familiar particles which play a part in the construction of atomic nuclei – the protons and the neutrons, for example. There is some evidence that the unstable particles found in cosmic rays and created by the huge machines are somehow linked with the forces which exist between the more stable atomic particles and which, for example, are the forces which hold atomic nuclei together. Even so, the precise way in which this task might be accomplished by the unstable particles now being discovered is still only poorly understood. But there are still more important questions. What are the rules that govern the existence of atomic particles? What decides that one atomic particle is stable and another not? In the end, will the answer to that question depend on some new discovery about the

Launching of a radiosonde balloon from a Dutch weather ship near the Arctic Circle. After the war meteorological forecasting was coordinated on a world basis for safer travel

Infra-red photo of a hurricane from a weather satellite; the circular white mass (lower centre) is Hurricane Celia, 200 miles from Texas on 3 August 1970. The Great Lakes can be made out (upper centre)

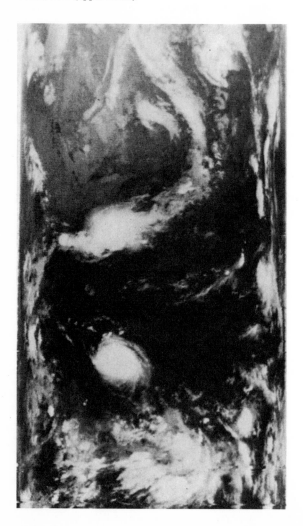

nature of the physical world, or about the character of the basic laws of physics? Following this line of speculation, a great many physicists in the past few years have been driven to the view that there will be no explanation of the puzzles which abound in the study of the most unstable and tiny elements of matter until an explanation has been found for the behaviour of the universe as a whole and in particular some of the puzzling features which have kept the cosmologists on the edges of their chairs for the past decade or so.

Continental drift

In the past few years there has already been a remarkable transformation of the generally accepted picture of how the surface of the earth has evolved. Since before the Second World War, it has been clear that the earth is some thousands of millions of years old. In the years after the war, by studies of radioactivity in ancient rocks, it has been possible to establish the age of the earth at something like 4,500 million years. For most of this time, however, it is quite clear that the earth was very different from what it is now. For much of the time, for example, the atmosphere was thicker and quite different in chemical constitution – more water vapour than at present and substantial quantities of exotic gases such as ammonia and methane as well. So far as can be told, the solid crust of the earth began to make its appearance something like 1,000 million years ago – this at least is the age of the oldest rocks which can be identified. But it is now also clear that the solid parts of the earth's surface were very different from what they are now and that, indeed, the continents as we know them have only existed for a little more than 100 million years – one-tenth of the length of time during which it is known that solid continents have been present on the surface of the earth and two per cent of the length of time during which the earth as a whole has been in existence.

What has brought about this change in the understanding of how the earth itself has evolved? The most striking of the recent developments is the way in which the theory of continental drift has come about. The origins of this exciting notion go back to the beginning of the century and the German scientist Alfred Wegener, who first put forward the notion that Africa and South America may once have been joined together, chiefly on the grounds that the opposing coasts of the South Atlantic could be imagined easily to fit one against the other. For a long time Wegener's theory was ridiculed. Only after the war, when people began making studies of the magnetism embedded in ancient rocks, supposedly a sign of how the ancient magnetism of the earth was pointed, did it become clear that there have indeed been changes in the relationships of the several continents to each other. For a great many years after the Second World War, these facts were something of a puzzle and attempts were made to explain them by the supposition that the North and South Poles – the magnetic poles – had wandered substantially from their present positions in the course of time.

These investigations also provided conclusive evidence that the earth's magnetism has not only changed in direction in the period of time covered by the rocks deposited on the surface of the earth but it has also turned itself inside out with surprising rapidity: now it seems to be accepted that at least in the recent geological history of the earth there has been one reversal of the magnetism every 200,000 years or so. By themselves, however, these investigations of the history of the earth's magnetism could not provide sufficient support for a theory as novel and radical as that of continental drift. The theory was only firmly established when oceanographers were able to provide direct evidence of how the continents may be driven about the surface of the earth by processes occurring at a considerable depth in the earth's crust.

The strange feature of the floor of the deep oceans known as the Mid-Atlantic Ridge provided, in the early sixties, the most valuable example of these processes in action. The Mid-Atlantic Ridge is in fact a long range of mountains rising several thousands of feet above the floor of the deep oceans, itself something like five miles below the surface of the sea. One of the sur-

A 70-foot carbon dioxide laser at Essex University which produces temperatures of up to two and a half million degrees centigrade: lasers have varied potential, including the controlled fusion of hydrogen atoms for power

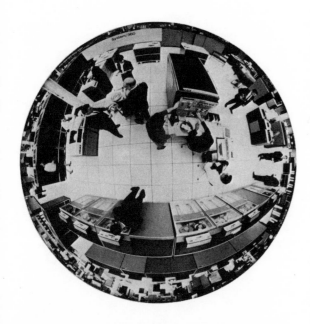

The computer revolution: (*above*) large IBM System/360 complex at NASA; (*below*) computer printout of a street map for the St Louis Police Department

prising features of this mountain range is that it seems to be for practical purposes symmetrical on the east and the west – on both sides of the mountain the sides fall away evenly from the central peaks. But the ridge is also more or less continuous – it runs from Iceland in the north down into the South Atlantic to a point at which it bifurcates south of St Helena, one part turning eastwards round southern Africa and the other moving towards the tip of South America and Antarctica.

From the beginning it was apparent that the Mid-Atlantic Ridge was associated with all kinds of volcanic activity: Iceland itself is a volcanic mass, and the same is true of the other islands – the Azores and St Helena – through which the Mid-Atlantic Ridge passes. Moreover, the ridge has been known to be associated with earthquakes while the magnetic evidence has made its function clear. What seems to happen is that bands of rock which are magnetized in opposing directions lie like long ribbons on either side of the ridge but running parallel with it. The implication is that these bands of rock somehow made their appearance on the ocean-floor at times in the past characterized by magnetic forces on the earth as a whole which were alternately reversed and normal. By careful study of these ribbons of rock, it has now been possible to establish that the Mid-Atlantic Ridge is really a long gap in the crust of the earth through which material in the form of volcanic rock has been extruded upwards from below and then spread out over the surface of the ocean-floor.

This provides an intimation that the surface of the earth as such is much more malleable than had previously been supposed. It also implies a way in which the continents may be pushed apart from each other by forces sufficiently big to change the ambience of the surface of the earth. In the past decade the working out of this theory has been exceedingly rapid. To begin with, there has been a systematic mapping of the ocean ridges in oceans other than the Atlantic.

On the basis of these studies and magnetic observations collected in the past two decades, it has been possible to reconstruct the relative movements of the continents over the surface of the earth in the past several 100 million years. In the South Atlantic, for example, where Wegener first let his theory run riot, it now seems clear that the two continents began to separate about 170 million years ago, when a huge rift valley like that now running the length of East Africa began to appear. The process of separation was slow, but eventually the sea appeared in huge gulfs in the super-continent, and many of the deposits of salt now to be found beneath the sea off the coasts of Africa and South America are relics of this time. The gulf cut in the primitive continent seems to have broadened steadily, and for much of the past 100 million years the Atlantic has become more than an inch wider every year. Moreover, there is no reason to suggest that the separation of South America and Africa has now ceased – most probably the drifting apart of the continents continues. The implications of this valuable new theory for geology as a whole are understandably profound; to begin with, it now becomes possible to work out the history of the continents for the past 300 million years or so.

One startling implication of this work is that most of the major continents – South America, Africa, Antarctica and Australia – were once united in a single continent now referred to as Gondwanaland. Second, it is clear that India, once a member of the super-continent of Gondwanaland, has moved quite rapidly northwards, the length of the Indian Ocean, so as to drive up against the great land mass of Asia. The existence of the Himalayas can be attributed quite simply to the collision of two continents in the past 50 million years or thereabouts.

Elsewhere in the world, hitherto equally puzzling features of the earth's crust can also be explained more easily. The faulting of the earth's surface on the Californian coast which makes San Francisco something of an earthquake hazard is, for example, a consequence of the way in which the western edge of the United States is being sheared off as if it were a woodshaving being removed from a piece of wood by the cutting edge of a plane. The same process is responsible for the volcanic islands lying to the north of the

Right Space research under the sea, 1970: NASA set up an underwater research station to examine the biological effects of stress situations on small groups of people living in isolation

Below One of the largest US research vessels, the fifteen-metre-long *Aluminaut*, can descend to 4,500 metres

Bering Straits. In South America, however, the long chain of seismic earthquake activity more or less the whole length of the western coast is now known to be attributable to the way in which material from the Mid-Atlantic Ridge is forced against the western edge of the South American continent and is required to move underneath the surface of South America, presumably to be returned eventually to the deep interior of the earth.

From this point of view, the continents are merely pieces of solid rock floating on what seems to be a continually if slowly moving mass of somewhat different rock within which huge currents surge up and along the surface and then back into the interior. This concept goes a long way to explain a number of puzzling features of the geophysics of the earth, not least the way in which the heat is released in different amounts beneath the sea (where comparatively large quantities of heat escape to the surface) and beneath the continents (where heat is less easily to be found).

One of the most striking evidences of these tectonic processes still in action is to be found in East Africa and its conjunction with the Middle East. For one thing it now seems that the Rift Valley of East Africa is really the beginning of a process likely eventually to lead to the splitting off of Somaliland, Ethiopia and large parts of Tanzania; it looks as if the gulf is widest at the north where the Red Sea has for several thousands of years been invading northern Ethiopia and Somaliland. But it is also clear that a great many features off the east coast of Africa, the island of Madagascar and even the Seychelles group of islands, for example, are products of earlier splinterings of the African continent. And so it seems that just as new continents or at least new land masses are being created by volcanic activity above the mid-oceanic ridges – Iceland for example – so the older continents and Africa in particular are being worn away by the continuing processes of upheaval in the earth's crust.

Understanding primitive man

If the origin of the now familiar features of the earth has been so much clarified in the past few years, so too has been the origin of living creatures and indeed of life as such. One of the most impressive developments has been the way in which the history of the human race has been carried back in time to span close on 3 million years. Most of the exciting discoveries relating to the ancestry of man have come from southern East Africa. The chief effect has been to distinguish between some ape-like creatures which are almost certainly along the line of descent to man and other creatures,

Below C.S.Cockerell's 1956 model of the hovercraft, designed to carry medium loads at above economic ship speed (i.e. 20 m.p.h.). Beneath it is the world's first hovercraft – the sr-n1, utilizing the principle of an air cushion to reduce water friction. By 1966 British Rail were operating cross-Channel services

Tokyo monorail service, opened in September 1964: a link between Tokyo Airport and the city centre at an average speed of 37 m.p.h.

very similar in many ways to both apes and man, which appear to have been unsuccessful attempts at the evolution of the human species.

The excavations of pre-human skeletons from the Olduvai Gorge in Tanzania has been one of the most prolific sources of information. Chiefly because of the excavations of Dr Louis Leakey and his colleagues in Tanzania, it has become apparent that the length of time during which human beings have been evolving is much more like $2\frac{1}{2}$ million years than the quarter of a million years or thereabouts previously supposed to span the descent of man from ape-like ancestors to *Homo sapiens*. In the process it has also been possible to define with some accuracy the characteristics of the creatures on the line of descent to man. Some of the most distinctive of these are now known as the Australopithecenes, sometimes small and sometimes large but able to walk more erect than apes and carrying in their heads a brain considerably larger than that of the apes among whom they lived. Largely because of the richness of the deposits in southern Africa compared with those further north, there is now every chance that the past 20 million years or so in the history of the evolution of man will be written in some detail on the basis of palaeontological investigations.

But where did life as a whole begin? And how? This is a point on which biochemists and others have provided valuable evidence in the past few years. To begin with, it is now clear that the conditions under which living things were first formed were very different from those which now exist on the earth. The primeval atmosphere consisting mainly of ammonia and methane may, for example, have provided the chemical constituents needed to make biological molecules of a kind which are still to be found in living things. In the fifties, experiments in the United States showed that electrical discharges, similar to those which may be produced by lightning, could yield some of the primitive small chemical molecules from which more complicated biological material may have been derived. Since then, a great many experimentalists have been able to demonstrate that quite simple chemicals can in suitable circumstances be turned into complicated chemicals which are themselves related to the proteins and even the nucleic acids which play a vital part in living things. At the same time there has been a rapid deepening of understanding of the processes by means of which assemblies of inanimate chemicals can be thought of as functioning as if they were alive. In short, the stage now seems set for understanding just how it came about that living things first made their appearance. It is entirely consonant with this that, with the prompting of cosmologists and astronomers, there has grown up the belief that other kinds of living things than those known on the earth most probably exist elsewhere in the universe.

With scientific activity it is always hard to tell when discovery will rid people's minds of questions and when it will provoke questions that cannot yet be answered. The end of the nineteenth century was a time when scientists and their audience were inclined to think that most things had been understood. The twentieth century seems to have been one long recitation of the now familiar principle that most solutions to most problems create more problems. This, for example, is what has happened in high-energy physics. The discovery of the particles called mesons in the years after the war helped to explain some unexpected properties of cosmic rays but has created a whole range of questions about the reasons for the existence of matter in the forms in which it is known to exist. Similarly, molecular biology has made a great deal of biology rational but has also sharpened the challenge of how to explain, for example, the way in which living things develop.

Undoubtedly, the general public discontent with science as an intellectual pursuit owes something to this maddening opposition between discovery and conundrums. In ordinary circumstances, it would be reasonable to expect that a person with a great discovery to report would somehow also be able to lay at rest uncertainties about the nature of the real world and the likely direction of its evolution. The perpetual doubt which scientists create is by contrast infuriating. The fact that from these shifting sands must spring the appurtenances of prosperity must inevitably seem to the layman an assault on reason rather than an assault on the unknown.

The Great Adventure

German developments in long-range rocketry during the Second World War had given man, for the first time, the means to break away from his planet. Both the United States and Russia had eagerly recruited German scientists at the end of the war, but it was not until 1957, when the Russians launched the first satellite, that the space race really began. Initially, the Russians led the way: in April 1961 they put the first man, Yuri Gagarin, into space; and in August 1961 they consolidated their lead when German Titov made a flight of seventeen orbits in *Vostok 2*. The American reaction was hesitant at first, but in July 1961 President Kennedy gave his country a clear goal, to which all other aspects of space exploration were subordinated – the landing of a man on the moon before the decade was out.

Above The first earth satellite on display in Moscow; *Sputnik 1* weighed 180 lb and was launched on 4 October 1957

Left Yuri Gagarin strapped down in the *Vostok* on 12 April 1961 before the first flight into space; he returned safely after one orbit

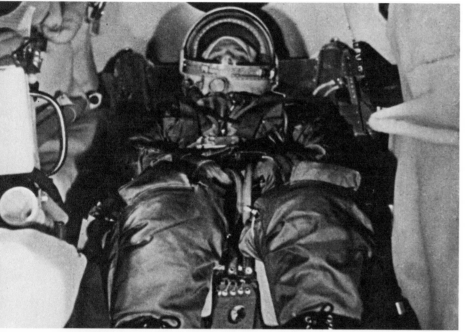

Below left Lunokhod: which the Russians claim provided as much scientific information in 1970 as the more spectacular American manned programme. The USSR made the first soft landings on the moon and Venus

Below TV picture of Russian *Cosmos 112* and *113* sputniks carrying out docking experiments (1968)

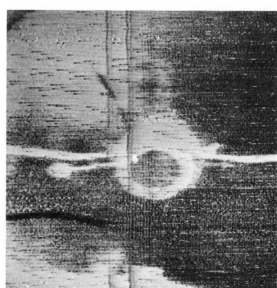

Left The scene at Grand Central Station on 20 February 1962, when John Glenn became the first American to orbit the earth

The first ten years in space 1957-67

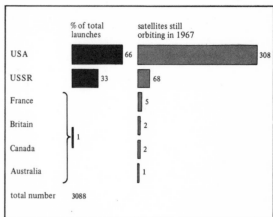

	% of total launches	satellites still orbiting in 1967
USA	66	308
USSR	33	68
France		5
Britain	1	2
Canada		2
Australia		1
total number	3088	

Left Man walks in space: Russian and American astronauts first walked in space in March and June 1965 respectively

One Small Step

President Kennedy's goal was achieved on 20 July 1969, when Neil Armstrong stepped on to the moon's surface. The epic journey of *Apollo 11* caught the imagination of the world and was the most spectacular achievement of the space race. But even as it was taking place, powerful forces were at work suggesting that future developments in space exploration should concentrate on simpler, less expensive, and more immediately useful projects. The enormous Apollo programme had been set up largely for reasons of prestige to provide a national goal, and it had overshadowed solid achievements in the development of communications, weather and scientific satellites. At a fairly early stage, the Russians had opted out of attempting to beat America to the moon, and they had concentrated on building up considerable experience in assembling manned orbital space stations and in developing robot vehicles which could be landed on the planets far more cheaply and safely than the American manned projects. As American doubts about the Apollo programme led to a progressive trimming of future flights, it came to be seen that a new approach would be needed for space exploration in the 1970s.

Above Cape Kennedy: Command Service Module for *Apollo 11* (right) which made the first moon landing. On the left is the spacecraft for *Apollo 12*

Above right The Stars and Stripes, first planted on the moon on 20 July 1969

Right Footprints on the moon: US astronauts Neil Armstrong and Edwin Aldrin, who took off in *Apollo 11* on 16 July 1969, touched down and collected rock and soil specimens on 20 July and splashed down in the Pacific four days later

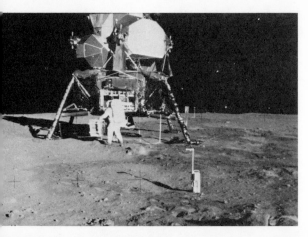

Left Edwin Aldrin takes down scientific apparatus from the lunar module after the 20 July landing. In the front of the picture is a 35 mm stereo camera

Below Against the background of a half-lit earth, the ascent stage of the lunar module rises on 21 July to meet the command ship piloted by Michael Collins in orbit

President Nixon (right) with the *Apollo 11* astronauts, Armstrong, Collins and Aldrin, who are in quarantine on 24 July aboard the recovery carrier USS *Hornet*. Nixon's comment: 'the world has never been closer together'

Friedrich Heer

Creeds and Ideologies

During the twenty-five years following the end of the Second World War a process was taking place which had been foreseen by critical observers in the nineteenth century such as Kierkegaard, Marx and Nietzsche. This was the decay of Christian belief and it was evident throughout the Christian Church. The vacuum thus created was rapidly filled by sects and political ideologies which had absorbed some of the essence and the fanaticism of the older religious-political Christian ideologies. Europe, and to an ever-increasing extent North America, began to absorb the religious ideas of the Near and Far East like a sponge. By 1960 many young American students and intellectuals were enthusiastic about Buddhist, Indian, Chinese and Japanese methods of contemplation; they were also beginning to show great interest in Francis of Assisi and were attracted by the early French wandering scholars. In fact they were creating an atmosphere similar to that of Paris or Berlin or Vienna between 1880 and 1900.

At the same time coloured gods began to emerge in the white continents of Western Europe and the USA. Red Indian gods and, in secondary forms, the cults and rites of Great Black Mother Africa were penetrating the Red-Indian, African-White world of South and North America. A new epoch of syncretism seemed to have begun: the white cities, nearly bursting with people conscious of their spiritual emptiness, were reminiscent of Rome in the first century AD when the gods of the Hellenist world began to advance from Asia Minor, conquering men and their places of worship.

'The crisis of Christianity' is an old theme of Protestant theology. During the period 1945-70 this crisis developed into a phenomenon of world significance within the Roman Catholic Church. Pope Pius XII (1939-58) had tried using disciplinary measures to suppress the spiritual unrest which had previously caused an explosion in the form of 'Modernism', and which at the time of the Second World War was being cautiously expressed in the works of certain French, German and Dutch theologians. When in 1942 the French Dominican, M.D.Chenu, was condemned by the Church on account of a paper which he had written in 1937, Cardinal Suhard, the Archbishop of Paris, said to him 'Don't be upset, Little Father, in twenty years time everyone will be speaking as you do now.' Twenty years later, Pope John XXIII (1958-63), realizing the danger of an explosion, tried to make the Church take 'a leap forward'. (Let us bear in mind the significance of 'great leap forward' ideology advocated by Marxist revolutionary thinkers, not least Mao Tse-tung.) John convened the Second Vatican Ecumenical Council. (Pius XII had often thought of convening a Council but he had been afraid of the possible consequences.) At Pope John's Council the advisers of the Council fathers, the cardinals and bishops turned out to be those leading theologians who had been the victims of the great purge of 1949-58 – who had lost their chairs (like Lubac), or been exiled into the desert (as Congar, who was sent away from Paris to Jerusalem); others had 'voluntarily' renounced their desire to discuss 'burning topics' in theology (as Karl Rahner and other members of the Society of Jesus).

The Second Vatican Council

The Second Vatican Council (11 October 1962 to 8 December 1965), described as 'a Council of transition' by D.A.Seeber and as 'the beginning of a beginning' by Rahner, was the first attempt by the Roman Catholic Church in the twentieth century to give an account of herself: the 2,500 delegates (who had been influenced by very uniform European-Latin modes of

In the West, the decline of all forms of Christian belief: in Russia and Eastern Europe, perhaps, a surviving link with the old order

Top The election of Pope John XXIII (1958-63)
Above Pope John; popular, approachable and far from austere, his brief papacy brought some of the Catholic skeletons out into the open

Poster for the Eucharistic Congress (1960)

thought, with the exception of the representatives of the Oriental Churches) learned, to their astonishment, that a certain amount of free expression was possible in the middle of papal Rome. For most of them this was an overwhelming experience.

At this Council something happened which was unique in the history of the Roman Church, inconceivable even in her own eyes – it was something 'unheard-of', 'unlawful', 'scandalous' in the view of conservative ecclesiastical theologians: heretics of the kind that had been persecuted for almost a thousand years, heretics who had often been proclaimed 'exterminated', who as recently as the nineteenth century had been attacked in papal encyclicals as 'sons of Belial', 'devil's brood', 'a blot in the history of mankind', were now taking part in discussions at the Council of leading representatives, as guests.

The 'arch-heretics' among this distinguished gathering were Pelagians (viciously persecuted since the fifth century), Waldensians (often brutally persecuted since the thirteenth century, and often proclaimed 'exterminated' in Italy), the spiritual heirs of Wyclif, and men of the Church of England who had been attacked by the papal church more for political than for theological reasons, Lutherans, Calvinists, members of Free Church congregations, Unitarians, Quakers and representatives of the Greek Orthodox Eastern Church. More than *two* worlds confronted each other here!

Most of the Council delegates, it is true, failed to grasp that 'Rome' was on the brink of revoking her ecclesiastical ideology. In her conception of herself there was only *one* true Christianity: this was embodied in the representative of Christ on earth – the Pope. *One* Christianity, *one* Church, *one* 'pure doctrine': Rome, the holy city, centred round the Holy Father, the Pope. Until this event – the presence of the 'heretics' as 'observers' at the Second Vatican Council – the Roman conception of 'the one holy, Roman Catholic Church' had allowed no recognition of Christians who thought differently or of non-Roman Christians, as Christians.

In Rome during 1962-5 an ideological self-renunciation took place *de facto*, not theologically; the thousand-year-old conception of the Roman papacy, the Roman Church itself, its whole teaching, its whole past was being challenged.

Roma locuta, causa finita: when the Church had passed judgement, the 'case' was finished as far as she was concerned. Thus the 'Jews, the murderers of God' had ceased to exist in ecclesiastical history. The heretics had been 'liquidated'. Now, however, in the middle of the twentieth century – and this was the great experience of Giovanni Roncalli, later John XXIII – the heretics, theists and atheists, Christians and non-Christians, Muslims, Jews, Buddhists and members of other religions were demanding of the Roman Church a new self-conception. Perhaps the Church herself would prove to be *de facto* no more than a 'sect'.

The chain of reaction, starting when the Council ended and developing swiftly into a revolutionary change in the Roman Church, began at this Janus-headed Council. The Council fathers were – as even Roman Catholic observers pointed out – solely concerned during the Council with efforts to enable *their* Church to achieve an *aggiornamento*, to adapt itself to the present. The Church should 'function' better, should use a 'modern' language, should consider 'worldly matters'. Thus it was soon shown how infinitely unworldly the vast majority of the Council delegates were. The unique atmosphere created by Pope John enabled questions and difficulties to be discussed at Council debates, which until then had been taboo.

The presence of distinguished theologians belonging to other Christian churches (and communities which no longer regard themselves as churches) forced a confrontation with Christian theologies and ideologies which Rome throughout its history had condemned. Pope Paul VI, who conducted the Council after the death of Pope John, considered the most important question to be that of the bishop's office: how could the pope maintain his absolute authority against the bishops and their demand to participate in decision-making?

182

The vast majority of the Council delegates found their horizons widened in a way that had never happened in their lives before. Cardinal König of Vienna, commenting on Archbishop Weber's (Strasbourg) exegesis, warned the Council against believing the Bible to be wholly free from error. In fact, he said, it contained 'a great many' historical errors, false renderings and unscientific statements. The authors of the Bible, he stressed, had had only limited knowledge of the historical information relevant to their time.

Cardinal Lercaro (Bologna) declared in a motion considered by many to be the most important at the Council, that the Church must divest herself of her 'old-fashioned attitude'. The Church, he said, was not a cultural museum; she must liberate herself from scholasticism. Lercaro attacked ignorance and spiritual narrow-mindedness; he demanded sober thought, the courage of the Church to embark on a new course and to recognize historical reality.

Archbishop Edelby, right-hand man to Patriarch Maximos IV of Antioch, explained that 1,200 years of development in the wrong direction could not be corrected in two years. Edelby related this to Rome's ancient struggle against the Greek Church. Many Council delegates were shocked when they heard German Council advisers, quoting Ratzinger and Rahner, declare at a press conference: 'Dogma is not a neatly tied parcel, but an open window.' Again and again the question arose which Cardinal Ottaviani, the head of the conservative Council fathers, had raised: did the Church go wrong earlier? Cardinal Alfrink, the spokesman of the Dutch Church, declared in the midst of the Council: 'After 2,000 years we stand before the people in a dubious light. We should also remember that more than 2,000 million people have never heard the Gospel preached.'

A Peruvian Indian in the High Sierra, where many, although nominally Catholic, believe in the old gods of the earth and sky as well

A Czech priest: the sign reads 'Forward to the victory of socialism'

Archbishop Hurley (Durban), one of the most independent of the Council fathers, challenged the Roman curial ideology that the Church 'is *in possession* of the whole truth': 'History shows us that men do not reach any significant truth without first having made mistakes. If you want to make man's freedom and his rights dependent on whether he has already penetrated to the truth, you are denying him the right to think for himself. . . . Man is not free *because* he is in possession of the truth, but *so that* he can search for truth. We must guard our right to search and to make mistakes [*ius quaerandi et errandi*]. He who has never erred, does not seek.'

Here Anglo-Saxon traditions of democracy and empirical thought were beating on the iron gates of the Roman Church. When the French Bishop Lefèbre, defending the absolute authority of the pope, argued that 'things have gone on for two thousand years like this and there is no reason why they should not continue to do so', an American bishop replied that the Catholic Church must learn what democracy is, and Catholics must master the art of 'disagreeing without being disagreeable'.

Conciliar consequences

Two controversial issues in the years following the Council were: the deep, magic power of the Church as a cult and (related to it) the maintenance of celibacy. When the Italian Archbishop Dante, the papal master of ceremonies, expressed his regret that the liturgy no longer included the veneration of relics, the Spanish Bishop Garcia answered that he hoped the Church might soon see her way decently to bury and forget such relics as the milk and the veil of the Virgin Mary, or the sandals of St Joseph. (Erasmus of Rotterdam had demanded this in the sixteenth century.) The eighty-four-year-old Patriarch Maximos IV of Antioch, refusing to speak in Latin – he belonged to the Greek rite – and ignoring Pope Paul VI's ban on the discussion on celibacy, remarked that the official standpoint of the Roman Church on sexuality was only comprehensible as the expression of a kind of bachelor neurosis.

The authorities in Rome were alarmed by an experiment taking place in Mexico: Prior G. Lemercier of the Benedictine monastery at Quernavaca, (originally from Belgium), was having his monks psychoanalyzed – those who volunteered, that is. Lemercier was supported by his bishop, Mendez Arceo – who at the Council suggested that the Church should recognize the discoveries of Sigmund Freud. Mendez Arceo also urged that the Church should be reconciled to the Freemasons and that she renounce her deeply rooted anti-Semitism. Could the Roman Church leap over her thousand-year-old shadow? The difficulty of this question was revealed in the debate on the Jewish question. The American Cardinal Cushing, speaking for a

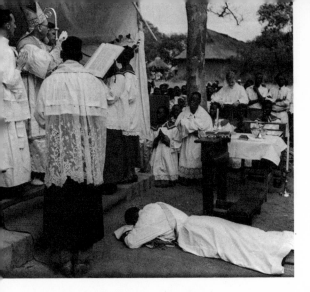

An African ordination ceremony, in which the ordinand falls at the feet of the officiating bishop

Below Pope Paul with King Hussein on his 1964 visit to the Holy Land
Bottom Communion for a Colombian worker in Bogota

majority of the Council delegates who were in favour of a Christian confession of murders committed by Christians against the Jews, declared that if the Jews were murderers of God, so were we all. The Council should, he suggested, admit that in the past and at the present time we had not always behaved towards the Jews as true Christians should. Many Christians had watched the sufferings of the Jews with passivity or indifference.

The statement on the Jews, condemning anti-Semitism, which was brought out at the wish of Pope John, dwindled during the Council, and above all, behind the back of the Council, into Article Four of the 'Declaration concerning the Church's relationship to the non-Christian religions "*nostra aetate*"', which was described by distinguished theologians as 'mean' and 'pathetic'.

Three directions emerged as a consequence of the Second Vatican Council. First, some bishops and cardinals tried to 'realize' the suggestions and proclamations made at the Council through cautious reform from above. Second, anxious conservatives tried to wipe out the memory of Pope John XXIII (by, for example, removing his portrait from Italian churches). They regarded the Council as a disaster, the beginning of the Church's self-destruction. Third, theologians saw the Council as, at best, the 'beginning of a beginning', for it had not faced up to the most important questions.

The situation was illuminated by an unprecedented development: the pope, Paul VI, was exposed to bitter criticism from theologians of 'his' own Church. Paul VI, a Hamlet figure (according to John XXIII), a sensitive, scrupulous man, sought to steer the Church on a path of moderate reform. To his alarm, things seemed to be getting out of hand: he was bombarded by 'outrageous', 'forbidden', 'free' opinions, and by demands for reform which he was convinced would question the very existence of the Church.

Paul VI said of the papacy: 'Here is the teaching function of the Church, the seat of its highest authority, its most sublime role: that of teaching, not an ordinary subject, but the Word of God, interpreting its true meaning, if necessary with infallibility . . .' (General Audience, 12 January 1967). A questionnaire sent to Dutch priests – 'What do you think of the concept of the infallibility of the Pope?' – can be seen as a reaction not only to Paul's absolutism but to his anxiety over the criticism of him by leading theologians. Here are some of their answers: 'This is the ultimate in regional narrow-mindedness – it is myopia, almost blindness. Infallibility is a technical term and is not appropriate.' 'A Renaissance term.' 'Irrelevant today.' 'A false construction bearing no relation to what most people today would call "infallible".' 'Irreconcilable with the Gospel.' 'Infallibility is part of that ecclesiastical view which treats men as children.' In 1970 one of the leading progressive European theologians, Hans Küng, a Swiss (it is not without significance that the *avant-garde* among Catholic theologians came from countries with a long democratic tradition) demonstrated in his book *Unfehlbar?* (*Infallibility?*) the untenability of the dogma of papal infallibility, a principle which had already been declared historically and evangelically erroneous by leading Catholic Church historians such as Ignaz von Döllinger during the turbulent First Vatican Council.

During the world-wide discussion within the Catholic Church of the encyclical *Humanae vitae* concerning marriage and sexuality, and forbidding the use of the 'pill', the pope was accused of having at the beginning of his pontificate expressed support for a 'dialogue within the Church' and 'a dialogue between the Church and the outside world' and then of making decisions without any dialogue having taken place. According to Walter Dirks in *The Pope against the Church*, his decision had been taken 'in favour of four as against seventy-one theologians in the commission, against the opinion of important bishops and cardinals . . . , contrary to the resolution drawn up by the lay advisory body, against the views of leading moral theologians, at least in Europe. . . . At no point in his letter does the pope admit the limitations of knowledge concerning individual human experience; he never asks, he always knows.'

The conflict between ecclesiastical Roman ideology and scientific knowledge is strikingly visible here: the pope 'made his decision not only against

A meeting of dissident priests; many in the sixties could no longer accept the doctrines of celibacy and papal infallibility

The rock of faith: the titular bishop of Libya on stage with his pop group Los Robis in Madrid. The bishop believes in proper understanding between the clergy and young people

the majority view, which of course could be mistaken, but in the face of scientific knowledge and in the face of social development. He is demanding that the faithful obey his decision which is hostile both to development and to reality.'

The significance of the arguments about Paul VI goes far beyond the immediate case. Today the whole magical, hieratic structure of the Church is being questioned: the pope as half-God, as 'more than man, but less than God' (as the medieval scholars regarded him), as the embodiment of Christ living on in the Church; bishops and priests as 'gods' (as they are described in a Psalm), as magic authorities who administer the magic sacraments.

The battle to rid Christianity of magic begins in the Roman Church with the battle to demythologize the hierarchy: 'hierarchical power must give way to the service given by the Church, clerical despotism to spiritual leadership; closed, rigid attitudes to an open approach to all reality; fear of freedom to courage to be committed; distrust to honourable cooperation; dependency (so much desired up till now) to Christian responsibility . . .' (Hans Küng).

Paul VI emphatically forbade the discussion of celibacy urged at the Second Vatican Council. In the discussions concerning Paul's encyclical *Sacerdotalis caelibatus* of 24 June 1967 which clung to the magic conception of celibacy, Catholic theologians argued 'that biblical words and images which were intended for the disciples of Jesus or other faithful believers are being irresponsibly exploited by the celibate officials of the Roman Church. . . .' This and other defects 'must be mentioned, since not until we consider the ideological vulnerability of *Sacerdotalis caelibatus* do we begin to get some idea of the true extent of the incredible nature of the circular. . . .'

They have pointed to the disastrous results for the Church of enforced celibacy, and – in self-criticism – 'Catholic theologians' extreme tactlessness on the subject of love, women. . . .' History has shown that the sexual fear prevalent in the later ecclesiastical communities has deformed Jesus' 'gloriously healthy and natural attitude to sexuality'. It was influences from outside the Church that led to celibacy. Even today Roman ideologists still adhere to the thesis put forward by a cardinal at the sixteenth-century Council of Trent: 'If priests were allowed to marry, the interests of their families, their wives and their children would tear them away from their dependency on the Pope.' Underlying this thesis is the assumption that there is a connection between celibacy and submissiveness to authority.

In *A Modern Priest looks at his Outdated Church* (New York, 1967) Father James Kavanaugh describes the priests' rebellion against the distortion and perversion of sex in a church run by celibates. 'I preached orthodoxy with the fanaticism of a madman . . . with her fear of sex, the clergy's sexual envy and her perverted ideology of sin, my Church has terrorized countless men and women to death.' Books of this kind were written in Central Europe fifty, eighty years ago by 'apostate' priests who had left the Church. Today these subjects are being debated within the Roman Church, most openly in Holland and South America. Here the conviction is being expressed that enforced celibacy must be abandoned: 'Soon there will be married priests. It must be so. The seminaries are empty. We are unable to continue with the traditional education of priests. Far too many people whom we cannot afford to do without – valuable creative people, are not becoming priests because of the celibacy rule. The priest of the future will be secularized, will be more worldly, a man of the world in which he lives and works. It does not matter whether he is married or not. . . .'

Celibacy and the Church's conception of sexuality are related to the magic concept of 'holy chastity', the concentrate of the divine seed within men and women who remain 'untouched'. For a long time the monk was regarded as the only true Christian, the Virgin Mary as the only true woman. During 1945-70 the movement within the Catholic Church in favour of ridding the Church of its magic waged a growing battle – against, for example, the magic, incantatory use of the Bible, against the image of the priest as a magician (a priest admits: 'the people still see us as magicians . . .'), against infant baptism, confirmation (regarded as a magic initiation, like those of

Above In Switzerland the first women were ordained as priests in 1963, but by the end of the decade they still did not have the vote in local elections

The Church moves with the times:
(*above*) a British cartoonist's view;
(*below*) no Surrealist montage, but a mobile church with stained-glass windows

primitive peoples), the Eucharist, the ordination (priest as medicine-man).

The 'layman' in the Church had no rights at all against this powerful and experienced hierarchy of Pope, bishops and priests. The 'lay uprising' within the Church was led largely by theologians during the period 1958-70. They pointed out that in the New Testament there is no clergy and no laity. Christ speaks to his 'brothers'. They discussed themes such as 'Is the Church to be believed?', and 'Is the Church becoming the tomb of God?' Robert Adolfs, prior to the Augustinian monastery in Eindhoven, Holland, who worked from 1954 to 1960 as a teacher and chaplain in the USA, maintained that the Roman Catholic Church had shown itself to be untrustworthy in its teaching and in its practice. The Church was now like an 'Indian reservation', a ghetto, alien to an advanced industrial society. Adolfs recommended that the Church's sacred centre – the focal point which Catholics claim to be the centre of the universe, St Peter's in Rome – be made into a museum.

'Not one of our deacons still believes in God' – this was said by the anxious head of a seminary to the Swiss Dominican, Gonsalv Mainberger. Today the leading theologians of the Roman Church are convinced that 'we are never in possession of the truth'. 'Expressed in theological terms this means that dogmas are basically evolutionary' (Schillebeeck). 'While dogma is based on thought and originates from an intellectual consideration of faith it cannot claim to represent an eternal truth.'

In *Dogma unter dem Wort Gottes* (1965), Walter Kasper of Münster, Westphalia, insists that dogmas are not literally the Word of God but a human-ecclesiastical way of referring to God's turning to mankind through Jesus Christ. 'Dogmas are necessary as guide-lines for life, as essential signposts for society and history. But they should be formulated in such a manner that they do not exclude their own demise – on the contrary, they should affirm it. Their death enables their inherent truth to live on. Rigid dogmatism is like the avarice of old men who cannot die' (W.Weymann-Weyhe). The Dominican Mainberger explains it thus: 'Belief is aimed at the truth. Truth is not the Bible and it is not dogma. Truth is the Word of God. The relationship of Bible and dogma to truth is similar to that between the rays of the sun, focused in a magnifying glass, and the sun itself, when the rays set paper alight. The setting alight of the paper is similar to belief. The paper burns and the burning represents the sun. Similarly, belief represents truth. The truth remains. Belief burns up. The dogmas are left as ashes.'

This is what frightens the conservatives: is not the Church burning down and – in the fire-storm created by the revolutionaries among the theologians – perhaps faith itself in Christ and the Gospel?

The answers given by critical Catholic biblical scholars to this urgent question are not reassuring. The scholars themselves were having to face the challenge of questions provided by 150 years of Protestant biblical research, questions which had been taboo in the Catholic Church until the death of Pius XII. In a 'remarkable upsurge in biblical, historical-critical theology' (S.Schulz), Catholic research had caught up with astonishing speed (Rudolf Pesch). This research revealed how little we really know about Jesus as a human being. 'Because virtually the last thing we know for a fact about Jesus is his death. After this we have only the historical evidence of those who claim to have seen him, but we cannot accept this evidence as historical fact.' The focal point of traditional Christian faith, the belief in the resurrection of Christ, was now wavering, even in the Church of Rome. Distinguished theologians admitted that the resurrection is untenable as an historical event; it can only be understood as an act of faith.

What does the Roman Church of Christ think about Jesus today? Paul VI maintained (4 January 1967): 'You must appreciate, my beloved sons, the importance of your being gathered here together, physically as well as spiritually, in one *place, where Christ's presence is most strongly felt*, which is in a sense unique because it *guarantees us* the orthodoxy of our view. *Here* is the Epiphany of Christ.' The reaction of Dutch priests to this Roman belief in Christ expressed by Paul VI is: 'No, that is magic.'

What does Jesus of Nazareth mean to progressive Catholics today? A Dutch questionnaire produced a multitude of different answers. But they

In the fifties and sixties Billy Graham, the American revivalist crusader, made bids for mass instant conversions to Christ (Earl's Court, London, 1966)

The Salvation Army: nearly a century of temperance, nonconformism and campaigns among the urban poor

have two things in common: firstly, they reject orthodox expressions such as 'Saviour', 'Son of God', 'Redeemer', 'Mediator', 'Good Shepherd', 'Messiah', 'Lamb of God', etc. Secondly, they take Jesus as a person very seriously: 'He is the truly human man. He chose humanity in all its forms, and so he embodies hope. That is what Jesus of Nazareth means to me.' 'He is the most profound realization of myself . . . the most profound level at which a man can live, which gives value to this life . . . this realization lives on in one.' 'He is the ideal of humanity, the norm of humanity. This means more to me than his divinity.'

These replies are quoted because they show the similarity between statements made by Dutch Catholics and those of Protestant Christians and non-Christians from all continents. Young atheist Russians, Polish agnostic intellectuals, elderly Japanese Buddhists, North American hippies and South American communist revolutionaries were united in this personal, intimate attitude to the young Jew in Jerusalem who fought against the temple of the Jewish high priests and against the bastions of the Roman occupying power. A German Catholic lay theologian saw him thus: 'Our religion continually pictures a gentle Jesus gathering round him a band of simple, though devout men. This image is a caricature, and a harmful one at that. Jesus himself was a revolutionary prophet. Today he would be described as an intellectual, indeed, as a left-wing intellectual' (H.R. Schlette).

What remains then, if we rid the Church of its magic and its ideology? A Franciscan answered: 'What the Church should do now is to exercise its proper function, to serve . . . to bring about a tangible "kenosis", a process of self-renunciation . . . a de-clericalization, a de-institutionalization, a pruning of much that is overgrown and outlived, a purging of concepts, a reappraisal of the Church service and of the ethics of the Church. The Church must apply the words of the Gospel to herself: "He that loseth himself shall find it." This is the true meaning of the statement "The Church must die, so that the congregation may be resurrected."' A professor of theology answered: 'Not only every Christian but every Church will have to die and be resurrected with Christ.' A Carmelite monk answered: 'Because many of us can no longer see the presence of Christ expressed in our everyday life, in the traditional Church service, we come to the radical conclusion that we must "tear down this temple".'

The hardest blow for conservative Catholics came from the newly emerging political theology which advocated that Christians should follow the example of Jesus the rebel and support the oppressed everywhere in the world. It even advocated the human right to make a *violent* revolution.

While in Europe this political theology often seemed merely academic, justifying the criticism that most revolutionary theologians had regular salaries with guaranteed pensions and sat safely at home while they urged others into action, the involvement of theologians and laity in South America showed that political theology could be a deadly serious matter. The theologian Camilo Torres, who acted as spiritual adviser to students, took part in guerrilla warfare and was killed. He is the 'Catholic Che Guevara'.

Rebellion *within* the Church and revolutionary opposition to political regimes are different matters, but they thrive in the same intellectual climate. The experiment of Don Mazzi in Isolotto (Savonarola 1954-69; the battle of a country priest against the Triumphalist Church of the Archbishop of Florence), the opposition of young priests in Spain and Latin America, the underground Church in North America and the priests in the Civil Rights movement . . . the individual aspects of these movements were very different. But they all shared a desire to do away with outdated ideological encumbrances and to achieve a relaxation in the Church's attitude to other Christian Churches, to atheists and to the old political opponents of the Church, the communists.

Conservative theologians demanded the expulsion of the 'Progressives' from the Church: 'In practice this means that the Church must if necessary sacrifice theologians in order to save the faithful. "It is better that men

At Salt Lake City, Mormon missionaries receive instruction; the practice of personal revelation has long since replaced that of polygamy

Below Mass baptism for Jehovah's Witnesses – the sect is an offshoot of North American Protestantism
Bottom At the top of Mont Blanc – the Last Post; a doomsday sect that miscalculated the end of the world for 14 July 1960

should suffer, rather than the truth"' (Ferdinand Piontek). 'It is the task of Catholic theology to present the revelation of Christ as the absolute truth and the perfect religion.'

The 'counter-revolution', 'the protest of the old', 'of the old faithful' (these included some young, militant Catholics) formed a number of organizations which pressed for a radical purge within the Church, a tightening of the rules of censorship, reintroduction of the Inquisition, and the denunciation of all 'innovators' to the local Roman Catholic authorities. Working for this end were the Confrontatie (Confrontation) in Holland, the Una Voce movement in Germany and Italy, which campaigned for the maintenance of Latin as the language of the Church, and in England the founding of the organization of priests in 1968 against 'neo-Modernism', called 'Obedience and Loyalty to the Pope'. In Italy the Una Voce movement began to conduct a powerful propaganda campaign in favour of a return to the spirit of the Council of Trent to counteract the 'demonic Council spirit' of the Second Vatican Council. In Germany and Italy conservative priests and their followers fought against the 'sovietization of the Church'. They preached fanatical faith in the pope. One of them said of Paul VI: 'I believe that one day he will be known as Paul the Great.'

Ecumenism and ecclesiastical reform

The German theologian J.B.Metz outlined the position of the Roman Catholic Church at an ecumenical congress in Philadelphia on 18 June 1969: 'There still exists in our Church a constitutional distrust of spiritual freedom. The Church is all too quick in entertaining doubts about the purity of the reformer's faith. . . . Even now the human rights which have been accepted in modern times have not been incorporated into the ecclesiastical rights.' The reformist theologians had begun with a 'first kind of courage', 'the courage to be non-conformist, to break with the accepted canon of prejudices, to swim against the current, to risk losing the support of officials and friends'. Metz demanded that the courage to be non-conformist be followed up by a 'second' courage, the courage of solidarity, the courage to risk being accused by the Church of 'jumping on the band-wagon. . . .'

During 1960-70 much was said about a 'crisis in the ecumenical movement'. The movement attempted to bring about a dialogue among the Protestant Churches and between them and the Roman Catholic and the Orthodox Churches, in order to achieve practical cooperation in 'worldly matters' (combating hunger, war and oppression), and a 'theological meeting of minds'. Within the narrow framework of its official ecclesiastical powers, the ecumenical movement achieved what it set out to do in the first half of this century. It brought about a more neighbourly relationship between the Churches. In December 1965 Rome and Byzantium solemnly revoked their mutual excommunication of 1054, in accordance with the decree of the Second Vatican Council. The revoking of the Bull was preceded by a meeting between Orthodox and Roman Catholic theologians in Constantinople. Catholic observers now attended meetings of the World Church Council of the Evangelical Churches, and Protestants attended Catholic conferences. In the secular sphere cooperation between the Churches was working successfully, for example in giving help in Nigeria or Vietnam. What was still unsatisfactory in the eyes of 'young Christians' was the refusal of the Church to celebrate joint communion services, and its hostility to 'mixed marriages'.

The Churches were, understandably, trying to protect themselves against 'too much openness'. Meanwhile a *new ecumenical movement* grew up, cutting across all fronts. It was not based upon committees and conferences, but on *practical* cooperation, in facing up to fundamental problems such as 'Can there still be a belief in God in the middle of the twentieth century? Is God as he is presented in the Old Testament, or in the New Testament?'

All the great Christian Churches made a discovery during the period. This was the discovery, or rather the rediscovery, of the Old Testament as the foundation of the New Testament. Theologians found, to their fascination, that the Old Testament has no 'next world', no 'supernatural' element.

Top Jews at prayer under the 'Wailing Wall' in Jerusalem, which became Israeli territory after the Six-Day War
Above The Maccabees: a Hasidic private police patrol formed to combat anti-Jewish violence in Brooklyn

A synagogue in Harlem: the rabbi holds the *torah* or holy scroll

The Kingdom of God is to be prayed and fought for here on earth, as a kingdom in which truth is lived and social justice practised. *Shalom*, the 'great peace' is a total peace embracing all aspects of social, political and human life. God is not 'above us', he is in front of us; he is the living future, the life of humanity in the future, he is the 'forward' dimension.

Catholic theologians pointed out that old concepts such as 'God', 'spirit' and 'soul' had become devalued. These derived from an age when primitive man believed that he was surrounded by gods, spirits and soul. But what did modern man mean by them? Or such words as 'revelation', 'sin', 'grace', or 'belief'? (Van de Pol). Protestant theologians now admitted (with H. Zahrndt) that 'we are experiencing today a theological monetary crisis of hitherto unsuspected dimensions. All the great sayings, the images and concepts taken from the Bible which the Church uses as a matter of course, are so much paper money in the eyes of most of our contemporaries, for they no longer appear to be covered by proper experience.'

According to P.L.Berger, 'all the Christian Churches have adapted themselves to the American way of life. Religion is used as a tranquillizer, as a drug. The Sunday God is used as the status symbol of the Church of the upper class, or of the middle class, of the black hemisphere. There are churches for whites, churches for negroes.'

The new theology

The more successfully the Churches appeared to have adapted themselves to the needs of an industrial society (this was before the crisis in American society became apparent, the crisis in the faith in 'democracy', 'progress', 'efficiency' and the 'victory of the children of the light' over the red, yellow, brown, black children of darkness) the less successful did God's adaptation seem. 'God is quite different' – the struggle of Anglo-Saxon, particularly American theologians during the decade 1960-70 to de-ideologize God, Christianity and religion was also a reaction to the deep unrest within American society, the society whose great hope seemed to die with the Kennedy era. To face up to this challenge, young theologians turned to the German Protestant theology which developed during 1918-33 as a reaction to the collapse of the old European civilization and its political order. These German theologians themselves came under fire from both left and right when, in Hitler's Reich, the question of God became a question of humanity.

'The Church should sing its Gregorian chants only if she is singing them for Jews and communists also.' Dietrich Bonhoeffer, who was hanged in the concentration camp of Flossenbürg, died a martyr, but not a martyr for his Church, rather for mankind. 'God is in reality.' 'God is in the centre of our lives, only beyond us.' 'The transcendent is not infinitely remote, but close at hand.' These statements were written in prison. Dietrich Bonhoeffer (1906-45), when he was only twenty-three years old wrote 'an ontological statement which no theologian should ignore' (R.R.Grunow) – 'A god who exists, does not exist.'

Rudolf Bultmann (born in 1884), in his attempt to 'demythologize belief' was trying to 'release the safety-catch of faith', to 'translate mythological statements into existential statements' (Macquarrier, *The Scope of Demythologizing*). Karl Barth, his great opposite (1886-1969) shared his conviction that religion is the opposite of faith. Religion is the 'shameless anticipation' of that which can only come from the unknown God. Since the beginning of the world the Church has 'done more to extinguish men's interest in God than to arouse it'. This 'atheism' is revealed as the true essence of *every* Church.

Paul Tillich (born in 1886 in Starzeddel, in Eastern Germany – from 1933 until his death in 1965 he taught as a professor in New York, Harvard and Chicago) did much to awaken American theologians from spiritual torpor. Tillich wrote that 'Conventional theism has created an image of God as a divine, utterly perfect being, ruling over the world and humanity. The atheist's objection to this perfect being is completely justified. We see no evidence of this being's existence, nor does it have any relevance to anyone.

God is not God without universal participation.' 'The Bible is not only a religious book; it is also an anti-religious book. The Bible fights for God against religion.' (Ernst Bloch continued and radically extended these ideas in his great work *Das Prinzip Hoffnung* and in *Atheismus im Christentum*.)

Much against his will, Paul Tillich was the father of the 'God-is-dead' theology ('That is going too far', he said, a few weeks before his death). Thomas Altizer states in *The Gospel of Christian Atheism* that he owes his Christian faith primarily to Tillich's ideas, and that his concept of the Gospel of Christian atheism is the logical conclusion of Tillich's theories.

In 1966 *Time* magazine publicized the 'God-is-dead movement' in a long article. The reaction this set off was reflected in subsequent issues of the magazine. Responses ranged from one extreme to another, from 'The existence of God is far above question' to 'The myth of God is dying and we must do all we can to help it along.'

The whole discussion was started off by the publication of Gabriel Vahanian's book *The Death of God*, in 1961. It is important to remember that this American debate took place within the context of Vietnam. The tragedy of American problems led to the rediscovery of the tragic dimension of human life, and thus raised the question of God, which until then had been left to European thinkers – and American poets!

The sub-title of Vahanian's book is *The Culture of our Post-Christian Era*. Vahanian reaches the conclusion that '. . . The death of God may be only a cultural phenomenon as though only our religio-cultural notion of God were dead. But this makes even more serious the question whether the transcendental views of man and his culture, as set forth in the Bible, have any chance of surviving the modern presupposition that God is dead.' William Hamilton's book, *The New Essence of Christianity*, was published in the same year. Hamilton tried to call to mind 'the few things that are certain'. In 1966, as the 'American crisis' was beginning to develop in the universities, T. J. H. Altizer's *The Gospel of Christian Atheism* was published. Altizer is convinced that to proclaim the death of God is an act of Christian faith; the radical Christian will admit that God died with Christ and that his death was final and irredeemable.

The American theologians who represented the 'God-is-dead' ideology have replaced the dead God by the real figure of Jesus of Nazareth. The underlying political idea was that conventional Christianity, the Churches and their bourgeois morality, had betrayed the Gospel, the joyful message of Jesus. This conviction led Pierre Berton (*The Comfortable Pew*, 1965), to break with all the Christian Churches. He passionately supported the concept of Jesus of Nazareth. During 1965-70 many books were written on similar lines (for example, Werner and Lotte Pelz, *God Is No More*).

The German 'God-is-dead' theologians are even more radical than the Americans. Dorothee Sölle (for the first time women were coming to the fore, in German Evangelical as well as Catholic theology) in her book *Stellvertretung* (1965), declares that God is dead, but that Jesus is his representative. Herein lies the possibility of Christian hope: 'Christ introduced a new way of living into the world, and therefore there is always hope. Christ's representation is the transcendental realization of hope.' Dorothee Sölle ends her book with the challenge: 'God has worked for us for long enough . . . now it is time that we did something for God.'

The American 'God-is-dead' theology was primarily a theology *of* the death of God. The death of God is itself the subject of this theology. The German 'God-is-dead' theology was on the other hand a theology that is a *consequence* of the death of God – the death of God is its condition.

'A God who can die does not deserve tears.' Harvey Cox, the author of *The Secular City*, claims that the Church's only future lies in becoming a Church of the future. Cox makes no mention of 'death' or 'eternal life'; he is not interested in heaven and hell or the 'beyond'. The theological destruction of the thousand-year-old Christian concepts of heaven and hell, and the 'loss of the beyond' are surely the most revolutionary achievements of this Euro-American Protestant theology. It has its parallel in Catholic theology in the work of Thomas and Gertrude Sartory.

Above Anti-Semitic slogans and counter-slogans in Brussels 1960: one of the periodic throwbacks to an apparently rejected creed

Below Anti-Semitism in the USSR, 1961: a Soviet cartoon accuses Zionist leaders of collaborating with the Germans during the war
Bottom Towards the end of 1970 demonstrators throughout the world showed their concern over the plight of Soviet Jews; here former concentration-camp victims parade in Jerusalem

In Senegal, Muslims kneel towards Mecca after the call to prayer which, in strict ritual, occurs five times a day; for the followers of Islam there is one God and Muhammad is his prophet

Above American Black Muslims: separatist and inward-looking for negro truth. Unlike the Black Panthers, most do not believe in challenging the white man's power structure

Right Hindus: mystical and transcendental, the mythology stresses the transience of earthly things

The dissolution of the ecclesiastical ideology of heaven and hell was now penetrating even the Greek Church, its firmest supporter. Paul Evdokimov, who was born in 1901 in St Petersburg, and became professor of moral theology at the Theological Institute of St Sergius in Paris in 1954, taught that 'Hell and paradise are not compensation, punishment or reward but represent the levels of life which men create for themselves, and from which they prepare their own fate.'

Paul Tillich wrote that 'a faith which interprets its symbols literally, becomes idolatry'. He had already replaced the traditional concept of the 'heights' (in the heights are the heavens) by the concept of 'depths'. He who seeks God must not turn his eyes away from the earth and gaze up into the sky, into an imaginary heaven. He must turn to the world and must become more deeply involved in it. Man will find God in the depths of reality, as the reason and meaning of all existence.

The progressive Protestant theology that emerged during 1960-70 was not interested in the old concept of the 'beyond'. It was concerned with 'pointing the way to reality, with showing people that they are responsible for the fate of the world'. Heaven and hell were interpreted as human realities: 'Hell is everywhere in the world where men feel that they have to work for their lives . . . where they shut themselves up and so begrudge others their lives and quarrel over the living space they must share. Heaven is everywhere on earth where men accept their lives as a gift, where they are thankful for their own existence. . . .'

Heinz Zahrnt, the most widely read German Protestant theologian of the postwar period (*Die Sache mit Gott*, 1966; *Gespräch über Gott*, 1968; *Gott kann nicht sterben*, 1970) suggested that 'the Church should be there on earth where there is heaven, in fact, it should contribute to there being more heaven on earth'.

During the last ten years the conservative opposition to these 'Godless'

Above Buddhist Zen monks chanting *sutras*; self-liberation through enlightenment to a hopeful *nirvana*

Below During the fifties and sixties the young in the West seized on Oriental religions to fill the Christian void. Zen Buddhist thought goes back to the legend of the Buddha, who when asked to preach held up a golden flower. Only one disciple understood

Evangelical university theologians was gathering strength. The conservatives were demanding of the Protestant bishops and the Church leaders that these new theologians be expelled from the Church. They were demanding disciplinary proceedings against vicars who refused to baptize their own children, who proclaimed from the pulpit that Christ's ascension was an *un*-Christian myth. The reactionaries within the Protestant Church were hostile to the Protestant political theology which they accused of creating 'an opening for the left'. But even the conservatives were forced to admit that nowhere had the Church failed more than in its influence on the young. 'To add the vacuum of the Church to the vacuum in young people's lives is no way out.' It was for example building more and more churches in West Germany for fewer and fewer people; 1,100 ugly, though expensive, churches were constructed in 1945-70. The empty churches reflected the disintegration of religious faith.

Religion in a secular society

During the period various factors combined to cause the decay of religious faith. The most pervasive was the a-religious technical-industrial society which required of its individual members the ability to be competitive and worldly. In this closed society there was no room for God, unless he was tucked away in the 'Indian reservation' of the Sunday service, or used as a tranquillizer. But even here he must compete with the psychiatrist. The natural sciences perhaps tended towards atheism, while history, psychology, sociology and comparative cultural anthropology relativized Christianity.

At the same time progressive theologians were trying to rid Christianity of its magic and its mythology. The vacuum which they created was being filled by other religious movements. The process was similar to that occurring in Africa, China and Asia with the departure of the white missionaries. Their place was taken by 'hot' religio-political movements. In Africa, at least, a black religious messianism appearing in the numerous new tribal churches and pan-African religious movements was part of a political messianism: God is an African God, 'if he is incarnated in Jesus he is a black man'. The negroes in South America, and those in the USA in the Black Power movement who were forming 'Afro-American' communities are naturally attracted to these messianic religio-political movements.

The vacuum in North America and Europe was being filled by Eastern influences; this was most apparent among young people. By 1965 over half the world population was under the age of twenty. The older generation seemed to be fighting a rearguard action against this 'invasion of youth'. The cold war between the generations was being waged all over the world. Between 1964 and 1970 there were over 2,000 disturbances at universities. Youth (fourteen-year-olds, nineteen-year-olds and twenty-five-year-olds often formed quite distinct generations, but presented a united front on basic issues) was challenging the authority of the old-established political leaders and 'super-father-figures' of the Western 'democratic' parties and the leaders of the Stalinist and post-Stalinist Party Churches in Eastern Europe; of the *Fachidioten* (those who concentrate on their subject to such an extent that they know, or care, little about anything else in the world); of the professors; of the 'experts' in the technical-military apparatus. The young believed that the older generation meant to exploit them, to sacrifice their lives in the cold and hot war. The old men's old gods were the gods of war. In America the Protestant and Catholic Churches, above all the Roman Catholic Church, had literally nothing to say when two atom bombs were dropped on Japan. Army chaplains of all denominations stood at the graves of young men in Vietnam, or wherever they were sent by their superiors. At the Second Vatican Council an American bishop declared that the USA was not only right to drop the atom bomb on Hiroshima, but had a duty to drop more bombs if it was a question of protecting the right to send children to Catholic schools, a right which would be endangered if the godless Soviet Union were to attack. When a Swedish Catholic (a woman) drew his attention to the New Testament, and insisted that the Gospel could exist even without Catholic schools, he shouted 'You are talking

Local magic: (*top*) Bacoulogui, a West African forest god; (*above*) consultation with a witch doctor in Malawi

A Voodoo priestess in Haiti draws a religious emblem with cornflower. The republic's president, Duvalier, was said to make use of Voodoo to destroy the ghosts of his political victims

high spirituality, I'm talking about realities.' *Realities* – this was what the *religious revolt* of the young was about. For the young were convinced that the old Churches were defending the *Realpolitik* of the old Establishment figures whose entire energy was spent on perfecting their super-weapons in preparation for the 'final solution of the human question' (to follow on from the final solution of the Jewish question). The heroic participation of young priests, from the Protestant and Catholic Churches, in the civil rights and the peace movement, still could not exonerate the old Churches and their old God in the eyes of this restless, awakening youth. For they saw the old gods demanding 'unprecedented sacrifices'; they, the young, were being sent to the battlefields of the old.

Eastern invasion

During the decade 1960-70 religious elements, mainly from Asia, began to exert some influence on the sub-culture, the 'counter-culture' of the youth opposition. Laotse, Buddha and Zen Buddhism contributed to the fresh formation of religious feeling. In 1954 the American poet Allen Ginsberg discovered Zen. In 1955 he wrote his *Sunflower Sutra*; in 1956 Jack Kerouac wrote *The Dharma Bums*. Epiphany was celebrated, the divine was seen in the midst of universal squalor and poverty, in the midst of physical and spiritual degradation. In his early poems Ginsberg had already intimated:

> all the pictures we carry in our mind
> images of the Thirties,
> depression and class consciousness
> transfigured above politics
> filled with fire
> with the appearance of God.

'God is a God of the present' (Meister Eckhart), 'rien qu'aujourd'hui' (St Teresa of Lisieux) – the new mysticism was rooted in the ordinary of the 'here and now':

> This is the one and only
> firmament . . .
> I am living in Eternity.
> The ways of this world
> are the ways of Heaven.

In the early 1950s the poets Gary Snyder and Ginsberg came to San Francisco from the east coast. Snyder had already developed his Zen model of life, based on poverty, simplicity and meditation. He had studied Zen techniques in Japan. In collaboration with D.T. Suzuki, Alan Watts played an important part in adapting Zen to American life, relating it to the restlessness of youth, so alienated from the parent generation. Through his books, his teaching, his television appearances and his continuous contact with young people he became known as the exponent of a new religious sensibility.

Allen Ginsberg, this ecstatic Jewish poet feeding on the fire of the prophets – an Amos – became America's prime Hindu guru. California is a melting-pot of religions; it appears to be emerging as America's destiny, the *femme fatale* of a nation which till then had been dominated by North American WASPS – White Anglo-Saxon Protestants. Suddenly there arrived on the scene a young Jesus, the friend of flowers and flower children, a friend of the hippies and of the young Franciscan rebels who dedicated their lives to the poverty of the Church and to peace. This young Jesus walked (as Hölderlin had longingly pictured it in his *Friedensfeier*) in the circle of his friends, the prophets, the Sufis, the blessed. 'May the baby Jesus open your mind and shut your mouth' (Charlie Artman). The great figures, the founders of the main religions, were interpreted in a totally unorthodox way as guides to a blessed life in *this* world and were reinforced by elements drawn from the thousand-year-old magic and archaic underground of ancient Europe, Asia, Africa and Indian America. In this religio-political context we see the *revival of an Indian America* – above all in North America – *in the eyes of the young generation*.

The battle for a new metaphysics to express the new world spirit is always

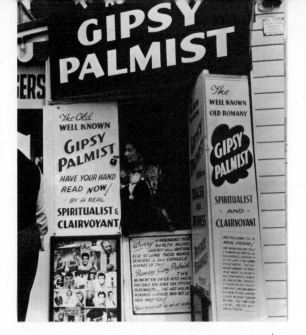

Above In the unreligious sixties primitive cults of witchcraft, astrology and fortune-telling took on a new fascination

Below Charles Manson, leader of an extreme hippie group, which murdered Sharon Tate and several others in 1970
Bottom The Manchester coven of witches looks for suitable altar sites on the Yorkshire moors; the brooms have a symbolic rather than practical function

first and foremost a language-battle: the battle for a new language – to conquer the old language of the old gods. *Kyrie eleison*: the Roman Catholic liturgy expresses the victory of the new Kyrios Christ over the old Kyrios, Nero. . . .

The young Christian theologians have destroyed their Churches' roots in the magic of the sacraments, in the cult, liturgy and ritual. In the face of this diffuse upsurge of restless youth, between 1960 and 1970, the difficult question arose: could the new society exist without magic or mystery (these are not the same), and without ritual?

In the mass society of the super-towns, in the lonely crowd made up of a horde of lonely individuals, millions of people took refuge in the practice of magic. Just as in the Hellenist cities of the late Roman Empire, in Alexandria, Antioch, Ephesus, Rome, and Marseilles, so in recent history witchcraft, black and white magic, began to be practised from Rio de Janeiro to New York, from Buenos Aires to London. In the 1960s magic rituals and practices began to re-emerge from their thousand-year-old underground existence. This process was closely connected with the 're-primivization, re-barbarization, re-infantilization', the reversion to puberty of the majority of adults who remain spiritually immature. Max Hork-heimer (*Eclipse of Reason, Dialektik der Aufklärung*), who is deeply know-ledgeable about the spiritual and intellectual climates of Europe and North America, has long contended that a narrow-minded, closed reason, an 'instrumental reason', a rationality based on specialized knowledge which limits itself to the fetishist worship of its own numbers, its 'pure facts', is not only no defence against the encroachment of irrational movements, but in fact actually promotes them.

Modern man was in imminent danger of sinking into an almost infantile barbarity. Technology even stimulated the growing recourse to magic. For magic is 'the technical manipulation of spiritual and emotional powers in order to achieve something', *to master it*; an object, an animal, a human being or a god.

More and more people tended to use technical products as magic: the television, the car, the machine (particularly in the household), drugs, alcohol. They created an artificial paradise by artificial means. And not least, man himself was exploited technically-magically like consumer goods, as a thing, a means to attain pleasure. Woman was exploited in this tech-nical age – the modern witch burns herself, by means of sexual technique, at the stake of inordinate sexuality. This underground existed against a back-ground of the old Churches and the old, secularized churches of education. These are helpless, as is the humanism preached in the universities.

Frustration was the keynote of the spiritual and intellectual 'underground' mentality of individuals, of the masses. The twenty-five years following the Second World War brought neither satisfaction nor peace. The war merely achieved, with barbaric means, a temporary cease-fire in the great conflict.

The hundreds of small wars, and the few large-scale ones that broke out between 1946 and 1970, might seem gradually to be merging into one great world civil war. In May 1969 helicopters used tear gas against students in

Top Czechs with the placard of their communist ancestor at the 1965 May Day parade
Above A Prague shop in 1950 offers a choice between Stalin and Christ; the Russian dictator liked to hear himself called 'little father of the people'

Poster of Mao, who has never discouraged the attribution of godlike powers to himself

Berkeley. In May 1968 the French police used gas grenades against school-children and students. For six whole months (June 1968–January 1969) Japanese students fought to defend the buildings of Tokyo University against police. In this confusion the old Churches seemed about to be replaced by a new religious mentality. This expressed a new 'world piety' which for the first time really was a *living ecumenism*, a 'spiritual banquet'. Goethe describes this in his *West-Östlichen Divan*:

Welch eine seltsame Gemeinde An Gottes Tisch sitzen Freund und Feinde	(What a strange community At God's table sit friends and enemies)

and:

Wer sich selbst und andere kennt wird auch dies erkennen Orient und Okzident sind nicht mehr zu trennen	(He who knows himself and others will also know this: East and West can no longer be separated)

The crisis of communism

The Orient and the Occident, the East and the West: the decay of ecclesiastical Christianity from 1945 to 1970 was matched by the parallel phenomenon in the *World Churches* of communism. The World Church of communism, presided over by the ruby-red stars of the Kremlin, in the fifty years of its existence underwent the process which the Roman World Church took a thousand years to get through. First, its orthodox doctrine was established on the foundations laid by the Church fathers: Marx, Engels, Lenin, and for a time, Stalin. Then decay set in; the one, holy doctrine was questioned by great heretics such as Trotsky and Tito. A Western Church was formed around Moscow, and an Eastern Church around Peking. The Eastern Church accused the Western Church, just as the Byzantine Eastern Church accused Rome, of committing a whole host of heretical deviations from the pure doctrine of original communism (cf. early Christianity). The collapse of the cult of the pope after the death of Pius XII, is comparable to the effect achieved by Khrushchev in his three speeches at the Twentieth Party Congress of the Communist Party of the Soviet Union in February 1956, in which he toppled Stalin from his pedestal. The de-ideologization within the Protestant and Catholic Churches was matched by the de-ideologizing which took place in the Soviet Union, in Poland, Hungary and Czechoslovakia. In order to prevent 'deviation' from the pure doctrine, Rome attempted to establish a Roman Catholic neo-orthodoxy. In the hopes of preventing a falling-off of faith, and of gaining support in its religious-political battle with Peking and the European dissidents, Moscow attempted to create a Muscovite neo-orthodoxy.

Many a stalwart champion in the battle for world revolution lost his faith in the 'death mills' of Stalinism, in the Spanish Civil War and in the prisons and labour camps of the Soviet Empire. In the 1920s and 1930s and again, after 1945, communist intellectuals in the West went through 'crises of conscience' that often ended in their leaving the party and turning against communism. But none of these crises were comparable to the avalanche which was set in motion by the revelation of the monstrous character of Stalinism in the Soviet Union and the communist-ruled countries of Eastern Europe. This really meant a collapse of faith; the world, history itself, seemed to lose its meaning overnight. One needs to have seen the look of despair in the faces of old and young communists in Russia, Poland and Hungary to understand the full tragedy of this loss of faith, which often ended in suicide.

In April 1956 *Nova Kultura* published a letter from an eighteen-year-old Warsaw student, Michael Bruk, describing the collapse of his faith in communism. 'I am ashamed for all of you, I am ashamed of myself, for being so stupid and gullible. I feel I can't cope any more, because I have lost my belief in everything. . . .' Even the official party newspaper, *Trybuna Ludu*, published letters from readers, all asking 'What should we believe? Whom should we believe?'

Banners of Cuban revolutionary leaders at a mass political rally

On 20 October 1956 the new Polish party leader, Gomulka, spoke about 'the tragedy of Poznań'. Workers had risen there. He said 'Silent, enslaved minds began to shake off the poisonous fog of deception, of lies, of hypocrisy . . . criticism of the past swelled into a great tidal wave. This criticism was of the violence, of the mistakes and falsifications that had been committed in every sphere of life. . . . But above all, the working people were demanding to be told the whole truth, no more half-truths. . . .'

Three days later the Hungarian revolution broke out. On 23 October, some 300,000 people marched through Budapest in a peaceful demonstration, singing the national anthem and songs of 1848, shouting 'Independence! Freedom!', 'Up with Polish-Hungarian friendship!', 'Down with Stalinism!', 'Imre Nagy for Prime Minister!' The huge bronze statue of Stalin in the Stalin Square was toppled by metal-workers from the 'Red Csepel' district (a working-class district on the outskirts of Budapest, with a militant, left-wing tradition), using their welding equipment. The statue fell to the ground and broke into pieces, symbolizing the fall of a god who has been exposed as an idol.

By 1970 the attempts made to introduce a 'humane' communism had been suppressed in Poland, Hungary and finally in Czechoslovakia. In Moscow, after long internal debates, a neo-orthodox ideology had triumphed, whose advocates believed that the Soviet Empire could only be defended against inner decay and against the Chinese by a strict closing of the ranks.

The ideological battle between the Eastern Church and the Western Church of communism broke out over the question of a 'holy war'. (Throughout the Middle Ages a controversy continued between the Latin Western Church which believed it was necessary to wage holy wars, crusades, and did so, and the Eastern Church, whose theologians did not recognize the crusade-theology.) In the conflict between China and the Soviet Union, the Red Eastern Church's position is comparable to that of the old, Latin Western Church – quoting Stalin as her authority.

In its statement of February 1963, the Chinese CP maintained that the quarrel had started with the CPSU's Twentieth Congress, and Khrushchev's betrayal of world communism. (In fact the quarrel went much further back, to the time of Stalin.) The Chinese accused Khrushchev of betraying 'proletarian internationalism'; because he denied the necessity of war, they tried to expose him as a heretic. Peking wanted to become the 'first Rome of World Communism' (L. Barcata), and the leader of the world revolution in Asia, South America, Africa and the Near East.

Lenin, Trotsky and a glamourized Che Guevara were the heroes of the French student rebels of May 1968, who pressed for educational reforms and an end to repressive aspects of the de Gaulle regime

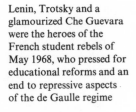

Rioting in New Delhi in 1966 between Hindus and Sikhs over the future of Punjab state, whose mixed ethnic and religious communities have lived in tension since partition

Ritual Buddhist suicide in Saigon in 1963 in protest against the religious discrimination practised by the Catholic Diem regime, which was overthrown shortly after

In 1958, the League of the Communists of Yugoslavia published its own heretical programme, Mao proclaimed his 'great leap forward'. In the two countries where, as in the Soviet Union, the native population had won power for the communists, two opposing versions of communism arose.

Even before the Twenty-Third Party Congress of the CPSU in the late autumn of 1961, the Chinese CP was beginning to launch its offensive against the 'deviationist and irresolute' cause of the CPSU and its followers in the West. The Chinese invited communist functionaries from other countries and built up a huge world-wide propaganda machine. They accused 'Comrade Togliatti and his friends' of making common cause with the 'Tito clique', of 'no longer being able to distinguish between just and unjust wars', of backsliding into 'bourgeois pacifism', of betraying the revolution out of a mistaken fear of war, of not supporting the 'national wars of liberation' and the 'people's revolutionary wars'.

The Chinese CP in its ideological propaganda accused Moscow of moving to the right, of making overtures to the USA and of betraying the world revolution. (The CPSU, on the other hand, accused the Chinese CP of being Trotskyist.) The most significant accusation was published on 7 February 1964, in the 'Seventh Comment of the Chinese Central Committee to the letter from the Central Committee of the CPSU'. This stated that 'All fraternal Parties, whether large or small, whether new or old, whether in power or not, are independent and equal. At no meeting of the fraternal Parties has there ever been any unanimously accepted agreement that there are ruling and subordinate Parties, that there is one Party that leads and others that follow, that there is one Party *to play the role of father*, and others who are the sons, or that the leaders of the CPSU should rule over the other fraternal Parties.'

'Every remark and every sentence uttered by Khrushchev, however absurd or incorrect, is an *imperial edict*. All the fraternal Parties must submissively listen and obey. Criticism and opposition are strictly forbidden. This is outright tyranny! It is the ideology of the feudal aristocracy, pure and simple.'

The primacy of the Moscow Communist Church was being challenged – in its role as infallible leader, as super-father-figure, as the papacy of the communist movement. Thus had the struggle for the primacy of the Roman pope begun after the Second Vatican Council.

Meanwhile, Mao Tse-tung was being built up as the yellow-red imperial divine emperor. In an as yet unparalleled pope-cult, he is extolled in a liturgical form of propaganda. His words have sacred power, literally – they help women to bear the pain of childbirth more easily, they cure people suffering from cancer, their recitation soothes the dying. Every day his words are repeated, sung and used as prayers, like the calender, the hours of the liturgy of old religious orders.

In the Ninth Comment of the Chinese CP to the open letter from the Central Committee of the CPSU, which is ascribed to Mao himself, it is stated that 'the question of educating the successors to the revolutionary cause of the proletariat is a question of life and death, a question that will be of fundamental importance for centuries, for thousands, for tens of thousands of years hence. Because of the changes that have taken place in the Soviet Union, the imperialist prophets are cherishing hopes of a "peaceful revolution" in the Chinese Party in the third or fourth generation. We will thwart the imperialist prophets.'

Mao, the 'Red Moses', whose march through Yenan has often been compared to that of Moses through the desert, sees himself as the prophet of the revolutionary communist faith that is to transform the world. In support of this faith he mobilized millions of young people in the 'cultural revolution' – they were to overthrow the high priests of the Chinese CP, the new mandarins of the party bureaucracy who had become sacrilegious. In fact, the Red Chinese leadership did have a preponderance of old men; in 1965 the average age of the Politburo was about sixty-seven, and that of the Central Committee and KCT about sixty-four.

The rebirth of the Red faith

Mao and his followers used the gigantic powers at their disposal to try to prevent the disintegration of communist ideology in China; they tried to fan the flames of faith by burning down the old Chinese culture. Temples and graves were destroyed; the 'new people' were to be torn from their roots in every way, from their ancestor-worship and from counter-revolution.

How did the ideologists of the Moscow Church attempt to counteract this upheaval?

'The ideological inheritance of the war was the combination of the cult of Stalin and Soviet imperialism' (K. Marko). After the fall of Khrushchev, and in view of the increasingly *public* conflict with the Chinese, the leading Soviet politicians, whose ideological repertoire was becoming noticeably poorer, and increasingly unable to bear comparison with the *docta ideologia* of the party clergy and scholars, retreated into a pragmatic *Realpolitik*. A kind of communist vulgar Catholicism is being preached to the masses. Stalin is being rehabilitated as the great wise father of the peoples of the Soviet fatherland. Patriotism is being inculcated as the great virtue. The gulf between the mass indoctrination of simple ideological formulae, and the subtle endeavours of leading party ideologists and philosophers who struggle to achieve an ideological understanding of the present world situation at the All Union Conference, is as great as that between the Thomist and Scotist scholars and the religious faith of the ordinary people in the fourteenth century. It is as great as the gulf between progressive theologians and the religious faith of Polish, Spanish and South American Catholics in 1970.

Enlightenment and counter-enlightenment, progress and reaction – they are confronted here in Moscow as they are in Rome, following the Second Vatican Council. They are often intertwined, they often exist within the same person, in for instance, a theologian, or a communist ideologist who is both enlightened and reactionary. Jean Danielou, SJ, who was made a cardinal by Paul VI, could here be compared to the communist ideologist, P. N. Fedoseev.

The tremendous setbacks suffered by the oldest conservative, and the youngest revolutionary, ideologies between 1945 and 1970 should not be ignored. The broad masses of society no doubt live out their lives beyond the pale of conscious ideologies. They content themselves with a few remnants, mostly highly secularized, of the older, religious, humanist, and political ideologies, long since robbed of their once explosive inner force. *Here*, at the very lowest level, a process of de-ideologization has begun, which is affecting more and more people. The inner vacuum within people is growing. According to your ideological standpoint, you can interpret this fact as a great opportunity, or as a threat to man's progress towards becoming human.

Top Religious riots between Protestants and the Catholic minority in Northern Ireland accompanied the depressive economic situation of 1969
Above Protestant, right-wing, Reverend Ian Paisley carried shoulder high by supporters during a rally in Belfast

Part Two

Nations and Frontiers

Arthur Schlesinger Jr.

The United States: Prosperity and Turmoil

The United States emerged from the Second World War relatively unified, powerful and confident, prepared to take an active part in the affairs of the greater world. This represented a striking change in the national condition. A dozen years before V-E day, America had been in collapse, with a quarter of the labour force out of work, factories gloomy and silent, crops rotting in the countryside, businessmen panicky, workers sullen and the sounds of revolution in the air. If Franklin Roosevelt's New Deal brought fresh hope after March 1933, it produced a rancorous reaction among an influential minority; the result was protracted political strife of bitter intensity. A profound mood of isolationism limited American contact with international problems. But by 1945 both internal conflict and international diffidence seemed to have passed. Entering the postwar world, the United States displayed an uncritical pride in the unity of its people, in the productivity of its economy, in the prowess of its armed forces, in the rectitude of its motives and in the global application of its liberal ideals.

The war itself, though it had spared the American mainland, had still been a searing national experience. Sixteen million – more than ten per cent of the total population – served in the armed forces, of whom three-quarters went overseas. Casualties rose above a million, with nearly 300,000 deaths in battle. (In the First World War, 4·7 million had been under arms, of whom slightly more than half went overseas and 53,000 died in battle.) At the same time the war uprooted people from familiar places, exposed them to new experiences and also awakened and released great latent energies in American society.

Defence spending achieved what New Deal spending had never been large enough to accomplish: it brought the long depression to an end. Between 1933 and 1945 the gross national product increased (in current prices) from $56 billion to a then-astounding $214 billion. By 1943 unemployment practically disappeared. Economic recovery substantially abated the fierce political divisions of the thirties. While conservative Congresses did away with New Deal emergency agencies, the basic New Deal structure of social and economic reform was now part of the landscape of American life. At the same time, the Japanese attack on Pearl Harbor had terminated the foreign policy debate that raged between interventionists and isolationists in 1939-41. The Senate's ratification of the United Nations Charter in 1945 with only two dissenting votes was in spectacular contrast to the rejection of the League of Nations a quarter of a century before.

Most marked of all was the confidence with which Americans looked to the future. The New Deal experiment in regulated capitalism now seemed a clear success. Dogmatists on both right and left had denied the possibility of a middle way between *laissez-faire* and socialism; but Roosevelt, scorning ideological absolutism, had proved otherwise. Confidence sprang too from the wartime sense of achievement and power and especially from the incomparable momentum of American science and technology. This technological dynamism found its supreme, and tragic, expression in the invention of the atomic bomb.

Living with the atom bomb

Roosevelt died on 12 April 1945 without knowing whether his decision to spend $2 billion on this fantastic venture would be vindicated. His successor was his vice-president, Harry S. Truman, a shrewd and diligent Missouri politician without experience in international affairs. But Truman, who was

Democratic Convention, 1964, solidly backing Lyndon Johnson and the Great Society

Cartoon of Truman, surprise Democrat winner of the 1948 presidential election and originator of the doctrine of 'containment' against the Soviet threat

Eisenhower and Nixon at the 1952 Republican Convention: they opposed Truman's Far East policy and were unresolved on civil rights

doughty, stubborn and courageous, rapidly developed a crisp authority in the executive side of his new role. Gradually he transformed a Roosevelt administration into a Truman administration. By the time he came to the Potsdam Conference in July 1945, Churchill found himself impressed by 'his gay, precise, sparkling manner and obvious power of decision'.

Three months after Roosevelt's death, with war over in Europe but continuing in the Pacific, the first atomic bomb was tested at Alamogordo in the south-west desert. Truman heard the news at Potsdam; his power of decision now faced a crucial test. Through the interception of Japanese cables, the American government knew that the Japanese regime was vaguely seeking a way out of the war. On the other hand, the joint chiefs of staff estimated that a conventional invasion of Japan would mean a million casualties to American forces alone. A declaration issued from Potsdam cryptically called on the Japanese to surrender or face 'utter devastation'. When Tokyo spurned the Potsdam Declaration, Truman made up his mind to go ahead. On 6 August 1945 the first atomic bomb fell on Hiroshima, killing nearly 80,000 people and reducing the city to ashes. The Japanese still stalled. Three days later the second bomb exploded over Nagasaki. At last the Japanese surrendered.

So mankind passed into the Nuclear Age. 'I realize the tragic significance of the atomic bomb,' Truman assured the American people; but it is not clear that he ever really did. The latest evidence suggests he may well have been right in supposing Japan would not have yielded in August without the bomb. But the decision was hardly so easy as Truman would ever after insist. For the atomic bomb represented a qualitative leap in the progress of man's capacity to destroy himself. The first nation to use so ghastly a weapon placed itself before the world in a position of fatal moral vulnerability. No one could ever be sure that the government that had once dropped the bomb might not do so again.

Inside the United States the impact of the bomb was no less unlucky. After the destruction so righteously wrought against Hiroshima and Nagasaki, some Americans found it easy to assume the role of the world's judge, jury and executioner. Others felt that, having created and used the bomb, America was permanently evil. And, while the evidence does not sustain the contention of revisionist historians that the 'real' reason for using the bomb was to intimidate not the Japanese but the Russians, perhaps the Russians may have thought this and regarded American policy even more suspiciously.

For here was the flaw in the American optimism of 1945. America was discovering that it was not alone on the top. Another nation, though far more grievously mangled by war than the United States, still had emerged with formidable military force, political influence and ideological self-assurance. By Marxist definition, moreover, the United States as the citadel of private capitalism was a threat to the security of Soviet Russia, and, by Leninist analysis, no accommodation with capitalist leaders could be anything more than an armed truce. The inordinate suspiciousness of Stalin intensified Soviet distrust of every American leader or policy. As for the Americans, though past dislike of Russia had been submerged during the war by honest admiration for the Red Army and sentimental effusions about the great Soviet ally, the anti-communist propensity remained just under the surface.

America and Russia had clashing conceptions not only of ideology but of international organization. The Americans were true to the old Wilsonian faith. Returning from the Crimean Conference in February 1945, Roosevelt expressed the hope that Yalta would 'spell the end of the system of unilateral action, the exclusive alliances, the spheres of influence, the balances of power, and all the other expedients that have been tried for centuries – and have always failed.' By this universalist view, all nations had an equal interest in the affairs of the world (except Latin America, where the United States deemed itself more equal than the rest); and security was to be assured by the United Nations.

The Russians, on the other hand, saw the world *only* in spheres of

Actual and projected population growth

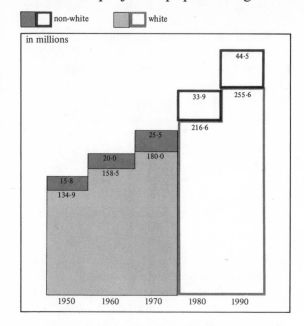

Per capita income 1969

in US dollars

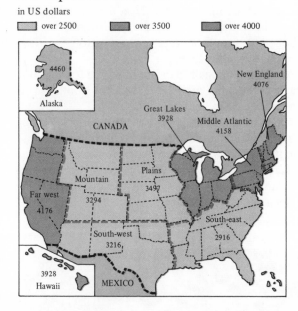

Las Vegas during the fifties: the gamblers' city

influence. Their physical safety, in their view, demanded that all states along or near the Russian border should have 'friendly governments'. Thus they had no intention of according other powers an equal role in Eastern Europe. In exchange for a free hand in his own zone of vital interest, Stalin, while not renouncing the making of mischief in other parts of the world, was prepared to allow America and Britain free hands in their zones, including the freedom to suppress communist subversion. His first concern was not the dominion of the world but the security of the Russian frontiers.

At the same time, the war itself was leaving great gaping holes in the international power equilibrium. With the Axis states vanquished, Europe wrecked and the colonial empires in dissolution, only America and Russia had the dynamism to fill the new vacuums of power. Both had grown accustomed during the war to thinking and acting on a world scale. Even without ideological disagreement competition for power would have propelled such energetic states into collision. America and Russia appeared in 1945 as the first truly global powers in history, exerting their influence everywhere, encountering no serious opposition, except from each other.

There thus developed what soon came to be known as the 'cold war', an intricate, reciprocal process, involving authentic differences in principle, supposed clashes of interest and a considerable range of misunderstanding. The Russians saw American universalism as a hostile intrusion into an area vital to Russian security; the Americans increasingly feared that the Russians were hardening their sphere-of-influence policy in order to use Eastern Europe as a springboard from which to assault Western Europe, now lying defenceless before them. Each superpower believed with passion that its own safety as well as world peace depended on the success of its own conception of international order. Each superpower, in pursuing its own principles, only confirmed the fear of the other that it was determined on aggression.

Hostility to the Soviet Union was not premeditated. Even as relations grew worse, the United States cut back its armed forces to almost an eighth their wartime size; by 1949-50, the defence budget was down to $13 billion. Nor did Washington heed those like Bertrand Russell who urged the use of the atomic bomb to compel the Russians to good behaviour. Still, disagreement fed on disagreement, and distrust bred distrust. In February 1946 Stalin alarmed the West by a truculent speech to the Supreme Soviet; a month later at Fulton, Missouri, Churchill, with Truman at his side, warned that 'an iron curtain has descended across the Continent'. When the United States that summer called for total control by an international authority of all materials and facilities involved in the production of atomic energy, the Russians turned this imaginative plan down as a threat to their security.

The Truman Doctrine and the Marshall Plan

At home, Truman made clear in a series of messages to Congress that he saw himself as the continuator and consolidator of his predecessor's New Deal. But the American people were less concerned about the long-run revision of their society than about the immediate prospects of their economy. Economists had predicted that the end of war spending would bring severe depression. The economy, however, showed unexpected resilience. Between 1945 and 1946, while government purchases of goods and services fell from $83 billion to $31 billion – a sum equal to almost one-quarter of the gross national product – the GNP itself declined by only $4 billion, and employment actually increased by 3 million. Contrary to prediction, inflation rather than depression proved the greater problem. Here Congress frustrated Truman's determination to continue wartime price and wage controls; prices shot up; trade unions went on strike; and by mid-1946 Truman seemed to have lost control. Conservatives disliked his liberal professions, and liberals criticized his faltering performance. 'To err is Truman' became a popular joke. Republicans asked the electorate, 'Had enough?' In November 1946, the Republicans carried both houses of Congress for the first time since 1928. The new Eightieth Congress proceeded to punish the trade unions by enacting the Taft-Hartley Law, to punish Roosevelt by

The supermarket, an American invention, made possible in the mid-fifties by improvements in food freezing and transportation

Below Pontiac status symbol, 1956 model
Bottom Flyover systems brought more speed and suburbs spreading into the countryside

passing a constitutional amendment forbidding third presidential terms and to punish Truman by ignoring his recommendations and overriding his vetoes.

While the administration floundered at home, the cold war deepened abroad. Communist pressure was mounting against Greece and Turkey; and early in 1947, Great Britain notified Washington that it would have to end financial support to a Greek government struggling against communist insurgents. The collapse of Greece, it was supposed, would embolden Moscow to press an offensive against Italy and France. Truman accordingly went to Capitol Hill in person to urge what later became known as the Truman Doctrine. 'I believe,' Truman said, 'that it must be the policy of the United States to support free peoples who are resisting attempted subjugation by armed minorities or outside pressures.' Some, within the administration and without, flinched at the sweeping language and open-ended commitment. But Congress responded to presidential evangelism and enacted the Aid Bill.

Britain's economic trouble was part of a general collapse that now threatened to bring down all Western Europe. Drastic action was imperative if the European democracies were to rebuild their economies and resist the communist offensive. In June 1947, the secretary of state, George C. Marshall, offered American support for a European recovery programme. 'Our policy,' he said, 'is directed not against any country or doctrine but against hunger, poverty, desperation and chaos.' The Russians, however, rejected the invitation to join in the programme and forced their satellites to do likewise – an action that completed the division of Europe and facilitated the enactment of the Marshall Plan by the American Congress. Marshall Aid – $12·5 billion in the next four years – helped restore the West European economy in a strikingly short time.

The Truman Doctrine and the Marshall Plan provided the foundations for a policy of containing communist expansion. But the containment policy soon provoked heated debate in the United States.

On the right, traditional isolationists, led by Senator Robert A. Taft of Ohio, doubted America's financial or moral capacity to sustain an activist international policy. On the left, the American communists and other Americans unwilling to surrender the idea of the innocence or virtue of Stalin had some strength within the labour movement and the liberal community. They found a leader in Henry A. Wallace, who had been Roosevelt's vice-president in 1941-5.

YEAH — SO HELP ME GOD!

LOYALTY OATH

Top Senator McCarthy from Wisconsin examines a communist rifle. The projections of his Senate Sub-Committee on Investigations branded 'communists' and 'homosexuals' as enemies of the US; many Democrats had apparently been 'traitors' for twenty years or more
Above A cartoon from the early fifties which typifies the suspicions and hatred whipped up by McCarthy's persecutions

Truman's second term

As the 1948 presidential election approached, Truman's advisers concluded that his only hope for re-election lay in a strong liberal programme. The president bombarded Congress with a series of reform proposals. Much of this was a reaffirmation of New Deal objectives; but in the field of racial justice Truman broke new ground. Though he was himself the child of the Southern folk-ways of a border state, he was a man of humane instinct. He was also aware of the considerable change in the position of black America wrought by the New Deal and the war.

The New Deal had rarely challenged the practice of segregation where locally established, but New Deal agencies had generally worked hard to give the black worker or sharecropper a fair economic break. Then the war, by creating full employment, increased economic opportunity for blacks and accelerated their migration from Southern backlands to Northern industrial cities. The war also produced declarations that were obviously incompatible with the continued subjection of black America: it was not easy to crusade against Hitler's 'Master Race' doctrine abroad and retain a white-supremacy doctrine at home. Recognizing the validity of black aspirations, Truman in 1946 appointed a President's Committee on Civil Rights and in 1948 adopted its racial justice programme as his own.

Many still considered him, however, a figure of derision. When Truman, doughty as ever, managed to secure renomination, it looked as if his party were disintegrating under him. Democrats alienated by his foreign policy defected in one direction to support Henry Wallace as the candidate of the communist-dominated Progressive Party. Democrats alienated by his racial policy defected in the other direction to nominate Strom Thurmond of South Carolina on the State Rights Democratic ('Dixiecrat') ticket. The Republicans again picked Thomas E. Dewey, who now travelled round the country with the complacent confidence of a man who could not lose.

Only Truman himself thought he had a chance. His tireless whistlestop campaign, marked by pungent attacks on the 'do-nothing, good-for-nothing' Eightieth Congress, soon began to rouse the voters. The Dixiecrat movement made him a hero among the blacks, while the Wallace movement eliminated communism as an issue between the major parties and kept the Catholics in the Democratic camp. To everyone's astonishment save Truman's own, he won a decisive victory.

Truman began his second term by promulgating an ambitious programme of social and economic reform. But his Fair Deal encountered strong opposition and soon trailed off in frustration. Developments abroad, moreover, began to shift attention back to foreign affairs. In June 1948 Stalin had clamped a land blockade round Berlin; the Western Allies responded by organizing a massive airlift. Though the Russians finally called off the blockade in May 1949, the Berlin crisis, on top of the 1948 communist coup in Czechoslovakia, convinced Western Europe of the need for a regional defence agreement. Washington welcomed the European initiative and, in an historic departure, agreed to become a fully committed member of the new military alliance. The North Atlantic Treaty Organization, established in April 1949, gained new significance when the Soviet Union that summer exploded its first atomic weapon, ending the American nuclear monopoly. In response Truman directed American scientists to create an even more fearful weapon, the hydrogen bomb.

So each superpower continued to corroborate the worst fears of the other. In retrospect, it seems probable that both were acting on essentially defensive grounds. Yet how could anyone be certain at the time? How, in particular, were the Americans to be sure in this strange period when Stalin's madness, as subsequently disclosed by his closest collaborators, had grown into unbridled paranoia? Could the Western democracies have relied upon Stalin's restraint had there been no Truman Doctrine, no Marshall Plan, no NATO, no response in Korea?

For the Far East was even more unstable than Europe. By the end of 1949 Chiang Kai-shek and his remaining forces withdrew to the island of Taiwan,

Federal government expenditure 1950-70

Legend:
- defence
- international affairs
- space
- agriculture
- commerce and transport
- housing, welfare and education

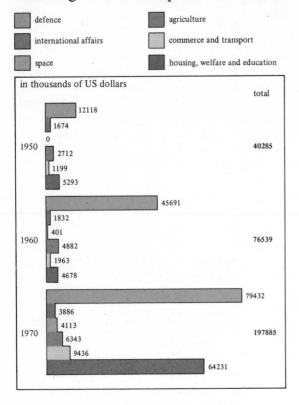

in thousands of US dollars

total

1950
- 12118
- 1674
- 0
- 2712
- 1199
- 5293

total 40285

1960
- 45691
- 1832
- 401
- 4882
- 1963
- 4678

total 76539

1970
- 79432
- 3886
- 4113
- 6343
- 9436
- 64231

total 197885

Civilian employees in the federal government 1940-70

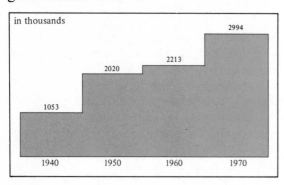

in thousands

- 1053 (1940)
- 2020 (1950)
- 2213 (1960)
- 2994 (1970)

Crime 1960-8

Legend:
- murder and manslaughter
- rape
- robbery
- assault
- burglary
- larceny (over $50)
- auto theft

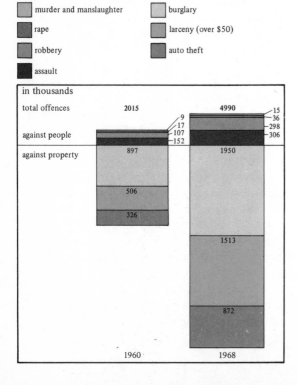

in thousands

total offences 2015 — 4990

against people
- 9 — 15
- 17 — 36
- 107 — 298
- 152 — 306

against property
- 897 — 1950
- 506 — 1513
- 326 — 872

1960 — 1968

leaving Mao Tse-tung and the communists in control of the mainland. Hardly had the United States absorbed this shock than on 25 June 1950 North Korean troops crossed the Korean dividing-line at the 38th parallel in a surprise invasion of South Korea. If the United States did not react in Korea, Truman believed, the Russians would sponsor similar thrusts elsewhere; and, without hesitation, he ordered American forces in Japan under General Douglas MacArthur to go to the defence of South Korea. At the same time he obtained a UN resolution authorizing collective resistance to aggression in Korea.

Truman's intention was to fight a limited war for limited objectives; but MacArthur's brilliant generalship recovered most of South Korea by October and raised the possibility of carrying the war into North Korea. Despite warnings that crossing the 38th parallel might provoke Chinese intervention, the UN gave MacArthur the new authority he requested. Seven weeks later, as the UN forces were advancing towards the Yalu River, the Chinese entered the war and forced the UN troops to fall back in disarray.

MacArthur blamed his defeat on Washington's decision to forbid attack on Chinese bases in Manchuria. He thereupon began a campaign, public as well as private, for the enlargement of the war. The campaign rapidly reached the point of insubordination. Truman, after showing exemplary and unaccustomed patience, finally recalled MacArthur in April 1951 – an act that set off an intense, if short-lived, uproar in the United States. After sober consideration, most Americans agreed with General Omar Bradley that general war against China would be 'the wrong war, at the wrong place, at the wrong time, and with the wrong enemy.'

Though Truman avoided serious military escalation, he was less successful in avoiding rhetorical escalation. The new China, for example, was perceived simply as an extension of Soviet power. Assistant Secretary of State Dean Rusk spoke of the Mao regime as 'colonial Russian government – a Slavic Manchukuo'. Soon the uprising of Vietnamese nationalism against French control was incorporated into the larger pattern. By 1954, the United States was paying nearly eighty per cent of the French costs of the war.

The intensification of the cold war had drastic repercussions within the United States. Many Americans demanded to know why their nation, deemed so powerful and so safe in 1945, should now appear in deadly peril. Some, resenting the complexity of history, found a satisfactory answer by tracing all trouble to the workings of the unsleeping communist conspiracy. There had unquestionably been communist penetration of the American government, the labour movement and the intellectual community, and there were now multiplying disclosures of communist espionage in Canada and other countries. Recognizing the reality of the problem and at the same time hoping to keep public reaction under control, Truman in 1947 set up a federal loyalty programme.

The charge in 1948 that Alger Hiss, a former official of the Roosevelt administration, had been a Soviet spy and Hiss's own conviction for perjury in 1950 increased popular apprehension. If Hiss, a man of unimpeachable respectability, was a communist agent, who might not be? A few weeks later Senator Joseph R. McCarthy of Wisconsin suggested that the State Department itself was full of communists. A storm of near-hysteria began to blow. Conservatives asked 'Who lost China?', as if China had been America's to lose, and replied that it was a group of officials in the State Department. Though Truman's loyalty programme had in some respects overridden traditional safeguards of individual freedom, it did not go nearly far enough for McCarthy and his followers; the McCarthy Committee began a grotesque career of free-wheeling investigation and accusation.

The 1952 election

As the 1952 election approached, Truman once again found himself in trouble. Revelations of corruption in his administration confirmed the popular notion of a 'mess in Washington'. The Republicans, seeking a candidate above politics, passed over Senator Taft and nominated General Dwight D. Eisenhower, a man held in widespread national affection and

Top A *Krokodil* comment on the American way of life; the capitalist complains that 5 million unemployed are spoiling his advertisements
Above Little progress was made towards social integration during the fifties but in September 1957 a high school at Little Rock was forcibly integrated
Below A backdrop design proclaims American union solidarity

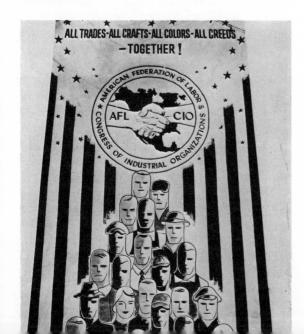

trust. Truman had taken himself out of the contest, and the Democrats turned to Governor Adlai Stevenson of Illinois. Though Stevenson proved to be an impressively literate and eloquent campaigner, the hope that Eisenhower could end the war in Korea and restore tranquillity at home proved too much for the Democrats.

Eisenhower, the first Republican president for twenty years, came to office promising to replace the Democratic policy of containment by a more aggressive policy of 'liberation'; and his secretary of state, John Foster Dulles, was the most dogmatic and sanctimonious of cold warriors. Yet Eisenhower's own instincts were pacific. Though he often seemed oblivious to problems until they reached the point of danger, his last-minute interventions were generally on the side of restraint. After protracted negotiation, an armistice terminated the Korean War in July 1953; and, when in 1954 Dulles and Vice-President Richard M. Nixon advocated American participation at the side of the French in the Vietnam War, Eisenhower killed the idea. The liberation doctrine vanished as a result of American inaction in the face of upheavals in East Germany in 1953 and Hungary in 1956. In the Suez crisis of 1956 the United States even joined with Russia against Britain and France in supporting a UN condemnation of Israel. Under Eisenhower American adventurism abroad tended to take a clandestine form, utilizing not the armed forces but the Central Intelligence Agency – as carried out in Guatemala, attempted in Indonesia and planned for Cuba.

In his circuitous and spasmodic way, Eisenhower genuinely strove to mitigate the cold war. The death of Stalin in 1953 gave new opportunities. Khrushchev was able to make a picturesque tour of the United States in 1959, concluding in amiable meetings with Eisenhower. But the Eisenhower administration's addiction to clandestine methods undercut the president's own conciliatory impulses; and the shooting down of a CIA U-2 espionage plane over Russia in May 1960 led to the collapse of a projected summit meeting in Paris and the revival of cold war recriminations.

The preference for inaction that often served Eisenhower so well in foreign affairs proved less fortunate in domestic policy. When Joe McCarthy proceeded to terrify the entire executive branch in his quest for communists, for many months the Eisenhower administration appeased and accommodated him. Encouraged by this complaisance, road-company McCarthys sprang up across the land. A horrid atmosphere bred by legislative investigations, loyalty oaths, blacklists, secret informers and repressive laws darkened the light of the Bill of Rights. But, if the Korean War had given McCarthy his great opportunity, the end of the war dissipated his emotional base. A series of televised Senate hearings in the spring of 1954, in which McCarthy tried to justify extravagant accusations against the army, gave him full and disastrous exposure, and the Senate voted his censure in December.

The Eisenhower administration also remained inert in the face of deepening social questions. The Supreme Court, under the leadership of Chief Justice Earl Warren, proceeded to take an active role in vindicating the rights of black Americans, notably when it outlawed racial discrimination in public schools in the 1954 case of *Brown* v. *Board of Education of Topeka*. But Eisenhower did little to execute the Court's decision until an attempt to nullify that decision in Arkansas in 1957 compelled him to send in the National Guard. That same year Congress forced the first Civil Rights Act since Reconstruction on the unenthusiastic president.

The administration remained even more passive before the problems of technological change. Eisenhower had two overriding domestic goals – to reduce the activity of the national government and to maintain the value of the dollar – and these prevented action to stop the decay of the cities, to preserve the natural environment, to eradicate poverty and to oppose the condition, brilliantly described by J.K.Galbraith in *The Affluent Society* (1958), of private opulence and public squalor. Eisenhower's archaic budgetary and fiscal policies succeeded only in slowing down the rate of economic growth (from 4·3 per cent in 1947-52 to 2·5 per cent in 1953-60) and causing sharp recessions in 1953-4 and 1957-8. The failure to tackle

The 1960 presidential election; it looked like a new era. The Democrats campaigned on an ambitious programme of social reform but Kennedy's extraordinary personal gifts were not to result in much of its legislation

John F. Kennedy, the youngest American president, with his wife

urgent domestic problems when they were still relatively manageable bequeathed a perilous legacy of unmanageability to the next decade.

For all this, Eisenhower's own popularity continued unabated. Though the Democrats regained control of Congress in 1954, Eisenhower defeated Stevenson once again in the presidential election of 1956.

The Kennedy era

As the 1960 election approached, the Republican nomination went to Nixon. John F. Kennedy, an attractive young senator from Massachusetts, then won the Democratic designation, defeating Lyndon B. Johnson of Texas, who became his vice-presidential running-mate. Kennedy contended that America had become stagnant and smug and that vigorous progressive leadership was necessary to 'get the country moving again'. In a series of face-to-face television encounters, Kennedy's superior poise and command destroyed the Republican argument that he was too young (forty-three) and inexperienced for the presidency. On the other hand, many hesitated to support a Roman Catholic; and, in the end, he emerged the victor in the closest popular vote since 1888.

The youngest man as well as the first Catholic elected to the presidency, Kennedy was an 'idealist without illusions', as he once described himself, with wide-ranging sympathies and a high sense of America's national and world responsibilities. He was still in part a child of the cold war, as his eloquent inaugural address showed: 'Let every nation know, whether it wishes us well or ill, that we shall pay any price, bear any burden, meet any hardship, support any friend, oppose any foe, in order to assure the survival and the success of liberty.' In this grandiloquent mood, he countenanced a CIA scheme, inherited from the Eisenhower administration, involving the dispatch of an expedition of Cuban refugees against the Castro regime. However, when disaster followed at the Bay of Pigs in April 1961, Kennedy cut his losses and assumed full personal responsibility.

This fiasco strengthened his scepticism about military advice and about American messianism. Basically Kennedy was an ironist, with a realistic sense of the limitations of superpowership. 'The revolution of national independence,' he said in 1962, was bringing a 'world of diversity' into existence, 'a world where, within the framework of international cooperation, every country can solve its own problems according to its own traditions and ideals.'

In this new world, he understood, both America and Russia must accept diminished roles. Nine months after his inaugural address he asked the American people to 'face the fact that the United States is neither omnipotent nor omniscient – that we are only six per cent of the world's population – that we cannot impose our will upon the other ninety-four per cent of mankind – that we cannot right every wrong or reverse each adversity. . . .' In this spirit, he abandoned the Eisenhower-Dulles hostility towards neutralism in the Third World, sought through his Alliance for Progress to strengthen the chances of progressive democracy in Latin America, cultivated the new nations of Africa and Asia and hoped through the Peace Corps to bring young Americans into partnership with the peoples of the Third World in their quest for national development.

To his conviction that in the long run 'the great currents of history are carrying the world away from the monolithic toward the pluralist idea', Kennedy added an intense concern over the short-run development of relations with the Soviet Union. Khrushchev's menacing speech of 6 January 1961, expressing a euphoric sense that communism was riding the crest of history, alarmed Washington, especially the passages displaying Soviet confidence that 'national-liberation wars' would soon deliver the Third World to communism. Persuaded that neither superpower had enough at stake in the remote Asian state of Laos to justify armed confrontation, Kennedy abandoned the Eisenhower effort to build a bastion of the West in the Asian jungle and turned to a policy of neutralization.

In June 1961 he met Khrushchev in Vienna and tried to persuade the Soviet leader that their two nations should refrain from actions that would

The Kennedy assassination, 22 November 1963: a psychopath, Lee Harvey Oswald, shot Kennedy as he rode in a Dallas motorcade; while in custody Oswald himself was killed by a Texas club-owner, Jack Ruby, in front of the TV cameras

A negro weeps at the spot where Kennedy died

upset the existing balance of international power and compel counter-action by the other. Khrushchev, still euphoric and perhaps misled by the Bay of Pigs into seeing Kennedy as irresolute, rejected the proposal for a global standstill and, except for Laos where he went along with Kennedy's proposal, adopted an intransigent attitude. In particular, he revived the perennial Berlin crisis by threatening to conclude a treaty with East Germany that would end Western rights of access to West Berlin. Kennedy's response – a rapid increase in American armed strength – evidently caused Khrushchev to think again. With the erection of the Berlin Wall in August, Khrushchev postponed his deadline indefinitely.

Blocked in Central Europe, Khrushchev looked elsewhere. In the summer of 1962, hoping to turn the American flank, he began to step up the delivery of Soviet arms to Cuba. When Kennedy warned against the installation of offensive weapons, Khrushchev repeatedly denied he had any such purpose. He was lying; ships carrying nuclear missiles were already on their way to Cuba. If Russia could carry out so spectacular a nuclear intrusion into the heart of what Moscow had always conceded as the American sphere of influence, other nations would wonder whether they could place any trust in Washington's protection and power.

When a U-2 overflight on 14 October 1962 revealed the presence of Soviet nuclear missiles, Kennedy decided to demand the immediate dismantling of the sites and the removal of the missiles. For thirteen days the world trembled on the abyss of nuclear war. But Kennedy took care to leave Khrushchev room for retreat, and the Russians finally removed the missiles in exchange for assurances that Kennedy would not invade Cuba, which he had no wish to do anyway. He now hoped that he had made to Khrushchev the point he had tried to make in Vienna – that neither super-power could afford to tamper carelessly with the delicate international equilibrium. With this in mind, he resumed his pursuit of *détente*.

In a speech at American University in Washington in June 1963, he asked the Russians to adopt more enlightened policies and added: 'I also believe that we must re-examine our own attitude . . . for our attitude is as essential as theirs.' He concluded with an appeal for a ban on nuclear testing. Khrushchev, calling it 'the greatest speech by any American president since Roosevelt', soon indicated that he would consider a partial ban, outlawing tests in the atmosphere, in outer space and under water. A treaty along these lines was negotiated in Moscow in July and ratified by the Senate in September.

In domestic affairs, where Kennedy was handicapped by his narrow margin of victory and by the power of the conservatives in Congress, he only partially attained the reform objectives of his New Frontier. However, an aggressive economic policy, culminating in the Tax Reduction Act proposed in 1963 and enacted in 1964, fostered the longest peacetime expansion of the American economy in recorded business-cycle history, with the GNP increasing at an average rate of 5·6 per cent. Noting that general fiscal stimulus did not reach down to the problem of the chronically poor, Kennedy began in 1963 to pull together the elements of a war against poverty; this too was enacted in 1964.

Right Unemployment: Kentucky miners stayed on in the deserted coalfields of Appalachia without work or the prospects of retraining

President Johnson signs the Economic Opportunity Act (1964): education and job-training programmes in the 'war on poverty'. The signature ceremony involved seventy-two pens, which were later handed out as souvenirs

His most dramatic fight was for racial justice. At first, Kennedy concentrated on executive rather than legislative action. With his brother, Attorney-General Robert F. Kennedy, as the key figure, the administration took steps to end segregation in interstate transportation and to secure the right of negroes to vote. In October 1962 Kennedy called out federal troops to protect the right of a black student to attend the University of Mississippi. But the black revolution, gathering momentum under the eloquent leadership of Dr Martin Luther King, demanded more. As the Kennedys began to understand the rising intensity of the problem, they threw the administration's full weight in 1963 behind the presidential proposition 'that race has no place in American life or law'. This effort won them strong support in black America and resulted in the enactment of sweeping new civil rights legislation in 1964.

In the fifties America seemed an old nation, complacent, weary, fearful of the future. Kennedy brought a message of discontent, and his words and actions set free an immense outpouring of critical energy. A new literature of protest examined hitherto shadowed or sacrosanct corners of American life and challenged hitherto uncontested premises. After a decade of torpor, America seemed headed for a decade of exhilarating movement when, on 22 November 1963, an assassin murdered Kennedy in Dallas, Texas.

Vietnam

Amidst world wide grief, Lyndon B. Johnson succeeded to the presidency. A politician of an older generation, Johnson had had unparalleled experience in the American Congress. A fervent New Dealer who had become more conservative in his middle years, he still retained an authentic concern for the poor, and, though he was a Southerner, for black America. While he soon rebaptized Kennedy's New Frontier under the name of the Great Society, he carried forward Kennedy's domestic programme with formidable legislative skill. Receiving the presidential nomination in August 1964, with Hubert Humphrey of Minnesota as his running-mate, he overwhelmed the right-wing Republican candidate, Senator Barry Goldwater of Arizona, and brought in with him enough Northern Democratic congressmen to assure, for the first time since 1938, a working progressive majority in the House of Representatives. This enabled Johnson in 1965-6 to compile an extraordinary record of legislation in such areas as medical care, aid to education, civil rights, housing and urban development and the fight against poverty and against air and water pollution; no Congress had been so productive on national questions since the days of the early New Deal.

Johnson's experience and progressive instinct in domestic affairs were unhappily combined with a devious, secretive and rather domineering

Right Civil rights marchers led by Ralph Bunche and Martin Luther King (right centre) demonstrate against voting discriminations towards negroes in Montgomery, Alabama, 1965

The assassination of the negro moderate leader, Martin Luther King on 4 April 1968 brought a nationwide wave of violence and looting; thirty people were killed and thousands injured or arrested. For many blacks King's death marked the end of liberal civil rights tactics. Scenes of disorder in Chicago (*below*) and Washington (*bottom*)

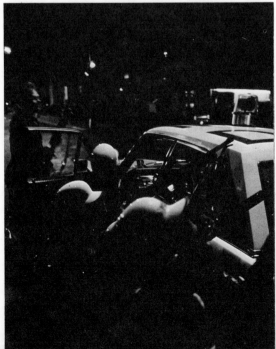

personality and with ignorance, inexperience and insensitivity in foreign affairs. These latter traits became evident in April 1965 when he sent 22,000 American troops to settle a civil war in the Dominican Republic – an action that revived the traditional mistrust of the United States throughout Latin America. But Johnson's penchant for overkill in foreign affairs found its most disastrous expression in the war in Vietnam.

Johnson was not, of course, responsible for American involvement in South-east Asia. After the expulsion of the French in 1954, the Eisenhower administration had made the Diem regime in South Vietnam a beneficiary of American political and economic support. In 1961 Kennedy decided to balance his neutralization of Laos by aiding the regime in South Vietnam, where prospects for military success seemed better. Beginning in early 1962, American 'advisers' were assigned to units of the South Vietnamese army and government; by the end of 1963, there were nearly 16,000 American troops in Vietnam. But the Vietcong continued to increase their numbers and extend their control. Kennedy, belatedly perceiving that Vietnam was as much a political as a military problem, urged Diem in vain to reform his regime. Then, three weeks before Kennedy's own death, a Vietnamese military junta overthrew and murdered Diem.

Kennedy never fully clarified his views on Vietnam. While regarding the United States as 'overcommitted' in South-east Asia, he said none the less that, the commitment having been made, America could not let South Vietnam fall to the communists. However, his memory of the French predicament a decade before had persuaded him that too large an infusion of white soldiers would only unite Vietnamese nationalism against the alien presence; and he had shown at the Bay of Pigs his capacity to refuse escalation and cut losses. 'In the final analysis,' he said of the South Vietnamese in September 1963, 'it is their war. They are the ones who have to win it or lose it.'

In any case, responsibility now passed to Johnson. By the end of 1963, only 110 Americans had been killed in Vietnam. Johnson ignored Vietnam in his State of the Union message in January 1964 and gave it hardly more than a hundred words in January 1965. When Goldwater advocated bombing North Vietnam during the presidential campaign, Johnson vigorously opposed the enlargement of the war. Then, early in 1965, told that the South Vietnamese army was on the verge of collapse, he sent American bombers to North Vietnam and American combat units to South Vietnam and thereby began the Americanization of the war.

Johnson's strategy was based on the conviction that, pounded long and hard enough, the enemy would eventually abandon the war. His generals kept assuring him that one more step of escalation would do the job, and,

A girl in a flower-power helmet with stickers on her face demonstrates against the Vietnam War; by 1968 more than half a million American soldiers were involved in the war, many of them near her age.

Brutal clashes between police and anti-war demonstrators marred the Democratic Convention in Chicago, August 1968; the 'doves' lost and the Convention endorsed Johnson's policies on Vietnam

step by step, America lurched deeper into the quagmire. By the end of Johnson's term there were 540,000 American troops in Vietnam. Nearly 50,000 had been killed in battle. More tons of explosives were dropped on that hapless country than on all the Axis states during the Second World War. Yet it was like trying to weed a garden with a bulldozer. Bombing failed to stop the movement of troops or supplies down from North Vietnam; and, instead of breaking the spirit of the enemy, if anything, it hardened Hanoi's will.

The enlargement of the commitment required an enlargement of the justification, and Johnson quickly obliged. 'History and our own achievements,' he said in 1965, 'have thrust upon us the principal responsibility for protection of freedom on earth.' What Kennedy had called 'their' war Johnson now saw as 'our' war. The revival of American messianism was accompanied by the theory that the 'free world' was confronted by a premeditated plan of Chinese aggression, of which the Vietcong and North Vietnam were only the spearhead. 'The threat to world peace,' cried Vice-President Humphrey, 'is militant, aggressive Asian communism, with its headquarters in Peking.'

Johnson's Vietnam policy continued for some time to have overwhelming public support. In the spring of 1965, however, a movement of protest, arising in the universities, soon found its most effective lodgement in the Senate Foreign Relations Committee whose chairman, Senator J.W.Fulbright of Arkansas, became a caustic and increasingly influential critic of the war. In February 1966 Robert F. Kennedy, now senator from New York, began a powerful campaign against further escalation and for a political settlement. The debate between 'doves' and 'hawks' intensified in the country with the approach of the 1968 presidential election.

In March 1968 Senator Eugene McCarthy, a dove, set back Johnson in the Democratic primary in New Hampshire, and the prospect of defeat in the Minnesota primary, along with the entry of Robert Kennedy into the contest, induced Johnson to withdraw at the end of the month, announcing at the same time the partial cessation of bombing in North Vietnam and the initiation of peace talks in Paris. But in June Kennedy was murdered, a few weeks after the death of Martin Luther King – two events that appalled the nation – and the nomination eventually went to Hubert Humphrey. The Republicans chose Richard Nixon. Nixon, with Spiro T.Agnew of

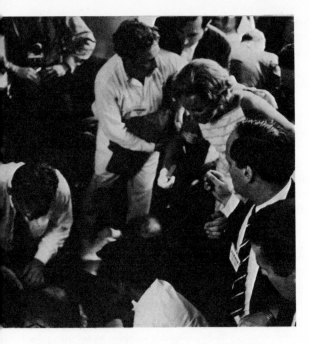

The assassination of Robert Kennedy, 5 June 1968:
his wife, Ethel at the front of the crowd in the
Ambassador Hotel, Los Angeles, where they had been
celebrating presidential primary victories in
California and South Dakota

'Nixon's the One': victory and confetti in the Philadelphia
motorcade following the 1968 election result

Maryland as his running-mate, was elected after an astonishingly close contest.

The new president soon began a programme of gradual troop withdrawal and announced the Nixon Doctrine limiting American commitments in Asia. At the same time, however, his policy of Vietnamization, by linking American withdrawal to the fortunes of the Saigon regime, clashed with Hanoi's insistence on a new government in Saigon and doomed the Paris negotiations to futility. Though casualties substantially declined in 1970, the American incursion into Cambodia and intermittent renewal of the bombing of North Vietnam suggested the futility of Nixon's hope that through military action he could bring the war to an end and preserve the unpopular Saigon regime.

By 1970 the Vietnam War had lasted longer than any war in American history, had caused more deaths in combat than any war except the Civil War and the two world wars and had cost the nation around $25 billion a year. It had produced a damaging inflation and new threats to the position of the dollar as well as a contraction of resources available for domestic development; Johnson's Great Society was an early casualty of his obsession with Vietnam. Even more serious was the spreading disillusion and disgust among the young over both the purpose of the war and the way it was fought – a mood that led some, especially after the dove revolt of 1968 failed to bring substantial change in the war policy, to question the efficacy of the American system of democracy. Demoralization spread into the army itself. The disclosure in 1969 of a ghastly massacre of Vietnamese civilians at My Lai in March 1968 showed how the war had brutalized some American soldiers, while by 1970 others were refusing to go into combat or solacing themselves with marijuana and other drugs or openly wearing peace symbols.

The Vietnam experience brought to a conclusive end the spirit of messianic confidence that had characterized America in 1945. By 1970 the American people were divided, the economy was in trouble, the armed forces were in discredit, the national motives were in doubt and liberal ideals themselves seemed implicated in the disaster. One result was an intensive re-examination of the bases of American policy in order to account for the horrible consequence.

On the left a tendency arose to ascribe everything – not only the Vietnam

War but the cold war and even American opposition to Germany and Japan in the Second World War – to the quest of American capitalism for world hegemony. It was true that American overseas investments had grown strikingly in the postwar period – from $8·4 billion in 1945 to $65 billion by 1968. If it was hard to argue that America went into Vietnam to gain markets or protect investments, the more sophisticated exponents of the economic thesis contended that, because defeat in Vietnam would jeopardize American markets and investments in other underdeveloped countries, economic interest therefore compelled Washington to a course of ruthless counter-revolution throughout the Third World. Close analysis of the figures showed, however, that two-thirds of American exports and seventy per cent of American investment went not to the Third World but to other industrial countries.

A more persuasive explanation saw Vietnam as the culmination of a number of pressures – pressures exerted by the vacuums of power created by the Second World War; by the doctrinaire execution of a perfectly honourable belief in a universal peace system; by the old evangelical commitment to America's regenerative mission to suffering mankind; by the liberal faith, fortified by the postwar experience of military occupation, in the American capacity to instruct and rebuild other nations; by the quite real menace of Stalinist communism; by the absolutist counter-ideology of anti-communism. And the specific pressure leading to active American intervention, especially in Vietnam, appeared to be the powerful military establishment, created in the Second World War, nourished in the cold war and at every stage the decisive influence in intensifying the Vietnam War – an influence operating, not at the bidding of American business, which by 1970 had predominantly turned against the war, but as an independent force in its own right.

The new crisis of confidence did more than generate a national desire to limit America's world role to areas clearly within the zone of American interests and capabilities. It also penetrated the domestic life of the nation. For the technological dynamism released by the Second World War had continued to disrupt and reshape American society.

The most spectacular technical accomplishment lay in the exploration of space. In 1961 Kennedy had proposed that the nation should land a man on the moon before the end of the decade. On 20 July 1969, as the world gaped before its television sets, Neil A. Armstrong stepped out of the *Apollo 11* lunar module into the moon's Sea of Tranquillity.

On earth America became the first nation to move from the Mechanical into the Electronic Age – the fantastic new epoch of electronic mechanisms of information, feedback and control, foreshadowed by television and the computer. This new age, founded on instantaneity, simultaneity and collectivity, promised to alter the very modes of psychological reaction and expectation; as Marshall McLuhan argued, the step-by-step, linear processes of thought instilled in a typographical culture might well give way to habits of instant perception and hopes of instant results. It also intensified the desire for visibility and self-assertion among previously submerged groups in the population. Following in the footsteps of the blacks other groups – students, women, the poor, Mexican-Americans, Indians, homosexuals – began to mobilize their strength in the quest for improved status.

The accelerating rate of technological change resulted in grave damage to the natural environment through pollution of air and water and through chemical disturbances of the balance of life; this produced what came to be known as the 'ecological crisis'. It enormously complicated life in the cities, now choked with traffic and filth, overflowing with tension and crime, deluged by the unemployed and the unemployable, vulnerable to crippling labour stoppages, lacking the funds to meet basic problems of urban management – hence the 'urban crisis'.

And the larger result of the injection of unprecedented and uncontrolled change into American society was to shatter the traditional framework of ideas, institutions and values. There thus arose the talk of the 'permissive society'. Speech, whether political or pornographic, was never more free

The sixties: a peace demonstrator with a flower in Washington

Kent State University students under fire from National Guardsmen in May 1970; four of them were shot dead

Right A construction workers' demonstration in New York City supporting Nixon and the war in Vietnam; by the late sixties the danger of breakdown in American society was openly acknowledged

Below Cartoon carried by the London *Evening Standard*, 5 October 1970

than in 1970. With regard to people's dress, appearance, behaviour or even their sexual activity, individual variations had never been more pronounced or individualism more unfettered. Many among the young seceded altogether, some entering into the aimless, timeless world of drugs and drifting, others seeking the physical destruction of what they considered a corrupt and hopeless society. It was a time of social and moral confusion, frustration, fear and violence.

All this presented a profound challenge to American politics. The urgent need was to bring the alienated and excluded groups into full membership in the national community; and this plainly required extensive revisions in the political, economic and social structure. The Nixon administration, however, showed in 1969-70 meagre recognition of the problem. Its economic policy slowed economic growth and increased unemployment without reducing inflation; and its political strategy aimed, not at national reconciliation, but at what Vice-President Agnew called the 'positive polarization' of the 'great silent majority' against the vociferous minorities. This strategy, with its emotional emphasis on 'law and order', failed markedly, however, in the mid-term elections of 1970, where the voters displayed a sober refusal to be panicked into extravagant national division.

If the internal crises seemed especially acute in the United States, it was probably not because of the peculiar depravity of the American economic system or of the national character but because the revolution wrought by science and technology had proceeded further in America than anywhere else. The crises afflicting America were crises of modernity, destined to afflict all states, whatever their systems of ideology or ownership, when they reached a comparable level of technological development. If the nation was in trouble, this was less the proof of decay than the price of progress. If governments could learn to manage the consequences of what Henry Adams had called the 'law of acceleration', the world might in time look back on the contemporary turmoil as the birth pangs of a new epoch in the history of man. In any case, the every-growing velocity of history posed the problems with which Americans would have to struggle in the decades ahead.

Karl Dietrich Bracher

Western Europe: the Quest for Unity

The concept and the development of Western Europe since the Second
World War are basically distinct from the traditional forms in which the
world of the European states arose and developed prior to the twentieth
century. It is true that extensive changes were already under way before and
after the First World War. But they were still, to a large extent, obscured by
older structures and illusions. It was only in the global aftermath of 1945,
accelerating the slowly developing process of change by the introduction
of new factors, that the real trends were clearly visible. Four highly significant developments most clearly illustrate the changed situation in Europe.

Above all we have the observation that world politics are no longer
Europe-centred, no longer conditioned by a balance of power essentially
concentrated in Europe. This observation is admittedly valid also for the
period between the two world wars, but the awareness of peoples and statesmen at that time lagged far behind the reality. The international influence of
the USA, the crises of the imperial colonial powers, the rise of Japan and
the Eurasian potential of Soviet Russia, formed the realities of the inter-war
years. The neglect of these realities was not least among the reasons for the
collapse of the attempt at reconstruction after the First World War and for
Hitler's disastrous rise to power. It is significant that the League of Nations
in effect was limited to the European sphere of power politics, and was
never able to do justice to the fact of a global extension of international
relations and interdependence of the political and economic problems of
all states. The First World War and its aftermath, the catastrophe of world
economic crisis and the spread of fascism were the expression of this international interdependence compared to which the traditional policies of
individual states played a very secondary role. But it was only the desolation
of 1945 which signalled irrevocably the end of the 'classical' politics of
sovereign nation-states in the modern era, which saw world history and
world politics as conditioned by Europe alone, by the conflicts and the
alliances of the European powers. In its place there appeared supranational
complexes which quickly divided Europe into two halves and, at the same
time, transcended it; they were dominated by two superpowers whose
policy-making had increasingly to take into account the newly created
states of the non-European world. Europe, from being the subject of international politics, had become its object, since American and Soviet troops
had come face to face in the centre of Germany and the development of the
UN had, for the first time, created a platform for voicing truly international
political ideas. In contradistinction to the upheavals from 1917 to 1919,
which brought down great empires, made far-reaching changes in regimes,
created new states, the second postwar period in Europe reconstituted the
system of states which had been steam-rollered by Nazi imperialism. Apart
from the Soviet annexation of the Baltic countries and of eastern Poland
the only significant change from the prewar situation was the destruction
of the German Reich; but despite this restoration of the nation-states their
traditional claim to sovereignty was not likewise restored. It was superseded by a polarization into Eastern and Western blocs dominating the
spheres of military power, economics and ideology.

Secondly, the drastic alteration in the international status of Europe had
a decisive effect, too, on the internal political structure of the European
countries. This can largely be seen as a function of the bloc formations of
external politics, which, in the train of the confrontation between East and
West, between Soviet and American hegemonies, also conditions the

Unity in Western Europe: an Italian poster (1947)
proclaims European recovery through peace and work.
The European Recovery Programme came to mean
Marshall Aid

Marshall aid to Western Europe 1948-52

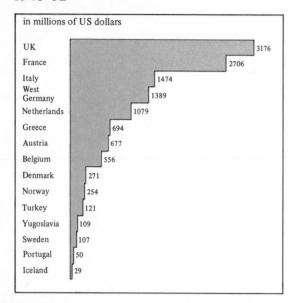

in millions of US dollars

UK	3176
France	2706
Italy	1474
West Germany	1389
Netherlands	1079
Greece	694
Austria	677
Belgium	556
Denmark	271
Norway	254
Turkey	121
Yugoslavia	109
Sweden	107
Portugal	50
Iceland	29

'Berlin emergency programme with Marshall Plan help' reads the sign over the building site; between 1948 and 1952 some $12 billion worth of American aid was distributed through the Organization for European Economic Cooperation, which was formed in April 1948 by the sixteen countries participating in the European Recovery Programme

domestic ideological scene. Even by 1946 the partition of Europe into liberal parliamentary systems and communist one-party regimes was already complete, and Western Europe was unambiguously divorced from Eastern Europe by its internal political structures. The amount of variation within these two fixed attitudes may be important for an appreciation of any particular state, its national characteristics and its political influence; but even in those countries which have managed to maintain some degree of independence somewhere between the two entrenched blocs, the internal political structure is, even so, conditioned by the confrontation of the major powers. Let us hasten to add, however, that outside the sphere of Soviet military power, that is to say, in the neutral countries (Sweden, Switzerland, Austria) it is the Western, not the communist form of government which has established itself. The exceptional case of Yugoslavia is counterbalanced by the preservation of a multi-party democracy in Finland.

In contrast to the inter-war period, when a multiplicity of powers characterized both international and internal politics and permitted a multitude of forms and attitudes among the European states, since 1945 the geographical concepts of West, Central and East Europe have been replaced by political considerations in terms of which Western Europe consists of the non-communist countries. In this sense then, of a political system which extends beyond the limits of geographical alignments, the term 'Western Europe' indicates that part of Europe in which political processes and political government rest on the basis of the will of the majority, in the form of multi-party systems with scope for changes of government and for opposition. Exceptions to this are the authoritarian systems of Spain and Portugal, which thereby demonstrate that an external adherence to the West is not necessarily identical with a domestic political system of Western democracy.

Thirdly, the socio-economic and cultural changes in this Western Europe which we are examining have largely been brought about by external factors; by the destruction wrought by the war, the disruption of population groupings and the withdrawal from colonial rule. In the long term, the process of reconstruction, with increased opportunities for modernization and industrialization, is overriding the traditional expressions of nation-state politics and making possible, indeed unavoidable, new forms of supranational cooperation. This process too, though doubtless sparked off and encouraged by military considerations as a sequel to the cold war (NATO), also involves the non-aligned states. This demonstrates that in the final analysis we are dealing with long-term, far-reaching developments, not explicable in terms of power blocs and foreign politics. We might say that the development of Western Europe rests on particular economic, social and cultural preconditions which, in the first instance reflected the existence of the Iron Curtain barrier; with new moves towards an East-West *rapprochement* a gradual convergence of these disparate systems appears to have entered the realms of the possible.

Finally, the system of government known as 'parliamentary democracy', having been shaken to its foundations between the wars, where it was not in fact destroyed by authoritarian fascist regimes, has shown itself to be surprisingly capable of regeneration. Again in contrast to the years after 1918, when the feebleness of parliamentarianism quickly became the most popular of bywords, and most of the new democracies fell victim within a short time to anti-parliamentary movements, the Western type of parliamentary democracy is becoming stabilized in a manner previously impossible and barely conceivable in the dark days of 1945. The events of the twenties and thirties have taught us to recognize in modern democracy a complex, constantly jeopardized and by no means perfect form of government. It is a form which, under the conditions of industrialization and technological revolution, of social mobility and shifts in intellectual climate, is exposed to a constant process of adaptation and adjustment. Two basic problems of modern democracy on the Western pattern emerge. Firstly, it is marked by deep tensions and contradictions: the tension between freedom and equality, between centralized government and maximum participation,

Per capita income 1958-68

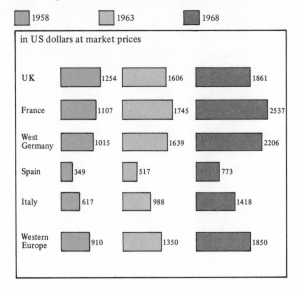

	1958	1963	1968
in US dollars at market prices			
UK	1254	1606	1861
France	1107	1745	2537
West Germany	1015	1639	2206
Spain	349	517	773
Italy	617	988	1418
Western Europe	910	1350	1850

Distribution of working population

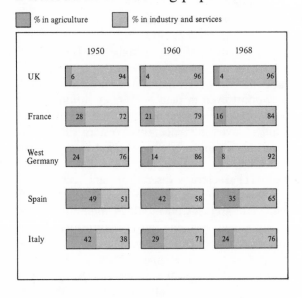

% in agriculture   % in industry and services

	1950		1960		1968	
UK	6	94	4	96	4	96
France	28	72	21	79	16	84
West Germany	24	76	14	86	8	92
Spain	49	51	42	58	35	65
Italy	42	38	29	71	24	76

Witch hunt 1962: angry farmers chase the European
sorceress (German cartoon). Agricultural problems proved
a divisive factor in moves towards European unity

between social order and individual freedom, between the principle of government by the people and the practice of representation, between direct democracy and the kind of parliamentarianism without which political decision-making and democratic rule in the larger states seem impossible. The second basic problem is the internal structural crisis of the parliamentary system itself. It is aggravated by the extension of state interference and control into ever wider areas of society, and a massive build-up of the administration. The shift of power from the legislative to the executive arm, the supplanting of parliamentary control by a movement towards bureaucracy, expertocracy and simple party rule jeopardize the efficiency and credibility of the democratic process.

In the period since the Second World War, these problems have continued to loom large in the construction and development of the Western democracies. But the problems which laid low most of the European democracies after 1918 were largely overcome; the problems of rendering the democratic system viable, capable of subordinating the political and social tensions of 'the age of the masses' to a stable and yet flexible order.

After 1945 there were three ways in which the preconditions for reconstructing parliamentary democracy in Western Europe were different and more favourable. First of all, in terms of *constitutional* arrangements, there was the painful awareness of past disasters to call upon, which was now framed in democratic constitutions and served to protect the parliamentary system, its effectiveness and its stability. This awareness is written into the West German system with particular thoroughness, but elsewhere too, as for example in the Fifth French Republic, it has led to the prevention of excessive political fragmentation, and to a stabilizing of parliamentarianism.

Secondly, *sociologically* the upheavals of the war and postwar period have resulted in a process of transformation and loosening of traditional social structures; the consequence is an increasing de-ideologizing and pragmatism in political parties. This promotes coalitions and cooperation between the various social and political groupings within the system, it softens the traditional divisions in the body politic and, finally, it strengthens the tendency towards two- or three-party systems, already underwritten by constitutional provisions and electoral procedure.

These tendencies have been particularly prominent in the development of West Germany, where the resettlement and integration of over 10 million refugees has had its effect; but equally in other countries a loosening of society, a new mobility, has facilitated the democratic process and simplified parliamentary decision-making; ideologically sharp oppositions have been diluted, democratically minded cooperation promoted, political conflicts blunted, all of which has facilitated practical compromises.

Thirdly, as far as *foreign policies* were concerned, the stabilization of the Western European democracies was guaranteed at an early stage by a network of alliances and cooperation, confronting Soviet claims to power in East and Central Europe. The driving force of European politics after the First World War was an unbridled nationalism, which by its very nature destroyed the internal foundations of democracy. At the same time the USA, which after all had decided the outcome of the war and had inaugurated the new order in Europe and the League of Nations, had withdrawn from international politics. It was quite different after 1945. The American policy of containment of communism placed Western Europe firmly within the framework of a far-reaching and intensive international cooperation, through the Marshall Plan and the NATO alliance. New facets of supranational integration were revealed in the shared institutions of the North Atlantic community; these provided a kind of protective umbrella for the new parliamentary democracies. Not that all this prevented the threat of internal political crises implicit in political fragmentation and the existence of strong communist parties, such as those of Italy and France. But at least it was possible to avoid a repetition of the prewar crises that led to capitulation and fascism.

In place of the tangle of national ambitions which had paved the way for the triumph of nationalistic dictatorships after 1918, the misery of post-

Clement Attlee, leader of the British Labour Party, during the May 1955 general election, won by the Conservatives; he resigned the following December

Funeral of the joint: housewives protest at the reduction of the meat ration in February 1951. By the end of the year electors had turned against Labour austerity

'You've never had it so good' was the Conservative slogan under Macmillan: the prime minister grouse shooting on the Astor's moor in Aberdeenshire, 1958

Second World War Europe engendered a realistic appreciation of the need for self-limitation of national sovereignty. The resistance movements had already generated far-reaching plans for closer cooperation and even political integration within Europe. The only appropriate reaction to the drastic situation of 1945-6 was to accept the reality of economic, military and political inter-involvement, not to pursue isolated national policies. It was a process to which the inevitable running-down of colonial empires contributed, tending to direct the attention of European states to the tasks of domestic reform and external cooperation. In the face of such problems the old nation-state tensions dwindled to insignificance, and the possibility of compromises in internal and external policies was very much increased. This was notably true of the West German democracy; here, after the breathing-space provided by the occupation, development towards stability could take place almost undisturbed under the umbrella of Western European and Atlantic alliances. This experience of economically and politically efficient parliamentary rule was a refreshing contrast to the inter-war years, when it was equated with crisis and collapse.

Trends of the postwar era

The development of the Western European countries displays a variety of characteristics which, for all the differences in national tradition, are common to all states in the group. Three main tendencies can be seen emerging in the immediate postwar period.

Nearly everywhere the left acquired such a powerful new impetus that one could speak of a general shift to the left. This was first seen in the great election victory of the British Labour Party in 1945, and is also revealed in the strength of communist and socialist parties in France and Italy, in the attempts to form anti-fascist left-wing coalitions in the early postwar years, in the part played by social-democrat governments in Scandinavia and in the enlistment of the left's support even in places where coalitions of the middle-class parties have been formed. However, in contrast to the course of events in Eastern Europe under Soviet influence, this Western shift to the left has nowhere led to a permanent union or fusing together of socialist and communist parties.

On the other hand, there was a characteristic discrediting and recession of the political right. Certainly it was only in Italy that a monarchy was replaced by a republic, but the surviving monarchies were modified and limited, in so far as they had not previously already become fully constitutional (as in Britain or Scandinavia). And even if there could be no question of a simple association of the right-wing parties with the stigma of Nazi collaboration, their ambivalent attitudes to the authoritarian and fascist ideologies and regimes was enough reason for the fact that the anti-fascist wave of the postwar years was directed mainly at the conservative right. And it was too early to forget the failure of conservative-liberal economic policies between the wars, such a powerful contributory cause of the crisis of the democracies. A restoration of the old capitalist order seemed ruled out, furthermore, by the need to continue into the years of postwar austerity the emergency measures taken by central government to support a war economy. The continuing trend towards planned economy and nationalization, towards politico-social reform in depth, seemed to confirm the dominance of socialism in Western Europe; the failures of capitalism and the ensuing collision-course of fascism must inevitably be followed by socialism; so at least the diagnoses and prognoses proclaimed.

The third tendency was that within a few years there was a general swing in political attitudes and the power balance in the Western European democracies, notwithstanding local variations. The most significant features of this new direction were the exclusion of communist parties from participation in government, the strengthening of the moderate centre, and in particular the rapid rise of Christian-democrat parties to the key positions in state and society. They represented a new element in the party structure of Western Europe; even if they had their roots in older forms of Church-affiliated organizations there were features of the new parties which removed

Top Macmillan as Guy Fawkes: Vicky cartoon,
5 November 1962, on the then explosive issue of Britain's
bid to join the Common Market
Above 'Where the seeds of the whirlwind have been sown,
scarcely more than the first blades are above the surface':
1969 cartoon on Enoch Powell, Conservative MP for
Wolverhampton, who seized on the race issue as a subject
for national debate

Harold Wilson press conference: prime minister from 1964
with a Labour majority of only three, which was increased
to ninety-seven by a shrewdly timed election in March
1966. Wilson lost support over the decline of the
economy, for which he had taken personal responsibility,
and over Rhodesia – yet it still looked as if he would
be returned in 1970. But the opinion polls were wrong
in the biggest upset since the 1948 American
presidential election

them entirely from the old framework – the affirmation of parliamentary democracy, the receptiveness to Christian-socialist stimuli and the diminished importance of conservative clerical traditions, all leading to a popular party of the centre open to offers of coalitions from all sides, and prepared to reconcile capitalism and socialism. This emancipated Christian-democratic movement united the interests of most middle-class elements. In this it received invaluable assistance from the support of the Church, which was the only form of strong authority to survive the total ideological collapse of the war period. In Germany and Italy, indeed, the Church was almost the only authority still intact and recognized by the occupying powers. Of no less importance to the rise of Christian democracy was its association with anti-fascist resistance groups and the new will to democracy emerging from the bloody demise of a totalitarianism sanctioned by the middle classes.

There was a chain of causes for the rapid scene-changing of political life in Western Europe. The almost total reversal after 1947 was accelerated as much by economic as by political and military factors. The close inter-meshing of internal and external politics is characteristic of the crucial developments of 1947-8. It led extraordinarily quickly from the open-ended, crisis-ridden postwar situation with its prospects of a socialist-style transformation of state and society, to the consolidation of parliamentary multi-party government and the restoration of liberal economic and social systems, accompanied by a resurgence of the centre and the right. With this reversal, soon reflected in the West German market economy and gaining immense popularity as the 'economic miracle', the signals were set for future economic-political development up until the present day.

The direction taken was decisive, and there was soon hardly any conceivable alternative to it. The facts appeared all too plain. The economic stabilization brought about by the Marshall Plan formed a glaring contrast to the calamities of communist economic policy in Eastern Europe. The confrontation of the superpowers, the USA and the USSR, was increasingly regarded as a trial of strength between the free and the planned social systems. Stalinist coercion, climaxing in the Prague takeover of February 1948 and the blockade of Berlin (June 1948-May 1949) was answered on the American side by reinforcement of the containment policy, by increased economic and military aid to Western Europe. The cold war effectively blocked the chances of socialist policies in Western Europe and resulted in the exclusion of communist parties from political leadership.

Western Europe's democratic stabilization was of course not simply the result of a dark capitalist-imperialist plot, as Soviet propaganda slogans proclaimed. It was not only communism but also the ideas of socialist reform and of an independent European development, that were discredited by the enforced sovietization of the Eastern camp. The consequence was anti-communist-orientated, bourgeois governments – in Britain among others, upon the defeat of the Labour Party (1951) – setting about the job of reconstruction with American economic support and military backing. Economic recovery and political stabilization tended to restore traditional structures, as did also the growing European and Atlantic cooperation. At the close of the forties the patterns were set for the further development of Europe up to the present. In the fifties and sixties it was particularly the democratic left which suffered from these patterns; its efforts to promote an alternative style of restoration remained ineffectual until sooner (in France) or later (in West Germany and Italy) it was forced to recognize the *fait accompli*. In these circumstances possible alternatives to the adopted course of confrontation between East and West, or conservative and socialist platforms, were never really tested for their viability. Hence the difficulty of deciding whether it is accurate to talk of the 'lost opportunities' of the postwar period, as many critical observers have done, or whether it was iron necessity that decided the division of Europe (and of Germany above all), as many who took an active part were convinced – a conviction shared by the greater part of the population under the impact of the threats and crises inherent in the cold war and, conversely, the incomparably greater freedom and higher living standards of the West. Again within the general picture

Top Ejector seats for reactionary governments – 1954
French cartoon on political instability
Above Rioting on de Gaulle's visit to Algiers in
December 1960; two years later Algeria was independent,
and one of the main problems leading to his
recall was solved
Below Opposition to de Gaulle increased in the late
sixties, but he hung on in the March 1967 national
elections with a slim majority (the emblem is the
Free France double cross of Lorraine)

were to be found many local variations of attitude among the Western countries involved. It was in West Germany above all that the politics of stability within confrontation were most powerfully expressed; the spectacle of Soviet coercion in Eastern Germany, and the vision of West German political rehabilitation and a rapid recovery from disaster, were particularly strong incentives there.

Problems in five countries: France

Against the background of general trends, the history of individual Western European countries is still essentially bound up with specific problems of *national* development and socio-economic conditions, for so long the chief factors in conflicting European politics. This was completely understandable. It not only indicated the weight of traditional attitudes and ideologies, lagging behind changed realities, but also corresponded to the very heterogeneous circumstances and interests of the peoples of Europe. The tension between individual state politics and those of Europe as a whole does in fact play a considerable part in inter-state relations as well as in the pursuit of national interests, and in forming opinion in Western European societies.

Though this tension was lessened by the consolidation of an economic union (EEC), it was yet a surprise to the protagonists of the union to discover that this progressive step did not automatically give rise to further political integration, for example a European federation. Despite official assertions of support, individual interests stood in the way of such an achievement.

Most prominent was the difference between the intact nation-states of Europe and the special interests of Western Germany, which was only able to secure guarantees of recognition and parity with the aid of supranational European policies. By way of contrast we can take France, whose policies were directed primarily towards rehabilitation after the catastrophe of 1940 and shoring up her position as an independent great power in the camp of the victors. That these two poles might be brought closer together was the essential precondition for any European programme. This first showed signs of happening after the changes of 1948. Initially, however, it seemed that the political system of the Fourth Republic, despite many constitutional changes and France's diminished status as a European and colonial power, was bent on reviving the style of the prewar Third Republic. There were admittedly new elements – especially Charles de Gaulle and the continuing importance of the Resistance – but they had an ambivalent influence on political developments.

A figure of supreme egocentricity, controversial and yet impossible to ignore, de Gaulle twice decisively stepped into a central role in French history: with the proclamation of resistance in 1940 and with the solution of the Algerian crisis. The latter set the seal upon the radical transformation of the tottering Republic into the Gaullist presidential regime of the Fifth Republic. But in 1945 he failed utterly in his attempt to use the respect he enjoyed as a Resistance leader to bring about an authoritarian modification of the parliamentary multi-party state. It was not until the explosive civil war atmosphere of 1958 that there was any real chance of success for the mixture of absolutist, traditionalist and democratic-plebiscitary ideas which the Gaullist movement conceived in the years after 1945. And the mystical glorification of the nation, which de Gaulle saw embodied in himself, revealed itself in the conditions of postwar Europe as a mere anachronistic interlude. The independent policy of *détente* with Eastern Europe certainly had some effect in the lessening of East-West tensions, but Gaullist nationalism could not be reconciled with the reality of an age of superpowers, either in military terms – through the French nuclear programme – or in economics, or in international politics. For the most part Gaullism was a negative and disruptive influence in European integration and on relationships with the USA and Britain. The historical role of de Gaulle in 1945 consisted in the fact that he incorporated the broadest possible anti-fascist coalition front, from right to left. On this basis the Resistance, embracing members of all parties from communists to conservatives, established its place as the main political support of the Fourth

De Gaulle: a strange mixture of absolutist and democrat, whose policies managed to contain both anachronisms and prophecies. In the early sixties he rode to some extent on the crest of improving French economic conditions; under his presidency France became the world's fourth nuclear power in 1960 and formed a front against Anglo-American influence in Europe

Student rioting in Paris, May 1968: a month of social and economic turmoil that involved a strike of nearly 10 million workers for higher minimum wages; among the students' demands were educational reforms, some of which they got, after de Gaulle's referendum and brief continuance in office

Republic. Complicated and unstable the structure of parliamentary compromise in the Republic may have been, but on this basis it survived the onerous encumbrance and divisions of the Indo-China War and truly paved the way for the economic recovery which the Fifth Republic could exploit for stabilization and for its own ambitious ends. Equally significant was the fact that it was the political weight of the Resistance, well disposed towards European thinking, which gave reality to the first faltering steps towards European unity, in which the French vote was necessarily decisive. Out of the tensions between nationalistic Gaullism, permanent communist opposition and European cooperation, the latter arose to assert itself as a determining force.

It was a confusing course which French domestic politics ran from de Gaulle's gesture of resignation (1946), via the ousting of the Communist Party, to the NATO alliance and to the Coal and Steel Community of the Six (initiated 1950), and, after the breakdown in 1954 of the European Defence Community (signed 1952) finally to the Paris Agreements (1955) and the European Common Market (1957). But whatever the setbacks suffered by this course before and after the return of de Gaulle in 1958, there was no basis for comparison with the methods and objectives of French policies after the First World War. All attempts to give precedence to policies of great-power prestige in preference to a concrete programme of domestic renewal and supranational cooperation, ended like de Gaulle's cherished objectives in a cul-de-sac. This course of events appears all the stranger when one reflects that the question of a political majority in France remained extremely complicated. In the first elections for the constituent assembly formed to establish a constitution (October 1945) three almost equally powerful blocs confronted each other: Communists (twenty-six per cent), Socialists (twenty-four per cent) and MRP (twenty-six per cent). The trade union movement also remained (as in Italy) divided into three factions.

Here too a new Christian-democratic movement (MRP) was able to play a vital part. As well as the conservative middle class, liberal and moderate-leftist elements were attracted to it on the basis of the common Resistance tradition. In contrast to earlier Christian parties, which had gone into operation against the liberal and laicizing France of 1789, the MRP attempted to reconcile democratic and republican, Christian and conservative, liberal and socialist traditions within a popular party of all classes. While the socialists profited little from their support of most governments and continually lost adherents, the communists were not considered eligible to participate in any coalition, the liberals had shrunk to a mere splinter group and the Gaullists after 1947 led the intransigent right, the MRP under Robert Schumann successfully diverted France into a European policy which, despite the delicate parliamentary majority situation, could count on the agreement of a pragmatically minded population. The new initiative was favoured by the leading role played at the same time by Christian-democrat-dominated governments in Italy, the Benelux countries and in the newly founded Federal Republic of Germany. Undeniably the movement was also conditioned by the conservative middle-class nature of the pro-European philosophy: even the non-communist left hesitated for a long time to associate itself with it, and most of all the moderate unions.

MRP foreign ministers remained on this course. Admittedly their party, unlike kindred parties elsewhere in Europe, was put under pressure and weakened by Gaullist competition for the hearts of the conservative middle class. Its vital function in the decisive events of 1948-52 was not followed by a spectacular rise comparable to that enjoyed in the same years by the CDU in Bonn. The MRP was in the end almost annihilated by the polarization between the left (communists) and right (Gaullists). Even the attempts at a firmer course of reform under the left-liberal liquidator of the Indo-China War, Pierre Mendès-France, who was responsible for a successful drive to modernize the social and economic structure (which later benefited the Fifth Republic), could not arrest the galloping deterioration of the Republic. Sceptical observers drew parallels between the fate of the centre in Weimar and de Gaulle's seizure of power – except that the latter was no Hindenburg

The division of Germany after 1945

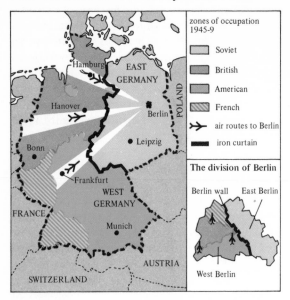

zones of occupation
1945-9

Soviet

British

American

French

air routes to Berlin

iron curtain

The division of Berlin

Postwar damage in Berlin; in June 1948 the Western
powers decided to turn their zones into a state and
to give it the potential for economic growth

Berlin a decade later: the prosperous Kurfurstendamm

and very far from being a Hitler. On the contrary, he succeeded (1958-61) in
pacifying the army, disenchanted and in some sections ready for a *coup d'état*.
And above all, the political public in France, for all its criticism of the failed
Fourth Republic and broad sympathy for the conservative stability of the
Gaullist presidential regime, was not ready to make an apolitical surrender
to dictatorship. So much became clear, when the reverse side of the Fifth
Republic's stability revealed itself; behind the façade of modernization and
nationalist great-power policies there lurked stagnation and blindness to
reality. The great crisis of 1968 and the final resignation of de Gaulle
demonstrated the existence of a vital democratic culture, capable of withstanding Caesarism and fascist tendencies, of setting a strong Communist
Party on the course of reform and of binding almost all political forces in
the country to the republican tradition of 1789. Unlike Italy or Germany,
France can boast of a basic consensus behind the often confusing impression
of political and ideological fragmentation.

It must be conceded that economic interests and calculations, increasingly
threatened by de Gaulle's costly nationalistic autonomy, contributed a
great deal to this healthy French consensus. Here is yet another token of the
significance which pro-European economic policies have for the domestic
structure and development of states. Here is the real nucleus of the hope
that economic involvement will exert a growing pressure towards political
integration. It was possible to see even in the year of de Gaulle's death (1970)
the beginnings of an adaptation, however hesitating, of the Gaullist system
to democratic and European postulates. The general had himself already
dismantled the anti-American policy; the curt double veto on Britain's
entry to the Common Market, this too rooted in personal resentment, has
made way for concrete negotiations; and in the historic decisions of France,
the painful renunciation of her colonial empire, and her European and
bilateral cooperation with West Germany, de Gaulle was forced to swallow
his own words. His conception of a nation-based Europe *des patries* led by
France could be seen as a delaying tactic; the steps already taken under the
Fourth Republic remained decisive.

Italy

Much less dramatic was the development of Italy, even though numerous
government crises and permanent economic and social structural problems
beset both domestic modernization and policies towards Europe. The
revival of democracy was burdened not only with the fascist inheritance, but
also with a long history of foreign occupation, the continuing existence of
feudalism, the deep discrepancies between the industrial north and the
agrarian south; as a recently unified country, Italy like Germany had special
difficulty in acquiring a democratic sense. True, and unlike Germany, Italy
had succeeded in putting a timely end to fascism and war (September 1943).
But this only succeeded in deepening internal divisions; while in the north,
against the rump of Mussolini's republic, a partisan movement was gathering
strength, committed to radical political and social reforms, in southern and
central Italy by the end of the war the pre-fascist establishment had long
re-established the old order in all its aspects.

The monarchy, discredited by fascism, was indeed finally dislodged by
means of a plebiscite, with fifty-four per cent in favour (June 1946), although
it was only in the north that there was a majority vote for the Republic. But
the Democrazia Cristiana (DC), as a broadly representative party with right
and left wings constituting a new element in Italian politics as elsewhere,
failed to detach itself from the conservative Church to the same degree as
did Christian-democrat parties in other countries. Its power base was rooted
in the underdeveloped south and it enjoyed an uninterrupted reign,
generally with the support of right-wing coalitions.

The hopeful reconstruction of state and society, which was demanded
particularly by the Resistance forces (*resistenza*) of the north after the end of
the war, was halted by this mighty bastion. The DC possessed in Alcide De
Gasperi a talented exponent of the anti-fascist centre, well able to play the
factions off against each other and finally to out-manœuvre the communists

and left-wing socialists (May 1947). Political forces were divided, as in France, into three chief camps, of which the DC, the central party of the right, was by far the strongest (thirty-eight–forty-eight per cent); the Communists could muster about twenty-five per cent and the Socialists fifteen–twenty per cent (six per cent Social Democrats). The experiment of an anti-fascist all-party government under Ferruccio Parri (June-December 1945) came to grief over plans for reform, and the shift towards a non-socialist pro-European policy relegated the strong left to permanent opposition and set the seal on a crisis-ridden maintenance of the *status quo*. Not until 1962, with the *apertura a sinistra* (opening to the left) under Amintore Fanfani (DC) was there any attempt to pursue long-overdue social reforms and modernization on a broad basis.

The Christian-democratic and pro-European policies pursued by De Gasperi until his death in 1954 brought in their train a belated Italian 'economic miracle'. But its benefits were very unevenly distributed; failure to solve the problems of the underdeveloped regions and to reform an antiquated educational system as well as an excessively bureaucratized civil service that was partly corrupt and partly over-extended, aggravated the old animosity towards the state widely found among the Italian people, and the already deep schisms of political and social life. The much-needed reform of the federal structure was never carried out; fragmentation of opinion and immobility characterize the situation to this very day. The responsibility for this is borne not least by dissension within the once-powerful Socialist Party, whose divisions and reunions have been a constant feature of postwar politics. Essentially, it is only due to Italy's participation in Europe that a crisis, such as happened in 1922, was avoided and a coalition of the left triumphed over communists and neo-fascists to initiate at least a democratic reform of society.

Benelux

The smaller democracies of Western Europe had their own specific problems and interests. In the Benelux countries, as in Scandinavia, constitutional monarchy on the British pattern was retained. The disputes about degrees of collaboration with or resistance to the Occupation, the tension between continuity and change in political structuring, the anti-reaction to communism and the problems of socio-economic reconstruction and reform – these major questions of postwar development were in the Benelux countries bound up with the discussion of national and international perspectives.

This applied particularly to Belgium, where the war and postwar crises had newly activated the old rivalry between Walloons and Flemings. The seemingly outdated conflict was intensified by socio-economic differences in the development of the two sections of the community. While the old coal-mining areas in Wallonia, predominantly socialist, anti-clerical and pro-French by tradition, went into permanent economic crisis, the agrarian Flemish region, conservative and Catholic in character, was gaining the upper hand by dint of economic modernization. A particular cause of strife was the capital, Brussels, situated in the Flemish area, but French-speaking. The Flemish claims were a response to the cultural predominance of the French-Walloons; the prolonged conflict surrounding King Leopold III (who abdicated in 1951) and the collaborationism of some Flemish groups added fuel to the flames. Thus the distribution of power among Christian-Socialist (thirty-five per cent), Socialist (thirty per cent) and Liberal (twenty-two per cent) parties was complicated by radical pro-Walloon or pro-Flemish parties; it was only with great difficulty that the large parties, ruling in fluctuating coalitions, could succeed in maintaining the country-wide unity of the political scene. Belgium's determined move into Europe, which made the country (along with neighbouring Luxembourg) the centre of most European institutions and also (after de Gaulle's anti-American verdict) of NATO, could not solve the main problem, a functional reform of the Constitution.

The Netherlands, on the other hand, successfully overcame heavy war damage and the loss of their Indonesian Empire. The prescription consisted

De Gaulle with Adenauer: their friendship augured the end of the long enmity between their countries

Below Chancellor Brandt; in 1969, for the first time in nearly fifty years, chancellor and president were both social democrats
Bottom An ex-Nazi, Emil Maier-Dorn, tries to whip up support for the extremist right-wing NPD, founded in 1964 by von Thadden

Italian anti-fascist demonstration, Genoa, 1960, in the middle of a period of government crises

Russian slavery: an Italian anti-communist poster of the late fifties, when the two main socialist movements moved closer together after the Russian denunciation of Stalin

of a timely economic modernization, especially of agriculture, and a determined pro-European policy, aimed at a supranational union including Britain. The chief problem remained admittedly the traditional division into socially and denominationally exclusive bodies, the basic structural principle of the political system. And in contrast to the rest of Western Europe, no broadly based Christian-democratic party arose. Apart from the Catholic People's Party (about thirty per cent), the moderate Labour Party (about twenty-five per cent) and the Liberals (about twelve per cent), the political spectrum included two separate parties representing the Protestant middle class: the Anti-revolutionary Party and the Christian-Historic Union (about ten per cent each). Correspondingly, trade unions were divided into socialist, Catholic and Protestant. But note that this historical peculiarity of Dutch political culture, a conservative 'freezing' of society into integrated organizations representing sectional interests, allows no comparison with the class society of Italy or France, or with the cultural division of Belgium. The remarkably unified bearing of the Dutch population under the German occupation was as little damaged by it as the course of reform which subsequently made the Netherlands a particularly strong partner in Europe.

The Bonn Democracy and Western Europe

In the rapid development of Western Europe the 'German question' has played a dual role. The immediate postwar tasks were those of coming to terms with the aftermath of war, organizing reconstruction and securing a basis for the necessary cooperation. They were intimately connected with the problems the Allies faced in their occupation of Germany. The policies of the Marshall Plan and of containment after the turning-point of 1947-8 made the connection abundantly evident. From this point onwards the initially negative and restrictive Allied supervision of West Germany evolved into a system of positive control through cooperation and partial integration. This was the substance of the negotiations and agreements leading from the Western European Union, to the foundation of the Federal Republic, the Iron and Steel Community and NATO, the Paris Agreements and the European Common Market.

On the other hand, the birth of pro-European policies and movements, based on plans conceived by the Resistance movements and aiming for political integration, opened bright prospects for a supranational solution of the 'German question'. Economically and politically the European idea acquired a powerful function as substitute for the defunct German national state. It filled the vacuum which collapse and disillusion had left in the minds of most Germans. The policies of the first Federal chancellor, Konrad Adenauer (1949-63), were founded from the beginning on this aspect of European politics. The inward-looking arguments of the social-

228

democrat opposition seemed to most West Germans to offer no viable alternative, in view of the realities of power policies in the early forties.

The German problem of division, then, contributed in large measure to the acceleration and stabilization of Western European integration. The immediate interests of the West German population were thereby served. This meant that the proclaimed object of German reunification became remote and eventually unreal, however emphatically the government and the majority might continue to cling to it. But the real interests were quite clear; the ostensible priority of reunification could be seen with the passage of time as a mere ideological postulate. It ideologically justified the setting up of the West German state, which in reality sensibly coincided with material and defence needs. And the decision in favour of restoring an only slightly modified version of the liberal-capitalist order was also determined by such considerations. *Dirigisme*, socialism and nationalization smacked of dictatorship and of wartime and postwar austerity. Actual examples of socialist planned economies in Eastern Europe offered little attraction.

West Germany did indeed come off better in European developments from 1947 to 1970 than any other Western European country. There were, to be sure, problems peculiar to West Germany; but they were balanced out and masked by stability – a consequence of the rapid economic recovery, the concentration of a disillusioned population on work and private success, the long term of office of Konrad Adenauer (that cunning tactician) with the aid of an improved party system. The Federal Republic avoided constitutional weaknesses which at an early stage spelt out the downfall of the Weimar Republic. Acquaintance with a more smoothly functioning parliamentary system led to a positive attitude to democracy itself, lacking in 1918. It was a system that built a bridge from the tradition of the German authoritarian state to a stable multi-party democracy, via the leadership of a 'grand old man', a chancellor with authoritarian traits. The historical fragmentation of party life was replaced by a concentration of political groupings into two parties of almost equal size (CDU and SPD). Alongside the big parties there was room for only one other – the Liberals (FDP), and they

Postwar development in Italy has included the building of *autostrada* linking the main centres in the country

Below Turin, the Fiat city: Italy's 'economic miracle' in the mid-fifties was on the late side, and its benefits unevenly distributed

Dutch Provos meet at Maastricht: the torn-up newspapers express their anarchist views

Flemish demonstrators in Brussels: in spite of legislation during the sixties, clashes continued between the conservative and mainly Catholic Flemings and the socialist, anti-clerical and French-speaking Walloons

had less than ten per cent – a constellation which increasingly resembled the cooperative British and American party systems rather than the old factional party divisions of the Continent.

Such was the consummation of the parties' long development away from ideology and towards pragmatism, attested after twenty years by the smooth change-over from CDU to SPD government (in the election of 1969). But the Bonn party system was never exposed to any crisis as grave as the permanent crisis of Weimar. Observers should bear this in mind when tempted to infer political stability from election returns alone.

As the old generation gives way to the new, the international scene changes; the crisis of the reunification concept, the problematic aspects of the Bonn state are today becoming more apparent than they were in the years of seemingly self-evident integration and development as a part of the Western world. They are a function of the special problem which the state was inevitably faced with at its very inception.

The starting-point for the Federal Republic was the destruction of the state founded in 1871 – this itself had from the beginning, and especially after the losses of the First World War, been aware of its insufficiency as a nation-state. The events of the Weimar Republic and the Third Reich, leading to the collapse of 'greater Germany' aspirations, demanded a complete refurbishing of the German concept of the state. But the rethinking incorporated in the Bonn Constitution was not unambiguous enough to preclude extremely varied interpretations. The unsolved problems related to foreign policies and their limitations as well as soul-searching at home about the format of the new state.

On the question of state frontiers, the Federal Republic regarded itself as an interim arrangement on the way to reunification; instead of accepting the *de facto* frontier along the Oder-Neisse line, the Federal Republic based its map-drawing on the territories of the German Reich in 1937, whose sole legal successor the Republic claimed to be. In this there was a contradiction of the external political facts, which could only become increasingly embarrassing. Internally, the Republic was, to be sure, once and for all defined as a constitutional and social democracy of the federal type; but even then, opinions differed widely as to what concrete meaning was to be attributed to the concept of a free and constitutional democracy. The range of interpretations stretched from the socialist and the liberal to the traditionalist; Bonn democracy was explained or criticized in the light of well-worn criteria derived from the old paternalistic, bureaucratic state. Again and again this came to the fore in the subsequent disputes about reunification and rearmament, state security and emergency legislation, electoral reform and federalism. The founding of the state in 1949 was in fact far from representing a democratic revolution from below, and a large proportion of the population, exhausted and disenchanted after the Hitler years, remained apathetic to the demands of democracy, which clearly depends on the cooperation of all.

The result was a strange juxtaposition; in contrast to Weimar, there was an assured, even militant constitutionalism, but it coexisted with the largely passive demeanour of the population, prepossessed with economic development and defence against Soviet power. In view of the recent past, this was understandable. But this passive acceptance was a long way from the kind of democratic feeling for the state that is capable of withstanding political crisis.

Four chief problems may be isolated. Firstly, the Federal Republic's self-definition as a provisional arrangement, designed to reach its ultimate dimensions only through national reunification or through supranational solutions. Secondly, the state's establishment confirmed the partition of Germany: the result was a tension between national and state identity. Thirdly, the centring of the political consensus upon the cold war confrontation, with its attendant dangers of over-sensitivity to all international changes. Finally, the discrepancy between pragmatic acceptance of Western European policies and the *status quo*, guaranteeing the Federal Republic's economic success, and the demand for revision and an independent policy towards the East.

Top Swedish airforce 'Dragons'; neutrality was
backed with formidable armed forces
Above Poster battle in Sweden: the Social Democrats'
slogan was answered by the opposing Folkpartiet;
'Gladly a medal, but pension *him* first!' meaning the
veteran Tage Erlander, Social Democrat prime minister

However true it is that these problems are still with us at the present day,
it is equally true that the political self-awareness of the West German
population has changed greatly in the last twenty years. This happened not
only under the influence of the advances or setbacks of attempted policies,
but also through the supplanting of the old generation and the widening of
political experience. This is reflected in the results of numerous opinion
polls. While in 1951 forty-five per cent of West Germans thought the best
era was under the Kaiser before 1914, and forty-two per cent even preferred
the Hitler period, by 1963 only sixteen per cent still plumped for the Kaiser
and ten per cent for Hitler! Two-thirds of the people now believed that
Germany had never had it so good – and they identified this success with the
Federal Republic.

Since the most positive reaction came from the younger generation, the
Federal Republic in 1963, having been in existence for the equivalent of the
Weimar Republic's life-span, could count on the steadily increasing support of its citizens. The notion that Germany could regain her former world-
political role declined in like measure. In 1954 half of the West German
population still believed in it; but ten years later the proportion had dwindled
to twenty per cent. It became clearer from year to year that the turning-
point of 1945 was a far sharper, clearer cæsura than the defeat of 1918,
which was never really accepted. The heavier national losses that resulted
from the Nazi catastrophe were far more readily accepted, and democracy
was this time not made arbitrarily responsible for them. This was, however,
only achieved by ignoring important questions; integration with the Western
European Alliance strengthened the sovereignty of the Federal Republic
but complicated relationships with East Germany and the Soviet bloc;
goodwill towards democracy depended upon steady economic progress
and stable government. The renunciation of ambitious foreign policy
rested upon the continuance of NATO protection and the well-defined inter-
relationships of the cold war.

During the sixties the Federal Republic faced severe trials; the end of the
Adenauer era, *rapprochement* between the United States and the Soviet
Union, the thawing of the cold war, differences among the Six. The prevailing uneasiness indicated the vulnerability of the Federal Republic, and
both old and new weaknesses of German democracy were revealed. The
crisis came to a head in the entry upon the political stage of the nationalistic
NPD, on the one hand, and on the other, the rapid growth of radical feeling
among students which questioned the whole existence of the Federal Republic.

The seriousness of these developments has been somewhat exaggerated.
The latest results of opinion polls among students, and of analyses of NPD

Tyrolean demonstration: Austrians demand government measures to bring about South Tyrolean autonomy. The cartoon shows an Italian pulling a hat over the eyes of a Tyrolean

Male hands are raised in a Swiss local election; early in 1971 women were at last given the vote in general elections, but they still were unable to vote in local elections

prospects, afford a very limited account of the symptoms of crisis which have appeared since the fall of Chancellor Erhard was followed by the problematic experiment of a grand coalition government. More serious is the over-sensitive political response to the mere threat of any economic upsets (as in 1966–7). This applies also to the question of reunification, the relationship with the German Democratic Republic and West German-Eastern bloc relations in general.

The flattering spectacle of East German refugees flocking over the border to join in the affluence of the Federal Republic supported the West Germans in their single-minded pursuit of material rewards to the detriment of their interest in democracy. Above all, no changes, either economic or social, had been great enough to challenge the conventional political wisdom. The merest glance at party structure and voting habits reveals the extent to which traditional social and religious groupings still determine political attitudes in West Germany and militate against a flexible and open democracy.

Two important problems complicate the issue of Germany's future; the persistence of apolitical and Utopian thinking; and the twists and turns of international relations, which have long since outgrown the simple framework of the cold war. Thus every reform programme, even in the name of political progress, is regarded as ambivalent. There is always the danger that government control will be extended along the apparently innocuous non-party lines, and develop towards an undemocratic ideology of the state.

The European concept after 1945 opened up vistas which were particularly significant for the Germans, after the partition of their country and the loss of national tradition. This led to a reliance on the national achievement of European unity as a solution to the problem of Germany's lost national identity. But this hope collided with both the continuing tendency of foreign states to see things in terms of their own national interests and with the continued domestic claims for reunification. Supranational policies are impossible without the cooperation of other states.

Long-standing German reservations about the party system, combined with disappointment in and mistrust of the new government 'establishment' of the second German democracy, have revealed a critical political situation. This democracy is in constant jeopardy, so long as its only security lies in continuing prosperity. It can only endure to the next generation if the 'interim arrangement' can throw off its lingering taboos and emerge as a responsible state. Whether or not this is attained depends primarily on the recognition that the aim of reunification, in so far as this has been the keynote of an independent national policy for Germany, must not exclude some form of competitive cooperation between the two parts of Germany. Indeed, the very concept of stability, till now based on a consensus of anticommunist opinion among West Germans, today needs adjustment and 'normalizing'. (The unrest of the younger generation may have something positive to contribute here. Apart from their impetus towards social reform they also bring the Federal Republic into line with an international movement.) It will take a happier acceptance of change in both external affairs and in domestic government to prevent further identification of one permanent ruling party with the state.

The Federal Republic's constitutional orientation *ab initio* comprehended such possibilities of change. They are the only real hope of overcoming the burden of the past, whether it be traditional German political attitudes, or the recent cold war entrenchment. The Adenauer era can now clearly be seen as a period of transition, during which the government won support for the system largely by ignoring the basic problems, from partition to *Ostpolitik*. With the changing scene of the sixties, the system itself came in for heavy criticism. With the questionable experiment of the 'Grand Coalition' (1966) the spectre of Weimar arose in the form of extreme polarization and anti-democratic feelings on both left and right. But Bonn is not Weimar. The parliamentary victory of the Social Democrats in 1969 was a crucial watershed. For the first time in forty-five years the highest offices of state were filled by Social Democrats; the chancellorship by the controversial '*émigré*' Willy Brandt, and the presidency by the thorough-

Right General Franco shakes hands with Prince Juan Carlos, grandson of Alfonso XIII, who was exiled by the Republicans in 1931. In July 1969 Franco named the prince as his successor

Summer in Greece, 1964; tourism was a major prop of the economies of Spain, Portugal and Greece and a factor in relaxing their regimes

The leaders of the 1967 Greek army coup, which resulted in the restriction of civil liberties and the flight of King Constantine to Rome

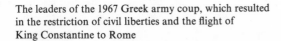

going Democrat Gustav Heinemann. The new leadership, and with it the viability of the system, will stand or fall by whether it finds a solution to the basic problems of internal reform and a stabilization of *Ostpolitik* which will fully recognize the painful consequences of 1945, and the *de facto* frontiers of modern Germany. A German policy of oscillation between East and West is, however, out of the question. The Federal Republic owes its entire allegiance to Western Europe and must rely on the progress of the programme for European unity to which it owes its existence and well-being. Only when the European Union becomes a complete reality can German reunification be re-examined. But, even then, this will depend on changes in world politics which are barely conceivable at present. The immediate problem is a European one. And since the resignation (and subsequent death) of that great stumbling-block, de Gaulle, two main tasks have come to the fore; to strengthen economic cooperation with the aim of creating a United States of Europe, and the expansion of the EEC to include Great Britain and other candidates for entry. Today these aims seem to be contradictory or even mutually exclusive. The entry of Britain with her ancient democratic traditions and pride in sovereignty might very well prove a barrier to complete political integration. But the process of integration, in any case, stands or falls by the will to create a Parliament of Europe, and Britain's political experience could be a powerful contribution to this joint act of faith, once she has brought herself to clear the hurdle of economic integration, which, ten years ago, still seemed too high. The European parliamentary movement will call for a massive sacrifice of sovereignty from all participants. In the final analysis, all will depend on whether the individual nation-states of Europe will find in the seventies the resolution to dismantle the remaining barriers which stand between them and continue the great Western European movement which has created such an encouraging distinction between recent postwar history and the misery of the second and third decades of this century.

Commonwealth
Parliamentary Conference,
Westminster Hall, London,
September 1961; twenty-
seven nations became
independent in the
postwar period to 1970

Patrick Keatley

The Commonwealth and Britain: Changing Realities

To paraphrase Voltaire, if the Commonwealth did not exist, it would be impossible to invent it. The global association of sovereign states had, by 1970, transformed itself so fundamentally as to bear only superficial resemblance to the six-nation club of a quarter of a century before.

No one could pretend this evolution had been planned or directed. This, perhaps, is the key to its sinewy strength; its surprising ability to adapt, to survive in a climate of increasing hostility in Britain and to keep on growing.

That this should have happened, particularly during the decade that embraced Sharpeville, UDI in Rhodesia and three British initiatives to join the European Common Market, is a political fact of life that never ceased to confound critics. It became fashionable during the quarter of a century after 1945, at least in Britain, to distinguish the long list of obvious anomalies in the Commonwealth that was taking shape, and to regard it as a ramshackle structure destined to disintegrate when the trumpets of crisis were sounded.

What escaped the eye of these critics is that, in the other sovereign states of the Commonwealth, especially in the twenty-seven nations which gained their independence during the period, those shaping policy and forming opinion were coming to an opposite view from the sceptics and the pessimists in Britain. Leaders of the newly sovereign states of Asia, Africa, the Caribbean and the Mediterranean began to see something taking shape which had practical value for them both as a forum for diplomatic cooperation, and as a mutual aid club for economic development.

Canada: counterweight to Britain

In this they were joined by one of the 'white dominions' of the prewar Commonwealth, Canada, which saw the new association as a useful counterbalance to the economic and diplomatic power of her neighbour, the United States. In a nuclear world dominated by two superpowers, the Canadians found themselves increasingly vulnerable. 'Living next door to Big Brother' was the catchphrase of the new era, and it was unnerving for successive prime ministers from St Laurent onwards to realize that the traditional counterpoise on the other side of the Atlantic had become lighter and less dependable. Britain could no longer counterbalance the USA.

Canadian foreign policy, from the time that a department of external affairs had been set up by Dr O. D. Skelton and his team of young academics – Lester Pearson among them – in the 1920s, had postulated a North Atlantic triangle embracing Ottawa, London and Washington. Prime Minister St Laurent, with Mr Pearson as his successor-designate on foreign policy, led Canada into NATO as a founder-member in 1949. The threat of Soviet power was the prime motivation, of course, but policy-makers in Ottawa were shrewdly aware they were gaining a diplomatic counterpoise to Washington by having a foot in Europe.

Canada's relationship to 'the Old Country' (as it still exists in common speech and newspaper headlines) was rapidly changing. Canadian Mutual Aid to Britain in the war years, the equivalent of the American Lend-Lease, had worked out at $234 per capita – a figure rather higher than that in the United States. Canada had emerged at the end of the war with a nuclear military capability – an option not so far exercised – and the possessor on the victorious side of an army, navy and air force that made her – temporarily – the fourth-strongest military power in the world. Ottawa arranged a 2 billion dollar loan to Britain, responding to an appeal from Mr Attlee in

235

Per capita income 1958-68

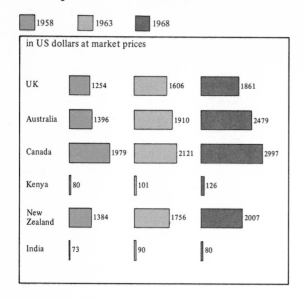

London, the Canadian equivalent of Marshall Aid, and proceeded to re-shape its diplomatic thinking for the new world that was coming into view.

If, by 1970, Canada appeared to be making a takeover bid for the Commonwealth, it was not for reasons of arrogance but by improvisation out of despair. The failure of the Labour government under Harold Wilson to deal with racialism in Rhodesia in the five years after UDI was followed in 1970, when the Tories returned to power under Edward Heath, by another apparent deviation from the racial principles of the Commonwealth over the issue of arms sales to South Africa.

But if Britain was abdicating her historic headship, her implicit role as *ex officio* chairman of the global association, the Canadians were not in fact attempting a takeover. It was the Afro-Asian powers of the Commonwealth, and the Caribbean, who sought to thrust Canada into the vacant chair. In practical terms, it was not so far-fetched. The junior partner, whose watchword in the First World War had been 'Ready, aye, ready' was approaching Britain's status as a middle power. Her population of 22 million was still rather less than half, but GNP was already two-thirds of Britain's and would surpass it well before the end of the century. In the Aid-India consortium under the Colombo Plan, Canada's contribution was running at a level slightly higher than that of Britain; in Commonwealth Africa it was the Canadian army and air force that stepped in with training teams for Ghana and Tanzania when those of other Western powers had become unavailable or politically unacceptable.

Canada was flexing her muscles for a larger role on the world stage, in economic if not so much in military affairs. But she had no great-power aspirations: bridge-building, mediation and peace-keeping was what emerged under Pearson when his Liberal Party was in power. It had also been followed by Diefenbaker during the years of Conservative rule in Ottawa; this included the strong leadership from Canada to hammer out the principle of non-racialism at the Prime Ministers' Conference in London in the spring of 1961. That meeting ended with the decision of South Africa to withdraw from the Commonwealth, and Diefenbaker returned home to a spontaneous welcome from a huge crowd gathered at the airport.

Most of the Commonwealth countries of Africa and the Caribbean were still a year or two away from independence, but the leaders of their national movements drew two conclusions about the role of Canada as it was developing in the 1960s. First, the principle of majority rule for the Africans of Rhodesia, and non-racialism as a mainspring of Commonwealth philosophy, was a policy that had bipartisan support in Ottawa and would

Commonwealth independence 1947-66

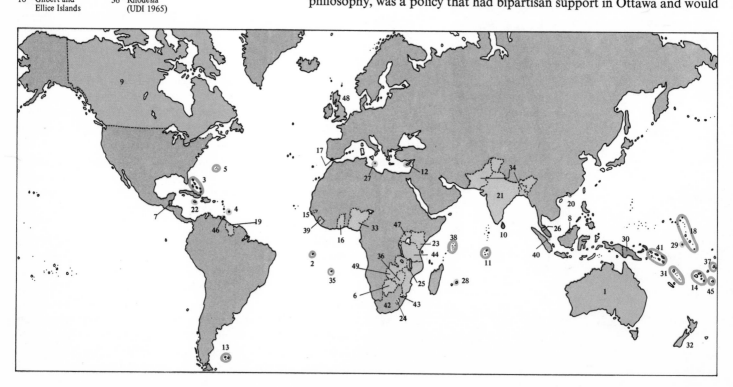

be pursued consistently by Canada, regardless of which party was in power.

Second, the emerging economic strength of Canada, and her growing diplomatic prestige in crises such as Suez at the United Nations, meant the balance of forces was rapidly shifting within the new Commonwealth. From the time Lord Rosebery had first improvised the phrase at a speech in Adelaide during his Australian tour in 1884 – 'the Empire is a Commonwealth of nations' – through two great wars to the era of Attlee and Churchill, there had never been any question of the primacy of the UK. Just as she had been the hub of Empire, so she remained the unchallenged hub of Commonwealth in the initial period after 1945. Even India, which severed the last imperial links when she became a republic in 1949, remained a sleeping giant in terms of any power game within the Commonwealth association. The monarch, at the initiative of Mr Nehru himself, assumed the mystic title of 'Head of the Commonwealth'. The actual phrase had originally been devised by a distinguished Pakistani lawyer when he was a member of Chatham House in London and carried with it no definable duties.

It was the decade that began with the crisis over South Africa that saw Canada emerge, involuntarily, as the challenger to Britain in the counsels of the Commonwealth. Where there had been a single, dominant power in the organization, there were now, indisputably, two. Britain, already eased out of great-power status in the world arena, had at least had the consolation of being the sole holder of this post in the Commonwealth. Now she had the galling experience of having to share the leadership with a young challenger whose diplomats were not only eager, crusading and energetic, but better off to boot.

There were few consolations to be derived from the one undisputed role that remained to Britain as hub of the residual and shrinking colonial Empire. Whitehall felt, understandably, that Canada might take on a little of the drudgery of the colonial development burden, and there had been tentative talk in Ottawa in the 1950s about the possibility that Caribbean territories might gain their independence through association. The idea was even canvassed that British Guiana or Jamaica, where Canada had major aluminium investments, might become the eleventh and twelfth provinces of the Canadian federation. There had been practical links during the war when the Canadian army took over the defence of Jamaica and the RCN linked up with the RN on the West Indian patrol as well as the North Atlantic.

Constitutional involvement with British colonies proved, however, to be politically unpopular within Canada and the emphasis was put on development aid instead. When the West Indian Federation was set up in 1958, Ottawa came in with a considerable package of christening gifts concerned mainly with education and communications. Two handsome cargo liners were built and dispatched; someone with a wry memory for the hymns of Victorian imperial times chose an apt pair of names: MV *Dominion Palm* and MV *Dominion Pine*.

In 1966, the same summer that the Colonial Office in London was formally wound up, and amalgamated in the Commonwealth Relations Office, the Canadian prime minister embarked on an exercise that should, in theory, have been welcomed in London as evidence of burden-sharing. Mr Pearson invited the premiers and chief ministers of all thirteen Commonwealth territories in the West Indies to come to Ottawa, including the nine that were still British dependencies. The upshot of the conference was a stepping-up of Canadian aid in the Caribbean – Pearson shrewdly reckoned that the taxpayers would accept the idea more readily when they had seen these hitherto remote political leaders on Canadian television, and learned a little about their Commonwealth cousins and their problems of poverty.

However, such is the perversity of human nature, this diplomatic initiative by Canada was viewed in Whitehall with edgy hostility rather than gratitude. Ottawa absorbed the lesson, for there was no wish to rub the British the wrong way, and Canadian initiatives thereafter were focused on sovereign states of the Commonwealth. Burden-sharing in the dependencies was not to be expanded, at least for the time being.

The first Prime Ministers' meeting to be attended by Asian leaders in 1948: Sir Godfrey Huggins (Southern Rhodesia), D.S.Senanayake (Ceylon), Liaquat Ali Khan (Pakistan), Dr H.V.Evatt (Australia), King George VI, C.R.Attlee, N.A.Robertson (Canada), E.H.Louw (South Africa), Peter Fraser (New Zealand) and Jawaharlal Nehru (India)

Commonwealth Prime Ministers' Conference, 1969: (left centre) Harold Wilson and Arnold Smith are seated among the hardliners on racial issues – Kaunda of Zambia (next to Smith) and Obote of Uganda, with Nyerere of Tanzania (on Wilson's far side)

The diplomatic development of the Commonwealth in the past two decades takes coherent form only when this curious and involuntary role of Canada has been sketched in. It is one of the two dynamic forces during this period, the other being the thrust of nationalism in Asia, Africa and the other imperial realms, leading in the space of two decades to the dismantling of the greatest empire the world has ever known. On both counts Britain found herself challenged: first for her constitutional authority in the colonial territories; and, as these evolved into sovereign status and Commonwealth membership, challenged by Canada for her diplomatic primacy.

What has confused the thinking of most of us is that the run-down of Empire and the build-up of Commonwealth have been going on simultaneously for the past quarter of a century as two parallel but distinct operations. This has been forcefully set out by Professor Nicholas Mansergh in *The Commonwealth Experience*, where he demonstrates the many different forces at work.

As with all political questions, this can best be analyzed by identifying responsibility. The dismantling of Empire is, and must be, the sole responsibility of ministers in London. Ultimately, it falls upon the prime minister of the day, which is why Harold Macmillan accepted and discharged the task of dealing with Cyprus, Nyasaland, Malaysia and other thorny colonial problems.

But the building up of the Commonwealth, creating the Secretariat in 1965 and investing a global association of thirty-one nations – as it had become in 1970 – with purpose, budget and personnel, was a task involving all its members. By the time of the 1964 Commonwealth Prime Ministers' Conference in London, when Rhodesia was the main topic on the agenda and two-thirds of the delegations were from the 'brown nations', it was clear that the organization had established as rule number one the conviction that the peoples of all Britain's dependencies were entitled to expect full political rights, regardless of race, when Britain was transferring power and responsibility to local hands at the time of national independence.

Did this bedrock rule of the Commonwealth apply to Rhodesia? Or had power been transferred in all but name to the white settlers in Salisbury in 1921, when their leader, Sir Charles Coghlan, had struck his bargain with Churchill as colonial secretary? In those far-off days, Southern Rhodesia had been given the right to run her own parliament (all white) with a civil service (all white) paid wholly from local funds as were the white-officered army and police. When one of Churchill's successors. L.S.Amery, granted the settlers the right to establish their own (all white) air force in 1925, the final seal of political control was put in place.

Top Lester Pearson, prime minister of Canada (1963-8) when Canadian influence on the Commonwealth was growing
Above Pierre Trudeau: flat opposition to Britain's decision to resume arms sales to South Africa in 1970
Below Queen Elizabeth II attends Canadian centenary celebrations in July 1967

A rump – white and royal?

Nations, like individuals, live by their illusions. There is a deep instinct for self-deception in most of us, particularly if it makes us feel safer and more comfortable. Lewis Carroll defined it as painting roses. After the Rhodesian illusion, where Churchill devised the face-saving formula of calling the territory a 'self-governing colony' the issue next arose with India's decision to become a republic in 1949. The Balfour Formula, stemming from the Imperial Conference in London in 1926 and enshrined in the Statute of Westminster five years later, had referred to countries united in 'common allegiance to the Crown and freely associated as members of the British Commonwealth of Nations'.

It had been possible for the two years after 1947, with India independent under a governor-general, to turn a Nelsonian blind eye to the adjective 'British' in that definition as it applied to several hundred million people in India, not to mention Pakistan and Ceylon. But now there was to be a president in the same magnificent quarters that had once housed Mountbatten as imperial viceroy. If Britain did not shift, India would withdraw from membership. The other Asian nations would opt out; the Africans would never opt in, when they had a choice; the Commonwealth would become in the words of one irreverent commentator in Canada 'a rump –

Australian troops in South Vietnam make an assault landing from American helicopters; Prime Minister Harold Holt was a strong supporter of Johnson's policies in South-east Asia

New Zealand Royal Tour 1953–4: the Queen waits for parliament to assemble before delivering the speech from the Throne

white and royal, but a rump nevertheless'. It was a prospect that thoroughly disturbed Ottawa and Wellington, although Canberra pressed no views on the Attlee government.

In the event, the Balfour Formula was jettisoned, the adjective 'British' disappeared from the phrase about the Commonwealth of Nations, the king's style and titles were drastically altered, and the ingenious new phrase defining him as 'Head of the Commonwealth' (without specifying rights or duties) was provided in order to sweeten public opinion in Britain. It was a watershed of Empire, and of Commonwealth. The deep emotional motivations behind it all have been well assessed by Colin Cross in *The Fall of the British Empire* (Hodder and Stoughton, 1968):

Correspondence between the King and Attlee shows that one motive impelling the Cabinet was the belief that if India left the Commonwealth it would assist the spread of Communism in Asia.

A broader consideration . . . was that the British could not bear to admit that their world influence was shrinking. They wanted to keep some of the forms of the former Empire alive, even after the reality had died. It was palatable for the British to regard India as not just another sovereign nation; [they] were willing to go to extreme lengths to maintain this fiction, even to that of changing the titles of their monarch.

For the sake of just such an illusion successive British prime ministers in the 1960s asserted that final responsibility for Rhodesia lay with the government in London. The pledge was given repeatedly at the conferences of Commonwealth prime ministers and presidents and was similarly asserted at the UN. Predictably, the result was not to deflect criticism but to invite it.

Thus, the bedrock rule of the Commonwealth on race equality, as it had been emerging from the campaigns for national independence in Zambia, Tanzania and other African territories in the early 1960s, was now applied retrospectively to Rhodesia. It was understandable not only in logic, as a piece of constitutional legality, but also in terms of personal links. It is sometimes forgotten how closely the African leaders were thrown together in the ten years of the unsuccessful experiment of the Central African Federation, an experiment that ended with R.A. Butler's conference at Victoria Falls and the break-up in 1963. Kenneth Kaunda, for example, while a political prisoner in Northern Rhodesia in that era, once found himself bundled roughly into a lorry and taken down to Salisbury City Gaol and its less sympathetic staff of Afrikaaner warders.

He recalled this in conversation with me in Lusaka in 1967. There, speaking as President Kaunda of the Republic of Zambia, he was answering my question as to why he and Commonwealth colleagues like President Julius Nyerere of Tanzania should continue to hound British ministers in London for action to deal with the unresolved state of rebellion in Rhodesia. Why not let the defiant white regime under Ian Smith go one way, while Zambia would go another?

As his first point, Dr Kaunda cited the standard British government assertion that it accepts sole and final responsibility for Rhodesia. But his second point was personal:

My old friend Daba Sithole [the Rev. Ndabaningi Sithole, leader of ZANU] is in the City Gaol where I was, probably in the same block of cells. I cannot let him rot there, and keep my conscience. Joshua [Mr Joshua Nkomo, the then leader of ZAPU] is in Gona Camp, down in the lowveld. I cannot let him rot either. I must do what I can to press the British, who have responsibility and the military power, to act in the Rhodesian tragedy.

These personal links are a recurring phenomenon in the process of Empire-into-Commonwealth. Some years after Indian independence had been achieved, Nehru quietly relayed his personal thanks to the anonymous men in the Republic of Ireland – colleagues no doubt of De Valera – who had organized the printing and shipping of the pamphlets that had been used by the Congress Party to bring about the end of the Raj. It was, indeed, the unused section from De Valera's draft for an Irish republic within the Commonwealth, sometimes known as Document Four, that was used by India as the basis for her own draft when becoming a republic in 1949.

Mountbatten with Nehru and Jinnah at a meeting in June 1947, when he put forward the British plans for transference of power to India and Pakistan the following August

On partition, Muslim refugees in New Delhi crowd on to a Pakistan-bound train; total migration both ways probably amounted to more than 12 million

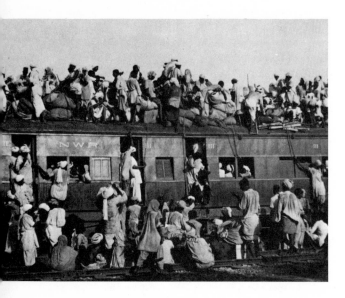

This same Commonwealth principle on race equality, again applied retrospectively, came into action on the South African arms issue after the Conservatives were returned to power in the British General Election in June 1970. The new prime minister, Edward Heath, had given two pledges undertaking to resume the sale of arms in the Tory Campaign Guide, and these had been repeated by the man who became his foreign and Commonwealth secretary, Sir Alec Douglas-Home, in a BBC broadcast forty-eight hours before polling day.

In the months that followed, leading up to the summit conference of Commonwealth prime ministers and presidents at Singapore in January 1971, it was evident that Mr Heath took an entirely different point of view from most of these other leaders. Again, the dispute turned on the basic question of responsibility.

Was not the British prime minister entitled, as he asserted in heated exchanges with other Commonwealth leaders by letter and in personal interviews, to take a sovereign decision on the sale of arms to South Africa, calculated wholly in terms of British national interest? Mr Heath was quick to add that the Conservative government in London had no truck with racial discrimination at home and gave no support to South Africa's apartheid policies. His intent was simply to supply arms which he conceived to be 'within the spirit, as well as the letter, of the Simonstown Agreement'. This related to the arrangement, concluded by a Tory minister, Mr Selwyn Lloyd, in 1955, providing for the continuing use of the naval base at Simonstown, near the Cape, after it had ceased to be a full-scale operation of the Royal Navy and had reverted to South African control.

On 18 December 1970 there was an important statement from the man who had been prime minister of the Labour government when it held office from 1964, and was now leader of the opposition, Mr Harold Wilson. He said he and his ministers had examined the Simonstown Agreement and the 1967 revisions, and had taken the most detailed advice from the government departments in Whitehall concerned, including the legal advisers. They had been in agreement that there was no requirement to sell arms, and the fact that the South African navy had continued to engage in the annual exercises with the Royal Navy, provided for in the 1955 Agreement, indicated that Pretoria accepted this too.

Mr Heath, preparing for his departure to Singapore, totally rejected this argument. There were both implicit and explicit obligations to supply arms under the Agreement, he said, and he had come to this conclusion only after consulting the government's legal advisers. Were these the same advisers consulted by Mr Wilson? Mr Heath would not say.

But apart from these legalistic arguments, apart from the unavailing lobbying efforts by Afro-Asian governments (including those of the Commonwealth) to get Security Council action at the United Nations, what was central to the new crisis over South Africa was that the Commonwealth faced once again the bedrock issue that had shaken the summit conferences of 1960 and 1961 in London.

The British prime minister was asserting a right of total sovereignty in foreign affairs by any member state of the Commonwealth. The case in point happened to involve the sale of arms, a form of commercial policy notorious for high emotional potentialities.

The other Commonwealth governments, led by Tanzania, Zambia and Canada, were asserting the second principle alluded to earlier: that the members of the Commonwealth bear joint responsibility for the running of their organization. This includes, by definition, joint acceptance of rule number one on racial equality. The sovereignty of individual nations is, therefore, diminished to the extent that member governments do not give support to regimes that are opposed to the principle of race equality and are working actively to prevent it being achieved.

It follows that a member unwilling to observe this rule should recognize the conflict of interests and withdraw from membership. Alternatively, the other member states have a right to enforce the expulsion or suspension of the offender. The trouble, as the 1970 arms crisis revealed, is that the

Top President Makarios with General Grivas, the
Greek Cypriot who launched a terrorist revolt in
April 1955 against the British. Unsuccessful retaliatory
measures included the deportation of Makarios
to the Seychelles
Above Jomo Kenyatta, released from prison in 1961
after a seven-year term for organizing Mau Mau

The Commonwealth: 1956 Low cartoon in *The Guardian*

association had never anticipated such a situation and had no machinery of
enforcement. After all, in the 1961 crisis over South Africa and apartheid,
a previous British Tory prime minister, Harold Macmillan, had proven
realistic when it came to the final decision. In his capacity as chairman at the
London conference that year, he had accepted the consensus of the meeting
and was content merely to express – publicly – his regrets to the South
African prime minister at the way things had worked out.

Caught unprepared, with neither code nor machinery for disciplinary
action, the Commonwealth association as it existed in mid-1970 resorted to
the only available alternative: the techniques of diplomatic pressure.

Of these, the most interesting and easily the most effective was the
'accidental leak' employed by a group of Commonwealth governments
who managed to keep their identity anonymous. Evidence suggests that
African and Caribbean leaders were involved. On 26 July 1970 there
appeared in *The Sunday Times* in London a report containing virtually the
full text of a letter that the Canadian prime minister, Pierre Trudeau, had
sent to Mr Heath at 10 Downing Street. Inquiries in Ottawa revealed that
it was authentic, although the Canadians professed ignorance as to how it
had got out. The key passage contained these words:

> I must tell you frankly that I have serious misgivings about your decision to resume
> sales of certain types of arms to South Africa . . . I fear attention is more likely to be
> focused on the fact of the resumption of sales, in the face of the 1963 UN Security
> Council resolution, than on the nature of the supplies involved, or the limitations you
> envisage concerning the purposes for which they could be used.

Mr Trudeau came to the central point of Commonwealth principle involved
when he declared that the supply of arms of any kind or any quantity 'will
be interpreted by many Commonwealth governments as an implicit gesture
of acquiescence in the policy of the South African government towards the
African population of the country'.

It was clear what the practical considerations were that lay behind
Canada's action. As at the time of Suez, the unilateral action of a British
prime minister threatened the break-up of a diplomatic grouping – the
Commonwealth – that lay at the basis of Canada's global policy. The power
network that acted as the counterpoise to the Americans, and potentially a
shield against Canada's two Arctic neighbours, China and the Soviet Union,
at some date in the future, was in danger of being destroyed.

There were emotional factors too. Heath's obstinacy, and his apparent
insensitivity to the outlook of African leaders like Kaunda and Nyerere who
had served prison sentences under white gaolers, brought back anxious
memories of similar difficulties in getting through to Sir Anthony Eden at
the time of his disastrous adventure at Suez in 1956. To find a Tory prime
minister in London thus putting the whole Commonwealth network at
hazard was compared by a Canadian diplomat to 'finding your uncle
convicted for rape'. At the Singapore summit, as at Suez, the member
nations were confronted with the unlikely situation of the founder-member
flouting the rules and being unaware that she was doing so. Not surprisingly,
a number of Commonwealth presidents turned their minds to using the
Singapore meeting to devise a book of rules and means of enforcement.

In retrospect, it is still difficult to identify the point where Britain's
Commonwealth partners went wrong, if they did go wrong, in delineating
the shape and philosophy of the new, mutually operated association.
Mansergh refers frequently to the 'time-lag' in British adjustment to the
idea that the Empire was dissolving and that something very different was
taking its place. Kierkegaard has described it as the tendency of peoples,
and nations, down the ages 'to think backwards while living forwards'. A
perceptive analysis of this national state of mind, at the end of the imperial
era, came from Professor F.S.Northedge of the London School of
Economics writing in *International Affairs*, in January 1970:

> The British, because of their ancient security from foreign invasion, their remoteness
> in mind – if not in distance – from the complexities of European politics, their long-
> assured supremacy at the apex of the international pyramid of power, are peculiarly

Ghana portraits of the Queen and Nkrumah in preparation for her visit to Accra in November 1961

Below Kenyatta as prime minister on Kenyan Independence Day, 12 December 1963, with Prince Philip *Bottom* Kaunda and Duncan Sandys, colonial secretary in May 1964, when Zambian independence was announced for the following October

prone to assume that in all essentials the world is still much as it always was; and that Britain, despite all the evidence to the contrary, will still manage to come out on top, almost without effort.

The political nostalgia underlying these insular notions has affected Britain more than any other of the old European Great Powers. Britain's retention of her sovereignty during the Second World War, while most lost theirs, fostered the illusion that Britain was still free to shape the world closer to her heart's desire.

Professor Northedge goes on to cite the habit of ministers and diplomats in Whitehall of taking a 'condescending attitude towards other countries now equal in rank to Britain'. He was writing before the June election and the change of occupancy at 10 Downing Street, but he could have been describing exactly the impact of Edward Heath as prime minister on the Commonwealth leaders who were to meet him on the arms issue in the flurry of personal diplomacy that led up to the summit at Singapore.

'I have informed the British prime minister that in arming South Africa, he is proposing to arm our enemy', said the cool-headed foreign minister of Nigeria, Dr Arikpo, a distinguished university administrator in private life, when he had made his fruitless call at No. 10 in October 1970. Trying to convey the anxieties of non-white nations in Commonwealth Africa, he said, was like trying to make a dent in a hill of glass. There was no apparent way to get through to the man.

It was the same Edward Heath, of course, who had led the team of fifty officials and experts in the unsuccessful negotiations at Brussels in 1961-3 when Britain under the Macmillan government made her first application for membership of the Common Market. After those efforts had failed, I found an occasion to ask one of the commissioners of the EEC about them. He is an old friend, an anglophile with fluent English, as much at home in London as in the three EEC capitals where he grew up. He was very tactful, but I noted his words down, for they seemed to go to the heart of the matter. He said: 'What we have in common in the EEC is that all six nations went through military defeat and occupation. I think that teaches you a certain humility.'

The austere, bachelor politician who had come to the levers of power at 10 Downing Street in mid-1970 was not particularly well equipped in terms of temperament for diplomacy requiring a leap of empathy. His tactics with Commonwealth leaders revealed a woeful deficiency when differences of culture and continent were involved. As the crisis on South African arms intensified, the Trinidad prime minister, Dr Eric Williams – himself an Oxford man like Mr Heath and holder of an economics doctorate – sent a strongly worded cable to No. 10 asking the British prime minister not to treat responsible Commonwealth leaders 'with contempt'. He also took the unusual course of making part of this cable public – usually a sign of desperation when the ordinary private channels of diplomacy are failing.

Churchill's blind spot

There is an Ashanti saying in the hill country in Ghana, that a wise man travelling through thick jungle uses a high point to look back the way he has come before he tries to chart the way ahead. If we apply this to the Commonwealth, in the context of the arms crisis, then Singapore becomes our convenient summit. What can we learn from the path we have travelled – we, the 800 million peoples of thirty-one sovereign states of the Commonwealth?

First, that this is hardly a logical organization in the sense that applies to other international groupings. Some, like the UN, are global-comprehensive; others, like the EEC or OAU, are regional. If they are selective, like the ANZUS, SEATO or NATO pacts, then there is an agreed policy line such as defence, binding all members. Some Commonwealth nations, incidentally, belong to the three just cited; there is no clash because the Commonwealth is not a diplomatic, military or economic bloc.

The Commonwealth does not fit any logical pattern for the elementary reason that it was never planned. It has, therefore, the pragmatic strength one expects of any spontaneous human initiative. Patrick Gordon Walker

Meeting of the ill-fated British Caribbean Federation at Lancaster House, February 1956. The federation lasted for only four years

British administrators and the Tonganese royal family (including Queen Salote, left centre) at a banquet; Tonga was one of the few remaining British protectorates by 1970

in his book entitled simply *The Commonwealth* says the member nations share a common heritage that embraces the territories of settlement, like Canada or Guyana, as much as those where the Colonial Office simply defined the frontiers and administered, as in Africa. They show immense diversity in language, culture and geography; but there is an underlying unity that springs from the common experience of nation-building, of the search for an identity. It is perhaps noteworthy, although Mr Gordon Walker tactfully ignores this point, that one nation alone in all the Commonwealth territories scattered across twenty-four time zones and six continents, has missed this shared experience. This, of course, is Britain. Secure behind her Channel moat since the boot of the last military invader trod her beaches nine centuries ago, she alone has not known what every other Commonwealth country went through in the heyday of Victorian Empire. (Even New Zealand had her troubles, leading to the demand for the withdrawal of British troops after the Maori massacre; and the nationalist grandfather of W. L. Mackenzie King fled from the British redcoats who put down the 1837 rebellion in Upper Canada with rifle and cannon.)

There is no such phrase as 'an English nationalist' although the political lexicon of the Commonwealth bulges with Indian nationalists, Irish, Ghanaian, Zambian, Jamaican and other nationalists. Amritsar was not unique. In the four countries I have just named the visitor may be taken along, as I have been myself, to 'the place where our people died from British bullets'. Those words were spoken to me in Kenya by the late Tom Mboya. When his president, Mr Kenyatta, wrote his memoirs he called the book *Suffering Without Bitterness*.

This was Winston Churchill's blind spot. He was a great English patriot, of course, but he had never been an English nationalist. Very simply, it had not been necessary. The same factor presumably explains the unimaginative outlook of his counterpart in the 1970s, Edward Heath. When Mahatma Gandhi was released from prison by the viceroy, Lord Irwin, and invited to come and talk about calling off the passive resistance campaign, Churchill exploded with this description of the scene, as he visualized it from London: 'The nauseating and humiliating spectacle of this one-time Inner Temple lawyer, now seditious fakir, striding half-naked up the steps of the Viceroy's Palace, there to negotiate and parley on equal terms with the representative of the King-Emperor.'

What most Commonwealth leaders share is that they, or their predecessors, were at one point stripped of the thing all of us prize most – their dignity – before the political prize of national identity was secured. Churchill, as minister, could order the shooting of Erskine Childers during the Irish troubles 'as a traitor' because he could not accept the fact that the English civil servant had become the Irish nationalist on the run.

It was perhaps significant that Churchill, when he returned to office in the Tory victory of 1951, installed his personal friend Oliver Lyttleton at the Colonial Office and apparently ordered the wind of change to stop blowing in Great Smith Street. This can only be asserted by inference, since no Cabinet minute or CO memorandum has yet seen the light of day, which would confirm this was the policy. But there had been the famous declaration from Churchill that he had not become the king's first minister 'in order to preside over the liquidation of the British Empire' and this policy was now implemented with characteristic vigour. Not one yard of British soil received independence, or approached it, in the second Churchill era, 1951-4.

Instead, this era saw the launching of the doomed experiment of the Central African Federation, after the final round-table conference at Lancaster House in January 1953 presided over by the Marquess of Salisbury as minister. (He was later to emerge, in the era of Ian Smith's proclamation of UDI, as president of the Anglo-Rhodesian Society in London, and to resign when Smith proclaimed a republic.) The six Africans from the member territories of the new Federation, the two Rhodesias and Nyasaland, boycotted the final session and wrote to *The Times* explaining why, saying the federal plan was an act of political irresponsibility. The one hundred remaining delegates, all white to a man, then solemnly proceeded

Macmillan in Swaziland, shortly before his historic 'wind of change' speech in Cape Town, February 1960; he was the first British prime minister in office to visit the African territories

Above right Vicky cartoon on the Prime Ministers' Conference, 1961, after which Verwoerd announced the departure of South Africa from the Commonwealth

Last attempts at a Rhodesian settlement: Ian Smith (right) leaves Harold Wilson on board HMS *Tiger*, 4 December 1966, after two days of talks aboard the British cruiser in the Mediterranean

to federate three territories containing 9 million Africans and 285,000 settlers. The Archbishop of Canterbury, and Mr Attlee as leader of the opposition, added their voices to the chorus of warning at Westminster, predicting (rightly) that the dragon's teeth for future bloodshed were being sown. Lyttleton, oblivious, introduced the legislative bill in March, declaring: 'This is a turning-point in the history of Africa. If we follow this scheme I believe it will solve the question of partnership between the races.'

There were still those alive in London at that time who had heard Asquith introduce the bill for South Africa's independence forty-four years earlier, with glowing predictions of white liberalism expanding into African emancipation. In the Churchill-Lyttleton initiative, tinder had been lighted for a political explosion that would demolish the rickety Federation before ten years were out, and would reverberate so as to endanger the very fabric of the multi-racial Commonwealth of the 1960s.

Louis Napoleon advised that 'in politics, one should never say never', but Bourbons, as we also know, learn nothing and forget nothing. There was one more bitter harvest to come from the Churchill era before it ended. The legions were leaving Egypt, at the behest of the unknown young Colonel Nasser who had come to power in Cairo, but their banners were not to be borne north as far as the Channel. They would be raised once again, no further away than Cyprus, now earmarked in Churchillian planning as the permanent base for the rest of the twentieth century and beyond.

This policy flew in the face of the incipient Cyprus nationalist movement that had been sending civilized delegations of lawyers and clerics to London since 1928. Yet the British minister of state, Henry Hopkinson of the Colonial Office, solemnly went into the House of Commons on 28 July 1954 and declared: 'It has always been understood and agreed that there are certain territories in the Commonwealth which, owing to their particular circumstances, can *never* [my italics] expect to be fully independent. Nothing less than continued sovereignty over this island can enable Britain to carry out her strategic obligations.'

The Cyprus nationalists drew the only possible conclusion – the same one now sadly accepted by the African nationalists of Rhodesia, South Africa and the Portuguese territories in Africa – that the time for talking had ended and the time for military hardware had begun. Heavily laden fishing-boats began touching down on quiet beaches in the spring of the following year. On 1 April, precisely on schedule, the military campaign against imperial rule was launched. Mr Hopkinson was elevated to the House of Lords. By 1959 the round-table talks were under way in Geneva and London and in 1960 the last governor, Sir Hugh Foot, brought in to do a political rescue job, was sailing for home. A few months after independence President Makarios, as a separate and deliberate act, made formal application for his country's membership in the Commonwealth. It was unanimously accepted.

Constitutional precedent had been set, under several headings. Cyprus was so small, relatively speaking, with its population at that time only just

244

exceeding 600,000, that there was some talk of 'two-tier membership' within the Commonwealth association. This was rejected by the prime ministers and presidents at their next summit conference, after an extended study by a sub-committee over several months. The idea re-emerged in 1968 when the Pacific trust territory of Nauru, with only 6,000 inhabitants, achieved independence after fifty-one years of Australian administration.

After consultation, Commonwealth governments agreed to accept the island republic as the first territory in a new category of 'special members'. This would enable Nauru to receive the flow of documentation from the Secretariat in London, and to attend such meetings of the technical, professional and development aid agencies of the Commonwealth as might be relevant to her needs. A nominal sum of £1,000 per annum was set as her contribution to the total Secretariat budget of £650,000.

In a middle position, still fluid at the end of 1970 are the six Associated States of the Commonwealth in the Caribbean. Antigua, St Kitts, Dominica, St Lucia, St Vincent and Grenada, with populations varying from 50,000 to 100,000, have advanced to a status that has been described as 'a blank cheque for independence'. They have assumed full control of their internal affairs and there is an exact formula, involving a two-thirds majority for an independence bill in their own parliaments, which provides the automatic right for them to claim final sovereignty without further reference to London, apart from formal notification. The protection of the RAF and the Royal Navy would then, presumably, cease and they would apply for membership in the Commonwealth and the UN. *Pro tem* the Associated States take part in most Commonwealth activities barring the prime ministerial summits; their budgetary contributions are being determined.

The unscrambling of the residual British Empire is turning out to be an untidy, *ad hoc* affair. It is also one where the sovereign members of the Commonwealth are finding themselves increasingly involved. The Gibraltar Referendum, for example, on 10 September 1967, which gave a very high majority vote in favour of separate existence and against amalgamation with Spain, was seen to be fair because of the active presence of the four-man observer team provided, at British government request, by the Commonwealth Secretariat in London. The choice, determined by the Secretariat and not by Whitehall, embraced senior ambassadors loaned by New Zealand and Kenya, administrators from Jamaica and Pakistan and a Nigerian diplomat heading the servicing unit.

This same Nigerian official, Mr E.C. Anyaoku, was assigned the delicate task of serving as secretary to the Wooding Commission, headed by a Caribbean judge, that went to St Kitts and Anguilla in 1970 to take evidence and prepare a report on the separatist movement which had been causing trouble and distress since 1967. The request came, once again, from the British government; it was the Commonwealth Secretary-General, Arnold Smith, and his staff who took on the responsibility of seeing that the observers were impartial, thorough and helpful.

It had been Mr Smith, together with his Ghanaian deputy, Mr A.L. Adu, who had done so much to bring about quiet mediation behind the scenes in the Nigerian civil war. The tangible outward sign of this was the Kampala summit in May 1968, with President Obote of Uganda providing a neutral meeting-place and hospitality. It was the first encounter by the two sides since the fighting had begun a year before, and it led to the whole series of subsequent meetings organized by the Organization of African Unity (OAU) through its secretariat in Addis Ababa. The war ended with the collapse of the rebels, before mediation could succeed. But it was undeniably true that the joint agency serving all member governments in London had been able to bring balm to Nigeria's wounds – what Mr Nehru in an earlier crisis had called 'the healing touch of the Commonwealth'.

The Secretariat, in the years that followed its foundation in 1965, carried out other exercises in diplomatic assistance to Britain, involving the provision of observer teams at crucial elections in dependent territories. British Guiana in 1966 was one example. And even earlier, when Singapore was separating from Malaysia, in 1965, the 'healing touch' was brought to

Ghanaian students in Accra demonstrate against British policies on UDI and demand the release of African political leaders imprisoned in Rhodesia

British 'invasion' of Anguilla, 1969; the government's decision to send in hundreds of paratroopers to deal with the local troubles of this tiny West Indian island provoked derisory press comments

bear by Arnold Smith as Commonwealth Secretary-General at a time when he had little more than a set of empty rooms at Marlborough House in London and a staff of three. The full story has not been written, and may never be, but it kept both countries in the Commonwealth association, with diplomatic relations established from the start of Singaporean independence, when neither of these aims had appeared possible.

Further diplomatic assignments for the Secretariat presumably lie ahead, since it is now British policy to dismantle the rest of the colonial empire, embracing some 10 million people in twenty-one dependent territories. Rhodesia with its 5 million and Hong Kong with nearly 4 million account for the bulk of this population. Typical of the problems that remain is the colony of the Gilbert and Ellice Islands with its 55,000 people living on thirty-seven islands or atolls, scattered over 2 million square miles of Pacific Ocean. But the policy line is clear, conceived in terms of the inhabitants and stated unequivocally in 1965 by Sir Hugh Foot, the former Cyprus governor, now ennobled as Lord Caradon and serving as minister-delegate at the United Nations: 'We believe that no nation, no people, and no race should be dominated by another. We believe every nation should be free to shape its own destiny. We believe colonialism should be ended as rapidly as possible. We believe that in the small and scattered territories which remain, we should apply these principles.'

The wind of change was now blowing over the far Pacific; terrain where de Gaulle, in one of his lofty phrases, had referred slightingly to French dependencies as 'the specks of dust' – with no political future. France, with no equivalent for the Commonwealth and its tradition of vigorous sovereignty for each member and the joint Secretariat wholly independent of Whitehall control, might be unable to comprehend. But the Commonwealth had set the pace in Africa, forcing the French to match it, and might do the same again. It was not perhaps without significance that when the member states of La Francophonie were setting up their new organization with headquarters in Paris, they sent to Canada for their first secretary-general, Jean-Marc Leger.

He was, needless to say, an old friend of his compatriot, the Commonwealth Secretary-General at Marlborough House in London, Arnold Smith, the Canadian diplomat originally seconded to that post by Lester Pearson. The two men have had meetings in London and Paris and the two secretariat

Mutual aid between members of the Commonwealth has been one of its most tangible benefits for many countries: (*top*) agricultural students visit an English farm; (*above*) an Australian field surveyor helps to build a trunk road through the jungle in Malaysia; (*bottom*) the 'Canada Dam' at Mayurukshi in India – a large irrigation project which is helping to transform agricultural methods

offices aim to cooperate in matters of education, youth and development problems. Two Commonwealth governments, Canada and Mauritius, are also members of the Francophone Association.

A gigantic farce?

When it comes to an assessment of where the great turning-point occurred in the quarter of a century of Commonwealth development that followed the Second World War no two experts will agree. Much depends on a man's outlook. If he is an unrepentant Tory romantic, like Sir Arthur Bryant, he will regret the passing of an imperial era that could produce from Lloyd George the statement in 1922 – after the Chanak incident – that: 'The instrument of policy of the Empire is the British Foreign Office.' It was these hankerings for long-lost grandeur that doubtless impelled 'A Conservative' to write in a celebrated article in *The Times*, as a preliminary to the 1964 summit conference, that 'the Commonwealth has become a gigantic farce'.

The staff of 167 civil servants, seconded from two dozen member governments, working at the Commonwealth Secretariat headquarters in London, would not agree. It is doubtful, in fact, if any of the Tory romantics know, or want to know, of the immense extent of the global network of self-help that was created in the five years to 1970. Lester Pearson, borrowing from an academic in Malaysia, called it the lattice that has replaced the old hub-and-wheel; the Duke of Edinburgh took up the phrase and used it in his London speech of 3 June 1965 welcoming the decision to establish a secretariat.

In medicine, law, the substantial scholarship scheme that provides 1,000 free places per annum for doctoral studies by graduates at universities in eighteen Commonwealth countries; in tsetse-fly and locust control; in the professional exchange plan of the Commonwealth Foundation; in science, agriculture and the imaginative 'ComTech' plan for technical assistance by experts girdling the globe on short assignments – in these projects and dozens like them, embracing 50 professions and 253 professional organizations, the Commonwealth is doing a practical and effective job that gets few headlines but is immensely valued by the governments of the poor, non-white member states. Botswana, for example, faced with the need to negotiate copper royalties with a huge international consortium after the first real strike of metal ore in her territory, turned to the Secretariat. Out came a team of economist, accountant and lawyer, of mixed nationalities, and the consortium ended up paying two million dollars more than it had originally offered. That was practical aid indeed.

The late Iain Macleod, as colonial secretary, identified one of the great turning-points as the Hola Camp scandal in Kenya, where eleven African political prisoners were beaten to death. In that same year, 1959, came the report of the Devlin Commission, headed by a Conservative judge, condemning the Tory government's handling of the Nyasaland emergency. The Protectorate had become 'doubtless only temporarily, a police state'. When Macmillan called his general election in Britain that year, with daily casualty lists being published in Cyprus and Kaunda behind barbed-wire in Zambia, it was predictable that a new minister would be taking over from Lennox-Boyd at the Colonial Office. He did, in the person of Macleod, while Macmillan himself was on his way in January of 1960 on a historic journey, the first British prime minister in office to visit his African territories.

Nagging at the back of his mind, Macmillan had visions of another Amritsar, or another Black Hole of Calcutta. The former would incense the two superpowers, America and the Soviet Union, united in their antipathy to the continuance of colonial rule. The latter would incense British domestic opinion and improve Labour's chances at the next election, or even provoke one. He had confided these thoughts to Macleod, who shared his anxieties.

These were the negative aspects of the problem: the process of de-colonization. But Macmillan, as he was to demonstrate when he reached Cape Town at the end of his tour, had been ruminating on the positive

Sport has become another of the factors which help to create links between Commonwealth countries: finish of the 100 metres at the 1970 Commonwealth Games held in Edinburgh

Kanhai scores a six during the Australian-West Indies series of cricket Test Matches

Pakistanis protest against the Commonwealth Immigrants
Act in February 1968 which severely restricted entry
to Britain

Australia, 'doorway to a bright future': a party of
400 British immigrants set off from St Pancras
Station on the first stage of their journey to
Brisbane in 1959

Migration to and from UK

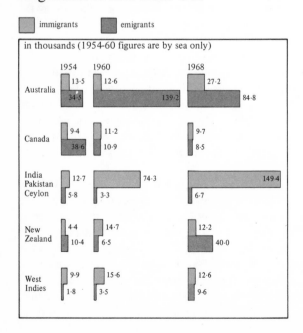

█ immigrants   █ emigrants

in thousands (1954-60 figures are by sea only)

	1954	1960	1968
Australia	13·5 / 34·5	12·6 / 139·2	27·2 / 84·8
Canada	9·4 / 38·6	11·2 / 10·9	9·7 / 8·5
India Pakistan Ceylon	12·7 / 5·8	74·3 / 3·3	149·4 / 6·7
New Zealand	4·4 / 10·4	14·7 / 6·5	12·2 / 40·0
West Indies	9·9 / 1·8	15·6 / 3·5	12·6 / 9·6

aspects as well. He correctly foresaw the role that the nascent Commonwealth, as an association of predominantly black and brown states, was
capable of playing in building a bridge across the racial gap. The battle
against discrimination was going to coincide with the battle against poverty.
He hoped, with persuasion, he might take Dr Verwoerd and South Africa
along this multi-racial highway. The alternative was the showdown on
apartheid at the 1960 London conference of Commonwealth leaders, where
Nehru and Tunku Abdul Rahman of Malaysia were going to demand
action against South Africa, and Diefenbaker of Canada was said to have
been coordinating strategy with them as well. The Commonwealth, as a
force directed against racialism had already acquired a diplomatic
momentum of its own.

The classic image of the imperial legions, ever in the forefront of the
public-school mind, was very much a part of Mr Macmillan's thinking. I
had noticed, observing him at close quarters in those years, that the tie he
wore alternated unvaryingly between Old Etonian one day and Brigade of
Guards on the other. This continued during his African safari, regardless of
the climate. In Cape Town came the historic words in his speech on
3 February:

Ever since the break-up of the Roman Empire, one of the constant facts of political
life in Europe has been the emergence of independent nations. . . . We have seen the
awakening of national consciousness in peoples who have lived for centuries in
dependence upon some other power. Fifteen years ago this movement spread through
Asia. Today the same thing is happening in Africa. The wind of change is blowing
through the continent.

There was a corollary coming; one that Macmillan reckoned would have
strong appeal to his South African hosts, the combined houses of parliament
meeting in the National Assembly building:

The great issue in this second half of the twentieth century is whether the uncommitted peoples of Asia and Africa will swing to the East or the West. Will they be
drawn into the communist camp? Or will the great experiments in self-government
now being made, especially in the Commonwealth, prove so successful . . . so compelling
that the balance will come down in favour of freedom, order and justice?

Macmillan's eloquence made not the slightest dent in apartheid. Six weeks
later, on 21 March, at Sharpeville, the massacre of sixty-seven Africans took
place at the hands of Verwoerd's police, using Sten guns. The Macleod-
Macmillan nightmare of a new Amritsar had come true, but fortunately not
in British territory.

The Canadian prime minister, John Diefenbaker, the leader of the Tory
Party and a man who had won a deserved reputation for taking briefs (at no
fee) for Indians and members of other minority races, made Macmillan's
point in a public speech when he arrived in London in May 1960, just before
the opening of the Commonwealth summit conference. He said the equality
of all races and peoples in all parts of the Commonwealth, including southern
Africa, must be the accepted major principle of the association: 'Unless we
accept that as a basic principle the Commonwealth, instead of becoming a
bulwark against the onrush of communism everywhere in the world, will
ultimately be greatly diminished.'

It was Diefenbaker's successor, Mr Pearson, when the Liberals returned
to power in Canada, who made the running at the 1964 summit conference.
He provided the bridge-building speech at the vital point, when the
arguments on Rhodesia kept delegates five hours beyond the scheduled
time for adjournment. The result was – at last – a communiqué that the
African Commonwealth leaders could accept. It set out the majority rule
principle for any independence deal with the Smith regime, although the
British prime minister, Douglas-Home, was one of the minority of three
(out of eighteen) leaders who jibbed at this. It boldly declared that all
Commonwealth governments, not just some of them, would never grant
diplomatic recognition to a white minority regime that declared UDI.
And this same 4,900-word communiqué, the longest in Commonwealth
history at that date, created the new Secretariat which would start

The Singapore Heads of Government Conference, January 1971 (Edward Heath in the foreground); arms for South Africa was the big issue

functioning – with its Canadian chief executive and with a multinational staff – in 1965.

The new attitude of the 'Brown Commonwealth' made the conference the landmark which it remains to this day. It marked the moment in time when the leaders of sovereign nations in Africa, Asia and the Caribbean, after very nearly deciding to opt out, came down on the other side and opted in. By doing so they took a step that, in constitutional terms, transcended any declaration of national independence at the time when British colonial rule had ended in their territories. This amounted to a Declaration of Joint Responsibility, if one were to formalize it with a title. The brown nations were serving notice that from henceforth they intended the Commonwealth association to serve their hard-headed national interests, by assuming new burdens and performing new functions. The practical instrument would be the Secretariat. As the London *Financial Times* shrewdly observed: 'Far from threatening to break up the Commonwealth, the African members showed they were anxious to make greater use of its potentiality.'

Canada, for reasons which have been set out here, had emerged as the mediator in this intercontinental grouping of nations. The mood of disenchantment with the Commonwealth had appeared to swell within Britain itself, almost in mathematical proportion to the new enthusiasm for the association among the other member states. Britain under Wilson, and again under Heath, renewed her application for EEC membership and began to look to Europe as the place to cut a diplomatic figure. The chairmanship of the Commonwealth was vacant, and was Canada's for the taking, if she would accept the hint from the Afro-Asians. Pearson ignored the hint, but he re-visited London after leaving office in Ottawa and chairing his development mission for the World Bank. His message, in the public speech he prepared for the occasion, was essentially aimed at Downing Street in the context of the unresolved policy of Britain towards Rhodesia and South Africa: 'If the Commonwealth does not condemn racialism wherever it shows itself; if it does not reject and fight discrimination; if any of its members base their policies on discrimination of that kind – then the Commonwealth is not going to survive in its present form or, indeed, in any acceptable form. Such a result would be tragic.'

With the arrival of the new Tory administration in Whitehall in 1970, led by a non-Commonwealth man in the person of Edward Heath, the imperial wheel had come full circle. Disraeli's bitter prediction of 1852 had become ironically true: 'These wretched colonies will all be independent in a few years, and are a millstone around our necks.'

It was in the diplomatic sense, on the central issue of race and southern Africa, that these territories had become a collective millstone; and not the economic sense Disraeli had anticipated. When Heath as prime minister flew to Singapore for the 1971 summit conference of thirty-one sovereign states, he was at pains to emphasize that 'Britain claims the right to her independence of action as well as any other member' and to do so on the basis of hard national self-interest. What he refused to face up to, or simply could not discern, was the clash between this policy of his on arms for South Africa, and the basic Commonwealth policy on race.

The Canadian author, Professor D. G. Creighton, has said mid-Victorian Britain, pursuing national interest in her own tariff policies, 'had in effect broken away from her own Empire'. Quoting this, Nicholas Mansergh wrote recently that: 'Overseas it was assumed that, in the later twentieth century she would likewise break away . . . from a Commonwealth over whose destinies, as chief among equals, she had long presided.'

The Empire which Britain had acquired 'in a fit of absent-mindedness' had been replaced by something with a dynamic of its own, and the rejection was mutual. Paradoxically, perhaps inevitably, the Britain of 1971 was the one member territory which was incapable of grasping the aims and ideals so clearly seen by the other thirty partners. Britain, under her new, austere prime minister, was not particularly welcome in the association she had helped to found. As the 1970s unfolded, she might even become no longer acceptable.

Aid to Commonwealth countries from UK 1950-69

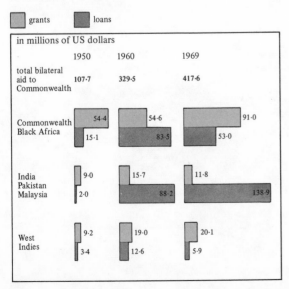

	grants	loans

in millions of US dollars

	1950	1960	1969
total bilateral aid to Commonwealth	107·7	329·5	417·6
Commonwealth Black Africa	54·4 / 15·1	54·6 / 83·5	91·0 / 53·0
India Pakistan Malaysia	9·0 / 2·0	15·7 / 88·2	11·8 / 138·9
West Indies	9·2 / 3·4	19·0 / 12·6	20·1 / 5·9

Iverach McDonald

The Soviet Union: the Permanent Enigma

In Russian eyes the years since the Second World War divide into three periods so separate and distinct that they might have been shaped by three entirely different regimes. In the first period – made up of the eight years from Germany's collapse in 1945 to Stalin's death on 5 March 1953 – the people knew great pride, great triumph, grief, utter weariness, increasing disillusionment with the rewards of victory and finally a renewed fear that the old nightmare of the prewar repression would return among them. In the next period, lasting eleven years until Nikita Sergeyevich Khrushchev was overthrown on 14 October 1964, they experienced stronger hope, pleasure in the first achievements in outer space, satisfaction that daily life was improving, but also bewilderment at home of Khrushchev's starts and alarms at home and abroad, from the virgin lands campaign to the Cuban crisis. They were years of promise, excitement and mental and physical upheaval. The third period since 1964, under Brezhnev and Kosygin, brought a relapse into normalcy – and if this seemed dull to outsiders it was reassuring and comforting to very many Russians and other Soviet peoples after everything they had lived through.

This last period, being without pyrotechnics, allows the basic continuity and stability of the Soviet state behind all the changes to be seen the more clearly. The one-party system of control that was Lenin's creation was as firm as ever. Industries remained nationalized. The farms were still run either directly by the state or by farmers' collectives. Trading, publishing, schooling, transport, almost all public activities, were under public control, which means under party, state or local direction. Most of the changes in the three periods since the war were changes only of degree and of method. That did not prevent their having had an enormous impact on the lives of the 200 million people of the Soviet Union.

Under Stalin

On 2 May 1945, when at last Berlin surrendered to the Soviet troops and the war ended, the Russian people back home were too exhausted, too hungry, too burdened by grief for the fallen to rejoice for long. In all, according to Soviet official announcements, over 20 million people of the Soviet Union were killed or died in the war. About 1,700 towns and 70,000 villages were laid waste. About 40,000 miles of railway track were destroyed. In its long survey for the fiftieth anniversary of the 1917 Revolution the Soviet Communist Party stated that the war had cost Russia no less than thirty per cent of its national wealth. 'Our workers, peasants, and intellectuals worked with the utmost self-denial in appalling conditions.' It was a sober statement of the truth. And for the Kremlin the truth was the more bitter because the United States had emerged from the war largely unscathed and stronger than before in every way.

When the end came it was soon clear how very differently Stalin and the ordinary Russian were looking to the future. The ordinary man and his wife knew that they had to rebuild the broken factories and houses; they put in extra hours after their normal working days. But, as they looked ahead, they wanted some reward and some assurance of relaxation. They took comfort in the knowledge that Russia was no longer alone but had allies. Capitalist encirclement must surely be over.

A first jolt came when the United States stopped lend-lease supplies to Russia as the war ended. A worse shock came in February 1946 with Stalin's announcement that the five-year plans were to go on. A whole series

Heirs of the Revolution pose in front of a relief at the Exhibition of the Achievements of the Soviet Economy which shows the Soviet people marching towards the bright future

Red Army troops in street-fighting at Yukhnov on the Moscow front in March 1942. About 1,700 towns and 70,000 Russian villages were devastated during the Second World War; over 20 million people were killed or died as a result of it. According to a Party estimate, the war cost Russia thirty per cent of her national wealth

Captured German battle standards in Red Square at the Victory parade in Moscow, 24 June 1945. It looked like the beginning of a new era for the Russian people; but disillusionment was to follow. Stalin's relationship with the Western powers deteriorated and rigorous war measures remained in force: arms before consumer goods

of them stretched out ahead, he said, which meant that the old furious pre-war and wartime pace would be maintained and that priority would be given to heavy goods, well in front of the consumer goods that people longed for. Worse still came with the evidence that Stalin and the Western powers were falling out, and that armaments were accordingly to be maintained at a high level.

Russia's internal exhaustion and weakness, and America's lead with the atomic bomb, go far to explain Stalin's mounting fears and suspicions as he faced the world. Outwardly all seemed well. Russia's prestige in the world was at its highest. Her frontiers were expanded as the reward of victory. At the Potsdam Conference of 17 July-2 August 1945 Russia received part of East Prussia from Germany and the western Ukraine and western Byelo-russia from Poland. She maintained her right to the Baltic states occupied and annexed in 1939. Even in the Far East, where her share in the victory had been small, she was promised that all her former territories ceded to Japan since the Russian-Japanese War of 1903-5 – including Port Arthur and South Sakhalin Island – should be returned to her.

More important than cessions of territory were her other gains in Central and Eastern Europe. The Eastern zone of Germany went to her as the Western zones went to the Western powers: that was to be expected. The more decisive gain came in the general agreement that Russia should have 'friendly governments' in the Eastern half of Europe. Stalin and his lieutenants sought guarantees of friendliness by imposing and carrying through communist-style revolutions led by communists and fellow travellers. The old prewar anti-Soviet *cordon sanitaire* was turned inside out to face westwards. When the Western powers protested at the suppression of democracy the Soviet government became the more determined to hold Eastern Europe as a closed preserve, free from Western poaching.

After a four-power foreign ministers' meeting in London in December 1945 many months of often venomous argument had to be endured before peace treaties were concluded early in 1947 with Italy and the ex-enemy states of Eastern Europe. On a peace treaty with divided Germany no progress at all was made and the subject was put into indefinite cold storage.

Stalin salutes the Guard of Honour formed by the British Scots Guards at Potsdam 1945, the conference that set the shape of postwar Europe and a decade of cold war. Germany and Berlin were divided; Russia was to have 'friendly governments' in the east. Stalin feared the strength with which America had emerged from the war and, in particular, the Bomb

Russia's territorial gains after 1945

| | Soviet dominated countries |
| | Soviet gains |

1	Finland	4	Lithuania	7	Ruthenia
2	Estonia	5	East Prussia	8	Bukovina
3	Latvia	6	Poland	9	Bessarabia

Relations between East and West went on worsening. Even the imaginative offer of economic aid by General Marshall, US secretary of state, in June 1947, served only to feed the suspicions. Stalin could not believe that the offer to include communist countries in the aid would sincerely be carried out: since when had capitalists pressed charity on to their business rivals? Alternatively, he suspected that, if positively meant, it was a plot to deflect their economies from the straight path of socialist planning. He refused to join the scheme and made Czechoslovakia back out after its luckless show of interest.

Stalin's fears mounted swiftly from this time. He was having to clamp down on real or fancied opposition groups from Central and Eastern Europe. In February 1948 some tactical mistakes by party leaders in the still largely democratic Czechoslovakia gave the Communist Party the opportunity to seize power with the help of factory guards and Russian moral support. So the last and most famous 'bridge between East and West' was broken. Hardly could Stalin congratulate himself on being safe behind a moat than he saw much of the security advantage thrown away. In June 1948 Yugoslavia (which had not needed the Soviet army to liberate it from the Germans) rebelled against Russian dictation and Stalin had it thrown out of the camp.

His fears that others might copy Marshal Tito were so great that he very soon launched the ghastly series of mock trials of communist and other leaders in Eastern Europe. But, most strongly of all, Stalin was alarmed when he saw the Western powers, mainly the United States, beginning actually to carry out Marshall Aid; beginning to put new life into West Berlin, and beginning to build up Western Germany. At a time when refugees were still streaming westward from drab and impoverished East Germany, Stalin calculated that he could not afford to let the West keep its bright shop window in West Berlin. So he began the slow, steadily increasing restrictions on traffic along the railways and the autobahn which ought to have exposed the helplessness of the West but which led to one of his own heaviest defeats. The unprecedented air lift by America and Britain, taking supplies to Berlin, was a bitter sign to him and to all Russians of the West's power and of its refusal to yield even a highly exposed position. In the five years he had left Stalin did not challenge the West so openly again.

He had more than enough to occupy himself at home. There his anxieties can be divided into the familiar three Marxist divisions of society into workers, peasants, intellectuals. The workers had much to their credit. The reconstruction and expansion of industry throughout the Soviet Union was driven forward so fast that the prewar level of production had been reached again by as early as 1948. By 1952 industrial production as a whole was claimed to be 2·3 times greater than in 1940. By 1960 the output of steel had gone up another 18·3 million tons from 1948 to 65 million tons. Oil had risen from 31·1 million to 148 million, electric power from 48·3 billion kilowatt hours to 292 billion kilowatt hours. New towns, new hydro-electric stations, new universities and schools were built in many widely separated regions. Housing and consumer goods were still lagging far behind.

For town-dwellers they were years of austerity. Among the peasants they were years of misery. The peasants, still making up about half of the population, were short of machinery, short of seed and short of men, owing to the terrible losses during the war. When in 1952 the industrial production was claimed to be 2·3 times greater than in 1940, agricultural production was said to have gone up by only ten per cent. Once again, as during the first five-year plans, the peasants were being kept on a miserably low standard of life in order to help to pay for the expansion of industry. The prices allowed on the produce directly procured by the state were so low (and in any case so few goods reached the countryside) that the collective farmers had no incentive to produce. Many of them fell back on a bare subsistence level of living, tending their own private plots and neglecting the collective lands.

The government responded with new taxes and restrictions. On 19 September 1946 a decree sought to compel peasants to work more on the

A West German cartoon at the time of the 1956 invasion of Hungary implicates Khrushchev in Stalin's crimes. Twelve years later (*right*) Russian tanks moved into the cobbled streets of Prague and put an end to the government's bold liberal policies. The Czech aim under Dubček: 'to give communism a human face'

A Moscow delegation comes to Mongolia – now claimed by the Chinese on the grounds that it was wrongly ceded in the time of the Tsars. Also disputed is the frontier Damansky Island in the Ussuri River (*bottom*) where Chinese guards confront Soviet armoured vehicles on the ice.
The 1969 Russian cartoon inscription (*below*) on the machine-gun magazine reads: 'Thoughts of Mao'

collective lands. In 1950 a further attempt to tighten discipline was made by decreeing that field work should be done not in small groups but in so-called brigades. Then, partly for the sake of efficiency but partly in the hope of stricter control, farms were amalgamated. Where in January 1950 there were over 250,000 collective farms, only 97,000 larger ones remained in 1952. Nikita Sergeyevich Khrushchev first came into international prominence when he began advocating the building up of 'agro-towns', large urban centres in the countryside; but as little came of this scheme as came from Stalin's grandiose plans for changing nature by planting huge belts of trees in southern Russia.

The war had left another legacy in the broad territories of the Soviet Union. In the Ukraine, White Russia, the Baltic states and the Caucasus national aspirations grew. How much direct collaboration there was with the Germans may never be known. What is known is that several nationalities were taken to Siberia or Central Asia *en masse*: the Volga Germans, the Crimean Tatars, the Kalmyks, and smaller Caucasians like the Checheni, the Ingushi, the Balkars and the Karachai; over a million souls in all. As late as 1970 the Volga Germans and the Crimean Tatars were still dispersed somewhere in the east. Ukrainian and Baltic national groups remained actively hostile to Moscow, sometimes up in arms, until after Stalin's death. Stalin employed his customary repressive methods, and more people were deported. (His successors faced the problem by sending more Russians into the republics, by making sure that key posts had a Russian either in charge or as the nominal second in command, and by opening more careers, through the provision of higher education, to youths among the minorities.)

The plight of the intellectuals, particularly the writers, became clear in 1946. Zhdanov – speaking with all the authority of a Politburo member and all the prestige of the defender of Leningrad – warned writers that they had to drop any pretensions at being independent critics of society. More journals were closed; more novels of painstaking correctness and dullness were given the Stalin Prize.

The attack on the writers was only the most open of the attacks on a broad front against independence of mind anywhere on any matters that could be classed as doctrine or accepted practice. The determination and savagery with which Stalin broke the strength and coherence of the Communist Party itself became known only gradually in later years. The central committee (its parliament) became a powerless shadow. The Politburo (its cabinet) became a meeting of timid ciphers. Men like Voznesensky who ventured to suggest improvements were shot out of hand.

These were the years when Stalin, distrusting everyone, was by-passing the official apparatus of power and was ruling his empire through his own secretariat, through the secret police under Beria and through the voiceless functionaries who obeyed without question. Labour camps were filled by the criminals, by the political dissidents and by those luckless enough to have made a mistake or had an accident in a factory. On 13 January 1953 sharp and direct alarm was caused in Moscow by the announcement that nine doctors, seven of them with Jewish names, had murdered Zhdanov and were plotting to kill military leaders. With its anti-Jewish overtones, the 'doctors' plot' seemed to portend a new and widespread wave of arrests.

Then came the overwhelming shock, with the news first of Stalin's stroke and then of his death on 5 March 1953. The Architect of Victory, the Great Teacher, the Friend of the Peoples, all-seeing and all-powerful, was gone without leaving an heir apparent.

Under Khrushchev

The bereaved lieutenants, evidently in a state of extreme nervous shock, seemed agreed on only one point. Never again: no single one of them would ever be given Stalin's supreme position. 'Collective leadership' was the order of the day accepted by all – except perhaps by Beria. How far he plotted to seize power in those early months after Stalin is still uncertain. Obviously the others distrusted his ambition. Certainly they feared the

Khrushchev with Castro during the Cuban leader's visit to Moscow in May 1963. The meeting resulted in a radical change of Cuban economic policy, which became closer to Eastern European models, and in a return to intensive sugar production. The missile confrontation six months before had drawn Castro further into the communist camp

Khrushchev's foreign policy focused greater attention on the newly independent African territories; this Soviet-Mali friendship meeting was held in May 1962. Russian involvement in Third World aid was at the expense of China: an ever-growing rift which was one of the major factors in Khrushchev's downfall two years later

private army which he commanded as head of the Ministry of Internal Affairs and the secret police. His arrest was announced in July and his death by shooting in December. In a far milder way the principle of collective leadership was invoked in getting rid of Malenkov. It was thought unwise that he should be both prime minister (he had been appointed on 7 March) and a leading member of the party secretariat: on 14 March he gave up the party post. He was to be turned out of the premiership also in 1955.

Nikita Sergeyevich Khrushchev was left dominant in the secretariat, and his whole career had fitted him to make the most of the opportunities. This shrewd, ebullient, pugnacious, unpredictable, near-genius was before anything else a party man. He had climbed his way up through it and had survived the purges. He had directed key branches in the toughest areas like the Ukraine before and after the war, and the Moscow region itself. He now led the movement to bring back the power of the party, and reassert its supremacy over the administrative bodies – the state ministries, the managerial ranks, the technological staffs, on which Stalin had relied.

As he strengthened his own position and looked around, Khrushchev saw a strong country that was becoming more powerful but was slowed down in its progress by the rigid system of centralized planning and control. He saw talented men unwilling to take initiatives through fear. He saw a peasantry work-shy and demoralized. He saw a system of Central and Eastern European satellite states in which only the party bosses believed. And, further afield, he saw that the Soviet Union was dangerously isolated in an unfriendly or openly hostile world. Even the Chinese communists were beginning to show minds of their own. In tackling these problems Khrushchev started with many of the right ideas. He had imagination. He had supreme confidence. He had courage. But, lacking the habit of disciplined thought, he overreached himself in almost every sphere and brought about his own downfall in October 1964. The squandering of his outstanding gifts was a tragedy for Russia and the world.

He set out first to show that the new regime stood for something better and more humane than Stalin's and Beria's. Many exiles and prisoners from the labour camps began to return home and were given flats in Moscow and other cities. Courts less frequently departed from the letter of the law; secret administrative tribunals were abolished. Ilya Ehrenburg in 1954 did more than publish a book called *The Thaw*: he gave a title to a wide political process and, more than that, gave a propulsion to the process. Dudintsev (*Not By Bread Alone*) and the young poets Yevtushenko and Voznesensky were able to publish works that had candour and social insight. Yet the clear sign that was awaited – the firm evidence that Stalinism was dead – finally came from the leaders in a curiously roundabout way.

Khrushchev gave his famous secret speech to the Twentieth Party Congress in 1956 intending that it should be leaked to party members (and many others) in Russia and to the East European communist leaders. Why not come out straightforwardly in public with the catalogue of Stalin's crimes and cruelties? Probably some of the old guard were against any speech at all. Probably others thought that ordinary people would put the blame not so much on the aberration of the 'cult of the personality' but on the system itself. And which of the post-Stalin leaders was entirely guiltless?

Probably also Khrushchev was reluctant to have the speech public for a deeper reason. Though he knew what went wrong under the old system, he was not sure what doctrinal and political guarantees were needed to prevent a relapse in times to come. Probably he felt instinctively that the speech was unbalanced, strong in diagnosis, weak in prescription. He was essentially a pragmatist. He could describe his ideal communist state of the future in general terms, but he was happier when forsaking political theory, and expressing his robust belief in 'goulash communism' as his critics called it, a system which he was convinced could provide more goods, food and services than capitalism ever could.

One of his first concerns was to loosen the system of centralized planning and control. Everyone could see that the system kept industrial production inflexible and gave the more powerful and older ministries an unfair advan-

Russians at the annual parade for the Revolution carry a
banner showing the North Vietnamese as war heroes.
American aid to the South was countered quickly and a
formal pact with North Vietnam signed in September 1967.
The people are waving at the Russian leaders, who are on
the stands of the Lenin Mausoleum

Kosygin, prime minister from 1964, meets Nasser, the
master of diplomatic balance between East and West.
The vast Aswan Dam project was mainly Russian financed.
But investment in the Middle East has had little return and
involved the almost total destruction of Russian arms and
equipment in the Six-Day War with Israel

tage over the newer ones that were producing synthetics, chemical products
and other modern types of goods. Not only shoppers but factory managers
found that there was no mean between scarcity and glut. Khrushchev's
answer in 1954 was to abolish many of the central ministries and decentralize
much of the planning. He set up over a hundred regional economic councils
(*sovnarkhozy*) which would work out what was needed for the region and
either produce it or import it from other regions in exchange for surplus
goods from their own area.

It seemed a good idea, but soon ran into difficulties. Men had become
unused to planning for themselves. They had few means of knowing what
other regions would offer at any one time unless they still used Moscow as
the great centre of information and direction. And, most ominously, many
of the comfortable bureaucrats in Moscow went in for a go slow strike
against the scheme, making difficulties in operating it and refusing to go
themselves to help to run the regional councils. After some years of uncertainty the number of regional councils was halved, and after Khrushchev's
fall they were done away with altogether in September 1965.

Throughout this time the armaments drive was still absorbing precious
resources and labour; and the same could be said about the space programme, although nothing boosted Russian morale or startled the world
more than the launchings of *Sputnik I, Sputnik II* and *Sputnik III* in 1957-8
or the news on 12 April 1961 that Yuri Gagarin had become the first man to
fly in space. Here, it seemed, was the supreme justification of directing
resources towards a desired end. The other side of the medal remained clear
to ordinary Russians in the prevailing lack of consumer goods. On a broad
view the chief credit in industry during the upheavals of the Khrushchev
years should go to the factory managers, foremen and workers, men and
women, in countless plants of many kinds who, in spite of all the schemes
and counter-schemes and cancellations, kept production rising strongly.
Where in 1953 the total Soviet production was only a third of the American,
in 1963 it was very nearly two-thirds.

In trying to put agriculture to rights Nikita Sergeyevich was even more
prolific in ideas. He began quietly enough, while Malenkov was still prime
minister, by paying more to the peasants for that part of the produce which
the government compulsorily procured and also for grain sold above the
quota. He further encouraged the peasants by reducing the taxes on their
private plots. His next move was far less quiet. In February 1954, he launched
the great virgin lands campaign to bring vast areas of Kazakhstan, southern
Siberia and south-eastern European Russia under grain. Over 300,000
people moved to the new areas; they were cheered by the first year's crop,
disheartened by the 1955 drought and cheered again by the 1956 yield. Not
content with that Khrushchev had his hardly less grandiose scheme in 1955
to grow maize for fodder in areas where it had not been grown before. In
1957 he capped his plans with a campaign to catch up with the United
States in milk, butter and meat.

Not one of these schemes turned out according to promise. Parts of
Kazakhstan soon resembled a dustbowl, though some of them later
recovered. The maize refused to grow where nature had not intended it.
And the Soviet Union was still short of meat and dairy produce. But the
government and the state became aware of farming as never before, and in
1958 the central committee of the party wound up the detested machine-
tractor stations which, by supplying the machines and men for ploughing and
harvesting, had virtually controlled the collective farms. Prices were again
adjusted to encourage the peasants. Even so progress was painfully slow.

It was in his dealings with foreign countries, communist and non-
communist alike, that the merits and the faults of Nikita Sergeyevich
showed most clearly. Very soon after Stalin's death, the whole Eastern
camp was shaken by the astounding, entirely unforeseen popular rising in
East Germany. It was put down by Soviet tanks on 16-17 June 1953. Yet
Khrushchev, Mikoyan and others were not blind to the underlying cause
of the upheaval. The Soviet Union had clamped down too hard. It had
driven tough trading bargains with their East European satellites; it had

'Sandal' missiles at the Moscow parade of 1963 celebrating the October Revolution. Missiles of this type had been installed in Cuba during the crisis of the previous year, and were subsequently withdrawn following American pressure

Below The satirical magazine *Krokodil* celebrates fifty years of the Red Army's conquering progress

enforced iron political discipline. Khrushchev argued that a little more freedom would induce greater loyalty and cooperation. He began to speak of different roads to socialism for different countries.

These were dangerous words to utter unless they were to be followed by real measures to allow such different roads. Rioting in Poznań in June 1956 – four months after Khrushchev's secret speech against Stalin – was followed by the confrontation between Gomułka and the Soviet leaders in October and immediately afterwards by the rising in Hungary, 23 October–4 November. The Soviet leaders, Khrushchev among them, who had conceded the calm and firm Polish demands for more independence, felt obliged to put down the Hungarian armed challenge to their European system. Soviet tanks and troops silenced the Hungarian insurgents while the world's attention was half distracted with the Anglo-French Suez adventure. The lesson of the suppression was clear: though the Stalinist system of economic colonization was to be eased, no country could break away from the military alliance.

Hungary could be stopped from breaking away. Poland could be half-placated. China could be neither stopped nor placated. Strangely enough the Russians were less startled by the rupture with China than most Western observers were. In Western eyes the Chinese communists' overwhelming victory in 1949 had appeared as one of the titanic and irreversible movements in the history of man. Tightly disciplined communist regimes, led by the Soviet Union, now held the strategic Eurasian heartland, with all its wealth in manpower and material resources, from the Elbe to the Yangtse. It was a glittering prospect of power. Yet from the beginning the Russian leaders were uneasy. Several of them would have preferred the Chinese communists to follow Stalin's advice to them and take over only northern China. That would have left a Nationalist China in the south as a convenient counter-weight to keep the communist north in order. More Russians were appalled when Peking announced that China already had 600 million people

The Russian space programme had some solid early success with the first sputniks (1957-8) and on 12 April 1961 Yuri Gagarin (*above*) became the first man in space, and a symbol of superiority over the Americans

Inside the COSMOS pavilion at the USSR economic achievements exhibition in Moscow, 1968

– three times the Soviet population, depleted by war. And what lay ahead? China might indeed have to rely on Russian technical and industrial help and advice in the early years; yet the time would come when the pupil could be much stronger, harder working, and possibly abler, than the teacher. Always in the Russian mind, beyond all the bitter doctrinal disputes that broke out with Peking – over whether war with the capitalist was really inevitable, and whether Lenin was partly outmoded – there lay this sense of strategic foreboding. The ally had become too big to be biddable.

Unfortunately for Moscow, Khrushchev had neither the knowledge of China nor the patience of character to keep talks going without an open rupture. Nothing was more just and fitting in his view, nothing was more outrageous and hostile in the Chinese eyes, than his sudden withdrawal of all the Soviet technicians and engineers from China in August 1960. The Chinese armed attack across the Indian frontiers in October 1962 was seen by the Russians as an act reckless beyond belief. They had been carefully wooing India since Khrushchev's and Bulganin's visit in the autumn of 1955. Now the Chinese would undo it all and push India into accepting more American industrial and military help. Russian anger and anxiety grew as the Chinese newspapers made adroit references to the Far Eastern regions which Russia had taken from China by means of 'unequal treaties' in Tsarist times. The rift became so wide by 1964 that it helped in Khrushchev's fall. His colleagues had decided that among the other disadvantages of keeping him was the evidence that there could be no hope of reconciliation with China so long as he was in power. He was not pliable enough.

In his dealings with other countries Nikita Sergeyevich was always proudly conscious of being the leader of a great world power, defined as one that made its influence felt in every part of the world. At his best he was sincerely aware of such a power's supreme responsibility for preventing another great war. Most of the time he seemed to mean what he said about peaceful coexistence in all his journeys abroad – particularly to Britain in 1956 and to America in 1959. One reason for preaching coexistence was that he wished to compete with the West in raising standards of living and knew he could not so long as so much of Russia's scantier resources was devoted to armaments. He also knew that a new world war would be annihilating, a horror to be dreaded at least as much by Russia as by the United States.

Khrushchev, however, was being increasingly attacked by China and by old-guard critics at home as a revisionist and reformist. He therefore was probably not at all sorry to prove his orthodoxy (as well as show his deep sense of affront) when he broke up the summit meeting in Paris in May 1960 because Eisenhower had been obliged to admit his awareness that a U2 spy plane had been sent over Russia. Neither, for the same reason, was Khrushchev averse to threatening President John F. Kennedy, when they met in Vienna in June 1961, with dire consequences if the West did not accept Russia's terms for a still-divided Germany. He had to show people at home that he was not beguiled by the West. Perhaps he overdid the act in Vienna. The young and still inexperienced president's surprised silence in the face of his bluster may well have misled Khrushchev into thinking Kennedy weak, and so have tempted Moscow into the disastrous mistake of putting the missiles into Cuba in October 1962.

Nikita Sergeyevich was partial to missiles. They were for him the great-power status symbol. He liked boasting about them. He threatened London with them at the time of Suez in 1956. Cuba, as he thought, gave him his real opportunity. Slip some of the Soviet missiles into Castro's Cuba and then announce (Khrushchev could do it himself in New York at the United Nations) to a badly shaken and humiliated America that they were there, pointing at American cities. Nothing could put up Russian stock more: nothing would give greater encouragement to revolutionary forces throughout Latin America.

Clearly enough Khrushchev miscalculated over President Kennedy's character and over the general American reaction. What is significant is

Above Stalin's funeral in Red Square. Khrushchev and
Chou En-lai, the Chinese premier (third from right), are
among those following behind the coffin
Below right Brezhnev and Kosygin, Khrushchev's
successors in 1964, take a May Day parade, with President
Podgorny on the right. A painting of the Social Realist
school (*below*) depicts Stalin, 'Architect of Victory and
Father of the Peoples', with Marshal Voroshilov. The work
can be viewed in the Tretyakov Gallery, Moscow

that, when he had to give way, he was much more blamed by many ordinary
Russians for weakness than for brinkmanship; more for pulling the missiles
out after the American ultimatum than for putting them there in the first
place. It was Russia, they felt, that had been humiliated.

Khrushchev lasted another two years. He tried hard to mend the broken
fences. He signed the nuclear test ban treaty; he opened talks with China;
he made overtures to Western Germany. Yet his prestige and authority
were not what they had been. In July 1957 he had been able to turn the
tables on his Politburo critics led by Molotov and Kaganovich. They had
objected to his regional economic councils and his general revisionist
tendencies. Outvoted by them in the Politburo he was saved by a sweeping
vote in his favour by the central committee – the body which he had himself built up to new influence as one part of his desire to revive the party.
But in October 1964 there was no second chance. He was dismissed for his
'adventurism', his 'hare-brained' schemes, his arbitrariness, his refusal to
take advice. A chapter almost tragic by reason of its bungled opportunities
and disappointed hopes was ended.

Under Brezhnev

Once again, as so often in Russian history, the new team began with the
watchword: never again. This time there would be real collective leadership.
It would be ensured by staid, middle-aged, hardworking men like Brezhnev
as first secretary of the party and Kosygin as prime minister. Since 1964 the
primacy of Brezhnev has become clearer, but in 1970, six years later, he was
not out of his colleagues' control as Khrushchev often had been.

The Twenty-second Congress of the USSR Communist Party in Moscow (*top*); the Politburo is the Party's cabinet, the Central Committee its parliament. Stalin ignored them all, but the Party grew in authority under Khrushchev *Above* 'Young Pioneers' toe the Party line in Red Square

Below The Party on stage in a play dealing with its early history, *Kremlin Chimes*

To bring order and symmetry back to the pattern of government was the first task of the new team of party men. By September 1965 they had restored the industrial ministries to their central directive role. The state planning commission became once again the only machine for planning. Yet the new men were aware of some, at least, of the drawbacks of planning, especially when every kind of production was given a fixed annual or quinquennial target which it had to reach as its prime task. The system of strategic planning which in its cumbersome way was effective during the early years of basic industrial construction was much more cumbersome and much less efficient when the market was more complex and more changeable. Consumers' needs were growing; their desires were growing still more; household goods were becoming more sophisticated and harder to produce.

Discussions on making the system more efficient had begun in Khrushchev's time and were carried forward. The Russian economist Professor Liberman and others argued that the profit motive would stimulate the necessary drive and imagination in an enterprise: it should be allowed to have a greater influence on a director's choice of what to produce in his factory. Others, like Novozhilov and Kantorovich, urged that advanced computers could be used more widely to simplify the complexities of planning which hitherto were insoluble. In his *Economic History of the USSR* (1969), Professor Alec Nove reports that some progress was very slowly being made:

Reforms so far implemented go some way in the direction indicated by the reformers. Enterprises have a wider autonomy, the number of planned indicators has been greatly reduced. There has been more freedom for enterprises to purchase inputs (without prior allocation by planners) from stores and depots. The importance of profits has been greatly enhanced.

A little later Nove suggests that we might be seeing only the first steps in a big change which could eventually lead the Soviet system towards what might be called 'market socialism'. It might be so. The figures of production for the first half of 1970 showed that the plan was being fulfilled – an improvement on the last half of 1969. But the urgent need for greater flexibility and variety was shown in press reports during that same period in 1970. Many consumer goods, whether household utensils or suits, were still hard to come by. Queues stood before meat-shops, and milk and butter were scarce in many towns.

Farming in fact was still in 1970 the backward sector in the Soviet economy. Khrushchev's reforms had left many peasants rather better off but rather more bewildered. To instil confidence the new leaders quickly put up prices for agricultural and especially dairy products, and they lowered prices for farm machinery. They made it easier for peasants to keep their own livestock once again. In other measures they gave the peasants a more assured income. Yet much was still to be done to get the farmers producing sufficiently to feed the towns. As a return to private farming could be excluded from Soviet thinking, the remedy seemed to lie in the provision of many more services, easier transport, better schools, better houses and many more labour-saving machines in the Soviet countryside.

A little flexibility and freedom – Brezhnev and Kosygin showed that they thought the prescription to be useful in the running of modern industry. The opportunity to use his powers of judgement was necessary, they would agree, to a man of education, whether factory director or scientist. As Soviet higher education spread still further, the number of men and women with minds trained to make judgements would grow. With all that, Brezhnev and Kosygin indicated that the exercise of judgement must stop short of criticizing the bases of Soviet policy or Soviet society.

Observers in the Soviet Union suggested that the ordinary man was not over-troubled by this deprivation. He was fairly content with the hopeful convention that, if he did not touch the government, it would not touch him. If he went in for political thinking at all, he tended to believe in the inevitability of gradualness; in the slow softening of the regime as material life improved. Even many of the writers themselves wished that their rebel

Tower blocks in Moscow; great progress has been made in building flats and offices in the postwar era

colleagues would not be so outspoken and persistent, fearing that the authorities would clamp further restrictions down on all authors. Besides, said the orthodox, the Soviet Union was at least spared the kind of freedom that in the West encouraged a flood of pornographic and worthless books sold merely for the sake of making money.

Nevertheless, a few writers went on speaking out, bravely courting arrest, boldly protesting against others' imprisonment and going to prison or labour camp themselves. The most talented writer of them, Alexander Solzhenitsyn, saw his books *The First Circle* and *Cancer Ward* published abroad but not at home; he was expelled from the Writers' Union (and then was awarded the Nobel Prize). Some, like Sinyavsky and Daniel, satirical and perceptive, were sent to prison. Others, much less well known in Russia, like Sakharov and Amalrik were more directly political. Criticisms of Soviet society were passed round in the so-called *samizdat*, self-publishing, form. Other news and views of the small opposition groups were circulated in the same underground way. Sometimes the police appeared to turn a blind eye. In general, however, the fight was remorseless, for neither side could give in.

The independent-minded writers were quite consciously in the high Russian tradition evolved in the literary protests of the nineteenth century. Severe censorship, the dearth of opposition parties, the Orthodox Church's lack of a secular mission all meant that the writers had to fill a void in society; they had to be the reformers, the priests, the prophets, men pursuing a calling apart from others, and ready to face persecution. On the other side the authorities gave warning that no one could set himself up as an independent critic of the party and state. Back in the twenties the writers fought for the right to be critics, and they lost, and the battle was not to be joined again. The same warning applied to Christian believers, whether Orthodox, Old Believers, Baptists or members of other sects; many of them in recent years sought to live according to their own lights apart from society, or they resisted orders to close religious houses and schools, and found themselves in the same trouble as the writers. It was the party, and the party alone, personified in the leadership, that decided how society should develop, and what society should read or not read. The supremacy of the party was the unbreakable law.

No dissidence at home, no dissidence in the European socialist camp: the force that was ever ready to back up the rule was exerted in Czechoslovakia during the night of 20-1 August 1968 with a ruthlessness that appalled much of Western opinion, made a mockery of many hopes of coexistence and threw many of the communist parties themselves into disarray and despair. In the weeks that followed – while Alexander Dubček and the other reformist leaders were being browbeaten in Russia, and free voices were being silenced in Prague and Bratislava – Westerners and Russians who

Rush-hour shoppers in GUM, the department store; there is still a severe shortage of consumer goods in Russia

Above Members of the council of elders at a collective farm in Tajikistan. Under Stalin the collectives had been unproductive and the low prices offered by the government had encouraged bare subsistence farming. Khrushchev's agricultural reforms placed more emphasis on the peasants' personal profit, but his policies were only partially effective and his 'virgin lands' scheme a total failure. In 1970 farming was still the backward sector of the economy despite lower prices for machinery

Cotton-picking in the Russian deep south, Azerbaijan

tried to converse found themselves separated by basically irreconcilable idealogical assumptions.

To many Westerners, the Dubček reforms, allowing for more freedom of discussion and choice within the structure of the Marxist socialist state, seemed to do no more than respond to the needs of an educated industrial society. Other Marxist countries, as they came to the Czechoslovak level, would surely feel the same need to soften the harsh discipline of the state. The Soviet defence of the invasion – setting aside the propagandist fantasies about a West German plot that had to be forestalled – was essentially strategic in its argument. It started from a survey of Russia's general position in the world as this had been left by Khrushchev and shaped by subsequent events.

The world picture, seen from Moscow, was one of anxieties and dangers. On their eastern flank a still hostile China was creating frontier incidents. The explosion of the first Chinese atomic device in 1964 remained as an abiding reminder of China's potential power. China was a continuous nagging threat, never to be ignored. In South-east Asia the dangers of a wider war had increased since the Americans had begun persistent bombing in North Vietnam – and begun it, incidentally, while Kosygin was actually in Hanoi. Russia was committed to sending arms to the North Vietnamese and, especially as Peking was accusing her of slackness in the revolutionary and anti-imperialist cause, she had to prove her zeal by keeping up the supply of arms. She faced something of a dilemma. Though in many ways America's apparently unending embroilment and consequent unpopularity in the world suited Russia's interest, there was always the risk of being dragged herself much further into the war than she intended.

In the Middle East her anxieties were worse. She had backed the Arabs because they possessed the general strategic advantages: the Arabs had the territory, the oil, the communications, the sea ports, the population. But Russia's returns from the support she had given had so far been worse than nil. In the Six-Day War of June 1967, precipitated after some provocative connivance between Moscow and Cairo, Israel had trounced the Arab countries and had destroyed or captured much of the war material which Russia had sent to Arab states. Moscow was facing the prospect of more cost and more anxiety in that region.

It is no wonder that Russia, desiring some basis of stability in those pre-Czechoslovakia days, sought for a measure of broad agreement with the United States. Here she made a little valuable progress. After Premier Kosygin had met President Johnson at Glassboro, half-way between New York and Washington, on 23 June 1967, Russia and the United States at the Geneva disarmament conference in August tabled drafts of a treaty on the non-proliferation of nuclear weapons. The treaty was signed on 1 July 1968 – less than two months before the invasion of Czechoslovakia. On the whole Russia had reason to be fairly satisfied with the state of Europe since the fall of Khrushchev. When Kosygin visited Britain in February 1967 he made an appeal for the disbandment of the NATO and Warsaw alliances, but it was hardly more than routine; tension between the two sides was certainly less. The chief development which seemed to arouse Russian suspicions at that time were some serious West German approaches to East European countries in the hope of establishing better contacts; Russia still distrusted German intentions at that time.

Such a survey brought little comfort for a Moscow ringed with potential troubles. What reassurance there was, apart from the tentative moves with America, could be found chiefly in Europe. For all these reasons, when Czechoslovakia began to cause acute anxiety, in the very strategic centre of the Europe that had been so quiet, the Russian leaders reacted with disproportionate panic.

They were faced with a movement they could neither measure nor understand. They did not think that Dubček was going deliberately to lead Czechoslovakia out of the socialist camp. They did not think of him as consciously disloyal to socialist principles. But he was breaking the unbreakable law: he was weakening the supremacy of the party. He was

Production under the economic plans

1946-50 fourth five-year plan
1951-5 fifth five-year plan
1956-8 sixth five-year plan (abandoned)
1959-65 seven-year plan
1966-9 seventh five-year plan

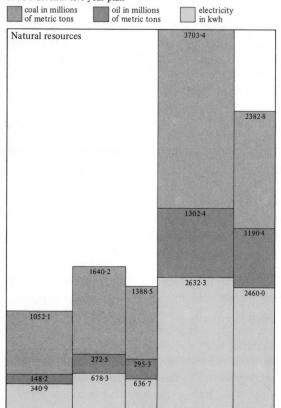

coal in millions of metric tons · oil in millions of metric tons · electricity in kwh

Natural resources

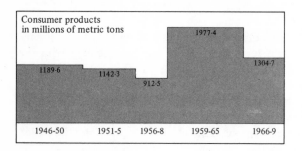

Consumer products in millions of metric tons

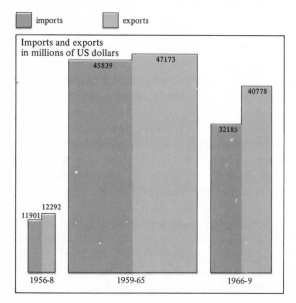

imports · exports

Imports and exports in millions of US dollars

allowing other voices to speak, other policies to be aired. The Russians felt they could no longer be sure how Czechoslovakia would develop. It *might* become anti-socialist. The Czechs and Slovaks *might* leave the camp. The Kremlin believed it was being asked to base Russia's security on an uncertainty. This was a risk that could not be taken.

Beyond that, the danger that Czechoslovak reformism would infect other Marxist socialist states was certainly in the minds of Ulbricht (East Germany), Gomułka (Poland) and other leaders. After all, East Germany, Poland and Hungary had already known popular revolts against the system; they did not want to take any more chances.

The same danger would almost certainly be in the minds of the Russians. Although they rejected the risk of political infection at the time as unworthy of consideration, and a slur on loyal Soviet solidarity, they were still denouncing reformism at the end of 1969 with the vehemence normally reserved for a real danger. In the *Theses for the centenary of Lenin's birth*, published 23 December 1969, the Soviet Communist Party attacked the whole concept of 'liberalized' socialism, 'which denies the guiding role of the Marxist-Leninist party, replaces socialist democracy with political liberalism of the bourgeois trend, reducing to nought the centralized planning and guidance of the national economy, so as to unleash anarchy in the market and competition.' In the largely de-politicized atmosphere of modern Russia any unorthodox idea seemed bad and disruptive. For every reason in August 1968 the clock had to be put back. Czechoslovakia was invaded.

From 1968, after a pause for reflection, Moscow followed a policy similar to Khrushchev's discreet post-Cuba aim of repairing the fences. Once again the dangers had become too great for comfort. So in its own state interests as a great power it set about negotiating agreements that could weaken the international memories, the suspicions and the tensions. This did not stop Russia from going on building up her arms. The survey published in London on 4 September 1970 by the Institute for Strategic Studies, under the title, *The Military Balance*, reported that the Soviet Union had then more land-based intercontinental ballistic missiles than the United States – 1,300 to 1,074. Though America still had the lead in sea-borne nuclear missiles Russia was fast increasing her power there. At sea in general the West was still superior, but the picture had been greatly changed by Russia's drive in recent years to build up its submarine fleet (in 1970 it had some 290 conventionally powered and 80 nuclear-powered submarines) as well as surface ships. 'Soviet fleets', says the Institute, 'are able now to challenge at every level of military and politico-military action' – and in several oceans. The leaders recognized that a great power must possess great power. When they talked with the Americans about reducing armaments they meant reducing them from a very high level indeed on both sides. Yet they would probably like some reduction. In 1969 they began the discussions with the United States on the limitation of strategic arms – the so-called SALT talks. In 1970 they helped to bring about the truce in the Middle East and arrange for the tortuous peace talks. In August 1970 they began a new effort to get talks moving in Peking.

It was on 12 August 1970 that they signed their most important agreement of this period: the treaty with Federal Germany, 'ending the war', as was said; the treaty renouncing the use of force and acknowledging present frontiers to be inviolable. Western observers could say that Moscow was hoping to turn Federal Germany away from concentrating too much on the European Economic Community, which the Russians naturally disliked, especially if the Community were to be enlarged by the inclusion of Britain. Offering Federal Germany opportunities in the East would help to divide and disperse the Community's energies. But the Russians had more direct interests in becoming more friendly with Federal Germany. These were to be found in the shortcomings of their own industry. Great though the progress had been, Soviet industry was short in many fields of advanced technology and the means of applying it. The treaty with Federal Germany, with its specific mention of economic and technical cooperation, would make it

'Keep at it,' says the sailor to the bricklayer in this magazine cover: the flags at the top bear the inscription 'Workers' vigilance in honour of October'

Above right A view of paraffin processing installations at a major oil refinery

easier for German technology to help in chosen Russian enterprises. It was thus in line with the broader Soviet move to enlist the skills of the best Western and Japanese enterprises to fill out some important gaps in their industrial planning. Other countries had not been ashamed to call in foreign experts and managerial skill. It need not be taken as a sign of failure if the Russians should do so.

Conclusion

By the end of 1970 the Russians and the other peoples of the former Tsarist empire had known few periods of respite from strain and hardship since 1914. Their state structure was stronger and much more centralized than the revolutionaries dreamed of fifty or sixty years ago. In general living conditions were still short of the first bright hopes, although recent years had brought swifter and surer improvements. The Second World War thrust the people back, and the Stalin system became a brake on their growth besides retarding them politically.

By 1970 there was curiously little political discussion that a foreigner could hear. The Revolution had become middle-aged and settled down. There were indeed many solid reasons – even good Marxist reasons – for the conservative air that at first sight might seem surprising. The very large numbers of administrators, directors and bureaucrats had a vested interest in the continuity of the regime without change or upheaval. Their interest was the more direct and compelling because, as a body, they had no private lands or fat directorships to fall back on if they fell from favour. Some of the younger bureaucrats were discussing and advocating administrative reforms. In general, however, there seemed little movement. Where in other countries the middle classes had traditionally been the liberals and reformers, in Russia it was the men and women of these influential ranks that seemed the most conservative.

All the peoples of the Soviet Union, peoples of many different nationalities, could take pride in their industrial strength; they could take advantage of the greatly expanded schools and universities; they could enjoy much shorter working hours and better social insurance than they had before the war; they could buy imported clothes and shoes of good quality; small Fiat-type cars were beginning to appear in Moscow. If the people and their leaders thought less about world revolution, or even about eventual communism at home, they thought more about the material progress that could be made in the next few years within the Soviet Union itself.

Neal Ascherson

Eastern Europe: Between Two Worlds

The term 'Eastern Europe' is used here in the contemporary and conventional sense: to denote all the territories which for one reason or another adopted a Soviet type of communism after the Second World War. It includes the new phenomenon of the German Democratic Republic, claimed still (though with fast-fading conviction) by Western Europe, and it leaves out Greece although the Greek destiny has been so closely connected to the affairs of the other, communist Balkan states. It includes both Yugoslavia and Albania, neither of them today members of the 'Soviet bloc'.

Since 1945, the experience of these states has been comparable, if not quite similar. They have passed through forced industrialization, collectivization of the land, membership of military, economic and political treaty organizations directed by the Soviet Union, and police terror. During the early fifties, they were largely isolated from the rest of the world. Since then, they have shared the experience – in very different degrees – of de-Stalinization and of a slow movement towards national independence, often based on the introduction of market-orientated economies. The nations of Eastern Europe are, in short, becoming less like each other.

This account starts, approximately, at the Liberations of 1944-5. But the area's common experience between 1945 and 1970, especially during the arduous years of Stalinism, would be in false historical perspective if no reference were made to the preceding twenty-five years. With the exception of Bohemia and Moravia, and of central Germany which became the GDR, Eastern Europe between the wars was a region of deepening social misery and apparently insoluble economic and political problems. An undernourished and disease-ridden peasantry, far too numerous for available land, was governed by generally corrupt and selfish cliques. There was little industry, much of it foreign-owned. The emergence of the successor states to the Austrian and German empires left large and often seditious minorities within the new national boundaries. The depression of the early thirties only accelerated the destitution of Eastern European societies, while their political difficulties were multiplied by the revival of fanatical nationalism. Using methods which caused much avoidable human suffering, the postwar governments and the Stalinist forced-industrialization programmes broke the back of these problems. The minorities were mostly expelled, rural overpopulation was drawn off into new cities, free and universal welfare and education were introduced and an industrial base was constructed in each state. It is against these achievements that the vices and blunders of the Eastern European national governments must be measured.

Since no order of precedence is particularly significant, I have set the national sections of this chapter in alphabetical order.

Albania

Two main factors have determined the policies of Albania since the war. The first is the fact that the Albanians, principally the communist partisans, bore the brunt of their own struggle to liberate themselves from Italian and German occupation. The second is Albania's remoteness from the Soviet Union and from the main strategic confrontation of East and West in Central Europe. These factors have encouraged and enabled a country with a population of less than 2 million to defy successively the Western powers and the Soviet Union. The need for economic aid, which might have allowed the USSR to bring Albania to its knees, has now been amply met by China.

The Albanian Communist Party was formed in 1941, under the leadership

Five-year plans in Eastern Europe (Roumanian poster, 1950): Soviet COMECON policies of specialist industrialization based on the natural resources available in each state, provoked opposition, especially in Roumania

266

PLANUL 5 CINCINAL

CONSTRUIM SOCIALISMUL
fărā burghezie şi împotriva ei

Marx in remote Albania, which escaped the Soviet orbit in 1961 and became China's ally in Europe

Below Chou En-lai on a visit to Tirana in Albania; relations were friendly during the Sino-Soviet split and considerable economic aid followed in the late sixties
Bottom The first railway to be designed and built entirely by the Albanians: it was completed in 1967

of Enver Hoxha, who has remained the dominant figure in Albania ever since. He received Anglo-American military aid in the war, but after the war, when highly un-Western elections confirmed the Communist Party's grip on Albania, Britain and the United States broke off diplomatic relations.

Yugoslav-Albanian relations were at first cordial. Stalin, however, was at this time encouraging the Yugoslavs to absorb Albania, and traditional suspicions between Albanian and Serb reasserted themselves. In 1948, at the time of Yugoslavia's breach with the Soviet Union, Albania sided with the Soviet Union and purged pro-Yugoslav communists from the party.

A period of enthusiastic Stalin-worship followed. In 1950, Western intelligence services made their only recorded attempt to destroy a Warsaw Pact regime by armed force. Parachutists were landed, but due to advance information given to Russia by the master spy Kim Philby, and passed on to Tirana, the Albanians were prepared and able to deal with the intrusion.

In the late fifties, relations with the Soviet Union deteriorated. Resentful of Soviet control, Hoxha and his associate Mehmet Shehu extended feelers towards China. An attempt by Khrushchev, who visited Albania in 1959, to divert this trend failed. In 1961, Albania moved into a position of open defiance, and Soviet military and economic aid was withdrawn. Albania left COMECON in 1962, and remained a merely nominal member of the Warsaw Pact until departing after the invasion of Czechoslovakia in 1968.

Albania was now totally isolated, facing the hostility of the NATO powers, the Warsaw Pact and Yugoslavia. A campaign of forced industrialization began, and education programmes attacked the backwardness of a principally Muslim population which, before the war, had been eighty-five per cent illiterate. Friendly relations with China were established, but the connection only became effective, in economic and military aid, at the end of the sixties.

The 'Chinese' orientation of Albania is to some extent superficial. There has been no cultural revolution, Hoxha being no doubt unwilling to risk such a loss of control, and the 'big revolutionary action' of 1966 was less a 'great leap forward' on any Chinese pattern than a general reorganization of government. Under slogans which are often Maoist, the Albanian leadership has tried to develop its own solutions.

The invasion of Czechoslovakia in 1968 was a profound shock to Albania. A Soviet attack on Yugoslavia and Albania seemed possible, and Enver Hoxha proceeded at once to deepen his contacts with China and to mend fences with neighbouring countries. A large Chinese military and economic delegation arrived in late 1968. Chinese aid, probably worth over $100 million, was arranged, and a military agreement which included some form of Chinese missile produced alarm in the West, although it has been concluded since that any Chinese effort to arm Albania with nuclear delivery systems is highly unlikely.

Albania radio, powerful and audible across the Continent, continued to denounce the Soviet leaders – including their Czechoslovak policy – as 'social imperialists and New Tsars', and to encourage the formation of anti-Moscow communist parties within Eastern Europe. Soviet efforts to appease the Albanians in late 1969, at the time of the twenty-fifth anniversary of Albania's liberation, were rejected.

Relations with Yugoslavia improved. Hoxha, while still insisting on his 'profound ideological differences' with Tito, suggested that the two peoples had glorious common traditions of struggle. On the Yugoslav side, the grievances of the Albanian minority in the Kosovo region were met by reforms. At the same time Hoxha established consular relations with Turkey (late 1969), and in 1970 concluded a trade pact with Greece. While maintaining its defiance of the Soviet Union and its link with China, Albania seems to be interested in taking part in a general drawing-together of Balkan states which feel endangered by Soviet policies.

Bulgaria

Modern Bulgaria in effect dates from 9 September 1944. This was the day on which the combination of a *coup d'état* and popular rising put a communist-

Top Russian troops enter Sofia in September 1944 and support the communist-dominated 'Fatherland Front' coup, which led to the deposition of the monarchy and several years of purges, show trials and Stalinist terror
Above Georgi Dimitrov, first prime minister of Bulgaria, which became a 'People's Republic' in December 1947; his schemes for Balkan economic union were short-lived

Below Bulgarian shipbuilding; at the end of the sixties the economy was improving rapidly

dominated 'Fatherland Front' in charge of the nation. Bulgaria, traditionally pro-Russian, had entered the war against the United States and Britain on Germany's side, but had resisted Nazi pressure to join the war against the Soviet Union. In September 1944, while the regents and a political group led by the Agrarians were preparing to offer peace terms to the British and Americans, the Soviet Union unilaterally declared war on Bulgaria, and the 'Fatherland Front' successfully carried out its rising the following day. Bulgarian troops joined the war against Germany under the direct command of the Soviet Union, and a bloody manhunt against opponents of the new regime was organized by the communist ex-partisan Anton Jugov, in which thousands lost their lives.

In 1946, the 'Front' won a majority at the elections, the king was deposed, and in December 1947 the National Assembly adopted a constitution which made Bulgaria a People's Republic. The first prime minister was Georgi Dimitrov, the veteran international communist who had headed the Comintern and spent the war years in the Soviet Union. The independent political parties were rapidly squeezed out of existence and Nikolai Petkov, leader of the Agrarian Union, was executed.

Dimitrov's short period in office – he died in 1949 – was partly occupied in an attempt to forward plans for a Balkan federation or customs union. Although pliant to Stalin's orders, Dimitrov appears to have seen these Balkan union schemes as a form of collective defence against Soviet pressure. The quarrel between Stalin and Tito finally obliterated the idea completely in 1948.

In 1949, Bulgaria staged a notorious series of show trials, with faked confessions. A group of Protestant pastors was tried early in 1949, and later that year there took place the trial of Traicho Kostov, who had been secretary of the central committee of the party and now, with his 'associates', stood accused of treacherous relations with the heretic Tito. Kostov withdrew his forced confession in court, and was executed shortly after being found guilty: a 'posthumous confession' was later confected to reduce the effects of his defiance at the trial.

Dimitrov's successor as prime minister was Chervenkov, a loyal Stalinist, but the experience of Stalinist dictatorship, though bitterly resented, did not destroy the Bulgarian people's historical loyalty to Russia. Curiously, it was to the Bulgarian leadership that Khrushchev chose to make his first revelation of the exposure of the crimes of Stalin, when he passed through Sofia in June 1955.

Chervenkov, the arch-Stalinist of Bulgaria, was replaced by Anton Jugov in 1956. Among other consequences of Khrushchev's attack on Stalin at the Twentieth Party Congress that year was the rehabilitation of Kostov. The powerful Todor Zhivkov, who had been first secretary of the party since 1954, absolved him from the charges and assured his widow a pension and his son an education in the Soviet Union. But effective de-Stalinization in Bulgaria had to wait until 1962. Jugov in 1958 had attempted to put into practice a Bulgarian version of the Chinese 'great leap forward', a huge programme for instant industrialization which ended in failure. In 1962, both he and Chervenkov were expelled from the central committee of the party and Todor Zhivkov became prime minister. The 'personality cult' was now denounced, political prisoners were released in hundreds and an impressive Bulgarian literature emerged to examine the tragedies of the recent past.

Zhivkov has remained in power ever since, the obscure 'Chinese plot' among army officers in 1965 hardly challenging his authority. Under Zhivkov, Bulgaria has remained more steadily loyal to Soviet policies than any other country in the socialist bloc, the German Democratic Republic included, but has gone some way to reduce the centralized direction of social life within the country. A new economic model, based on market pricing and the rentability of enterprises, was introduced after years of cautious testing in 1968, and both the economy and the standard of living in Bulgaria – still among the poorest countries in Eastern Europe – are beginning to improve rapidly.

The Russians ended the Nazi occupation of Czechoslovakia; three years later President Gottwald established a communist dictatorship, forcing the resignation of non-communist ministers

The Stalinist fifties: notorious for rehearsed and scripted trials, executions based on forced confessions and the bureaucratic decay of the economy in the hands of unqualified party veterans

Relations between Yugoslavia and Bulgaria remain a problem. Tension arises from the historic Bulgarian claim to what is now Serbian Macedonia, and after the 1968 intervention in Czechoslovakia a combined attack from the Soviet Union in the north-east and Bulgaria in the east was thought possible in Belgrade.

Mutual suspicions had declined slightly by 1970, although tactless speeches by leading Bulgarian personalities still refer to the 'Bulgarian' history of Macedonia. As the only imaginable context for a Bulgarian effort to change the frontier is a Soviet attack on Yugoslavia, it seems likely that the prospective pacts on European security will help to lay the dispute finally to rest.

Czechoslovakia

Czechoslovakia emerged from war and Nazi occupation relatively undamaged. With the exception of Eastern Germany, this was the only country in the post-1945 Soviet sphere of influence which possessed a highly developed industrial base and in which a large and long-established communist party existed. Both these facts played an important part in the ensuing twenty-five years.

Another factor was the tradition of Slav solidarity with Russia, especially among the Czech and Slovak intelligentsia; politically, this was reinforced by the betrayal of Czechoslovakia by Britain and France at Munich in 1938. After the war, when the exile government under President Beneš returned from London, the Communist Party won thirty-eight per cent of the vote at free elections in 1946, and its leader, Klement Gottwald, became prime minister. In February 1948, under the pressure of immense street demonstrations in Prague, twelve non-communist ministers in the cabinet resigned and Gottwald established effective control of the country. In June 1948, President Beneš resigned, and Gottwald succeeded him.

Czechoslovakia – the false dawn. Early in 1968, Dubček (here with President Svoboda) took over as first secretary of the party from the discredited Novotný. He instituted economic reforms, federal autonomy for Slovakia and lifted the ban on non-communist politics. Some six months later Warsaw Pact forces moved in to prevent the 'counter-revolution' and political resistance was slowly but inevitably crushed by Moscow

Above Mourning students carry the Czechoslovak flag through the streets of Prague after the Russian invasion
Right Street-fighting in Prague on 21 August 1968

There followed a period of rigid and ferocious Stalinist dictatorship. In politics and in the economy, Soviet models totally inappropriate to an industrialized country with a long tradition of middle-class democracy were imposed. Direct Soviet influence, especially in the security services, was willingly accepted. The autonomy of Slovakia was sacrificed to centralized dictation from Prague. Political prisoners filled gaols and labour camps. In the early fifties, a series of political show trials based on fantastic evidence and false confessions took place, of which the most notorious was the trial of Rudolf Slánský, first secretary of the party, and several others in 1952. There were many death sentences with Slánský among the victims. The population, totally cowed, was by now so confused that many Czechs and Slovaks believed in the guilt of those executed. No popular movement or change in leadership took place in 1956, following the revelations of Stalin's crimes at the Twentieth Congress of the CPSU.

In 1957, Antonín Novotný, first secretary of the party, became president. Direct Soviet intervention in Czechoslovak affairs became less frequent. Slowly oppositional forces began to build up strength within the party, looking either to the principles of the Twentieth Party Congress or to foreign experiments in Yugoslavia and elsewhere. Nationalist resentment revived in Slovakia during the sixties, where reformers came to see a more 'liberal' regime at Prague as the precondition for Slovak self-government; the first secretary of the Slovak Communist Party, Alexander Dubček, allowed some of this dissent to be expressed. Most significantly, the decay of the mismanaged economy was obvious to everyone. Resentment and frustration in the new technical intelligentsia, unable to use its qualifications, were among the most important social causes of what took place in the course of 1968.

Novotný's position was undermined from several directions. Fits of repression failed to silence criticism and debate among intellectuals. A first attempt to reform the economy along 'market' lines, planned by Professor Ota Šik, failed because the party leadership refused to accept the political relaxation and sweeping purges of 'unreformable' Stalinist placemen which it required. In 1967, Novotný made several fatal mistakes. He repressed the writers who were demanding relaxation of the censorship, gratuitously offended the Slovaks, and let the police beat up students in Prague protesting against their living conditions. The Russians did not defend him when he was replaced by Alexander Dubček as first secretary in January 1968.

Under Dubček, the reformers took control of the party. In the early months of 1968, Dubček allowed the full force of repressed longing for change to break through. Censorship ceased to exist, 'conservatives' and Novotný placemen lost their posts throughout society, and the party drew up a draft for a new 'socialism with a human face'. The Šik reforms were to be reapplied, Slovakia was to have full federal autonomy and the party's

Above An East German poster after the war points the contrast between the past and a thriving new workers' state; in fact the GDR, created out of the Soviet zone, did not advance economically until 1963
Below Brief rebellion after Stalin's death in 1953

leading role, as expressed in the April 'action programme', was to be one of 'informal, natural authority based on its working and managing ability and the moral qualities of communist functionaries'.

By the early summer, the Soviet Union and some of its allies, Walter Ulbricht in particular, had come to see this experiment as a menace to the internal stability of their own regimes. Late at night on 20 August, Warsaw Pact forces in overwhelming strength invaded Czechoslovakia. Although the Dubček leadership had refused to the last to believe that military intervention was imminent, the party and population resisted the invasion by operating the entire state and communications apparatus clandestinely. Underground 'legal' newspapers and broadcasts held the nation together. Although the army had put up no resistance and there had been little bloodshed, the invaders failed to install a 'collaborationist' regime. But on the political front, the resistance gradually collapsed. Dubček and his colleagues, taken under arrest to Moscow, agreed to emasculate the reform in return for a Soviet promise to evacuate interventionist forces when conditions had been 'normalized'. This promise was never kept. Instead, it was used as an ever-receding carrot to induce Dubček, temporarily back in power, to make increasing concessions. Censorship was gradually reimposed, the economic reform was blocked, the security police reasserted themselves. In 1969 Dubček himself was replaced by Dr Gustáv Husák and a full-scale purge of 'reformers' from the party and from all state or economic posts was carried through.

By late 1970, little of the 1968 reforms remained beyond the federal status of Slovakia. The economy, stripped of its managerial talent by the purges, remained in confusion. In the summer, however, small tokens of stabilization – a readiness to negotiate with West Germany and a slackening of the purges – made themselves felt.

The Czechs benefited less from twenty-two years of communist government than almost any other East European nation (Slovakia at least, a poor peasant country in 1945, was effectively industrialized in these years). Their priceless asset of skilled manufacture was wasted, their self-respect as a democratic community was shattered by the cancerous ramifications of the trials in the fifties and Czech culture, historically the main national element of continuity, was subjected to a destructive alternation of false dawns and brutal interruptions. The spring of 1968 was a moral revival as much as a political experiment. The prospects under Dr Husák, not a man given to illusions, are of a very cautious return towards an economic reform programme and – if he is sure of his own position within the party – of an equally cautious effort to win back, step by step, the cooperation of the intellectuals and the public. Like the slow consolidation of the Kádár regime in Hungary after 1956, it is likely that this could take many years.

German Democratic Republic

The German Democratic Republic is the state created out of the Soviet zone of occupation in Germany, when disagreements between the four Allies of the Second World War made it impossible for the central administration of a single but reduced Germany to continue. The Federal Republic was established in the Western zones in May 1949, and the German Democratic Republic was proclaimed in October the same year.

The events in the Soviet zone before the partition of Germany appeared inevitable but were not entirely typical of Soviet procedure in Eastern Europe. Massive dismantling of industry took place, and much of the zone's industrial equipment – with a large number of skilled technicians – was transported to the Soviet Union. Politically, the 'Ulbricht Group' of German communists who returned in the wake of the Red Army at first pursued a 'broad front' tactic, an anti-fascist alliance of socialist and bourgeois parties with a conventional social-democratic programme. In April 1946, at a fusion congress, the German Communist Party merged with the Social Democrats (SPD) in the Soviet zone to form the Socialist Unity Party (SED) which still governs.

As the cold war developed, and as it became clear that Western policy was

West German cartoon: Ulbricht announces total state security by evacuating the whole population to China and declaring the GDR forbidden territory (1961, following the creation of the Berlin Wall)

Escapes from East Germany to West Germany 1950-70

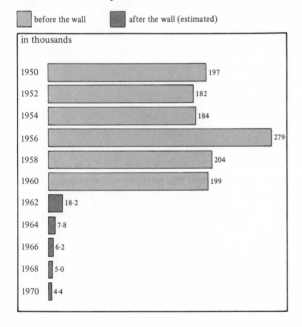

before the wall   after the wall (estimated)

in thousands	
1950	197
1952	182
1954	184
1956	279
1958	204
1960	199
1962	18·2
1964	7·8
1966	6·2
1968	5·0
1970	4·4

Below May Day parade of armour in East Berlin

to work by military and diplomatic pressure for a reunification of Germany which would mean the absorption of the GDR by West Germany, the SED imposed a stringently Stalinist discipline. Soviet influence, at first through the occupation authorities and later through the Soviet Embassy in East Berlin, was dominant.

A major crisis, still imperfectly understood, arose in 1953 after the death of Stalin. It would seem that the new Malenkov-Beria leadership in Moscow, interested in a possible German settlement with the West, pressed Ulbricht for a general relaxation of political and economic discipline and even contemplated replacing him by a more moderate leader. Ulbricht resisted, and his refusal to revoke increased work norms produced a spontaneous revolt in the working class in June 1953 which spread to other cities. Soviet armed intervention was necessary to repress the demonstrations, which paradoxically confirmed Ulbricht's cautious and restrictive policies.

In the course of the fifties, West Germany with the support of its allies shifted its policy from direct annexation towards attempting to prevent international recognition of the GDR as a state (the 'Hallstein Doctrine'). The NATO countries in effect banned travel from the GDR to their own territory. This isolation encouraged the survival of Stalinist policies in the GDR, and the development of a grim and mindless treatment of culture and information. The GDR, once committed to the reunification of Germany in socialism, now became preoccupied with defending its own state existence against Western or 'liberal' communist contamination. The events of 1956 found little echo in the GDR.

After the 'thaw' of 1955 in international relations had proved illusory, the GDR became involved in the fresh series of world crises which centred on Berlin. Although the GDR was now a heavily armed partner in the Warsaw Pact, the Soviet Union did not permit Ulbricht either to take an independent part in the Berlin crises or to control the access routes to West Berlin which ran through GDR territory. The promises made by Khrushchev in the late fifties to sign a separate peace treaty with the GDR were never fulfilled, and the titular sovereignty of the state remained much more qualified in practice than that of other Warsaw Pact countries.

In 1961, the exodus of GDR citizens to the West through the open Berlin border became a torrent, seriously threatening to drain the republic of its reserves of qualified manpower. With Soviet approval, GDR police and troops closed the border on 13 August 1961, later erecting a 'Wall' of concrete or barbed-wire which cut off East from West Berlin. This act, regarded by the West as a defiance of Berlin's four-power status, produced a head-on military confrontation between East and West, and by its sudden division of the city, created great hardship and personal suffering for the Berlin population. It proved, however, to be a turning-point in the development of the GDR.

After 1961, the 17 million Germans in the GDR were no longer able to dream either of reunification or of escape to the West. A sense of qualified loyalty to the economic and social achievements of the GDR slowly grew up, which – while resenting the oppressive style of SED leadership – was no longer accessible to West German radio exaggerations of the misery of the GDR and the wealth and liberty of the Federal Republic. After 1963, a new economic policy was launched which used a degree of market pricing and incentives to build up an industrial economy which is now the most advanced and successful in Eastern Europe. This was the 'East German economic miracle', which – considered as an effort against difficulties – bore favourable comparison with the *Wirtschaftswunder* of the Federal Republic.

The party itself, the SED, proved able to mobilize the traditional German resources of industriousness and ingenuity. Party members, while often swallowing whole the naïvely demonized picture of the outside world provided by the media, displayed and still display an enthusiasm and commitment rare in other Warsaw Pact societies. In part, this was made possible by the shrewdness of the Ulbricht leadership in the fifties; in spite of the relentlessly Stalinist style, the GDR was spared both show trials, followed

by death sentences, and party splits leading to extensive purges throughout the SED.

The physical and cultural exterior of the GDR remains drab; *Neues Deutschland*, the party daily, is one of the dullest newspapers in the world. A readiness for some degree of contact with the West, demonstrated in the grant of passes through the Wall for West Berliners at Christmas 1963, also petered out. A suggested meeting between Willy Brandt, as leader of the Social Democrats in West Germany, and GDR leaders came to nothing in 1966.

From the late sixties, however, improvements in the international climate began to affect the GDR's policies towards the outside world. Recognition by Arab, African and Asian countries raised the GDR's self-confidence. The main challenge, then as now, was the new *Ostpolitik* of the Federal Republic. For some years, and in the face of Soviet reluctance, the GDR successfully insisted that the price of better relations between the Warsaw Pact states and Bonn must be prior diplomatic recognition of the GDR and the withdrawal of nuclear weapons from the Bundeswehr. This policy collapsed in 1969-70, as the new Brandt government in Bonn signed bilateral treaties with the Soviet Union and Poland.

In the spring of 1970, two dramatic meetings between Chancellor Brandt and Prime Minister Willy Stoph took place at Erfurt in the GDR, and at Kassel in West Germany. They were inconclusive, the Ulbricht regime still fearing that inter-German contacts below the level of recognition could be used to undermine the security of the GDR. The violent reaction of the SED leadership to the Czechoslovak experiment in early 1968, and Ulbricht's consistent urging of military intervention upon the Russians and the other Warsaw Pact powers, reveal the lasting fear of the regime that West Germany remains secretly committed to the destruction of socialism in the GDR, and its belief that a more 'liberal' or 'revisionist' form of communism in Eastern Europe will infect the GDR and lower its resistance to West German penetration.

The GDR today presents the unique spectacle of a prosperous and modernized economy operated by a society whose self-expression is severely restricted. Internally, the SED now has an authentic power base, and the assumption that the regime is kept in power only by 'Soviet bayonets' is no longer tenable. The population's principal grievance today is the regime's almost total ban on foreign travel to the West, followed by resentment of the anachronistic and didactic management of information and culture. At the moment, it seems unlikely that either demand will be met, even partially, before a general European security settlement has persuaded the SED leaders that the system's survival is effectively guaranteed.

Hungary

Traditionally anti-Russian, strongly Catholic and with a heroic style of patriotism paralleled only, in Eastern Europe, by that of the Poles, Hungary emerged from the war in considerable moral and political confusion. Under the Horthy dictatorship Hungary had been an ally of Nazi Germany and, by accepting Transylvania from prostrate Roumania in 1940, had taken part in the German spoliation of Europe. A mixed resistance movement had, however, kept alive the spirit of independence, and only ss intervention prevented Horthy himself from seeking peace terms from the Allies in March 1944. An armistice was finally arranged early in 1945.

With large Soviet forces in the country the first postwar elections in November 1945 gave the Smallholders Party a heavy majority (245 seats to the communists' 70), and Zoltán Tildy, the Smallholder leader, became president. With Soviet assistance, however, the communists began to exert heavy pressure on the government which culminated in the events of 1947. Under a communist minister of the interior, László Rajk, the secretary of the Smallholders, Béla Kovács, was arrested by the Russians in February 1947. The leaders of a 'counter-revolutionary conspiracy' supposedly involving the Smallholder prime minister, Ferenc Nagy, were hanged.

Against a background of arrests and intimidation, elections in August

Top Hungarian poster after the war: the CP fights for nationalization of the mines
Above In 1956 a period of political relaxation and Khrushchev's denunciation of Stalin brought the overthrow of the Rákosi government and the October popular rising

Imre Nagy, whose neutralist government lasted a week after the Budapest rising; he was deported and executed in June 1958
Above right In Budapest, the death of a member of the security police during the Budapest rising

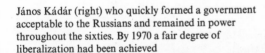

János Kádár (right) who quickly formed a government acceptable to the Russians and remained in power throughout the sixties. By 1970 a fair degree of liberalization had been achieved

displaced the Smallholders, and the communists (Hungarian Working Peoples' Party), who received twenty-two per cent of the vote, seized power. The following year there took place, as elsewhere in Eastern Europe, a merger between the remnants of the social democrats and the Communist Party. Under the leadership of Mátyás Rákosi, Hungary now entered the tunnel of Stalinism. In conditions of privation and police terror, the industrialization of the primarily agricultural economy was driven ahead through massive projects like the metallurgical complex at Sztálinváros. Agriculture was collectivized. The fertile and highly influential creative intelligentsia was reduced to silence or hagiography. Show trials struck down leading communists of the first postwar years, of whom the most prominent was Rajk, condemned and executed as a 'Titoist' in 1949. Gyula Kállai and János Kádár, to be respectively prime minister and party leader after 1956, were among those imprisoned. The Catholic hierarchy, despite its professions of loyalty to the regime in 1951, was not spared either.

A certain relaxation set in after the death of Stalin in 1953. But slight concessions – the release of some political prisoners, a move towards partial decollectivization of agriculture – did not dispel the sense of patriotic outrage which had accumulated under the monstrous distortions of legality and common sense imposed by Rákosi. Matters came rapidly to a head in 1956. Khrushchev's denunciation of Stalin and the Polish riots in June encouraged party intellectuals to fight for Rákosi's overthrow, which they achieved in July. Rajk was rehabilitated, but reform did not keep pace with popular excitement. The Budapest demonstration of 23 October touched off a popular uprising. On the thirtieth, a government headed by Imre Nagy came to power, promising a plural political system and the negotiated withdrawal of Soviet troops.

The Nagy government was not given time to bring under control the ever-strengthening discharge of popular excitement, ranging from a workers' council movement on the far left to traditional nationalist revivals on the long-suppressed right. After the fighting in Budapest, the Soviet armed forces had withdrawn; now their return began to seem likely. The Nagy government vainly proclaimed Hungary neutral and appealed for outside aid, but a counter-government was formed outside Budapest by János Kádár and on 4 November Soviet armour and troops entered the main towns and suppressed the rising by force. Hungarian casualties were high, and thousands crossed the border into Austria as refugees. Nagy and several colleagues were deported to Roumania by Soviet security police, and were executed in June 1958. Cardinal Mindszenty, the primate, took refuge in the United States Embassy in Budapest, where he still remained in 1970.

In 1961 the Kádár regime felt strong enough to end repression and move towards a 'New Course' of cautious modernization and reform. In the

A Polish flag flies over the ruins of Warsaw, January 1944

Below A meeting of the Warsaw Pact countries in Warsaw, 1955, when the Polish political situation was still unsettled following Stalin's death
Bottom The Poznań riots of June 1956 preceded the return to power of Gomułka, who had been imprisoned as a 'Titoist'

course of the sixties, old Stalinists were removed from the party, an amnesty for 1956 'offenders' was declared, a limited armistice with the Vatican was achieved and travel to the West became easier. In 1968, after three years of preparation, the 'New Economic Mechanism' was introduced, a fairly radical grafting of market pricing, the profit concept for enterprises and wage incentives on to a socialist economy redesigned to take account of the consumers' needs.

The Kádár regime has now achieved a considerable degree of liberalization both in the 'meritocratic' economic reform and in society as a whole. Care has been taken to do nothing which might irritate or alarm the Soviet Union; Hungary participated, with reluctance, in the Warsaw Pact intervention in Czechoslovakia. Four Soviet divisions remain stationed in the country. But the economic outlook is encouraging, and the press, though still controlled, is open to fairly uninhibited debate on internal affairs. Hungarian culture, especially in poetry and the cinema, has revived strongly. The last Party Congress in November 1970 produced reforms which make the party itself a less centralized and more democratic structure. After the Czechoslovak disaster, Hungary today leads the slow movement of Warsaw Pact states towards more open and efficient forms of society.

Poland

The history of Poland since 1945 has been, essentially, the history of the communist regime's efforts to reach a working compromise with three constants: first, the necessity broadly to satisfy the Soviet Union's requirements for a loyal member of the socialist camp, second, the need to construct, for the first time in Polish history, a sound economy based on a new social balance between industry and agriculture; third, the intensely Catholic and nationalist traditions of the population, which in history had often expressed themselves in a proudly antinomian disrespect for routine and regulation.

The prewar Communist Party was small, and its independent attitude led to its abolition by the Comintern and the murder by Stalin of several of its leaders, a disaster which has influenced the attitudes of Polish communists to Moscow ever since. The party was re-established after the German invasion of Russia, and a certain division grew up – also important in the subsequent history of the party – between those communists, including Władysław Gomułka, who remained in Poland and fought as partisans against the Nazi occupation, and those who spent the war in the Soviet Union and were later loosely called the 'Muscovites'. In 1947, the party established full control over Poland and the anti-communist political parties ceased to exist as effective forces. Bolesław Bierut, who had returned from his wartime sojourn in the USSR, became president. In 1948 the communists merged with part of the Socialist Party to form the Polish United Workers' Party (PUWP). Gomułka became its secretary-general.

Poland after the war was in chaos. One in five of the population had died as a direct consequence of the Nazi occupation, Warsaw was in ruins, and the industrial equipment of the country had been largely destroyed. The wartime Yalta Conference and the Potsdam Conference in August 1945 had agreed to move Poland bodily westwards to the line of the Oder and western Neisse. Immense areas of formerly German territory became Polish and the German population was expelled. The first postwar years were occupied by reconstructing war damage and by repopulating the new western and northern territories with Polish settlers drawn largely from the lost eastern lands.

Politically, a rigid and totalitarian Stalinism soon set in. Poles who had fought in the West or in the non-communist resistance (Home Army) were persecuted. In 1948, Gomułka was purged as a 'Titoist' and Bierut with a 'Muscovite' team took full control. The security services were under direct Soviet influence, although the regime managed to avoid the major show trials and executions which afflicted other East European countries in the fifties. The Catholic Church was harassed, and in 1953 Cardinal Wyszyński was arrested. The economy was directed towards forced heavy industrialization, at the expense of living standards, and agriculture was collectivized.

In 1956, following Khrushchev's denunciation of Stalin at the Twentieth Congress of the CPSU, this system disintegrated. Riots in Poznań in June were followed by changes in the leadership, and in October Gomułka returned to power as first secretary of the PUWP. The population prepared for armed struggle as Soviet tanks moved towards Warsaw, but Khrushchev, after failing to intimidate Gomułka on a hasty visit to Poland, decided shrewdly that the regime's ultimate loyalty to the Soviet bloc was not in danger. In November, as Soviet forces crushed the Hungarian rising, the Poles restricted themselves to expressions of horror and sympathy.

After 1956 Gomułka ruled Poland by a policy of balance between existing forces. At first he appealed to liberal communists and public opinion, in order to complete his victory over surviving Stalinist elements in the party. The land was redistributed to the peasants and a concordat was reached with the Church. The security services were partly disbanded and – for a few months – press censorship almost completely lifted. The 'Polish October' released a display of brilliant intellectual and artistic experiment which fascinated all Europe. But by mid-1957, the steady reassertion of party discipline had begun. The reformers, 'liberals' and exponents of a 'Polish model' of socialism were eased out of power.

Certain gains of 1956 lasted longer. Polish foreign policy became more independent, and a long series of efforts were made – the two Rapacki Plans, the Gomułka Plan, the offer of normal relations with West Germany – to reach a European security settlement on the basis of the *status quo*, and to persuade the West Germans to give up their claim to the western territories east of the Oder-Neisse line. Some effort was made to improve consumer industry and wage levels. In the first years after 1956, Poland accepted considerable indirect financial aid from the United States.

Gradually even these gains seemed to be dissipated. The German and European policy came to nothing, largely due to the irreducible hostility of Chancellor Adenauer. By the late sixties, the Polish government was returning this hostility with interest. Foreign policy now came to be based on an identification of interests with the German Democratic Republic, and when a new West German policy of conciliation began to emerge in 1966-7, Poland appeared in Bonn to be the most forbidding and unyielding nation in the socialist bloc with the exception of the GDR itself. A feeling of discontent, tinged with nationalist resentment, was general in Poland by 1968. The economy had achieved certain major targets, especially in reducing Poland's rural overpopulation and constructing a sound industrial

Gomułka (right) with Ulbricht; between 1966 and 1969 foreign policy showed solidarity with the GDR on Berlin and German issues

In December 1970 massive riots in Gdańsk and other Baltic towns followed the panic measure to raise food prices by about twenty per cent. Gomułka resigned, leaving intimidating problems

Gheorgiu-Dej, postwar leader of Roumania until his death in 1965: he achieved a measure of economic independence from the Soviet grouping COMECON

Below Roumanian postwar elections; the FND front included communists and trade unionists
Bottom Ceausescu, head of state from 1967, with de Gaulle in Bucharest: the end of the sixties brought a startlingly successful independent Roumanian foreign policy

base, but in the late sixties signs of crisis were everywhere. Consumption became erratic, and in 1967 meat prices were raised by seventeen per cent to counter a sudden shortage. The intellectuals were increasingly disaffected and the Church, still retaining a rather theocratic view of its status, put up powerful resistance to the state's attempts to limit its control over religious education.

Within the party, a nationalist and disciplinarian faction headed by General Moczar, minister of the interior, became powerful. Its attacks were directed against surviving 'liberals' and 'Muscovites', and against alleged 'Zionists'. Large numbers of Poles of Jewish origin lost their jobs and were pushed into emigration. In March 1968, a protest against theatre censorship was followed by student demonstrations in Warsaw, repressed with panicky violence. A general breakdown of order ensued. Massive and indiscriminate purges swept state and party organs. In the chaos, it seemed likely that Gomułka would lose his post to Moczar or one of his nominees.

The Czechoslovak crisis, however, intervened. The Soviet Union was already uneasy about the threat of Moczarism, and Gomułka, by agreeing to send Polish troops against Czechoslovakia in August, bought the full support of the Soviet leadership. At the Party Congress in November, public and backstage Soviet endorsement helped Gomułka to retain command; Moczar accepted candidate-membership of the Politburo which led to his political neutralization.

The position in Poland slowly stabilized. In May 1969, Gomułka unexpectedly moved away from his defensive solidarity with the GDR and offered West Germany an acceptable frontier treaty to recognize the Oder-Neisse border (signed by Chancellor Brandt in early December 1970). Relations with the Church also began to improve. A cautious economic reform was drafted in the course of 1969-70. Far less bold than counterparts in Hungary or the GDR, its first stage proposed to 'increase incentives' by drastic overhaul of certain key industries, often involving a reduction of inflated labour forces. This measure was due to take effect from January 1971, but in the autumn of 1970 popular rumours suggested that the reform would involve cuts in many salaries and possibly unemployment. There was a very bad harvest in 1970, and in the weeks before Christmas, a rush on food shops seemed to threaten the already inadequate stocks. In the second week of December, the central committee repeated the panic measure of 1967 and raised food prices by an average of twenty per cent.

The shock of price rises reacted with the anxiety of industrial workers for their jobs and wages. A protest march by shipyard workers in Gdańsk on 14 December led to furious fighting between workers and armed militia in Gdańsk, Szczecin and other Baltic towns in which scores – at a low estimate – were killed. On 20 December Gomułka and four other Politburo members resigned, and Edward Gierek, party secretary in Upper Silesia, became leader of the Polish United Workers' Party. Three days later a new government was formed and Józef Cyrankiewicz, who had been prime minister for twenty-one years, was replaced by Piotr Jaroszewicz.

The new leadership, composed of younger men with greater economic and practical experience, confronts an intimidating legacy. With the brief exception of 1956, the party has treated popular feeling with misgiving; fear that change would produce unrest reduced most reform projects to faint compromises. The large technical intelligentsia created by the party's own educational reforms became disaffected, while the working class came to consider itself abandoned. The sense of stagnation and the alienation of government from governed became so strong that even 'Moczarist' chauvinism seemed to find temporary popularity. For Poland today, the question is whether the post-Gomułka ruling group can overcome the party's ingrained mistrust of political relaxation, in order to make the economic reforms effective.

Roumania

As the end of the Second World War approached, Roumania found itself in an exceedingly exposed position. The pro-fascist Antonescu government

Selected consumer products in Eastern Europe and West Germany 1955-68

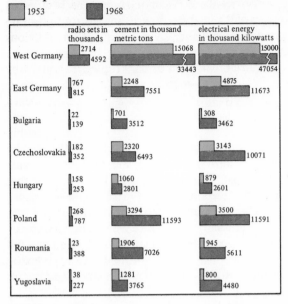

	radio sets in thousands	cement in thousand metric tons	electrical energy in thousand kilowatts
West Germany	2714 / 4592	15068 / 33443	15000 / 47054
East Germany	767 / 815	2248 / 7551	4875 / 11673
Bulgaria	22 / 139	701 / 3512	308 / 3462
Czechoslovakia	182 / 352	2320 / 6493	3143 / 10071
Hungary	158 / 253	1060 / 2801	879 / 2601
Poland	268 / 787	3294 / 11593	3500 / 11591
Roumania	23 / 388	1906 / 7026	945 / 5611
Yugoslavia	38 / 227	1281 / 3765	800 / 4480

(□ 1953 ■ 1968)

Distribution of net material production 1968

■ % from agriculture   ■ % from industry   ■ % from services

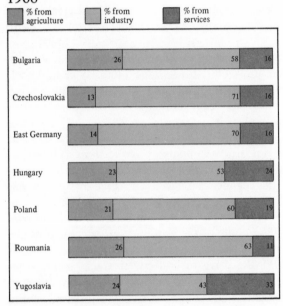

	agriculture	industry	services
Bulgaria	26	58	16
Czechoslovakia	13	71	16
East Germany	14	70	16
Hungary	23	53	24
Poland	21	60	19
Roumania	26	63	11
Yugoslavia	24	43	33

Total net material product (GNP) at constant prices 1950-68

■ 1950   ■ 1960   ■ 1968

1963=100%

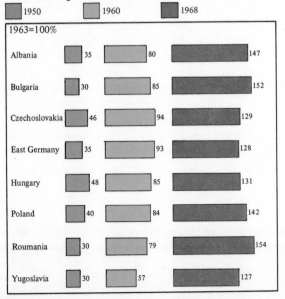

	1950	1960	1968
Albania	35	80	147
Bulgaria	30	85	152
Czechoslovakia	46	94	129
East Germany	35	93	128
Hungary	48	85	131
Poland	40	84	142
Roumania	30	79	154
Yugoslavia	30	57	127

had supported Hitler, and Roumanian troops had taken part in the invasion of the Soviet Union. In an effort to ward off the worst consequences, King Michael arrested Antonescu in August 1944 and declared war on Germany as the Red Army crossed the Roumanian borders. The Communist Party, decimated by persecution, seems to have then numbered scarcely a thousand members. However, Roumania had been assigned to the sphere of overwhelming Soviet influence by the Allied leaders, and in February-March 1945, backed by Soviet military pressure, the Russians obliged the king to dismiss Prime Minister Radescu and accept a new government headed by the left-winger Petru Groza which appointed communists to several key posts.

The Groza government was recognized by Britain and the United States in February 1946. In 1947 the king abdicated and a peoples' republic was proclaimed. At the same time, peace agreements settled the much-disputed frontiers of Roumania by confirming Soviet possession of Bessarabia and the northern Bukovina, to the north-east and north, and Bulgarian possession of the southern Dobrudja region. Roumania was, however, given back the hilly region of Transylvania to the west, unwillingly ceded to Hungary in 1940, and containing what now became a national minority of $1\frac{1}{2}$ million Hungarians. The effective leader of the country, as prime minister after 1952 and secretary-general of the party, was Gheorge Gheorgiu-Dej. He embarked cautiously on what, with great modifications, remains the national strategy today: the attempt to maximize Roumanian independence and reduce Soviet interference, while conciliating Soviet misgivings through stern internal discipline.

Sympathy, at first latent, began to grow between the Roumanian leadership and the equally independent Chinese. By 1960, Roumania was openly playing a mediating role in the incipient Sino-Soviet quarrel; an independent foreign policy was accompanied by the dethronement of Soviet culture as an ideal and, most significantly, by a drive to industrialize the nation and end Roumania's role as a supplier of oil and agricultural products to her neighbours. Efforts by Khrushchev to engineer the dismissal of Gheorgiu-Dej were vain. When he died in 1965, he was succeeded as secretary-general of the party by the young and energetic Nicolai Ceausescu, who also became head of state in 1967.

Under Ceausescu, Roumania became identified with a group of international principles: independence and sovereignty, non-interference in the internal affairs of states, the common interests of small nations of varying ideologies, the eventual dissolution of the two military blocs in Europe and the equality of status of all communist parties. Roumania established diplomatic relations with West Germany in early 1967, bringing about a major crisis within the Warsaw Pact, and in the same year became the only Pact state to maintain relations with Israel after the June War. Ceausescu defiantly preserved links with China, opposed the early versions of the nuclear non-proliferation treaty as the establishment of a nuclear monopoly by the superpowers and continued to oppose further integration of the Warsaw Pact and of COMECON.

The fatal year of 1968 produced something like a confrontation. Roumania outspokenly supported the Dubček regime in Czechoslovakia and refused to take part in the invasion that August. The crisis brought Yugoslavia and Roumania, with Czechoslovakia, into a close relationship which recalled the prewar 'Little Entente'. After August, the nation steeled itself against possible military intervention by the Soviet Union, while at the same time the Ceausescu leadership made some verbal concessions to the Soviet demand for professions of loyalty. For over a year, however, Roumania was successful in resisting Soviet pressure for Warsaw Pact manœuvres on its territory.

By August 1969, Roumania had sufficiently regained its confidence to invite President Nixon for a brief visit. But the extraordinary display of state independence was not a token of internal 'liberalization'. Although changes are being cautiously made, Roumania remains a centralized, autocratic and fairly severely policed society. Ceausescu's popularity rests on his appeal to patriotism, and on the gigantic campaign to transform Roumania into a technically advanced and highly industrialized nation.

A guarded 'cease-fire' in Soviet-Roumanian relations was reached in July 1970, when after two years of Roumanian procrastination a new twenty-year friendship treaty was signed with the Soviet Union. If this relationship can be held stable, and if the hectic pace of economic development does not over-reach itself and produce breakdown or bankruptcy, Roumania is likely to become even more influential as an independent force in European and world affairs.

Yugoslavia

Yugoslavia, like Albania, largely achieved its own liberation in the Second World War through a partisan movement which was at once intensely patriotic and devotedly communist. The resulting confidence and sense of independence led the Yugoslav leadership under Marshal Tito inevitably towards conflict with Stalin. The Yugoslav partisans discovered that it was their very ruthlessness and revolutionary impatience which Stalin resented. Tito overwhelmed remnants of opposition at elections in 1945 and established a communist system without delay. This haste, and Tito's aggressive attitude towards the West, upset the more gradualist tastes of Stalin, as did Tito's plans for a Balkan federation.

In 1947 the Yugoslavs took a leading part in setting up the Cominform, shadowy successor to the Comintern, and its headquarters were located in Belgrade. Tito's impetuousness continued to disquiet Stalin; Yugoslavia was involved in the Greek civil war, and in claims to parts of Carinthia and above all to the city of Trieste which created a minor but enduring East-West crisis with Italy.

The breach with Moscow came in 1948. The occasion was renewed discussion of the Balkan federation. On 1 March, the Yugoslav central committee rejected Soviet federation proposals and in June the Cominform finally condemned the Yugoslav leadership and called upon 'healthy elements' in Yugoslavia to replace it.

For a time, the Yugoslavs hoped for a reconciliation. They maintained rigorous discipline; there was a new campaign to collectivize agriculture. But an economic blockade by the socialist bloc, accompanied by Soviet-engineered plots against the regime, convinced Tito that this policy was vain. Yugoslavia gradually extricated herself from the Greek civil war, and replied to the torrent of Soviet and East European calumny with her own propaganda. In 1950, in the middle of the economic crisis created by the blockade, the system of workers' self-management through elected councils was launched, and in 1951 the drive to collectivize the peasantry was slackened, much of the land returning to private cultivation. Western economic support was sought, while Yugoslavia began to build up for herself a special international role as a leader of the 'uncommitted' nations.

There were two attempts at Soviet-Yugoslav reconciliation. Bulganin and Khrushchev visited Belgrade in 1955 and admitted Yugoslavia's right to seek a 'separate road' to socialism. This improvement in relations lasted only until 1957, undermined by the Soviet intervention in Hungary and by the ideological sparring between Tito and Mao Tse-tung (still then on reasonable terms with the Soviet Union). A second and equally inconclusive improvement took place in 1961-2.

Internally, the experiments in democratic socialism continued, all the more remarkable in that they were conducted in one of the poorest countries in Europe which was divided into autonomous republics. During the fifties, there was an overhaul of the central and republican parliaments, to make local interests more effective, and in 1963 a new constitution set up a five-chamber federal assembly. The principle of regular rotation of party and state posts was established.

Tito and the ex-partisan leadership remained supreme. But the disaffection of Milovan Djilas, one of the toughest of the leading team during and after the war, posed them with an embarrassing problem. Djilas, who eventually moved to a position nearer to social democracy than to Marxist-

Top Yugoslav communist partisans in Belgrade, 1945. Under Tito's leadership the breach with Stalin was not long delayed
Above Khrushchev, Gromyko (speaking), Bulganin and Tito (right) at the reconciliatory Belgrade 1955 conference; Khrushchev admitted Yugoslavia's right to a 'separate road' to socialism

Tito and Kennedy in Washington

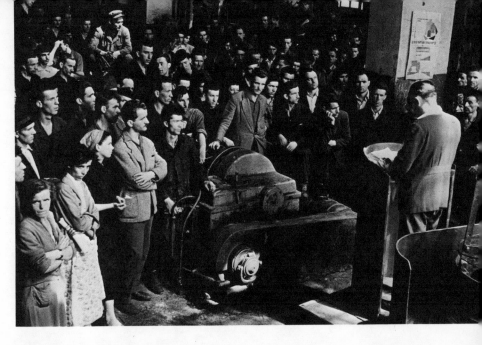

Workers' council at a Sarajevo metal factory; in the sixties successful industrialization widened the gap between the rich and poor republics of the country

Steel works at Zenica; from 1967 Western companies were allowed to invest in some Yugoslav state enterprises

Leninism, condemned Soviet repression in Hungary and scandalized his colleagues with the publication abroad of his book *The New Class*, which attacked the bureaucratization of communist societies. He was imprisoned in 1956 and again in 1962, when he had proposed the legalization of opposition and written his second political book, *Conversations with Stalin*.

In 1965, Yugoslavia embarked on an ambitious economic reform. Greater local democracy and factory independence was accompanied by 'liberalization' and the exposure of the economy to market pressures and competition. The general effect of the reform has been to make Yugoslav industry more competitive and raise consumer living standards in certain groups, but also to widen the difference between rich and poor republics. Unemployment in 1968 reached the figure of nine per cent of the labour force. Hundreds of thousands of Yugoslavs worked abroad, principally in West Germany. From 1967, Western companies were allowed to invest in Yugoslav state enterprises, though not to achieve a dominant holding.

In 1966, Aleksander Ranković, architect of the security police and a centralizing Serb conservative, was accused of conspiracy and removed from the leadership. The security apparatus was largely dismantled and attempts were made to reduce the appearance of 'Serb imperialism'. But tensions between the republics persisted after the Ranković affair. Tito himself, who had degraded Ranković, became concerned about centrifugal tendencies in Yugoslavia.

The events of 1968 deepened his anxiety. Student riots in Belgrade raised the demand for a more radical form of left-wing communism. The Soviet intervention in Czechoslovakia followed, and seemed to threaten Yugoslavia itself with invasion. At the Party Congress in late 1970, Tito attempted to solve both his problems by proposing a large collective presidency to act, hopefully, as a centralizing force and evade a succession struggle between the republics following his own retirement or death.

At the end of the sixties, Yugoslavia's relations with the Soviet Union were again improving. A special relationship with Roumania, the only Warsaw Pact country to condemn the Czechoslovak intervention, was constructed. Yugoslavia maintained its 'non-aligned' attitude by guarded *rapprochements* with Albania and China, Tito having steadily refused to endorse the Soviet Union's campaign – during the height of the Sino-Soviet dispute – for the total excommunication of China.

In twenty-five years, this backward Balkan country has become a force in world politics, through its boldly independent policies, and has achieved a prosperity envied by neighbours like Bulgaria or Greece. The very originality of the regime has created the unruly but positive controversy over its future direction. But too much reliance, perhaps inevitably, has been placed on the personality of Tito as the axis of national unity. Until his succession has been negotiated, the destiny and even the state existence of Yugoslavia remain uncertain.

Richard Harris

China:
the Coming Colossus

Nei-luan, wai-huan (internal disorder, external aggression) was the historical catch-phrase that summed up for the Chinese one stage of dynastic decay in their accepted cyclical view of history. So it was in the nineteenth century except that the aggressors were not seduced by the superiority of Chinese culture, as they had been at all previous turnings of the wheel of time, but brashly brought into action the better guns they had. The Chinese were slow to comprehend what this would mean. The century had almost ended, and China was despoiled, insulted and divided, before a new-born nationalism set about the country's regeneration.

Nationalists agreed that China's territorial integrity must be restored and China's equality with the West put beyond doubt: *fu ch'iang* (wealth and power) was the slogan that summed up this determination to get equal with the invaders and exact a proper acknowledgement from them both of China's virtue and of their misdemeanours. Sun Yat-sen, Yuan Shih-k'ai, Chiang Kai-shek and Mao Tse-tung all shared this view with all Chinese. There was no dispute about the ends, only a long period of confusion about the means. The Kuomintang (Nationalist) Party had included the communists in the early twenties but, after Sun Yat-sen's death in 1925 and the seizure of power by Chiang Kai-shek, a split came in 1927 and with the foundation of guerrilla-liberated areas civil war began. Japanese aggression overlaid this internal conflict and even for a time introduced a truce and the 'nationalizing' of the communist Eighth Route Army, but the war almost completely extinguished the national appeal of the Kuomintang and brought more power to the communists.

Civil war and the communist victory: 1945-9

The Japanese War divided China into three parts. The big cities of the east coast – Peking, Tientsin, Nanking, Shanghai and Canton – were in Japanese-occupied, puppet-governed territory. In the north the communists spread over the countryside as saviours of the peasants from Japanese brutality; in ten years after gaining power in 1935 Mao had remodelled and invigorated the party. From their exile in China's backward west Chiang Kai-shek and the Kuomintang came back east as carpet-baggers, quickly adding to the deep disaffection earned by their wartime performance.

Early in 1945, when he met Chiang in Chungking, Mao was still open to American mediation and a coalition government. This was the first time the two men had met since 1926. But six weeks of negotiation brought no agreement and Mao set aside his hopes: all he now insisted on for his party, ruling 100 million peasants, was a democratic square deal. When the war ended American aid helped Chiang, often against communist competition, in recovering territory vacated by the Japanese. Mao's hopes of the Americans faded, and when General George Marshall arrived in China at the end of 1945 as President Truman's emissary to try and bring the two sides together in a coalition government, the atmosphere was bad. In January 1946 a political consultative conference met but made no progress; early in 1947 Marshall gave up and left, blaming reactionary elements in the Kuomintang almost more than the communists for his failure. Within a few weeks the civil war was going again at full blast.

Thus the high hopes of the Americans, in a sentiment for China built up over more than half a century, were almost insensibly undermined. The pre-war isolationist power was now busy in the peacetime reordering of the Western world. The hopes in China, officially flowering when Pearl

A People's Liberation Army parade in support of the cultural revolution, Mao's massive purge of intellectuals and revisionists (1966-8)

Harbor brought America to China's side as an ally, were shown to be unreal by China's wartime corruption. Only eight years after Pearl Harbor China had a government, strong, dedicated, efficient, owing nothing to the country that had lavished its patronage and its earnest endeavours on China's salvation, and ready to spurn and revile this friend of yesterday. American chagrin at this sudden reversal cast its shadow over the whole quarter of a century following.

Indeed, China's critical years of change found all other great powers heavily engaged by the problems left by the war. The Russians, in their policy towards China, were even more hesitant than the Americans, having exacted at Yalta concessions from the China of Chiang that the China of Mao was forced in its turn to endorse. Stalin had stripped the north-east (Manchuria) of its industrial equipment as reparations from the Japanese, but the action showed a contempt for China that bruised the nationalist aspirations of the communists. Stalin's contact with them had been minimal in the decade after Mao took charge and he had discovered how independent and self-reliant Mao was. To the last he hoped that he would have to deal with a divided China rather than a united and determined country under Mao's rule.

Mao's transformation of the party in the Yenan period enabled him to deploy his highest skills as a strategist against an opponent much more numerous and much better equipped. Yet most Chinese began by being spectators of an ideological struggle between Chiang and Mao that scarcely engaged them. The battle was not, after all, to overthrow an existing, traditional order; that order had collapsed in 1911. But from his well-entrenched, self-supporting peasant bases Mao's tactics could be brilliantly exercised. The north-east was mostly in communist hands by the end of 1947 and in the latter part of 1948 the civil war turned wholly in favour of the communists, with the surrender of the Kuomintang armies in the north-east, the capture of two provincial capitals in north China, and the surrounding of a vast force in the Huai river basin in December which surrendered in January. The fall of Peking and Tientsin by January 1949 left the communists free to push southwards against a demoralized Kuomintang. The Third Field Army under Ch'en Yi went down the east side, the Fourth under Lin Piao down the centre, Liu Po-ch'eng's Second Field Army took on the south-west, while

Above China at war with Japan: infantrymen occupy a trench on the Salween front, 1943; (*below*) civilians turn over rail tracks in an effort to cut Japanese supplies
Bottom Peking falls to Mao's PLA forces on 31 January 1949 in the civil war with the Kuomintang

The Chinese masses acclaim the victory of the PLA forces (poster). During 1949 the communist armies moved south and south-west, taking the principal cities. The Nationalist government fled to Taiwan on 7 December 1949

The Chinese communist revolution 1945-50

- communist base areas July 1945
  areas under communist control
- by April 1947
- by July 1948
- by December 1949
- 1950 and after
- non-communist states
- communist states

P'eng Te-huai's First Field Army went north-west. The communists who in mid-1948 had expected two or more years of war now saw the end in sight.

So did all China. Chiang Kai-shek's military misjudgement had been compounded by economic anarchy. Wartime inflation had been quickly resumed, the more disastrous the situation began to look the more corruption thrived. Supplies brought in by the United Nations Relief and Rehabilitation Association (UNRRA) were siphoned off or rotted because of bureaucratic inertia. An absurd official exchange rate against a vast black market made fortunes for a few. When Chiang Ching-kuo, the president's son, was sent to Shanghai to run a ruthless currency revaluation his methods aroused open anger against a government that had lost all popular support. With the crossing of the Yangtse in April 1949, and the fall of Nanking, the capital, the civil war on the mainland was virtually over. Garrison after garrison surrendered to the communists.

In the last stages of the civil war Chiang had handed over the presidency to Li Tsung-jen, his deputy, while keeping all the strings of power in his own hands and preparing a retreat in Taiwan (Formosa). After moving to Canton, to Chungking and Chengtu, the Kuomintang was driven off the mainland and Chiang resumed the presidency in Taiwan in December 1949. It was not until April that the communists took Hainan island, but the attack planned against Taiwan itself had to be postponed because the soldiers training that spring in lakes near Shanghai for the amphibious landing went down in thousands with the debilitating Asian disease of schistosomiasis. In June, just as Mao was outlining plans for demobilization, the Korean War began and the expected final victory that would have completed China's territorial integrity with the inclusion of Taiwan was deferred for a quarter of a century, with profound effects on China's outlook.

A new regime: 1949-56

'Our nation will never again be an insulted nation. We have stood up,' said Mao Tse-tung at the People's Political Consultative Conference meeting in Peking ten days before the People's Republic was proclaimed on 1 October 1949. He spoke as a nationalist to an audience that fully shared his sentiments, an audience of all classes of Chinese who would accept their new leaders. The reputation that Mao and the communists had won in the wartime days at Yenan had brought the majority to their side; in hope, and not much in fear, since Mao had himself, much earlier in his career, foresworn violence in settling differences within the movement. The young had flocked to Yenan, the intellectuals had inclined to Marxism for decades, most city-dwellers were drawn by curiosity to an army that behaved as no other Chinese army had ever been known to do. Only the landlords, suffering roughly in land reform, were the victims of an inescapable rancour.

Most of all the new regime brought to life a constant Chinese contrast between *luan* (disorder) and *ho-p'ing* (peace). The year 1949 ended a century of *luan* from which all Chinese had suffered: much could be forgiven the men who imposed the peace. The call to salvation was sounded by the eager party cadres and it proved that security could be assured for all but the utterly contaminated. In the countryside landlords were only rarely found to be 'enlightened'; below them were the rich peasants who were 'struggled against' – and could survive; the middle peasants who could be 'united with' and the poor peasants who were the salt of the Chinese earth. In the towns only the 'bureaucratic capitalists' fell into an evil category and most of those with money abroad had already gone. The 'national capitalists' who stayed could respond to a patriotic appeal and mostly did. All things considered, order descended upon China with remarkable speed.

One could go further and say that the doctrine that was insistently, earnestly and encouragingly pumped into this battered society by the newcomers was welcome too. A people accustomed throughout their history to a doctrine of the state had lost their bearings for several decades past: now they were offered certainty and a doctrine to live by. The moral foundations of the new regime passed inspection and if doubts crept in from the beginning they could easily be silenced.

Land reform in 1951: the burning of the deeds (*below*), one of the measures designed to raise the peasants' political consciousness
Bottom Most communes display their achievements on wall posters; this one shows increases in bicycles, watches and sewing-machines on the Shenyang commune between 1957 and 1962

The priority was to win over the people and to teach them the new faith. But equally urgent were the demands of effective government in a country fought over for so long. Floods, drought and pests, aside from civil war itself, had brought famine and disaster to many. The Yellow and Huai and the Yangtse rivers had to be controlled. Transport was rudimentary and railways, unknown in west China, were soon under way. An agrarian reform law, a trade union law and a marriage law (women's liberation had struck the young Mao personally as one of China's needs) were passed.

Government was decentralized in 1954 by dividing the country into regions defined by the areas occupied at the end of the civil war by each of the field armies. There was a brief period of inflation before the new currency settled down. After a grim year in 1949 harvests began to improve, though grain distribution was uneven for many years thereafter. Land reform was carried out after 1951, still very much as a struggle spilling over into violence through which the peasants' political consciousness was supposed to be raised. The rounding up of Kuomintang army stragglers ('bandits') went on for two years before all the country was under control.

Absorbed in restoring the country the new government felt less concern with international relations. Mao's – unhurried – choice of 'leaning to one side' (of the Soviet Union) had been announced in July 1949 and the Soviet Union, Eastern European countries and such Asian neighbours as Burma, India and Pakistan were prompt to recognize the new regime. On his first journey away from China, Mao left Peking on 16 December for Moscow where ten weeks were needed to reach agreement on an alliance in return for which the Russians could stay in their base in Port Arthur and share in the economic exploitation of Sinkiang. $300 million was a very modest loan for China's economic development. Stalin, at least, was showing no generosity to the new China though in public no hints were then given of Chinese resentment. Mao personally was ready to acknowledge Stalin's supremacy since by doing so he earned a legitimate place in the hierarchy descending from Marx through Lenin. Moreover, in those early days the Chinese were glad to enjoy the sense of association with a communist world stretching across the Eurasian heartland in place of the Western world towards which their resentment could be unconcealed.

This was apparent when British recognition in January 1950 was met by a demand for a mission to 'negotiate' diplomatic relations. In the United States, where a White Paper recording the failure of American relations with the defeated Kuomintang government had been published in 1949, no alternative to eventual recognition of the new government was canvassed.

A country so obsessed with its own internal renewal, coupled with the determination to bring back under Chinese authority territories such as Tibet, Sinkiang and Taiwan, was in no mood to pursue foreign relations so long as the government felt secure. But the Korean War changed all that. No evidence suggests that the Chinese were a party to that war; much that they were ignorant of what was intended. They were hesitant in action and only intervened after explicit warnings. Much more damaging than the war itself, however, was President Truman's decision, the day after American troops landed, to interpose American power against an attack on Taiwan. This was the most direct interference in Chinese sovereignty and roused Peking to fury. The Chinese intervention in Korea roused the Americans too; when the armistice eventually came in 1953 Washington stood squarely behind the Chiang government which it had in 1950 virtually rejected, and treated the Peking government as a pariah that might be overthrown.

The repercussions of the Korean War within China were far-reaching. The promising settlement of government and people became punctured by suspicion lest surviving pro-American feeling should surge up. A 'resist America, support Korea' campaign was reinforced by a campaign against counter-revolutionaries – more a settlement of the 'blood debts' of twenty-two years of civil war than a drive against opponents of the regime as such. Executions that were more urban than rural led to about a million death sentences (830,000 was the figure given by Mao in a version of a speech made in Moscow in 1957 that leaked through Warsaw).

A poster covering the wall of a house in Chungking spurs the local population on to reach their allotted target in iron and steel production

In Canton railway workers repair a track near the Hong Kong border, but not before placing the Chairman's picture in a place of honour

Two further campaigns against corruption among government servants and in commercial circles brought heavier burdens, so did the ever more pervasive political indoctrination with meetings for criticism and self-criticism. The potency of shame (rather than guilt) in Chinese culture has been much exploited in techniques of conversion to the cause. Against this one must admit that adherence to the doctrine offered a security that all Chinese sought; even refugees from the mainland later confessed to their interviewers in Hong Kong how helpful they found the intensive therapy of the self-criticism meeting.

Peace instead of disorder was not accompanied by plenty. The men of Yenan were too spartan under Mao's leadership to pursue economic advance except at the price of the consumer's interest. The period of recovery (1949-52) and of the first five-year plan (1953-7) did provide a heavy industrial base and per capita figures of food production may have kept slightly ahead of population increase. By 1958 the calorie intake of 2,200 average was still minimal, though better distributed among the population than it would have been before the war. Taking an estimated per capita figure (in 1952 *yüan*) of prewar domestic product at 119, the figure for 1957 had reached 150 and by 1958 166, but that was to be the last year of steady advance for a decade.

In most spheres the years from 1953, when Stalin died and the Korean armistice was signed, were years of adjustment, self-discovery and progress. Ordinary international relations were scarcely in the minds of the leaders in 1949: the only diplomatic relations the Kuomintang had enjoyed were with Western powers whom China was importuning for return of lost privileges and territorial rights. The new China settled temporarily into the communist bloc and found itself up against American hostility and containment, but otherwise was slow to get outside a Marxist textbook view of other countries. In 1950 the *People's Daily* could still stigmatize the 'puppet Nehru', but by 1952 China was beginning to take note of neutralism among her Asian neighbours. In 1954 China assumed her place at the Geneva Conference and was an active agent in reaching a settlement. At Bandung in 1955 Chou En-lai made a wider reputation as an international statesman and sympathy for China in her exclusion from the United Nations grew.

Yet even in this decade China's approach to the world outside her immediate interest was ambivalent. On the one hand, the Western world could be ignored, even spurned by a China busy becoming its equal: on the other hand, acknowledgement of China's position was duly recorded: where else would a country's participation in an international congress in Holland of experts on coastal lighting have earned a headline in the country's leading newspaper?

But in vain pursuit of China's national interest the mixture of violent abuse and hopeful negotiation with the United States that began after Bandung (first at Geneva, later in Warsaw) got nowhere. Taiwan could not be recovered, and worse, it remained the seat of a government of China still occupying the United Nations Security Council seat. By comparison the continued British occupation of Hong Kong seemed scarcely a disadvantage; in many ways it acted as a tranquil political centre in the Dulles-inspired cold war front that China faced.

In September 1956 Peking welcomed delegates from all communist countries and parties to its Eighth Party Congress, the first to be held since 1945 in Yenan. A new party constitution was adopted with the 'thoughts of Mao Tse-tung' no longer included as a creed – perhaps in recognition of the dangers of a personality cult. Reporting to the Congress Liu Shao-ch'i said that 'the question of who will win in the struggle between socialism and capitalism in our country has now been decided.' Class struggle was receding as the country became more and more united.

A new party and governmental hierarchy could be seen to exist in China. In 1956 an able young man in China might, for the first time for as long as eighty years, have considered the ladder of the public service to be the natural one for him to climb; once again after long years of *luan* the old career was open to talent, given, as ever, the proper acceptance of the state doctrine.

China's foreign trade 1955-65

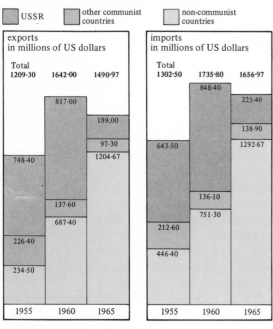

USSR | other communist countries | non-communist countries

exports in millions of US dollars

Total
1209·30   1642·00   1490·97

817·00
189.00
97·30
1204·67
748·40

137·60
687·40
226·40
234·50

imports in millions of US dollars

Total
1302·50   1735·80   1656·97

848·40
225·40
138·90
643·50   1292·67

136·10
751·30
212·60
446·40

1955   1960   1965   1955   1960   1965

Estimates of national income 1952-9

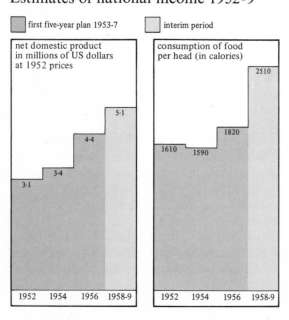

first five-year plan 1953-7 | interim period

net domestic product in millions of US dollars at 1952 prices

5·1
4·4
3·4
3·1

consumption of food per head (in calories)

2510
1820
1610   1590

1952 1954 1956 1958-9   1952 1954 1956 1958-9

Mao returns to the helm: 1955-9

Mao was a man who had always stood above and apart from his colleagues. 'Chu Teh was loved,' Agnes Smedley had noted in Yenan, but 'Mao Tse-tung was respected . . . his spirit dwelt within himself, isolating him.' He had imposed his ways on the party not simply as a leader but from above as a judge; he could not have succeeded in this if he had not also been an able manipulator of political power. He had based his revolutionary career on struggle – which was endless and enriching; but the motive force for the activist he wanted to call forth in his own image was rage, a well-stoked fire of hatred against exploiting landlords or intrusive imperialists: for Mao, resentment has always been the starting-point of action, as in the land reform campaigns when peasants were stimulated to 'speak bitterness'.

Conflict was necessary. The contrast of *luan* and *ho-p'ing* was not one that Mao could accept: his own political slogan of unity-criticism-unity meant a constant swaying movement from an apparent disorder to a new order and back again. Thus the holding of the Eighth Party Congress found Mao more of a spectator than a leader of the party in this moment of consolidation. He introduced the Congress only with a short speech. For most of the time since 1949 he had, as he put it later, been content to remain in the 'second line' while Liu Shao-ch'i and Teng Hsiao-p'ing in the party, and Chou En-lai in the government, had taken the lead. Perhaps he had felt that either the grasp of the administrator or the knowledge of the economic planner was beyond him. He had remade the party and in its first spell of ruling China it could be trusted to act in the Yenan spirit.

Nevertheless, Mao's hand had always been ready to touch the ideological tiller. Through all the years since 1949 there had been a 'red thread' provided by Mao. In 1951 an apparently innocuous film was attacked for a month in the press; in 1954 an elderly professor of literature was vilified for an academic study of the novel *Dream of the Red Chamber*. Hu Shih, the dominant literary figure in China between the wars, was the victim of another campaign in 1955, and Hu Feng, a Marxist writer and party member who demanded liberal freedoms for the creative, was pilloried and disgraced. The Mao who laid down his own line on literature and art at Yenan in 1942 was still convinced that cultural weakness let in the devil of revisionism.

By 1955 Mao was no longer satisfied with ideological intervention. He was deeply dissatisfied with progress in revolution on the land. Mutual aid teams and lower-stage agricultural cooperatives were not enough. In July he called an *ad hoc* gathering of senior party members (Mao has always shown a reluctance to work through institutional channels) and accused his colleagues of 'tottering along like a woman on bound feet'. That autumn and all through 1956 China was flung into a spasm of change in the countryside under the slogan of 'More, faster, better, cheaper.' Mao might have followed this initiative with others but for the dramatic change in 1956 of the Soviet Twentieth Party Congress and Khrushchev's assault on Stalin and the personality cult. For Mao this was damaging since it was only too easy for his colleagues to bring the same accusation against him, though they in turn had used Mao's charismatic appeal to the peasants to ensure their own success. So when the Eighth Party Congress met Mao's part was still muted and his backing in the party was less firm than it had been in the grand success of 1949.

But this scarcely deflected him from his task of bringing China back to an ideological path from which it might stray. The 'hundred flowers' policy had been launched in May 1956, before the Congress, with the aim of starting a struggle with China's sceptical – and usually foreign-trained – intellectuals to whom Chou En-lai had made an appeal in January 1956. Both the stimulation of the intellectuals and the guidance to the party were set forth in two important speeches by Mao on contradictions among the people in February and March 1957 which were followed by a deliberate stirring of criticism among the reluctant intellectuals. In the West Mao's opinions and the criticism made seemed a sudden and surprising injection of liberalism in the rigidity of communist practice. The criticisms freely published in the news-

Above 'We the Chinese workers are riding a fast horse to overtake John Bull in industrial production', says the poster outside Peking railway station
Below Sculpture as indoctrination; man bends under the exploiting feudal system. The cultural revolution finally disposed of the idea of culture for its own sake

papers seemed to confirm this until suddenly the line changed and the official press early in June turned on the critics. It may well have been the party bureaucracy that changed the tune while Mao himself would have been willing to allow more 'disorder' than the party bureaucrats relished, but Mao's aims were not those of a liberal; there was only one end prescribed to the free discussion: a voluntary and enthusiastic acknowledgement of the truth of the thoughts of the chairman.

The anti-rightist campaigns that followed – at first against the intellectual critics and in 1959 within the party itself – were the outcome of ideological stirrings by a man who was not content to see China congeal politically. His fear that the revolutionary impulse would be lost had, however, been first aroused in 1956 by Khrushchev's attack on Stalin. The momentary jolt to Mao's personality cult was only a minor aspect of that detonation. That China was not consulted was also regarded as an insult from an upstart in Moscow. The Chinese retort to the Russians on 5 April 1956 allowed some criticism of Stalin but rejected the manner of it. Mao had not only stepped forward to correct the path followed by his own party; he was now to do the same for the communist world cracking under uncertain Russian leadership. The troubles of Poland that autumn were blamed on Russian great-nation chauvinism; at first this was the charge against Russian activities in Hungary too, until China suddenly turned and urged Russian action against counter-revolution. In October and again in December two further blasts from China saying how the communists should run their affairs were not yet unfriendly in tone but unabashed in their criticism, and they foreshadowed the crack opening up in Sino-Soviet relations. When the fortieth anniversary of the Soviet Communist Party was celebrated in November 1957 Mao felt it his duty to journey to Moscow for the second time to 'wage necessary appropriate struggle' against the failings of the Khrushchev leadership.

Mao's suspicions of Russian tendencies under Khrushchev's leadership were matched by a distaste for China's first five-year plan (1953-7) that had been modelled on Russian methods and relied on Soviet technicians and industrial planners. The rush into agricultural cooperatives from 1955 to 1956 led by Mao was followed in 1958 by Mao's own recipe for speedy economic advance by an independent and self-reliant China – the great leap forward. The great leap marked Mao's hankering for a return to the spirit and the style of Yenan days coupled with a rejection of Soviet-style economic planning which could not enthuse the masses. Where did China's strength lie? In manpower. It should be mobilized and at the same time, instead of the countryside being drawn to the towns, rural organization should be one of self-help and small-scale industry. The answer was the commune, in effect replacing the *hsiang* (the lowest unit of local government in China) but making the commune not merely an administrative organ but the controller of economic life and welfare for the peasant. Thereby all trace of peasant proprietorship would soon be abolished and full-scale collectivization would organize manpower on a paramilitary basis. All communes would organize their own education, their own small-scale industry and provide their own medical needs. In moments of euphoria collective eating and even collective living were planned.

First tried out in north China in the spring of 1958, the communes were pushed through by an enlarged meeting of the party's political bureau in August. But almost immediately opposition was apparent and the scheme ran into difficulties. Enthusiasm for 'backyard steel' sometimes left harvests ungathered.

Mao's intervention had not been confined to the great leap and the communes. His moment of euphoria had been promoted first by the Russian sputnik in 1957 – at last it gave an assurance that Russian technology had passed the American – and by the recession in America that winter which was seen as an intimation of the certain collapse of capitalism. In August 1958 the induced crisis in the Taiwan Straits may have been intended to test Russian staunchness as an ally and American weakness as an enemy: however, the probing stopped when it was the Russians who proved to be weak and the Americans who were unyielding. When the central committee met in

American military aid to the Nationalist government produced this cartoon (1951): 'Mr Austin, standing in front of the US 7th Fleet, is impudent enough to say that the American imperialists are not invading the Chinese territory of Taiwan'

Chiang Kai-shek and his wife on Sun Moon Lake, central Taiwan, in 1966, the year of reelection to his fourth six-year term as Nationalist president

December plans for the great leap were discreetly cut back and Mao himself, aware of a failure he later confessed to, was shifted out of his chairmanship of the Republic and replaced in the following spring by Liu Shao-ch'i.

This was done delicately, with careful explanations lest there should be misunderstanding. Was it Mao's own wish, to give himself more time to deal with the 'policy and line of the party' and 'Marxist-Leninist theoretical work'? Six months later, when China was facing the first of three bad harvests, he told his colleagues that he:

knew nothing about industrial planning . . . however, comrades, in 1958 and 1959 the main responsibility has fallen on me and you should take me to task. I invented the smelting of steel. This created a great disaster. We have paid a price; blown some communist wind – comrades your stomachs will feel much more comfortable if you move your bowels and break wind.

Differences internal and external: 1959-65

Optimism over their national regeneration and their prospect of regaining control over lost territories had fortified the Chinese leaders all through the fifties. By 1959 most of their hopes had been disappointed to some degree. The country's economy had been set in confusion by the great leap. No kind of settlement with the United States seemed possible and the Kuomintang government in Taiwan seemed impregnable. China's relations with Russia were going downhill and the future of the communist world itself was beginning to look shaky. This was not a time when doubts about policy could be buried or Chairman Mao's leadership could any longer be accepted without question.

The growth of China

- ⬛ China before 1950
- ⬛ territory gained in 1950
- ⬛ disputed border territories
- ⬛ non-communist states
- ⬛ communist states

Rebellion in Tibet 1959: the silent siege of women. In the last hours before fighting broke out in Lhasa thousands of women virtually surrounded the Dalai Lama's Potala Palace as a protest against the Chinese presence in the country. Tibet had been 'liberated' in April 1951 when the Dalai Lama's representatives signed an agreement in Peking after the Chinese occupation.

When the central committee met at the mountain resort of Lushan in August 1959 there was a spokesman for the opposition – the minister of defence, P'eng Te-huai, who not only attacked the 'guerrilla style' of the great leap but was said to have passed on his comments to the Russians. The gulf between Mao and his colleagues now began to open and, having dismissed P'eng as defence minister, Mao chose Chou En-lai to inaugurate a new campaign against 'rightism' in the party. For the first time since 1949 real inroads were made in the upper ranks and many senior provincial figures lost their position. Ch'en Po-ta, Mao's secretary and intimate, said that the fate of socialism in China was in the balance. Lu Ting-yi, later to fall in the cultural revolution, admitted that the line of demarcation was 'to obey Chairman Mao or not'.

Despite this campaign against revisionism Mao had to retreat still further in face of difficulty. The bad harvest of 1959 was followed by a worse one in 1960, and in 1961 weather conditions were worse still, bringing real famine conditions in some parts of the country. The importation of grain from Australia, Canada and other countries solved the problem of feeding the coastal cities but for a time China's supply crisis was acute. The result was to entrench those in command in party and administration and confirm the policies that had been tacitly sanctioned after the failure of the great leap. The commune system had been remodelled back to what were almost the original cooperatives; free marketing of sideline produce was permitted; private plots were fully restored. While they tacked over ideological rectitude in the face of their leader the party leaders were not impeded in the practical policies they followed to rescue China from its difficulties.

Forced back into the 'second line', so that his colleagues could manage China's internal problems, Mao's conviction of his revolutionary vision found expression elsewhere – he could set himself to rescue the failing Russians from revisionism. The year 1956 had shown Khrushchev lurching unsteadily between the faults of 'great-power chauvinism' and dangerous concessions to counter-revolution. In November 1957, when the Soviet Communist Party's fortieth anniversary was celebrated, Mao had paid his second visit to Moscow. He was still ready publicly to admit that the communist fraternity needed a leader and that China, lacking 'even a quarter of a sputnik' was not fitted for the role. Obviously the sputnik had stirred Mao's hopes in many directions. America as *the* advanced country was an image deeply embedded in the Chinese mind, even in remote Yenan; so this dramatic intervention allowed Mao to believe that the tide was flowing strongly in favour of the communist camp. The East wind would prevail against the West wind, he said in his black-and-white, sloganizing way. Not only was this technological leap an advantage in the direct struggle of communists against capitalists, it became apparent to Mao that communist leadership of the emerging Third World was better placed to resist the nuclear threats of a counter-revolutionary America. The strategy he had employed in China came to life in the world at large: Latin America, Africa and Asia had a revolutionary countryside which could surround and finally conquer the capitalist cities. Already some of the pro-Western nationalist governments had been replaced by governments of the left either by election (Ceylon, 1956) or by a coup (Iraq, 1958). When similar displacements in Lebanon and Jordan were foiled by American and British intervention Mao saw the danger and the opportunity. American power must not be allowed to snuff out any of the revolutionary processes since the more countries in which anti-imperialist governments might come to power (as Castro in Cuba) the more would American power be weakened and China's prospects, nationally and internationally, be improved.

The Russians, with no outstanding territorial claims nor quite so tightly contained by American power as was China, could not share Mao's new belligerence, as they made plain in the Taiwan Straits crisis in the summer of 1958. China then realized that all hope of bringing Taiwan back into the fold must be deferred: the talks with the Americans had got nowhere and only the broadening front of the world's anti-imperialist masses would bring down American power. Yet in 1959 Khrushchev went to Camp David

The Sino-Soviet honeymoon (1949-56): a poster shows workers bringing gifts to their Russian advisers. Stalin's aid was in fact far from generous

Stalin and Mao form a common front against Western imperialism; Stalin, however, would have preferred a divided China. The association with Russia gave Mao legitimate descent from Marx and Lenin

and talked with Eisenhower – and then infuriated Mao by coming to tell him in Peking that peaceful competition with the capitalist world was the only answer. That was on 30 September, though earlier in that month the first border clash between China and India had drawn a neutral and reproving comment from the Soviet news agency Tass. The personal resentment between Mao and Khrushchev was now beyond repair. In April 1960 the Chinese took the occasion of the Lenin anniversary to launch a full-scale attack on Russian revisionism. Thereafter the assault was carried on at all communist meetings until a world gathering of eighty-one parties in Moscow in November could only patch up a communiqué that was plainly a collation of opposed views. To Mao this was all 'principled' inter-party struggle; if state relations were harmed it was the Russians' doing in breaking their agreement on nuclear aid to China in 1959 – to please the Americans – and in 1960 by summarily withdrawing 1,400 technicians and all their plans from China's industry. Trouble on the Sinkiang border in 1962, the Cuba crisis and the Chinese rejection of the test-ban treaty in 1963 all widened the gulf.

Rival public statements had brought a firm but conciliatory letter from the Russians in July 1963, which found Mao in no such mood. With immense zest he personally answered this letter in eight devastating attacks. In August 1964 he told a party of Japanese socialists that his war with the Russians was a 'paper war' and could go on for twenty-five years, but, more ominously in Russian eyes, he also recalled that he had taken up the question of Mongolia in 1954 with Khrushchev and Bulganin who refused to consider Mongolian independence as negotiable. In conversation with the Japanese (later reported) Mao expressed his resentment over the territories ceded to Russia in the nineteenth century. The Russians, Mao added to the Japanese, were already then concentrating troops along the border; rightly so, they must have thought in October, when China joined the ranks of nuclear powers with her first test.

Exultant in this ideological battle with the Russians Mao nevertheless had reason for alarm at the growth of revisionism in China itself. The party leaders had found as far back as 1956 at the Eighth Party Congress that the contradiction between the people and the bourgeoisie had been resolved. In 1957 the *People's Daily* claimed that the urgent task was 'uniting the whole body of the people for the development of production'. As 1962 found the country recovering from the post-leap disastrous years the impulse to put ideological struggle behind them and get on with the job grew stronger in the minds of the established leaders. At the central committee plenum in September 1962, however, Mao insisted on a new socialist education campaign in the country, but his attempt to regain full ideological command met resistance that he was too wily to try and overcome forthwith without careful preparation. Up to this point it is probable that differences in the Chinese party leadership had been settled by mutual concessions; after 1962 – when no further plenums of the central committee were called – disagreement may have been unconcealed.

The cultural revolution and its background: 1962-9

In the great leap and the commune system Mao had made his first attempt to remake Chinese society in accordance with his vision; decentralized, self-reliant, simple-living communities, combining agriculture and industry, running their own schools and medical services, egalitarian in all things, dedicated to class struggle lest the poison of the bourgeoisie were to arise. It was a society in which generals took their turn as privates, soldiers worked in factories, teachers hoed the fields, intellectuals were sent to immerse themselves in the rough life of the village. Thus might the divide between town and country, between intellectual and manual labour – so long-standing a social distinction in China – be abolished.

The disasters of the leap had not diverted him from his mission. And that mission was now more urgent if China was to be saved from revisionism. China was lapsing into its old habits before his eyes. A party hierarchy was asserting its differences from the masses it ruled; special schools for the

At the height of the cultural revolution in 1967, Khrushchev and Liu Shao-ch'i appear on this poster caricaturing the 'supreme twosome of revisionism' (Liu has to some extent been reinstated). When Mao's Great Leap Forward in 1959 turned into a considerable economic step backwards, Liu had for a short time looked like a possible rival and successor. Khrushchev's policy of peaceful competition with the West provoked bitter hostility

Major border incidents in 1969 brought battles between Russian and Chinese: Chinese border guards on the disputed Damansky Island

children of higher party cadres were even being set up. The material incentives that had helped to pull China out of the bad years from 1959 to 1961 were filtering through society; in parts of the country peasants were even withdrawing from cooperatives and going back to private agriculture. Not least, Mao was able to note how in Peking itself, and in all of the regions into which China was divided – six administrative and thirteen military – as well as in the loyalties that survived in the old provinces, centres of regional power were solidifying. In getting going the cultural revolution Mao proclaimed the need to educate a new younger generation whose loyalty to Maoism would guarantee that China would not be diverted from its true revolutionary path when he was dead. But he saw plainly that he could not do this without facing direct conflict in the party and for this he would need the assurance of power.

He had prepared his ground ever since Lin Piao, his close disciple and faithful follower, had been appointed to the defence ministry. For Mao the army had always been the true source of revolutionary ardour; in Mao the romantic militarism of Yenan days lived on. So it had been Lin's task to combat revisionist tendencies within the army and to give it back its simple Maoist faith – in gestures such as abolishing ranks.

In September 1965 Mao began his challenge to the party establishment, using a technique of appointing to the task of new indoctrination in Maoism those he suspected of being half-hearted in the task, expecting that they might thus expose themselves. Hence the cultural revolution was at first put in the hands of P'eng Chen, the powerful party boss of Peking; later Liu Shao-ch'i and Teng Hsiao-p'ing were ordered to send out work teams to further the cause of socialist education.

So it went on through 1966, first with P'eng Chen's empire undermined, then with Liu Shao-ch'i, Teng Hsiao-p'ing and the party secretariat manœuvred into a corner. Military moves coupled with the rivalry of coup and counter-coup were rumoured in July, by which time Mao's determination was fully apparent to all his senior colleagues. His next challenge had been prepared some time before with the formation of a party group to guide the cultural revolution. Soon the Red Guard cadres were ready behind the scenes; a ferment in universities and schools was prepared by Maoist activists; and in August 1966 Mao was able to call the first plenum of the central committee since 1962 and drive through a packed meeting changes in the political bureau which gave him command of the standing committee,

the elevation as his undisputed second in command of Lin Piao, and the adoption of a sixteen-point decision on the cultural revolution which set forth the need, prescribed the criticism, told the party to learn from the masses and promised to train successors in the thoughts of Mao Tse-tung so that China would be saved from future corruption after the leader's death.

An intensive inflation of Mao's personality cult – his thoughts 'may be likened to the ceaseless movement in the skies of the sun and moon and the endless flow of the rivers and streams on earth' – showed what a small minority stood beside him. Aside from Lin, raised to a special position above all others, and Chou En-lai, whose readiness to side with Mao at all points of crisis dated back to the Yenan period, those who emerged as the core group of the cultural revolution leadership were Ch'en Po-ta, Mao's personal assistant, K'ang Sheng, the elderly, ex-Comintern security chief and not least Chiang Ch'ing, Mao's wife, soon to prove herself the most vindictive persecutor of her husband's old colleagues. In rally after rally all through the autumn 11 million Red Guards came to Peking, were reviewed by Mao and Lin and were launched into mass campaigns of criticism, vilifying traditional China and using 'big character' wall posters to denigrate revisionist party leaders. The high ideals of the Maoist vision were soon belied by the manner of the assault. Fighting between factory workers and Red Guards was reported; the puzzled masses were loath to march against local leaders; from all parts of China a period of confusion and violence was reported. This was the period when destruction preceded construction.

Soon the mass criticism campaign of the Red Guards was followed by the encouragement of rebellion at every focal point in society – in schools and universities, which had been closed down in 1966 to free students for their Maoist tasks, in factories, in hospitals – in every conceivable institution where activists could point the finger of criticism against a 'revisionist' leadership. In some cases Mao's oldest colleagues were submitted to the ordeal of brutally humiliating mass meetings.

The new regime that began to emerge substituted revolutionary committees for the discarded party committees at every level from the province downwards; three-way alliances, these were called, in which the army stepped in as the strongest and usually controlling element, with such old party cadres as passed the Maoist tests forming the second element. The third element was the new young rebels, almost always in a small minority. All through

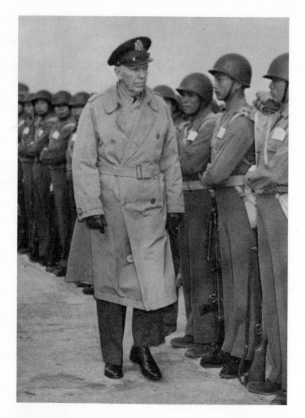

General Marshall, sent by Truman to China in 1945 to reconcile the communists and the Kuomintang, found the Nationalist reactionaries as intractable as the People's Liberators

Below The paper tiger of American imperialism; US policies, which consistently backed a government that existed only in name, must take some of the blame
Below right Between battles in Laos, the Pathet Lao relax with the *Thoughts of Mao*

美帝国主义从刚果滚出去

Anti-American rally in Peking staged to support the 1964
Congo rebellions

1967 and early 1968 the revolution went on, swinging backwards and forwards, evicting first those exposed as revisionists or opponents of Mao, then
left-wing extremists who had been leaders of the revolution. At times an
intense hysteria gripped cities such as Peking and Shanghai and this brought
out a xenophobia which exposed the diplomatic corps to frequent humiliation and violence. There were Russian and Chinese clashes in Peking and
Moscow. In Hong Kong rioting promoted by cultural revolutionaries led to
anti-British actions in Peking such as the burning of the British mission and
the detention of Anthony Grey, Reuters' correspondent, as a hostage.
China's ambassadors were recalled for 'teaching'; China's coexistence with
countries such as Burma broke up and incidents caused trouble with
Cambodia, Nepal and some African countries.

It was not until the summer of 1968 that a turning-point at long last came.
Provincial revolutionary committees had been slowly formed – against
evident regional resistance – but in September 1968 the process was speeded
up and the much-promised Ninth Party Congress was mooted. The Red
Guards had turned out to be a disappointment, proving as subject as their
elders to the 'lure of power and prestige'. The movement of intellectuals to
the countryside not only sent doctors and nurses by the thousand but an
often discontented and ill-disciplined youth by the million.

All this necessarily frightened the Russians. The Sino-Soviet dispute
developed into a great-power confrontation on the frontier with both sides
massing troops. A point of acute crisis followed the Soviet invasion of
Czechoslovakia when the full implications of the confrontation were

apparent to both. Early in 1969 major incidents on the border at Chen Pao Island on the Ussuri and, later that year, on the politically more brittle and strategically more vulnerable Sinkiang border, brought the crisis to such points of mutual allegation and threats of action from the Russian side that, after talks in Peking between Chou En-lai and Kosygin, Chinese and Russian delegations met in October 1969 for talks which were still in progress at the end of 1970 and which seemed by then to have averted the worst danger of 1969.

Conclusion: 1969-70

The long-promised Ninth Party Congress was not held until April 1969, a sign of the difficulties that the cultural revolution leadership had had with recalcitrant provincial leaders – no doubt military as well as civil. And afterwards the communiqué and the published speech by Lin Piao said nothing about the future but only went over the past as if to justify all that had happened in Mao's struggle against his old colleagues. It was assumed, however, that the party would now be restored, a purged party but still a recognition of the proper authority of the party.

However, it was not until December 1970 that the first province held its party congress and elected a new party committee. Seven more provinces and Shanghai (one of the three independent municipalities) followed in the next three months. These all showed that the new party committees were no more than replicas of the regional balance of power that had emerged in the cultural revolution. Without exception the military dominance exhibited in the revolutionary committees was reproduced in the new party committees. Shanghai, the one centre where radical revolutionaries had won power in the cultural revolution proved this by also being the one place with radical dominance of the new party committee.

So a new model communist party reshaped by Mao is not in sight. The army's temporary control continues behind the screen of a supposedly rehabilitated party.

The temper of the country seemed to be mixed during these first two years after the cultural revolution. As a result of the confusion the Chinese were in the early stages much less disciplined, much more apathetic, often slipshod in their work, much more given to petty crime. Executions of criminals reported from all parts of the country seemed a sign that the remarkable public discipline under communist rule in China had been seriously weakened. But by the end of 1970 the appearance of a new unity in the country struck foreign visitors.

It seemed that most people in the country, as if glad to have thrown off the years of confusion, violence and embittered struggle in the cultural revolution, were only too ready to turn to less ideological tasks. Under the still firm leadership of Chou En-lai economic development again became a priority, trade fairs regained their old briskness and Chinese missions abroad, commercial and political, took on a new colouring. As if aware how much the image of China had suffered from the cultural revolution, Chinese representatives behaved with uncommon politeness and showed a marked willingness to make contacts.

But not all the damage caused by the cultural revolution had yet been repaired. China's intellectual and artistic life had not recovered even the limited freedom it had enjoyed in the fifties or early sixties. The 'cultural revolution' was not a misnomer. Ever since 1949 Mao's concern with literature, films, plays and art as propaganda media serving the masses had been consistent, and in the end disastrously repressive. Backed, if not prodded, by his wife, Chiang Ch'ing, the reformer of the classical Peking opera, Mao left China at the end of the cultural revolution with virtually no new culture at all. A handful of the plays based on revolutionary themes that Chiang Ch'ing had revised was all that was in the repertory. So far as is known no new films, plays, novels or other literary work had seen the light of day in China since 1966. The cultural revolution sneered at most aspects of the art of the past; and drove into silence the poets, novelists and artists.

One of Mao's oldest supporters, Prime Minister Chou En-lai (right) on a visit to Hanoi and President Ho Chi Minh in 1960

Mao with defence minister Lin Piao, who is expected to succeed Mao on his death

If one compares the cultural revolution with the great leap there is one vital difference that may have saved Mao from defeat in his second great attempt to transform China as it had brought him near to defeat in the first: the fortune of good harvests. Against the three bad harvests in a row following the great leap there were five good harvests in a row during and after the cultural revolution.

A China ruled by regional power, predominantly military; loyal to the national leader, subscribing to the current orthodoxy, and responding as it feels best to the exhortation of the centre – that is as much as one can say about China's political structure in 1970 and it is remarkably similar *pari passu* to what one might have said about China at any time in the last thousand years. Certainly the political hiatus induced by the cultural revolution continues.

If, however, one recalls the nationalist objectives from which the Chinese revolution sprang, and were to ask how far China had gone in her regeneration, the answers would have to be rough and ready: a considerable way in economic development but far less than might have been achieved if Mao's obsession with getting his political style adopted had not so often obtruded. The result was a rise and fall in the graph of production: up until 1958, down after the great leap and the bad harvest years, up again after 1962, down again after 1966, up again after 1969. But overall China's economic growth in the sixties must have been small. Agricultural production in the face of population increase gave the Chinese the security of an adequate food ration more justly and efficiently distributed than they had known in Kuomintang days but not noticeably more plentiful. Aside from the slender material gains, even that greatest blessing of the new regime, the peace in place of disorder that descended on China in 1949, was sadly disrupted by the cultural revolution. Basically the peace remained a gain but public opinion may have lost some of its confidence.

Questions about China and the world are more easily answered. The China that offered the world – and above all the Third World – its revolutionary leadership was a world of Mao's imagining. He gave a revolutionary ideal to many of the young everywhere but his hopes of revolution in the Third World under China's example were disappointed and for a very good reason: just as Mao had to adapt Marxism to China's national needs so revolution of the Maoist type has to be adapted to the needs of other countries in Asia or Africa or Latin America. People's wars did not flourish; China's example was not followed – except in an area of complete cultural kinship like Vietnam. What did remain an unsolved problem, sticking out in a vain appeal in every document from Peking, was the demand for Taiwan. For this major stumbling-block to China's equanimity American policy towards China must take much of the blame, though not quite all. In the context of a quarter of a century many of China's difficulties must be attributed to an unwillingness to understand and to work with an international system. The shift towards recognition of the Peking government by Canada and Italy at the end of 1970 might have begun a move that would end by this government taking the permanent Chinese seat in the Security Council. Only then would China's view of the world become clear.

As for the Soviet Union, one may recall the atmosphere of 1949 and suggest that a China then newly but confidently communist thought it could establish relations with an existing communist world without having given much thought to the complications that might arise in having a Russian neighbour. In 1970 the serious problems that remained were those of two great powers abutting on each other, while the communist partnership survived as the context for an insoluble and by now meaningless quarrel.

Such problems made little dent in a China as self-reliant in 1970 as it was in 1949. It had briskly returned to its objectives of economic and military equality with any other great power and had shown with the formidable progress of its nuclear programme what the country was capable of when impediments were removed. The impediments may be less in the next quarter of a century than they have been in the last, but China's era of change internally, and of adjustment externally, will certainly take that.

Red Guards, fanatically Maoist teenagers, study a *People's Daily* editorial: At the height of the cultural revolution they were incited to 'anti-bourgeois' violence

A Shanghai detachment of the PLA gives a dramatic performance eulogizing the Army's part in the cultural revolution

Tulio Halperin Donghi

Latin America:
the Struggle for Progress

In 1945 few of the problems now demanding urgent solution were yet conspicuous in Latin America. True, in Mexico, Central America and the Andean countries, from Ecuador to Bolivia, a dual society existed, not only in socio-economic but in more immediately visible cultural terms; and only in Mexico was a serious attempt being made to unify Indian, European and mestizo in a new cultural synthesis seeking to balance the non-European elements with the preponderant European ones. Even where the 'two nations' could not be identified with different ethnic groups, the economic and social gap between them was staggering; only in some areas of Argentina, Brazil and Uruguay, and in enclaves like the Costa Rica highlands, had something emerged that was comparable to the 'balanced' societies of the world where a large middle class acts as a buffer in social conflicts, and some of the worrying aspects in this process, so frequently discussed in later years, were already apparent. In later years Latin America was to become obsessed by the feeling that even rapid and widespread economic and social changes served merely to maintain the modest improvements already established, and that they might, because of basic instabilities, actually worsen the situation. In the 1940s, however, such fears were absent. Serious ills were acknowledged to exist. But it was believed that they could be cured, given the will to do so, without imposing any intolerable strain upon the social structure.

Not surprisingly, therefore, observers of Latin America assumed that conflicts in the immediate future would centre round the issue of constitutional democracy versus military dictatorship; and that all the progressive forces would identify themselves with democracy, encouraged by the defeat of European fascism after twenty years of apparent triumph – a triumph that had provided a ready answer for those Latin Americans inclined to believe that only under constitutional regimes could their countries achieve international respectability. Nor was it surprising that more cynical observers should feel that the real problems would stem from the changed position of Latin America in a world dominated by the United States. The Second World War had apparently put an end to European influence in Latin America: American hegemony was taken for granted.

These forecasts were not altogether incorrect. For some years after 1945 the critical moment when the political order would begin to suffer from the frailty of its economic foundations was not reached. Until then the most prominent political task of the postwar era was still that of completing the political changes launched in some Latin American countries – such as Argentina, Uruguay, Chile and Mexico – before the 1929 world crisis, and expanded in the wake of the slump and the economic and social adjustments it forced on the sub-continent, namely, the incorporation of always larger social groups to active political life. The first ten postwar years were then absorbed by the completion of a phase already initiated.

The postwar decade

The postwar years were dominated by the problems linked with the enlargement of the politically active sections of the population. In Mexico that enlargement was effected through revolution (after 1910); in Uruguay through a reorientation in the policies of the dominant Colorado Party, linked with the powerful personality of Batlle (president in 1903-7 and again in 1911-15); in Argentina through an electoral reform (1912) which offered a real freedom of vote to citizenry and allowed the opposition

The Indian poor, unaffected by industrialization and changing governments: illiteracy rates may be as high as ninety per cent

Russian cartoon on American activity in Latin America

Crowds in Guatemala celebrate the overthrow of communist-influenced President Jacobo Arbenz in 1954; among other reforms he struck at the canned fruit interests of the US, who helped arm the 'liberation forces'

Radical Party to reach national power in 1916; in Chile by gradual enlargement of the number of voters, preceded by popular reorientation of the hitherto unprogressive liberal coalition in 1920, and a coming to the fore of the progressive sectors within the army.

Everywhere the advent of an invigorated democracy reflected the rise of social groups insufficiently represented within the framework of the oligarchic republicanism, and favoured further advances by these groups, at least by giving them access to bureaucratic posts. In almost all large- and medium-sized Latin American countries the depression of the 1930s created new difficulties for exports and diminished the ability to import, thus favouring some industrial development and giving an unexpected advantage to crops that found a market within the national boundaries against those orientated towards exports. The economic changes had large social effects: urbanization accelerated, and in the cities a more complex social pattern was evolving. Improved public hygiene increased population in the less modern areas, whereas in some more modernized and prosperous areas it was checked by the advance of birth-control.

The political heritage of the thirties was complex and ambiguous. It was also contradictory, in that political changes moved in opposing directions in different countries. In Argentina in 1930 and in Uruguay in 1933 a genuine experiment in broadly based democracy was interrupted, by a military revolution in Buenos Aîres, by a presidential *coup d'état* in Montevideo. In Chile, following the dictatorial regime of General Ibáñez, an intricate series of events brought in a substantially conservative constitutional regime. In Peru it was left to the army to overthrow President Leguia, a civilian dictator who had steered a fairly independent course. For a short period an *entente* between the army and Aprismo (a political movement launched in the twenties by university students with a programme of political democratization and somewhat vague revolutionary social change) was still possible. But, after the rise of Sanchez Cerro, a quasi-fascist political leader from the army, who defeated the Aprista candidate Haya de la Torre, and after the assassination of the elected president by a killer with Aprista sympathies, after an Aprista rebellion in the north, bloodily suppressed by the army, the anti-Aprista stand of the military became the basic fact of political life in Peru for the next four decades. It was left to the oligarchic groups to benefit from the rift; Marshal Benavidez, who replaced the assassinated Sanchez Cerro, was a veteran of traditional politics.

In Mexico, in Cuba, in Colombia and in Brazil the breaking of the old political order was on the contrary to prove irreversible. In Mexico during the twenties political stabilization made decisive advances. During the thirties General Cárdenas (president in 1934-40) ventured upon a widespread redistribution of land and the nationalization of the assets of foreign oil companies. The new impetus was, however, short-lived; in 1940, sensing the misgivings his radical leanings evoked in public opinion, Cárdenas chose as his successor the most politically moderate of his followers. Once again revolution was to become almost indistinguishable from conservatism. In Cuba during the twenties the Old Republic, weakened by the blurred party loyalties among conservatives and liberals alike, assumed a dictatorial character under Machado, a businessman and politician with a previous career in the Liberal Party. In 1933 Machado was overthrown, and for a few months Cubans were allowed to hope that a period of long-needed political and social reform was to begin. This hope was crushed by American pressures; Colonel Batista, a former army stenographer, emerged as the power-broker between the pre-1933 political machines and the communist labour organizers, American influence and an increasingly vocal nationalist feeling.

In Colombia in 1930 the Liberal Party triumphed, and in 1934 a new and liberal republic was proclaimed. In order to sustain it, the liberals had to build a solid majority in a staunchly Roman Catholic country; they counted on rapid urbanization and on the growing urban labour force. But, as in Mexico, 1940 brought a turn to the right, and the liberals began to steer a middle course between their new-found popular supporters

The Bay of Pigs: Castro's prisoners after the unsuccessful US sponsored invasion of 1,200 men in 1961

Fear of another Castro led to American intervention in the Dominican Republic in April 1965 when 20,000 marines were sent to encourage – with some success – supporters of the discredited and assassinated dictator, Trujillo

Anti-American demonstration in Caracas, Venezuela, by Castro supporters in 1960, a time of deteriorating US-Cuban relations

and the business interests with which the party had long been associated.

In Brazil a much more complex development followed the successful revolution launched in October 1930 by the Liberal Alliance. The Alliance was a loose front of veteran politicians from the marginal states, ready to merge their personal grudges with the deeply rooted grievances of urban public opinion, until then ignored by a political establishment supported by rural electoral machines. The overthrow of the Old Republic was not followed by a well-defined new political equilibrium. The impatience of certain young army officers who were committed to radical changes – even if not always sure of the nature of the changes they wanted – kept pace with the disillusionment of certain politicians, who turned in despair towards the fascist model to build a unifying national movement. However, these forces would not abandon their obstinate particularism, even in the face of the rival movements which flourished in the post-revolutionary climate: the fascist-inspired Integralismo and the communist-led ALN (Alliance for National Liberation). Finally, it was left to the Liberal Alliance's President Getulio Vargas to find a way out of the muddle. After ruthlessly suppressing communism and before turning against Integralismo, he established a centralized dictatorship – the Estado Novo.

Yet when political radicalization reached exhaustion, and a more conservative mood triumphed, this large support for the *status quo* offered no guarantee of its durability; and soon the war imposed new strains. The war created a new economic context, and a growing identification between internal conflicts and the world-wide struggle.

The economic effects of the war varied greatly. Mexico had to face a quasi-famine in certain moments and regions. In Chile a less severe shortage of foodstuffs favoured a still incipient inflationary process. In Cuba, Brazil and Argentina, the stimulating effects of war – also present in Mexico and Chile – outweighed the adverse ones. The political effects of the war, also diverse, were everywhere a challenge to the situation prevalent on the eve of the conflict. In Mexico a growing impatience with economic difficulties favoured the spreading of Sinarquismo – a movement that blended Christian-millenarian expectations with more mundane fascist sympathies. The consequence of the wilting of the popular support gathered by Cárdenas was the progress among the official party's leaders of less other-worldly conservative tendencies. In Brazil, after some hesitation, Vargas aligned his country with the United States and became their main ally in South America, though aware that this switch had suddenly outmoded the Estado Novo and that his own identification with that quasi-fascist experience was now suspect.

In Brazil, as in Mexico, a strong leadership facing no organized opposition was able to cope with the additional tensions caused by the war. In other countries these tensions further weakened the dominant political forces, faced with a solidly entrenched opposition. In Peru in 1940 Marshal Benavidez was able to impose the election of a successor, Dr Manuel Prado, who was totally identified with the *limeno* political and economic oligarchy. Even so, the potential influence of the Apristas on the electorate had not been weakened by a decade of almost continuous persecution.

Similarly, in Cuba the return to a more sincere application of the rules of representative democracy favoured the heirs of the revolution of 1933 against Batista.

In Colombia, in Chile, in Uruguay and even more in Argentina the world war had additional effects besides giving a momentary edge to representative democracy against rival solutions. In Colombia after 1934 the Conservative Party had lost all hope of regaining power through the polls. For a party that in the previous five decades had regarded its predominance as a permanent fact of Colombian political life the temptation to deny legitimacy to the Liberal republic was great. The warring tendency – so strong in both parties – was reinforced by the example of a world in flames; Franco's victory in Spain offered to some conservatives a viable model of the future. The liberals suffered from their attempt to be both the party of the working class and of the business interest; as the war began to impose

South American governments

- presidential democracy
- military rule
- dictatorship
- colony

increasing hardships upon the poor the call for unity became less effective.

In Chile in 1938 the alliance of conservative parties was defeated by a Popular Front, in which the Radical Party (a mainly middle-class movement) was supported not only by the working-class parties, socialist as well as communist, but by the fascists and the followers of the former military dictator, General Ibáñez. The Front soon disappointed the contradictory hopes it had awakened; it had no revolutionary programme and Chile's economic position left little room for pacific social reform. In 1941, in the presidential elections called after the death of the radical president, Aguirre Cerda, the rightist parties supported the candidacy of Ibáñez, who was only narrowly defeated by José Antonio Rios, a leader of the right wing within the Radical Party. After four years in government the left-wing coalition, brought to power amid hopes and fears of radical change, had become the defender of the *status quo*. For the Chilean left the postwar prospects were dismal.

In Uruguay the consequences of the war were less perturbing but no less far-reaching. Under the pressure of the world crisis the coalition that had sustained the Terra dictatorship was dissolved. The majority section of the Blanco Party, called by Terra to share the spoils of the *coup d'état* of 1933, was traditionally hostile to American influence. This attitude and the growth of quasi-fascist sentiments among some of its leaders resulted in a stubborn defence of Uruguayan neutrality. In order to impose a pro-American line against such resistance the reconstruction of Colorado unity was unavoidable. This development favoured the political heirs of Batlle; in 1942 President Baldomir, successor and brother-in-law of Terra, staged a *coup d'état* with Batllista support, promising a return to full electoral freedom.

But it was in Argentina that the repercussions of the world conflict were most complex. In this country the neutralist conservative regime adopted increasingly authoritarian attitudes. By 1943 all sensible Argentine politicians were agreed on the foreseeable outcome of the war, and even the more fascist-minded conservatives were eager to support the anticipated victors. A number of army officers, however, did not concur. In June 1943, while the neutralist President Castillo was busy organizing the rigged elections that were to transfer power to the pro-American successor he had already selected on behalf of his party, a military takeover imposed a return to neutrality (abandoned in 1944 under pressure applied by the United States) and changed the basic terms of the Argentine political order. It was too late to impose military dictatorship; by breaking its alliance with the conservatives, the army had, however, won a freedom of action that it was reluctant to relinquish to the ineffectual political opposition.

Other countries were beginning to experience radical transformations, influenced by internal rather than by world events. In Venezuela the death in 1935 of Juan Vincente Gomez, the rural dictator who had ruled the

Postwar Mexico – stable, under civilian, if not democratic, rule: the 1958 elections returned Adolfo Lopez Mateos as president for a six-year term

Right The year of the Mexican Olympics, 1968, brought violent student demonstrations and street fighting; the government guaranteed university autonomy and a reappraisal of some sections of the penal code

country since 1909 supported by a clique of army officers, opened the way to more enlightened forms of despotism. The change in the political climate, however, failed to satisfy the opposition, who emboldened by the new liberalization, denounced it as a sophisticated attempt to attain, under new guises, the essential objectives of the Gomez dictatorship: defence of the social and economic *status quo*. In Bolivia and Paraguay the protracted Chaco War (1932-5) brought together social sectors that had long ignored each other. In both countries some officers saw in the army the natural representative of the masses. In Paraguay, almost twenty years of strife, opened by the military revolution of February 1937 and punctuated by a civil war (1947), initiated a new political order, in which the army monopolized political power. In Bolivia the emergence of 'military socialism' was to open the way for one of the most baffling social revolutions of the postwar years.

After the war, the evolution of a world order very different from that predicted by Allied propaganda was to have widespread consequences in Latin America. In the immediate aftermath the progress towards democratic-representative regimes was accepted as the trend of the times; and communism (identified with the Soviet Union, temporarily accepted by its allies as a great power with legitimate world interests) experienced a significant expansion. Soon, however, the cold war began to influence politics in Latin America. Communism, after its short period of respectability, was shunned, and the weight of the United States, anxious to organize the 'free' world, was more and more imperiously felt. The impatience of the United States towards the political instability of Latin America found a sympathetic response among those who were eager to equate the defence of Western democracy with that of their own regime. True, the favourable consequences the United Nations victory had for the prestige of representative democracy were apparently opening a way for the masses. However, the process proved to be far from simple.

The adaptation of liberal institutions to a mass democracy is more easily successful when gradual: too protracted tensions between the few inside and the many who would like to be there lead to a reciprocal denial of legitimacy. In Argentina the Radical Party saw themselves as the political embodiment of the entire nation; their conservative rivals, theoretically denied a legitimate place in the political system, were soon to show how far they were ready to go in order to deny the radicals the place given them by the preferences of the enlarged electorate. Even in opposition, Peruvian Aprismo not only claimed a monopoly of political legitimacy but adopted styles reminiscent of European fascism. The very fact that these indulgences did not hinder the realignment of Aprismo on social-democratic positions shows the vigour of those eclectic inclinations ingrained in Latin American ideological tradition.

Latin American politics displayed tactical as well as ideological eclecticism. In October 1945 the military coup staged in Venezuela indicated some of the possibilities: here the junior officers who expelled the *andino* generals were supported by the principal opposition party, Acción Democratica. Romulo Betancourt, leader of the party, and then viewed by right-wing opinion in Latin America and the USA as a dangerous crypto-communist, became head of government. It is true that in its new role Acción Democratica did not modify its political programmes and ideology (close to those of Peruvian Aprismo) but the way it took power determined the use it made of that power. From a movement committed to all-out (although non-violent) opposition to the existing order grew a party ready to compromise. When in 1948 a new military coup forced Acción Democratica into secrecy, the response was not a return to opposition to the existing order, but rather its explicit acceptance, seen as the unavoidable price the movement had to pay to be tolerated in power.

In Peru Aprismo drew a similar conclusion. In 1945 not military intervention but public opinion forced a partial normalization of electoral procedures upon the reluctant government of President Prado. The Apristas waived the right to offer a candidate to the presidency; they supported an independent candidate, Dr Bustamente y Rivero, not noted in the past for

Top Chilean elections 1970: Eduardo Frei (*above*), Christian Democratic president for six years, had embarked on moderate social reforms, but was replaced by Salvador Allende, the first elected Marxist president in South American history

Below Allende election meeting: a programme of nationalization of foreign interests as a measure against Chile's ailing economy

any Aprista sympathies. They were able to reorganize their party under a new name and thus gain control of parliament. But the hostility of the army and the non-Aprista political forces did not diminish; the president was the arbiter between Aprismo and its powerful enemies, whom he seemed increasingly inclined to favour. A 1948 coup established General Odria as dictator; Aprismo, already outlawed by President Bustamente, was suppressed even more ruthlessly than in the thirties. Too weak to organize a successful upheaval, unable to win the allegiance of significant groups within the armed forces, Aprismo acknowledged the need to conciliate the right-wing politicians. Here again a movement sought to make political democracy palatable to its foes by turning it into a means of social conservation. As a consequence of this new attitude, both Aprismo and Venezuelan Acción Democratica reappraised the unequal link of their countries with the United States; these movements, once proud of their anti-imperialist intransigence, wanted now to be considered the firmest friends the United States had in Latin America.

These curious developments sprang from a quite accurate assessment of the margin of freedom left to popular movements under the aegis of the cold war. The pervasiveness of its influence could be detected in the fate of the communist parties where these had been able to win popular support: in Cuba and Brazil, and especially in Chile, where in 1946 an alliance of the communists and the left wing of the Radical Party had won after proposing to the voters a return to the sources of the Popular Front. Only one year after his victory, the radical President Gonzalez Videla outlawed communism on the assurances of American diplomats who convinced him that the Third World War might break out within the next three months. In Brazil too communism was outlawed, and in Cuba violent means were used to eliminate its hold upon the labour movements.

It is not surprising, then, that the non-communist left-wing parties chose to adapt to the new political climate. If the lessons received in adversity were useful, the experience of power was even more effective in dampening reformist zeal. In Cuba the heirs of the hope born from the 1933 uprising, after years of condemnation of Batista's corrupt ways, were allowed to win in 1944 by the reluctant strong man, whose hand was being forced by the Americans – only to organize an equally corrupt electoral machine that kept them in power until 1952. These movements naturally lost the confidence of the electorate. Equally serious, the enemies they had made in the past remained basically suspicious and hostile; even when they went further than was convenient for their popularity in placating the right, the army and the State Department, it was not easy for them to evoke a benevolent response from these three centres of authority.

The comparison with other movements which, precisely because they did not offer uncompromising defiance of the *status quo*, were able to change it, is instructive. For a decade the successes of Peronismo in Argentina and the heirs of the Varguista political tradition in Brazil offered a clear contrast with the failures of the popular movements in Venezuela and Peru.

As has been mentioned, in Brazil too a return to electoral democracy seemed unavoidable in 1945. Faced with the danger of Vargas profiting from this democratic wave as he had profited from the quasi-fascist one eight years earlier, the army expelled him from the presidency with the public blessing of the US embassy. A new urban popular force, the pro-Vargas Labour Party (catering for the working-class clientele organized by the state-sponsored unions) was soon to be strengthened by the outlawing of communism. But the return to a federal organization restored rural Brazil to political dominance. Though Vargas owed his re-election to the presidency in 1950 to the support of the Labour Party and some regional organizations, once in power he was forced to come to terms with an opposition firmly entrenched in parliament.

In Argentina the balance established by the return to free universal suffrage was extremely unfavourable to the popular parties. The leaders of the 1943 military revolution were far from eager to relinquish power to the Radical Party (the main popular opposition), and preferred to organize a

Above A 1950 Peron rally. The extraordinary husband-and-wife rule of the Argentinian dictator (*right*) and his wife Eva, who died in 1952, brought eventual economic disaster and a military coup in 1955

Below A further military coup in Argentina in June 1966 installed an army dictatorship under General Juan Carlos Ongania

Getulio Vargas, effective dictator of Brazil for nearly twenty years, committed suicide in 1954 after economic failures and the loss of support among army generals, who felt that the old man was losing his grip

Tanks patrol Rio; the army finally took over in April 1964 after President Goulart's inability to deal with spiralling inflation and drift to the political left

In June 1968 a student-dominated protest march in Rio: the flag reads 'Down with dictatorship – the government belongs to the people'

new political coalition, with weak roots in the traditional parties. It succeeded beyond its own expectations, thanks to the ingenuity of the vice-president, minister of war and labour secretary, Colonel Juan D. Peron, who, through lavish welfare legislation, was able to win the allegiance of the working class and a majority among rural voters. The audacity of its social reforms (especially when compared with the performance of past governments) was considered by Latin-American public opinion as the distinctive feature of Peronismo, even if at least some Argentinians were alienated by its increasingly authoritarian tendencies.

In Bolivia political renewal was more agitated. In 1943 the old political leaders were purged and a new military regime successfully sought the support of the new anti-oligarchic parties (particularly the middle-class anti-imperialist Revolutionary Nationalist Movement – MNR – and the Trotskyite Workers' Revolutionary Party – POR – comparatively strong among tin-miners). The experiment was short and dismal. The restoration of 1946, however, was also far from solid; in 1951 the MNR obtained a narrow electoral victory. It was denied power but in 1952 regained it thanks to a new popular revolution. The army, divided against itself, emerged with weakened influence; even militarily the militia of mine workers effectively balanced its power. In this context the nationalization of the tin-mines and a sweeping agrarian reform were rapidly carried out. The peasants' unions were now dominant in the countryside, and their support gave the regime additional leverage against the militant miners. Externally, the new regime soon adopted a policy of total support to the United States, repaid by the economic aid on which the very survival of the Bolivian revolution was soon to depend. Here, as with the popular parties of Venezuela and Peru, pro-American policies were inspired by a realistic if unheroic appraisal of the situation the revolution faced.

In Guatemala in 1944 a coalition of junior officers and disgruntled young civilians attempted to establish a reform regime. Under Colonel Arbenz, after 1951, the government of Guatemala not only extended its agrarian reform plans to American-owned lands but showed a growing disenchantment with the cold war mystique in striking contrast with the crusading zeal of the neighbouring dictatorial regimes. These policies, not unexpectedly, won for the regime the support of the local Communist Party and the animosity of the State Department. In Caracas the American nations agreed to declare that Guatemala was a Soviet beachhead in Latin America. This anomalous situation was corrected by an invasion launched from neighbouring Honduras; the bastion of militant and dedicated communism was easily suppressed by a small force of dissident Guatemalan military men with a little air support.

The political climate of the late forties and early fifties thus imposed quite rigid limits upon the reforming regimes. These were, moreover, the exception in a stagnant political landscape. After 1948 Peru and Venezuela were ruled by military dictatorships, soon legitimized by rigged elections. In Cuba a reforming party, preparing for the 1952 presidential election, proclaimed a campaign against corruption in public life. But Batista, realizing that this would eliminate him as a serious presidential candidate, staged a military coup and, facing a small but determined opposition, resorted to a repression of unprecedented savagery; the prosperity in the sugar-exporting sector of the economy bolstered his political ambitions.

In Mexico the stability of the revolutionary – but increasingly less revolutionary – regime seemed assured. Under Miguel Aleman (1946-52) the country entered a phase of rapid industrial expansion. After 1952 a mild social and rural reorientation began; real wages slowly rose and a large-scale irrigation programme led to a steady rise in agricultural production. This political stability, and the ability to maintain consistent economic policies, were a tribute to the hard-headed political skill of the Mexican rulers.

Stability, rather than reform, seemed then to be the main political ambition of the times. Colombia was to enjoy neither, in the decade after the conservatives returned to power in 1946. A few years later, Gaitán, the leader

President Betancourt (1959-64) managed to become the first elected civilian in Venezuelan history to finish his term of office; he is shown (*above*) with bandaged hands following an assassination attempt.

Below The Bolivian president, Victor Paz Estenssoro aimed at rapid economic development and the integration of the Indians; in spite of US support, he was replaced by a military junta under General Ortuno in 1964

Right Bolivian stamp to mark the nationalization of the mines in 1952, during the first term in office of Paz Estenssoro

of the ousted liberals was assassinated. Political violence, hitherto sporadic, became general; and the government reacted in turn with brutal severity. In 1953, when the dead amounted to hundreds of thousands, the army imposed its own peace. General Rojas Pinilla seized power, with the support of moderate conservatives, and the thankful approval of the impotent liberals. But he soon began to manœuvre so as to weaken the established parties and launch a third force to support him in power. This menace to their political monopoly brought about the reconciliation of conservative and liberal leaders. In 1958, when the Church and the army joined the opposition, Rojas Pinilla fled the country, opening the way to a coalition of the traditional parties, the National Union government. The system of loyalties that gave the leadership of both such a solid grip on their followers nullified any attempt to transform them.

Status quo with violence, *status quo* with internal peace were the alternatives in these postwar years. It is easy to explain this conservative trend by referring to the international situation. There is, however, another even more important explanation: even political experiments seriously committed to social reforms were comparatively indifferent to the economic framework in which society evolved. But during the fifties the optimism implicit in this indifference lost its justification. In 1954 Vargas committed suicide; in 1955 Peron was overthrown. In Chile Ibáñez, after a landslide victory in the presidential elections of 1952, was unable to fulfil his promises of rapid social change amid universal economic prosperity. These political catastrophes reflected the growing economic difficulties faced by programmes based on income redistribution. A continuous economic expansion was required to make them possible without intolerable social tensions, and – after the war, the first postwar prosperity and the Korean boom – the limits of this expansion were obviously reached in more than one Latin American country.

Continued redistributive endeavours resulted in increasing inflation, which at least in Chile and Brazil was in danger of getting out of control, and in other countries was a source of growing concern. Inflation was produced by the competition between different sectors for a share in a gross national income that had ceased to grow as quickly as in the past. But any attempt to face the economic problems would entail the victory of the industrial over the agrarian sector, of the propertied over the popular classes, or vice versa. In both cases the failure of the conciliatory solutions was implicitly recognized; from then on any economic policy would have to single out one social sector which would bear the burden of economic rehabilitation.

A more tense political climate and a victory for the solution which could develop the widest appeal could be expected. These expectations, however, were soon proven wrong: the era of social conciliation had not prepared the masses for militancy; it had not decisively weakened the traditionally dominant elements. It had, moreover, encouraged the emergence of new, politically uncommitted elements, especially within the industrial sector. But the real and growing economic difficulties had not yet reached a critical stage when almost everywhere the notion was accepted that the basic structures of the Latin American social and economic order were not viable. This sudden change in attitude is attributable to two fresh factors. One was the social revolution in the most unexpected corner; by 1961 Cuba was ruled by the principles of Marxism-Leninism and was building a socialist society. At that time a new president had won election in the United States by denouncing the complacency characteristic of the Eisenhower era. In Latin America the *Pax Americana* suddenly seemed a glossy and brittle surface. The *status quo* it now appeared had no future; revolution was inevitable and the only question was who would lead the way. Under these double auspices the frantic years of fear and hope were opened.

The years of fear and hope

The change in the political climate during the sixties was produced not only by Castro and Kennedy, but by the chronic difficulties of most of the Latin American national economies. These difficulties now seemed

Above Propaganda posters in Peru, October 1948, following the takeover of General Odria, who maintained power for eight years

Left Peruvian president Belaunde Terry (1963-8) whose settlement with American oil interests led to a nationalist military coup in the name of revolutionary government

In Nicaragua, a demonstrator murdered by police while campaigning for secret ballot: in spite of the assassination of the dictator Somoza in 1956, his family continued to run the country along much the same lines

ominous not only because the proclamation of revolutionary political alternatives suggested that the limits within which economic hardship would be tolerated were narrowing, but also because some ambitious programmes for economic recovery without social and political upheavals had conspicuously failed. The prelude to the tense sixties was the lack of success of what had been called *developmentism*. The *developmentist* solutions sprang from a revived awareness of the dependent character of the Latin American economies. Even after industrialization, the typical Latin American country depended on imports from the metropolitan economies, but the world trade structure inhibited any export boom to allow it to pay for imports. What Latin America needed was better integrated national economies. Industrial structures had to be completed; at the same time an expansion of the internal market was needed to free industry from the threat of stagnation. This meant that the income level of wage- and salary-earners had to be maintained. But how could national economies unable to sustain the quite modest gains from the past afford such a gigantic transformation?

These difficulties explain the emergence of a debased version of the *developmentist* programme which gained widespread, though temporary popularity. It proposed policies explicitly tailored to the interests of investors from outside the area; furthermore, it satisfied the ambitions of internal groups – among others a working class hungry for jobs and middle classes hungry for consumer durable goods. It must also be kept in mind, in order to understand the support these policies found in quite unexpected quarters, that neo-liberalism, and not a more ambitious version of the *developmentist* gospel, was seen as the real alternative to them. Neo-liberalism meant a return to the past, to the primary economy dominated by the export sector. Not only those who still controlled this sector, and were less and less willing to finance an industrial sector facing growing difficulties, shared in the nostalgic mood which nourished the neo-liberal revival. In 1958, in Chile, the unthinkable happened, and a conservative candidate, Jorge Alessandri, won the presidency in a four-cornered contest, on the simple programme of freeing the economy and thus stopping inflation; in the same year the Uruguayan Blanco Party, after almost a century of subordination to the Colorado government party, won a frontal battle against the Batllista tradition of state economic intervention. In a country which had enjoyed general prosperity as an exporter of rural staples in the pre-1929 world, the nostalgic yearning for the good old times attracted mass support even more easily than in Chile.

Developmentism was doomed by its readiness to embrace all sorts of expedients, and also because its successes were too brief to last between one general election and the next. This was the case in Brazil, where President Kubitschek, victor in 1955, as the chief of the social democratic-labourite alliance, had promised to give the country fifty years of progress in a five-year span. Although this exorbitant promise was not literally fulfilled, Brazil did for some years have one of the highest growth rates in the Western world. This impressive performance, however, had been facilitated by coffee prosperity; in the final years of Kubitschek's tenure of office, in a less favourable international trade climate, the partners in the *desenvolvimentista* adventure – landowners, industrialists, workers – returned to their more usual role as rivals in the distribution of income, and inflation, never quelled (the government had hoped that the problem would take care of itself), began again to gather momentum. In 1960 the electorate passed judgement on the *desenvolvimentista* experience by electing Janio Quadros, a colourful politician who had only scorn for any economic goal beside the fight against inflation. But the electoral verdict was not unambiguously conservative. In the vice-presidential election Joao Goulart, candidate on the social democratic-labour ticket, was elected; Janio's political message was complex and confused, because he also preached a wholesale condemnation of 'petty' politicians from right and left and – quite unexpectedly – a foreign policy orientated towards the Third World neutralism. The incoherence of this programme for change reflected the moods of a public more aware of the

Top Cuban artillery in action during the US Bay of Pigs invasion, 1961
Above Castro at a mass rally in Havana; after three years of guerrilla warfare, he instituted the most sweeping social revolution in Latin American history. All businesses were nationalized, rentals severely restricted and private ownership of farming land reduced to thirty per cent

By 1970 Castro had vast popular support and had not lost the authentic Cuban quality of his revolution

irrelevance of the solutions adopted after 1930 than sure about the orientation to be taken from then on.

In Argentina, after the fall of Peron, a dissident leader from the former opposition party, Arturo Frondizi, sought in *desarrollismo* a way out from the escalation of political and social strife. After his election, in 1958 with Peronista support, it was evident that the army leaders could get rid of him as soon as they chose, and that little support could be expected from the Peronistas, busy reconstructing their political organization for the next election. So whereas in Brazil *desenvolvimentismo* was interpreted in a generally pro-labour context, in Argentina it became distinguishable from liberalism only in its even more intense eagerness to attract foreign investment. The economic success was less marked than in Brazil, and – perhaps as a consequence – was followed by a less shocking anticlimax. The more important difficulties, however, were political: in 1962 the Peronistas won so many provincial elections that the army leaders thought it wise to put an end to the Frondizi regime. In Argentina the failure of *desarrollismo* produced the return to a division between a popular force based on the trade unions, and a sizeable middle- and upper-class minority, of variably conservative feelings, enjoying the decisive support of the army. But the failure also fostered a mood of desperate disillusioned pessimism.

It was then not only because the Cuban revolutionary leaders had chosen, after repelling an American-sponsored invasion, to enter the Eastern bloc, that communism began to look less exotic in the Latin American landscape. In this context of growing unrest the Cuban revolutionary government, expelled from the pan-American organization and submitted to a diplomatic quarantine which only Mexico was bold enough to ignore, understandably turned to extreme left-wing solutions; for in Latin America there was apparently no place for less extreme ones. So the hope spread that the tactics that had led to victory in Cuba would be equally successful elsewhere. But this ignored the vital fact that the revolution which had swept Cuba had not initially been socialist, and that this circumstance had had some bearing upon the very large consensus it had awakened in the island (and upon the vacillating policies adopted by the United States; after all, although the Cubans might not care to be reminded of this, they had ousted Batista only after the United States imposed an embargo of military supplies to his regime). No similar response could be expected in the continent after the Cuban revolution; even less where the regimes to be overthrown, even if socially conservative, were not politically oppressive. The aid offered by Cuba to the guerrilla movements was not strong enough to compensate these negative factors. The history of the *guerrillero* attempts was accordingly unimpressive. Only in Guatemala, where extreme political oppression did exist, were the guerrillas able at least to hold their own. In Colombia some of the surviving local guerrilla chieftains accepted the new revolutionary banner, without changing their tactics and their quite modest goals. In Peru in 1964 the army crushed attempts to channel peasant unrest in a guerrilla movement. In Bolivia in 1967, during a period of deep political crisis, Ernesto (Che) Guevara was not able to foment a rural insurrection and was killed by a force lavishly supplied by the United States. In Venezuela, where the conflict was further embittered by the *odium theologicum* now dividing Castro and Betancourt, the guerrilla movement after a promising start experienced a progressive decline.

The menace of guerrilla war accelerated the consolidation of a sort of holy alliance of all the defenders of the *status quo*. It is, however, easy to exaggerate the importance of the *guerrillero* threat in inspiring this turn to the right. The conservative trend was already detectable before 1960, and the realignment of United States' policies in the mid-sixties was stimulated by events in South-east Asia rather than in Latin America. The return to a policy of open intervention in the hemisphere (exemplified by the Santo Domingo expedition in 1964, which saved the military regime from total popular defeat) stimulated in any case the rightward trend; some of the politically least reputable, but also more reliable, among the traditional friends the United States had south of the Rio Grande were reassured by the

Brazilian anti-communist posters in 1955 point a choice between liberty and slavery

Below Death of Guevara, who was killed by Bolivian troops on 9 October 1967: an air force official indicates the bullet entry to press photographers. Guevara, Castro's former chief lieutenant and industrial minister, had tried to start Cuban-type risings in Venezuela, Colombia, Peru and Bolivia. The Bolivian government were more shaken by the publication of his war diary which had mistakenly been released by a government minister, than by any Guevara-inspired revolt: a total military cabinet was appointed in July 1968
Below right Guevara, myth and martyr, in a demonstration in Venezuela, 1968

return of their powerful protector to more normal behaviour. And the widespread fear evoked by Cuba and the *guerrillero* menace dimmed the protests among the less conservative supporters of the American hegemony after its unexpected return to a political style based on the use of naked violence.

Yet not every reaction was crudely reactionary. Among them should be included a new awareness of the need for some kind of rapid alleviation of social problems, evident not only among centrists but even from among the right. (In the early sixties from Lima to Santiago de Chile, Buenos Aires and Rio de Janeiro, it was the right-wing politicians who suddenly discovered the housing problem, and launched vast building programmes, in most cases with American financial assistance.) Another aspect of this new awareness was the discovery of the political potential hidden in the marginal populations, among whom the guerrillas had hoped to gather support. This deliberate appeal to still politically and socially marginal elements was to be a common feature in the most typical political developments of the early and mid-sixties; the disastrous attempt at re-launching the Varguista experience in Brazil, and the political emergence of Christian Democracy in Chile and Popular Action in Peru.

In Brazil, after a period of economic austerity, President Quadros attempted to regain popularity by stressing his independent international policies. A superficial reconciliation with the Varguista sectors followed, which caused deep bitterness among the right-wing supporters of the president. Quadros resigned, alleging that he was under military pressure. For the conservative forces and for the army leadership, committed to friendship with the United States, Vice-President Goulart was even less acceptable than his predecessor; if Quadros had been unpredictable, the heir of Vargas's following in the working class, the assiduous visitor of the socialist countries, was perhaps only too predictable. In subsequent manœuvres Goulart pressed for the enlargement of the franchise to include the illiterates (of course this reform could only be beneficial to him if the traditional deference system in the countryside was destroyed) and – to loosen the pressure of the army officers' corps – also the non-commissioned officers, who were to be allowed to participate in the elections.

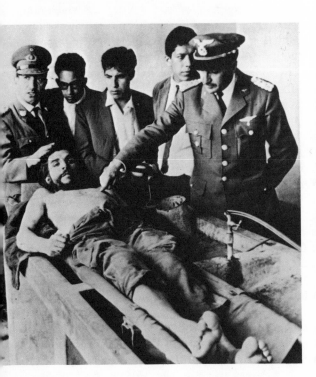

ENSEÑAR A LEER Y A ESCRIBIR
A UN ADULTO O A UN NIÑO
NO ES EMPRESA DIFICIL
SI SE PONE EN ELLO ENTUSIASMO
CONSTANCIA Y AMOR A LA PATRIA
CAMPAÑA NACIONAL CONTRA EL ANALFABETISMO

Mexican poster campaign against illiteracy: 'It is
not especially difficult to teach a child or an adult
to read and write if this is done with enthusiasm
and the spirit of patriotism'

Proportion of population at school

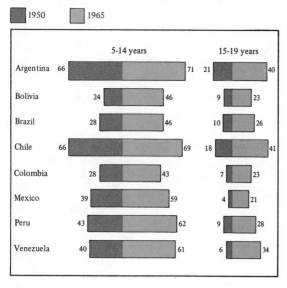

■ 1950   ■ 1965

	5-14 years		15-19 years	
Argentina	66	71	21	40
Bolivia	24	46	9	23
Brazil	28	46	10	26
Chile	66	69	18	41
Colombia	28	43	7	23
Mexico	39	59	4	21
Peru	43	62	9	28
Venezuela	40	61	6	34

Population of major cities 1968-9

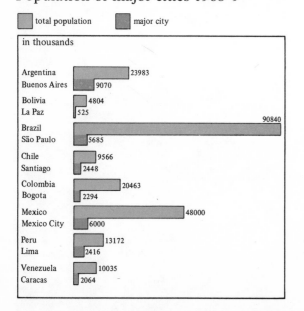

■ total population   ■ major city

in thousands

Argentina	23983
Buenos Aires	9070
Bolivia	4804
La Paz	525
Brazil	90840
São Paulo	5685
Chile	9566
Santiago	2448
Colombia	20463
Bogota	2294
Mexico	48000
Mexico City	6000
Peru	13172
Lima	2416
Venezuela	10035
Caracas	2064

These reforms were thus essentially political, and the president – himself a prosperous landowner – did not envisage any sweeping social reforms. But his indifference to reform, in an increasingly adverse economic situation, contributed to his downfall. The overthrow of Goulart, staged by a coalition of the traditional political class and the army leadership, was easy and bloodless. The outcome was slightly more surprising (at least for the politicians who had sought the aid of the army); the military were now in power, and meant to keep it.

An intermediate solution was adopted, but a thin constitutional veil covered what was in fact a ruthless military dictatorship. A stern anti-inflationary policy was imposed, and after four extremely difficult years a kind of prosperity returned to Brazil. This change in the economic climate did not engender a milder political attitude; repression seemed – in 1970 even more than in 1964 – basic in determining the actions of the Brazilian military government.

In Peru, in 1963, a new popular party, Acción Popular, reached power with the backing of the army, with Rafael Belaunde Terry as its presidential candidate. The victory of Belaunde, favoured by a reorientation of the volatile Lima electorate, was, however, based on the extension of party politics to the Indian south of the country, until then controlled by local notables. It was there that Belaunde was able to organize a following big enough to rival that of the Apristas in the predominantly mestizo north. In the more politically active areas he appealed to the sub-proletariat left outside the Aprismo-controlled labour unions. Thus patronage systems of a markedly rural style vied with each other for the voter of the slum and shanty-town dwellers of Greater Lima. Although the promises of reform which Belaunde had lavishly offered had been couched in conveniently vague terms, the expectations they awakened were vast and difficult to satisfy. The programme of public works sponsored by the new president satisfied some pressing needs by creating new jobs, but it was expensive; the limits of Peru's ability to borrow foreign capital were soon reached; and his opponents could cite the current economic difficulties as a proof of the soundness of the economic liberalism practised by Belaunde's predecessors.

These disappointing results were aggravated by the bitterness which the timidity of Belaunde's social reform caused among his more radical supporters; the land system was left practically untouched, and rural unrest (on which, as already mentioned, the extreme left had unsuccessfully tried to graft a *guerrillero* rebellion) was mercilessly crushed. In 1968, when Belaunde was finally ousted by his former military supporters, he had already made a far from honourable peace with his enemies on the right, and nothing but a military coup could stop the electoral victory of Aprismo in 1969.

In Chile a less hastily conceived realignment was also less than totally successful. In 1964 the Christian Democrats were able to go to the country as a valid alternative to both the right-wing coalition then in power (in that they offered an even more effective barrier to the progress of the left-wing alliance) and to the left wing itself (in that they were allegedly in a better position to implement the quite moderate reform programme then supported by the left). They reached power as representatives of the whole non-Marxist section of the Chilean body politic. They wanted to gain solid support in the countryside, by agrarian reform and by a rise in agricultural wages, and also appeal to the urban lower-working class and other marginal groups. This could only be done by weakening the protection enjoyed in the past by the politically organized social groups (urban middle class, unionized working class, landowners and industrialists). From the economic and social viewpoint, the Christian-Democratic experiment (facilitated by several years of copper bonanza in world markets) was quite impressive. Politically it did not yield the rewards President Frei and his followers had hoped to reap. It brought about the resurrection of the old right wing as a refuge for resentful opponents among the middle classes, and a consolidation of the Marxist left, that not only held its own in the working- and middle-class electorate, but found some supporters among the political newcomers on whose allegiance the Christian Democrats had counted.

310

In Latin America generally the drift of the rural poor into the towns continued and few profited from it; less than one-tenth of the continent's population have completed primary education

Below An Indian village near Cuzco in Peru, where politics has little relevance
Bottom Brasilia (view from the Presidential palace): the new national capital since 1960, planned on an extravagant scale

None of the attempts at reconstruction launched during the early and mid-sixties was thus wholly successful. The political scene revealed the dissolution of previous alignments without the appearance of alternative solutions – except that of total revolution. In Venezuela, after a protracted agony, the Acción Democratica regime gave way in 1968 to its Christian-Democratic former allies, far more conservative in inspiration than their Chilean opposite numbers. In Colombia the programme of the conservative-liberal alliance became one of mere self-preservation amid general stagnation. In Argentina a more subdued experiment in constitutional government, begun in 1963, soon faced the prospect of a Peronista comeback, as unacceptable to the armed forces as in 1962. Even in Mexico, after one of the longest periods of political stability in its history, the widespread opposition disclosed by student demonstrations during 1968 was perhaps a first intimation of mortality for a by then only nominally revolutionary regime. The government's response was swift, harsh and for the moment effective; the appearance of national unanimity behind it and its party was, however, possibly deceptive.

Nowhere did political dissolution go so far as in Bolivia. Its experiment in social revolution financed by the Eisenhower government was intrinsically fragile. The return to power of Paz Estenssoro, in 1960, could not reverse the tendency. In 1964 his bid for re-election, due less to personal ambition than to the absence of any other candidate able to rally general support in the hopelessly divided government party, led to an intensification of factional struggles, and a rise in the influence of the army. The outcome was a military coup, and a protracted contest between right and left, within the army and the nation, with growing support from the USA for the rightist elements.

Conclusion

None of the problems that loomed so large in the early sixties was solved by 1970. In countries with slow population growth – as Uruguay, Argentina or Chile – the economy was no more able to provide jobs for the newcomers to the labour market than in Colombia, Brazil or Peru, where the population explosion was often blamed for economic difficulties and social tensions. But stagnation or too slow growth was not the only problem: even where there was some growth, its effects were mixed; the adaptation of Latin America to a productive style matured in countries where capital was abundant and labour was scarce tended to aggravate economic instability. And in expansion and stagnation alike the weakened Latin American economies tended to fall back on progressive de-nationalization. Business concentration and the influx of new technology worked against them and in favour of the local branches of international enterprises. This process, deplored even by conservative economists, was very difficult to stop, except by a return of the state to industrial and extractive activities. Such a return was everywhere visible. But even when ideological opposition to the state as entrepreneur was abandoned, the problem of how to finance its entrepreneurial activities remained intractable.

New and equally alarming problems appeared even less easy to master. Why then did the sense of urgency characteristic of the early and middle sixties gradually vanish? At the beginning of the decade circumstances indicated a sudden crisis; however, it became evident that, if the dysfunctions were even more serious than had earlier been thought, it was both necessary and possible to live with them. But this orientation towards less activistic policies reflected also a change in external circumstances. One factor was the shift of revolutionary Cuba towards the very type of export economy so widely condemned in Latin America, and the only moderate success that rewarded this unexpected economic course. Even if valid in the Cuban context, the decisions of the Castro regime revealed that the solutions adopted there were less and less relevant to Latin America as a whole. Still more important were the changes evident in the United States' foreign policy; the discovery of the limitations of power was soon reflected in the attitudes of the US towards Latin America. The Nixon administration was markedly less ready to stimulate open confrontation than its predecessor.

Oil complex in Venezuela, at Maracaibo. Both copper and oil were US-owned by 1970; but the future for foreign developers was very much in the balance

Exports 1966-7

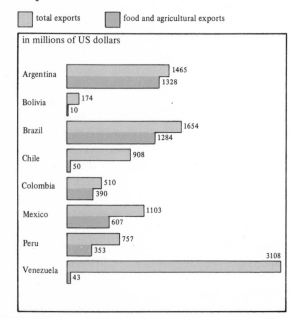

	total exports	food and agricultural exports

in millions of US dollars

	total exports	food and agricultural exports
Argentina	1465	1328
Bolivia	174	10
Brazil	1654	1284
Chile	908	50
Colombia	510	390
Mexico	1103	607
Peru	757	353
Venezuela	3108	43

Chuquicamata in Chile – the world's largest copper-mine, 10,000 feet high in the Atacama Desert

The alleviation in tensions was soon felt in the political developments of the late sixties. The comparison between policies of the Brazilian military regime and those of Argentina is suggestive. Even if the Argentine army hierarchy, in deposing in 1966 the constitutional government and establishing an open-ended period of military dictatorship, was following the Brazilian example and even improving on it, its use of power was different. They viewed the national predicament with less alarm than their Brazilian colleagues; they had suppressed party politics not because civilian rule could not cope with problems too serious to be left to the politicians, but because party strife was aggravating the quite manageable problems the country faced. This comparatively relaxed attitude was reflected in the quite mild use of repressive measures and in a readiness to come to terms with political and social sectors which, it was thought, were prone to foolish behaviour, but not intrinsically evil. If perhaps the new leadership was wise to present the country's situation in less apocalyptic terms than had been fashionable before the coup, it did not, however, follow that the modest political talents of the new leaders would succeed where more experienced politicians had failed.

The lack of expertise and clear long-term aims, characteristic of the Argentine military regime, contrasts with the political skills revealed by the Peruvian military after 1968. The new post-Belaunde government's allegiance to economic nationalism was much more than a device to attract popular support: the US-owned oil-fields were nationalized and a radical agrarian reform expropriated the – mainly foreign – sugar estates and mills to the north. A gradual takeover of large- and medium-sized industrial enterprises by the workers was instituted, and – perhaps more important for the short term – quite high compulsory rates of reinvestment were decreed. These sweeping economic reforms were introduced without social strife. It is too soon to forecast the future course of the Peruvian experiment, but what has already happened in that country since 1968 is of very great significance.

Land use 1969

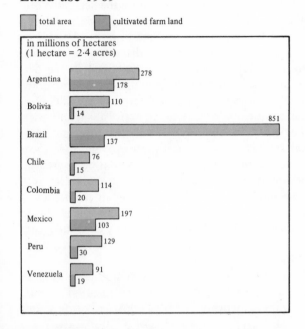

total area   cultivated farm land

in millions of hectares
(1 hectare = 2·4 acres)

Country	total area	cultivated farm land
Argentina	278	178
Bolivia	110	14
Brazil	851	137
Chile	76	15
Colombia	114	20
Mexico	197	103
Peru	129	30
Venezuela	91	19

In Mexico government officials teach *peons* to improve the quality and quantity of their crops

Even in Peru the new mood did not arise from any clear-cut prognosis of the Latin American crisis; the Peruvian rulers remained reticent about their ultimate aims even though their supporters began to fear that their silence might signify ignorance rather than discretion. In other Latin American countries the mood was still less clearly defined; almost everywhere, however, a diminished rigidity in political alignments was detectable. In Chile the failure of the Christian-Democratic experiment led to a neither unexpected nor premature victory of the left; thanks to the division between Christian-Democratic and conservative votes, Dr Salvador Allende was elected president. This mature parliamentarian was to govern with the support of a minority left-wing parliamentary bloc within which the Radical Party representatives were as numerous as the communists. After some weeks of panic, with the wealthy frantically leaving the country, a calmer atmosphere prevailed. Even if heightened tensions are expected from any further reform, this dispassionate forecast of future conflicts is quite different from the almost Pavlovian simplicity of the reactions formerly stimulated by the prospect of a coalition with communist support winning a presidential election in a Latin American country.

This ideological thaw was also evident in the reactions towards more indigenous forces, which had been put outside the pale of political respectability. In Argentina the anti-Peronista parties were now ready for an understanding with their old Peronista foe, which seemed to relish its new role of spearhead in the struggle for old-fashioned constitutional democracy; at the same time the military regime, in need of some political support – or at least forbearance – singled for its favours the still-numerous Peronista movement. In this way the former political outcast became indispensable in any pro-government or anti-government coalition. Similarly in Colombia, after the presidential tenure of the liberal Lleras Restrepo, who attempted to change the liberal-conservative coalition into a 'front for national transformation', the supporters of General Rojas Pinilla placed their candidate only a few thousand votes behind the government candidate, the conservative Misael Pastrana Borrero. But they took their quasi-defeat with comparative good grace, and the marginal victors soon showed a commendable modesty. It is true that any other tactics would have been self-defeating: even so, this coolness suggests that the acute tensions reflected in the recent past in all sorts of political holy alliances were now subdued.

This revision of outlook is, however, no sure sign of new and stable political solutions. Though attempts at the overthrow of the existing political and social order through guerrilla warfare are less frequent and more obviously illusory, the adoption of violent tactics by extremist movements (or by extreme fringes of moderate movements) seems likely to be a lasting heritage of recent experiments with armed struggle. In this context is to be understood the phenomenon of the so-called 'urban guerrilla', crushed in Brazil and Venezuela, moderately successful in Argentina and extremely powerful in Uruguay (where the continuing deterioration of the economy is a cause of widespread resentment among the formerly prosperous urban middle classes), it entails, however, only a minor breakdown of the existing order, and even in Uruguay a bid for power by the activists of the left would meet sure defeat. There is a perhaps more serious aspect in it: armed rebellion is but one expression of a more general phenomenon, namely, the growing estrangement of large sectors from the existing order. The change seems less remarkable because its manifestations are comparable to those everywhere present in the Western world, but the surface similarity (confrontation in the universities, modish new leftism in intellectual circles, political radicalization among the clergy), is somewhat misleading. What is conspicuously absent in Latin America is the sturdy political and social balance which elsewhere has soon reduced neo-leftish groups to political marginality. These episodes in Latin America reveal new stages in the erosion of an order menaced by its own shortcomings. The grave problems that destroyed the viability of the conciliatory policies are always there, unsolved and more urgent than ever; even without seriously attempting to solve them, living with them may in itself become increasingly difficult.

Ali A. Mazrui

Africa: the Age of Nkrumah

Perhaps the most basic dialectic in Africa's history since the Second World War has been between the quest for continental autonomy and the pull of a continuing relationship with Europe. The first came to be symbolized by Kwame Nkrumah's version of pan-African nationalism. The second was best illustrated in French-speaking Africa, and exemplified in the personality of Charles de Gaulle and its impact on Francophone Africans. The conflict between the goal of a self-reliant Africa and the cosmopolitan ideal of 'Euro-Africa' is part of a wider dialectic between nationalism and internationalism in the postwar world. In this essay we shall, therefore, first relate this wider dialectic to the genesis of African self-assertion, and then focus on the interaction between Nkrumah and de Gaulle in relation to Africa.

In idealistic and emotional times, the study of symbolic leaders helps to define the dominant moods of the era. The 'Age of Nkrumah' in Africa was characterized by self-conscious nationalism. To examine his role is thus to shed light on political Africa as a whole. Similarly, to study de Gaulle from 1958 to 1969 as a shaper of Francophone Africa is to capture the centrality of his influence upon France in the post-imperial age.

In the tug between nationalism and internationalism, nothing was more pertinent than the formation of the United Nations Organization in 1945. When the UN came into being, independent Africa consisted of only four countries: Ethiopia, Liberia, Egypt and the Union of South Africa. Yet it was ambivalent. Ethiopia had only just emerged from Italian occupation, exhausted and humiliated though proud. Liberia remained tied to the apron strings of the United States. Egypt, though technically sovereign, had a British military presence, and was ruled by a deficient and dependent monarchy. South Africa had attained autonomy within the British Empire, first with a Pact of the Union in 1910 and then with the Statute of Westminster in 1933. But South Africa had attained independence without attaining freedom. It is true that at that time Africans, coloured and Asians had more of a semblance of a say in the affairs of the nation than they later had. African interests were formally represented in parliament, and political participation by the non-white population, though modest, was nevertheless guaranteed by tradition and law. Racialism was already at the base of South Africa's political system, but the highly structured policy of apartheid had yet to come into being. At that momentous meeting in San Francisco to form the UN, South Africa was clearly the most influential African state present. The Second World War as a global experience reactivated both internationalism, as the world searched for means to prevent wars, and nationalism, as the colonized peoples of the world sought to liberate themselves. The participation of India, Ceylon, Burma and the African colonies in the war against Germany, Japan and Italy were important factors behind the reawakening of Afro-Asian militancy. The question of dismantling the British and French empires following the war was in the air at the same time as the issue of forming a world organization. And whatever the subsequent failings and perplexities of the UN, it was in the early days to play a momentous part in the decolonizing and regrouping of the peoples of the world.

From the point of view of African nationalism, 1945 is a historic year for two conferences. One of these was indeed at San Francisco, even if Africa was grossly under-represented and her interests hardly recognized. The other took place in Manchester, England. This is sometimes referred to as the Fifth Pan-African Congress, but it is possible to regard the Manchester Congress of 1945 as the first genuine Pan-African Congress.

Market day in Conakry, capital of Guinea. One day (so a Guinean story runs) President Touré went among the people to find out what they wanted: 'Here's what I want to know,' said a farmer, 'this independence is all very well and we're quite pleased with it. But when's it going to end?'

Ghanaian women wearing Nkrumah patterned dresses: in 1961 he became Ghana's first president and acknowledged leader of the pan-African movement

Below Julius Nyerere, president of Tanzania and skilful exponent of the doctrine of economic aid from all quarters and dependence on none
Bottom Zambian coat of arms: a republic from 1964 under President Kaunda, with the second largest copper exports in the world

The distinction between pan-negroism and pan-Africanism can be critical. Pan-negroism was that movement, ideology or collection of attitudes primarily concerned with the dignity of the black people wherever they might be. Pan-negroism brought sub-Saharan Africans and Afro-Americans together. Pan-Africanism, on the other hand, became a continental movement within Africa, and from its point of view the Arabs of North Africa were more important than black Americans. Indeed, Tom Mboya of Kenya used to argue that the proof that pan-Africanism was not a *racial* movement lay in the fact that the Organization of African Unity (OAU) included both Arab and black states.

Historically, pan-Africanism was born out of pan-negroism. It was black Americans like W.E.B.DuBois and West Indians like George Padmore who helped to make pan-Africanism globally conspicuous. But while the foundation of pan-negroism remained an affinity of colour the basis of pan-Africanism became an attachment to a continent.

Until 1945 the pan-negro movement was led by black Americans and West Indians; Africans had only subsidiary roles. At an earlier conference following the end of the First World War, pan-Africanists like Du Bois appealed to the powers at Versailles to let the African colonies be ruled or administered by fellow black people imported from the New World. In these earlier phases there was a paternalistic streak in black Americans and West Indians in their attitude to their black African brothers. They saw themselves as a higher stage of 'civilization' – and therefore qualified to take charge of their parental continent until the parent was civilized.

But although there was this paradoxical filial paternalism among black Americans and West Indians, the greatest of them were deeply concerned about Africa's future. They saw the liberation of the black peoples in their own part of the globe as inseparable from the liberation of Africa.

With 1945 the balance of diplomatic effectiveness among the blacks began to shift. Two participants in the 1945 Pan-African Congress in Manchester came to exercise significant influence over the fortunes of their own countries, and of the continent as a whole. These two were Kwame Nkrumah, who was later to preside over independent Ghana, and Jomo Kenyatta, destined to be the founding father of the Kenyan nation.

The Manchester Congress addressed itself to questions of equality and dignity for the black man. Commitment to actual African liberation was still couched in modest terms. The ambition was clearly there and was beginning to find expression. But the immediate emphasis was on social equality, respect for African dignity and an end to racial segregation.

Yet the Manchester Congress was a forum of nationalism, just as the San Francisco Conference was an exercise in internationalism. Indeed, pan-Africanism as a movement is at once nationalistic and international. It has remained nationalistic in its commitment to the dignity of the black man and the well-being of the African continent. But, by involving different states and black people from different regions of the world, pan-Africanism has included a profound international dimension. The internationalism of this movement has been a regional or racial internationalism. It has been either pan-continental or pan-pigmental. But the internationalism envisaged at San Francisco was global.

Yet, from the African point of view, the interaction between nationalism and internationalism symbolized by the two conferences continued in other forms and other areas. It is probably safe to say that few African nationalists had, in fact, read the UN Charter. And those who had read it were less interested in the specific procedures for assuring world peace than in the reaffirmation of 'faith in fundamental human rights, in the equal rights of men and women and of nations large and small'. In spite of this, the UN Charter did become a kind of global bill of rights for the underprivileged.

For Africa, the 'Age of Nkrumah' began in 1945, since 1945 was the year when he assumed a leading role in the Manchester Congress. In that year also, de Gaulle had just left England to return to liberated France. We might best capture the dreams of both personalities for their countries by tracing them back to their 'exile' in Britain in the 1940s.

Exile and return

To study Nkrumah and de Gaulle together is to study the nature of nationalism itself. In de Gaulle we saw the nationalism of a big power trying to reassert itself after a period of decay and decline. In Nkrumah we saw the nationalism of weaker countries seeking to rise from the depths of insignificance. In de Gaulle we saw the sense of history in proud austerity; in Nkrumah a sense of the future in impatient dynamism.

Each loved his own country and the continent in which it was situated. In other words, there was in de Gaulle both French nationalism and European nationalism; just as there was in Nkrumah both Ghanaian and African nationalism. But the balance within the two men was different. It is true that de Gaulle aspired to eliminate or mitigate the American hegemony in Europe, to ignore the ideological gulf between the East and West. De Gaulle dreamt of a Europe extending harmoniously from the Urals to the Pyrenees. But he was a French nationalist first and a European nationalist second. He could not see France merged into a larger entity in which France would lose its historic distinctiveness. De Gaulle's united Europe was, in his own words, 'a Europe of the fatherlands'.

But, if de Gaulle was French first and European second, Nkrumah was African first and Ghanaian second. This combination was both Nkrumah's strength and weakness. His dreams captured one of the fundamental urges of modern Africans. Nkrumah became the spokesman of the most ambitious school of pan-Africanism. He also became the ultimate symbol of the defiant assertion of African dignity in a hostile neo-imperial world. But his commitment to Africa was not matched by a similar consideration for Ghanaians. Within Ghana he drifted towards policies of 'muddling through', and left Ghanaians much poorer and, as individuals, less free than he found them. It would be foolish to say that Nkrumah did not love Ghana. A man of such political sensitivities could not escape the more immediate patriotic ties. But he did put greater emphasis on African dreams than on Ghana's realities.

Both men schemed for their country's independence in the 1940s in England. For de Gaulle it was the earlier 1940s, when a beaten France was under German occupation. De Gaulle without a power base was the voice of free France outside France. Stubborn and proud, he became profoundly unpopular with President Roosevelt and with Prime Minister Churchill.

De Gaulle, then, worked isolatedly in wartime Britain for the liberation of France from Nazi rule, and with allies who were on the whole rather exasperating and exasperated. In 1945 he returned to his country, to a hero's welcome. In 1945 Nkrumah was scheming in a different direction. He was helping to organize the Manchester Congress as a move for the liberation of Africa.

And yet, even then, there was an issue which was to lie at the heart of Nkrumah's relations with de Gaulle's France: the participation of French-speaking Africans in the pan-African movement. The nearest thing to the representation of French-speaking Africa at the meeting in Manchester was the presence of Dr Raphael Armattoe from Togoland. But Armattoe was very much a detached guest among African militants. At Manchester Armattoe equivocally remarked: 'It is sometimes questioned whether French West Africans have any feeling of national consciousness, but I can say that French West Africans would be happier if they were governing themselves.' Nevertheless, Armattoe went on to add that French West Africans 'sometimes envy the British Africans their intense national feeling.'

Nkrumah was puzzled by this Francophone aloofness, but he resolved to challenge it. De Gaulle had just returned to France. Nkrumah followed soon after. His mission was to reawaken in French-speaking Africans a commitment to African liberation.

Nkrumah had by then become the secretary of the West African National Secretariat. His activities included organizing meetings, working for the Coloured Workers' Association of Great Britain and trying to start a

Top Mau Mau violence in Kenya (1952-6), the most savage expression of anti-British feeling to accompany decolonization in Africa
Above Jomo Kenyatta, first Kenyan prime minister, on independence in 1963

Tanzanian cartoon attacks the threat of 'neo-colonialism'

African independence 1954-69

independent 1954		independent 1969		dependent
1	Algeria	17	Guinea	33	Rhodesia
2	Angola	18	Portuguese Guinea		UDI after 1965
3	Botswana	19	Ifni	34	Rwanda
4	Burundi	20	Ivory Coast	35	Senegal
5	Cameroon	21	Kenya	36	Sierra Leone
6	Central African	22	Lesotho	37	Somali
	Republic	23	Liberia	38	South Africa
7	Chad	24	Libya	39	South West Africa
8	Congo	25	Madagascar	40	Spanish Sahara
9	Dahomey	26	Malawi	41	Sudan
10	Egypt	27	Mali	42	Swaziland
11	Equatorial Guinea	28	Mauritania	43	Tanzania
12	Ethiopia	29	Morocco	44	Toga
13	French Somaliland	30	Mozambique	45	Tunisia
14	Gabon	31	Niger	46	Uganda
15	Gambia	32	Nigeria	47	Upper Volta
16	Ghana			48	Zambia

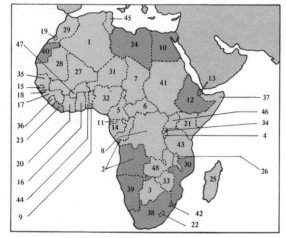

Left Sékou Touré, who took Guinea into independence from France in 1958; all French aid was abruptly withdrawn by de Gaulle

Below Anti-independence supporters in the French Somaliland referendum of 1966

nationalist newspaper, *The New African.* It was in an attempt to involve French-speaking Africans in pan-African activities that Nkrumah crossed the Channel and went to see African members of the French National Assembly. This, of course, was one of the major differences between French and British policy. The French system allowed for the possibility of Africans becoming members of the National Assembly in Paris, and, through involvement in metropolitan politics, developing an empathy with the imperial power unknown among English-speaking nationalists. For the British, on the other hand, there could be no question of a Nkrumah sitting in the House of Commons as a member of the British parliament. The system did not permit such political interlocking. Perhaps in that lay part of the explanation as to why French-speaking Africans were less rebellious against their metropolitan power than English-speaking Africans were beginning to be.

Nkrumah wanted to remind these members of the French National Assembly of the greater cause. He managed to meet Sourous Apithy, Léopold Senghor, Lamine Gueye and Houphouët-Boigny. Unlike him, they were not firebrand nationalists. But at that stage they were capable of respecting the Nkrumah version of African nationalism. As a result of Nkrumah's visit Apithy and Senghor later went to London to 'represent French West Africans at the West African conference' which Nkrumah organized.

Both Nkrumah and de Gaulle had become national symbols while in exile in England. In the case of Nkrumah, his organizational skills and his journalistic efforts finally came to the attention of political figures in the Gold Coast. It was not long before Nkrumah received letters from Ako Adjei and J.B.Danquah urging him to go back to the Gold Coast and become general secretary of the new United Gold Coast Convention. After some heartsearching, Nkrumah accepted. In November 1947, Nkrumah left London to return home to the colonial Gold Coast.

Both de Gaulle and Nkrumah soon became disenchanted with politicians. In January 1946 de Gaulle summoned the members of the government to a meeting. With characteristic abruptness, de Gaulle declared that he had had enough. He was withdrawing forthwith and handing his resignation to the president of the National Assembly. But he also believed that one day the nation would again look to him for salvation after the chaos which the parliamentarians were likely to leave.

In the case of Nkrumah, the disenchantment with the politicians who had invited him was for different reasons. It was not so much that they were selfish and irresponsible. It was more because, as distinguished lawyers of the Gold Coast, they seemed not populist enough or radical enough for the next phase of Ghana's struggle for independence.

Then the pressures from the younger and more proletarian parts of Nkrumah's following began to be felt. One day Nkrumah was confronted by an excited crowd which wanted him to resign as general secretary of the United Gold Coast Convention, dominated by lawyers, and form a more radical party of his own. 'Resign' the crowd shouted – 'Resign and lead us!' Nkrumah suddenly felt that they meant it. He made up his mind to resign not only the general secretaryship but also his membership of the United Gold Coast Convention. Standing on the platform, surrounded by an expectant crowd, he asked for pen and paper. Then, using somebody's back as support, he wrote out his official resignation and read it aloud.

The enthusiasm of the crowd was deafening. A woman supporter jumped up on to the platform and led the singing of the hymn 'Lead, Kindly Light'. Nkrumah relates: 'What with the strain of it all and the excitement, the singing of this hymn was more than I could take. I covered my eyes with my handkerchief, a gesture which was followed by many . . . the impact of all this made me suddenly humble and lonely, and the tears that came were shed not from sorrow but from a deep sense of gladness and dedication.'

Disenchantment impelled de Gaulle and Nkrumah towards different courses of action. For de Gaulle it led to his swift withdrawal from active politics, until recalled from obscurity by the events of 1958. With Nkrumah,

however, disenchantment with the politicians of the United Gold Coast Convention led not to a withdrawal but to a greater democratization of his political base. He stopped being secretary to a middle-class nationalism and engaged himself in a movement of 'verandah boys'.

Colonialism by consent

The end of the Second World War initiated two processes which have left their impact on the second half of the twentieth century. One was decolonization on a grand scale. The other was the inauguration of the Nuclear Age, ushered into fiery existence at Hiroshima and Nagasaki. Nkrumah and de Gaulle clashed in their policies in both these areas.

The conflict between them over decolonization was, as we indicated, foreshadowed by the relative Francophilia of French-speaking Africa in the 1940s. The confrontation came fairly soon after de Gaulle's return to power. The year 1957 saw Nkrumah's assumption of power as the head of an independent government. The year 1958 saw de Gaulle's grand resumption of authority in France.

Top Algerian riots; in the mid-fifties the French had nearly half a million soldiers in the country
Above Demonstration by the militant National Liberation Front formed in 1954 in Algeria

Rumours spread of an impending military coup in Algeria. France was anxious, the Western world was anxious, the Eastern bloc waited. The Algerians wondered, engaged as they were in a bitter war for independence. Soldiers were blaming the politicians in Paris for their own failure to subdue the National Liberation Movement in Algeria. A military coup was a tempting solution. Only one man, it seemed, could save France from civil war or a military takeover. The nation started clamouring for him. By the end of May, after one false start, President Coty had extended the invitation to de Gaulle just in time to save the country from the army's threatened seizure of power. De Gaulle formed the last administration of the disintegrating Fourth Republic. On 1 June 1958 the National Assembly gave him a comfortable majority in his task of restoring the nation to stability.

De Gaulle was determined to create a new republic, and he was going to ask all Frenchmen, and all subjects of France in the colonies, to vote 'Yes' or 'No' in a massive referendum. Internally in France he was going to reduce the power of the National Assembly, and strengthen the executive so as to restore order and authority.

It was over his colonial policy that he clashed with Nkrumah. De Gaulle visited the colonies offering them a stark choice. France's subjects in the West Indies and in Africa, excluding Algeria, were going to be offered independence if they wanted it. But if they chose independence, de Gaulle made clear, it would have to be total independence – the severance of every tie with France, political, financial, economic and educational.

The alternatives were agonizing for French-speaking Africans. Would they be able to survive economically? Could the educational system support itself if French teachers departed? Would their welfare services, then subsidized, be able to continue? Would their products, accorded easy access in France, find alternative markets? Would their nations be viable at all?

Below In the July 1962 referendum, Algerians voted overwhelmingly for independence, which was proclaimed: de Gaulle's ambitions for France remained imperial though no longer colonial

Nkrumah had declared that the independence of Ghana was meaningless if it was not accompanied by the independence of the rest of Africa. In 1958 Ghana was still the only black country south of the Sahara to have won independence from Britain or France. Here, in the de Gaulle referendum, lay the possibility of having several additional black African states emerging into independence. Nkrumah sent out feelers to different African political leaders, offering to help the vote for independence.

Nkrumah perceived what was at stake in the referendum. African chiefs had formerly sometimes been given the impression that they had a right to decide for themselves what was going to happen to their territory. In fact, as a rule, the sovereignty accorded by the imperial powers was the right of self-alienation. The African had the right to surrender his rights to someone else. Solemn treaties were sometimes drawn up between Queen Victoria and tribal potentates. Thus the doctrine of colonialism by consent was born. This exercise in negotiation in the British imperial tradition lasted a long time. In the beginning the British negotiated with chiefs and kings in their own compounds in Africa in order to prepare the way for colonization.

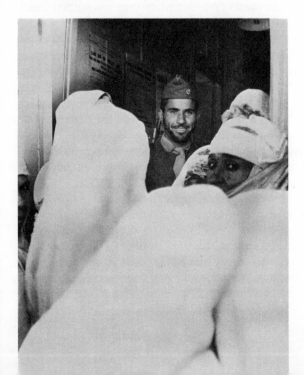

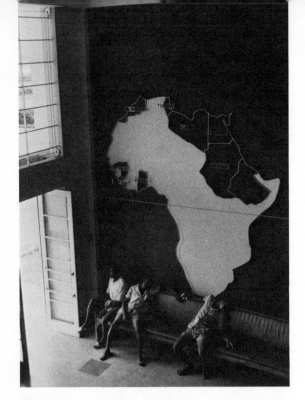

Top Three boys taking a rest under the map of Africa in Ghana's Parliament building
Above The Ghana-Guinea-Mali Union, proclaimed in December 1960 by the three countries' presidents; but it was never to be effectively finalized

Fifty years later Britain was negotiating with politicians, sometimes at Lancaster House in London, in order to prepare the way for decolonization. In French-speaking Africa, the doctrine of colonialism by consent assumed concrete, if brief, realization with the de Gaulle referendum of 1958.

Nkrumah's contacts varied from one country to another. In Niger, for example, he seems to have sought the support of Djibo Bakary, a Marxist-orientated politician and journalist, and one of the main organizers of the communist-orientated trade union movement. Earlier in 1958 Djibo was among the most vociferous advocates both of a new French West African federation and of immediate independence from France. When the referendum came he announced that he would campaign for an anti-imperial vote. He seems to have announced this even before Sékou Touré of Guinea reached a similar decision.

But in the momentous referendum of 1958 colony after colony preferred to retain the imperial link. In Niger itself the vote in favour of the French community was by no means overwhelming. Only Sékou Touré in Guinea managed to mobilize the electorate to vote 'Yes' in favour of independence. Those who had fallen short of this courageous 'Yes' deeply disappointed Nkrumah. But that there was one African country which had stood up to General de Gaulle and said 'We are not French' – this was enough to atone for much of the disappointment.

And yet Guinea did pay heavily. De Gaulle was a man who took his own words seriously. He had said that a vote for independence was a vote for total severance. French facilities, French personnel, French equipment, were pulled out of Guinea – lock, stock and barrel. It is reported that even telephones were wrenched from the walls and taken away to France. Nkrumah realized that what Sékou Touré needed above all else in that shock was to know he had friends. Nkrumah not only promptly congratulated Touré and the people of Guinea for their vote; he made a financial grant to tide Guinea over during the initial period of independence. Nkrumah made available to Guinea a loan of £10 million, and the two countries planned closer association.

Two months later Ghana and the Republic of Guinea made formal moves to unite. They described their union as a nucleus for a union of African states. They also envisaged it as an alternative to de Gaulle's vision of a French community. Nkrumah planned to draw more and more of the French colonies from the French orbit into the mainstream of pan-Africanism and African unification.

After the referendum and the vote to remain under France, some people assumed that the colonies would remain colonies indefinitely. But de Gaulle's vision soon allowed for the granting of formal sovereignty to the colonies, though with the retention of close economic and cultural ties with France. Nkrumah was not satisfied with these concessions. But at that time he was more interested in promoting African unity than in ending French neo-colonialism in West Africa.

The next convert after Guinea to pan-Africanism was Mali. And the Ghana-Guinea-Mali Union came into being, again more ambitious in intent than in effect. The Union of African States, as it was called, envisaged a common currency which never materialized. There was a proposal that each country should have a resident minister serving in each other's capitals, but this was never fully worked out. There were abortive plans to coordinate internal economic and social policies. The residual solidarity was of periodic consultation on African and international affairs by the three presidents – Nkrumah, Sékou Touré and Modibo Keita.

Then Nkrumah turned his attention to Upper Volta, seeking to woo the Voltaic nation away from the domination of Houphouët-Boigny and de Gaulle. There was even a ceremony of 'knocking down the wall' when Nkrumah and the Voltaic president, Maurice Yameogo, declared their determination 'by concrete measures quickly to achieve the total independence and effective unity of Africa' – and as a first step they agreed to knock down a wall, specially erected for the purpose. This was to symbolize

the agreement that 'freedom of movement for persons and groups shall be the rule'. More prosaically, there was an agreement for the equitable refund of customs dues collected on re-exports from Ghana to be paid into the Upper Volta treasury. Nkrumah's economic agreement with Upper Volta cost Ghana £3,500,000. Nkrumah saw it as a stage towards the inclusion of Upper Volta in the Ghana-Guinea-Mali Union. But his co-presidents in the Union were less optimistic about Voltaic participation. Indeed, the presidents of Guinea and Mali pointedly stayed away from the wall ceremony. On the whole Touré and Keita were right in their pessimism about the seriousness of Upper Volta's intentions; Nkrumah was wrong in his optimism.

The drift towards subversion

Meanwhile new issues intruded to divide Ghana from the majority of French-speaking countries. On some de Gaulle had firm opinions. Pre-eminent among these was the future of Algeria. When the soldiers hailed de Gaulle's assumption of power, they thought he would guarantee victory and retain Algeria as part of France. De Gaulle did regard that as one major possibility.

In the Arab world the Algerians had a lot of support, including support among those countries which had been under French rule. But in Africa south of the Sahara the cause of the Algerians was inadequately understood. Nkrumah was among the first to urge Algeria's separation from France. As he put it in an address to the United Nations in 1960:

> France cannot win a military victory in Algeria. If she hopes to do so, then her hopes are false and unrelated to the realities of the situation. . . . From whatever angle you view this problem Algeria is African and will always remain so, in the same manner that France is French. No accident of history, such as has occurred in Algeria, can ever succeed in turning an inch of African soil into an extension of any other continent.

De Gaulle was contemptuous of the UN, especially of its capacity to deal with the situation in Algeria. Nkrumah had bitter feelings about big-power control of the UN, especially in relation to the problem of the Congo at a time when Lumumba, Kasavubu and Tshombe were struggling for political survival and power. In some ways de Gaulle was right in his estimate. It was certainly unlikely that the UN could have resolved the crisis. Perhaps the UN was a symbol of bigger things than it could accomplish. It was an aspiration. Nkrumah's vision of the world had room for such an organization, and envisaged more effective African participation in the

Top African stained glass, by a leading young Ethiopian artist, Abework Teclé
Above Dancers at a 1966 Festival of the Negro Arts in Senegal which involved thirty-nine countries, including representatives from Britain, France and the USA as well as African and Latin American nations

Right The Organization of African Unity – opening session, May 1963: thirty founding members had as their object to 'promote the unity and solidarity of the African states'

world body. But de Gaulle's imagination did not include such global supra-nationality. He was against the UN involvement in the Congo, let alone in Algeria.

Most French-speaking African states were solidly behind de Gaulle, and strongly critical of the Nkrumah school of African nationalism. The solution of the Algerian problem was in their eyes to be left for ultimate negotiation between Algeria and France. The rest of Africa and of the world should keep out.

Meanwhile the concept of 'Euro-Africa' was consolidating itself economically as well as diplomatically. The Treaty of Rome of 1957 which set up the European Economic Community had been concluded before de Gaulle's resumption of power. That treaty had associated French colonial territories with the European Economic Community. But by 1960 most of French-speaking Africa had become formally independent. 'Euro-Africa' received a new stimulus when the association was envisaged as between a sovereign Africa and a sovereign Europe.

De Gaulle wished to impose outer limits to this association. When Harold Macmillan initiated British moves to enter the EEC, de Gaulle had reservations, not only about British entry, but also about the place of Nigeria, and later the East African Community, within the EEC. But in the initial stages of bargaining the French government was militantly protective of the interests of former French Africa.

In the face of these developments, and especially after his experience with Upper Volta, Nkrumah became even more disillusioned by the former French colonies. He became convinced that many of them were no more than, to use his own words, 'client states, independent in name'. Their luke-warm attitude towards the FLN in Algeria was only one manifestation of their continued dependence on France.

As Nkrumah became disillusioned, he adopted the alternative policy of supporting dissidents from French-speaking countries. Ghana became a

Nkrumah's speech to Parliament in 1962 in which he declined the life presidency of Ghana

Decapitated statue of Nkrumah during the bloodless army takeover in 1966; opposition to his policies had grown after a serious fall in the world price of cocoa (Ghana's chief revenue) and the foreign debts which resulted from lavish industrial development schemes

haven for rebels from Francophone Africa. This factor, perhaps more than any other, aroused the anger of the French-speaking African states at their meeting in Nouakchott in February 1965; and it made them threaten to boycott the meeting of the OAU scheduled to take place in Accra later in 1965. The price which they exacted for their attendance in Accra was a new 'good neighbour' policy to be followed by Ghana, especially in regard to the rebels from French-speaking Africa. Ghana might still give political asylum, but she was no longer to afford the rebels a public platform for their grievances, or a training-ground for their resistance.

Although Ghana did make some gestures to her neighbours along these lines, and was keen to ensure the success of the OAU Accra Conference, all indications remained that Ghana would find it hard to maintain good neighbourliness. The general evidence suggested that Ghana under Nkrumah was prepared to alienate most of the current regimes of Francophone Africa, in the hope of a more militant pan-African partnership in the future. Nkrumah seemed to believe that time was on the side of the radical French-speaking Africans.

In assessing Nkrumah's impact on relations between African states, we might divide the continent into three categories – Arab Africa, English-speaking black Africa, and French-speaking black Africa. Nkrumah did try to establish closer ties with each. Within twelve months he contracted two symbolic marriages. One was his own personal marriage to an Egyptian girl. The other was the token territorial union between Ghana and Guinea on 23 November 1958.

But Nkrumah's subsequent role in bringing together different sections varied according to the section. In relations between Arab Africa and black Africa, his influence was, on the whole, unifying. But in relations between English-speaking black Africa and French-speaking black Africa Nkrumah was, on balance, a divisive force.

If France had continued on her downward trend following the Second

Léopold Senghor, president of Senegal, on a visit to the Elysée Palace in 1961, shortly after independence. Senghor, a poet of some standing, has published several volumes of French verse on *négritude* themes

Above Over 20,000 Kenyans at a pre-independence general election rally held by Tom Mboya, later Kenyatta's minister for economic planning

Right Three East African heads of state, Nyerere, Kaunda and Kenyatta together in Mombasa for the commissioning ceremony of a new ship of the East African National Shipping line in 1969

Tanzanian national servicemen on the march with African freedom posters

Below Rebels in Angola, where the Portuguese stubbornly – and expensively – resisted independence movements in the sixties
Bottom Ian Smith, prime minister of white-dominated Rhodesia: for many Africans, British attitudes over UDI were one more nail in the colonial coffin

World War, the mystique that she held for many Francophone Africans might well have disappeared. The relationship between France and the majority of Francophone African states depended, not simply on economic factors, but also upon the apparently mystical spell which France could still exert. If economics were all that mattered, Guinea and Mali would not have attempted to assert themselves. Upper Volta would not have come so near to pursuing an area of autonomous foreign policy. But while French aid and concessions in trade remained paramount, there was in addition simple attachment and awe.

It is especially with regard to this element that de Gaulle was so important. His success in reconstituting the pride and prestige of France helped to maintain the emotional bonds between France and those she had ruled. English-speaking Africans in the colonies had once also felt the magic of imperial splendour. When independence came it was inevitable that some of this should evaporate, yet much could have been saved if post-imperial Britain had succeeded in dramatizing the new dignity suitable for the post-imperial era.

Britain, however, did not produce a de Gaulle. England's spell was broken after the bonds of the Empire were severed. But France's spell retained its hold partly because de Gaulle had assumed power at that critical moment in the period of decolonization. The act of disengaging from Empire was made to appear as a grand design of French magnanimity. De Gaulle succeeded in creating the impression that France in imperial decline was, at the same time, France in an international ascendancy. So Francophone Africans continued to follow him with awe. Nkrumah's rival designs to liberate French-speaking Africans and bring them into the main-stream of pan-Africanism were doomed to failure for the time being.

Two nuclear visions

As with decolonization, so over the new problem of nuclear power, Nkrumah and de Gaulle clashed. Again much of the divergence was con-nected with their different conceptions of nationalism. For de Gaulle the acquisition of nuclear status was inseparable from a resurgence of France as a world power. He directed the technocratic and scientific resources of the country towards the fulfilment of this ambition. He looked forward to a European self-reliance in defence. But he wanted to ensure that France was not a mere puppet to American nuclear strategy. To the dismay of his Western allies de Gaulle started demanding a reform of the NATO Com-mand. He also refused to allow American nuclear weapons to be stock-piled in France except on condition that they should be under French control.

By contrast, Nkrumah was committed to the elimination of nuclear weaponry. Nkrumah was consistent in this, going back to some of the positions taken on the eve of independence with regard to the general implications of the Bandung Conference of Afro-Asian countries in 1955. Nkrumah was capable of censuring both the West and the East on matters connected with nuclear power. In September 1961 the first world conference of non-aligned powers was held in Belgrade. One of their aims was to reduce world tension and, if possible, eliminate the hazards of nuclear confronta-tion. There was also considerable unease about the spread of radiation from nuclear tests. And yet, in spite of the Belgrade meeting, the Soviet Union decided to resume nuclear tests in a way that seemed almost a calculated insult.

At the time they could not risk an open censure of the Soviet Union with-out risking a big cleavage within their ranks. The communiqué of the conference did not therefore specifically condemn the Soviet Union. But some of the leading figures at the Belgrade Conference, including India's Nehru and Egypt's Nasser, did express disapproval. And Nkrumah de-clared emphatically that the Soviet tests had been 'a shock to me'. Nkru-mah's position was that disarmament was necessary not only because of the destructive madness of the armaments race, but also because it reduced the world's capability to deal with poverty and underdevelopment. In pursuit

Right The Sharpeville massacre: 72 killed and 186 injured, when police opened fire on an African demonstration against the pass laws on 21 March 1960. UN repercussions proved ineffective

Below An anti-apartheid poster mocks white South African fears
Bottom South African prime minister Verwoerd, responsible for the extensions of apartheid in the sixties, was assassinated on 6 September 1966, but apparently without political motive. The assassin was white – and judged insane

of this aim Nkrumah's government set aside funds for an assembly to be held in Accra, in June 1962, to which were invited representatives of organizations throughout the world whose aim was the establishment of world peace. The preparatory committee for this assembly in Accra agreed that the agenda would include 'the examination of such fundamental problems as hunger, disease, ignorance, poverty and servitude, with a view to utilizing for social purposes resources now misused as a result of the armaments race'.

But the most direct clash between Nkrumah and de Gaulle came over the issue of French nuclear tests in the Sahara. In 1960 France entered the Nuclear Age with the explosion of a nuclear device. Ghana became the platform from which not only African protests but also protests from other world liberal organizations could be launched against the French experiment. In December 1959 and January 1960 an international team of representatives from Africa, Britain, the United States and even from France itself, attempted to enter the testing-site at Reggan in the Sahara. Their starting-point was Ghana, under the leadership of the Reverend Michael Scott. But the team was prevented from proceeding beyond the borders of Upper Volta. They were confronted by armed guards under the control of French authorities. The guards sealed off the area and confiscated the team's vehicles and equipment.

Just as Nkrumah believed that Ghana's freedom was incomplete so long as any part of Africa was still under foreign rule, so he believed that Ghana's safety was not secure while any part of Africa was used for nuclear purposes. Nuclear fall-out was no respecter of boundaries. Neither was Nkrumah's plan for pan-Africanism. These two positions merged into an outcry of protest as de Gaulle pursued his plan.

Nkrumah called for positive action against French nuclear tests. As soon as the tests took place, Nkrumah froze French economic assets within Ghana. When France exploded a second bomb, Nkrumah recalled his ambassador from Paris. And in April 1960, he called a conference in Accra to discuss 'positive action and security in Africa'. He did so in consultation with other African states. Many of the French-speaking ones were dubious, if not hostile. But, for once, Nigeria and Ghana saw eye to eye. Nkrumah hoped to urge greater exertion by African peoples themselves to proclaim their indignation. His attempts to mobilize large-scale protest movements were not successful, though he gained a wide audience for his views.

Once again it was a clash of nationalism. Nuclear status for de Gaulle became a functional alternative to imperial status in the world. De Gaulle, who had come into power partly with the purpose of consolidating France's control over Algeria, was moving in the direction of recognizing the inevitability of decolonization. The part of the Sahara which he used for his nuclear test was, in fact, in Algeria – one of the last services rendered by colonized Algeria in the grand design of French power. De Gaulle played it well. He gradually disengaged from the notion that Algeria was French;

and he began enigmatically to sing the song that Algeria was Algerian.

But he could not wait until decolonization was complete before embarking on an alternative path to France's grandeur. Grandeur based on an empire was gone; the new prestige must be based on technological power and global diplomatic strategy. In an important sense de Gaulle's France became the first major power to opt for non-alignment. Nkrumah, on the other hand, saw the Sahara nuclear tests as a violation of the sanctity of Africa's soil. He also saw it as a manifestation of big-power arrogance. As Nkrumah put it:

General de Gaulle is reported to have said recently that while other countries have enough nuclear weapons to destroy the whole world France must also have nuclear weapons with which to defend herself. I would say here . . . that Africa is not interested in such 'defence' which means no more than the ability to share in the honour of destroying mankind. We in Africa wish to live and develop. We are not freeing ourselves from centuries of imperialism and colonialism only to be maimed and destroyed by nuclear weapons. (*I Speak of Freedom*)

But in the next few years Nkrumah began to think more deeply about the meaning of nuclear science for the contemporary era. De Gaulle had decided that the honour of France could not be safeguarded without French entry into the Nuclear Age. Could Africa's honour be safeguarded without a similar nuclear initiation? Nkrumah began to dream about pan-African participation in nuclear science. His conception was still different from that of de Gaulle. Nkrumah did not dream of building an African nuclear capability to rival that of the big powers. But he did dream of developing a nuclear technology effective enough to give Africa status in the world.

But while de Gaulle linked nuclear science to French patriotism Nkrumah preferred to link it to socialism. At the ceremony at which he laid the foundation-stone of Ghana's Atomic Reactor Centre in Kwabenya near Accra, he said: 'We must ourselves take part in the pursuit of scientific and technological research as a means of providing the basis of our socialist society. Socialism without science is void. . . .'

The reactor was an extravagance which Ghana could ill afford. Nkrumah related it to socialism, but in effect, as in the case of de Gaulle, nuclear status was related to nationalism. African dignity began to be associated in his mind with African participation in scientific research.

On 24 February 1966 Nkrumah was overthrown by a military coup. Three years later de Gaulle stepped down from power after a defeat in a referendum. It was a military crisis in 1958 which brought de Gaulle into power, and a constitutional verdict which led to his fall from power. In the case of Nkrumah the means were reversed. It was a military act which threw him out of power; just as it was a constitutional judgement which brought him into power in an election in Ghana more than a decade earlier.

The interplay between the military and politics defined interaction between these two historic figures. Nuclear power and its dimension for security; empire and neo-colonialism and their implications for freedom. These were the areas within whose bounds the African and the Frenchman had moments of contact and conflict. And the stream of world history flowed on.

Top A pre-independence picture of Patrice Lumumba, first prime minister of the Congo, imprisoned by the Belgians for inciting riots in 1959
Above Riots in Leopoldville; Belgian withdrawal brought chaos and the murder of Lumumba on 17 January 1961

Below Tshombe, responsible for the secession of the rich province of Katanga in July 1960

Towards the future

Nkrumah's views about the nature of neo-colonialism and external manipulation have gained wider acceptance among intellectuals in Africa since his day, though they may not have transformed the policies of government on the continent. An important area of discussion in the whole relation of Euro-Africa has hinged on the need for development and external assistance. The French record of aid to her former colonies, making her the largest world contributor in relation to her own gross national product, has been part of the picture which unfolded under de Gaulle's leadership. Sometimes Nkrumah shared the belief held by other African nationalists that the very act of receiving aid – be it from the East or the West – was fundamentally neo-colonialist. Nkrumah's answer to the dilemma was

something we might call the 'Doctrine of Balanced Benefaction' – the idea that the best defence against neo-colonialism is to diversify one's bene- factors. Nkrumah could himself obtain from the World Bank and the Western powers assistance to build the Volta River Project and from the Soviet Union money for the generation of power in some sectors of the project. This was viewed by Nkrumah as 'neo-alignment in action'. And yet he underestimated the liberating potential of the EEC for Francophone Africa. Reliance on a community of six could mean greater economic sovereignty for French-speaking Africans than reliance on France alone.

After Nkrumah's fall the torch of African self-reliance passed to Mwalimu Julius K. Nyerere, president of Tanzania. Tanzania has taken a decisive lead in trying to live up to the doctrine of 'Balanced Benefaction'. Over the years the country's benefactors have included the US, the USSR, com- munist China, West Germany, East Germany, Israel, Egypt and others. Even on specific projects Tanzania has sometimes, either by accident or design, ended up dividing one project between two ideological camps. The preliminary survey for the Tanzania-Zambia Railway was to be paid for by the West (Britain and Canada) whereas the actual railway was to be financed by mainland China.

In many ways the person nearest to being an ideological successor to

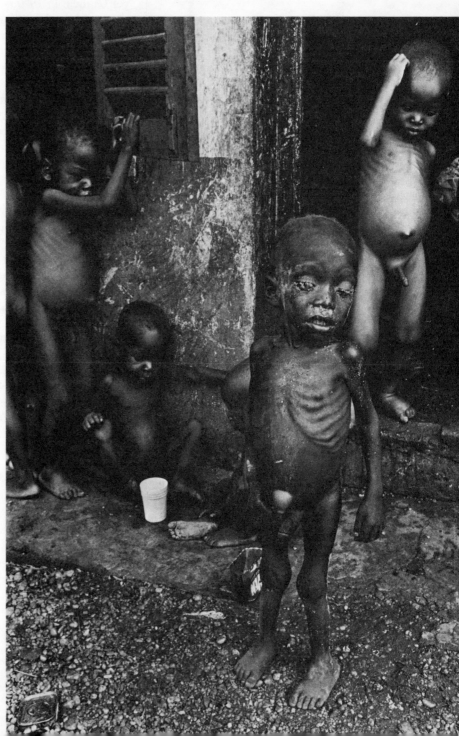

Top Colonel Ojukwu, Biafran military leader; civil war broke out on 6 July 1967
Above Biafran troops surround Nigerians

Left General Gowon, head of army and government in Nigeria from July 1966; his appointment was followed by massive tribal rioting and the secession of Biafra in the following year

Right Starving children in Biafra; the plight of civilians as Biafra was more and more tightly besieged aroused world-wide concern

Population 1969

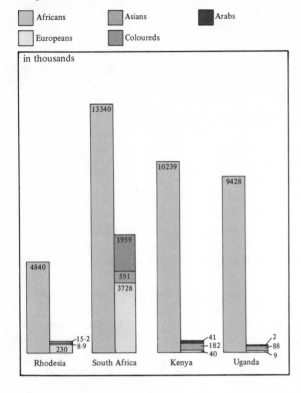

Legend:
- Africans
- Asians
- Arabs
- Europeans
- Coloureds

in thousands

	Rhodesia	South Africa	Kenya	Uganda
	4840	13340	10239	9428
	230	1959	41	2
	15·2	591	182	88
	8·9	3728	40	9

Bamboo stalls and modern buildings in Lagos, Nigeria:
a typical African urban contrast

Per capita income 1958-68

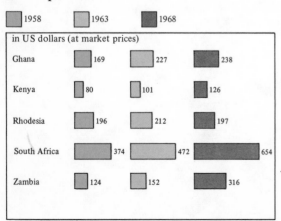

Legend:
- 1958
- 1963
- 1968

in US dollars (at market prices)

	1958	1963	1968
Ghana	169	227	238
Kenya	80	101	126
Rhodesia	196	212	197
South Africa	374	472	654
Zambia	124	152	316

Nkrumah is indeed Julius Nyerere. Domestically he has represented a radical school of social transformation; and continually he has figured as the most militant voice of pan-Africanism. The two roles overlapped over the issue of Rhodesia in 1965. The foreign ministers of the African countries had given Britain an ultimatum to bring down the regime of Ian Smith, or face a break of diplomatic relations. When the time came for African states to implement their resolution, the great majority backed down. Among the countries within the Commonwealth only Nyerere's Tanzania and Nkrumah's Ghana carried out the ultimatum. Nyerere announced his severance of relations with Britain first. He was delighted when news reached him that Nkrumah had followed suit.

History may not repeat itself, but there are occasions when the future is strikingly reminiscent of the past. It was Nkrumah who rose to the occasion and went to the aid of Sékou Touré of Guinea in 1958 when de Gaulle ruthlessly cut Guinea off and left her destitute. In November 1970 a different kind of threat faced Guinea. This time a contingent of mercenaries, the bulk of whom were seemingly Portuguese, threatened the independence of Conakry, the capital of Guinea. The first African country to rise materially to the occasion was Nyerere's Tanzania. In 1958 Nkrumah had provided £10 million to help Guinea when French imperialism abruptly moved *out* of Guinea. In 1970 Nyerere provided 10 million shillings to Guinea when a new form of imperial threat was attempting to come *into* the country.

But has there been a successor to Charles de Gaulle as well? Within Africa the nearest equivalent has in fact been the president of the Ivory Coast, President Félix Houphouët-Boigny. There was a period of overlap. Sometimes the overlapping, curiously enough, included areas of policy shared with Tanzania. Pre-eminent among these was the issue of Biafra while the war in Nigeria still raged. De Gaulle's sympathy for Biafra was well known, though he did not go as far as extending French recognition. But Houphouët-Boigny of the Ivory Coast did extend recognition, in the hope of strengthening the secessionist province's ability to maintain a separate identity. Before the Ivory Coast, Nyerere's Tanzania had set the precedent of recognizing Biafra. On the issue of Biafra de Gaulle himself, de Gaulle's prospective successor in Africa and Nkrumah's ideological successor did, for different motives, share a policy orientation.

There were other areas of overlap between de Gaulle's own influence and the neo-Gaullist influence exercised by Houphouët-Boigny. Even the test of strength over the allegiance of Upper Volta, and Nkrumah's attempts to erase the boundaries separating Ghana's economic life from the economic life of Upper Volta, was in the end a contest for influence between Nkrumah and Houphouët-Boigny. And Houphouët-Boigny's influence on Upper Volta finally prevailed.

An issue of broader international implications concerned the Republic of South Africa. De Gaulle had not shared either the aim of totally isolating South Africa or the belief that UN resolutions were to be taken seriously. On the contrary, many of the UN moves to isolate South Africa encountered French opposition. De Gaulle's legacy to France had therefore entailed accepting the reality of a racialist South Africa, and ensuring that French interests did not suffer in response to any pan-African pressures against the Republic. The record of French sales of planes, submarines and military equipment to South Africa was part of the diplomatic bequest left by de Gaulle to his successors. And South Africa could be at the heart of Europe's relations with Africa.

In 1970 the Conservatives returned to power in Britain, and the issue of British resumption of the sale of arms to South Africa began to bedevil Anglo-African relations. The question arose – why bring such pressures on Britain when France was conducting a very profitable trade in arms with South Africa? At a meeting of the Organization of African Unity in Addis Ababa in September 1970 there was an attempt to frame a denunciation of France in terms comparable to those levelled against Britain. But again the old identification between French-speaking Africa and metropolitan France asserted its political efficacy. French-speaking Africans vigorously resisted

Africa industrializing: a shoe factory in Senegal. Although the pace of industrialization has been quite fast in some African countries, only South Africa has reached even the level of industrial development of prewar Italy

Mining output south of the Sahara 1950-68

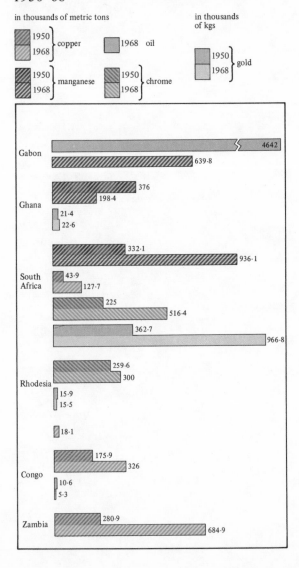

any public condemnation of France. There was no doubt that French-speaking Africans were more protective of the reputation of France than English-speaking Africans were in relation to Britain. The whole history of assimilation and integration which France had once pursued in relation to her colonies continued to affect the diplomatic postures of Francophone states within the African continent.

The Ivory Coast's president, Houphouët-Boigny, began to appear as among the leading Gaullist influences on this issue. In October 1970 Houphouët-Boigny became the first black African spokesman to suggest an actual meeting of heads of African states to discuss a re-evaluation of Africa's approach to South Africa, and a possible initiation of a dialogue with the white-dominated regime. French-speaking Africans were among the first to rally to his support. Niger's President Diaro Hamani joined the debate by asserting that negotiation was not inconsistent with the continuation of the struggle against apartheid. After all, there were discussions going on round a table in Paris about the ending of the Vietnam War, while the war itself continued.

But the issue of South Africa remains part of the larger question of Europe's relations with Africa. Even after de Gaulle we continue to have a convergence of issues involving South Africa, relations between French-speaking and English-speaking Africa, and the role of France in Afro-European relations. The signing of a commercial treaty between South Africa and the Malagasy Republic in November 1970, which encompassed the promotion of Madagascar's tourist industry by South Africa, was symbolic of the Gaullist legacy of pragmatic self-interest.

Conclusion

This essay started from the premise that one important dimension in politics is the interaction between politically significant *persons*. But our decision to focus on de Gaulle and Nkrumah had additional reasons. For French-speaking Africa has remained the clearest illustration of the continuing pulls of relationship between Africa and Europe. French-speaking Africa attained formal independence under de Gaulle, and the very architect of the Fifth Republic's relationship with the former colonies was de Gaulle himself. Nkrumah was a most symbolic figure in a nationalistic sense. He was profoundly representative of the African aspiration for continental autonomy. His endeavour to loosen the ties which Francophone Africa retained with France was symptomatic of this deeply felt ambition.

Behind both figures was the massive fact of the Nuclear Age, and the belief by both ultimately that some kind of participation in the science of the age was an important pre-condition of national dignity. The nationalism of Nkrumah and the nationalism of de Gaulle both clashed and converged in the fields of science and imperial relations.

After their departure from the political scene further changes took place in Africa. In 1970 Nkrumah was writing memoirs and radical tracts from Guinea, the country he had once helped when de Gaulle cut it off, and which gave him sanctuary when he was overthrown in 1966. Would Nkrumah one day be recalled from his enforced retirement as de Gaulle was recalled in 1958 to save France from new internal perils? The parallels between the two leaders might by no means have ended, though for the time being it appeared unlikely that Nkrumah would ever again be called upon to hold power in Ghana. When de Gaulle died a French literary figure said of him: 'He was a man of the day before yesterday, and a man of the day after tomorrow.' De Gaulle had combined grand anachronisms with inspired visions of the future. Nkrumah's sense of history was not as developed as de Gaulle's mystical nostalgia. Few would describe Nkrumah as 'a man of the day before yesterday' in that sense. But in his vision of a united Africa, in his ambition to loosen the apron-strings which tied Africa to her imperial past, in his dream of placing Africa at the heart of world affairs, and in his growing conviction that Africa must marry her culture to the new science, it may be movingly true that Kwame Nkrumah, like Charles de Gaulle, was indeed 'a man of the day after tomorrow'.

Walter Laqueur

The Middle East: the Permanent Crisis

The First World War resulted in the breakdown of the Ottoman Empire, the Second World War decisively weakened the position of Britain and France in the Middle East. The year 1945 therefore constitutes a watershed in the history of the area, even though the full impact of the changes that had taken place were felt only several years later. No Middle Eastern country had actively taken part in the war. Turkey had declared war on Germany and Japan in late February 1945; within a month the Arab countries were also at war: they all wanted to be represented at the Inaugural Conference of the United Nations.

The war years had been, on the whole, a quiet period in the Middle East. Between 1941 and 1945 no violent changes of government, no major upheavals, no mass uprisings against foreign occupying powers had taken place. The signing of the armistice in Europe spelled the end of this truce. In May 1945 fighting broke out between Syrian and French forces; in Palestine Jewish extremist forces resumed the armed struggle against the Mandatory power which had been suspended by and large during the war. The following year anti-British riots erupted in Baghdad, and the Anglo-Egyptian treaty was repudiated by a new Egyptian government.

Turkey and Iran

The repercussions of the postwar Soviet offensive were most acutely felt in Iran and Turkey. Iran had been occupied since 1941 by the Soviets and the Western Allies. As the war ended, the Western powers evacuated their forces, whereas the Soviet Union announced that it had no intention of doing so, because (as Stalin claimed) the Baku oil-fields had to be protected against possible Iranian sabotage. The explanation was threadbare, but the Soviet intention to retain a foothold in Iran or, at any rate, to extract a maximum of concessions, both political and economic, was real enough. The emergence of Soviet-sponsored secessionist governments in northern Iran was a direct and dangerous threat to the central government. At the same time, a general strike took place in the Abadan oil refineries; tens of thousands of members of Tudeh, the Iranian communist party, demonstrated in Tehran, and tribal insurrections occurred in the south of the country. The Iranian government, faced with total breakdown, was compelled to make substantial concessions to the Russians, such as the recognition of an autonomous regime in Azerbaijan, the establishment of a Soviet-Iranian oil company and the appointment of three Tudeh leaders to the cabinet. Upon achieving these gains, Stalin bowed to Western pressure and decided to withdraw his troops from Iran. But the Soviet position in Iran had only temporarily improved; deprived of direct Soviet support, the local separatist regimes collapsed, and the Tehran government won an overwhelming victory in the general elections. The Soviet demand for the establishment of a combined Soviet-Iranian oil company was rejected by the Iranian parliament, and the Tudeh party was outlawed after an attempt on the life of the Shah in February 1949. The Soviet Union threatened retaliatory action, including even military intervention under the Soviet-Iranian treaty of 1921, but the world situation clearly did not favour such action, and Stalin gradually accepted that his schemes had failed for the time being.

Strong pressure was brought by the Soviet Union on Turkey as the war ended. Moscow demanded a new regime for the Straits which would have made the Soviet Union responsible, together with Turkey, for their defence.

A refinery on the Persian Gulf; oil revolutionized the economy of the Middle East and by 1970 accounted for ninety per cent of export earnings in Iran, Iraq, Saudi Arabia and Libya

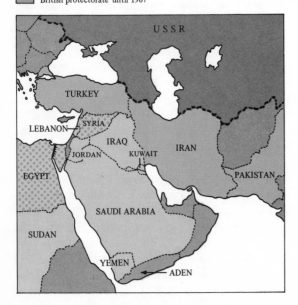

Atatürk's successor as leader of the Republican Party, I. Inönü (*left*), president of Turkey until 1950. He was followed by the Democrat, Adnan Menderes (*below*), who was in power until the army coup in 1960, when he was executed for not keeping his liberal promises. Turkey joined NATO under Menderes who is shown here on his way to a NATO meeting in 1957

Arab alliances

	Arab league since 1945		United Arab Republic
	CENTO members 1959		1958-61
	British protectorate until 1967		

At the same time it demanded that Turkey should cede to the Soviet Union some of its eastern provinces. Large Soviet forces were concentrated along the Turkish border, when Russia terminated its treaty of neutrality and non-aggression with Ankara and refused to renew it. Soviet pressure compelled Turkey to keep hundreds of thousands of soldiers under arms, a strain which had ruinous consequences on the Turkish economy. To prevent the collapse of Turkey, American aid was extended under the Truman Doctrine and the Point Four Programme. By the time Turkey joined NATO in 1950 its military position had become less critical. In that year the Soviet drive in the general direction of the Middle East petered out; it had been a strategy aimed at probing the strength of Greece, Turkey, Iran and their Western allies, rather than part of an overall grand design. For a full-scale Soviet offensive the situation was clearly not ripe, nor could Russia, greatly weakened as it was by the ravages of war, have coped with such an enterprise involving direct conflict with the West. The Soviet drive to the south was resumed, in a very different international constellation and with much more success, in the mid-fifties.

Once the outside danger was averted, domestic problems began to dominate the political scene in Turkey. The Republican Party, which had ruled the country under Atatürk and, after his death, under Ismet Inönü, showed signs of decline and exhaustion. There was widespread criticism of the traditional *étatiste* policy which concentrated political and economic power in the central government; in the countryside the resistance against the anti-Islamic edicts of the Republicans had never quite ceased. The Democratic Party, the main opposition group, founded in 1946, thus had a fairly broad popular base. In the general elections of 1950 it gained an absolute majority. Its leaders, Celal Bayar and Adnan Menderes, became president and prime minister respectively, and they ruled Turkey for almost exactly a decade. Under Menderes agricultural development took a great step forward, but in other respects his economic policy was, to put it mildly, less than well planned: rapid inflation took place, the currency was undermined and many of the new business ventures failed within a few years. By 1958, after two years of drought, the Turkish economy faced immediate collapse which was averted only by substantial Western loans. These acted as a temporary palliative; while they did not effect radical or lasting improvement, they paved the way for another period of erratic economic growth in the 1960s.

Menderes' policy alienated influential sections of the population, above all the urban middle class, many army officers and intellectuals. By the end of his reign most of the élite had turned against him, claiming that the Democrats' promises of 1950, such as the undertaking to liberalize political life, had not been kept. In 1960 Menderes was overthrown, as the army leadership refused to call out troops to quell student disorders. Political power passed at first into the hands of a military junta, but as the officers had no desire to perpetuate an army dictatorship, civilian rule was soon restored. The elections of 1961 resulted in Inönü's return to power for four years. He was defeated as the Justice Party, under Demirel, gained much popular support. This was a new political force, closer in its orientation to what Menderes had stood for than the Atatürk tradition.

The Mossadeq oil crisis

Except for the coup of 1960 which resulted in the execution of Menderes and several of his closest collaborators, political change in Turkey was peaceful in the postwar period. Developments in neighbouring Iran were, in contrast, far more dramatic and violent in character. After the Soviet threats to Iran had receded, the position of the Anglo-Iranian Oil Company, which controlled the country's oil industry, became the most important political issue. After the murder of Prime Minister Ali Razmara, a former army chief-of-staff, by a religious fanatic in March 1951, Muhammad Mossadeq came to power. Mossadeq was a political leader firmly committed to the nationalization of the oil industry. This was a popular demand; it was argued in Tehran, not without justification, that the main part of the

The Shah of Iran: he pursued policies of land reform and industrialization in one of the Middle East's most backward countries

Military aid from the US is openly proclaimed in the valley of Sefid Roud, Guilan

oil profits had gone abroad, and that mainly foreigners, not Iranians, had benefited from the exploitation of the natural wealth of the country. The crisis reached its climax in late summer 1951 when oil production virtually ceased. In October 1952 Iran severed diplomatic relations with Britain after various initiatives to find a compromise solution had failed.

Mossadeq's policy did not succeed because he overrated the importance of Iranian oil for the European market. The oil companies could easily step up production in other parts of the world; by 1953 it was clear that Iran, deprived of its oil royalties, was suffering more than any other party from the shut-down of the industry. When, in July 1952, Mossadeq asked the Shah for near-dictatorial powers to cope with the situation, he met with a refusal. But Mossadeq still had the support of the street, and after a few days of demonstrations and riots the Shah was forced to recall Mossadeq. Once again Mossadeq overplayed his hand: after various dramatic ups and downs, culminating in the flight of the Shah to Rome in August 1953, Mossadeq's government was overthrown by a royalist coalition headed by General Zahedi. The new government and its successors throughout the 1950s were conservative in character. The Mossadeq interlude remained, however, not without consequences; the consortium of oil companies which replaced the Anglo-Iranian Oil Company had to sign agreements with the government providing for a much larger contribution to the Iranian treasury. As Iranian oil production almost quintupled between 1950 and 1970, annual payments to the Iranian government amounted to about $1 billion by 1970.

Oil revenue thus became the key factor in Iran's economic development. Once the financial crisis of 1961 was overcome, industry in Iran made rapid progress and the mechanization of agriculture got under way. This striking advance (annual growth was more than once in excess of ten per cent) greatly contributed to the modernization of one of the poorest and most backward countries in the world. Equally important were the social reforms promulgated in the early sixties. They aimed at eradicating corruption, improving tax collection and breaking the domination of the great land-owners. The agrarian reforms helped to break up the traditional social structure in the countryside and resulted in the end of the share-cropping system and the emergence of a new class of small landowners.

The political aim of the Shah in promoting these measures was to gain the support of the peasant majority against the power of the big landowners. But there was considerable resistance. The mullahs, champions of Muslim orthodoxy, claimed that tampering with the system of land ownership, let alone giving women the right to vote, was contrary to the principles of Islam. Some of the tribes again rebelled, and the merchants, hit by the imposition of higher customs duties, also turned against the government. There was disaffection among the intelligentsia because of the lack of political freedom. The anti-corruption drive was bound to cause resentment among the state bureaucracy while the communists and Dr Mossadeq's followers were opposed to the government anyway. The Shah and his advisers thus had to pursue their policy against great opposition from both conservative and revolutionary forces. Politically the regime remained vulnerable, for although technocratic reforms could provide an answer to economic and social problems, political stability depended in the long run on the government's success in gaining the active support of the élite and in bringing about a community of purpose between the leaders and the people.

With all their difficulties Turkey and Iran had certain advantages as they tried to cope with the problems facing them which the Arab countries lacked. In their relationship to the outside world Turks and Persians showed, on the whole, more confidence and maturity; this may be not unconnected with the fact that in their long history they never entirely lost their independence. The Arabs were less fortunate, which helps to explain certain specific features in Arab political behaviour, such as the strong anti-Western resentment, as well as the division of the Arab world into ten major or minor units. Up to 1970 attempts to unite the Arab world failed, despite the fact that all Arab leaders at least paid lip-service to the idea.

In Syria, spies hanged and labelled with their crimes in the main square of Damascus

A former Ba'ath chief of state, Dr Atassi, speaking in the Syrian parliament building; in 1966 the party came under army control

The rise of a new élite

As the Second World War ended, foreign influence was still strongly entrenched in most Arab countries. Political power was in the hands of kings, emirs and imams, and the big landowners who constituted the ruling stratum. Modernization had made great strides in the main urban centres such as Cairo, Alexandria and Beirut, but it had barely touched many rural areas in the region. Islam, too, was still a political factor of paramount importance. There had been during the late 1930s considerable sympathy for the Axis powers among the Arab intelligentsia, particularly the younger generation. These radicals were attracted by Germany and Italy because these powers spearheaded the struggle against Britain and France. Fascism also seemed to embody a more effective road to the political emancipation of the Arab world than parliamentary democracy, which had failed in many European countries and which was thought to be totally unsuited to Middle Eastern conditions.

With the military defeat of the Axis powers the attractions of fascism vanished, but the underlying emotions and the intense desire for political change were bound to re-emerge in a new form after the end of the war. Some turned to a socialism which had, however, little in common with what was commonly known under that name in the West; others opted for the Muslim Brotherhood or other extremist Islamic groups. The radical nationalists were not interested in splitting fine ideological hairs but wanted, each in his own way, to remove a system that was manifestly bankrupt and to restore pride and dignity to the Arab homeland. The moderate politicians who headed consecutive Egyptian governments at the end of the war were forced to resign by popular opinion (in so far as they were not assassinated, like Ahmad Maher and Nuqrashi), because they did not press with sufficient fervour for a revision of the treaty of 1936, an abomination in the eyes of all Egyptian nationalists. The British were willing, in principle, to evacuate Cairo and Alexandria and, by 1949, also the Suez Canal, but they were opposed to the union of the Sudan with Egypt, as demanded by Cairo.

The leading political force inside Egypt at the time was still the Wafd; in the elections of January 1950 it gained an overwhelming victory and, for the next two years, again formed a government. Its leader, Mustafa Nahas, was widely respected as a central figure in the Egyptian national movement; but he was an elderly man, at the end of his political career, and popular respect did not extend to some of his closest colleagues. To the younger generation the Wafd, too, had become part of the Egyptian establishment, lacking purpose and militancy. Gradually the Wafd lost control; there were recurrent riots culminating in the widespread destruction of Black Saturday, 26 January 1952. King Farouk deposed the Wafd, declared martial law and for another six months succeeded in clinging to power. On 23 July, he in turn was overthrown by a coup carried out by a group of young army officers under the leadership of Gamal Abdul Nasser; Major-General

Muhammad Naguib, who at the time appeared as the head of the junta, was a senior officer who had been drawn into the conspiracy only at a late stage to give it more respectability in the eyes of the army and the country at large.

Farouk was criticized for his greed and for the corruption, bribery and the general decline of public morals which had permeated public life in Egypt under his rule. His personal failings had certainly greatly contributed to the fact that the monarchy was held in such universal contempt by the time it collapsed. It is not certain, however, whether the verdict of posterity will be as harsh as that of his contemporaries. With all its sins of omission and commission, Farouk's regime had certain redeeming qualities: it provided, within limits, expression of popular will; the country was not run by the army and secret police; leadership was ineffective, but, in a way, it did not pretend to be anything else.

The political system in Syria had broken down even earlier than in Egypt; in Iraq the monarchy lasted for six more years after the deposition of Farouk. Parliamentary democracy was no more of a success in Syria than in

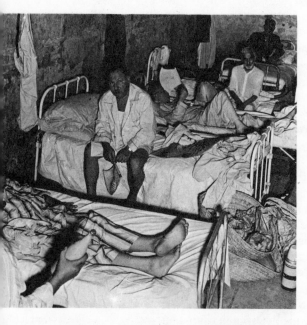

Top Iraqi political prisoners after General Qassem's 1958 coup included a former premier and a foreign minister; the Royal family were executed. General Qassem (*above*) lasted five years and was killed by a military junta which showed his crushed body on Baghdad television, but was overthrown by another army group nine months later

Right After a coup at the defence ministry

other parts of the Arab world, with the exception of Syria's neighbour, Lebanon; no political party commanded a majority or showed leadership ability. There was growing discontent in the country, and consequently the call went forth for the proverbial strong man. In March 1949 Colonel Husni Zaim took over; he lasted five months more than his successor, Sami Hinnawi, who was in power for only four months. Adib Shishakli, who was next in line, cooperated with the politicians and remained at first in the background, until in November 1951 he deposed the civilians and became military dictator. Shishakli, in turn, was ousted in February 1954 by yet another army coup, which for an interim period restored civilian rule to Syria.

The Egyptian and Syrian examples were bound to have repercussions elsewhere in the Arab world: in July 1951 King Abdullah of Jordan was assassinated, in 1958 his Hashemite cousins in Iraq were killed, and in 1962 the Yemenite army deposed Iman Badr. The situation in Jordan was not immediately affected by the murder of Britain's most faithful ally among the Arabs; within a few years, however, Britain was to lose also all its influence in Amman. In Iraq the events of 1958 triggered off a chain of coups and counter-coups which, except for one brief interval, lasted to 1970. Iraqi politics had a flavour and style of its own, including public hangings and purge trials. The royal family and Nuri Said, the prime minister, were brutally killed, but the leader of the insurrection of 1958 did not fare differently: five years later, in February 1963, the crushed body of General Qassem was shown on Baghdad television. Yet nine months later it was the turn of those who had overthrown Qassem; they were removed by another military junta headed by Abdul Salem Aref.

Thus, by the late 1950s political power in all the major Arab countries had passed into the hands of the new élite, personified by captains, majors and colonels who, alone or in little groups, had established their rule in the name of the popular will. The rise of this new class was a fairly common phenomenon in the underdeveloped countries during the postwar era; its roots were by no means specifically Arab or Middle Eastern. But there is no doubt that the Arab-Israeli conflict contributed to the spread of the ferment in the Arab world and exacerbated it. The coups in Syria were a direct outcome of the Arab League's defeat in the war against Israel. The idea of an armed coup against Farouk was first hatched by young Egyptian officers who had taken part in the disastrous Palestinian campaign.

The emergence of Israel

For the Zionists, too, the immediate postwar period was the moment of truth. The Zionist movement, aiming at the establishment of a national home for the Jewish people in Palestine, had adopted during the war a resolution in favour of a Jewish state (the Biltmore Programme). The destruction of European Jewry seemed to have provided cruel justification for the Zionists' warnings about the dangers of anti-Semitism; as the war ended, a shelter had to be found for the remnants of the holocaust so that they could start a new life in safety far away from the countries which had become cemeteries for their families and friends. The Balfour Declaration

Top Exodus 1942, an illegal Jewish immigrant ship boarded by the British Navy in Haifa harbour. As an example the Jews were deported to German refugee camps; a harsh and heavily criticized measure
Above David Ben Gurion, first prime minister, reads the declaration of the State of Israel on 14 May 1948, with Chaim Weizmann as first president

Right The first Arab-Israeli war broke out on the first day of the new state, which was invaded by Arab armies; after UN intervention armistice agreements were signed, January-June 1949

Territorial gains of Israel 1945-56

▪▪▪▪ boundary of British Palestine Mandate 1920-48
☐ Israel under UN partition
☐ gained by Israel after war with Arabs 1949
☐ occupied by Israel during Suez War 1956
☐ Arab states
⚓⚓ furthest advance by Israel during Suez War

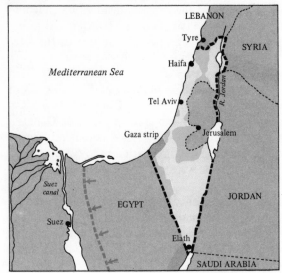

Below Palestinian Arab refugees who lost their homes during the war; the number of displaced is a matter for bitter dispute
Bottom King Hussein of Jordan; the civil war of 1970, caused by the problem of the Palestinian Arabs, nearly brought about his downfall

(November 1917) in favour of a Jewish national home had once been the declared policy of successive British governments. But as the Mandatory power gradually realized that it faced an irreconcilable conflict between Jews and Arabs, it dissociated itself from the letter and spirit of the obligation it had once taken upon itself.

Jewish immigration to Palestine was limited to 1,500 a month in 1945; thousands of illegal immigrants were deported to Cyprus or, in some instances, returned to Europe. Anti-British feeling among the Jewish population of Palestine found an outlet in acts of terrorism which previously had been the preserve of right-wing extremist groups. In June 1946 the headquarters of the Jewish Agency were occupied by British troops and most of its leaders arrested. Attempts to find a compromise failed: the recommendations of an Anglo-American Enquiry Commission were rejected by the Palestinian Arabs, who also refused to attend a Round Table Conference in London in September 1946. The Zionists announced that they would participate only if the discussions aimed at the establishment of a viable Jewish state.

After both sides had rejected the British proposals for a federal settlement, the British government in February 1947 submitted the whole issue to the UN. A Special Committee for Palestine (UNSCOP) was appointed, which in September 1947 recommended the partition of the country. Later that month the British government announced that it was planning to terminate the Mandate and would withdraw its administration and troops from Palestine in the near future. Both the United States and the Soviet Union declared their support for the partition plan, which in late November 1947 was endorsed by the necessary majority of the United Nations General Assembly.

The Palestinian Arabs were bitterly opposed to partition and immediately after the UN vote launched a guerrilla campaign against the Jewish community, which retaliated with counter-terror. The military efforts of the Arabs were mainly directed against the lines of communication of the enemy and they succeeded in cutting off Jerusalem from the rest of the country. On 14 May 1948, when the British Mandate came to an end and the state of Israel was proclaimed in Tel Aviv, the chances for its survival were very much in the balance. On that very day the armies of Egypt, Syria, Iraq and Jordan crossed into Palestine, and the Jewish military forces, ill-equipped and insufficiently trained, seemed hardly in a position to resist.

The Arab armies, however, did not show much fighting spirit, and, having underrated the determination of the Jewish population, proved unable to occupy the centres of Jewish settlement in four weeks of fighting. Following UN intervention a truce was proclaimed on 11 June and a month later, when the Arab League unwisely refused the UN request for an extension of the truce, its forces were routed along all fronts. There was more fighting in October 1948, which resulted in Egyptian defeats in southern Palestine and the Israeli conquest of central Galilee. In February 1949, after protracted discussions in Rhodes under the auspices of a UN mediator, an armistice between Israel and Egypt was signed, which was followed later that year by armistices with Israel's other neighbours.

As a consequence of this war about 750,000 Arabs lost their homes; their exact number and the circumstances of their flight have remained a matter of bitter dispute. Their place was taken by Jewish immigrants from Europe and the Middle East; half a million arrived within three years of the establishment of the Jewish state. For the Palestinian Arabs the war of 1948 was an unmitigated disaster: having rejected during the 1920s the idea of a binational state based on parity and in the thirties various projects for a miniature Jewish state, and having *a fortiori* opposed the UN plan, they were now faced with a Zionist presence on a much larger scale.

The military defeat was, in fact, a painful blow to the whole Arab world: certain of victory, the Arabs had been defeated by a small people whose martial qualities they had never highly regarded. The Arab leaders refused to recognize the state of Israel or to conclude a peace treaty; they regarded their reverse as temporary, the result of bad leadership, lack of cooperation and insufficient preparation. For the next seven years an uneasy and incomplete truce prevailed between Israel and the Arabs; the latter imposed a total boycott on Israel, closed the Suez Canal to Israeli shipping and encouraged and assisted irregular Arab forces in their frequent forays over the armistice lines into Israeli territory. These acts of hostility were accompanied by many speeches and solemn proclamations by Arab leaders about their preparations for a holy war against the Zionist intruders which would throw the latter into the sea and destroy their state. The Israeli reaction was predictable; they opted for preventive war when at the time of the Suez crisis there was an opportunity to do so with a fair chance of success.

The Suez crisis was triggered off by the American and British decision in July 1956 to withdraw financial help for the building of the Aswan Dam in retaliation for the anti-Western policy pursued by Colonel Nasser. The Egyptian leader immediately reacted by nationalizing the Suez Canal, a step that was viewed with alarm in London and Paris, where it was feared that Egypt would eventually close the canal in an attempt to cut off the oil supplies from the Persian Gulf, which were vital to European industrial development.

Diplomatic efforts to settle the crisis failed; Britain and France found no support in the Security Council, and American assistance was at best half-hearted. Following the breakdown of negotiations, military action against Egypt was discussed between London and Paris. At a later stage of these

King Farouk of Egypt, deposed 23 July 1952 by a group of army officers led by Nasser: charged with corruption, bribery and ineffectual leadership and held responsible for the general decline in public morals.

Right Nasser's most cherished project – the Aswan Dam built during the sixties with massive Soviet aid

A Russian cartoon celebrates Nasser's seizure of the Suez Canal on 26 July 1956; the capitalist banner reads 'Shares of the Suez Canal Co. Ltd'

Right Sunken ships block the canal at Port Said after the Anglo-French-Israeli invasion three months earlier

Nasser's funeral in September 1970 brought huge demonstrations of mourning

talks Israel was called in. Israel was only too willing to cooperate since it felt acutely threatened by Colonel Nasser after the blockade of the Straits of Tiran and the increase of armed incursions during 1955-6.

On 29 October 1956, the Israelis attacked the Egyptians, routed them within a few days, and reached the Suez Canal. Thereupon the British and French governments announced that they would intervene to separate the two armies. Their forces landed in Suez and Port Said, but the execution of the plan was little better than its conception. Britain and France faced growing resistance at home and on the part of the other superpowers; they were isolated in the UN. Facing a twofold crisis, the British government stopped military operations one day after the Israelis had accepted the UN ceasefire order.

The Anglo-French action had been based on a series of miscalculations. Far from attaining its goal, it resulted during the coming years in the loss of their last positions in the Middle East and North Africa. Nasser's regime emerged immensely strengthened from the attack: the fact that he had successfully resisted two major European powers gave him enormous domestic credit and made him a hero even beyond the confines of the Arab world. The defeat of the Egyptian army by the Israelis was explained as the result of collusion between them and the Western powers; on their own, it was argued, the Israelis would never have dared to attack, and, had they done so, they would have been defeated in no time. The Israelis gained precious little from this ill-starred venture; following heavy American pressure Prime Minister David Ben Gurion had to give to his troops the order to withdraw from all the territories they had occupied. As a result of the war Israel regained freedom of shipping in the Straits of Tiran and won a respite of eleven years. But Arab enmity towards Israel and the desire for a war of revenge certainly did not lessen; the Arab leaders were still not in the least willing to accept the existence of a Jewish state.

The Six-Day War

The third round in the Arab-Israeli conflict opened in May 1967. In the meantime the Arab armies, particularly those of Egypt and Syria, had been greatly strengthened by massive deliveries of modern war material from the Soviet Union. They felt confident that they had gained overwhelming superiority and that in the final battle in the not-too-distant future the enemy would be crushed. Whether Nasser was tricked in May 1967 into premature action by his Syrian or Soviet allies cannot be established with any degree of certainty, but the fact remains that he gave orders to reimpose

The Six-Day War

The Six-Day War in June 1967 was one of the most decisive military victories in the twentieth century. Within six days Israel had routed her enemies and had made territorial gains which gave her shorter and more defensible borders. But the prospects for peace in the Middle East remained bleak: only a fundamental change of heart among the Arabs and Israelis or the cooperative intervention of the great powers seemed likely to divert the conflict in the Middle East from exploding once more.

After the war (*below*): burnt-out Egyptian tanks and lorries litter a road across Sinai to Suez, June 1967

Shadow of an Israeli jet (*right*) as Arabs take cover
Bottom From Moscow, a predictable response to the war

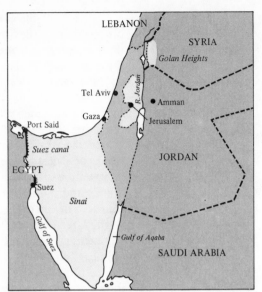

Israel after the Six-Day War 1967

⬛ Israel before the outbreak of hostilities
⬜ territories gained by Israel

Top left General Dayan, with his chief-of-staff General Rabin (right) march into the old city of Jerusalem through the Lion's Gate, 7 June 1967
Above Palestinian Arab refugees in an emergency camp set up in east Jordan after border fighting early in 1968. Some have been homeless for twenty years

Left Armed guard on the holy 'wailing wall' in the old city of Jerusalem, captured by the Israelis

A meeting of the Arab League (*above*) founded in March 1945 to promote Arab unity, but politically unsuccessful since decisions were only binding on those who accepted them

Below Nasser with Tito on posters in Damascus; attempts to unite Arabs under Egyptian leadership proved a failure

Bottom An anti-Israeli cartoon in Cairo

a blockade on the Straits of Tiran and asked the UN to withdraw their observers from the armistice lines. These actions and the troop concentrations were accompanied by solemn declarations on the part of Nasser and the other Arab leaders about an impending attack against Israel.

The Israeli government initially vacillated, but when it appeared that there was no international support for the restoration of the *status quo ante* by political means, it decided to go to war. Within six days in early June, following the destruction of the Arab air forces, the Israelis completely routed the Arab armies and occupied the Sinai peninsula, as well as the whole of Palestine west of the Jordan river and the Golan Heights. The intervention of the great powers prevented the total destruction of the Arab armies and the fall of Nasser, which, in the face of so decisive a defeat, seemed a distinct possibility.

The Israeli military victory did not, however, bring peace with the Arabs any nearer; if Israel's new borders were easier to defend, the long-range political and military problems facing it were certainly no less grave. The new territories occupied by Israel were inhabited by one million Arabs who, for obvious reasons, were not enthusiastic supporters of the Jewish state. Moreover the defeat of Egypt and Syria was a heavy blow to Soviet prestige, and it induced the Russians to involve themselves in the Arab-Israeli dispute to a much greater degree than before. The Arab armies were rebuilt by the Soviet Union within two years and when it appeared that the delivery of planes, warships and tanks alone did not have the desired effect, many thousands of Soviet military experts were dispatched to Egypt and Syria to man missile bases and support the Arab war effort in other ways, both direct and indirect.

The armistice between the Arabs and Israel lasted only a few months; after October 1967 there was almost constant fighting along the Suez Canal and other sections of the front. The war of 1967 also gave fresh impetus to the activities of the Palestinian-Arab irregular forces (Fatah and others). Militarily they were insignificant, at least as far as Israel was concerned, but inside Jordan and to a lesser extent in Lebanon they became a political and military factor of great importance. The Soviet involvement changed the whole character of the Arab-Israeli conflict; what had previously been a regional conflict, one among many, turned into an issue directly affecting the interests of Russia and America, and thus the global balance of power.

Nasser and Arab unity

What were the policies, what were the achievements of the new élites which in the 1950s seized power in the Arab world? The Free Officers in Egypt had at first no clear concept of the conduct of domestic and foreign affairs. Only after the brief Naguib interlude, when Gamal Abdul Nasser took over, did a clearer pattern gradually emerge. In foreign affairs Nasser pursued in the beginning a policy of neutralism, trying, not without success, to play off West against East, while at the same time extracting from both a maximum of financial aid to shore up Egypt's shaky economy and to underwrite its ambitious development projects.

In his pan-Arab policy Nasser was less successful; however great his popularity, his relations with the other Arab states were bedevilled by constant strife, and his attempts to bring about Arab unity under Egyptian leadership failed. Iraq under the old regime had been one of Egypt's main opponents, but relations with General Qassem were even worse, and those with his successors in Baghdad not much better. In January 1958 the Syrian politicians, afraid of a left-wing takeover, persuaded Nasser to come to their aid and to merge the two countries within the framework of the United Arab Republic. The union lasted until September 1961, when the Syrians, having regained their self-confidence and angry at the behaviour of Nasser's proconsuls in Damascus, expelled the Egyptians from their country. Syrian, Iraqi and Egyptian leaders met anew in Cairo in March 1963 and discussed for six months the advantages of a federation among themselves, but once again the talks broke down amid mutual recriminations. Egypt's support for the revolution in the Yemen led to its intervention

Yasser Arafat, leader of the Palestinian guerrillas who hijacked airliners in 1970 and fought the twenty-five-day civil war in Jordan

Below A guerrilla poster supports Gaza 'revolutionaries'

An El Fatah sniper on a police station captured in Amman, where much of the fighting took place; the ceasefire engineered by Nasser was his last act of statesmanship

in the civil war which had broken out in the Arab peninsula; this in turn caused the severance of relations with Saudi Arabia (November 1962) and the dispatch of an Egyptian expeditionary corps, which, unable to operate in unfamiliar terrain, suffered a series of humiliating setbacks.

Not only did Nasser find the road to a great empire under his leadership barred by rival interests, but he also encountered resistance from the Western powers to his more ambitious schemes. This brought him into growing conflict with the United States, and his policy veered more and more towards the Soviet Union, which alone among the big powers was willing to provide not only political support, but also unlimited quantities of arms supplies. In his domestic policy as well, Nasser took a sharp turn to the left in 1961 – as he himself stated in a speech at the time – to protect the revolutionary regime from feudalism, monopolies and exploiting capitalism. Some 400 banks, factories and public utilities were nationalized; maximum land ownership was reduced to 100 *feddan* and workers were promised a share in profits. As a result of these decrees large sectors of the Egyptian economy passed into the hands of the state.

In accordance with the provisions of the National Charter of 1962 half of the seats in parliament were allocated to workers and peasants. Yet in the last resort the country was not run by the parliament, nor even by the state party, the Arab Socialist Union, established in the mid-fifties in an attempt to provide broader popular support for the government. Most members of the Free Officers group which had overthrown Farouk in 1952 were purged during the fifties and sixties. Power firmly rested in the hands of Nasser and the army and police chiefs belonging to his entourage. From time to time the democratization of the regime was promised, but this was invariably made dependent on the termination of the state of war with Israel. When Nasser died in September 1970, deeply mourned by many Arabs, his position was unchallenged and there was no obvious candidate for a successor.

Nasser had succeeded in eradicating Western influence in Egypt but as his regime became increasingly dependent on the Soviet Union there was a distinct danger that his country would become part of the sphere of influence of this world power – geographically much nearer than Britain or America, and for that reason inevitably more formidable and more difficult to resist. Some long-overdue social reforms were carried out by Nasser's government, above all in the system of land ownership. These efforts were hampered not so much by active or passive resistance as by the basic poverty of the country, the lack of natural resources and Nasser's decision to give priority to military expenditure. However, work on the Aswan Dam was completed in time, some industrial progress was achieved and the Suez Canal was managed reasonably efficiently until its closure in 1967. If the population explosion was not brought under control and there was no striking progress in the economic situation, at least there was no marked further deterioration. Massive Soviet aid and substantial annual payments from the oil-producing countries helped to keep the Egyptian economy afloat after the defeat of 1967, and the discovery of oil-fields in the Western Desert came as an unforeseen and welcome boon.

Despite the discrepancy between Nasser's promises and his achievements, Egypt was a model of political continuity and stability in comparison with the rest of the Arab world. Internal war in the Arab peninsula had been endemic ever since 1962; the withdrawal of the last British troops from Aden in 1967 further exacerbated the struggle for power among conflicting local interests, between 'moderates' and 'radicals', and also among the radicals themselves. Syrian policies during the 1960s consisted of a series of military coups and counter-coups. Power gradually passed into the hands of the Ba'ath, a radical national socialist party which, founded in the 1940s, had adherents among the intelligentsia in many Arab countries; it was in effect the only all-Arab party. However, the old civilian leadership of the party was ousted in 1966 by a group of officers who not only propagated more extremist slogans, but claimed to be the only true proponents of Ba'ath doctrine and policy.

Top Royalist soldiers in Yemen, where a republican revolt against the monarchy led by General Sallal broke out in September 1962. Sallal received Egyptian and Soviet aid and is shown (*above*) in a Russian armoured car after proclaiming a new constitution in May 1965

King Faisal of neighbouring Saudi Arabia, who supported the Yemeni monarchy

This claim was contested not only by the old Syrian leadership, but also by the influential Iraqi branch of the party. A movement which had been launched to bring about unity in the Arab world thus ended in an ideological and political free-for-all with accusations of betrayal freely bandied around. But for the Israeli danger it might well have ended in a general war. Both Syria and Iraq were plagued by minority problems; the war against the Kurdish minority, which had lasted on and off for many years, sapped much of Iraq's strength. The governments of Syria and Iraq carried out agrarian reforms – a problem less urgent there than in Egypt – promoted industrialization with modest success and nationalized some key sectors of the national economy.

General Qassem's regime, which succeeded the Hashemites, was nationalist and populist in inspiration. At first it veered sharply to the left and collaborated with the communists against Nasser's partisans and other left-wing groups. Later it turned to the right: special revolutionary courts and the popular militia, which had earlier played an important role, were dissolved. Eventually the regime turned into a personal dictatorship, though to everyone's surprise Qassem managed to hang on for five years before being overthrown by a Ba'athist revolt. In 1958 the communists had persecuted and, on occasion, massacred their rivals; in 1963 the Ba'ath retaliated in kind. But the Ba'athists remained in power for only nine months and were replaced by yet another military dictatorship under General Aref. His regime was less clearly ideologically motivated, more moderate and, on the whole, less ambitious; Abdel Rahman Bazzaz, who served as prime minister under him – the first civilian in many years – promised elections and tried, not too successfully, to reduce the influence of the army officers in the government. When Aref died in an accident (April 1966), his brother took over. The second Aref lasted for two years and was overthrown by Generals Baqr, Amash and Taqriti, Ba'ath sympathizers who advocated extreme nationalism and what they called a specific Iraqi road to socialism (their critics called it fascism); they were at the same time opposed to both Nasser and the Syrian rulers.

Israel made the most of the respite which it had gained in 1956. If the early fifties had been a period of austerity and economic stagnation, the boom of the sixties resulted in high growth rates in both industry and agriculture. The four prime ministers who governed Israel since its beginning (Ben Gurion, Sharet, Eshkol, Golda Meir) all belonged to Mapai, the Labour Party, which in coalition with several minor groups ruled the country all along and provided political continuity unequalled elsewhere in the Middle East. The country faced major political and social problems such as the conflict between the state and organized religion, and the uneasy relations between immigrants from Europe and those from the Middle East. But for the permanent state of siege, which inhibited the outbreak of open conflict, these and other bones of contention might well have put Israeli democracy to a serious test. Basic decisions concerning the Zionist character of Israel, Israel's relationship to world Jewry and the future development of the state were carefully evaded. The outside threat facing the new state was of decisive importance in the transformation of an anonymous crowd of new immigrants from many countries, who often had little in common with one another, into a community showing solidarity and its own specific national consciousness. At the same time the state of siege and the mentality produced by it inevitably had less desirable effects on the cultural, social and economic development of the country.

Social and economic developments

No survey of the recent history of the Middle East would be complete without reference to the social and economic developments which took place after the end of the Second World War and which in a long-term view are of greater importance than many of the political changes. While the majority of the population in Egypt, Syria, Turkey, Iran and the Arab peninsula was still employed in agriculture, urbanization made rapid progress throughout the period under review; the traditional image of the 'romantic Orient', of

The bodyguard of Sheikh Zayed of Abu Dhabi, one of the new oil sheikhdoms

camels, Bedouins and harems, became more and more a thing of the past. A high annual birthrate (three per cent or more in Syria, Iraq, Egypt and other countries) coupled with a declining deathrate made for rapid population growth and created serious problems in countries such as Egypt with limited land reserves. Some experts advocated the development of heavy industry as a panacea, but the absence of metallic ores presented an obstacle difficult to overcome.

The prospects for light industry were more promising, but in this respect, too, there were inhibiting factors such as the lack of capital, the weakness of local purchasing power and a low technological level that could only gradually be surmounted. Land reform did away with absentee landlordism and helped to break up the largest estates. The state invested heavily in agriculture to introduce more modern methods of cultivation and to extend the area of cultivable soil. Despite this, productivity in agriculture remained low by world standards, partly because of adverse climatic conditions and inferior soil and the prevalence of various diseases and pests, partly as a result of the fragmentation of land holdings and the lack of capital and skills.

Oil became the region's main source of income and also accounted to a large extent for the prominence of the Middle East in world affairs. In 1938 less than six per cent of the world's oil production was in the Middle East – almost all of it in Iran and Iraq. By the late 1960s the Middle East, including Libya, accounted for more than one-third of world production. It had about seventy per cent of the proved world reserves in crude oil and produced eighty per cent of the oil requirements of Western Europe. The striking development of the Middle Eastern oil industry took place in the 1950s with the phenomenal increase in output in the known areas and the discovery of major new oil-fields, such as those in the Kuwait Neutral Zone in 1953 and in Libya in 1959. By the late sixties more than 100 million tons yearly were produced in Iran, Saudi Arabia, Kuwait and Libya. Abu Dhabi, a small sheikhdom on the Persian Gulf, where not a drop of oil had been produced as recently as 1961, exported 20 million tons eight years later.

Oil revolutionized the economy of the Middle East. Ninety per cent or more of the export earnings in Iran, Iraq, Saudi Arabia and Libya, not to mention the smaller states, were by 1970 derived from it. Kuwait grew from a sleepy fishing village into a modern city of half a million inhabitants, only one-third of whom were Kuwaiti nationals. Their average yearly income was $5,000, the highest in the world. Kuwait provided free education and health services, whereas the citizens of Saudi Arabia, whose revenues were approximately of the same order, began to profit substantially from this wealth only after King Saud had been ousted in 1964. Most of the Middle Eastern oil production was dominated by seven leading Western companies ('the seven sisters'), but independent newcomers from all over the world began operating in the late fifties and received a growing share of the rapidly increasing market.

British soldiers patrol in Aden before independence in November 1967

Oil drums in Abu Dhabi; oil brought wealth to Abu Dhabi, where not a drop was produced until 1961

World production of petroleum

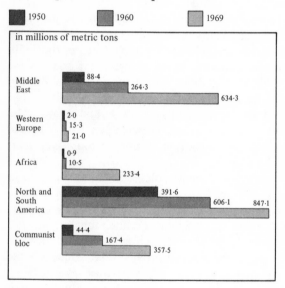

■ 1950	■ 1960	■ 1969

in millions of metric tons

Middle East	88·4 / 264·3 / 634·3
Western Europe	2·0 / 15·3 / 21·0
Africa	0·9 / 10·5 / 233·4
North and South America	391·6 / 606·1 / 847·1
Communist bloc	44·4 / 167·4 / 357·5

GNP of Middle Eastern countries 1958-68

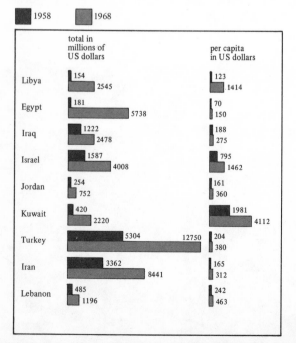

■ 1958	■ 1968

	total in millions of US dollars	per capita in US dollars
Libya	154 / 2545	123 / 1414
Egypt	181 / 5738	70 / 150
Iraq	1222 / 2478	188 / 275
Israel	1587 / 4008	795 / 1462
Jordan	254 / 752	161 / 360
Kuwait	420 / 2220	1981 / 4112
Turkey	5304 / 12750	204 / 380
Iran	3362 / 8441	165 / 312
Lebanon	485 / 1196	242 / 463

Oil operations in the major producing countries were on a profit-sharing basis; the great breakthrough in this respect was the decree of the Saudi government in 1949 demanding fifty per cent of Aramco's income after payment of United States tax. Thereafter most of the oil-producing countries pressed successfully for a higher share of the profits. As a result operating costs rose steadily, and the companies were forced to relinquish most of the concession areas in which no drilling had been made. For example, the Iraqi Petroleum Company was compelled by General Qassem to give up ninety-nine per cent of its concessions. The attempts to cut off the flow of oil to Western Europe during the Suez War of 1956 and again during the Arab-Israeli War of 1967 were, however, unsuccessful; the boycott was not total, and if Western Europe needed Middle Eastern oil, the oil-producing countries had come to depend on their revenues even more. In view of the abundance of oil resources in other parts of the world it quickly emerged that oil as a political weapon was less effective than many had thought. During the late 1960s the Soviet Union began to reveal a growing interest in Middle Eastern oil; as consumption in the Soviet Union grew at a faster rate than production, Moscow signed agreements with Iran and Iraq concerning the exploration and import of oil and natural gas.

Middle Eastern oil was cheap in comparison with oil produced in other parts of the world; some of it, notably Libyan oil, had also a lower sulphuric content, which made it particularly desirable. Though Middle Eastern oil would not retain its importance for ever, its future thus seemed assured for many years to come. But the fact that it was so unevenly distributed, and that most of it was found in sparsely populated areas (Kuwait and the Persian Gulf principalities, Libya, Saudi Arabia) was the source of much political upheaval. It exposed the small countries to pressure from their more powerful, but economically weaker, neighbours. Syria at various times stopped the flow of oil through the pipelines; the conflicts between Iran and Iraq, and the tension between Egypt and Saudi Arabia were not unconnected with oil politics and interests. The oil resources, actual and potential, of the Persian Gulf, were bound to attract the Soviet Union just as they had attracted Britain during an earlier period. Paradoxically, the long-term prospects for the political independence of the Middle Eastern countries might be brighter but for their oil resources.

Ominous undercurrents

While political developments in Turkey, Iran and Israel followed their own peculiar pattern, a common denominator could easily be detected for events in the Arab world. A new class and a new generation came to power with the establishment of military dictatorships in the leading Arab countries. This new élite felt the need for a more daring approach to both domestic and foreign policy. It desired quick results and greatly resented and envied the West, which had dominated the Middle East for several generations and still retained influence through its defence pacts and economic links. The Soviet Union, on the other hand, was thought of as a powerful but distant country whose support against the West was more than welcome. Moreover, since the Arab countries, unlike Iran and Turkey, had no common frontier with the Soviet Union, they did not feel directly exposed to Soviet pressure.

The young officers in Egypt and Syria, in Iraq, Sudan and Libya came to power on a wave of intense nationalist feeling and rising expectations. The historical function of this group has been variously interpreted as being that of an agent of modernization, an advocate of military socialism or as the vanguard (or the instrument) of the new middle class. None of these definitions contains more than a grain of truth; it would be more correct to say that the army came to power because the old élite had failed. The new rulers broke the power of the landlords, expelled foreign nationals and carried out various social reforms. But they failed to establish a firm mass basis for their rule; except in Egypt, where the movement was headed for two decades by a popular leader, their rule did not bring stability to the area. Altogether more than thirty *coups d'état*, successful and unsuccessful,

Muslims of the Ansar sect pay homage to the Mahdi El Hadi. In Sudan the Mahdi no longer has any ruling power.

Women's liberation in Egypt still has a long way to go; a nurse instructs women and children in health principles

occurred in the Arab world after the end of the Second World War. There was some economic progress; however, since a high and growing percentage of the GNP was used for the purchase of arms and other military purposes, the overall achievement was modest.

Radical Arab ideology varied in detail from country to country, an admixture of left- and right-wing elements, of Arab nationalism and Islamic tradition. Communism made substantial progress during the fifties and sixties but, internally divided, it did not achieve a decisive breakthrough in any country. Nevertheless, in view of the weakness of the existing social and political structures and also the absence of a real mass basis for the military dictatorships, it remained a serious contender for power.

Ominous undercurrents could be detected during the 1960s throughout the Arab world. While the conflict between the radicals and the moderates was partly submerged by the hostility against Israel, there were manifestations of a deep-seated malaise: dissatisfaction with established ideologies and institutions was growing as democracy seemed unattainable and planned-economy measures failed to produce spectacular results. The breakdown of old-established beliefs and values and the absence of new ones to replace them provoked a spiritual crisis deeper and more intractable than the transient political problems. There was a very real danger that the growing sense of despair would lead to the search for ultra-radical solutions which could only lead to anarchy and ultimately to further despair. Despite hope that this vicious circle would somehow be broken, there were few tangible signs to substantiate such optimism.

With the retreat of the West, the Middle East became a power vacuum in global politics. This was bound to affect the Soviet Union, since the drive to the south had been a constant factor and one of the traditional directions of Russian foreign policy. The Arab-Israeli conflict facilitated the spread of Soviet influence throughout the Arab world. Feeling these winds of change, Turkey and Iran began to veer towards neutrality in their foreign policy. Europe's inability to assert its interests in the area also helped to facilitate the spread of the Soviet sphere of influence. Only unity and internal stability could have provided a reasonable guarantee to preserve its independence, but on these counts the Middle East scored low.

Economic progress and the rate of modernization in Iran was impressive, and substantial advances took place in Turkey during the sixties. But the starting-point in both countries had been low, and it was doubtful, furthermore, whether economic progress by itself would decisively contribute towards a solution of the political problems besetting these countries. No lasting solution was in sight in 1970 for the crisis in the Arab world and the Arab-Israeli conflict. While the objective importance of the Middle East in world affairs was limited, during the fifties and sixties it had become one of the world's main zones of conflict. As Soviet military pressure in the Arab world, in the Mediterranean and the Indian Ocean increased, and as its political implications became more obvious, a new and more dangerous phase opened in the history of the permanent Middle Eastern crisis.

347

Peter Reeves

The Indian Sub-continent: Dilemmas of Democracy

India and Pakistan were independent of British rule in August 1947 and Ceylon followed in February 1948: the twentieth century's most significant revolution, that of the overthrow of the European domination of the Third World, had effectively begun. The South Asian successor states had been pioneers in the nationalist upsurge which brought that revolution to fruition and the influence of the Indian National Congress and its leaders, in particular, had extended throughout the colonial world. Their independence was significant, too, because of the degree of political development which had already taken place within them. Representative systems based on direct elections had been built up since 1920. Ceylon had had elections on adult suffrage and a Board of Ministers with responsibility for much of the island's government since 1931; British India had had provincial autonomy since 1937. Their political development even in this short first twenty years of independence has a significance that goes beyond the immediate and vital question of their own future as independent nations. Their differing experiences of the problems of political transition are crucial to our understanding of political development in the 'new nations'.

Independence

The Second World War saw major confrontations between the South Asian nationalist movements and the British colonial governments which brought the independence of the sub-continent to the point where negotiations were required not to determine whether there would be a transfer of power but how it could be done and when.

Elections immediately after the war in British India confirmed the dominant positions of the Indian National Congress in the 'Hindu majority' provinces and the Muslim League as the overall voice of the Muslim community. Proposals made in 1946 for a three-unit federation, which would ensure Muslim control in the areas claimed for Pakistan while maintaining a central Indian government, crumbled away. And the evidence of Congress-League conflict and intransigence within the Interim Government formed by Lord Wavell, the viceroy, confirmed the judgement that there was no real possibility of cooperation between the Indian parties. Lord Mountbatten, the new viceroy, moved quickly, therefore, after his appointment in March 1947, to get a solution on the basis of a truncated Pakistan by the division of the Punjab and Bengal, both of which had Muslim majorities but also sizeable Hindu and (in the Punjab) Sikh minorities in fairly clearly demarcated areas. The result was that when partition came in mid-August, there was a wholesale 'transfer of populations' in these two areas. Sizeable refugee populations were built up in both countries. Attacks on refugee trains and groups, the sad culmination of years of communal bitterness, were extensive, particularly on the Punjab border. The effects of this partition period are a vital part of the context within which India and Pakistan have lived in the past twenty years.

Ceylon's transition to self-government was, by contrast, relatively easy. Aided by developments in British India, the island's political leaders, led by D.S.Senanayake, used Ceylon's strategic position in wartime to get acceptance of their demands for self-government and their constitutional proposals. The Ceylon Tamils, about eleven per cent of the population, looked for parity in any future state but they were not strong enough to force the issue. The new constitution at first merely expanded the legislature and the responsibility of the elected members for executive government, while it

A Calcutta bricklayer; Indian industrial progress under the five-year plans started by Nehru has been very gradual; life for most workers has not changed

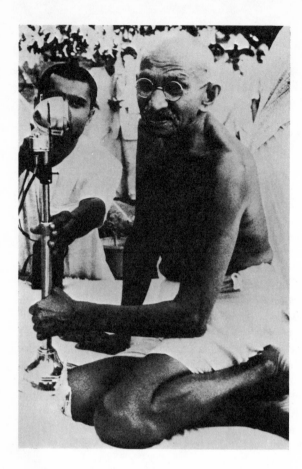

Gandhi, the advocate of *Ahimsa*, non-violence, and a leading figure in Indian independence, gained in August 1947 after nearly thirty years of civil disobedience campaigns on his part. Gandhi built up India's ruling Congress Party, but was heavily criticized for reactionary anti-industrial attitudes

Gandhi's funeral pyre after his assassination by a Hindu extremist on 30 January 1948

retained the governor-general's control over defence and external affairs, but Senanayake's formation of a new broad-based nationalist coalition, the United National Party, in 1946, opened the way for agreement on full self-government in June 1947. By February 1948 Ceylon was independent.

Relations between India and Pakistan

Indian and Ceylon had differences over the future of the immigrant Tamil plantation workers, numbering about 500,000, whom India agreed to take back over a period of fifteen years from 1965. But it was relations between India and Pakistan which were most difficult. The reasons, with partition as a background, are not far to seek. Attitudes derived from past communal propaganda had built, despite the work of men of goodwill on both sides, mutual distrust which was refurbished by communal clashes throughout the period. And there was, unfortunately, a seemingly endless supply of issues which arose between the two because of the complex geopolitical relationship which existed between these two nations carved out of the same area.

The partition boundary award itself caused a great deal of bitterness, particularly in Pakistan. It made possible immediate problems such as the dispute over the supply of water from the eastern rivers of the Indus basin which rise in India but flow into the 'canal colonies' which are the basis of the prosperity of the parts of the Punjab which went to Pakistan. The dispute began in 1948 and was settled only in 1960 by a $900 million World Bank-backed scheme for the construction of new canals in Pakistan to replace the water from the Indian rivers. By the end of the 1960s a new problem of the same kind had arisen in the east because of India's desire to build a barrage at Farakka which would increase the flow of the water through the Hooghly – the river on which Calcutta relies and which was silting rapidly. These works would have a serious effect on East Pakistan's rivers and could cause problems which would require works even more costly and complex than those of the Punjab to repair.

There were further problems derived from the difficulty of demarcating borders in the arid western areas or the riverine country of the east. The fighting in the Rann of Kutch in early 1965 was a case in point. This was a mudflat wasteland on the Gujerat-Sind border where Pakistan laid claim to a sizeable amount of territory (of which it was eventually awarded about ten per cent by an international tribunal). The fighting there was largely a probe by Pakistan to test India's military readiness and resolve. The major clash came on the more sensitive Kashmir front in August 1965. There, India and Pakistan had been deadlocked since the fighting of 1947-9 which had followed the maharaja's unwise dithering over accession to one or other of the new nations. (The maharaja was a Hindu but his people were overwhelmingly Muslim.) The result of fighting in the state left India with the Vale of Kashmir and most of Jammu, while Pakistan held some mountainous northern and western areas which it called *Azad* (Free) Kashmir. Despite

Above Nehru, first Indian prime minister, until his death in 1964 led a united Congress Party: 'a socialistic pattern of society' and 'non-alignment' in foreign affairs

Left Ceylon moved smoothly into independence under D.S.Senanayake, leader of the UNP, a coalition of key social groups. He died in 1952

Pakistani pictures of *Quaid-i-Azam*, 'the great leader', Jinnah, who led the country through independence and partition; his death in 1948 proved the first step to chaos and army rule

repeated UN attempts at mediation and calls for a referendum, by the end of 1970 no progress had been made towards a settlement. India in fact integrated its areas closely into the Indian Union and firmly put a stop to campaigns by Sheikh Abdullah for a sovereign Kashmir, independent of both. Pakistan claimed that the original accession in October 1947 was engineered by India and maintained that India should give the Kashmiris the right of self-determination. And in August 1965 it attempted to reopen the situation militarily, emboldened by the fact that it had an alliance with China – with whom the Indians had a bruising encounter in 1962 – which gave it the advantage of being able to threaten India with the possibility of attack on two fronts. Action by 'freedom fighters' from Azad Kashmir was followed by Indian retaliation against Pakistani outposts and a subsequent Pakistani drive with heavy armour into Jammu. India then countered, unexpectedly firmly, by moving tanks across the Punjab border towards Lahore and Sialkot. In the event the Chinese did not enter the arena and heavy fighting in the Punjab was finally brought to a halt on 23 September by a UN ceasefire. The Tashkent Declaration of 10 January 1966 effected the withdrawal of troops to positions held before 5 August 1965.

While Tashkent cleared up the immediate problems of the 1965 war, it neither brought the Kashmir dispute nearer resolution nor found any effective new ground for the changing of attitudes. The reception that the Declaration received in the sub-continent, especially in Pakistan, suggested in fact that there was indeed little support for compromise. Until there was a fundamental shift in attitudes, both nations were thus condemned to largely wasteful military expenditure and the ill-effects of the bitterness which tinged all of their relations.

Parties and political systems

The South Asian nations inherited systems of representative government from their colonial past, and the choice of political leaders in all three countries was overwhelmingly in favour of maintaining such systems after independence. India and Ceylon both had, throughout the period, constitutions which provided for direct election on adult suffrage and for cabinet government. Pakistan moved towards a similar system but was unable to sustain it by the late 1950s and a martial law regime took over. After a decade of martial law-cum-presidential rule, however, the politicians had successfully reasserted the claims of a 'constitutional' system by 1969-70. Such representative systems placed great stress on the emergence of parties which could operate the electoral, legislative and executive machinery. In the development of viable party systems, therefore, lies the explanation of their very different political experience since independence.

Any discussion of South Asian politics has to bear in mind that these are complex societies with problems of governance which place political systems – and perhaps representative ones in particular – under considerable stress. The 'good government' which colonial officials often believed made up for the lack of 'self-government' in these countries was in fact achieved only by shelving or circumventing or 'putting down' problems of social conflict and regional disparity which the indigenous governments have no option but to face – and to solve.

It is the communal structure of South Asian society which has been politically significant. Each country has a majority community which has regarded the nation as the centre of its own nationalistic aspirations: Hindus in India and Muslims in Pakistan and Sinhalese Buddhists in Ceylon. But these majority communities are nowhere so homogeneous or closely organized as to be sure of acting together. On lines both of regional (i.e. linguistic and 'ethnic') differentiation and internal social stratification (most importantly in terms of caste), there is in fact considerable fragmentation among the majority which has made 'majority' political action uncertain. Only in Ceylon has majority sentiment effectively become the basis of the system. In Pakistan the question of an 'Islamic' state has been a constant torment and has been cut across by regional differences, particularly between West and East Pakistan; while in India the dominant 'secular state' ideology, plus the difficulty of effectively bridging the linguistic and cultural differences between north and south, has limited Hindu-nationalist groupings like the Jana Sangh.

Each nation also has a number of sizeable minority groups whose presence made it difficult for the majority to express its 'nationalism' with impunity. Thus there are Muslim and Christian communities in both India and Ceylon, and Hindus in both Ceylon and Pakistan. There are also small pockets of Buddhists in both India and Pakistan, and the Indian groups have been swollen in recent years by the conversion of 'untouchables' particularly in Maharashtra. India also has Sikh, Jain and Parsi communities of considerable importance. And in all three countries there are, as distinct from these religious communities, ethnic groups such as the 'tribal' people and groups of mixed racial background – the Anglo-Indians in India and Pakistan and the Burghers in Ceylon.

There have been considerable possibilities for social conflict in these societies. Self-aware communities, often with distinctive cultures, often identified with particular economic activities, have easily enough seen their interests threatened by another such group – or been seen to threaten another. This is hardly a situation unique to South Asia, but the possibilities of conflict are greater there because of the complexity of the situation. There were communal riots, often of major proportions, in all three nations during the period 1945-70: the West Bengal/East Pakistan riots of 1949-50, the Tamil/Sinhalese riots of the late 1950s, the Ahmedabad (India) riots of 1969, to mention only the most prominent examples. Such outbreaks seemed almost inevitable in a situation where communities formed the most obvious basis for political mobilization. Electoral politics had (since the turn of the century) heightened the sense of community in the sub-continent and given politicians the opportunity, and the need, to develop a communally based electoral support. In colonial times in British India, some of the problems were sealed off by the provision of separate communal electorates (although there was still no shortage of communal bitterness). In Ceylon these were dispensed with after 1931 but there, too, communal feelings remained strong. After independence, India did away with the system and this made it possible for more normal processes of political bargaining at the local level to be more effective than formerly. However, where, as often was the case, minorities were particularly concentrated in one area or region, it was possible for particular parties to be so clearly based on one group that social conflict was built into the system at other levels. In Kerala, where Christian and Muslim minorities were important (and where large Hindu caste groups such as Nairs and Ezhavas had also organized themselves politically and used their numerical strength for political advantage) it was particularly difficult to get workable coalitions. Similarly, the position of Hindus in East Pakistan or Tamils in the northern and eastern provinces of Ceylon was sufficient to give those groups greater influence than their numbers would have at first suggested.

Conflicts over the choice of a national language to replace the English of colonial times indicated very well the social problems. Language was the most obvious indicator of cultural differences and was also the most immediate economic variable because it was the key to employment, particularly in 'government service'. In Ceylon there were struggles between Sinhala and Tamil, with Sinhala winning out by the 1960s. In Pakistan the Bengali-speaking East Pakistanis prevented the adoption of Urdu as the sole national language; and Urdu had to find a special place for itself in West Pakistan where the regional vernaculars are Panjabi, Sindhi and Pashtu. India had an even more complicated situation. Hindi and 'related languages' (each of which would claim separate status in fact) took in an area across the north with some forty-five per cent of the population, but beyond this area there were strongly developed regional languages with sizeable populations behind them: Bengali, Marathi, Tamil and Telegu all of which were spoken by 40 million or more people (about seven per cent of the population); Gujarati, Oriya, Malayalam and Kannada, each of which was spoken by some 20 million people; and several smaller groups such as Assamese and

Jinnah, speaking in Karachi, August 1947, after Lord Mountbatten (on his right) had transferred powers of government to Pakistan

A dead Hindu in Calcutta is surrounded by Muslims armed with wooden laths in the religious riots of 1946. Social and religious hostility between Hindus and Muslims caused the partition of India into two separate states

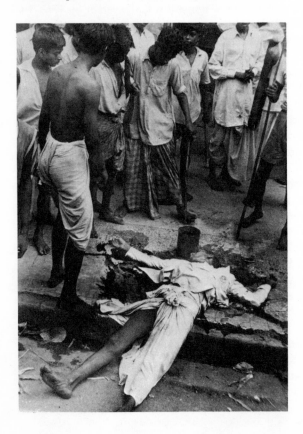

The partition of India and Pakistan

- ■ boundary of British India
- ⌒ˋ demarcation line between India and Pakistan 1947
- ▨ Punjab
- ▨ Bengal
- ▢ Hindu dominated territory
- ▢ Muslim dominated territory

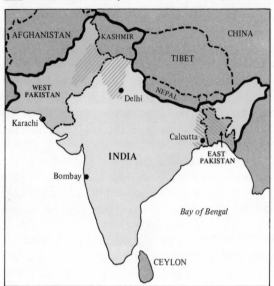

Religious groupings in India and Pakistan

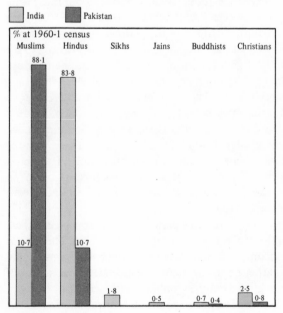

- India
- Pakistan

Kashmiri. Opposition from these regional groups, particularly in the south, to the decision to use Hindi as the official language in place of English from 1965 was considerable, and there was widespread rioting in Madras as the deadline approached, as a result of which the south secured the right virtually to dictate the time for the general introduction of Hindi.

The changing shape of Congress

The continued strength of the Indian National Congress was the key to India's political development. Four general elections were held between 1952 and 1970 and in each the Congress emerged as the most important single party. For the first three elections the Congress held about seventy-five per cent of the seats in the Lok Sabha, the lower house of the central parliament, and about sixty-six per cent of the state assembly seats. The break came in 1967 when its share of the vote fell and it lost a considerable number of seats at the centre and in the states. It was still able to form a government at the centre but in six states it was ousted completely and in another three its attempts to take office were short-lived. This decline of the Congress electoral position was related to splits in the state-level parties before the elections which resulted in the formation of 'breakaway' Congress groups such as the Bangla Congress in Bengal and the Janata Congress in Orissa. It was also related to the fact that most seats were won in Indian elections by relative majorities in many-sided contests, so that a small shift in votes in a number of constituencies could lead to a dramatic loss of seats. This fact was used constructively by the opposition parties in the 1967 elections: agreements ensured less 'wastage' of votes among themselves and they were able to unseat a good many congressmen. In Madras, the Dravida Munnetra Khazagam (DMK: the Dravidian Progressive Federation), the party of Tamil regional nationalism, spearheaded such an alignment and reduced the Congress seats in the state legislature from 130 to 49. Additionally, after the election, there was a loss of Congress control from defections resulting partly from sheer opportunism and partly from the need of local and factional leaders to find new sources of influence with which to maintain their followings.

This loss of Congress predominance caused instability in several northern states but there were also benefits in the sharp change in the configuration of Indian political life which had come about. Parties like the DMK, in particular, which had been discouraged in the past by the apparent problem of attaining power and which had talked of secession, needed this reassurance that the system did allow for changes of regime. (This was important in the light of the moves which the central government had made in 1959 against the communist government in Kerala.) While Congress's predominance was an asset in ensuring the transition to independence, there were real dangers for the system as a whole in Congress *immobilisme*. Moreover, centre-state bargaining became a more realistic (if more difficult) process with the greater differentiation that was introduced among state governments.

The Congress derived its influence and strength from a base of support built up throughout the country from 1920 onwards. At independence it had the support of a wide range of social groups: tenants and small landholders, industrialists and merchants, and a large part of the urban-professional 'middle class'. Its nationalist build-up, moreover, had been effected by drawing into itself local and district leaders – to whom it added other local notables once independence was assured. It had also the monopoly of leaders responsible for the attainment of independence and many of its rank and file members possessed great prestige as 'freedom fighters'.

No other political group could match the Congress on these counts. The communists (CPI) were open to attack because of their wartime stance which required them to support the British as a means of helping the Soviet Union; the Hindu Mahasabha, while active, failed in the postwar elections to make any impression; and the Hindu activist group, the Rashtriya Swayamseyak Sangh (RSS: National Volunteer Association), while it had an effective local organization, had not attempted to operate as a political party up to that time. Events in the late 1940s tended to confirm this situation, moreover:

Cartoon aimed at the small Indian Swatantra Party on the right of Congress

Communist slogans in the state of Kerala, a surprise victory for the communists in 1957. The CPI split into two in the early sixties and the rise of a third Marxist-Leninist party in 1968 weakened them further on a national basis

the CPI's attempt at armed peasant rebellion in the Telengana region of Hyderabad state (now part of Andhra Pradesh) and the apparent complicity of the Mahasabha and the RSS in the assassination of Gandhi in January 1948, placed all three under a cloud. The RSS was in fact banned officially until July 1949. The most likely rival came from the socialists within the Congress itself. Organized as the Congress Socialist Party from 1934, they broke away in 1948 but were decisively beaten in the by-elections which followed. This did not finish them as a party but it did prevent a rapid build-up of socialist forces for the first general elections.

In the years which followed, the CPI grew into a substantial force but splits in the party in the mid-1960s made its position more difficult. The socialists, too, were hampered by splits, defections and unsuccessful efforts at mergers. The most successful socialist party in the late 1960s was the Samyukta (United) Socialist Party which built itself on populist themes such as Hindi chauvinism. Until 1967 the Congress was also aided by the fact that there was no Hindu-nationalist party in a position to challenge it effectively. The Mahasabha declined in importance and the Bharatiya Jana Sangh (Indian People's Party), formed in 1951 by the RSS and Syama Prasad Mookerjee, an ex-president of the Mahasabha and a member of Nehru's cabinet from 1947 to 1950, took time to develop. It suffered the early loss of Mookerjee who died in detention in Kashmir in 1953 as the result of a Jana Sangh *satyagraha* campaign, but the organizational ability of the RSS leadership and the persistence of local units gradually broadened the basis of the party and in 1967 it gained a substantial position in the northern states. Its electoral position had not by 1970 been made absolutely secure (there was a marked swing-back against it in the Uttar Pradesh mid-term elections of 1969) but it looked the most likely alternative to Congress in *north* India.

One man does not make a political party but one man can make a great difference to a party's appeal. In this sense, Jawaharlal Nehru's position was a determining factor in Congress development in the 1950s. An uneasy truce with Sardar Patel kept it together until Patel's death in December 1950 and this enabled Nehru to lead an undivided (if not wholly united) party into the 1952 elections, and to keep it together until his death in 1964, partly at least by allowing its internal inconsistencies to continue. In that period the Congress needed to make decisions about its social strategy but these were difficult because of the party's success. At the Avadi session in 1955, Nehru secured acceptance of a resolution calling for the realization of a 'socialistic pattern of society' and in 1959 at the Nagpur session, he used threats of his own resignation to force through a resolution calling for the general adoption of cooperative farming. The problem was that it was clear that such prescriptions would be largely ignored at the state level. Although Congress lost some ground by adopting such policies, many groups which opposed them were unwilling to leave the dominant organization which they knew, or believed, they could manipulate to their own advantage. There was, for instance, no effective nation-wide response to the formation of the conservative, 'private enterprise' Swatantra [Freedom] Party formed in 1959 in the wake of the cooperative farming resolution (although it did have a considerable strength in some states).

But Congress was weakened over the period. Continuously in office, seemingly sure of electoral victory, it grew complacent and lax. The lack of a strong external threat encouraged internal conflict, the basis for which lay in the existence, from an earlier period, of strong local leaders. Factionalism became the dominant mode of Congress politics with struggles between those in office and out of office. The proposal of the Madras chief minister, K. Kamaraj Nadar, in 1963, that a number of central cabinet ministers and state chief ministers should retire and work to strengthen the organization (the so-called 'Kamaraj Plan') was ostensibly a response to this situation (although it was also a way for the High Command to neutralize some of the more difficult leaders). Kamaraj himself came to the presidency of Congress and it was in that position that he carried out the role of 'kingmaker' when, after Nehru's death in 1964, he was able to ensure the succession of Lal

Shastri, Nehru's aide, succeeded him as prime minister for two years until his own death brought another leadership crisis in January 1966. He is shown spinning yarn, the symbol of independence

Shastri's successor, Mrs Gandhi, Nehru's formidable daughter, managed to keep the Congress Party united despite challenges to her leadership from the right-wing Desai, twice passed over as prime minister. *Below* A pair of bullocks, Congress election symbol

Bahadur Shastri as prime minister. Shastri, an experienced cabinet minister and party official, had been 'Kamarajed' from the central cabinet but had been brought back as Nehru's chief aide in his last months and Kamaraj used his personal position to defeat Morarji Desai who had been more conveniently side-tracked by the 'Plan'.

Shastri's death in Tashkent in January 1966 brought a second succession crisis dangerously soon after the first, but Kamaraj once again called the moves which brought Nehru's daughter, Mrs Indira Gandhi, to the prime ministership over the luckless Morarji. Desai had to accept the position of deputy prime minister and finance minister, until the slump in the 1967 elections gave him a chance to challenge Mrs Gandhi's position – once more unsuccessfully. Matters were brought to a head after the death of President Zakir Husain in 1969: Mrs Gandhi's announcement of plans for bank nationalization and her subsequent support for an independent candidate, V.V.Giri, for the presidency in opposition to the official Congress candidate, allowed Desai and the 'established leadership' to move against her. Each side expelled the other and two Congress parties faced each other, both aware that to lose the name would be to appear to have lost the fight.

This split was a contest for office but it was also a contest about policies. It was a part of the shift which had not come earlier but which, after the defeats of 1967, became increasingly important as the means of making more specific the party's social strategy. Coming at this stage, moreover, there was a possibility that the 'left' Congress of Mrs Gandhi would be able to find the basis for viable coalition among other leftist parties. The split in the Communist Party into CPI and CPI (Marxist) parties, and the problems of the Praja Socialist Party (PSP) which was losing ground to the Samyukta Socialist Party in many areas, raised the possibility of an alignment of CPI, PSP and Mrs Gandhi's Congress, just as the other Congress party was likely to ally with Swatantra and Jana Sangh. These tentative groupings were tested in the Kerala mid-term elections in late 1970 and showed the leftist group to be well placed in that state at least. Its continuation or development remained an open question.

There was no question that the old Congress system would return. What had emerged at the centre was a collective leadership drawn from different regions and sections. Mrs Gandhi, to the surprise of her critics who had consistently underrated her political astuteness, was the central figure in that group by 1970, but there was no indication that the group could not survive without her. The Congress had started the task of making choices in 1969-70; the 1970s would see how genuine those choices were.

Ceylon: the rise of Sinhalese nationalism

The basis of Ceylon's smooth transition to national status was the position and influence of D.S.Senanayake. A long-time member of the Ceylon National Congress, he left that body after the war in protest against the admission of communists, and organized the key political organization of the transition period: the United National Party (UNP) from a merger of his own Congress followers, S.W.R.D.Bandaranaike's Sinhala Maha Sabha (formed in 1937), elements of the Ceylon Muslim League and with even some support from Ceylon Tamils. Although it included important nationalist figures, the UNP was not the party of national independence in the same sense as the Indian National Congress. Its significance lay rather in the fact that it was a coalition of key social groups. It did not attempt to impose too firm a discipline on the constituent parts of the alliance: Bandaranaike's Sinhala Maha Sabha was not disbanded, for instance. None the less, in providing the means of intercommunal government, the UNP fulfilled an essential task for newly independent Ceylon. It won the 1947 elections easily against the fragmented opposition of two factions of the Trotskyist Lanka Sama Samaj Party (Ceylon Equal Society Party) and the Ceylon Communist Party. In the northern and eastern provinces, where the Ceylon Tamils were the major group, the Tamil Congress won decisively and allied itself to the UNP.

The break came in 1951 with a rift between Senanayake and Bandaranaike.

Top Pakistani posters in Ayub Khan's 'basic democracies' election of 1959, an attempt to legitimize his coup of the year before, which involved the election of 80,000 'basic democrats' who would then choose the president
Above After 1962 Ayub sought closer ties with China as a result of American arms shipments to India (left, Chou En-lai, right, Liu Shao-ch'i). Ayub's regime fell in February 1969, after losing army support

An Indian view of political conflicts between the very different East and West divisions of Pakistan

Worried by UNP concern for intercommunal policies at the expense of Sinhalese interests and aware that he had increasingly little chance, despite the fact that his Sinhala Maha Sabha was the largest group in the UNP, of taking over leadership from Senanayake, Bandaranaike decided to leave the party. He disbanded his former group in 1951 and set up a new party, the Sri Lanka (Ceylon) Freedom Party (SLFP), based on Sinhalese upper- and middle-class support and Buddhist religious associations. Sinhalese communalism, with a 'radical', populist posture, was thus brought into the centre of the political stage. It did not immediately sweep the field. D.S. Senanayake died in 1952 and was succeeded by his son Dudley. An election followed almost immediately and although the SLFP made a useful showing the UNP maintained its dominance. The SLFP began therefore to force the pace and the remainder of the 1950s witnessed an alarming growth of communal tension, at times exacerbated quite deliberately by the SLFP and the *bhikkus* (monks) who were its prime allies.

Dudley Senanayake resigned in 1953 as a result of deaths during a food riot and John Kotelawala, the nephew of D.S. Senanayake, took over as prime minister. He had to face this rising tide of Sinhalese-Buddhist sentiment. In 1955 there came an SLFP call for 'Sinhala Only', i.e. the reversal of the earlier two-language formula which had guaranteed the use of Tamil along with Sinhalese. Sinhalese passions rose rapidly and Kotelawala, in an unsuccessful attempt to keep pace, broke the UNP's earlier two-language position. In the elections of 1956 the UNP lost to the SLFP-dominated people's Mahajana Eksath Peramuna (MEP: People's United Front), which brought one of the Trotskyist factions into alliance. These Sinhalese moves also produced a shift among the Tamils and the moderate Tamil Congress was replaced by the more militant Federal Party.

The MEP government, with Bandaranaike as prime minister, pointed the way to increased communal conflict. Tamil campaigns against the 'Sinhala Only' Bill, introduced in June 1956, brought the danger of Sinhalese nationalist retaliation and Bandaranaike tried to conclude a pact with the leaders of the Federal Party in March 1958. This, however, produced the very violence that it was meant to allay. The *bhikkus* forced Bandaranaike to repudiate the pact and thus effectively destroyed his credit with both sides. Faced with continuous rioting from 24 to 27 May 1958 the governor-general, Sir Oliver Goonetillike, declared a state of emergency which lasted until March 1959 and which had subsequently to be reimposed after the assassination of Bandaranaike by a disgruntled *bhikku* in September 1959.

The third phase of Ceylon's political history was a period of slowly emerging coalitions in the 1960s. The SLFP suffered from the loss of Bandaranaike and in the first elections after the state of emergency (held in March 1960), the UNP under Dudley Senanayake gained a narrow majority over the SLFP. This government was dissolved after only a month and in the elections of July 1960 the SLFP swept to a comfortable majority. Bandaranaike's widow, Mrs Sirimavo Bandaranaike, had entered the arena. From that time, she and Dudley Senanayake were the pivots round which Ceylon government-making revolved. In 1965 the position was reversed to place Senanayake at the head of a 'National Government' with the support of most groups except the LSSP faction led by Dr N.M. Perera. That group had joined Mrs Bandaranaike's government in May 1964 – and thereby caused a defection in the SLFP which brought down the government. They stayed together none the less and in May 1970 the tide flowed back strongly for them. The SLFP rose from 41 to 99 seats in the 151-member house and the LSSP rose from 10 to 19 seats; the UNP on the other hand fell from 66 seats to 17. The basic electoral reason for this dramatic swing was the same as in India: small shifts in votes which caused marked swings in terms of seats. In 1970 it was reported that Christians, Tamils and Muslims felt aggrieved that the UNP had not done sufficient about their grievances over Sinhalese, and they were in a position, although minorities, to affect the voting in some areas. The UNP gained more votes than the SLFP in 1970 (1·87 million to 1·81 million) but it took 73 fewer seats. Clearly, while there were some differences in programme and policy, these two parties had a more or less equal hold on

Rioting in Colombo, Ceylon, over equal status for Tamil, the minority language, with the official Sinhalese. Language problems are also part of social conflicts in India and Pakistan.

Below Ceylon's Communist Party holds its May Day parade; by 1970 left-wing parties had very definite influence on government policy.
Bottom Mrs Bandaranaike, the world's first woman prime minister, in 1960, after her husband, who had been in power for four years, was assassinated. Her campaign image: 'The Mother'

the Sinhalese vote. The communal riots of the late 1950s had put some restriction on the overt use of communal appeals and so undermined the SLFP's main potential advantage. The UNP, on the other hand, found that it had inadequate answers to the basic economic problems for while it could work to increase food-grain production, it could not hold down prices and so there was little chance that it could win over many SLFP supporters.

In governmental terms, the support of the left for the Sinhalese parties became a crucial factor. As the left was fragmented and not in a position to form a government on its own account, its constituent elements were, after 1955-6, prepared to ally with either the UNP or SLFP. The effect earlier was to produce governments that were noticeably ill at ease with each other. By 1970 it appeared that the SLFP was being drawn 'leftwards' although it was noticeable that the most radical parts of the new government's programme, such as nationalization of banks and state direction of plantations came under LSSP ministers.

Pakistan: the road to martial law

Pakistan seemed likely to follow the same path as India at independence. That is to say, it also had a party of national independence – the Muslim League – which, while it had not been so long in existence as Congress, had demonstrated its hold over the Muslim community in the 1940s. The constituent assembly that was formed from the members of the 1946 Indian constituent assembly representing 'Pakistan' areas, was dominated from the start by the League: there seemed no reason why Pakistan should not go ahead under the League as India did under the Congress. But the position was in fact very different. Although there had been a Muslim League since 1906, the party which won independence and partition was largely the post-1935 creation of Muhammad Ali Jinnah. Significantly, too, the Muslim-majority provinces, Bengal and Punjab, and the North-West Frontier Province were the last to be brought into the League fold; and even then there were strong regional groups which either opposed the League or co-operated only reluctantly. The League had been strong enough to sweep aside any Congress claims to represent the Muslims but once it achieved Pakistan its position changed radically. It held the trump card of being the party that won independence and it had Jinnah – *Quaid-i-Azam*, 'the great leader' – at its head; but its organization was to an important extent in the 'wrong' areas. It was re-formed in December 1947 as the Pakistan Muslim League but this did not go far towards reconstructing the party at the local level. The urgency had gone out of the situation to a considerable extent and the League's leaders reverted, if only slightly, to the notion that politics was something that 'leaders' did and that followers would accept.

Even this might have been satisfactory with Jinnah at the head, for he was in a position to sustain the political momentum. But Jinnah died in September 1948 and with him died much of Pakistan's hope for a smooth

Kashmir

▼▼▼ 1949 India-Pakistan ceasefire line
☐ Kashmir
▨ seized by China 1962
■■■ international frontiers in 1948
▨ claims given up by China and Pakistan in 1963

Below A Pakistani view of India and the West. Indo-Pakistani differences led to war in 1965
Below right A town in Kashmir after shelling by Indian troops

transition. He was 'succeeded' by the only other national-level figure produced by the Pakistan movement, Liaquat Ali Khan. But Liaquat lacked the stature of Jinnah; he led the country as prime minister but he could not direct it as Jinnah had done as governor-general. He was assassinated in 1951 and in that period he was able to make relatively little progress with the launching of the new state. By the time he died the constituent assembly, bedevilled by the problem of making an 'Islamic' state, was a long way from formulating definite or acceptable proposals.

Liaquat's death meant the end of the League as an effective party. 'Muslim League' remained as a convenient label for the group in power; and that group increasingly took decisions in private and used the assembly merely for its own ends. Opposition parties grew up under strong regional leaders who had been excluded from, or had no entry to, this central oligarchy. The Awami [People's] League under H.S.Suhrawardy and the Krishak Sramik [Peasants' and Workers'] Party under Fazlul Huq in East Pakistan and the Awami League in West Pakistan under men such as G.M. Sayed and Abdul Ghaffar Khan, had some influence regionally but they were not in a position to oust the central group which understood its own weakness only too well and took care not to hold elections which might give the regional leaders an opening. The result was political frustration, especially in East Pakistan, the more populous of the two wings, which felt itself treated unfairly in political settlements and much of its economic life being taken over by West Pakistanis. There was another danger point, illustrated by rioting in Lahore in 1953, in the increasing activity of the party of Islamic orthodoxy, the Jama'at-i-Islami, which was in the forefront of the demands that Pakistan should become unequivocally an Islamic state.

Discontent and disturbance opened the way for increased central control. Iskandar Mirza, formerly a soldier and 'political officer' on the frontier, and then minister of the interior, emerged as the strong man of the government. The constituent assembly was dissolved just as it agreed on a draft report and fresh (indirect) elections were held for a new set of members. When this new assembly met in January 1956 it was presented with the government's proposals for a constitution and was forced to keep to a strict timetable in its 'debate'. The first independent constitution, passed in February and inaugurated in March 1956, was hardly an expression of popular will. It made Pakistan a republic, with the president as head of state and with cabinet government maintained at both the centre and in the provinces. Iskandar Mirza, now governor-general, became the first president and, pending elections, the existing assemblies became those provided for by the constitution.

The conduct of affairs became increasingly chaotic under this sytem and in October 1958 Mirza used this as the excuse for proclaiming martial law. Before the month was out he himself was sent into exile and Ayub Khan, the commander-in-chief, assumed the presidency. Martial law lasted until June 1962. Steps were taken to disqualify from public life politicians who had been active in the 1950s and in 1962 a new constitution was introduced which put the seal on the changes in the basis of Pakistan's political system which Ayub had already introduced and which were designed to ensure that the politicians would not have the chance to re-establish themselves. A system of local councils, the Basic Democracies, established in 1959, was to act both as local government and as the electoral college for the new assemblies and – so that he could claim 'popular' backing – for the president himself. The president was now, moreover, the head of the government as well as the head of state.

With many of the former political leaders disqualified and because he had need of an organization of his own, Ayub Khan allowed the political parties to reappear in 1962. Ayub himself assumed control of a reconvened Pakistan Muslim League (sometimes called the Convention Muslim League because there was another 'Council Muslim League' which rejected Ayub). In the presidential election in 1965 Ayub found himself confronted by five combined opposition parties (COP). The alliance nominated Miss Fatima Jinnah, the sister of the *Quaid-i-Azam*, and campaigned strongly for a return to a fully representative system. Ayub won comfortably enough in the electoral college; he gained sixty-three per cent of the Basic Democrats' votes but he lost heavily in East Pakistan and in Karachi, the largest city.

The chance for the opposition political groups came in 1969. The Tashkent Declaration of January 1966 lost Ayub support in the army and among even his own political supporters and this allowed popular dissatisfaction to be heard and to grow into demands for a return to 'democracy'. Disorder mounted as politicians and students took to the streets and as it did so Ayub's power-base fell away. The army decided that Ayub should be allowed to fall and in February 1969 he went, to be replaced by a new military government headed by General Yahya Khan who was pledged to introduce constitutional government at some future date but who was prepared immediately to use the full weight of the armed forces to put down trouble. Elections were eventually set for August 1970 but were then shifted to December 1970. These, the first general elections on a popular basis in Pakistan's twenty-three-year history, provided an important opportunity for the parties, the Awami League led by Shaikh Mujibur Rahman in the East and Z. A. Bhutto's Pakistan People's Party in the West, to begin again the task of building a representative system.

Challenge from the left?

Given the difficulties which had been faced and the problems which remained, why had these representative systems not been challenged or more affected by the movements with revolutionary objectives? Economic problems

Above Indians demonstrate against the Chinese suppression of the 1959 rebellion in Tibet and queue (*right*) to enlist for the Chinese border war two years later

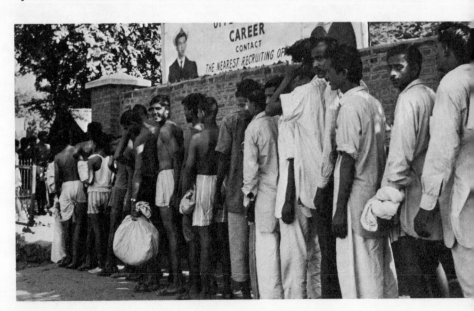

Distribution of working population

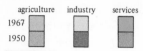

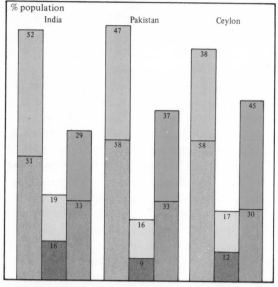

abounded in South Asia; inequality was a fact. There had been economic growth since independence, as a result of planned development, private investment and international aid programmes but this had done relatively little to raise the general standard of living. Familiar groups did very well out of what development there was – millowners, contractors, industrialists, farmers with large holdings, capital and personal knowledge of farming techniques – but their success merely enhanced existing inequalities. Large and rapidly expanding populations, overwhelmingly rural in character so that there was great pressure on available arable land resources and high under-employment in agriculture; low levels of productivity, particularly in agriculture, which meant recurrent problems of food supply and large imports of food-grains; and severe imbalances in the economic structures of all three nations as the result of the long colonial connection with industrialized Britain: these remained the outstanding features of the South Asian economies, despite the efforts which were made to develop them. In Ceylon the dependence on plantation industries and in Pakistan the relative lack of industrial resources added further special problems. And yet, despite this base of economic hardship, movements for revolutionary change had had no clear success by 1970. This was due partly to the character of the 'revolutionary' parties which had operated and partly to the problems that confronted attempts to mobilize mass support.

Of all the groups in the sub-continent with revolutionary aims, the Communist Party of India had the widest base and the largest membership at the beginning of the period. Its development over the following two

Part of the Bhakra Dam project, which will provide irrigation for 6,500,000 acres of land. Most of it was completed by 1970

Right Break for lunch outside the Durgarpur steelworks

Food production per capita

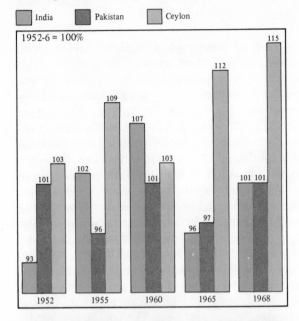

India | Pakistan | Ceylon

1952-6 = 100%

decades, however, changed its character and potential greatly. The party survived earlier pressure from the colonial government and had expanded considerably during the war when it was allowed to exist legally and so had a chance to strengthen its organizations among students, workers and peasants. Hard hit in the early years of independence when it attempted to lead armed peasant struggle in Telengana, it recovered under the leadership of Ajoy Ghosh and established itself as the main opposition party in parliament until the late 1960s.

This success was directly linked to Ghosh's strategy of 'constitutional communism', which saw the possibility of the party coming to power through the parliamentary system and which had its first fruits in the victory in Kerala in 1957. It was officially adopted at the party congress at Amritsar in 1958, but it was never wholly accepted by the left wing and Ghosh's death in 1962 made possible the gradual widening of the rift within the party. By the end of the 1960s there were two competing parties, neither of which was able to retain the former strength of the undivided party so that the leadership of the opposition passed to the right-wing Jana Sangh and Swatantra parties. The position was further complicated from 1968 onwards by the rise of a third, Marxist-Leninist, party.

The marked regional character of Indian communism was also important. Kerala, Bengal, Andhra to a lesser extent, and Bombay city were consistent strongholds of the party but in the rest of the country, while there were organizations, the party was either relatively weak or preferred to work mainly through other bodies. It had therefore, perhaps most significantly, a relatively weak base in the densely populated northern states with large peasant population like Bihar and Uttar Pradesh.

Ceylon had a number of competing left-wing parties. The Lanka Sama Samaj Party (LSSP), founded in 1935, and led by Philip Gunawardena and Dr N. M. Perera, was a Trotskyist party. A Stalinist group expelled at the beginning of the war eventually founded the Communist Party of Ceylon in 1943 and in 1945 the LSSP itself between Gunawardena and Perera. This tripartite pattern was basic to Ceylon left-wing politics until 1963 when the CPC also split into two parties. There were periodic attempts at the formation of a left united front, but these invariably broke up as one or other of the Trotskyist groups moved towards alliance with one or other of the major Sinhalese parties, the UNP or the SLFP. In 1952 the alliance between Gunawardena and the CPC was broken after the elections of that year and Gunawardena later moved towards the SLFP and formed a coalition (the MEP) for the 1956 elections. Gunawardena became minister for agriculture in the MEP government and was able to introduce some measures of land reform before the coalition, never particularly easy, broke down. Gunawardena retained the MEP label for his own group which was of diminishing importance over the 1960s. In 1963 there was an attempt to get the CPC, LSSP and MEP together but this time Perera's LSSP broke and joined Mrs Bandaranaike's government in May 1964, with Perera himself becoming finance minister. The coalition was defeated in December 1964 because of defection within the SLFP, and in the elections which followed the SLFP-LSSP coalition lost to a new UNP-MEP coalition. Perera stayed in alliance with Mrs Bandaranaike, however, and in 1970, with the larger 'pro-Moscow' section of the CPC also in alliance, the SLFP-LSSP coalition returned to power. The left in Ceylon had thus become part and parcel of the governmental system, able to exert a very definite 'leftwards' tug on policy but hardly a revolutionary force.

Communism in Pakistan had a much more difficult history. Heavily defeated in an attempted putsch in 1951, the party was outlawed from 1954 and was thus closely circumscribed for the whole period. It was estimated in 1968 that there were some 2,700 members of the illegal party in East Pakistan and some 750 members in West Pakistan and that developments in India after 1967 would strengthen the party, particularly in the East. But up to 1970 much of the work of the left devolved upon Maulana Bhashani's National Awami Party, which broke away from the Awami League in 1954 in order to pursue a more anti-Western line in foreign policy. Bhashani concentrated on the East Pakistani peasantry and talked in Maoist terms

The old way to crush sugar-cane; sugar was partially decontrolled in 1967-8 to stimulate falling production and forty per cent of the total output was put on the open market

A Delhi poster suggests that the ideal size of the Indian family is four; government family planning centres have been set up in much of the country

A roadside tap in Calcutta. Cholera epidemics recur in India and account for about 200,000 deaths annually; one of the main causes is the short supply of filtered water

although he himself was closer to the traditional 'Islamic socialist' spokesmen who arose from time to time among the Muslims of the sub-continent. The approach of the 1970 elections reportedly caused dissensions within the party as the younger, doctrinaire leaders argued against Bhashani's decision to participate in the elections.

Mass mobilization

Urban workers formed only a small proportion of the South Asian populations. They provided a relatively advanced section of left-wing organization through their unions but there were considerable problems. Unions tended to be tied to political parties in competing alignments which served the interests of the parties rather than the workers. The various Indian 'trade union congresses' were a case in point: the All-India TUC affiliated to the CPI; the Indian National TUC affiliated to the Congress; and the Praja Socialist Party's Hind Mazdoor Sangh. Similarly in Ceylon the split in the CPC brought in its train the formation of rival trade union federations. Workers were, moreover, subject to strong 'traditional' influences outside the factory: the xenophobic Shiv Sena in Bombay, which was aimed particularly against south Indians, was disquietingly effective among workers in the city.

In these overwhelmingly rural countries, however, it was the peasantry which was the major force available for mobilization. The problems here were even greater than among workers however. The sheer size and the scattered nature of village populations made the task an immense one. It was even more difficult in view of the fact that class consciousness and class institutions had hardly developed in the rural areas. The 'traditional' institutions of caste and community remained of paramount importance. The nationalist movements did little to disturb these and they had, since independence, been reinforced because in electoral politics the leaders of such groups were the most accessible entry points for party workers. (These were not necessarily the older leaders – new, more specialized 'brokers' often developed to deal with these new forms of political bargaining.)

The distribution of power in the rural areas was likewise an obstacle to peasant organization. Precise regional structures varied widely, but the stable colonial regimes of the sub-continent everywhere allowed strong landholding groups, landlords and secure tenants (it made little difference in practice), to dominate rural political life. Land-tenure reform programmes after independence were concerned in the main to strengthen the secure tenants and the smaller landlords at the expense of both the larger landlords (who posed problems of local control which the newly independent governments often wished to avoid) and the smallest tenants and agricultural labourers. Ten years after independence, Charan Singh, who played a leading part in the programmes of the Indian state of Uttar Pradesh, neatly underlined the counter-revolutionary strategy in a pamphlet entitled *Agrarian Revolution in Uttar Pradesh*:

The political consequences of the land reforms are no less far-reaching. Much thought was given to this matter, since the drafters of the legislation were cognizant of the need to ensure political stability in the countryside. By strengthening the principle of private property where it was weakest, i.e. at the base of the social pyramid, the reforms have created a huge class of strong opponents of the class war ideology. By multiplying the number of independent land-owning peasants there came into being a middle-of-the-road, stable rural society and a barrier against political extremism. It is fair to conclude that the agrarian reform has taken the wind out of the sails of the disrupters of peace and the opponents of ordered progress.

Other rural changes, such as the introduction of new forms of local government (*panchayati raj* in India and the Basic Democracies in Pakistan), and the development of cooperative institutions, worked to further, at least in the short run to enhance, the position of the already strong.

The clearest signs of a revolutionary movement came from India and from the traditional areas of communist strength, where the CPI (Marxist-Leninist) had made, since 1968, determined efforts at peasant insurrection. Activities began in the Bengal area called Naxalbari and the movement was popularly dubbed 'Naxalite'. There is no doubt that this was the most

In East Pakistan bodies in the fields were a common sight after the 1970 hurricane, the worst natural disaster of the century; the government was heavily attacked for not making the most of relief supplies

Population growth 1950-69

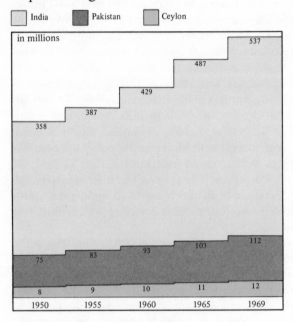

| | India | | Pakistan | | Ceylon |

in millions

				537
			487	
		429		
	387			
358				
75	83	93	103	112
8	9	10	11	12
1950	1955	1960	1965	1969

Age distribution in India and USA 1960-1

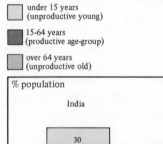
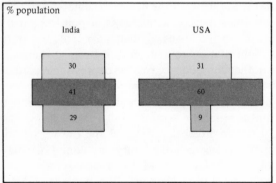

☐ under 15 years
(unproductive young)

■ 15-64 years
(productive age-group)

☐ over 64 years
(unproductive old)

% population

India   USA

30	31
41	60
29	9

serious attempt at peasant action since Telengana in the late 1940s but by 1970 it was not clear that it had made great inroads into areas where communist organization had not previously been markedly successful. Even in the areas of strength Naxalite activities brought further direct conflict among communist groups because the other communist parties were among the groups forming state governments. The politicization of the peasant might, as in the past, produce *jacquerie* in favourable circumstances, but find greater difficulty in maintaining a sustained campaign.

Conclusion

Towards the end of the 1950s, Selig Harrison pointed (in a book of this title) to these first years of independence as being, for India, 'the most dangerous decades'. This certainly was, and continued to be true – and for the other South Asian nations as well. What seemed equally true, after a further ten years' experience, was that India and Ceylon had shown resilience in the face of the dangers and that the political changes of these first two decades had begun to create political systems within which the continuing challenges could be met. Even in the case of Pakistan, where breakdown was obvious, there was a clear demand for a representative system; faced with the difficult task of creating a nation from two such widely separated and disparate regions it would hardly have been surprising if the country had had an even more troubled history. There were, however, no conclusive developments: the future for South Asia remained very much an open question. But it is possible to see the developments of the years 1945-70 as having moulded some important areas of the political life in the Indian sub-continent.

363

J.A.C.Mackie

South-east Asia: Warring Ideologies

When the Second World War ended in August 1945, the whole of South-east Asia except Thailand was still formally subject to colonial rule. But the colonial empires had been irreparably shaken by Japan's occupation of the region in 1941-2, by her granting or promising independence to most of the former colonies and by the emergence in Indo-China and Indonesia, within a few days of Japan's surrender, of vigorous independence movements which were to wage the wars of liberation that led to the overthrow of Dutch and French power. These events provided the impetus for the nationalism and anti-colonialism which have proved to be the most dynamic political forces in the region since that time.

As a consequence independence was attained during the next twenty years by the Philippines (1946), Burma (1948), Indonesia (1949), Cambodia, Laos and Vietnam, the latter divided *de facto* into North and South (1949-54), Malaya (1957), Singapore, Sabah, or British North Borneo, and Sarawak (1963), through merger with Malaysia, though Singapore was later ejected from Malaysia to become an independent state in 1965. By then only the tiny colony of Portuguese Timor remained to be emancipated, although the even tinier Sultanate of Brunei clung to its anomalous status as a self-governing British protectorate, after rejecting an invitation to become part of Malaysia.

Decolonization has had far-reaching effects on all these countries in the quarter of a century since Japan's defeat, even including Thailand, in so far as British semi-colonial influence over her governments has been supplanted. The political institutions sustaining colonial rule and the 'colonial caste structure' of society, with white foreigners assuming the top positions as of right and the 'natives' confined to the lower levels by the myth of white superiority quickly began to crumble. Nationalism flourished both as a concomitant of the struggle for independence and as a manifestation of a new self-assertive quest for national identity. Previously unknown forms of political mobilization called into being social forces previously dormant or kept in check by the colonial powers. One consequence was the mushroom growth of representative institutions and political parties, arising from the aspiration to base the authority of the new governments upon the consent of the governed, although neither democracy nor political parties anywhere lived up to the high expectations of their advocates but were gradually emasculated by authoritarian governments in Burma, Thailand, Indonesia and Vietnam. Another consequence was the depressing record of violence, conflict, repression, insurrection, attempted revolts and *coups d'état*, which seemed to justify the assertion that South-east Asia was one of the most unstable parts of the globe.

The contrast between these unsettled decades and the outward tranquillity of the region during the previous half-century of colonial rule may seem to demand some profound explanation. Melodramatic phrases have been invoked such as 'South-east Asia in ferment', 'the Balkans of Asia' or 'turbulent Asia awakening from its sleep of centuries'. But on a less high-flown plane the apparent turmoil and upheaval can be explained largely by reference to the interaction of several distinct historical processes.

First and foremost were the political adjustments to the ending of colonial rule, the shaking out of a new balance of forces throughout the region. Decolonization started a chain reaction which, by 1970, had by no means worked itself out. Second, the regional power balance also began to change, though the presence of American forces in the region

After colonialism, the cold war: *Krokodil* attacks the American presence in South-east Asia

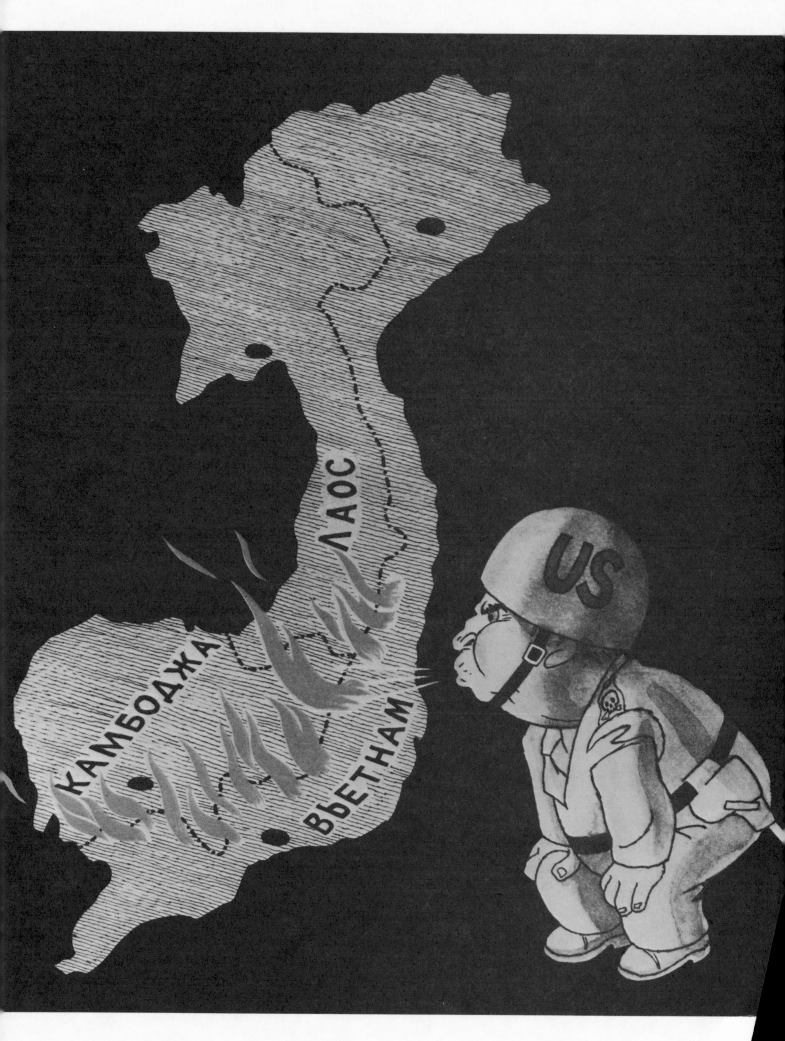

A soldier carves the word independence on a Burmese stamp issued in 1948. The party responsible for independence, the AFPFL, came into prominence at the end of the war in the struggle against the Japanese

postponed the development of the 'power vacuum' that some strategists anticipated, while the British checked the only attempt made to tilt the balance, Indonesia's 'confrontation' of Malaysia in 1963-6. Chinese and Russian influence, political and ideological rather than military, became new significant factors. Third, social and cultural changes were occurring in every country, especially in the towns, where the alchemy of modernization and political mobilization was most far-reaching. (But much of the social ferment associated with urbanization, education, greater social and occupational mobility and new criteria for élite status stemmed from the final decades of the colonial era: they were concomitants rather than consequences of decolonization. Cutting across and complicating these sources of tension was a conflict of ideologies, not merely the challenge of international communism, but also the rival claims of Islam, Buddhism, Christianity and other beliefs in countries where 'primordial ties' (kin, religion and language) were still very strong. It is hardly surprising that communism exerted an appeal in quarters where Marx or Lenin, perhaps even Mao, would least have expected it – to the socially and culturally dislocated, to the semi-educated rather than the intellectuals (though Marxism attracted the latter strongly), to peasants with traditional inclinations towards millenarianism, even to some hill-tribesmen of Burma and Thailand. Doctrines of revolution, violent or peaceful, were much in vogue, though neither Moscow nor Peking gave much assistance, except in Vietnam.

But to depict the decolonization process simply in terms of instability would be misleading. Another aspect was the consolidation of the new élites – except in the former French colonies of Indo-China, where the war of national liberation had not yet ended – as these countries settled down from the shock-waves which accompanied the collapse of colonial authority in 1941-2, the Japanese occupation and the violent struggles which accompanied the gaining of independence. In general the second postwar decade was far more settled than the first, when none of the new governments was securely established and the lineaments of the new states had not been settled, so that there was still ample scope for power plays by all sorts of challengers – communists, Muslims or Buddhists. The legitimacy of the various élite groups was less well founded in the early years of uncertainty than later when the institutional framework crystallized. And while the years between 1963 and 1970 were hardly tranquil in South-east Asia, there were many indications that the established élites had further tightened their grasp of political and economic power. Although new tensions were arising as a result of population growth, urban unemployment and inequalities of income, the threat of communism was not nearly as alarming in 1970 as in 1948-50. Nearly all the governments of the region were more secure than in the fifties, commanding more potent instruments of repression and far from hesitant to employ them. Changes of government were less numerous in the last decade than previously and, where they occurred by *coup d'état*, they signified little more than factional reshuffles. In Singapore Lee Kuan Yew's metamorphosis from a left-wing socialist inveighing against colonialism in the fifties to a middle-of-the-road pragmatist ten years later symbolized the trend.

The years of anti-colonial struggle: 1945-55

For the peoples of South-east Asia the years in which they threw off the yoke of colonialism are enshrined in their national folklore as an epoch of heroic deeds, of unprecedented sacrifice, excitement and revolutionary upsurge. Cold-blooded historians may tend to reduce the story to an analysis of power politics, but even they will find themselves enmeshed in the emotions of that turbulent era when 'power rolled into the street' for a brief interval between the collapse of the Japanese and the establishment of a new authority.

Our story must start therefore, with an account of how independence was won and how the new governments established themselves in conditions of confusion and uncertainty. The response of the colonial governments was of crucial importance. Where the transition had been peaceful, or

Indonesia about to break the bonds of Japanese occupation (poster). Independence was proclaimed in August 1945 in the confusion of the Japanese surrender and brought Dutch 'police actions'; legitimacy was achieved four years later

Malayan independence celebrations. Independence was finally won on 31 August 1957, after twelve problematic and violent years

South-east Asian alignments

- ▓ countries under communist influence
- ☐ SEATO countries
- ▨ ASEAN countries
- ▬ Malaysia

comparatively so, as in the Philippines, Malaysia, Singapore and Cambodia, relatively little dislocation ensued and former indigenous élites were not seriously troubled in establishing their authority. Where it was revolutionary, as in Indonesia, Vietnam, both North and South, and (to a lesser extent) Laos and Burma, old sources of authority were challenged and new ones weakened by the manifold problems of establishing legitimacy. Nationalism was more volatile in the latter group of countries, while communism posed a much greater threat there, as a rival ideology and as a political force.

To illustrate these points, I can only sketch some of the main landmarks from several significant countries. Others will have to be neglected, since it is impossible to do justice to all the tangled themes of this complex period in a brief compass. The challenge of communism in the various insurrections of 1948, following the international communist movement's espousal of Zhdanov's 'two-camp' doctrine, is one such theme. Another is the growth of non-alignment and the sense of Asian solidarity in a world-wide struggle against colonialism expressed in the Afro-Asian Conference at Bandung in 1955, an occasion that symbolized the end of colonial rule in South-east Asia (except in a few special cases) and the triumph of Asian nationalism.

Because French, Dutch and even British interests and influence in South-east Asia contracted so rapidly after the mid-fifties, while the shadows of America, Russia and China seemed to loom so large, it is easy to forget that in the first postwar decade it had been quite the opposite. The Dutch, French and British returned to their colonies after the war as administrators, soldiers, planters and businessmen, to resume their 'interrupted mission' of bringing civilization to the subject peoples of Asia – while not forgetting their own pockets. The Americans were unique in promptly granting independence to the Philippines in accordance with a promise made ten years earlier, but even they insisted on special privileges for American business, which aroused great nationalist resentment and the accusation (not seriously warranted, but not easy to dismiss) of 'neo-colonialism'.

In Burma the British authorities, after an unpromising start, soon came to terms with Aung San and the Anti-Fascist People's Freedom League (AFPFL), which had sprung up during the drive against the Japanese in the latter stages of the war. What was at stake there was not the principle of self-government so much as the constitutional measures required for it, in view of the special problems of incorporating ethnic minorities such as the Karens, Shans, and others whom the British had previously administered separately from the Burmans. In Malaya, as we shall see, the British moved much more slowly until 1955, also because of the peculiar problems created by a plural society; but there, too, they readily conceded the principle of ultimate self-government. By thus avoiding a direct conflict with the forces of anti-colonialism and nationalism, the British and Americans were able to exercise a moderating influence upon nation-building at its most critical stage and then quietly remain in the background long after the transition to independence.

In Indonesia and Indo-China, however, independence had to be fought for. By initially opposing the nationalist leaders and later trying ineffectually to undermine them by divide-and-rule tactics, the Dutch and French manœuvred themselves into inflexible policies of military conquest from which there was ultimately no retreat short of humiliating capitulation. The consequences were not only costly for them, but ruinously disruptive for their former colonies.

Soekarno and Hatta proclaimed Indonesia's independence on 17 August 1945 in the confusion of the Japanese surrender. The authority of the new Republic of Indonesia was quickly accepted across most of Java and Sumatra, though not without challenge, so that the Allied forces which landed a few weeks later saw the need to deal with it and urged the returning Dutch to do so too. Only grudgingly did the Dutch agree to negotiate with the new regime, however, though the Republican leaders accepted the necessity to reach a compromise with them. The Linggadjati Agreement of March 1947 provided *de facto* recognition of the Republic's

Ho Chi Minh, North Vietnamese president (seated) plans his tactics during the French war in 1950

authority over Java, Madura and Sumatra and the eventual establishment of a sovereign federal state under the Dutch Crown, in which the Republic would be the main constituent element, along with several Dutch-sponsored states in the outer islands. But the agreement was too ambiguous and complex to survive in the suspicious atmosphere of the times and in July 1947 the Dutch launched a military attack (euphemistically called a 'police action') against the Republic to enforce their demands. They quickly seized the main plantation areas and confined the Republic to the poorest, most crowded parts of central Java, around Jogjakarta. This brought the United Nations into the dispute, through a Security Council resolution calling for a ceasefire and the establishment of a Good Offices Commission, which endeavoured to bring the two sides together again on the basis of the Linggadjati principles. By the end of 1947, however, the Dutch were confident that they held the upper hand: they showed little willingness to make concessions to the Republic, but pressed on with their scheme of establishing a set of federal states ('puppet states' in the eyes of their opponents) through which they hoped to maintain their control.

In December 1948 the Dutch launched a second 'police action' with the aim of eliminating the Republic altogether. This time their strategy backfired, for they aroused widespread guerrilla resistance within Indonesia and a hornet's nest of international condemnation, which compelled them to renew the negotiations that led, in December 1949, to complete independence for a federal United States of Indonesia, in which the Republic leaders quickly achieved pre-eminence by virtue of their better nationalist credentials. The federal structure almost immediately crumbled under pressures for a unitary Republic of Indonesia during 1950.

Indonesia's revolutionary struggle had liberated an upsurge of revolt directed initially at old-established authorities who had supported and been supported by the Dutch, particularly the old colonial officials and the 'feudal' rulers (who in some areas were slaughtered in an outburst of 'social revolution'). Youth groups in the towns and militant Islamic leaders in the countryside seized the opportunity to take action on their own account in the name of 'the people'. The Republican government exercised only a precarious hold in its early months, until it was able to bring the various guerrilla groups together into a regular army and channel mass actions through political parties which were prepared to work within a more orderly framework. Challenges to its leadership occurred on several occasions, the most important being the revolt launched by the Communist Party at Madiun in September 1948. Even after 1949 the legitimacy of the government was frequently questioned – by advocates of a Darul Islam or Muslim state, by regional revolts (of which the 1957-8 challenge to Soekarno's authority from Sumatra and North Sulawesi was later to undermine the parliamentary system) and by some elements in the army. While the rules

Paratroops land at Dien Bien Phu to begin the battle that finished the French in Indo-China and resulted in a divided Vietnam

Diem attempts to justify his policies as president of South Vietnam; he led an autocracy propped up by US aid

South Vietnamese tribesmen take an oath of allegiance to Diem's government

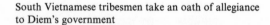

of parliamentary democracy were observed fairly well during the early fifties, with general elections being successfully conducted in 1955, there was no strong commitment to the institutions and values of liberal democracy even among the élite. These institutions were adopted mainly because they were familiar to the Western-educated leaders who were determined to show that they could work them as well as the Dutch, for the anti-colonial struggle was waged in the name of democracy. The men who dominated Indonesian politics during the first decade were mainly those who had the appropriate education and administrative skills to operate the machinery of government they inherited from the Dutch. Later, however, disillusionment with these institutions and challenges to the authority of those who were in charge of them were to mark a further stage in the rejection of the colonial past.

In Indo-China, the French were even more shortsighted than the Dutch. The First Indo-China War of 1945-54 proved to be longer and much more bitterly fought than the Indonesian conflict, ending inconclusively at the Geneva Conference with the ill-fated partition of Vietnam and an uneasy political balance in Laos and Cambodia which was later upset in the course of the Second Indo-China War after 1965.

Ho Chi Minh's leadership of the Indo-China Communist Party and the Vietnamese independence movement is one of the epic stories of Asian nationalism. The fact that he was a communist and that the Vietminh, which he had set up in 1941 as an underground anti-Japanese movement, was largely controlled by members of the Indo-China Communist Party, though outwardly a broad nationalist front, should not distract attention from the fact that it was his appeal to his countrymen as a nationalist in the fight against foreign dominance that gave him and the Vietminh their great political strength. (In Laos and Cambodia, by contrast, communists played little part in the resistance to French attempts to restore control.) The French helped to force the Vietnamese nationalist movement into the hands of the Vietminh by their refusal to give more than desultory consideration to negotiations with Ho in 1946, when he was still willing to compromise. By resorting to force at the end of 1946, they plunged Vietnam into seven years of inconclusive warfare between well-armed French regulars and poorly-equipped Vietminh guerrillas, warfare in which the French were impregnable in the towns and the strongly-held delta areas of the Red River and the Mekong, but the Vietminh virtually unassailable in the interior, especially in the north, near the China border. The fighting had two fateful consequences for Vietnam. It emphasized a division between the northern and southern regions (which had ancient historical roots and was accentuated by the failure of the Vietminh in 1945 to achieve the same degree of influence around Saigon as it established in Hanoi), since the main conflict was in the north. This, in turn, meant that the Vietminh were able to obtain aid from the Chinese communists after their victory in 1949, which led to increasingly open communist dominance of the Vietminh and, by 1953-4, to the entanglement of the conflict in the broader power struggle between America and China, through American aid to the French.

The French belatedly attempted to devise a political counter to the Vietminh in 1949, by conceding the outward forms of independence to a Vietnamese government under the former Emperor Bao Dai, a strategy similar to the Dutch federalist policy in Indonesia and equally ineffective in disguising the realities of continued foreign dominance. The 'Bao Dai experiment' failed to draw sufficient nationalist support away from the Vietminh to create a convincing alternative, though the new Republic of Vietnam obtained some international recognition. In the Protectorates of Cambodia and Laos, which also became Associated States in the Indo-China Federation and the French Union, the degree of independence granted was far from complete or satisfactory to the rulers.

A military and political stalemate developed in the years 1951-3, which was finally broken by the Geneva Conference of April-July 1954 and the battle of Dien Bien Phu, which reached its climax just as the conference was beginning. The French defeat at Dien Bien Phu, the one great pitched battle of the war, in which General Giap enticed the French army into a remote,

The Vietnam War: early in 1965 American intervention transformed a guerrilla combat into a major international confrontation. Punitive bombing raids against the North followed and failed; (*top*) US propaganda against communist aggressors; (*above*) North Vietnamese with the wreckage of an unmanned reconnaissance plane

Below A South Vietnamese strips and searches a prisoner

unfavourable, mountainous terrain, was decisive in convincing them that the war could not be won. It also had the effect of drawing the Americans to the very threshold of intervention in the battle with air strikes and nuclear weapons, a course fraught with danger for world peace at a time when both the Russians and the Chinese seemed anxious for an end to the Indo-China conflict and were urging the Vietminh to accept a temporary partition of Vietnam rather than risk a widening of the war. The battle of Dien Bien Phu hastened the fall of the Laniel government in France and the accession of Mendès-France, who had long advocated a peaceful settlement. At the Geneva Conference, the new French government and the Vietminh agreed to a ceasefire and a provisional partition of Vietnam at the 17th parallel, with a regroupment of forces on either side. This Agreement on the Cessation of Hostilities was signed by France and the Vietminh alone, while all the other participants in the conference, except the United States and the State of Vietnam (Bao Dai's government), agreed verbally to a final declaration which outlined the political features of the settlement – eventual reunification on the basis of nation-wide elections within two years, with an explicit denial that the military demarcation line constituted a political or territorial boundary. The Americans and South Vietnamese were later to insist that they were not parties to the Agreement and hence not bound by its provisions, when they refused to accept North Vietnam's call for elections in 1956. By that time, the French had abandoned almost all interest in Indo-China and were neither willing nor able to exert any pressure on the South Vietnamese government of Ngo Dinh Diem, which was entirely dependent on American financial and political support.

In Malaya, too, the transition to independence was marked by violence, but the attempt by the Malayan Communist Party (MCP) to generate an anti-colonial war against the British failed, mainly because, as an essentially Chinese movement, it was unable to win significant support from the Malays in a communally divided society. The guerrilla uprising which broke out in May 1948, generally referred to as 'the Emergency', dragged on for nearly twelve years and delayed any substantial progress towards self-government in Malaya until the mid-fifties, after the communist offensive had been contained. It was a grim struggle in the early years. The conflict arose out of the frustration of Chinese hopes for rapid progress towards self-government along democratic lines in the immediate postwar period. The Malayan Union scheme put forward by the British in 1945-6 had seemed to portend a reversal of the old policy of ruling through the Malay sultans, while virtually excluding the Chinese from political influence. But the scheme aroused such a storm of protest among the Malays that it was abandoned, though it precipitated the emergence of the United Malays National Organization (UMNO) and a hitherto unprecedented sense of Malay nationalism. Up to that time the only significant nationalist currents in Malaya were the small radical group associated with the Malay Nationalist Party, vehemently inclined towards Indonesia in its inspiration and strongly anti-colonialist ideology; and a more urban labour movement, supported

Prince Sihanouk of Cambodia, overthrown in March 1970,
failed to walk the tightrope between the power blocs;
his willingness to allow large sections of northern
Cambodia to be used as Vietminh bases alarmed
pro-Americans among the Cambodian élite. Yet a united
Vietnam is unlikely to allow Cambodian independence

Cambodian anti-American cartoon

largely by Chinese and Eurasians, in which the MCP found its support. In
1948, a Malayan Federation was established which confirmed the powers
of the Malay sultans and the political dominance of the Malays, to the
dismay of the MCP, which then switched from a peaceful united-front
strategy to a more militant revolutionary struggle against colonial rule.

Little need be said about the guerrilla conflict, which consisted primarily
of attacks on plantations, tin-mines and government centres in the hope of
paralyzing the economy and terrorizing those workers who did not cooperate
with the communists by supplying or assisting them. At first, the guerrillas
in the jungle were able to obtain a good deal of support from the Chinese
either through sympathy or intimidation. Gradually, however, after tough
measures had been taken to deprive the guerrillas of their links with the
Chinese community, including the resettlement of Chinese squatter communities away from the jungle areas, the British were able to contain the
communist threat. At the same time, they began to make political moves
towards independence which cut the ground from under the feet of the
communists. The formation of the Alliance Party in 1952, consisting of
UMNO, the Malayan Chinese Association (MCA) and Malayan Indian
Congress, provided the single broadly based organization which the British
regarded as an essential pre-condition of independence. By skilful manœuvr-
ing so as to win an indisputable claim to the mantle of nationalist leadership
in the negotiations with the British which preceded the first national
elections in 1955, Tunku Abdul Rahman gained a sweeping victory for the
Alliance, which paved the way for complete independence in 1957. Singapore remained separate, however, and still under British rule.

The new élite who came to power in Malaya were not former revolutionaries or militant nationalists like their counterparts in Indonesia. Among
the Malays there was a striking continuity with the traditional ruling class
that had provided most of the administrators under British rule, Western-
educated in most cases, though generally from aristocratic families: but
political, administrative and educational attainments now began to count
for much more than birth. Although the sultans lost most of their political
power with independence, nothing like the Indonesian 'social revolutions'
of 1946 occurred in Malaya and the Malay aristocracy quickly adjusted to
the new circumstances. Likewise, the leadership of the Chinese and Indian
communities remained in much the same hands as before the Second World
War. The democratization of politics later produced new challengers to
leadership in the various communities among the opposition parties, but
these posed no threat until the 1969 election. From the outset the Alliance
represented essentially a mechanism for political reconciliation and bargaining between the established leaders of the three ethnic communities.
The stability that Malaya enjoyed in the decade after independence, in spite
of the troubles of 1948-57, can be attributed in large part to that fact.

The somewhat different pattern of events in the Philippines is also
interesting in this respect. There, the old *ilustrado* élite of landowning
families who dominated Manila's political and social life, in addition to
their own provinces, had achieved their favoured status under the conditions of Spanish and American rule. They survived the transition to
independence remarkably unscathed, despite the demoralizing effects of the
Japanese occupation (for the issue of 'collaboration' was more bitterly
divisive in the Philippines than anywhere else) and the challenge of the
communist-led Hukbalahap peasant movement in Central Luzon, which
nearly shook popular confidence in the government of the young republic
in its early, unsettled years. Yet the Huks were successfully contained, as the
result of a skilful (and lucky) campaign led by President Magsaysay, which
destroyed their military potential, and of his genuine desire to eliminate the
real grievances of the tenant farmers of Luzon which the Huks had exploited.
Magsaysay modified the pattern of Filipino politics by directing his presidential campaign of 1953 to the common villagers in a bid for their votes,
something that the élite politicians had never before felt necessary. But
neither he nor any other Filipino politician achieved much success in trying
to push badly needed land reform measures through a landlord-dominated

TAKE OFF STRIP...

... AT CLOSE RANGE

Russian cartoon comment on American influence in Thailand: Thailand from the mid-fifties became solidly pro-American

In Laos the neutralist leader, Prince Souvanna Phouma (*left*) tried to unite a triangular coalition including communists and the right; a triangular civil war broke out in 1961 (*below*) and by the end of the decade the communist Pathet Lao still held the south-east in contravention of the terms of the 1962 Geneva settlement

Congress, or to mobilize the poorer peasants as a political force demanding fundamental social changes. The élite recovered its dominance over the two-party political system and third parties never prospered. On the other hand, the Huks never succeeded in gaining significant support outside the Luzon rice plain just north of Manila, and they degenerated, after 1953, into a small semi-bandit organization.

Deflated expectations: 1955-63

The first postwar decade had been characterized by optimism and achievement, as well as upheavals and violence. By contrast, the years following the Bandung Conference were comparatively peaceful until 1963, although bleak and dispiriting in other respects in most countries of the region. Hopes that independence would bring greater liberty, social progress and economic development began to turn sour. National problems were not being solved. Democracy came to grief in Burma, Thailand and Indonesia in 1958-9: it was never seriously attempted in South Vietnam under Ngo Dinh Diem or under the communist regime in the North. Only in Cambodia and Malaysia (which came to include Singapore, Sabah and Sarawak in 1963) could one feel much optimism that conditions were improving.

In the domestic politics of the South-east Asian countries in this period, two general features deserve attention. One was the concentration of political power in the hands of narrow élite groups, contrasting with earlier tendencies towards a broadening of political participation or greater scope for counter-élites to seek mass support. (Wealth, social influence and educational opportunities were also coming to be more narrowly confined within the circles of those who had political influence.) Military coups in Burma and Thailand put an end to democratic politics there. Soekarno's introduction of 'Guided Democracy' in Indonesia dispensed with elections (because they would have benefited the Communist Party at the expense of the other political parties) and thus operated to keep political power within the grasp of the Djakarta political élite which had established itself during the previous decade, confining the military and Communist Party counter-élites to a circumscribed role in the political system at this stage, from which neither could easily bid for greater power. Even in Malaya and the Philippines, where democratic institutions survived, Western education and administrative capacity was the key to élite status in the former, while in the latter the *ilustrado* families which dominated the two identical Filipino political parties were able to absorb the impact of Magsaysay's potentially unsettling politicization of the peasantry.

The other noteworthy feature of these middle years was the rejection of Western democratic institutions in favour of indigenous forms of political organization, which may be regarded as a further step along the path of decolonization and the throwing off of the colonial heritage. Examples of this were the 'Burmese Way to Socialism' of Ne Win's Revolutionary Council in 1962; Soekarno's 'Guided Democracy' and 'Socialism *à la* Indonesia' as manifestations of a distinctly Indonesian national personality; Ngo Dinh Diem's diffuse doctrine of 'Personalism' as a uniquely Vietnamese political philosophy; or Prince Norodom Sihanouk's characterization of his Sangkum Reastr Nijum (People's Socialist Community) as something superior to more orthodox political parties.

In Burma the satisfactory working of representative government until 1957 had been due in large part to the dominance of the AFPFL, the party that had been responsible for independence. With some difficulty, it managed to cope with rebellious ethnic minorities and communist insurgents, as well as increasing economic problems. But troubles developed after a split in the AFPFL in 1958: there was widespread disillusionment with politicians for their factionalism, self-seeking, and corruption. Finally U Nu called in General Ne Win to establish an army caretaker administration that would restore law and order so that elections could be held. After eighteen months in office Ne Win handed back power to the civilians in accordance with the election results; but soon the government again found itself so beset by problems that in March 1962 the army intervened to overthrow U Nu's government and assume power through a revolutionary council. The new regime set out to create a new and purer form of socialist society, less tainted by the liberal-democratic and Western features that had persisted through the fifties, under the aegis of a Burma Socialist Programme Party. Most large businesses were nationalized and the Indian and Chinese grip on economic life was broken, at the cost of considerable economic disruption. Burmanization of the government proceeded more openly, to the disadvantage of the minority Shans, Karens and so on. Most of these measures proved as unsuccessful as those of the AFPFL regime, yet opposition to the government's authoritarian methods posed no great threats to it until towards the end of the sixties, when Ne Win himself admitted that a more conciliatory approach to the problem of national unity was necessary.

In Indonesia the rejection of the Dutch legacy was carried further at the end of the fifties. The nationalization in 1958-9 of all Dutch investments, plantations, banks and trading firms (in response to the Dutch refusal to yield in the still unsettled dispute over West New Guinea), marked the end of Dutch economic overlordship. The step was taken in the midst of a tangled political crisis arising out of a regional challenge to the central government in 1957-8, which undermined the moral authority of the parliament and political parties, for it was not they but Soekarno and the army leaders who finally resolved the crisis and who then devised the new lineaments of a 'Guided Democracy' more suited to what they regarded as Indonesia's needs. Soekarno proclaimed the 'return to the 1945 Constitution', which gave him almost unlimited executive powers and confined the political parties to a subordinate legislative role; it also provided scope for considerable participation in government by the military leaders, though Soekarno played off the army against the political parties (principally the Communist Party), so as to maintain a commanding position in the balance of power.

Soekarno carried Indonesia's reaction against the West much further than this in his strident nationalism, his emphatic rejection of 'liberalism' and capitalism and his almost obsessive concern with an ideology suited to the requirements of Indonesia's 'national identity'. Domestically this entailed a plethora of socialist slogans, plans and regulations and preference for a strong state sector of the economy rather than an indigenous middle class; but the gulf between his aspirations and achievements was huge, for the Indonesian bureaucracy proved incapable of managing the grossly over-regulated economy, which deteriorated steadily as inflation accelerated throughout the years 1957-65. While problems mounted at home, Soekarno devoted more and more attention to Indonesia's international role, entering into closer relations with Russia to gain the arms which enabled him to force the Dutch to give way at long last on the West Irian issue in 1962, then 'confronting' Malaysia and the British in 1963-5 on the basis of his new foreign policy doctrine of eternal struggle between 'the New Emerging Forces' and the imperialist-colonialist nations. All this helped to create a stronger sense of national unity, which must be recognized as Soekarno's great historic contribution to Indonesia, but the restless thrust of his ideology had a profoundly unsettling effect, weakening the authority of the administrators and realists in relation to the slogan-wielders and ideologues of the left. However, the full consequences and costs of his extravagant fantasies were not felt until after 1963.

The military takeover in Thailand by Marshal Sarit in 1958 did not represent an abrupt break with past traditions, for army leaders had been prominent in the oligarchy that had held power in Bangkok ever since the 1932 coup against the absolute monarchy, while the National Assembly has rarely constituted much more than a fig-leaf of constitutional respectability. Political parties had seemed to be assuming some importance between 1945 and 1951, but they had few substantial roots and declined during the fifties under the premiership of General Phibun Songkhram, when left-wing opposition was frequently suppressed in the name of anticommunism. Marshal Sarit and his successor, General Thanom Kittikachorn, did without the assembly and such frills as elections between 1958

Agriculture and industry average 1960-5

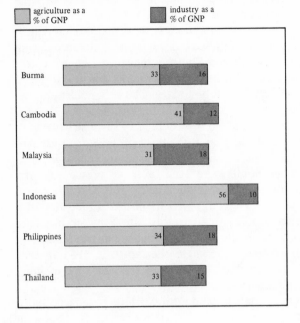

	agriculture as a % of GNP	industry as a % of GNP
Burma	33	16
Cambodia	41	12
Malaysia	31	18
Indonesia	56	10
Philippines	34	18
Thailand	33	15

Annual growth of GNP 1958-65

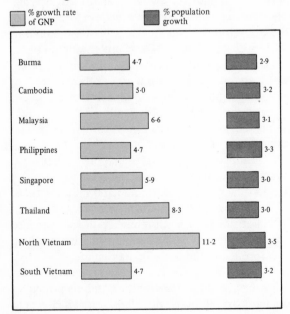

	% growth rate of GNP	% population growth
Burma	4·7	2·9
Cambodia	5·0	3·2
Malaysia	6·6	3·1
Philippines	4·7	3·3
Singapore	5·9	3·0
Thailand	8·3	3·0
North Vietnam	11·2	3·5
South Vietnam	4·7	3·2

'The Emergency' in Malaya – a patrol of the Malay Special Police. In 1948 communist guerrillas began a jungle snipers' war in which 11,000 lives were lost over a period of twelve years; harsh measures were taken against the Chinese Malays who supported the guerrillas

$ 1,000/=

凡任何一位馬共人員能
够脫離森林把一挺布連鎗帶
出來,或是帶領保安隊伍去將
他所知道收藏的布連鎗發掘
出來,都可獲得一千元的賞金.

獲得一千元賞金
開始新的生活!

Left British notice to terrorists during 'The Emergency': 1,000 Malayan dollars for handing in that gun

Education and language are explosive issues in the plural Malaysian community (cross-section, *below*), which includes Malays, Chinese and Indians. In 1969 race riots led to the suspension of parliamentary government after a decade of deceptive tranquillity

and 1968, without arousing much disapproval. Sarit was not an attractive dictator, but he proved to be effective, in so far as Thailand began to achieve one of the most rapid economic growth rates in South-east Asia in the early sixties, despite the corruption and concentration of wealth within the military and administrative élite. His successor began to move back toward slightly more representative constitutional arrangements in the late sixties. But the striking feature of Thailand's political history since 1945 was the continuity in both policies and personnel within the national leadership, except for a few notable feuds, such as that between Phibun and Pridi or Sarit and General Phao Sriyanon. Since the mid-fifties, the élite has been broadly united behind the government on its policies of anti-communism and support for America and SEATO, with only a few voices from the political wilderness calling for a more non-aligned foreign policy.

In Vietnam, a few years of calm followed the Geneva Conference during which the division between North and South, intended merely as a temporary line of military regroupment in the Geneva Agreement, hardened into the equivalent of an international boundary. The communist government in Hanoi obviously anticipated victory in the elections of 1956 as a prelude to reunification of Vietnam and it was taken by surprise when Ngo Dinh Diem, who had replaced Bao Dai at the head of the Saigon government, refused to regard the Geneva Agreement as binding on him. By 1958 communist guerrillas in the South were again exerting pressure on the Southern government by attacks on rural officials: the National Liberation Front (commonly known as the Vietcong) was established in 1960 and from that time on the guerrilla conflict grew steadily into a major problem. Although the communists originally had little support in the South (for most Vietminh guerrillas had withdrawn to the North in 1954-5), they gradually gained recruits as a result of the Diem government's increasingly unpopular and repressive measures.

Diem was a nationalist of long standing, an old Hué mandarin and a Catholic, who revealed impressive qualities of leadership in 1954-5 in consolidating the authority of the Southern government. But he failed to establish any firm political base or attract popular backing, despite the trappings of a democratically elected National Assembly and the passive support of the anti-communist élite in Saigon. As the regime's dependence on American backing increased (US aid, military and civil, totalled $1,800 million between 1955 and 1961 and was $700 million in 1962 alone), Diem became more and more autocratic, cut off from public opinion and intolerant of opposition. Power became concentrated largely in the hands of his Catholic brothers, whose harsh treatment of the Buddhist protest movement in mid-1963 precipitated the military coup which led to the overthrow and death of Diem in November of that year. His fall ushered in a period of even greater political instability, followed by intensified Vietcong activity in the South and the American decision to intervene in force in 1965.

In the background to these developments in the late fifties lay the shadow of the cold war. The growth of Russian and Chinese diplomatic influence and the increasing strength of local communist parties in Indonesia, South Vietnam and Laos aroused fears on one side – but so did the prospect of deeper American intervention in regional affairs in the name of her SEATO commitments, which was invoked in 1962 to justify sending US forces into Thailand during a communist advance in Laos. Yet it can hardly be said that the communists were making much headway over all. They were defeated thoroughly in the Philippines, Malaya, Singapore and Burma. Even Khrushchev's diplomatic initiatives (the most spectacular was his visit to Indonesia in 1960 and offer of lavish economic and military aid to Soekarno, in the hope of embroiling him in conflict with the Dutch and Americans in West Irian) did not gain the Russians much political influence with either the governments of the region or the communist parties, which were reluctant to become embroiled in the Sino-Soviet dispute.

China's influence in the region did, however, increase in the years after the Bandung Conference. Peking laid great stress on the Bandung principles of peaceful coexistence as a basis for relations with all nations which would

Above Royal Marines during the clashes with Indonesia which followed the creation of Malaysia in 1963; (*below*) Malays in predominantly Chinese Singapore burn an effigy of Lee Kuan Yew; (*bottom*) national service for men in their twenties in Singapore followed Soekarno's growing militancy in Indonesia

dissociate themselves from the imperialist camp. She modified her earlier policy of trying to woo the overseas Chinese, urging them now to become good citizens of their country of residence. She achieved some success in drawing the Cambodian and Laotian governments into closer relations and settled an unresolved frontier problem with Burma in exemplary fashion. However, in 1959-60 she ran into momentary trouble with Indonesia (which paradoxically was the only country attempting to negotiate a mutually satisfactory settlement of the problem of dual nationality of her overseas Chinese), over the latter's move to exclude alien Chinese storekeepers from rural areas. China gave way, after initially attempting to browbeat the Indonesian government into withdrawing the regulation, and gradually re-established cordial relations with Soekarno as he swung towards a militantly anti-imperialist foreign policy of 'confrontation' of Malaysia and the British in 1963-5.

What made the activities of the communists seem disturbing in the second postwar decade was not so much their appeal to the impoverished masses, as the apparent inability of the non-communist governments in most countries of the region to achieve political stability or economic progress. And China, at the time of her great leap forward towards industrialization, loomed in the background as a reproach and an attractive alternative. Not that the only communist government in South-east Asia, North Vietnam, was achieving any great success in raising its national income, despite grandiose talk of industrialization, planning and land reform; the land reform programme was accompanied by peasant revolts and severe disruption. Without substantial communist bloc aid her economy would have been in severe difficulties – but this was not widely realized in most of South-east Asia, where the unity and purposefulness of communist countries was greatly admired in countries plagued by political disunity and governmental indecisiveness.

Changing alignments: 1963-70

Events in South-east Asia began moving toward new patterns in about 1963, a year marked by Ngo Dinh Diem's fall from power in Saigon, the death of Marshal Sarit in Thailand and by Indonesia's resort to armed 'confrontation' of the newly created states of Malaysia. Not long before, the Ne Win government had seized power in Burma and begun the process of isolating Burma from the outside world (a traditional stance for that country) which resulted in her withdrawal from an active part in regional politics. Shortly afterwards the whole framework of international politics in the region began to change as a result of the intensification of the Second Indo-China War through American military intervention, the widening of the Sino-Soviet split and the cultural revolution in China, the Sino-Indonesian rift which followed the overthrow of Soekarno in 1965-6 and the destruction of the PKI, the most serious setback to communist prospects in the region since 1948. While there was no spectacular change in the foreign policies of the strongly anti-communist SEATO governments, Thailand and the Philippines, or of the more determinedly non-aligned ones, Indonesia, Burma and Cambodia, the differences between them began to blur as cold war alignments became less relevant to the world of the sixties. And, since 1968, governments of all complexions have had to take stock of the implications of America's probable withdrawal from further military involvement in Asia.

The failure of American intervention in Vietnam highlights the points that have already been stressed here – the diminishing capacity of outside powers to shape the course of South-east Asian history (compare also Russia's singular lack of influence over Indonesia and North Vietnam, despite her considerable expenditure of funds there, or China's inability to prevent developments adverse to her interests in Indonesia and Malaysia) and the growing importance of local power factors. The other international conflict in this period, Indonesia's 'confrontation' of Malaysia, was an attempt (unsuccessful, as it turned out) to hasten the departure of the British and demonstrate Indonesia's importance in the new power balance.

Above Soekarno in 1949: the creator of a national identity for Indonesia and president for nearly twenty years; his foreign policy became stridently 'anti-imperialist' as the country's economy ran riot

Below The burning of American books in Djakarta, 1965, and an anti-SEATO demonstration

After Soekarno's fall, his successors tried to establish a more modest framework for regional cooperation through ASEAN (Association of South-east Asian Nations) in an attempt to minimize the influence of outside powers.

In domestic politics, new forces or new patterns were evident. The colonial legacy of political and administrative institutions continued to erode in Burma and Indonesia as their governments experimented to find more suitable forms of organization. Yet despite outer changes of form or personnel, there were still no substantial changes of social structure in any country: on the contrary, the élites which inherited power from the colonial rulers seemed more securely in control than ever and less likely than before to be challenged by rival aspirants (except the military, in the two or three states where they did not already share power). Even in the Philippines, where social tensions seemed in 1969-70 to be increasing to a point where radical reforms in the political structure were necessary, revolution still seemed to be out of the question. In fact many observers have remarked that in both Thailand and the Philippines the problem was too little propensity to change rather than too much.

Indonesia's 'confrontation' of Malaysia was itself a projection of tensions in the Indonesian political system. Soekarno launched his campaign against the Malaysia scheme soon after an uprising in Brunei in December 1962 (before which Indonesia had raised no objection to it) arguing that it was a neo-colonialist stratagem of the British to perpetuate their economic and military control. (Paradoxically, confrontation probably delayed the British military withdrawal.) Initially Soekarno's opposition to Malaysia was a combination of bluster, propaganda, threats and covert assistance to dissidents in Sarawak and Malaya, coupled with a diplomatic strategy of trying to draw Tunku Abdul Rahman away from his dependence on the British into closer association with Indonesia and the Philippines in 'Maphilindo', a vaguely formulated political association proposed at the Manila Conferences of mid-1963. However, the circumstances of Malaysia's formation in September 1963 antagonized Soekarno to the point where Indonesia refused to recognize the new state and severed commercial connections between the two countries. Confrontation was then intensified in the form of military incursions into Sarawak and Sabah (and ineffective probing raids into Malaya a year later), along with a diplomatic-cum-propaganda offensive to force Malaysia to return to the Manila Agreements as interpreted by Indonesia. The wrangle dragged on until 1966. Militarily it was a minuscule affair by comparison with the Vietnam War; the British, with 40,000 troops in Malaysia, had little difficulty in containing the Indonesian forays. The main danger to Malaysia was the threat that confrontation would engender internal subversion and racial conflict, as it nearly did in mid-1964, when the race riots broke out in Singapore, partly because of Indonesian provocation.

The most far-reaching effect occurred inside Indonesia. By alienating the British and American governments to the point where they cut off their foreign aid programmes to her, confrontation weakened the pro-Western elements there and paved the way for a steady increase in communist influence during the two years after September 1963. This in turn made it increasingly difficult for Soekarno to call off confrontation by seeking a negotiated settlement, since the PKI was using the issue as a means to prevent any *rapprochement* with the West. By late 1964 Soekarno turned increasingly towards Peking for support (having by this time antagonized the Russians as well as the West), which caused mounting alarm among anti-communists in Indonesia, particularly the army leaders.

Tension between anti-communists and the PKI was increasing for a number of reasons in 1964-5, and it exploded in an outburst of violence in rural Java after the attempted coup of 1 October 1965, which was followed by the destruction of the PKI and the collapse of Soekarno's system of 'Guided Democracy'. The army, under General Suharto, gradually assumed power and pushed Soekarno aside, reversing his pro-communist policies (including 'confrontation' and the *entente* with China, with whom Indonesia's relations now deteriorated to breaking point) and keeping tight control

The Party building in Djakarta after the abortive coup in 1965 which led to Soekarno's fall from power

General Suharto, leader of the 1965 military takeover of Indonesia, at a remembrance day ceremony for its victims

over all political parties. The PKI was destroyed as an organized political force and there was no longer any substantial counterbalance to the army's power, though President Suharto sought to avoid the impression of complete military dominance by associating civilian elements with his regime, particularly the 'technocrats' whom Soekarno had spurned. He was dramatically successful in curbing the rampant inflation of 1965-6 and in reducing the temperature of political life which the excitements of those years and Soekarno's millenarian ideology had inflamed. While it can be argued that Suharto was only able to stabilize the situation with the help of substantial Western economic aid (to which the reply is that no Indonesian government, whether of the right or the left, could have stood on its own feet economically after the ruinous disruptions of 1959-65), Suharto made impressive progress towards restoring the economy and administrative structure. The Indonesian revolution at last reached its Thermidor. Although further changes were probably inevitable before any but a precarious political and economic equilibrium was reached, the pressures for change in the seventies were likely to stem from rather different sources and problems from those operating in the Soekarno era.

Malaysia enjoyed relative tranquillity until May 1969 when race riots broke out which led to the suspension of parliamentary government and aroused doubts about the continuation of the Alliance Party's formula for racial harmony and economic progress. The 'Alliance pattern' had worked well enough during the previous fifteen years to resolve the most immediate problems facing the new nation, even the potentially explosive problems of national language and education policy, but only so long as there was no serious challenge to the moderate leaders of the two communities from the more extreme communal parties. (Non-communal parties failed to take root, except in a few minor cases.) The growth of the opposition parties was probably bound to bring communal polarization sooner or later, but challenges to the Alliance were sidetracked in the early sixties by the Malaysia issue, involving the incorporation of preponderantly Chinese Singapore and the preponderantly non-Chinese (but also largely non-Malay) population of Sabah and Sarawak in the Federation. The Alliance was able to win a landslide victory in the 1964 election by exploiting the fears created by Indonesia's 'confrontation' of Malaysia. It also rebuffed Lee Kuan Yew's bid for political leadership on the basis of a 'Malaysian Malaysia' (i.e. equal treatment of all races and an end to special privileges for the Malays), which amounted to a bid for the Chinese vote. Towards the end of the sixties, however, the parties in the Alliance found it increasingly difficult to gain the allegiance of the younger and more impatient Malays and Chinese, who were dissatisfied with the

Burmese police round up suspect communists after the unsuccessful 1948 rebellion against the AFPFL government which had seen the country through independence

Portraits of U Nu, Burmese prime minister, and General Ne Win on a visit to Peking; the prime minister had invited the general to help deal with a split in the AFPFL and was replaced by him in 1962

compromises of 1957 accepted by their elders. The drift of Malay votes away from UMNO candidates in the 1969 elections caused great alarm among the Malay politicians, creating the atmosphere of tension and uncertainty in which the race riots broke out, followed by the imposition of emergency rule. While the government had a measure of success in preventing further outbreaks of violence after that and in persuading the parties to accept an agreement to avoid debate on the controversial issues of language and Malay rights, as a pre-condition for the restoration of parliamentary politics at the end of 1970, it was obvious that the moderates of both races would thenceforth find it much more difficult to attract electoral support in competition with communal extremists. The political structure that had persisted since 1957 was no longer taken for granted. What effects this would have on the extraordinarily stable social and economic structure (about which the Malays, being poorer, felt much aggrieved) remained to be seen.

The Second Indo-China War had the effect, first of involving the USA more closely than ever before in the fate of South-east Asia, then of producing disenchantment and a desire to disengage. The intensification of the Vietnam conflict in 1964-5, resulting in American air attacks on North Vietnam and the commitment of 400,000 US troops in the South must be traced back to the train of events which started with the overthrow of Ngo Dinh Diem in November 1963. The shaky military rulers who seized control during the next two years were hardly more successful than Diem in establishing a representative government capable of standing up against the National Liberation Front. Tensions between Catholics and Buddhists remained a serious obstacle to political unity and the war was going badly for the South when America intervened in early 1965, transforming what had been a guerrilla struggle into a major international confrontation.

The South Vietnamese government was stabilized somewhat in June 1965 under a military directory led by General Nguyen Van Thieu and Air Vice Marshal Nguyen Cao Ky, who were still in power in 1970. Ky took firm measures against the militant Buddhist organizations soon afterwards and silenced them as a political force. But the regime did not succeed in achieving more than an outward veneer of legitimacy and popular backing, despite a more liberal constitution and elections under restricted conditions (which included a ban on advocacy of neutralism or negotiations with the communists) in 1967. Because of its obvious dependence on the USA, it could not rival the nationalist appeal of the NLF and the North. Desertions from the South Vietnamese army were numerous, although they declined somewhat after 1966 as its military effectiveness improved.

The rationale for American intervention in Vietnam was to defend the South against aggression or subversion by the North Vietnamese, acting through their agent, the National Liberation Front (Vietcong); the struggle was often described as 'a critical test of the communist technique of military subversion'. According to this theory the conflict was not a war of national liberation or a civil war, as its critics alleged, but aggression by one state against another. Since this interpretation depends mainly on how one looks upon the Geneva Agreement and South Vietnam's refusal to hold elections for the unification of the whole country in 1956, it is not worth delving into the argument here. Whatever the rights or wrongs, the politically important factor was that the communists stood for both unification and nationalism – the expulsion of foreign troops – whereas the government in Saigon was upholding a state of affairs which presupposed partition and dependence on outside support to continue the war. The American strategy was to punish the North by bombing raids in the hope that it would order the Vietcong to call off their campaign, while simultaneously conducting 'search and destroy' operations to eliminate the Vietcong from the countryside. But the fallacy of this approach was that while the NLF may initially have been controlled from the North, it became more and more obvious as the war progressed that the NLF was a Southern resistance movement, recruited and led mainly from the South. In 1967, North Vietnamese combat divisions accounted for less than one-tenth of the NLF forces, estimated at nearly 300,000. The indiscriminate damage and slaughter wrought by the

Filipino police interrogate a Huk; the communist-led peasant movement was a political threat in the early independence years

A spry-looking Lyndon Johnson on a visit to Manila as vice-president; the Filipinos consistently supported American policies in South-east Asia

American military machine was itself a major factor alienating Vietnamese nationalists. If the war did nothing else, it enormously extended the popularity of the Vietminh in the South, where originally they had been handicapped by the long-standing differences between the two regions.

The unexpected vigour of the Vietcong's Tet offensive in February 1968 emphasized that this was a war the Americans could never win. It was followed soon after by President Johnson's decision not to seek re-election and to begin peace talks in Paris. His successor made it even clearer that he wanted to end the war and reduce America's involvement in Asia. The Nixon Doctrine, ambiguous though it was, almost certainly signified the end of the cold war epoch in US Far Eastern policy. Although there had been little progress in the Paris peace talks up to the end of 1970, the withdrawal of American troops was proceeding steadily and some American officials even seemed willing to consider a political settlement that would eventually lead to the reunification of·Vietnam under the North preferably with, but if necessary without, the assent of the Saigon government.

Cambodia and Laos were directly affected by the course of events in Vietnam. The overthrow of Prince Sihanouk in March 1970 was influenced by Sihanouk's willingness to turn a blind eye to *de facto* Vietminh occupation of large tracts of Cambodia territory in the north for supply routes and military sanctuaries: this led to apprehension among the Cambodian élite about the consequences of his foreign policy. Sihanouk had alienated the Cambodian élite in a number of ways, but this was probably the decisive factor in his downfall. He had attempted to walk the tightrope between the communists and the Americans, even though he had few illusions that he or Cambodia could retain their independence once Vietnam was reunited. His fall was largely due to the fact that he was felt to have gone too far in accommodating them and turning his back on the Americans. His restoration seemed improbable. But the events which followed his overthrow showed how precarious was Cambodia's independence and territorial integrity. A show of force by Vietminh-supported guerrillas, not initially numerous or strong, was more than General Lon Nol's army could handle: American and South Vietnamese forces were called in to help, thus subjecting the country to occupation by her most feared neighbours. The new government's authority was shown to extend very little beyond Phnom Penh. Time alone would tell whether Lon Nol could reach an accommodation with the communists and keep at bay the Vietnamese and Thais who proffered help. But the episode showed with brutal clarity that Cambodia's capacity to resist Vietnamese pressures without international backing was likely to be even less than it was before French intervention in 1884.

In Laos, the effects of the Vietnam War were less clear-cut. The coalition government established by the 1962 Geneva Conference began to collapse in the following year, when the Pathet Lao withdrew. From 1965, the prime military concern of the Pathet Lao was to maintain control over the remote eastern and southern areas commanding the Ho Chi Minh trail, denying access to government forces. The result was a polarization of political forces in Laos, pushing the neutralist Souvanna Phouma and the rightists closer together against the communists. Souvanna Phouma accused the North Vietnamese of invading and making war upon Laos, but did not abandon hopes of restoring the tripartite coalition government if only the Vietnam War could be brought to an end. Neither the Pathet Lao, with their base among the more backward hill-tribes to the east, nor·the government forces, appeared able to establish ascendancy, even with outside support. The survival of Laos as a political unit, for which restoration of the coalition government seems an essential condition, depends as much on foreign powers, especially the USA and North Vietnam, as on local political forces.

The end of the Vietnam War would mark the end of a century-long era of foreign interference in what was once Indo-China. Adjustments in Laos and Cambodia to the self-evident fact of North Vietnamese dominance of the region seemed, therefore, inevitable. That this would extend to a communist takeover in these countries or a resumption of the nineteenth-century Vietnamese advance into their territories, was far more problematical.

Chie Nakane

Japan: the Modern Miracle

The rapid economic growth of postwar Japan, which by 1968 attained the second largest gross national product in the 'free' world, seems to the rest of the world almost miraculous. The Japanese are of course not superhuman, but ordinary people, ninety per cent of whom identify themselves with the middle class, and their major concerns are directed to their everyday life: they try to get along with their co-workers and to maintain their families at the appropriate standard, with the expectation that this will rise as an index of increased proficiency and seniority. Their strongest desire is that they should not be left behind their colleagues, but rather be a little ahead of them. I believe that it has never been their prime concern to attain such a goal as making Japan a marvel for the world. They are not used to viewing themselves in such a world-wide perspective, although they have been conscious that the West was ahead of them and other Asian countries behind them. The Japanese have for a long while striven to approach the living standard of the West. What was meant by the Western standard or pattern was not quite clear to them, but obviously they had in mind the process of industrialization. This attitude on the part of the Japanese people did not lead to a conscious challenge to the West, but rather to a quietly determined effort to set themselves free from 'backwardness' or the 'legacy of feudalism'. What looked like nationalism or racism might have occasionally appeared in their remarks or behaviour, but these were not the expression of their basic attitudes, even though the government tried hard to instil patriotic fervour in the people. While the Japanese people were carrying on their life according to the usual daily rhythm, they suddenly began to realize that their country had become a 'third superpower'. Having heard foreign commentators wondering how Japan could have achieved such a fantastic growth, their Japanese counterparts have hurriedly joined them in a search for explanations. There have already been a considerable number of books and articles dealing with this issue; a number of factors and reasons have been put forward which single out specific Japanese features in various fields in the process of Japan's economic growth. However, the nexus of these reasons seems not to be so simple.

It is my conviction that if Japan's growth deserves to be called a modern miracle, the secret lies in a system which is somewhat different from that of other countries. Before discussing this main issue, it is necessary to outline the major factors which have offered advantageous conditions for Japanese industrial growth.

Solidarity under the US umbrella

Japan was perhaps one of the few countries during the quarter of a century from 1945 to 1970 which was able to enjoy internal solidarity without unexpected interference from other countries. Japan was placed in a position of dependency on the United States by the provisions of the Mutual Security Pact which was signed at the end of the US military occupation after the Second World War. During this period Japan hardly played a significant role in world politics. Diplomacy always meant dealing with the United States. Foreign policy could have been more dynamic, but the government always preferred a policy tightly connected with that of the United States.

The American military occupation following Japan's defeat in 1945 lasted longer than was originally anticipated, owing to the victory of the communists in China in 1949 and the outbreak of war on the Korean

Soka Gakkai rally: a fanatic organization in Japan which grew up after the war and is heir to the tradition of self-sacrifice. Militant Buddhists, they have been mostly recruited from the growing urban population and they form the third party in Japanese politics, called Komei-to

Hiroshima survivors two hours after the explosion on 6 August 1945. The atom bomb destroyed more than half the city and killed over 70,000 people; nearly as many died at Nagasaki three days later

Hiroshima victim with keloid scars caused by intense heat

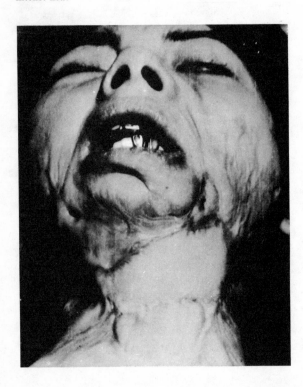

peninsula in 1950, as a result of which the American military effort involved the use of Japan as a rear base. It was not until 1951 that the military occupation ended and a peace treaty (which became effective in 1952) was signed.

During the occupation, the new constitution (effective in 1947) was written, which prohibited the nation from ever having a defence force or engaging in war. The constitution was in fact violated in 1950 when the Japanese government established a small 'self-defence' force by the order of the late General Douglas MacArthur who, as commander-in-chief of the Allied occupation, exercised almost absolute authority in these postwar years. This force, though subsequently enlarged, was in 1970 costing Japan only 0·9 per cent of her gross national product (prior to 1945 the defence force had taken seven per cent of the gross national product and the cost of maintaining Japan's colonies had amounted to three per cent of the gross national product). This low level of expenditure for national defence under the protection of the United States nuclear umbrella was an important contributory factor in promoting economic growth. So likewise was the large-scale American expenditure in Japan during the Korean and Vietnam wars: this investment greatly stimulated Japanese industry.

Guarded thus by the United States externally, Japan was able to concentrate upon internal order. The unconditional surrender and subsequent American occupation produced changes in various fields, including public administration and the educational system, some of which entailed a considerable dislocation of traditional style. Many institutions were reorganized along American lines. The people's ideas and values were in a sense changed from 'feudal' to 'democratic'. However, in spite of such a series of radical changes, the basic political and social structures remained fundamentally unaltered. Facing new systems, the people might be puzzled by actual day-to-day dealings, but they did not find any difficulty in maintaining their basic patterns. Except for a handful of top people, they were after all in contact with their own people, not Americans. They soon found out how to operate in new ways by modifying them to the Japanese style.

The most important fact was that the Japanese bureaucracy was little affected by these postwar changes. The Japanese political structure was revived like a phœnix from the ashes of defeat. Civil servants were restored to their posts (although many posts were reorganized and newly created by the introduction of American techniques) and vacancies were filled as soon as the war was over, to be constantly replenished with the best young brains which the Japanese educational system was able to produce. (Only right at the end of the period did the government begin to have a little difficulty in recruiting enough civil servants from the intellectual élite, because of the rival attractions of employment in industry.) These civil servants, whose origin goes back to the Tokugawa feudal system, have always played an important role in the operation of the state. Regardless of the quality of ministers or members of parliament, the driving force of the state has always been its able administrators. Although there were various organizational changes in the administrative system, the officials maintained the same essential, prestigious role. The general public soon grasped that they were the same set of people although they were now called 'public servants'. The degree of dependence of the people on them was also not at all altered. The effective function of the government administration is correlated with various organizations on the non-governmental side, the nature of which is characterized by an easy acceptance of government policies, as I shall explain later.

It should be also stated that the continued existence of the emperor, thanks to the policy of the American occupation, certainly contributed to the maintenance of stability in postwar Japanese society. Although the emperor became the 'symbol of the state and the unity of the people' (as stated in the 1947 constitution) from having previously had the powers of the sovereign regarded as the supreme holy figure, the characteristics of the postwar emperor were more akin to those of pre-modern days, if we look back over the long history of Japan. During the period from the Meiji

The bombed Hacchobori district twenty-five years later, when astonishing economic growth had put Japan well on the way to becoming a 'third superpower'

Restoration to 1945, owing to the policy of the leading statesmen of the time, the emperor had occupied a rather unusual place in Japan's history. The supremacy of the Japanese emperor derived from his *de jure* status at the apex of the religious (ritual) and social hierarchy of the Japanese people, not from the actual accumulation of political and economic power during the course of history, in which the emperor differs greatly from kings elsewhere. The essence of his power was his existence in the line of the legitimate succession. He was rarely *de facto* ruler: even before 1945, he was rather a titular sovereign. Probably for this reason the people soon overcame the postwar change in the role of the emperor, although it seemed to be very drastic and sensational at the time.

Phases of postwar development

The twenty-five-year postwar history of Japan can be divided into two periods, the dividing line of which was roughly drawn around 1955: the former represented the aftermath of defeat, and the latter the period when Japan's development was set on a definite track.

After the war, the economy began to register an average annual growth rate of ten per cent. The earlier period was characterized by the strong leadership of the prime minister, Shigeru Yoshida, which lasted seven years with short intermissions. Yoshida, an ex-diplomat who displayed all his professional skills in dealing with the United States, particularly with MacArthur, believed that the maintenance of a close relationship with the United States was the only way to achieve Japan's postwar development. This became the basic policy of his successors.

Yoshida was one of the most senior politicians who was not purged at the end of the war – he had been a peace advocate during the war years – and he played a vital part in steering Japan through the difficult period of near-starvation and humiliation under American occupation (1945-50). Towards the end of his premiership in 1951, the Korean War broke out, which brought Japan an economic boom. Industries revived and new enterprises mushroomed, although many of them started with a very insignificant paid-up capital and depended largely on banks for finance, even working capital – a device which became typical of Japan's postwar economy. It was in these transitional years that Japan's postwar industries began to sense and exploit the chances for future expansion. As a result of this initial boom the people, now fed and clothed with newly produced materials after the long strain of impoverished postwar years, became ready to work at top capacity, their incentive for work accelerated by prospects for a better life.

However, the end of the Korean War signalled an economic depression. It coincided with an ugly scandal over shipbuilding contracts, which finally

The Japanese army: the small 'defence' force permitted by the US in 1950 was later enlarged but took only a very small proportion of the national budget

General MacArthur, supreme commander, became the virtual ruler of Japan during the years of American occupation

Below US troops surround the American Embassy in Tokyo at the beginning of the occupation

A Japanese CP cartoon shows the figure of Yoshida, prime minister for seven years after the war, as an imperialist lackey in front of Eisenhower and Dulles

forced the resignation of Yoshida. In 1954 Yoshida was replaced by Ichiro Hatoyama, who resigned two years later owing to illness. Tanzan Ishibashi, his successor, was in the post for only two months because of illness and he was replaced by his deputy, Nobusuke Kishi, who held the premiership till 1960.

This period, between the resignation of Yoshida in 1954 and 1956 when Kishi took over the premiership, was a critical phase for it was then that the basis of the ensuing period of growth was established. The economic White Paper of 1956 stated: 'The postwar period is gone. Growth through rehabilitation has been completed. The coming growth will be supported by modernization.' In spite of the frequent changes in the premiership during this period, it was then that Japan's political structure took on the characteristics of today's political scene. For in 1955 the Liberal-Democratic Party was established, uniting all the then-existing conservative parties in what was to prove a powerful anti-socialist coalition, even though it actually originated as a counter-faction against the Liberal Party of which Yoshida was the leader.

At the same time trade unions became markedly more active. The depression after the Korean War, which produced a good deal of unemployment, offered fertile ground for the development of unionism. In the political spectrum, they joined the leftists who had been opposed to the Security Pact. In the process trade unionism developed into a nation-wide organization. Thus in 1955 Akira Iwai was elected to be secretary-general of Sōhyō (the largest association of unions consisting in 1970 of 428,000 members; it has been the central core of the union organizations in Japan) and held the post for fifteen years. Centred on Sōhyō, many groups of unions joined forces in the controversies over reform of the police and of the educational system. These forces finally culminated in a large movement of leftists against the Security Pact and the Kishi cabinet.

In order to overcome some of this opposition, negotiations were conducted in 1957-8 which led to the signing in Washington of a new agreement on 19 January 1960. This treaty stated: 'Each party recognizes that an armed attack against either party in the territories under the administration of Japan would be dangerous to its own peace and safety and declares that it would act to meet the common danger in accordance with its constitutional provisions and processes.' Other changes in the new pact involved the elimination of the use of American troops to put down domestic uprisings, and the specification that the treaty could be amended or abrogated after ten years by giving one year's notice. (In November 1969, the joint communiqué between President Nixon and Prime Minister Sato was announced by which the 1960 treaty was automatically extended.)

The ratification of the 1960 treaty was marked with the eruption of large-scale demonstrations and violence in Tokyo and other cities. Socialist, communist, labour and student groups were particularly active. There was also general anti-American sentiment. In the face of this widespread protest the Japanese government felt obliged to withdraw its invitation to President Eisenhower to visit the country and Prime Minister Nobusuke Kishi was compelled to resign.

Japan entered into a third phase when Hayato Ikeda assumed the premiership after the resignation of Nobusuke Kishi. Ikeda had learned a lot about the people's psychology through Kishi's stormy administration and from his own bitter experience of being forced to resign from the post of finance minister after his unfortunate remark that 'the poor eat barley instead of rice'. So at the very beginning in taking over the premiership, he reacted to the demonstrations by adopting what he called a 'low posture'. It was his proposed policy to divert popular attention to economic growth, avoiding issues likely to invite leftist opposition. His platform was an economic plan aimed at doubling the national income in ten years, and the government succeeded remarkably in its objective.

During Ikeda's premiership the economic life of the people progressed conspicuously through active investment and industrial expansion following the 'Jimmu boom' (December 1954 to June 1961) and the 'Iwato boom'

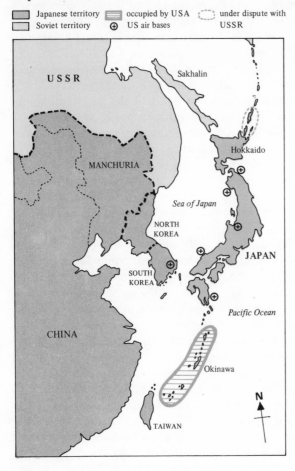

Japan since 1945

Japanese territory · occupied by USA · under dispute with
Soviet territory · ⊕ US air bases · USSR

A Japanese victim of an American air raid during the
Second World War takes part in a demonstration against
US air bases in Japan (1962)

(July 1958 to December 1961). Electric commodities such as television sets, refrigerators and washing machines were purchased by a majority of households. After 1962 automobiles for family use became regarded as a necessity rather than a luxury. The desire to provide higher education for Japanese youth and to have holiday trips rapidly increased. An accompanying phenomenon was the steady reduction of the national birthrate. The national average of household members, which had hovered around 4·9 persons since the first national census in 1920, sagged to 4·54 in 1960 from 4·97 in 1955, dropped to 4·05 in 1965, and to 3·72 in 1970.

Partly in preparation for the Tokyo Olympics year of 1964, highways and many large buildings including office blocks and fashionable hotels were constructed. It was also during this period that the agricultural sector began to diminish in importance. The ratio of the agricultural population to the total population stood at 38·5 per cent in 1955, but it dropped to twenty-three per cent in 1960 and 19·3 per cent in 1969. Industrial development not only brought a heavy concentration of workers in cities and the appearance of underpopulated areas, but also spurred the construction of factories in rural areas. As a result, villagers took factory jobs and commuted from their homes, causing a heavy drain on the farming population.

Prime Minister Ikeda retired late in 1964 and died shortly thereafter without seeing the full results of his policy. His designated successor, Eisaku Sato, continued Ikeda's policy with a slight modification, proposing 'stability and harmony' since the goal of Ikeda had already been realized and symptoms of some discrepant trends had begun to appear. Indeed there was another semi-recession. In March 1964 the Bank of Japan adopted a tight monetary policy with a view to improving the nation's balance of payments position. Demand for monochrome television sets had reached saturation-point by that time. There was a tendency for over-production, not only in home electric appliances but also in machinery and steel. Against such a background stricter monetary policies seemed inevitable.

There were apparent danger-signs of a large increase in stored goods, a drastic production cut and a great fall in corporate profits. But until October 1964, when the Tokyo Olympics ended, thanks to the construction boom the recession was postponed. It then began to spread to various areas of the economy during the spring and the summer of 1965. However, prosperity returned in November 1965 and at the end of 1970 was still generally vigorous. The rate of increase in consumer spending for fiscal 1970 was expected to reach eleven per cent, twice as high as the 5·5 per cent of fiscal 1965. Investments for fiscal 1970 were expected to expand by about twenty per cent compared with fiscal 1969. A warning note was sounded, though, in the economic White Paper of 1970: 'The Japanese economy is experiencing unprecedentedly long prosperity which is favourably affecting every aspect of the economy. By the same token, however, elements have arisen to restrict this prosperity'; and so the Paper called for a 'shift from quantity to quality'. The disturbing features of the Japanese economy, despite its continuing high growth, could be listed as environmental disruption, worsening inflation and isolation in the international society.

On the whole, since the second phase centred on 1955-6, Japan's economy has shown steady growth. Japan's share of world trade jumped from only 1·4 per cent in 1955 to 6·2 per cent in 1968. The Japanese GNP soared from $10,900 million in 1955 to $140,000 million in 1968, the second highest in the non-communist world.

In the twenty-five years after the end of the war, the Japanese economy implemented ten economic programmes. Aside from those programmes which aimed at postwar economic rehabilitation and economic independence, and considering only those after 1955 when the economy had returned to normal, these included the Hatoyama cabinet's Five-Year Plan for Economic Independence (fiscal 1956 to fiscal 1960), the Kishi cabinet's New Long-term Plan (1958-62), the Ikeda cabinet's Plan to Double National Income (1961-70), and the Sato cabinet's Mid-term Economic Plan (1964-8), Economic and Social Development Plan (1967-71), and New Economic and Social Development Plan (1970-5).

Top In the mid-sixties, the Japanese emerged as the world's leading shipbuilders; government structure and policies favoured heavy industry
Above The Yokosuka thermal power station which supplies Tokyo; by the late sixties Japan had the fourth largest electric generating capacity in the world

However, the Japanese economy usually developed far faster than was estimated in these programmes and the original plans had to be continually revised, usually at an early stage. For example, the income-doubling programme projected a GNP of $72,222 million, an international balance of payments surplus of $200 million with exports of $9,300 million, and imports of $9,800 million by its target year of 1970. Yet these targets were nearly all achieved by 1967. In fiscal 1970 the GNP was expected to reach $200,000 million, far surpassing the target figure of the income-doubling plan; the international balance of payments surplus was expected to reach $1,000 million, five times the target figure; and exports and imports were expected to reach about $19,000 million, or twice the original target.

The causes for such high economic growth, besides those outlined in the first section, included the agrarian land reform; the dissolution of the great family combines known as the *zaibatsu*; the enactment of anti-monopoly legislation; and the rapid improvement of workers' willingness and productivity as the result of the enactment of the three basic labour laws, including the Labour Standards Law. Japan's 102 million population provided not only a vast home market for industrial commodities, but also an abundant labour supply. Moreover, most of these workers were well educated. During the postwar years, the rate of the compulsory education constantly remained as high as ninety-nine per cent, and the rate of higher school education has much increased. In 1950 forty per cent of junior high school graduates advanced to senior high schools, and this rate of post-compulsory education soared to eighty-two per cent in 1970. A similar progress could be noted in college and university education. In 1969, 21·4 per cent of the total population of the age group (2·4 times that of 1959) were attending colleges and universities – the second highest rate in the world, surpassed only by the United States.

In addition, business's strong willingness for equipment investment and the high national savings rate (twenty per cent of income) were vital factors. Various reasons for the high savings rate may be offered. Above all, it has never been a general habit of the Japanese to acquire jewellery or land as investments, or to deposit money in banks outside the country. At the same time, perhaps because Japan has been always poor in resources, there have been fewer extremely rich men than in the West and elsewhere. Extravagant luxury has been frowned upon; their traditional pattern of life is rather plain. Hence the unusually high savings rate, as compared to other countries.

The government undertook cautious policies of protective foreign trade while encouraging exports, made capital available to large enterprises in the form of over-loans utilizing the relationship between city banks and the Bank of Japan, the central bank which was tightly connected to the government. The very high rate of loans to and investments in Japanese enterprises was also related to the Japanese value orientation, and to trust in the Japanese system (which derives from the stability of the state organization traditionally independent from that of any other countries). People in a country where resources are meagre tend perhaps to believe in flow rather than in stock in economic activities. This tendency was encouraged by defeat in the war; the widespread destruction of property compelled Japanese businessmen to start from almost nothing. Such deprivation stimulated enterprise, given the inner stability of Japanese society.

Stable power constellation

In addition to the factors already mentioned that have promoted economic growth, there is a more basic cause, less apparent in most other countries: namely, the operation of a stable, effective system of governmental and other institutions, particularly those developed since around 1955. In exploring this issue, I would like to consider first the structure of power at the top, and second the structure of the mass of society.

To begin with the political field, the Liberal-Democratic Party after its establishment in 1955 dominated Japan's political life, monopolizing prime ministers and cabinet members. Its power in 1970 was flourishing all the more. The party gained an overwhelming victory in the general election of

Above By 1967 the output of the steel industry had overtaken all countries except the US and the USSR and accounted for about 12·5 per cent of the world's crude steel. Progress in chemicals (*right*) was also very fast, with the main concentration on synthetic resins and non-cellulose-based plastic materials

By 1970, Japan had the second largest automobile industry in the world: for about eight years cars had been a necessity for average families rather than a luxury

December 1969 (302 seats). Eisaku Sato, who succeeded Ikeda in 1964, was elected president of the Liberal-Democratic Party for a fourth term on 29 October 1970, and would remain in power for a total of eight years, the longest span in office since the establishment of parliamentary government in Japan in 1890. The existence of such a dominant party does not always contribute to the democratic operation of parliaments, but in this case it did much to maintain stability in the operation of the state.

Such political stability, furthermore, was enhanced by the tendency to strengthen the relationship between top politicians and senior civil servants. Not only did the Liberal-Democratic Party and civil servants jointly form the driving force of the government, but also there were informal functional links between the two through their leading personnel. Many cabinet members and leading politicians had previously held high administrative posts in the central government. Examples of this type are the recent two successive prime ministers, Ikeda and Sato. This career sequence has become recognized and approved, being called 'the élite course', and the number and power of this kind of politician have been increasing. An earlier instance is presented by Yoshida who was an ex-diplomat. Yoshida did much to produce ex-civil-servant politicians, including Ikeda and Sato. However, during the time when Yoshida was prime minister, ex-civil servants were still not dominant among politicians, and he had to exercise considerable skill in striking a balance between officials-turned-politicians and so-called 'party' politicians who had entered politics from the beginning, or those who entered politics from fields other than the bureaucratic world.

Senior officials not only moved into politics but also, in far greater numbers, into the industrial field. It has been an informal practice among civil servants that if one of those who passed the state examination for senior civil servants in the same year became the director of a bureau or the highest post for their branch (normally in his early fifties), the rest of his year group would resign from their posts, accepting offers of top executive posts from industrial enterprises and associations. Thus politics and industry became linked with government offices through informal, effective networks forming the top sector of the state, in which the dominant power of the central government could be all the more strongly exercised. Such a tendency may be criticized by those who are outside the system, but it is clear that it contributed to stabilizing the power structure in Japan.

The mutual dependency between business and government has indeed distinguished Japan's politico-economic structure ever since the Tokugawa

Festival plaza, Expo 1970 in Tokyo

Commodity exports 1953-68

■ 1953 ▢ 1960 ▢ 1968

in millions of US dollars

	1953	1960	1968
cameras, watches, precision instruments	13·6	96·0	440·5
radio, TV, tape recorders	1·2	183·0	1152·8
toys	23·5	90·0	113·4
vehicles	5·3	107·4	712·9
ships	80·4	288·1	1084·1
iron and steel	141·9	388·1	1712·5
total exports	1953 1274·0	1960 4055·0	1968 12970·0

GDP and per capita product 1953-67

▢ Gross Domestic Product ▢ per capita

% 1968 = 100

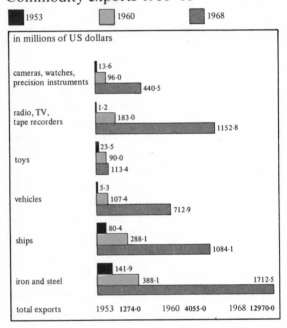

	1953	1960	1967
Japan	40 / 45	75 / 77	131 / 127
UK	77 / 81	94 / 96	112 / 109
USA	75 / 89	89 / 93	122 / 116

feudal age. In Japan, power and wealth have been always held by different kinds of people, or two sectors separately: civil servants (*Bushi*) and industrialists (*Shōnin* or merchants). Since the activities of the latter have been confined within the scope of Japan's political system, business has been always ready to accept the government's final decision, irrespective of the fact that business influence could play a significant role in the political and administrative sectors. And it has been the government's role to protect industry whenever this seems necessary.

Industrialists, owing to the maintenance of such a significant relationship with the government, have naturally developed their organization accordingly in order to deal with the government. The organization of industry has been always hierarchical: the same kind of enterprises are organized into groups with the largest firms at the top and the smallest at the bottom. Many such groups are again organized hierarchically according to the order traditionally conceived: for example, the association of banks stands at the top, then comes the association of steel, and so on. There is also an association of industries, known as Keidanren (Federation of Economic Organizations/Japan) which represents the power of Japan's industry. The stability of the organization in the postwar industrial field is seen symbolically in the fact that Taizo Ishizaka, president of Keidanren, remained in office for twelve years after 1957 when he was first elected.

One of the reasons for the flourishing power of the Liberal-Democratic Party derives from their close link with these top industries from which the major part of the political fund comes. Government economic policy, which has been so successful in increasing the gross national product, has been invariably orientated to the side of large industrial enterprises, disregarding the mass of the people. Thus a tightly knit triangular relationship between civil servants, politicians and industrialists forms one solid power constellation in Japan. This power constellation has been more and more institutionalized and closely linked to the educational system, particularly during the postwar period.

The nation-wide hierarchical organization found in industry is also to be seen in other fields, and education is no exception. In Japan, universities are informally organized in a hierarchical order, at the apex of which stands the University of Tokyo. The development of such a hierarchical order (informal but well understood) has become more and more obvious in the course of postwar history, as in the case of industry: postwar changes by the forced introduction of the American system seemed to have no effect on this structural order inherent in the traditional Japanese culture. In fact, the graduates of the University of Tokyo occupy the majority of the posts of the top sector in various leading organizations. It is also important to note that top-rank universities and major local universities are state institutions, the budget of which is dependent entirely on the ministry of education, although it is customary for many students and professors in these universities to declare themselves leftists or anti-government. Nevertheless, the majority of scholars among the members of the government advisory committees are professors of top state universities. Thus the educational system serves to select and train those deemed suitable to climb the ladder to the top sector.

Given such a situation, Japanese journalism has an especially important function. Indeed, one cannot be unaware of the significant contributions made by nation-wide broadcasting and daily newspapers. The network of NHK (Japan Broadcasting Corporation), which by 1970 could claim the largest station and equipment of any broadcasting corporation in the world, covers the entire territory of Japan: according to a survey carried out by NHK recently, there was no single local area where NHK radio broadcasts did not reach, while NHK television coverage reached ninety-seven per cent of the total potential audience. As for the daily newspapers, the three major dailies, *Asahi*, *Mainichi* and *Yomiuri*, maintain a circulation of around 5 million each. These papers are subscribed to by all kinds of people from top to bottom: local people may subscribe to a local paper, but most of

them are also subscribers to one of the big three. The information networks carried on by broadcasting and daily newspapers play an important role in linking the general public with the top sector. They voice the complaints against the government of those without power, and sometimes shape public opinion. On the other hand, they can become a medium to propagate proposed government policies which may influence readers in the way which the government is aiming at. They have been both the voice of the populace and of the government, sometimes ambiguously. They have also served to promote consciousness of national as distinct from local concerns.

Nation-wide organizations like NHK and Asahishinbun are thus structurally comparable to the Universities of Tokyo and representative top enterprises: they possess very high prestige and their internal organization is very bureaucratic. They have in consequence aroused opposition from people who have felt themselves excluded. However, such rigid organizations are not necessarily due to the exclusion of the people from privileged sectors. It is rather the social structure and the social value orientation of the Japanese that encourages the growth of these institutions, although the people themselves are not really aware of the mechanism.

Organization of men and their values

The solid structure of the top sector corresponds to the social structure which places individuals in a fairly stable system. It is a deeply ingrained habit of the Japanese people not to change their employment once they become full members of a group or institution.

Given such a system, a man feels impelled to work with the same colleagues until his retirement. His world tends to be bounded by his place of work. His concerns and involvements are naturally directed to the affairs of this small world, in which he finds himself secure, yet at the same time exposed to competition with his colleagues for a chance of promotion. Replacement of members of the group is only done by the retirement of older members and the entry of fresh young members; as a result it becomes a cohesive corporate group whose members develop a sense of oneness in relation to members of other comparable groups. It is advantageous for a man to remain in the group in which he starts his career and moves up step by step. It is very difficult for him to move from one group to another, because he can rarely succeed in breaking through the vertical links already established between individuals within their groups. The system entails a high degree of institutionalization and solidarity within the group. Here is the basis on which the lifetime-employment seniority system has developed. Other groups engaged in a similar type of work become a kind of enemy. Hostility enhances competition and competition again enhances hostility.

Individual incentive for work thus rests upon the consciousness of being a member of a group which is exposed to competition from other similar groups. At the same time, the individual also competes with his colleagues, since they are all striving for promotion. There is, of course, more prestige attached to a higher post, which influences his social life not only in the office. This kind of incentive produces a high standard of work-involvement. If a man is not physically or mentally handicapped, he has the chance of becoming a member of a group even though he might be dropped in other societies because of the inferior quality of his work. His promotion may be delayed, but he will do his best in such an atmosphere of group solidarity. Although competition is fierce, group solidarity sustains morale even among the less successful. The self-respect of an apparently mediocre man is saved by the seniority system: late-comers will be placed under him, so that even he may enjoy the sensation of recognized seniority. It is astonishing how an individual in any sector of society is proud of himself (the basis of which lies in the fact that he is higher than someone else) and is challenging his colleagues in order to get ahead of them.

It is my conviction that this kind of socio-psychological situation is decisive in making the Japanese work harder and more productively than workers in other industrial societies. The system contributes to prop up the less able in a group, and at the same time pull down those who have

Top Electrical appliances were one of the big boom sectors of the economy in the sixties
Above A cabdriver who doubled his trade by installing TV; intense competitiveness marks Japanese society at all levels

Japanese police, masked and helmeted, crack down on cars with too high a carbon monoxide content in their exhaust gases. By 1970 air pollution – largely ignored in general legislation – became a serious problem

Lunch break in a transistor factory; the library is for employees to increase their technical knowledge

Two workers at the Yawata Steel Company; the paternalistic employers provide bachelors' rooms on the premises. Complete loyalty to the company is expected

exceptional ability. Those who value group action tend to ignore differences of individual merits. Group activities produce the kind of lively climate which invites individuals consciously or unconsciously to contribute something to. Probably because of such a group habit, the Japanese seem to be always ready for action, and they feel happier doing something concrete, rather than thinking or doing nothing particular.

In the group structure, relative rankings are individually determined and each person takes his place within a firmly established hierarchical system. Such a system works against the formation of distinct strata within a group. In this kind of society ranking becomes far more important than any differences in the nature of the work or the status group. Indeed, ranking functions as the principal controlling factor in social relations in Japan. The Japanese are not generally class-conscious, but they are very much concerned with the relative prestige of their own group, which derives from the ranking hierarchy of similar groups. It seems to be of greater importance to the Japanese to be ranked higher than to make more actual profit. They are more concerned with social prestige or esteem than with specific economic gains. Groups or institutions seem more important than individuals. This is also made manifest by the mushrooming of grand modern office buildings in contrast to the poor housing conditions for individual families.

Ranking is the result of the competition among similar groups. Competition, which produces the apparent independence and isolation of each institution, at the same time entails the establishment of a hierarchical order among similar institutions. Indeed, a hierarchy is to be found in every field; and once an order is established, it will persist over a considerable period of time in spite of ups and downs in particular circumstances.

The solidarity of a group is found on various levels; it may be a section of a department or a department of an institution. The formation of intra-group factions and the development within a given field of activity of a number of similar independent groups possessing no means of controlling or accommodating each other are distinctive features of the Japanese situation. Japanese organizations regularly suffer from what they call 'sectionalism'. It is a well-known phenomenon in Japanese society that they tend to fight with people in other similar groups and ignore a potential common enemy outside their immediate concerns. This kind of organization precludes horizontal relations. The existence of competing equal powers constitutes an unstable situation in Japan; stability always resides in imbalance between powers, one dominating the other. There is no successful functional group built on a coalition or federation of sub-groups. All groups inevitably develop the vertical type of organization structure.

The characteristics of Japanese society assist the development of state power. Because competing groups have difficulty in reaching consensus, they have little authority in dealing with the state administration. Competition and hostile relations between groups facilitate the acceptance of governmental organization; and, since the group is organized vertically, once the state's administrative authority is accepted it can be transmitted without obstruction down the vertical line. In this way the administrative web has become more thoroughly woven into Japanese society than perhaps any other in the world. Here is the fertile ground which allows the development of the top power constellation described in the previous section.

It is important to see, in the context discussed above, the radical student demonstrations in Japan, the climax of which was reached in 1968-9, and which were not only a sensational event in Japan, but were also widely treated in the world's press. There have been reasons enough for young people to become anti-establishment; their protests were both anti-government and anti-superiors in organizations (professors and directors of boards). The explosions of their feelings and frustrations were indeed radical, but they were carried out within the framework of the structure described above. The coalitions of students' groups from different universities (even different faculties and departments of the same university) were short-lived and they did not succeed in winning the support of the workers

In Japan education and government structure is interdependent; teachers and academics sit on the ministry of education committees: (*above*) children practising *katizome* handwriting
Right Universities are strict hierarchies; the most prestigious is the University of Tokyo

Food supplies in Japan, UK and USA 1966-8

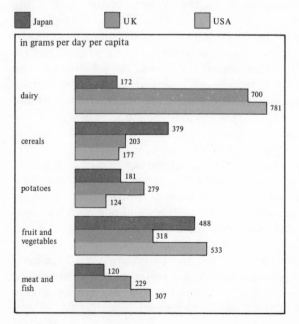

■ Japan □ UK □ USA

in grams per day per capita

dairy	Japan 172, UK 700, USA 781
cereals	Japan 379, UK 203, USA 177
potatoes	Japan 181, UK 279, USA 124
fruit and vegetables	Japan 488, UK 318, USA 533
meat and fish	Japan 120, UK 229, USA 307

who mostly remained critical of the students. Moreover, the radical attacks carried out by each university followed very similar patterns, copying that of the University of Tokyo where the first and most sensational attack was made. They became almost a ritual in the course of time. Now, many feel that the festive season is over. Certainly they have brought results. For example, the need for reforms in the educational system, and improvements of curriculum and of professor-students relationship have been widely accepted by those concerned. However, the students, except for a minor percentage, admit the failure of their movement and show no interest in the materialization of such reforms. Many of them are eager to graduate and to be employed by their former enemy, the establishment.

Other problems and sectors

As one can easily predict from the structure of the top sector, government economic policy has favoured the interests of large enterprises, rather than the healthy development of the people as a whole. The mass of the people were left out from a proper share of the gains of Japan's economic growth. This may explain the fact that in 1969 national income per head stood sixteenth in the world, while GNP was second in the non-communist world. Even public investments have been concentrated upon the development of particular areas such as roads and ports, which directly benefit industrial enterprises and only indirectly concern the people's welfare. Transportation problems have been dealt with mainly with an eye to the interests of the automobile industry, health problems from the viewpoint of the pharmaceutical and food industries.

The unfortunate results of these one-sided economic triumphs were becoming more and more obvious by the late 1960s. The achievement of the second-largest automobile production in the world was accompanied by a mounting toll of traffic accidents; pollution of air and water, resulting from the great development of the heavy and chemical industries, was left uncared for. By 1970 the results of this failure of concern were at last coming to the fore.

The rapid growth of the gross national product led to increased incomes, which stimulated demand and high prices, which in turn caused higher wages. Thus, the pattern of a vicious wage-price cycle began to take root in the Japanese economy. The inflationary trend became real with the rise of wholesale and consumer prices in the late sixties. To cope with this, the government and the Bank of Japan adopted a tight monetary policy in September 1969, the first time such a policy had been adopted in the favourable international balance of payments situation. Unlike previous situations which followed the process of moving from an overheated economy to increased imports, to deterioriation of the international balance of payments situation and then to tight money, this tight monetary policy in a favourable international balance of payments situation encouraged

Prime Minister Sato (left)
with the emperor and
empress in 1967; the
Liberal-Democratic Party
dominated the postwar
political scene

Early in 1952 Japanese communists demonstrated against
the Mutual Aid Pact with the US which ensured the
presence of American troops; but violent tactics
antagonized the public and led to the loss of all communist
seats in the October elections

a growth of exports and resulted in a paradoxical stimulation of inflation.

In addition to pollution and inflation, a number of other areas were left out of the economic growth of the country. The strikingly poor state of social welfare, housing and other facilities for living, education, medical care and public utilities lagged far behind the standard of an advanced industrial state. For example, in 1970 the proportion of social security outlay to the national income stood at only a little more than six per cent compared with fifteen to twenty per cent in Western Europe. The sewage system reached only eighteen per cent of the population as against ninety-six per cent in England (a time-lag of 100 years). This is in ironic contrast to the famous super express train between Tokyo and Osaka, which covers 300 miles in three hours.

Such one-sided economic growth may be attributed to the government policy subjected to the interests of industry. Leftists may say it is the evil of monopolistic capitalism, sacrificing the interests of the mass of the people. However, in my opinion, it also reflects the Japanese people's sense of values and way of life. People who live in a system where competition among peers is intense, are forced to be always looking ahead, and are interested in the rapidity rather than the quality of the achievement; the emphasis is directed to overt rather than covert areas. As a result many important matters have been left in abeyance. It is indeed a serious question, because such unfortunate facts are not simply the outcome of a particular policy, but closely related to Japanese culture and social structure. The inadequate welfare system is a conspicuous example.

Traditional welfare in Japan used to be carried out by a small group to which one was attached primarily through economic activities, such as a household, a local corporate group which might consist of several neighbouring households of peasants, or a set of dependent households centred on the master's household. This tradition is distinctly maintained in the modern setting, since it is maintained by the company or institution in which workers are employed. Therefore, those who work in a large institution, whether in industry or government, are well cared for: the institution offers health services, housing as well as housing loans, holiday accommodation, facilities for playing sports, and so on. Regardless of status,

Japan in 1969 had its share of student unrest:
(*top*) *zengakuren* demonstrate violently against the
visit of an American ship on its way to Vietnam;
(*above*) Tokyo clock-tower during student occupation

qualification or income, employees of such well-established institutions form the core and the dominant sector of Japanese society. For them national welfare services are hardly needed. However, those who work in unstable small companies, or who do not belong to an established institution or any kind of an effective functional group (including a fairly large number of people who might have left their native community and are not yet able to find a proper job) are left uncared for; and such people form a lower or peripheral sector of the society. Among them the physically handicapped, the needy, the aged and orphans are of course included. Since the problems of these peripheral members are not connected to the interests of politicians, they have been neglected by them.

At the same time, in Japan, institutions like the Christian charity or voluntary service groups characteristic of the West hardly exist. Nor does the social custom of aiding the weak, as seen rooted in India, exist in the fibre of Japanese society. The general attitude of most people is that they do not take care of those who are outside of their own group. In their daily behaviour much less sympathy is evident for the handicapped than in other countries. They usually remain cool towards those with whom they have no relations in their communal life. Even if they felt like giving a helping hand to others, there has been no institutionalized customary method of doing so. Therefore in Japan more than elsewhere the official administrative network of the central organization is needed to meet the problem. Indeed, criticism of and expectations from the government in these regards, are extremely high. Help for the handicapped and weak is insistently demanded in the Japanese press and various journalistic activities, yet it is still extremely difficult to attain. Apart from the reluctance of politicians to take up the problem, one major impediment to such relief projects is that responsibility is parcelled out among different departments in several ministries, such as health and welfare, justice, labour and education. Procedural and organizational matters, even more complicated than one might suppose, are involved in making policy decisions, mapping out plans and applying for budget appropriations. This makes it difficult for functional measures to be taken for the unfortunate. It goes without saying that the same difficulties apply to tackling pollution and foreign-aid policies.

Geishas outside a Tokyo bar

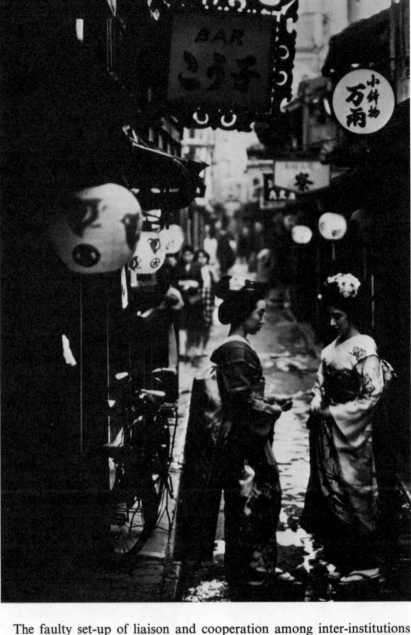

The Westernization of sex – a strip club

The faulty set-up of liaison and cooperation among inter-institutions stems from the basic social structure of Japan and the pattern of human relationships that forms its nucleus. And this phenomenon can be seen not only among government ministries but also in almost all fields in Japan. In my view, the defects of what I call 'vertical society' with its isolated and closed groups, pervade the administrative, industrial, educational, academic, artistic and all other realms of society. It lacks effective flexibility in dealing with new social problems. The amount of unnecessary energy expended for this reason is enormous. This, I fear, will be actualized, sooner or later, as a seriously retrogressive feature of Japanese society. This Japanese system certainly contributes to the efficient working and development of particular enterprises or groups, but it does entail inertia and indifference in the face of certain rapid social changes.

These cultural and structural defects of Japanese society are evident in attitudes to the problems of developing countries. The people's concerns, which induce them to look far ahead, make them appear unsympathetic to those whom they have economically left behind. Have they really thought of the affairs of developing countries? In the words of an Indian critic: 'Indians and South-east Asians generally feel that the Japanese are selfish, that they make every deal with an eye on maximum benefit to themselves and their country – be it a commercial transaction or a foreign-aid deal – and that they lack warmth of human or even neighbourly feelings.' (Durga Das, 'Japan's role in Asia', in *Indian and Foreign Review*, vol. 7, no. 18, 1 July 1970, p. 11.)

The Japanese attitude reflected in such an impression may be attributed

Golf introduced by the Americans has now become a popular sport; a triple-decker driving range in Tokyo makes the most of the space available

Traditional Japanese sports still maintain their popularity: (*below*) *Sumo* wrestling; the cloth banner proclaims the prize, and the referee (second from right) dresses in traditional clothes; (*bottom*) *Kendo* – fencing Japanese style

to their pattern of life at home, where competition among peers in the same organization as well as among similar organizations is so keen. Their major concerns are directed to the immediate interests of their own organization: often not even to the nation as a whole, let alone the affairs of other nations. The primary concern of the Japanese on the spot, whether in Japan or South-east Asia or Latin America, is the well-being of their own company or department, which is closely connected to their step up the promotion ladder: such individuals rarely have sufficient sympathy and energy in reserve to think of the interests of the country and people with which they are dealing.

It is an ironic fact that the social structure and value orientation, so instrumental in the economic development of the country, have negative effects in dealing with other countries. The Japanese system works effectively for the majority of Japanese (leaving out weak minorities) in the situation of isolation, but it has fatal drawbacks in dealing with non-Japanese societies. In addition the relative geographical and historical isolation of Japan has made the Japanese inexperienced and perhaps insensitive in dealing with international affairs. Japan has never played a significant role in international politics during the postwar period. It is indeed regrettable that Japan has not been able to improve even her most important foreign problem – her relationship with China. In this connection, only the following two achievements are worth mentioning here. One is the Japan-Korea Treaty signed in 1965, by which Japan restored diplomatic relations with Korea. Another is the reversion of Okinawa, which was one of the largest issues in postwar Japan. In the joint communiqué between Prime Minister Sato and President Nixon signed on 21 November 1969, the agreement was made to return the administrative rights over Okinawa to Japan in 1972. The prospect of it certainly involves an increase in the responsibilities of Japan in maintaining the peace and security of the Far East.

The period under the American umbrella is over and, fully grown-up, Japan has begun to be exposed to the sceptical eyes of the rest of the world. In 1970 the standard outlook in Japan could be stated as follows. As a country with a favourable international balance of payments, Japan's international responsibilities have also become heavier. The days are gone when the government can be excessively protective towards domestic industry. Japan must now tackle the problems of increasing imports, promoting capital exchange, increasing economic aid to the developing countries and effectively utilizing the foreign currency reserves which have continued to accumulate. Among the élite and intellectuals in Japan, there are not a few who are deeply concerned with Japan's obligation to contribute to the world, particularly in fostering the development of Asia. However, these thoughtful ideas and opinions are often overruled by the force of group dynamics, in which day-to-day interests of groups are felt to be more important than dealings with foreign countries. Therefore, the basic issue is how to overcome the cultural and structural drawbacks of Japanese society. The time of the real trial for Japan has come.

Marcus Cunliffe

Epilogue

During a war people need to believe that something better will emerge. Peace, of course, is one of the things they crave: an end to the fighting. But they need to believe that from the conflict may emerge a 'just and lasting peace' – an end, that is, not only to the immediate struggle but to all wars. Their sacrifices, they are told and wish to think, will not have been in vain. Suffering will have been justified by the creation of a better world. From the rubble and ashes a phœnix is awaited.

So it was, at least for the winning nations, in the latter stages of the Second World War. Freedoms, charters of human rights, an entirely different international organization from the battered old League of Nations: these were drawn up clause by clause, with every appearance of serious and permanent intent. In retrospect, how did our world actually fare from 1945 to 1970, measured against these documented aspirations?

Most of the young and many of the not-young, from the vantage point of 1970, would probably answer that once again, as so often in history, the war might have done something to accelerate social change but had done little to generate a more generous spirit among mankind. It had its ironies, and perhaps unexpectedly beneficial consequences for some parts of the world. Among the so-called 'victorious' nations, Russia endured miseries equal to those of the defeated nations; in China, the fighting helped to hasten the downfall of the Kuomintang; Britain's resources were so strained that she declined into the second rank of nations, far behind the United States and Russia. Britain, France, Belgium and the Netherlands, as a result of the war, lost most of their grip on their vast colonial empires (Portugal, relatively untouched by the war, still retained its hold on its African territories a quarter of a century afterwards). Of the defeated nations, Germany and Japan, their industrial areas laid waste, were forced into prodigies of improvisation and innovation, and by 1970 were considerably wealthier than Britain. They had accomplished this economic miracle in spite of their lack of a nuclear capacity or conventional armed forces – or (another irony?) was this in part *because* of the lack?

As for the grand schemes of world betterment, it was arguable that these had amounted to little or nothing, that the quarter of a century had been a dismal further chapter in the long record of human selfishness and stupidity. By 1970 the UN was threatened with actual as well as metaphorical bankruptcy. As with the old League of Nations, member states clung to their individual sovereignties. In the UN and its agencies one could easily gain the impression that unanimity on an issue signified that it was of no importance whatsoever. World peace? Instead there had arisen the cold war. The superpowers had divided the world into armed camps, and had devoted astronomical sums of money to the invention and stock-piling of weapons capable of destroying one another, and much of the rest of the world, within a few minutes. The dread of thermonuclear annihilation haunted the imaginations of the sensitive. And they were enraged by the apparent insensitivity of the men in power. Reflecting upon Hiroshima, the American physicist J. Robert Oppenheimer, who had been director of atomic research in the secret centre of Los Alamos, said: 'In some sort of crude sense, which no vulgarity, no humour, no overstatement can quite extinguish, the physicists have known sin; and this is a knowledge which they cannot lose.' Or as a colleague said to him, after watching the first successful nuclear explosion, with its awesome mushroom cloud: 'Now we're all sons of bitches.' They were almost more horrified, during the next fifteen years, by the apparent readiness of a new breed of government-employed intellectuals to 'think the unthinkable': to produce calculations for instance of an initial death-rate of 25 millions in the United States, following a Russian nuclear attack, with a further 25 million fatal casualties from fallout – and to maintain nevertheless that it was possible to 'win' such a contest by killing even more Russians.

Even if this appalling threat remained in abeyance, more conventional weapons were put to use in an unending series of conflicts all over the globe. And these weapons, it was widely believed, had made war more ghastly than ever before. Men, women and children were fried alive with napalm. Their towns and villages were pulverized with high-level bombing. Their country-side withered under the weird rain of defoliant chemicals. All this, it was often said, indicated that the superpowers, especially the United States, were in the hands of what the American radical C.Wright Mills called the 'crackpot realists'. In *The Power Elite*, Mills charged that his country's policies were dictated by an interlocking directorate of army generals, big corporations and executive appointees. America, according to another observer, had become *The Warfare State*. In other words, it was dependent upon a war economy. This was the theme too of a deadpan satire entitled *Report from Iron Mountain*, which was presented as an analysis from a research 'think-tank' team. Their report showed, with apparently irrefutable logic, that the United States simply could not afford to risk an outbreak of peace. Not merely its economy but its entire social structure was geared to the construction of destruction.

Inhabitants of the poorer and particularly the non-white nations could feel that their own hopes had been betrayed by the affluent white nations. They had achieved formal independence in most parts of the once-colonial world. They had not achieved stability or prosperity. After the glorious spree of the independence ceremonies had come the let-down: the realization that their economies were still subordinate to those of the 'have' nations, that the immense gap in wealth between the 'haves' and the 'have-nots' was narrowing hardly at all, and that their internal problems – which they interpreted as legacies of colonialism – would be greeted with scant sympathy, or else with attempts at 'neo-colonialist' direction and intervention.

In the affluent nations still other nightmares presented themselves. Of these the worst – as the phrase implies – was the 'population explosion'. In 1900 world population was about 1,600 million. By 1950 the figure had climbed to 2,500 million, and the rate of increase per decade was a little over twenty per cent. The reason – one more item for the ironist – was that improvements in medicine and hygiene had brought about a remarkable decline in the death-rate. By 1960 the world population total had reached the 3,000 million mark, and the rate of increase per decade was well over fifty per cent. By 1970 there were more than three times as many people living in the poor countries as in the rich ones, and their birthrate was twice as high. If increase continued at this scale, the world's population would almost double every thirty years, or eightfold with each century. Almost exactly this, it so happens, had occurred in the United States from 1800 to 1900. But in those days the growth was a source of pride, not alarm – as perhaps it might still be to some extent in China, though no longer in India. Once upon a time there seemed to be room for everybody, though men with a taste for privacy might speculatively express their dislike for numbers, as Ralph Waldo Emerson did in the middle of the nineteenth century: 'Enormous populations, if they be beggars, are disgusting, like moving cheese, like hills of ants, or of fleas – the more, the worse.' Where would the dehumanized multitudes of the by-no-means-distant future manage to live? Where would their food come from? How could the poor be persuaded to reduce their frightening fertility? How could one maintain the belief in human worth, along with the conviction that there were simply too many people in the world?

So dwellers upon our earth, in 1945-70, could well believe that most of the immemorial problems of history were still present, and that some in the process of apparent solution had only spawned new and worse problems. By 1970 there was a widespread sense of claustrophobia, of congestion, of living as if in an unventilated room with no way of getting rid of the garbage. There were frightening stories of a progressive and possibly irreversible deterioration in the earth's atmosphere; of polluted air, earth and water. Delegates at international assemblies began to complain in the same language of congestion: there were too many nations, too many special interests to be reconciled, too many speakers determined to be heard.

Partly because of the fascination of the approaching, chiliastic date of AD 2000, but perhaps more because of the multiplicity and ominousness of the world's problems, the 1960s saw a crop of attempts at serious prediction of the future. In Paris, Bertrand de Jouvenel established a *Futuribles* project. In the United States, under the direction of Daniel Bell, a group called the Commission on the Year 2000 compiled voluminous reports, and other books appeared with such titles as *The Next Ninety Years* and *The Most Probable World*. Bell's group produced by far the most comprehensive material. On the whole, however, reviewers of their condensed report were unenthusiastic or even scornful.

One possible explanation is that the Commission on the Year 2000 avoided the apocalyptic vein (except here and there in a conjectural 'scenario'): their tone was cool and they showed no desire to make the reader's flesh creep. After about 1880 nearly every ambitious account of the future was distinctly gloomy: utopias were replaced by dystopias. The twentieth-century intellectual developed an appetite for bad news. He tended to mistrust reassuring prophecies, and was ready to believe the worst about the future. True, the high hopes that the mass of mankind entertained of future betterment have usually turned out to be excessive: the example of 1945-70 is before us. On the other hand, most of the dire prophecies have also turned out to be wrong. Thus, it was widely predicted that female suffrage would overturn society and politics: the actual results were almost laughably unspectacular. In the 1930s the declining birthrate in countries such as France aroused alarm and brought forth a stream of pessimistic extrapolations: the demographers soon proved to be wrong. Again in the 1930s, it was believed by military experts as well as by the general public that future wars would be won in the air, and that bombing would make cities uninhabitable. This calculation induced the Germans initially, and then the British and the Americans, to devote a large part of their war effort in 1939-45 to bombing raids. They caused enormous destruction and loss of life. But when the war was over, it became clear that the effects of bombing had been far less calamitous than the experts anticipated. Life continued in the stricken cities, and the morale of the inhabitants was even in a way raised by the awareness of shared horror. (The same lesson was reinforced by the failure of the United States to halt North Vietnam through airpower, for all the immense tonnage of bombs dropped in Vietnam.)

Similarly, some of the predictions of imminent catastrophe made after the war happily remained unfulfilled. To the extent that the predictions functioned as warnings they may have contributed to their own falsification. At any rate, the superstitious belief that the world's climate had been altered for the worse by atomic explosions was unfounded. So were certain more sophisticated announcements that milk and other products had become dangerously radioactive. On a number of occasions – the sealing off of Berlin by Russia in 1948, the Suez crisis of 1956, the Russo-American clash over Cuban missile sites in 1962 – the world seemed to be on the brink. But it drew back. The lesser wars that did break out, providing a steady rumble of catastrophe, were lamentable and horrible. But most of them were, so to speak, traditional, even if the West saw them otherwise: civil wars, border conflicts, wars in the name of liberation. Often the innocent suffered: this was nothing new. The weapons employed were often dreadful; but it was doubtful whether the quantum of suffering exceeded that of previous centuries – for instance, of the Thirty Years' War that ravaged parts of Europe during the seventeenth century. In our era starvation was rife in too many corners of the world. But in proportion to population, there was probably a good deal less famine than in earlier epochs. By 1970, the avoidance of ultimate disaster over a twenty-five-year period began to suggest that perhaps the much-derided theories of the nuclear strategists contained a degree of good sense. Perhaps the 'ultimate deterrent' *had* deterred; perhaps the Dr Strangeloves were after all not in control, and the 'fail-safe' devices might have been both foolproof and knaveproof.

During these twenty-five years one might, with reservations, note other signs that a kind of progress had been achieved. Thus there were considerable advances in the care and cure of disease. Poliomyelitis – infantile paralysis – had for instance been overcome. And the explanation for the alarming rise of world population, as we have seen, was a consequence of improved sanitation, diet and medical care. Hundreds of millions, though probably still a minority of the world's total, experienced a distinct lift in living standards. For the young especially, in the affluent nations, there was greater actual freedom than people of their age had ever known – freedom from early and unremitting toil, from bondage to one patch of ground; freedom to study, to travel, to campaign. In other words, a number of the era's chief causes for anxiety were in fact not evidence of retrogression but of progression – of advances for which, alas, a price had to be paid. It was possible to maintain that the price was too great – a plethora of blessings becomes a curse, as in the case of the automobile in metropolitan centres. It could be said that the emphasis on improvement of material standards was in itself corruptingly materialistic. But it was unhistorical and superficial to argue that the modern world's problems were merely the consequence of greed, cruelty or lack of forethought. Some sprang from the best of intentions. If they represented a failure accurately to predict outcomes, the real lesson could even be a source of comfort to those concerned by the apparent victory of machines over men: the future remained as unpredictable as ever. The staff of the IBM office in Tokyo put up a notice during the 1960s that read:

MAN – SLOW, SLOVENLY, BRILLIANT
IBM – FAST, ACCURATE, STUPID

The machine only did what it was told. Computers served to eliminate infinitely dreary tasks of filing and classifying that had once had to be performed by wretched clerks and petty bureaucrats. The awe in which they were held during the 1950s was largely dissipated by their failure to render any fundamental assistance to the conduct of American operations in Vietnam, despite their widespread use. Human beings could be both evilly and gloriously intractable. The point is nicely illustrated by the story of a girl who supplied particulars of herself to one of the computerized 'dating' agencies that enjoyed a vogue in the 1960s. The machine digested her information and soon gave her the name and address of a young man guaranteed to be compatible. The girl, however, was shy and told a friend that she did not intend to keep the appointment. When the friend remonstrated with her she answered: 'If we are so perfectly matched, he won't turn up either.'

One world? Yes and no. A better world than hitherto? Again, yes and no. Since they were human beings, very few of those alive in any year between 1945 and 1970 would have professed themselves entirely happy or entirely reconciled to their lot. On this there was almost complete unanimity. On what was to be done to remedy matters, individually or collectively, there was the widest and wildest variance. The celebrated opening lines from Charles Dickens's *A Tale of Two Cities* seemed as apposite as ever:

'It was the best of times, it was the worst of times, it was the age of wisdom, it was the age of foolishness, it was the season of Light, it was the season of Darkness, it was the spring of hope, it was the winter of despair, we had everything before us, we had nothing before us, we were all going direct to Heaven, we were all going direct the other way. . . .'

Bibliography

The Scope of Our Times

Aron, R. (ed.), *L'histoire contemporaine depuis 1945*, Paris 1969
Bell, D., *The End of Ideology*, New York 1961
Bellow, S., *Mr Sammler's Planet*, New York 1970
Booker, C., *The Neophiliacs*, London 1969
Findlay, J.F. (ed.), *Contemporary Civilization*, Issue 4, Glenview, Illinois 1967
Knapp, W., *A History of War and Peace, 1939-1965*, London 1967
Lerner, D., *The Passing of the Traditional Societies*, Glencoe, Illinois 1958
Morin, E., *L'esprit du temps: essai sur la culture de masse*, Paris 1962
O'Neill, W.L. (ed.), *American Society since 1945*, Chicago 1969

War and Peace in a Nuclear Age

Aron, R., *Peace and War: A Theory of International Relations*, London 1967
  (first published as *Paix et Guerre entre les Nations*, Paris 1962)
Brodie, B., *Strategy in the Missile Age*, Princeton, New Jersey 1959 and Oxford 1960
Buchan, A. (ed.), *Problems of Modern Strategy*, London 1970
Gurr, T.R., *Why Men Rebel*, Princeton, New Jersey 1970
Halle, L.J., *The Cold War as History*, London 1967
Hoffmann, S., *Gulliver's Troubles or the Setting of American Foreign Policy*, New York 1968
James, A., *The Politics of Peace-Keeping*, London 1969
Laqueur, W., *The Struggle for the Middle East*, London and New York 1969
Lee, J.M., *African Armies and Civil Order*, London 1969
Ra'anan, U., *The USSR Arms the Third World*, Cambridge, Mass. and London 1969
Snow, E., *Red China Today*, London 1970
Ulam, A.B., *Expansion and Coexistence*, New York and London 1969

Problems of the 'Have-not' World

Bendix, R., *Nation-Building and Citizenship*, New York 1964
Breese, G., *Urbanization in Developing Countries*, New Jersey 1966
Chaliand, G., *The Peasants of North Vietnam*, London 1969
  (first published as *Les Paysans du Nord-Vietnam et la Guerre*, Paris 1968)
Debray, R., *Revolution in the Revolution? armed struggle in Latin America*, London 1968
  (first published as *Révolution dans la Révolution?*, Paris 1967)
Fanon, F., *The Wretched of the Earth*, London 1965
  (first published as *Les Damnés de la Terre*, Paris 1961)
First, R., *The Barrel of a Gun: political power in Africa and the coup d'état*, London 1970
Geertz, C., *Agricultural Involution: the process of agricultural change in Indonesia*, Los Angeles 1968
Jenkins, R., *Exploitation: power structure and the inequality of nations*, London 1970
Kiernan, V.G., *The Lords of Human Kind: European attitudes towards the outside world in the Imperial Age*, London 1969
Mangin, W. (ed.), *Peasants and Cities*, New York 1969
Myrdal, G., *Asian Drama: An Inquiry into the Poverty of Nations*, New York and London 1968
Myrdal, G., *The Challenge of World Poverty*, London 1970
Russett, W., Alker, H., Deutsch, K., and Lasswell, H., *World Handbook of Social and Political Indicators*, New Haven, Conn. 1964
Segal, R., *The Race War*, London 1966
Wolf, E., *Peasants*, New Jersey 1966
Worsley, P., *The Third World*, revised ed., London 1967

The Conception of a World Economy

Cooper, R.N., *The Economics of Interdependence*, New York 1968
Diebold, W., *The Schuman Plan*, New York 1959
Gardner, R.N., *Sterling-Dollar Diplomacy*, revised ed., New York 1969
Halm, G.N. (ed.), *Approaches to Greater Flexibility of Exchange Rates*, The Bürgenstock Papers, Princeton 1970
Hirsch, F., *Money International*, revised ed., London 1969
Johnson, H.G., *Economic Policies Toward Less Developed Countries*, Washington DC 1967
Kindleberger, C.P., *American Business Abroad*, New Haven, Conn. 1969
Kock, K., *International Trade Policy and the Gatt, 1945-1947*, Stockholm 1969

Machlup, F., *Remaking the International Monetary System*, Baltimore 1968
Patterson, G., *Discrimination in International Trade, The Policy Issues*, Princeton 1966
Tew, B., *International Monetary Cooperation, 1945-1965*, 8th ed., London 1965
Triffin, R., *Europe and the Money Muddle*, New Haven, Conn. 1957

Problems of Prosperity

Ali, T., *The New Revolutionaries*, New York 1969
Ardagh, J., *The New French Revolution*, London 1968
Brzezinski, Z., *Between Two Ages*, New York 1970
Crick, B., and Robson, W.A., *Protest and Discontent*, London 1970
Dahrendorf, R., *Society and Democracy in Germany*, London 1968
De Bell, G., *The Environmental Handbook*, New York 1970
Galbraith, J.K., *The Affluent Society*, Boston 1958
Harrington, M., *Toward a Democratic Left*, Baltimore 1969
Howe, I., *Beyond the New Left*, New York 1969
Jacoby, N.H., 'The Environmental Crisis', *The Center Magazine*, Vol. III, No. 6, November/December 1970
Laqueur, W., *Europe since Hitler*, London 1970
Riesman, D., *Abundance for What?*, New York 1964
Sampson, A., *The New Europeans*, London 1968
Toffler, A., *Future Shock*, New York 1970

Race and Racialism

Banton, M., *Race Relations*, London 1967
Barber, J., *Rhodesia: the Road to Rebellion*, London 1967
Bennett, L., *Before the Mayflower: A History of the Negro in America 1619-1964*, Baltimore 1966
Brookes, E.H., *Apartheid: a documentary of South Africa*, London 1968
Carmichael, S., and Hamilton, C.V., *Black Power*, London 1968
Grimshaw, A.D. (ed.), *Racial Violence in the United States*, Chicago 1969
Mason, P., *Patterns of Dominance*, London 1970
Report of the National Advisory Commission on Civil Disorders, Washington DC 1967
Rose, E.J.B., and associates, *Colour and Citizenship*, London 1969
Schuman, H., 'Americans and Race: Freewill or Determinism', *New Society*, 4 June 1970
UNESCO, *Apartheid*, Paris 1967
Van den Berghe, P., *South Africa, a Study in Conflict*, Los Angeles 1967

Mass Pleasures

Halloran, J. (ed.), *The Effects of Television*, London 1970
Hoggart, R., *The Uses of Literacy*, London 1957
Hopkins, H., *The New Look*, London 1963
Macdonald, D., 'Masscult and Midcult', *Partisan Review*, New Jersey 1961
Melly, G., *Revolt Into Style*, London 1970
Miller, J., *McCluhan*, London 1971
Montgomery, J., *The Fifties*, London 1965
Nuttall, J., *Bomb Culture*, London 1968
Sissons, M., and French, P. (eds.), *Age of Austerity*, London 1963
Thompson, D. (ed.), *Discrimination and Popular Culture*, London 1964
Tunstall, J. (ed.), *Media Sociology*, London 1970

The Arts: Reductionism and Pluralism

Butor, M., *Inventory*, London 1970
Delevoy, R.L., *Dimensions of the Twentieth Century*, Switzerland 1965
Holthusen, H.E., *Avantgardismus und die Zukunft der modernen Kunst*, Munich 1964
Jacobus, J., *Twentieth-Century Architecture 1940-65*, London 1966
Lucie-Smith, E., *Movements in Art since 1945*, London 1969
Mellers, W., *Caliban Reborn*, London 1967
Meyer, L.W., *Music, the Arts and Ideas*, Chicago 1967
Paz, O., *Marcel Duchamp or the Castle of Purity*, London 1970
Ponente, N., *Modern Painting: Contemporary Trends*, Switzerland 1960
Russell, J. and Gablik, S., *Pop Art Redefined*, London 1969
Stuckenschmidt, H.H., *Twentieth Century Music*, London 1969

The World of Science

Armytage, W.H.G., *The Rise of the Technocracy*, London 1965
Cotgrove, S. and Box, S., *Science, Industry and Society*, London 1970
Goldsmith, M. (ed.), *Technological Innovation and the Economy*, London 1970
Landes, G., *The Unbound Prometheus*, London 1967
Shils, E. (ed.), *Criteria for Scientific Development*, Chicago 1965
Taton, R., *Science in the Twentieth Century*, London 1966
Williams, B.R., *Technology, Investment and Growth*, London 1967

Creeds and Ideologies

Altizer, T.J.J., *The Gospel of Christian Atheism*, Philadelphia 1966
Berton, B., *The Comfortable Pew: A critical look at Christianity and the religious Establishment in the New Age*, New York 1965
Cobb, J.B., *Living Options in Protestant Theology*, Philadelphia 1962
Kavanaugh, J., *A Modern Priest Looks at his Outdated Church*, New York 1967
Macquarrie, J., *The Scope of Demythologizing*, London 1960
Metz, J.B., Moltmann, J., and Oelmüller, W., *Kirche im Prozess der Aufklärung*, Munich 1970
Paloczi-Horvath, G., *Youth up in Arms: A political and social world survey 1955-1970*, London 1971
Pethybridge, R. (ed.), *The Development of the Communist Bloc*, Boston 1965
Roszak, T., *The Making of a Counter Culture: Reflections on the Technocratic Society and its Youthful Opposition*, London 1970
Sölle, D., *Stellvertretung. Ein Kapitel Theologie nach dem Tode Gottes*, Stuttgart 1965
Vahanian, G., *The Death of God: The Culture of our Post-Christian Era*, New York 1961
Weymann-Weyhe, W., *Ins Angesicht widerstehen*, Olten/Freiburg 1969
Zahrnt, H., *Gott kann nicht sterben*, Munich 1970

The United States: Prosperity and Turmoil

Acheson, D.G., *Present at the Creation*, New York 1969
Cooper, C.L., *The Lost Crusade: America in Vietnam*, New York 1970
Eisenhower, Dwight D., *Mandate for Change*, New York 1963
Eisenhower, Dwight D., *Waging Peace*, New York 1965
Evans, R. and Novak, R., *Lyndon B. Johnson: The Exercise of Power*, New York 1966
Feis, H., *From Trust to Terror: The Onset of the Cold War, 1945-1950*, New York 1970
Kahin, G. McT. and Lewis, J.W., *The United States in Vietnam*, New York 1969
Konvitz, M.R., *Expanding Liberties: Freedom's Gains in Post-War America*, New York 1966
Lubell, S., *The Future of American Politics*, New York 1952
Lubell, S., *The Hidden Crisis of American Politics*, New York 1970
Schlesinger, A.M., Jr., *A Thousand Days: John F. Kennedy in the White House*, Boston 1965
Sorensen, T.C., *Kennedy*, New York 1965
Truman, H.S., *Memoirs*, 2 vols., New York 1955-6

Western Europe: the Quest for Unity

Beck, R.B. *et al.*, *The Changing Structure of Europe*, Minneapolis 1970
Black, J., and Thompson, K. (eds.), *Foreign Policies in a World of Change*, New York 1963
Bracher, K.D., *The German Dictatorship*, New York 1970
Bracher, K.D., (ed.) *Nach 25 Jahren. Eine Deutschland-Bilanz*, Munich 1970
Calmann, J. (ed.), *Western Europe: A Handbook*, 1967
Chapsal, J., *La vie politique en France depuis 1940*, Paris 1966
Graubard, St. (ed.), *A New Europe?*, Boston 1964
Grosser, A., *L'Allemagne de notre temps*, Paris 1970
Hoffmann, St. (ed.), *In Search of France*, Cambridge, Mass. 1963
Kogan, N., *A Political History of Postwar Italy*, New York 1962
Laqueur, W., *Europe since Hitler*, London 1970
Mayne, R., *The Institutions of the European Common Market*, London 1968
Willis, F.R., *France, Germany, and the New Europe 1945-1967*, Stanford 1968

The Commonwealth and Britain: Changing Realities

Britain and the Process of Decolonisation, COI pamphlet RFP 5865, London 1970
Commonwealth, journal of the Royal Commonwealth Society, London
The Commonwealth in Brief, COI pamphlet PB 4736, London 1970
Commonwealth Secretary-General: Third Report, London 1970
Commonwealth Yearbook 1969, London
Cross, C., *The Fall of the British Empire*, London 1968
Gordon Walker, P., *The Commonwealth*, London 1962
Ingram, D., *The Commonwealth Challenge*, London 1962
Kirkman, W.P., *Unscrambling an Empire*, London 1966
Mansergh, N., *The Commonwealth Experience*, London 1969
Miller, J.D.B., *The Commonwealth in the World*, London 1958
Robinson, R.E. and Gallagher, J., *Africa and the Victorians*, London 1961

The Soviet Union: the Permanent Enigma

Crankshaw, E., *Khrushchev*, London 1966
Deutscher, I., *Russia After Stalin*, London 1953
Deutscher, I., *Stalin: A Political Biography*, London 1949, enlarged ed. 1967
Ehrenberg, I., *The Thaw*, London 1955
Freeborn, R., *A Short History of Modern Russia*, London 1966
Kennan, G.F., *Russia, the Atom and the West*, London 1958
Kennan, G.F., *Russia and the West Under Lenin and Stalin*, London 1961

Khrushchev, N.S., *For Victory in Peaceful Competition with Capitalism: Speeches and Statements*, London 1960
Molotov, V.M., *Problems of Foreign Policy: Speeches and Statements*, Moscow 1949
Nove, A., *An Economic History of the USSR*, London 1969
Schapiro, L., *The Communist Party of the Soviet Union*, London 1960, revised and enlarged ed. 1970
Ulam, A.B., *Expansion and Coexistence: the History of Soviet Foreign Policy from 1917-67*, London 1968
Werth, A., *Russia: Hopes and Fears*, London 1969

Eastern Europe: Between Two Worlds

Auty, P., *Tito*, London 1970
Bethell, N., *Gomułka*, London 1969
Brown, J.F., *Bulgaria under Communist Rule*, London 1970
Ceausescu, N., *Romania on the Way of Completing Socialist Construction*, Bucharest 1969
Djilas, M., *Conversations with Stalin*, London 1962
Fischer-Galati, S.A., *The Socialist Republic of Rumania*, Baltimore 1969
Hangen, W., *The Muted Revolution*, (GDR), New York 1966
Kuron, J., and Modzelewski, K., *A Revolutionary Socialist Manifesto: open letter to the [Polish] Party*, London 1968
Lendvai, P., *Eagles in Cobwebs: Nationalism and Communism in the Balkans*, London 1970
Pano, N.C., *The People's Republic of Albania*, Baltimore 1968
Pryce-Jones, D., *The Hungarian Revolution*, London 1969
Schöpflin, G. (ed.), *The Soviet Union and Eastern Europe*, London 1970
Schwarz, H., *Prague's Hundred Days*, New York 1969
Shawcross, W., *Dubček*, London 1970
Stehle, H.-J., *Nachbar Polen*, Frankfurt 1963

China: the Coming Colossus

Donnithorne, A., *China's Economic System*, London 1967
Gittings, J., *Survey of the Sino-Soviet Dispute*, London 1968
Ho P'ing-ti and Tsou Tang (ed.), *China in Crisis*, Chicago 1968
Huck, A., *The Security of China*, London 1970
Lewis, J.W. (ed.), *Party Leadership and Revolutionary Power in China*, London 1970
Lifton, R., *Revolutionary Immortality*, London 1969
Pye, L., *The Spirit of Chinese Politics*, London 1968
Schram, S., *Mao Tse-tung*, London 1966
Schram, S., *The Political Thought of Mao Tse-tung*, London 1969
Schurmann, F., *Ideology and Organization in Communist China*, 2nd ed., London 1968
Schwartz, B.I., *Communism and China: Ideology in Flux*, Cambridge, Mass. 1968

Latin America: the Struggle for Progress

Baer, W., and Kerstenetzky, I., *Inflation and economic growth in Latin America*, Homewood, Illinois 1964
Frank, A.G., *Capitalism and underdevelopment in Latin America*, New York 1967
Hirschman, A.O., *Journeys towards progress. Studies of economic policy-making in Latin America*, New York 1963
Jaguaribe, H., *Economic and political development*, Cambridge, Mass. 1968
Johnson, J.J., *Political change in Latin America. The emergence of the middle sectors*, Stanford 1958
Lambert, J., *Amérique Latine: structures sociales et institutions politiques*, Paris 1963
Petras, J., and Zeitlin, M. (ed.), *Latin America. Reform or revolution?*, Greenwich, Conn. 1968
Prebisch, R., *Hacia una dinámica del desarrollo latinoamericano*, Mexico 1963
Silvert, K.H., *The conflict society: reaction and revolution in Latin America*, New York 1966
Véliz, C. (ed.), *Obstacles to change in Latin America*, London 1965
Wionczek, M.S., *Latin American economic integration: experiences and prospects*, New York 1966

Africa: the Age of Nkrumah

Carter, G.M. (ed.), *National Unity and Regionalism in Eight African States*, New York 1966
Foltz, W.J., *Military Influences on African Foreign Policies*, New York 1966
Grinnell-Milne, D., *The Triumph of Integrity: a Portrait of Charles de Gaulle*, New York 1962
Jack, H.A., 'Non-alignment and a Test Ban Agreement: the role of the Non-aligned States', *Journal of Arms Control*, Vol. I, No. 4, October 1963
Legum, C., *Pan-Africanism: A Short Political Guide*, enlarged ed., London 1965
Le Vine, V., 'New Directions for French-speaking Africa?', *Africa Report*, Vol. 10, No. 3, March 1965
Mazrui, A.A., *On Heroes and Uhuru Worship*, London 1967
Mazrui, A.A., *The Anglo-African Commonwealth: Political Friction and Cultural Fusion*, Oxford 1967
Mazrui, A.A., *Towards a Pax-Africana: A Study of Ideology and Ambition*, London 1967
Nkrumah, K., *Africa Must Unite*, London 1963
Nkrumah, K., *Ghana: The Autobiography of Kwame Nkrumah*, New York and Edinburgh 1957
Nkrumah, K., *I Speak of Freedom: A Statement of African Ideology*, London 1962
Padmore, G. (ed.), *History of the Pan-African Congress*, second ed., London 1963
Rotberg, R.I., and Mazrui, A.A. (eds.), *Protest and Power in Black Africa*, New York 1970
Wallerstein, I.M., *Africa: The Politics of Unity*, New York 1967

The Middle East: the Permanent Crisis

Be'eri, E., *Army Officers in Arab Politics and Society*, Jerusalem 1969
Cremeans, C.D., *The Arabs and the World*, New York 1963
Fisher, S.N., *The Middle East: A History*, 2nd ed., New York 1968
Issawi, C., *Egypt in Revolution: An Economic Analysis*, Oxford 1963
Karpat, K.H. (ed.), *Political and Social Thought in the Contemporary Middle East*, New York 1968
Kerr, M., *The Arab Cold War, 1958-64*, London 1965
Khadduri, M., *Republican Iraq*, London 1969
Laqueur, W., *The Road to War*, London 1968
Laqueur, W., *The Struggle for the Middle East*, London 1969
Lewis, B., *The Middle East and the West*, London 1966
Longrigg, S.H., *Oil in the Middle East*, 3rd ed., London 1968
Seale, P., *The Struggle for Syria*, London 1965

The Indian Sub-continent: Dilemmas of Democracy

Ali, Chaudhuri Muhammad, *The Emergence of Pakistan*, New York 1967
Ali, Tariq, *Pakistan: Military Rule or People's Power?*, London 1970
Bettelheim, C., *India Independent*, London 1968
Brecher, M., *Nehru. A Political Biography*, London 1959
Brines, R., *The Indo-Pakistani Conflict*, London 1968
Khan, Ayub, *Friends Not Masters. A Political Autobiography*, London 1967
Kochanek, S., *The Congress Party of India*, Princeton 1968
Ludowyk, E.F.G., *The Modern History of Ceylon*, London 1967
Mason, P. (ed.), *India and Ceylon: Unity and Diversity*, London 1967
Maxwell, N., *India's China War*, London 1970
Morris Jones, W.H., *The Government and Politics of India*, London 1964
Myrdal, G., *Asian Drama. An Inquiry into the Poverty of Nations*, New York and London 1968
Sayeed, Khalid bin, *The Political System of Pakistan*, Boston 1967
Scalapino, R.A. (ed.), *The Communist Revolution in Asia*, New Jersey 1969
Smith, D.E. (ed.), *South Asian Politics and Religion*, Princeton 1966

South-east Asia: Warring Ideologies

Bastin, J.S., and Benda, H.J., *A History of Modern Southeast Asia: Colonialism, Nationalism and Decolonisation*, Englewood Cliffs 1968
Fall, B., *The Two Viet Nams*, London 1963
Feith, H., *The Decline of Constitutional Democracy in Indonesia*, Ithaca 1962
Grossholtz, J., *Politics in the Philippines*, Boston 1967
Gullick, J.M., *Malaysia*, 2nd revised ed., London 1964
Kahin, G. McT., *Nationalism and Revolution in Indonesia*, Ithaca 1952
Kahin, G. McT. (ed.), *Government and Politics in Southeast Asia*, 2nd revised ed., Ithaca 1964
Lancaster, D., *The Emancipation of French Indochina*, London 1961
Shaplen, R., *Time Out of Hand. Revolution and Reaction in Southeast Asia*, New York 1969
Tilman, R. (ed.), *Man, State and Society in Contemporary Southeast Asia*, New York 1969
Tinker, H., *The Union of Burma*, 4th revised ed., London 1969

Japan: the Modern Miracle

Allen, G.C., *Japan's Economic Expansion*, London 1965
Dore, Ronald (ed.), *Aspects of Social Change in Modern Japan*, Princeton 1967
Guillan, R., *Japon-Troisième Grand*, Paris 1969
Hedberg, H.H., *Den Japanska Utmanigen* (The Japanese Challenge), Stockholm 1969
Kahn, H., *The Emerging Japanese Super State: Challenge and Response*, New Jersey 1970
Komiya, Ryutato (ed) Rober S. Ozaki (tr.), *Postwar Economic Growth in Japan*, Berkeley and Los Angeles 1966
Lockwood, W.W., *The State and Economic Enterprise in Japan*, Princeton 1965
Maruyama, Masao, *Thought and Behaviour in Modern Japanese Politics*, (edited by Ivan Morris), Oxford 1963
Nakane, Chie, *Japanese Society*, London and Berkeley 1970
Okita, Saburo, *Causes and Problems of Rapid Growth in Postwar Japan and Their Implications for Newly Developing Economies*, Japan Economic Research Center, Tokyo 1967
Passin, H. (ed.), *The United States and Japan*, New Jersey 1966
Vahlefeld, H.W., *100 Millionen Aussenseiter – Die Neue Weltmacht Japan*, Düsseldorf 1969

Biographical notes on contributors

Neal Ascherson was Central European Correspondent for *The Observer* (London) from 1963 to 1968 and has been their East European Correspondent since 1968. He has published *The King Incorporated: Leopold II and the Age of Trusts* and is at present writing a book on the West German *Ostpolitik*.

Karl Dietrich Bracher was Research Associate and Head of Department at the Institute for Political Science, Berlin, and Lecturer and Professor at the Free University of Berlin between 1950 and 1958. He has been Professor of Political Science and Contemporary History at the University of Bonn since 1959. He was a Fellow at the Center for Advanced Study, Stanford University, from 1963 to 1964 and a Member of the Institute of Advanced Study at Princeton University from 1967 to 1968. From 1965 to 1967 he was President of the German Association of Political Science. He is the author of a number of works on Germany; and his *The German Dictatorship* has recently been published in English.

Richard Cooper has been Professor of Economics at Yale University since 1966. He was Deputy-Assistant Secretary of State for international monetary affairs from 1965 to 1966, and is a consultant to government and industry. He was co-author of The Brooking Institution study, *Britain's Economic Prospects*, and his other publications include *The Economics of Interdependence*.

Marcus Cunliffe has been Professor of American Studies at the University of Sussex since 1965. Before that he was Professor of American History at Manchester University. He has travelled and lectured in a number of countries, but with a particular interest in the United States, where he was a Fellow of the Center for Advanced Study in the Behavioral Sciences, Palo Alto, California, from 1957 to 1958, and a visiting historian at Harvard University from 1959 to 1960 and at the Graduate Center of the City University of New York from 1970 to 1971. His publications include *The Literature of the United States, George Washington: Man and Monument, Soldiers and Civilians: The Martial Spirit in America, 1775-1865, American Presidents and Presidency*, and a short humorous book, *The Ages of Man*. He is now completing a study of comparative approaches to the United States, and a history of the world in the second half of the nineteenth century.

François Duchêne has been Director of the Institute for Strategic Studies (Britain) since 1969. Among the positions he has held are Press Attaché for the High Authority of the European Coal and Steel Community from 1952 to 1955, Paris Correspondent of *The Economist* from 1956 to 1958, Director of the Documentation Centre of the Action Committee for the United States of Europe from 1958 to 1963 and Editorial Writer for *The Economist* from 1963 to 1967. Among his publications are *Helmeted Airman* – a study of W.H. Auden, and he edited with an introduction *The Endless Crisis*.

Tulio Halperin Donghi was Lecturer in Latin American History at Harvard University from 1967 to 1970. Since 1970 he has been Professor of Latin American History at the University of Oxford. Among his many publications are *Historia Moderna de América Latina, Tradición Política Española e Ideológica* and *Revolucionaria de Mayo*.

Richard Harris is a specialist on Far Eastern affairs for *The Times*. Among his publications are *Independence and After* and *America and East Asia: A New Thirty Years' War?*

Ronald Hayman has been an actor and theatre director before becoming a full-time writer in 1966. He has been reviewing poetry for *Encounter* since 1968 and contributes to the *London Magazine* and the Arts pages of *The Times*. Among his publications are *Techniques of Acting* and a biography of Sir John Gielgud. He has just finished a critical study of Ionesco and is currently at work on an anatomy of the English theatre.

Friedrich Heer is Professor of the History of Ideas at Vienna University. He is the author of a number of important works on the Middle Ages and the history of ideas, and his publications include *The Medieval World, The Intellectual History of Europe, The Holy Roman Empire* and *God's First Love*. In 1961 he was appointed chief literary adviser to the Vienna Burgtheater.

Fernando Henriques has been Professorial Fellow and Director of the Centre for Multi-Racial Studies at the University of Sussex since 1964. He was Lecturer in Social Anthropology at the University of Leeds from 1948 to 1964 and Dean of the Faculty of Economics and Social Sciences at the University of Leeds from 1960 to 1962. His publications include *Family and Colour in Jamaica, Jamaica, Land of Wood and Water, Love in Action* and *Prostitution and Society*.

Patrick Keatley is Diplomatic and Commonwealth Correspondent for *The Guardian*. Over the past fifteen years he has travelled extensively for *The Guardian*, with the emphasis on Commonwealth and Afro-Asian affairs, while based in London. He covered the negotiations leading up to independence for Ghana and Malaya in 1957, and the similar negotiations for other Commonwealth countries which followed, as well as summit conferences of Commonwealth prime ministers and presidents, including Lagos and Singapore. He has toured India and Pakistan on extended lecture tours and has made a special study of southern Africa. His book, *The Politics of Partnership*, deals with the unresolved problems of white minority rule in Rhodesia and South Africa.

Walter Laqueur is Director of the Institute of Contemporary History (Wiener Library) in London and Professor of Contemporary History at Tel Aviv University. Until recently he was Professor in the History of Ideas and Politics at Brandeis University, Mass. He is co-editor of the *Journal of Contemporary History* and has written extensively on nineteenth- and twentieth-century history. His books include *Russia and Germany*, *Young Germany*, *The Fate of Revolution* and *Europe since Hitler*.

Iverach McDonald has been Associated Editor of *The Times* since 1967 and has worked for *The Times* since 1935. He has travelled extensively in the USSR, the Far East and America and he reported all the Allied conferences after the war. He was last in the Soviet Union in November 1970.

J.A.C.Mackie has been Research Director of the Centre of Southeast Asian Studies at Monash University, Australia, since 1968. He was Senior Lecturer-in-Charge of the Department of Indonesian and Malaysian Studies at the University of Melbourne from 1958 to 1966 and Reader-in-Charge from 1966 to 1967. He worked in Indonesia as a Colombo Plan economist and his publications include *Problems of the Indonesian Inflation*.

John Maddox has been Editor of the magazine *Nature* since 1966 and he edits the Nature Times Science Report in *The Times*. From 1955 to 1964 he was Science Correspondent for *The Guardian* and he was Assistant Director of the Nuffield Foundation and Co-ordinator of the Nuffield Foundation Science Teaching Project from 1964 to 1966. Among his publications are *The Spread of Nuclear Weapons* and *Revolution in Biology*.

Ali A. Mazrui is Professor of Political Science and has been Dean of the Faculty of Social Sciences at Makerere University College of East Africa, Uganda. He has lectured widely in Britain, North America, Asia and Africa, and among his publications are *The Anglo-African Commonwealth: Political Friction and Cultural Fusion*, *Towards a Pax Africana*, *On Heroes and Uhuru Worship* and *Violence and Thought*.

George Melly has recently written *Revolt into Style*, an authoritative work on pop culture in the 1960s. He was a jazz singer with the Mick Mulligan band for over twelve years and left the jazz world as a full-time performer in 1961 to concentrate on writing and broadcasting. He was television critic for *The Observer* from 1966 to 1970 and has recently become their film critic. He writes the balloons for the Flook cartoon strip in the *Daily Mail*.

Chie Nakane is Professor of Social Anthropology at the Institute of Oriental Culture at the University of Toyko. She was formerly Lecturer in Asian Anthropology at the School of Oriental and African Studies, University of London, and Visiting Professor in the Department of Anthropology at the University of Chicago. She is author of *Kinship and Economic Organization in Rural Japan, Garo and Khasi – A Comparative Study in Matrilinear Systems* and *Japanese Society*.

Peter Reeves has been a Lecturer in History in the School of African and Asian Studies at the University of Sussex since 1966. Before that he taught in Australian and American universities. He has published several articles on twentieth-century Indian history and is at present working on a book on landlords and politics in the Uttar Pradesh from 1920 to 1970.

Arthur Schlesinger Jr. has been Schweitzer Professor of Humanities at the City University, New York, since 1967. He was Professor of History at Harvard University from 1954 to 1961 and Special Assistant to President John F. Kennedy from 1961 to 1964. Among his many publications are *The Crisis of the Old Order*, *The Coming of the New Deal*, *The Politics of Upheaval*, *A Thousand Days: John F. Kennedy in the White House* and *The Bitter Heritage: Vietnam and American Democracy*.

Lucy Webster has been Research Manager of the International Division of the London Press Exchange and is now Managing Director of Export Market Research Ltd. She has published various articles on multi-country research. She is responsible for a number of studies which seek explicit strategy for developing adequate world institutions and she is Council Vice-Chairman of the World Association of World Federalists.

Peter Worsley is Professor of Sociology at Manchester University. His previous publications include *The Trumpet Shall Sound* and *The Third World* and he has contributed to *Out of Apathy*, *The Structural Study of Myth and Totemism*, *Populism* and *Régis Debray and the Latin American Revolution*.

Illustration acknowledgments

The photographs and illustrations in this book were supplied and are reproduced by kind permission of the following:

African National Congress: 36/3, 104/3, 352/2
Ajans Ekspres: 332/2
Architectural Association: 152/3, 153/1, 153/2, 154/1
Anderegg: 344/1
Architectural Review: 152/1
Arnaud, Odette: 194/1
Art Institute of Chicago: 159/2
Associated Press: 28/2, 64/1, 240/2, 242/3, 244/1, 342/1, 389/3
Australian News and Information Bureau: 239/1, 247/2
Barley, Bruno: 124/2, 339/3, 343/3
Galerie D. Bernador, Geneva: 143/2
Berry, Ian: 322/2, 335/3
Black Star: 32/2, 111/2, 232/1, 344/2, 347
British Printing Corporation: 36/2, 46/3, 67/2, 71/2, 79/3, 122/1, 133/2, 191/2, 217/2, 219, 221, 224/1, 254/1, 273/1
Bundesrepublik Press and Information: 272/2
Camera Press: 24/1, 27/1, 27/3, 28/1, 28/3, 30/2, 31/2, 33/1, 37/1, 38/2, 38/3, 40/2, 41/1, 45/1, 49/2, 52, 54, 55/1, 56, 57/2, 60/2, 61/1, 75, 77/1, 80, 82/2, 82/3, 85/3, 87/2, 88/2, 89/2, 90/2, 91, 92/1, 93/2, 96, 97/2, 99/2, 102, 103/2, 105, 110/1, 111/1, 112/3, 113/1, 115/2, 116/2, 117/1, 117/3, 117/4, 118/2, 121, 123/2, 124/1, 124/3, 125/1, 125/2, 128/2, 129, 130, 131, 133/1, 134/1, 134/2, 135/1, 137/1, 165/1, 167, 168/1, 171, 177/2, 184/2, 185/1, 186/1, 187/3, 190/2, 190/3, 192, 193/2, 195, 197/2, 205, 207/1, 210/1, 211/2, 212/1, 213/2, 213/3, 214/1, 217/1, 224/2, 227/3, 230/1, 231/1, 232, 238/1, 238/2, 241/1, 217/1, 245/1, 252/1, 255/3, 257, 258/1, 259, 262, 268, 269/2, 269/3, 270/1, 271/1, 271/3, 275/3, 277/1, 278/3, 282, 286/2, 287, 289/1, 290/2, 293/1, 295, 296, 297/2, 299, 301/1, 303, 305/2, 306/2, 307/2, 308/1, 308/2, 309/3, 311/1, 311/2, 312, 313, 315, 316/1, 318, 319/3, 320, 321/1, 321/2, 324/1, 324/2, 325/1, 325/3, 326/1, 327/1, 327/2, 328, 333, 334, 335/1, 335/2, 337/2, 338, 340/1, 344/3, 345/2, 346, 349, 350/2, 351/2, 351/3, 354/2, 355/1, 356/2, 357/3, 360/1, 362/1, 363, 367, 368, 369/1, 371/1, 372/2, 372/3, 374/3, 375/1, 376/3, 378/2, 379/1, 381, 382, 383, 385, 389/1, 389/2, 390, 391/1, 392/1, 393, 395/1, 395/2
Campaign for Nuclear Disarmament: 22
Canada House: 246/3
Capa, Cornell: 261/3
Cartier Bresson, H.: 394/2
Central Office of Information: 234, 247/1
Central Press: 32/1, 110/3, 185/2, 199/2, 341/3
Central Zionist Archives, Jerusalem: 336/1
Challon, François: 309/3
Commonwealth Office: 237/1, 240/1
Commonwealth Secretariat: 246/2
Communist Party (James Klugman Collection): 272/1, 274/1, 286/1
Conservative Research Department: 70/2
Coppens, Martien: 156/3
Cossack Vodka: 139/3
Council for the Advancement of Arab-British Understanding: 343/2
Cowan, John: 346
Crickmay, Anthony: 150/1
Cuban Embassy: 47/3, 53/3, 197/1
Cummings, *Daily Express*: 187/2
Daily Telegraph: 229/1
Davidson, Bruce: 95/2
Effel, Jean: 224/1
E.M.I.: 135/2
English Stage Company, Royal Court, London: 156/2

Enthoven and Mock: 153/3
Epoca: 190/1
European Community Information Service: 64/2, 68/1, 69
Felici Photo, Rome: 182/2
Fiat, Turin: 229/2
F.A.O.: 51/1, 51/3, 246/1
Ford Motor Company: 84/2
Fortune: 77/2
Fox Photos: 339/2
France-Soir: 340/3
Robert Fraser Gallery, London: 156/1, 157/1
John Freeman Ltd: 336/3
Furnas (J.R.Nonato): 50/1
Gamma – Raymond Depardon: 330, 345/1
Garland, *Daily Telegraph*: 223/3
Gazette d'Anvers: 68/2
Gemini News Service: 343/1
General Dynamics: 174/1
General Motors Corporation: 206/2
Grass, Gunter: 155/1
Greek Embassy: 233/3
Gregory, Alfred: 131/2, 362/1
Grosvenor Gallery; London: 142/1
Guardian: 78/2
Hamilton, Richard: 157/4
Heath, *Sunday Times*: 82/1
Help the Aged: 86/2
Hillelson, John: 35/3, 95/2, 113/2, 124/2, 214/2, 216/1, 226/2, 254/2, 261/3, 271/2, 322/2, 330, 335/3, 339/3, 343/3, 344/1, 345/1, 394
Hsinhua News Agency: 53/1, 53/2, 284/2, 284/3, 297/1
Illingworth, *Daily Mail*: 103/3
Illustrated London News: 238/3
Indian High Commission: 47/1, 355/2, 355/3
Institute of Contemporary Arts: 149/2
I.L.O.: 50/2
I.P.S.: 99/3
International News Photos: 294/1
Japanese Information Service: 71/3, 175/3, 386, 387, 388, 391/2, 395/3
Kahia, Abelhamia: 44
Kasmin Ltd: 148/3
Kenya Information Service: 51/2, 241/2, 317/2, 323/2
Keystone Press: 30/1, 32/3, 33/2, 33/5, 39/1, 45/3, 46/2, 66/1, 78/1, 84/1, 87/3, 103/1, 104/2, 106/1, 109, 110/2, 115/1, 128/1, 132/2, 133/3, 138/3, 139/1, 139/2, 163, 164/3, 166/1, 170/2, 173/1, 174/2, 176/3, 182/1, 183/1, 186/2, 187/1, 188/1, 189, 191/1, 191/3, 193/1, 194/2, 198/1, 222/1, 223/3, 225/1, 227/1, 233/1, 233/2, 248/1, 249, 253/1, 260/1, 261/1, 274/2, 276/2, 284/1, 301/3, 304/2, 305/1, 306/1, 316/2, 317/1, 321/3, 322/1, 323/1, 323/3, 324/3, 326/3, 327/3, 329, 350/1, 351/1, 352/2, 357/1, 358/2, 362/2, 375/2, 376/1, 376/2, 377/2, 384/1, 384/2
King Features Syndicate: 217/2
Laure, Jason: 112/1, 213/2
League for Democracy in Greece: 25/2
Lehmann, Monica: 152/3, 154/2
Leo Castelli Gallery, New York: 157/3
Library of Congress: 204/1, 207/2
Lichfield, Patrick: 344/3
London Express: 37/2, 98/2, 106/2, 112/2, 119/1, 210/2, 216/2, 227/2, 302/3, 305/3, 307/3, 308/3, 359/2
© Los Angeles Times Syndicate: 217/2
Trustees of David Low, *Evening Standard*: 58/2, 68/3, 241/3

Lukas, Jan: 181, 184/1, 196/1, 196/2, 250, 260/2, 270/2
McCullin, Don: 33/4, 34, 35/1, 39/2, 58/1, 101, 107, 118/1, 327/4, 370/3
Gallerie Maeght, Paris: 146/3
Magnum Distribution: 226/2, 254/2, 261/3, 271/2, 394
Marlborough Gallery, London: 140, 146/1, 148/2, 159/3
Marc, *The Times*: 169/3
Marron, Fred: 307/2
Meridiane, Bucharest: 267
Moger, Mrs Byron J.: 137/2
Mondatori: 169/2, 183/2, 190/1
Moro, Rome: 219
Musée d'Art Moderne, Paris: 143/1
NASA: 172/2, 173/2, 178/1
National Film Archive: 126/2, 127, 136/2, 144, 145, 151/2
National Theatre: 142/2
New World: 42
New Zealand High Commission: 239/2
Newcombe, Morris: 151/1
Novosti: 25/1, 73/1, 79/2, 176/1, 176/2, 176/4, 255/1, 256, 260/3, 261/2, 263/2, 265/2, 269/1, 276/1, 293/2, 370/2, 372/1
The Observer: 122/2, 168/2
Pakistan Embassy: 352/1
Paris Match: 36/1, 183/3, 185/3, 211/1, 230/2, 326/2
Penguin Books: 44
Pictorial Press: 252/2
The Pioneer: 354/1, 356/3
PIX: 112/1
Paul Popper: 31/1, 38/1, 48/3, 55/2, 66/3, 79/1, 86/1, 132/1, 182/3, 194/3, 199/1, 209/2, 222/3, 222/4, 224/3, 225/2, 228, 231/2, 242/1, 245/2, 275/2, 291, 300/2, 301/2, 302/1, 307/1, 309/1, 310/1, 311/3, 342/1, 356/1, 357/2, 369/2, 375/3, 384/3, 392/2
Psywar Society: 370/1, 374/2
Radio Times Hulton Picture Library: 188/2, 243/2, 304/1, 374/1, 378/1
Revolution Newspaper: 36/2
Rheinisches Bildarchiv: 157/2
Riboud, Marc: 216/1
The Ring: 133/2
Ben Rothenburg, Israel Publishing Co.: 337/1
Roumanian Embassy: 278/1, 278/2
Rowan Gallery, London: 147/1, 158/2
St Louis Post Dispatch: 66/2
Scarfe, G.: 125/3
Science Museum, London: 175/1, 175/2
School of Slavonic and East European Studies, University of London: 27/2, 40/1, 49/1, 70/1, 72/1, 73/2, 85/1, 209/1, 255/2, 258/2, 265/1, 300/1, 339/1, 340/2, 365
Sewell, William: 196/3, 285, 290/1, 292
Seymour, David: 226/2
Simplicissimus: 71/2, 221, 254/1, 273/1
Snark International: 33/3

Solomon R. Guggenheim Museum, New York: 147/2
Spencer, Jasmine: 45/2, 46/1, 48/2, 267, 289/2, 317/3, 342/3, 371/2
Spencer, Terence: 328
Der Spiegel: 122/1
State of Israel Government Office: 336/2, 341/1
Suddeutscher Verlag: 25/3, 55/3, 71/1 (Courtesy Krupp), 114, 275/1, 377/1
Sun Photo: 237/2
Suschitzky, W.: 60/1, 93/1, 94/2, 126/1, 138/2, 206/1, 206/3, 360/2, 361
Sycholt, August: 102/2
Tanjug News Agency: 280/1, 280/2, 281/1
Tass: 263/1
Tate Gallery, London: 146/2, 148/1, 149/1, 158/1, 158/3, 159/1
Teatr-Laboratorium 33-40: 150/2
De Tijd: 46/3
Time: 85/2, 88/1, 125/3
Timbers, John: 150/3
Transworld Features Syndicate: 87/1, 94/1, 95/1, 117/2, 136/1, 137/2, 138/1
Ullstein: 31/2
UK Atomic Energy Authority: 164/2
United Nations: 24/2, 62, 92/2, 172/1
UNRWA: 341/2
United Press International: 108, 119/2, 132/3, 164/1, 198/2, 242/2, 244/3, 248/2, 276/3, 277/2, 304/3, 309/2
United States Information Service: 29, 41/2, 48/1, 67/1, 72/2, 154/3, 160, 165/2, 166/2, 168/3, 169/1, 170/1, 173/3, 177/1, 178/2, 178/3, 179, 202, 212/2, 213/1, 220, 226/3, 273/2, 280/3, 359/1, 379/2
Usine-Universite: 89/1, 90/1
Uzzle, Burk: 35/3
Vicky, *Evening Standard*: 104/1, 223/1, 244/2
V.S.O.: 50/3
Warner Bros: 134/3
Washington Reporters: 213/3
Webb, John: 158/2
World Bank: 65, 99/1
W.H.O.: 59, 61/2, 61/3, 97/1, 98/1, 164/2, 347/2
Yugoslav Embassy: 281/2
Zambian Information Office: 316/3
Die Ziet: 79/3

If we have unwittingly infringed copyright in any picture or photograph reproduced in this publication, we tender our sincere apologies and will be glad of the opportunity, upon being satisfied as to the owner's title, to pay an appropriate fee as if we had been able to obtain prior permission.

Picture Research by Jasmine Spencer
Maps and diagrams drawn by Design Practitioners Ltd

Index

Figures in italics indicate illustration references